THE CHINESE ECONOMY
Transitions and Growth

Barry Naughton

The MIT Press
Cambridge, Massachusetts
London, England

MIT Press books may be purchased at special quantity discounts for business or sales promotional use. For information, please e-mail special_sales@mitpress.mit.edu or write to Special Sales Department, The MIT Press, 55 Hayward Street, Cambridge, MA 02142.

This book was set in Times Roman by SNP Best-set Typesetter Ltd., Hong Kong. Printed and bound in the United States of America.

Library of Congress Cataloging-in-Publication Data
Naughton, Barry
  The Chinese economy : transitions and growth / Barry Naughton
     p.   cm.
  Includes bibliographical references and index.
  ISBN-10: 0-262-14095-0—ISBN-13: 978-0-262-14095-9 (hc.: alk. paper)
  ISBN-10: 0-262-64064-3—ISBN-13: 978-0-262-64064-0 (pb.: alk. paper)
  1. China—Economic policy.   I. Title.

HC427.95.N38   2006
338.951—dc22
                                                          2006046840

10 9 8 7

Contents

Contents

Acknowledgments

This book grew gradually out of a course on the Chinese economy that I have taught annually since 1988 at the Graduate School of International Relations and Pacific Studies (IR/PS) at the University of California, San Diego. My biggest debt of gratitude is to the school itself, which for almost twenty years has created a stimulating, cross-disciplinary environment where there is always lively discussion and where a high value is placed on careful empirical work. The students in the China class have greatly enriched the content of this book by raising questions, challenging viewpoints and interpretations, and suggesting entirely new approaches. I have been especially fortunate to have enjoyed the help of a series of outstanding research assistants, who have helped in many ways to prepare this volume. Qi Yuan synthesized materials and drafted text that evolved into chapters in the current text, while Kourtney Heinz reviewed and carefully edited every bit of text available to her. Sun Shuyan and Cheng Yue were kept busy for a year locating, synthesizing, and updating material. Adria Hou, Laura Kaelke, and Ning Xia also made significant contributions.

I owe a double debt to those scholars who both influenced my understanding of China over the years and then made specific suggestions on the presentation and revision of the manuscript. Louis Putterman took an interest in the project early on and has made numerous valuable suggestions that I wish I had adopted when they were first made. Charles Gitomer gave me an enormous amount of assistance in drafting the chapter on agricultural production and technology. Carsten Holz, Gary Jefferson, and Thomas Rawski each reviewed part or all of the manuscript and provided valuable comments and corrections. In addition, four anonymous referees for MIT Press made many valuable suggestions.

More broadly, a work like this draws on, and inevitably borrows from, the work of many scholars across the whole field of economics in China. These debts are too extensive, and in some cases too unconscious, to be adequately acknowledged. It is a pleasure nonetheless to be able to recognize at least some of these intellectual debts. First and foremost, I'm grateful to those who were my teachers. Michael Montias provided a way of approaching comparative economic systems that gave me a solid platform for approaching China throughout its decades of multiple changes. Nicholas Lardy provided me and several other China scholars with the richest and most thorough understanding of the Chinese economy possible. There are a few pieces of this text that I can trace back all the way to the very first seminar, on Chinese economic history, that I took with Nick Lardy, while the influence of his most recent work on the Chinese financial system is obvious in the later chapters. I owe a different kind of debt to James Tobin, who encouraged me to plunge ahead with the study of China's economy and then charged my interest by explicating with absolute lucidity his own rigorous and realistic work.

In the text, I've tried to indicate where the analysis is dependent on specific scholars, but I doubt that I have been able to express fully the extent to which my work has relied on a number of economists and China scholars. In addition to those named in the previous two paragraphs, they include Loren Brandt, Diao Xinshen, Joseph Esherick, John Giles, Jean-François Huchet, Daokui David Li, Li Shantong, Justin Yifu Lin, Albert Park, Dwight Perkins, Qian Yingyi, Mary-Françoise Renard, Carl Riskin, Scott Rozelle, Terry Sicular, Dorie Solinger, Song Lina, Sarah Y. Tong, Wang Hongling, Christine Wong, Wu Jinglian, Shahid Yusuf, Zhang Xuejun, and Zhou Xiaochuan.

My colleagues and friends at the Graduate School of IR/PS at the University of California, San Diego, provided the intellectual energy and the personal companionship that make it enjoyable to undertake long projects. Andrew MacIntyre, Chris Woodruff, and Stephan Haggard have helped keep things stimulating and fun for years. I'm especially grateful to John McMillan, who influenced my work and peaked my interest while he was at IR/PS, and who continues to do so from a few hundred miles up the coast. Susan Shirk has been a special help as a friend and colleague with whom it is always fun to try out new ideas and approaches. The steady support and enthusiasm of Kwan So have been essential in creating this vital environment.

The editors at MIT Press have been patient and unfailingly supportive. John Covell has been an enthusiastic advocate for this book from the very beginning, and Nancy Lombardi has carried through the editing with care and tolerance.

This is the first book I've written that I think might have some intergenerational appeal. My father, perhaps, would have been tempted to pick it up and read it through if he had had the chance. Kieran and Claudia will hopefully find it interesting when they are a couple of years older. The book is dedicated to them.

INTRODUCTION

The Great Wall.

From Transition to Development

The Chinese economy displays both unmatched dynamism and unrivaled complexity. Since the early 1980s, China has consistently been the most rapidly growing economy on earth, sustaining an average annual growth rate of 10% from 1978 through 2005, according to official statistics. Moreover, as every schoolchild knows, China is the most populous country in the world: its population surpassed 1.3 billion people in 2004, despite a declining birthrate. Rapid growth and huge population have long implied that China would eventually emerge into the front ranks of world economies. In the new millennium, this promise is already becoming a reality. China's gross domestic product (GDP) reached US$2.225 trillion in 2005, valued at the prevailing exchange rate. Thus, China has grown past the two $2 trillion economies of the United Kingdom and France to become the world's fourth-largest economy. Since 2004, China has also been the world's third-largest trading nation, after the United States and Germany. The Chinese economy naturally attracts superlatives.

Yet China is also struggling to emerge from poverty. The World Bank "promoted" China from "lower income" to "lower middle income" status at the end of the 1990s. China's GDP is only about one-fifth the size of U.S. GDP, even though it has four times the population. Its 2005 GDP per capita (measured at exchange rates) is $1,700, comparable to that of the United States around 1850 (valued at today's prices), and compared to $40,000 for the United States today. Moreover, China encompasses diverse regional economies that range from extreme poverty to relative prosperity. In large stretches of rural China peasants still struggle on the margins of subsistence, while in Shanghai, Beijing, and Guangdong a modern information economy is taking root. Coal-fueled boilers, reminiscent of the early stages of the industrial revolution, coexist with domestically designed nuclear power plants and a manned space program. Bureaucratic state-owned enterprises dominate some sectors but compete both with tiny, hardworking household businesses and with multinational corporations whose managers are trained in the latest business school techniques. This diversity drives a dynamic economy but also makes it difficult for us to see China whole.

Ultimately, China's diversity can be traced to two incomplete transitions. First, China is still completing its transition away from bureaucratic socialism and toward a market economy. Second, China is in the middle of the industrialization process, the protracted transformation from a rural to an urban society. China is in the midst of "economic development," the process that transforms every aspect of an economy, society, and culture. These two transitions are both far from complete, and so China today carries with it parts of the traditional, the socialist, the modern, and the market, all mixed up in a jumble of mind-boggling complexity.

THE DISTANCE TRAVELED

In the more than 50 years since the founding of the People's Republic of China (PRC) in 1949, China has undergone an unusual and tumultuous development process, passing through revolution, socialism, and Maoist radicalism, and then gradualist economic reform and rapid economic growth. The PRC government after 1949 at first created stability and economic growth, and rapidly left behind an era of war, civil war, and widespread poverty, but it then inflicted terrible suffering on its own people, particularly during the Great Leap Forward (GLF) famine. Subsequently, the dislocation of the Cultural Revolution turned life upside down for many Chinese. Since the beginning of economic reform in 1978, China has jettisoned most of the ideological baggage of socialism, and has again traversed a tremendous distance. This time the ground has been crossed with a remarkable improvement of living standards, a general easing of social conditions, and relative social stability. The objective of the transition process—a moderately prosperous society with a market-based economy—is now tantalizingly close to being realized.

It is striking just how far China has come in the past 25 years. Few predicted, when China began to tentatively reform its economy in the late 1970s, that a gradual transition process would take hold and continue to move forward without some kind of traumatic rupture with the past. Yet that is exactly what has happened. Economic and political ideologies have changed completely, and many have been discarded. Institutions have been reshaped. The material basis of the economy has been completely rebuilt. Moreover, it is now clear that the Chinese approach of incremental reform and steady economic progress has succeeded in practice. Following an approach that has been called "crossing the river by groping for stepping-stones," China has evolved in the course of a quarter century from one of the world's most isolated socialist states to a powerhouse of the global economy. While there have been undeniable stresses and strains associated with this transformation, perhaps the most remarkable fact is that this enormous distance has been traveled with relatively little large-scale conflict and relatively lower social costs than other transitional economies. Never before have so many people moved out of poverty or near poverty in such a short time.

THE DUAL TRANSITION

Today, as China approaches middle-income status, Chinese institutions are becoming more similar to those in other countries, especially those in other developing countries. In some respects this trend toward convergence is making China easier to understand. Just as China's economic institutions are coming to resemble those in other developing countries, so too the challenges China faces are shifting, and increasingly they resemble those faced by other middle-income developing economies. In the recent past, the sharpest challenges that China faced were those relating to the *transition* from a socialist command economy to a market economy. Today, many of the initial challenges of market transition have been overcome. The market is now the predominant economic institution in China. As a result, the challenges of transition are gradually being replaced by the challenges of *development*: the need to invest in human skills and physical infrastructure, the need to create effective institutions, and the need to protect underprivileged and vulnerable sections of the population. These new challenges are still severe; they are not necessarily easier to handle than the earlier challenges of transition. Indeed, the ultimate success of China will depend on its ability to create stable, efficient institutions, to cope with social pressures, and to upgrade the quality of human skills.

The drive for economic development is especially evident today, but it has in fact been a nearly constant theme in China's modern history. The socialist system was adopted during the 1950s in part because the leaders assumed that it would be the quickest way to make China a rich and strong country. The disasters of the GLF and the Cultural Revolution led to disillusionment with socialism as a development strategy and to the growing conviction that the market could be a superior instrument of development. Thus transition to the market was launched in tandem with a renewed commitment to fostering economic growth. The twin challenges of underdevelopment and transition were interwoven at all stages of the transition process. When China began its market transition process, in 1978–1979, the biggest challenges were the simple availability of key commodities, such as grain and oil, as well as the virtual nonexistence of basic infrastructure. It was not certain, at that time, that China would be able to speed up its economic growth simply because it was not clear that there was enough grain to feed the people, or enough electricity to run the factories, or sufficient export commodities to swap on world markets for vital supplies. None of these fundamental supply uncertainties exists today. China has in fact been able to grow its way out of its early crises and steadily increase the momentum of growth. Almost alone among the transitional economies, China was able to maintain—and indeed accelerate—growth during the transition process.

Growth has changed not only the material basis of the economy, but also the standards by which we judge it. Thirty years ago widespread poverty was simply taken for granted in China; even under socialism, the poor were "always with us." Today the persistence of 100 million people in severe poverty in China is no longer seen as inevitable or acceptable. Moreover, while transition has led to improved living standards for nearly all Chinese, it has also led to increased economic uncertainty and risk for many. Urban Chinese now grapple with unemployment and a health insurance system with gaping holes. Rural Chinese, who never enjoyed real economic or health security while tied to their home villages, have now been thrown into even more precarious economic environments as they migrate in search of opportunity. Growth has been accompanied by deteriorating income distribution and a society that is increasingly perceived as unfair. These problems may, in fact, be more difficult to resolve than those created under socialism. But, in principle at least, growth has now for the first time created the material resources that makes it possible to address problems of poverty and privation.

CHINA'S GROWTH PERFORMANCE

China's growth performance over the past 25 years has been extraordinary. Why China? Why now? A general survey textbook cannot hope to allocate responsibility for China's growth performance to different components. But it is possible to put China's growth into a broad context that makes it much less mysterious and more understandable. China's dramatic growth today is the result of a unique historical confluence of three factors: structural, transitional, and traditional.

First, China displays a number of structural features that are associated with rapid growth because they correspond with rapid growth of inputs into the economy. China invests a high proportion of national income annually, and a healthy share of investment is devoted to crucial physical infrastructure with public-goods properties. China's population is at the stage of social development where growth of the modern labor force is exceptionally rapid. Some of the rapid labor-force growth comes from the "demographic dividend," in which declining birth rates bring down dependency rates. The modern sector of the labor force is growing especially rapidly as the rural-urban transformation reaches a high point, where urban areas can absorb proportionately large flows of labor from the rural economy. Today, large investments in higher human capital are being made that build on the broad base of health and skills created under socialism. Thus China is in the position that the inputs of physical capital, labor, and human capital are all increasing rapidly.

Second, China is reaping the economic benefits from a successful transition from socialism to a market economy. There is substantial literature on the transition from socialism, and still significant disagreement about the lessons of that experience. The competing virtues of "big bang" versus "gradualist" approaches to transition will probably be discussed for years. Still, there are two simple points that derive from China's experience about which nearly everyone should be able to agree. First, the market is the superior way to organize economic transactions. At virtually every point in China's transition, growth acceleration has been associated with the opening of markets and with increasing competition. Most recently, China's round of market-opening measures to prepare for accession to the World Trade Organization (WTO) at the end of 2001 led directly to a further acceleration of growth (from 2002 through at least 2005). Whatever else can be said, China's experience shows that markets work and should be at the heart of any country's development effort. Second, China's experience provides no support for "market fundamentalism." That is, China's experience provides no support for the argument that, since the market is a superior mechanism, the full panoply of market institutions should be set in place as quickly as possible in as many realms as possible. On the contrary, China's experience shows that steady expansion of human and institutional capabilities, consistent and predictable incentives and property rights, and some government coordination to make up for market failures are as important as the steady expansion of markets. At a given moment, the development of market institutions may not necessarily be any more important or urgent than the development of other types of institutions and capabilities.

Successful transition has positioned China to reap some of the benefits of socialism past (relatively broad-based education and health, for example), while avoiding the trough of recession that wiped out those benefits for many other transitional economies. These transitional factors interact with structural factors: the investment rate is high largely because the domestic saving rate is high; and the domestic saving rate is high largely because Chinese households and firms have experienced general macroeconomic stability and growth in the wake of a successful economic reform.

Third, and finally, China is reaping the growth benefits from the revival of some of its traditional economic relationships. The highly commercialized and entrepreneurial society that grew up along with the dense traditional agricultural economy has now sprung back to life in many parts of China. This rebirth gives China the ability to capitalize on features that are associated with growth in many economies: a long history of state operation, rich institutions and a history of trust, and familiarity with commercial procedures. The old, densely populated civilizations of Asia—China and India—are reclaiming the global economic position they held for many centuries (cf. Bockstette, Chanda, and Putterman 2002). China's economic rise has been assisted by the re-emergence of traditional commercial ties with Chinese in Hong Kong, Taiwan, and Southeast Asia. These links facilitated China's opening to the global economy. Globalization, in turn, is enabling the resource-poor and labor-abundant economies of China and India to take advantage of their long-standing advantages. Resources can be accessed globally at far less than their domestic cost; a broad range of labor-intensive manufacturing and service industries provide opportunities for labor-abundant economies; and the backlog of advanced technologies that was always theoretically available is now being enthusiastically exploited by both China and India. Contemporary developments have allowed China to take advantage of its commercial and institutional legacies.

BECOMING A "NORMAL" COUNTRY

In the past China's economy had many peculiar features. The institutions of China's economy under socialism were utterly distinctive. China was an outlier among developing countries because of its socialist institutions. But China was also an outlier among socialist countries because it had adapted socialist institutions to the problems of a poor, predominantly rural economy. Because China was big and relatively isolated, it developed its own vocabulary and terms of reference for many economic issues. Moreover, China's uniqueness was not merely a matter of institutions: actual economic outcomes were also distinctive. China under the planned economy was *sui generis*: a "model" for some and a nightmare for others, there was no doubt that China followed its own distinctive path.

For example, if we use standard economic indicators to examine China's economy on the eve of reform, in 1978, we observe many paradoxical features. Overall, China was still quite poor, with a per capita GDP estimated by the World Bank to be the equivalent of $674 in constant-price (year 2000) purchasing-power-parity (PPP) U.S.-dollar equivalents. This figure means that China's income level was fairly typical of a low-income developing country at that time. However, according to prices of that time, 44% of China's GDP was produced in industry, which was *much* more than other low-income countries. Moreover, China's energy consumption per dollar of GDP was several times that of other low-income economies. So China appeared to be "overindustrialized." But in the same year, only 18% of China's population lived in cities, which is considerably less than the average low-income country. Thus China appeared to be "underurbanized." At the same time, literacy and life expectancy were quite high for a country at that income level, so China appeared to have an exceptional human development record. China did not appear to fit any normal pattern. Undoubtedly, difficult valuation problems make any simple comparison difficult, and both the estimate of China's GDP in 1978 and the valuation of its currency are problematic. An upward adjustment to the GDP data would make the energy consumption and life expectancy more normal, but would make the urbanization rate even more abnormal. Moreover, in order to begin opening up its economy, China would soon begin *devaluing* its currency after 1978. In fact, there is no simple way to reconcile these facts about China in 1978: China was simply different, uniquely shaped by its own history and economic system.

By 2003, China's GDP per capita had reached $4,726, again in constant-price (year 2000) PPP U.S.-dollar equivalents, according to the World Bank. This figure is now fairly typical of a lower-middle-income country. Moreover, today most of the other indicators have fallen into line with typical patterns. For example, at current prices, 40.5% of GDP is produced by industry (including mining and utilities). This proportion is still high, but after all, industry has grown rapidly—much more rapidly than GDP for 25 years—and China has become the "workshop of the world." Energy consumption per dollar of PPP GDP is still above what it should be, but it is now similar to developing-country averages and clearly within the normal range. Cities have grown rapidly, and the urbanization rate, reaching 41%, has about "caught up" with the expected level for a developing country of China's income level. Life expectancy and literacy, while still respectable, are no longer very much higher than what one would expect from a country at China's income level. China in 1978 was an extreme outlier in numerous respects; it is today, in nearly every respect, much closer to "normal" patterns.

This convergence to "normal" institutions and patterns of development in most respects makes China easier to understand. Certain features stand out more clearly, as China becomes more open and easier to analyze. Chinese economic growth is rapid and unusually persistant; investment rates are very high; the contribution of manufacturing to GDP and to growth is very high; and the increase in China's participation in the world economy is dramatic. More broadly, the rapid upgrading of Chinese capabilities in a wide range of fields is extremely impressive.

Of course, China's size, diversity, and rapid growth—as well as the complex legacy of its past—continue to pose challenges to our ability to understand its unique institutions, economic strategies, and current challenges. The Chinese economy is difficult to pigeonhole because it is simultaneously an intensely competitive market economy and an economy subject to particularly severe distortions. Government regulations, state ownership, corruption, incomplete markets, and imperfect institutions seriously distort economic incentives. Yet at the same time, entry of new competitors and fierce competition among individuals, companies, and regions constantly erode the blockades and barriers erected by the privileged few. Communist Party political power means that economic institutions and policy-making processes are largely closed to outsiders and that there is no free press to probe inconsistencies. China is unusually nontransparent. Economic data are sometimes worthless and must always be used with caution. This volume predominantly uses official data, but throughout considers data reliability and discards some implausible data (see Chapter 6 for discussion of GDP data). Despite dramatic improvements in openness, China's economy retains distinctive institutions and sometimes reports contradictory or implausible information, which make it difficult to analyze.

CHINA TO THE FUTURE

The challenges facing China are still severe. Popular accounts repeatedly tend to either overestimate or underestimate China, and sometimes individual accounts veer from overestimation to underestimation in the space of a single paragraph. It is important not to lose sight of the formidable challenges, the constant sense of predicament, and the endless range of difficulties facing China. Because China has been emerging so recently from extreme poverty, it still possesses inadequate human and physical capital: education and technology levels are low, and much of the transportation and industrial infrastructure remains to be built. Institutions that support a high-productivity economy are either nonexistent or else created very recently and established on shaky foundations. Of course many challenges are ultimately traceable to the single great overwhelming fact of China: the enormous pressure of human numbers on an intrinsically limited supporting environment. It is only because China also has enormous reserves of human ingenuity and resourcefulness that it can have any hope of surmounting the difficulties facing it.

During most of the 1990s, it was perhaps more common to underestimate China. The shock of the 1989 Tiananmen student demonstrations and their brutal suppression caused many observers to downgrade their forecasts for China's future. Since the beginning of the twenty-first century, though, it has perhaps been more common to overestimate China. Overestimation often involves seeing China as an economic competitor, and perhaps as a potential strategic rival, to the United States. China's economic success has paradoxically convinced many that China is some kind of economic superpower, instead of a struggling developing country. This view reflects a major misunderstanding both of the nature of the economic links between China and the United States and of the magnitude of the challenges facing China. Placing China in a developmental context should make it clear not only that China faces formidable challenges, but also that Chinese policy-makers generally recognize the same problems and challenges that outside observers see. However, they do not always have the institutional or other capacity to deal quickly with challenges. Over the past 25 years, though, the Chinese government has been able to achieve a necessary minimum of essential policy changes. It is certainly *not* the case that the Chinese have done everything right. Quite the contrary: there have been as many failures as successes in China's economic and transition policy over the past two decades. But crucially, for the past 25 years the most important obstacles have been removed, and the absolutely essential changes that were necessary to allow the process of development as a whole to go forward have been achieved. Of course, there is no guarantee that this statement will continue to be true in the future, but these accomplishments show that the Chinese political system has a striking ability to target a few critical issues and mobilize talent and resources to address these issues when it is absolutely necessary to do so. This provides the system with a degree of resilience that is one of its key strengths.

We know from the experience of other successful developing countries that as a country reaches medium developed level, that country's contributions to world welfare begin to increase. New resources of human ingenuity are brought to bear. For example, as Japan made the transition from developing to developed economy, a steady stream of new techniques of manufacturing, new products, and new and traditional cultural influences began to flow out of

Japan. Today, American residents use and appreciate Japanese products and ideas that range from the sublime to the trivial on a daily basis. The same change is just beginning to become true for China as well. As China develops, its contributions to world welfare will increase in ways that are impossible for us to foresee. Over the next century, scientific and medical discoveries, new products and services, and a revitalized cultural contribution will come out of China. China will be taking up more space in an increasingly crowded world, but its contributions to world society will also increase rapidly. In the pages that follow, we aim to provide a comprehensive picture of the Chinese economy, building from the ground up. We will try to explain China's remarkable rise and peer into the future as effectively as possible.

USING THIS TEXTBOOK

The chapters of this book are organized in a bottom-up fashion. The first half of the book covers endowments, legacies, economic systems, and general issues of economic structure, labor, and living standards. The second half covers specific sectors, beginning with agriculture and progressing through industry and technology, foreign trade and investment, and macroeconomics. The final chapter covers the environment and sustainability. The book is designed to be a platform, covering much of the essential information about the Chinese economy and thereby serving as a starting point for further in-depth study of any specific topic.

The chapters in the book make frequent cross-references but are intended to stand alone as well. Thus classes should be able to assemble the chapters in different sequences, to accord with preferred approaches to the material. If the chapters are covered in order, the result is a strong China focus, with the opening chapters on China's geography and history first. This "program" is appropriate to a course specifically on China's economy or as part of a course on East Asian economies. An alternative "program" to cover the material would be to begin with Chapters 3 and 4 (the socialist economy and transition economy), then skip to Chapters 12 and 13 (township and village enterprises, and ownership and corporate governance in industry). This program gives a stronger emphasis on market transition and would be appropriate to a comparative class on economic systems. Those wishing to emphasize China's opening and integration into the world economy may wish to start with Chapters 16 and 17 (international trade and foreign investment). Of course, many other programs or approaches to the material are possible. The book presents many charts and graphs. The raw data for these graphics is available on the

Web site, http://irps.ucsd.edu/Chinese_economy, along with supplementary materials and updated data.

BIBLIOGRAPHY

Suggestions for Further Reading

For further reading related to specific economic topics, see the suggestions for further reading following each individual chapter. Among overviews in English, Lin, Cai, and Li (1996) is useful, and is especially good on the socialist era. Wu Jinglian (2005) is the best and most comprehensive account of Chinese economic reform currently available. Stepping outside the strictly economic sphere, Johnson (2004) manages to capture a realistic feel of life in contemporary China through three detailed and moving accounts. For a lively account of China's rise from a business perspective, see McGregor (2005). Naughton and Yang (2004) discuss the range of outside estimates of China's progress and future as of the mid-1990s.

A wide variety of academic journals now carry articles on the Chinese economy. Several high-quality Chinese journals carry economics articles, and today most economics journals have at least a few scholarly articles with significant China content. Of the Chinese journals, a (very) short list includes *The China Quarterly* (London: Cambridge University Press); *China Journal* (Canberra: Australian National University); and *China: An International Journal* (Singapore University Press), accessible at http://muse.jhu.edu/journals/china/index.html. Of the economics journals, the most consistently interesting China-related articles come in the *Journal of Comparative Economics*. A more specialized journal focusing entirely on China, the *China Economic Review*, carries many essential articles.

Sources for Data and Figures

The majority of the data in this text are drawn from official Chinese sources. There are many problems with official Chinese data, but to date nobody has produced an alternative set of data with a convincing claim to superiority. The strategy followed in this book has been to use the official data, but also to point out some of the most important deficiencies in those data. I have tried to use the most accessible data sources possible: in practice, this means relying on the *Statistical Yearbook of China* (*SYC*) whenever possible. The *SYC* is published annually (typically in November) by the National Bureau of Statistics (NBS). It is widely available and has the distinct advantage of having English headings for all tables. There is a great deal of continuity in the coverage of the *SYC* from year to year, which means that certain types of data can be readily updated from the *SYC*, and other types of data are consistently omitted. The *Statistical Abstract of China* (*SAC*), also published annually by the NBS (typically in June) has slightly different coverage, which can be useful, and no English headings. Many key statistics are released in February in the "Annual Economic Report," which is available at the NBS Web site, e.g., at http://www.stats.gov.cn/tjgb/ndtjgb/qgndtjgb/t20050228_402231854.htm.

Official Chinese GDP data for the years since 1993 were revised in late 2005. The economic census carried out on December 31, 2004, revealed a larger count of small-scale service businesses than had been anticipated, and the 2004 census was then used to adjust GDP data retrospectively through 1993. The newly revised data, from NBS (2006), have been used throughout this text, combined with GDP deflators from earlier statistical sources, such as *SYC*.

Some chapters use data drawn primarily from other sources. The NBS has overall responsibility for data collection and analysis, but data within specific sectors are often collected by specific ministries. Cooperation between those ministries and the NBS sometimes leaves something to be desired, and ministries may define their data coverage in ways that are influenced by the administrative authority. For example, data on township and village enterprises come primarily from the Ministry of Agriculture; data on urban labor come primarily from the Ministry of Labor and Social Security; and data on science and technology come primarily from the Ministry of Science and Technology. Each of these organizations has a Web site, and each cooperates with the NBS to publish statistics. But coordination is not seamless (cf. OECD, 2005, chap. 5). The discussion of the quality and coverage of Chinese data is extensive. Good places to start reading about the issues are Rawski (2001), Xu (2004), and Young (2003).

For comparative international data, I have followed the same principle of using the most accessible data sources when possible, which in practice means having first recourse to the World Bank, *World Development Indicators* (*WDI*), accessed online at http://devdata.worldbank.org/dataonline/. In cases where *WDI* data are inadequate, I have indicated an alternative source and the reason for using it.

U.S. GDP in the mid-1800s: Johnston and Williamson (2005).

References

Bockstette, V., A. Chanda, and L. Putterman (2002). "States and Markets: The Advantage of an Early Start." *Journal of Economic Growth* 7(4):347–69.

Johnston, Louis, and Samuel H. Williamson (2005). "The Annual Real and Nominal GDP for the United States, 1790–Present." Economic History Services, October, http://www.eh.net/hmit/gdp/.

Johnson, Ian (2004). *Wild Grass: Three Stories of Change in Modern China.* New York: Pantheon Books.

Lin, Justin Yifu, Fang Cai, and Zhou Li (1996). *The China Miracle: Development Strategy and Economic Reform.* Hong Kong: Chinese University Press.

McGregor, James (2005). *One Billion Customers: Lessons from the Front Lines of Doing Business in China.* New York: Wall Street Journal.

Naughton, Barry, and Dali Yang (2004). "Holding China Together: Introduction." In Naughton and Yang, eds., *Holding China Together: Diversity and National Integration in the Post-Deng Era.* New York: Cambridge University Press.

NBS [National Bureau of Statistics] (2006). "Woguo Guoneishengchan Zongzhi Lishi Shuju Xiuding Jieguo [The Results of Revision of China's Historical GDP Figures]," January 9, http://www.stats.gov.cn/tjdt/zygg/t20060109_402300176.htm.

OECD (2005). *Governance in China.* Paris: Organization for Economic Cooperation and Development. Chap. 5 on institutional arrangements for statistics, http://www.sourceoecd.org/governance/926400842X.

Rawski, Thomas (2001). "What Is Happening to China's GDP Statistics?" *China Economic Review*, 12:347–54.

SAC (Annual). *Zhongguo Tongji Zhaiyao* [Statistical Abstract of China]. Beijing: Zhongguo Tongji.

SYC (Annual). *Zhongguo Tongji Nianjian* [Statistical Yearbook of China]. Beijing: Zhongguo Tongji.

World Bank. (Annual). *World Development Indicators.* Washington, D.C.: The World Bank. http://devdata.worldbank.org/dataonline.

Wu, Jinglian (2005). *Understanding and Interpreting Chinese Economic Reform.* Singapore: Thomson.

Xu, Xianchun (2004). "China's Gross Domestic Product Estimation." *China Economic Review* 15:302–22.

Young, Alwyn (2003). "Gold into Base Metals: Productivity Growth in the People's Republic of China During the Reform Period." *Journal of Political Economy* 111(6):1220–61.

I LEGACIES AND SETTING

Plowing with traditional tools in Dengfeng, Henan 1982.

1 The Geographical Setting

China is the most populous nation, and it is also one of the largest countries, with the third-biggest landmass, after Russia and Canada. Its land area is 2% greater than that of the United States, which it resembles geographically. The two countries cover similar latitudes and a similar range of climatic conditions, and these similarities lead to numerous parallels between regions in the eastern half of both countries. The climate of Guangzhou (Canton) is like that of Miami, and the climate of the Northeast (Manchuria) is similar to that of Minnesota. The great difference between China and the United States is that China is far more rugged and more of the land is inhospitable. Most of China consists of hills, mountains, and high plateaus, broken by river valleys and a few plains and basins. In the west, China borders on the vast deserts of inner Asia. Mount Everest, the highest mountain in the world, is on the China–Nepal border, while the Turfan depression in Xinjiang, 155 meters below sea level, is the third-lowest place on earth. Only 25% of China is less than 500 meters (1,640 feet) above sea level, compared to 60% of North America and 80% of Europe. Although China historically was a nation of farmers, only a small proportion of the land is arable. The largest plains in China cover only a fraction of the area of the vast central plain of the American Midwest. China is big, rugged, and diverse.

China has only a single seacoast. Moreover, China's eastern seaboard is not particularly accessible. Most of the southern part of the coast is rugged and hilly, so that the occasional good harbors tend to be cut off from the inland regions. In the north, especially between the Yangtze and the Shandong Peninsula, the coast is low and swampy with few good harbors. Reflecting these geographic conditions, China's traditional economy was inwardly oriented. There were outward-oriented, seafaring subcultures, but these tended to be fenced off in the southeast coast, which was economically peripheral. China thus contrasts sharply with northern Europe and with Japan, Taiwan, and Korea, with their strong seagoing and commercial traditions. The lack of a coastal orientation contributed to China's late start in economic modernization. Indeed, China's links to the modern world economy really began to multiply only when foreign-dominated Treaty Ports were forcibly implanted into China's key economic regions after 1842. Even today, the vast interior places huge demands on China's economic capacity and will have lasting ramifications on future development. Since 1999, China has been committed to the Western Development Program, targeting investment and giving policy preferences to the western and inland regions. This government program reflects the fact that the west lags economically, while the coasts have surged ahead and have been firmly linked to the ocean transport web and the global economy.

1.1 LANDFORMS

The entire Chinese landmass tilts from west to east. The Himalayas are a young mountain range, still rising by several feet per century because of the collision of the Indian subcontinent with the Asian landmass. This mountain-building process shapes the whole topography of China, creating a series of mountain ranges that are high and rugged in the west and taper off to low hills in the east. Broadly speaking, the land of China forms three great "steps" in elevation. The top step is made up of the frigid Tibetan Plateau, which *averages* more than 4,000 meters (over 13,000 feet) above sea level and contains the world's highest mountains. The second step consists of a series of plateaus and basins with an elevation of between 1,000 and 2,000 meters (between 3,000 and 7,000 feet). These include the basins in arid north-western China (such as the Tarim and Junggar basins), the Inner Mongolian Plateau and Loess Plateau in northern China, and the Yunnan-Guizhou Plateau in southwestern China. The third step consists of the plains and low hills of eastern China, where the elevation is generally below 500 meters. Even in the east, ranges of relatively low mountains create barriers to north–south transport.

The three most important rivers in China, the Yangtze (Changjiang), Yellow (Huang), and Pearl (Zhujiang) rivers, all flow from west to east in accord with the basic topography. Even the great rivers of South and Southeast Asia, including the Mekong and Ganges, originate within China on the Tibetan highland and initially flow east before turning south and cutting through mountain ranges on the way to the southern seas (see Figure 20.2, p. 501). The western half of China is high and arid, and the population is sparse. A line drawn from the town of Aihui in the northeast province of Heilongjiang to Tengchong in the southwest province of Yunnan (the Aihui–Tengchong line; Figure 1.1)

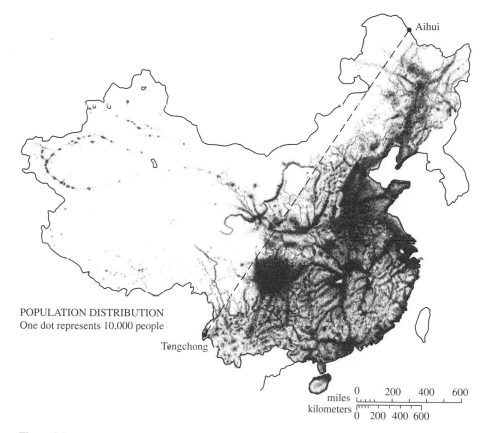

POPULATION DISTRIBUTION
One dot represents 10,000 people

Tengchong

miles
kilometers

0   200   400   600

0   200 400 600

Figure 1.1
Population distribution representing 10,000 people and the Aihui–Tengchong line

divides the area of China in half. But only 6% of the population lives in the
dry, mountainous west; 94% of the population lives in the eastern half of the
country. The area west-northwest of the Aihui–Tengchong line has a population density of only 11 people per square kilometer, about one-quarter the
world's average. Within this vast area, the Tibetan Plateau contains a quarter
of the land area of China but less than 1% of the population. The northwest
region supports about 4.5% of the population, mostly in a few basins and scattered oases. Shortage of available water sharply limits the population potential of the western regions. East-southeast of the Aihui–Tengchong line, the
country is lower in elevation, and water is comparatively abundant. This half
is considered "monsoon China," receiving abundant watering by the summer
rains. The population density in this area is 260 people per square kilometer,
about six times the world's average population density.

Table 1.1
Land and population, 2002

	Land area (1) (million hectares)	Arable land (2) (million hectares)	Arable percent (2)/(1) × 100	Population (million)	Arable per capita (hectare)
China	933	143	15.3	1,280	0.11
India	297	162	54.4	1,049	0.15
United States	916	176	19.2	288	0.61
Russia	1,689	123	7.3	144	0.86

A hectare is a square 100 meters on each side, equal to about 2.5 acres.

China's hilly and complex terrain means that relatively little of the land is suitable for cultivation. The good agricultural land lies in the fertile plains and valleys of the major river systems, separated from one another by hills and mountains. Only 15 percent of China is arable (Table 1.1), and there is very little land potentially suited for cultivation not already exploited. The United States has more arable land than China but less than one-fourth the population. Per capita arable land in China is only one-tenth of a hectare, or one-quarter of an acre. This is the size of a modest suburban home lot in the United States. Over the centuries China has adapted to land scarcity with a labor-intensive agriculture that wrests more total food grain from the soil than any other country.

1.2 CLIMATE AND WATER

The climate of China is dominated by the southeast monsoon, which sets the distinctive pattern of wet summers and dry winters. In winter there is little rain or snow anywhere in China. A high-pressure zone is established over central Asia, creating a steady flow of cold, dry air over all of eastern China. But in the summer, heating of the entire Asian landmass creates a low-pressure area over central Asia that draws tropical maritime air, saturated with moisture, into southeastern China. As this air encounters mountain ridges and cooler air masses, rains fall abundantly on southern China. As a result, the coast stays relatively cool while the inland basins become very hot, particularly in the "four furnaces" of central China (Chongqing, Wuhan, Changsha, and Nanjing) and in the western deserts.

As the summer monsoon moves northwest, it loses strength and delivers less rain (Figure 1.2). Overall the north is dry while the south is lush and drained by numerous waterways. The difference is reflected in an ancient saying about traditional means of transport: "South, boat; North, horse." Usually, the monsoons push over the belt of mountains between the Yangtze and Yellow River

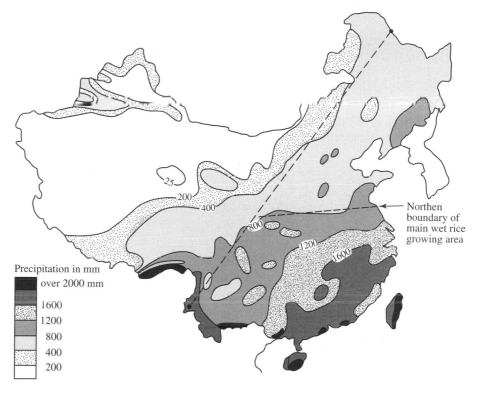

Precipitation in mm

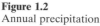

over 2000 mm

1600
1200
800
400
200

Northen
boundary of
main wet rice
growing area

Figure 1.2
Annual precipitation

basins, providing modest summer rains in northern China. In bad years, however, the monsoons are too weak to cross over to the Yellow River valley and become stuck over the central mountain belt. In those years, north China is struck by drought, while the rains hover over southern China, flooding the countryside. This central mountain range, then, creates another fundamental dividing line between south China, with abundant water, and north China, which is chronically short of water.

In fact, China is an arid country overall. In the Northwest, the margin of human habitation is defined by a continual tug of war with the desert, which threatens to advance, rolling over farmlands. The Aihui–Tengchong line marks this frontier between adequate and insufficient water. In the north, the Yellow River flows almost entirely through arid and semiarid country. The vast population of northern China creates enormous demands on Yellow River water. One of the great rivers of the world, 4,800 kilometers long, but of only moderate total volume, the Yellow River literally runs dry in many years, as withdrawals take *all* the available water. A record was reached in 1997, when there was no water in the downstream stretches of the Yellow River for 226 days (Liu 1998, 899). Furthermore, the Yellow River carries a heavy load of dissolved mud and sand, 1.6 billion tons every year, and drops one-fourth of it on the riverbed. This raises the river bed about 10 cm each year, so that today the river—held between a line of dikes on either side—flows along an elevated path, always threatening to flood the surrounding, lower countryside when water does come. By contrast, in lush southern China, the Yangtze is only a little bit longer than the Yellow River but carries 20 times as much water. The Yangtze flows abundantly year-round, carrying one-third as much total sediment as the Yellow River. Even the Pearl River system carries six times as much water as the Yellow River. All the rivers rise and fall in rhythm with the monsoon. Reaching their lowest point around February, the rivers rise steadily until August or September, at which point they flow mightily, barely held within their dikes and covering vast floodplains.

In relation to its enormous population, China is short of arable land, forests, and water, ensuring that China's environmental problems will be extremely severe. When account is taken of the highly uneven distribution of resources and population—especially the scarcity of water in the north and west—it is clear that enormous problems of environmental degradation challenge China. Indeed, China will inevitably be in a kind of permanent environmental crisis for the next 50 years or so, as economic growth pushes up against the limits of what the land can support (Chapter 20).

1.3 PROVINCES AND REGIONS

The most familiar way to divide China's vast space is into provinces. China currently has 31 province-level administrative units. Some Chinese provinces have more people than most countries: Henan, the most populous, hit 97 million in 2004, while Tibet has the smallest population, with only 2.7 million. China maintains an official distinction between provinces (22), municipalities under national supervision (4), and autonomous regions of ethnic minorities (5). These all have province-level "rank" in the national administrative system, and we will use the term "province" to refer to all of them. Some provinces have identities that trace back more than two millennia; two of them, however, are recent creations: Hainan Island was carved out of Guangdong Province in 1988; and Chongqing Municipality was separated from Sichuan Province in 1997. In addition, there are now two special autonomous regions (SARs) of China, Hong Kong (since 1997) and Macau

Figure 1.3
China's provinces. Includes provinces, autonomous regions, and municipalities with provincial rank. SAR, Special Administrative Region

(since 1999). These are never treated as provinces. Figure 1.3 shows the provinces of the People's Republic of China.

Provinces are not always the most natural way to divide up China's economic space. Another approach, following anthropologist William Skinner, is to divide Chinese territory into "macroregions" defined by the rugged topography. Each macroregion spreads over more than one province and consists of a densely settled core area and a less densely settled and often hilly periphery. Although it is possible to divide all of China into macroregions, not all macroregions are equal: we will look at several of the most important (Figure 1.4). The most important macroregion is North China. The North China Plain is by far the largest flat land area in China, and it contains a little over one-quarter of China's total farm land as well as slightly over one-quarter of the total population (in Figure 1.4 densely populated core areas show up as dark

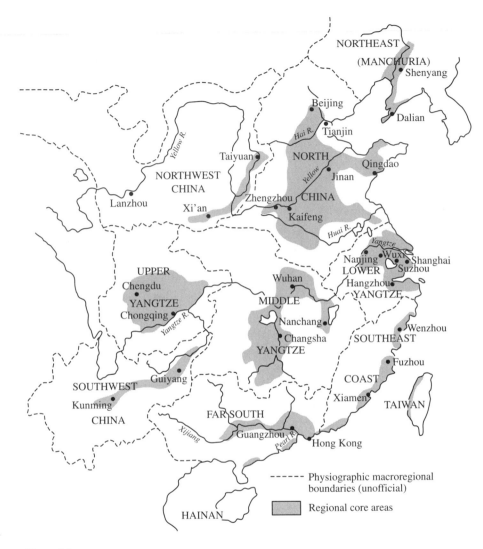

Figure 1.4
Macroregions and major cities of Eastern China

areas). The national capital, Beijing, serves as the urban center of North China, and along with its sister city, Tianjin, has a total population of around 20 million. Size, location, and the national capital make North China the most important region of China. In spite of the importance of the Beijing–Tianjin metropolis, the Plain as a whole is predominantly rural, with large villages spread thickly and fairly evenly over the entire expanse. Many areas in the plain are not irrigated; as a result, they are dependent on unreliable rains and subject to periodic droughts and floods. The primary staple crop is wheat, although some areas do well producing economic crops such as cotton and peanuts. While sheer size gives North China a predominant importance among China's regions, it is rather average in terms of development levels. The 27% of total national population that lives there produces 30% of the industrial output and 31% of the crop output of the entire nation.

The most developed part of China is the Lower Yangtze macroregion. At the center of the region is the metropolis of Shanghai, economically the most important city in China. Ten percent of China's population lives in the Lower Yangtze, but the region produced 21% of China's GDP in 2003. Incomes are higher and urbanization rates significantly greater than in any other area of China. Indeed, in recent years industrial production has spread so rapidly into the countryside that many areas classified as rural are more realistically thought of as urbanized countryside. For centuries, this was the richest part of China, and during the last decade its growth has been well above the national average, so the Lower Yangtze is regaining its predominant role in the Chinese economy. The Yangtze River Delta, covering 50,000 square kilometers, is one of the great river deltas of the world. Wet rice cultivation is dominant, and typically two or more crops are harvested per year. The country is lush and green, with water everywhere. The intensely cultivated countryside, comprising 7% of China's arable land, produces 10% of crop output.

Adjacent to the North China Plain, and tied to it by numerous economic links, is the region of the Northeast, or Manchuria. The Northeast is a region of abundant natural resources: 9% of China's population here cultivates 17% of the arable land, and rich reserves of iron ore, coal, and petroleum have made the Northeast the center of China's heavy industry. Since the beginning of the twentieth century, Chinese settlers have been braving the harsh winters to reclaim farmland from the northern forests of this region. The relative abundance of land has encouraged relatively high levels of agricultural mechanization and made the region an exporter of food grains and soybeans to the rest of China. The industrial center is at Shenyang, in Liaoning, which is surrounded by a ring of eight medium-sized industrial cities, including Anshan, site of China's oldest steel mill. But over the past two decades, the Northeast has struggled: the number of factory jobs in state-run industry has shrunk; the region has lost the important role it played in the national planned economy; and growth has lagged. From being a richer part of China, the Northeast has become average, 9% of the people producing 10% of GDP in 2003.

The economies of the North, Northeast, and Lower Yangtze macroregions have had very different trajectories in recent years. Historically, the link between the North China Plain and the Lower Yangtze made China into a single economic entity: the Grand Canal was built to ship the food grain surpluses of the lower Yangtze to the national capital region in the northern plain. Today, the Beijing–Shanghai link still defines the central axis of the economy. For a period in the mid-twentieth century, the mineral and land resources of the Northeast, along with the creation of its heavy industrial base, led it to be highly integrated into socialist, industrializing China. But in the past 20 years, the Northeast has become somewhat marginalized, losing its centrality to the Lower Yangtze. These three interacting regions make up the bulk of the Chinese economy; together they contain 46% of China's population and 51% of its farmland, and together they produced 55% of GDP in 2003.

The remaining Chinese macroregions are much less tightly integrated into a single national economic system. The provinces in the middle reach of the Yangtze—Hubei, Hunan, and Jiangxi—entered the reform era at Chinese average levels of development but have lagged behind the rapidly growing coastal regions. These provinces hold 13% of China's population but produced only 9.5% of 2003 GDP. The land is generally irrigated and intensely cultivated: it contains only 10% of China's arable land but produces 14% of the crop value. In contrast to the Lower Yangtze, where the agricultural economy is extremely diversified, the Middle Yangtze primarily produces grain. This grain monoculture enables the region to export significant surpluses of grain to other regions of China. The major urban center is Wuhan, which has trade and industrial roles that extend beyond the region.

Following the Yangtze further upstream, one arrives in Sichuan, a huge inland basin entirely surrounded by high mountains that is the core of the Upper Yangtze macroregion. Fertile and densely populated, there is no similar geographical feature anywhere else in the world. The Sichuan basin is now divided into two provinces, Chongqing municipality and Sichuan Province, which together have a 2004 population of 118 million. There is no natural route into or out of the Sichuan basin, and even the Yangtze River, as it flows out of Sichuan, cuts its way through spectacular and treacherous mountain gorges. This is where the huge and controversial Three Gorges Dam across the Yangtze was built, and the gorges are being inundated by a gradually filling reservoir. Chongqing and Chengdu (the capital of Sichuan Province) divide between them the functions of urban centers for the Upper Yangtze macroregion. Near the Sichuan basin, and linked to it by extensive economic and transport ties, is the Yunnan-Guizhou plateau, labeled the Southwest China macroregion in Figure 1.4. The Chinese government usually lumps the provinces of Yunnan and Guizhou in with Sichuan and Chongqing to form a greater Southwest China region. These four provinces have diverse topographies, but all have a dense population and a common low income. The GDP per capita is only about half the national average: 15.5% of China's population here produces 8.5% of GDP.

Figure 1.4 shows two macroregions along the southeast coast. Both these macroregions have long been oriented outward toward ocean-borne trade, while most of China was oriented inward. John King Fairbank suggested that "maritime China" was a distinct region and subculture within Chinese civilization. Maritime China is the homeland of most of the Overseas Chinese who left China before 1949. It is cut off from much of the rest of China by the mountain chains that define a narrow coastal strip. There is little hinterland, and communication was traditionally up and down the coast by boat. The one large core area along the coast is the fertile Pearl River Delta, the heart of Guangdong Province. The Pearl River Delta has long supported an extremely rich diversified agriculture and a correspondingly dense population, with both Guangzhou and Hong Kong serving as urban centers.

In recent years the rapid growth of an externally oriented economy in southeast China has transformed this region. Maritime China has always been a complex region, with many dialects and complicated overseas relationships. Over the past 25 years, the different segments of maritime China have grown together, increasingly constituting a single economic powerhouse. Investment from Hong Kong and Taiwan has built factories and new trading relationships. Of course, Taiwan and Hong Kong were traditionally parts of maritime China, but their close cultural, economic, and geographic ties with the other regions of maritime China were temporarily broken under Maoist China after 1949. As a result, those parts of Maritime China within the PRC's boundaries were surprisingly poor and backward at the end of the 1970s, and one of the first priorities of reformers after 1978 was to reestablish traditional economic links among parts of Maritime China. The early phases of China's economic opening after 1978 are largely the steps in the reconstitution of these traditional links.

Four special economic zones (SEZs) were set up in 1979–1980 to attract investors to China. Each SEZ strategically targeted a particular group of maritime Chinese as its primary source of investment. The largest SEZ, Shenzhen, was set up adjacent to Hong Kong to attract spillover investment from what was then still a British colony. The gradual dismantling of the barriers that separated Hong Kong from the rest of the Pearl River Delta has meant that multiple urban areas are progressively growing together, transforming the entire eastern delta into a single integrated economic region. Meanwhile, the Zhuhai SEZ was set up across the Pearl River, next door to the Portuguese colony of Macau. Up the coast, the Shantou SEZ was established near the Chaozhou (Teochiu) ethnic homeland to attract investment from this group, which is especially important economically in Southeast Asia. Finally, the Xiamen SEZ was designed to revive overseas links among the south Fujian (Minnan) people. People in Taiwan speak the same variety of Minnan that is spoken around Xiamen, from where most of them emigrated after the 1600s. The Minnan have long been an oceangoing, trading people, and the distinctive Minnan dialect of Chinese is spoken also in extensive commercial networks throughout southeast Asia, as well as in Taiwan and Fujian itself. As China opened up, investment from Taiwan increased dramatically, and Taiwan has begun to serve as one of the economic centers of the whole southeast region. Thus Taiwan and the Pearl River delta today serve as the dual cores of Maritime China.

The remainder of China's population is spread across the relatively arid regions of the north and northwest. A northern plateau region—consisting of Shanxi, Shaanxi, Inner Mongolia, Gansu, and Ningxia—contains almost all of these people, amounting to 10% of China's population. These people farm 18% of China's arable land, but the land is arid and of poor quality. This region accounts for 8% of the crop output and only 6% of industry. The population in the plateau region is concentrated in a few fertile river valleys—the Wei River in Shaanxi around Xi'an, and the Fen Valley in Shanxi around Taiyuan. To the west of this plateau country, people live primarily in oases or isolated fertile valleys in the northwest or are nomadic herdspeople. As one ascends to the high plateau of Tibet and Qinghai, one finds vast stretches of virtually uninhabited land.

1.4 MINERAL RESOURCES

Overall, China is a land-scarce and labor-abundant economy. With 20% of the world's population, China occupies 7% of the world's land area. China's share of world mineral wealth is roughly proportional to its share of land area, such that mineral reserves per capita are typically half or less of world averages.

Even reserves of coal, which China mines and burns in abundance, amount to only 11% of total verified world reserves. China has developed the world's fifth-largest petroleum industry, but verified reserves of petroleum and natural gas amount to 2.3% and 0.8% of the world total. There are, however, rich deposits of nonferrous minerals such as tin and copper, and especially tungsten and rare earth.

The distribution of mineral and energy resources in China is extremely uneven. Fossil fuels are predominantly in the north, which has 90% of the oil and 80% of the coal reserves. Hydroelectric potential is substantial, where there is water (the south) and relief (the west): 68% of the hydropower potential is in the Southwest macroregion. The rapidly growing southern coastal regions have virtually no energy resources. Geographic constraints, therefore, dictate that China must develop in a labor-intensive and, ultimately, knowledge-intensive path. Moreover, unrelenting environmental problems will make economic trade-offs more difficult and complex for the foreseeable future.

1.5   CONCLUSION: REGIONAL DIFFERENTIATION

Since the beginning of China's market transition, economic growth has been much more robust in the coastal provinces than in inland provinces. To some extent this difference reflects catch-up growth on the part of the coastal regions. Arguably, all three of the Far South, Southeast Coast, and Lower Yangtze macroregions were held back during the planned economy period. These macroregions entered the reform era significantly underperforming their potential, and it is not surprising that they have since grown faster than the national averages. But after 25 years of rapid growth, these southern coastal regions are now both richer and faster growing than the rest of the country. Not surprisingly, the coast-inland gap has been widely recognized as a fundamental feature of the Chinese economy. In 1999 the Chinese government officially launched the Western Development Program to give preference to western and inland provinces in investment projects and other economic development policies.

By itself, however, the idea of a coast-inland gap is too simple to capture the complexities of China's economic geography. In the first place, there is a north–south gap in growth rates that is just as significant as the east–west gap: the south is growing much faster. Indeed, the Chinese government implicitly recognized the north–south gap when it rolled out the Northeast Revitalization Program in 2003, designed to help the Northeast restructure heavy industries facing resource depletion, loss of customers, and the need for down-sizing. More fundamentally, it is inevitable that the coastal regions will emerge as the dynamic center of China's economy. This observation is especially true given China's dramatic reengagement with world trade and the high degree of openness China has achieved (see Chapters 16 and 17). Ironically, during 2005 the Chinese government even began to extend preferences to central China. In a sense, then, whereas the coastal regions received preferential poli-cies early in the reform era, from 1979 through 1999, today every region except the coast is the beneficiary of preferential policies. Each of these preferential policies is different, to be sure. But even put together, these regional devel-opment programs will not alter the fundamental shift that is occurring from China's traditional inward orientation to its new globalized and outward-looking economy. After all, the coastal provinces are not just a "strip" on the edge of China: 41% of the population lives in the coastal provinces. In a broader accounting, the five macroregions adjacent to the coast contain 59% of China's total population. It is reasonable to hope that the effects of eco-nomic growth along the coast will naturally diffuse to areas within a single macroregion.

By contrast, it may take a long time to ignite growth in the macroregions that are distant from the coast. In the far west, the half of the country west of the Aihui–Tengchong line contains only 6% of the total population, and these people are far from the spreading impact of coastal development. In fact, China's greatest development challenges are not in the vast and empty far western regions. Instead, they are in the areas where a dense population pushes up against the limits of water and what the land can provide. The line that defines these limits is precisely the Aihui–Tengchong line, slicing through the middle of the country. In a broad belt, running through Inner Mongolia, Shaanxi, Gansu, Sichuan, Guizhou, and Yunnan, China's most intractable problems of poverty are concentrated. It is in this belt that a huge population struggles to eke out a living from an ungenerous land. This is a belt of envi-ronmental degradation, including deforestation and soil erosion, and of espe-cially severe economic challenges: environmental, social, and economic problems all come together in this region. Geographical conditions and the associated environmental challenges will continue to shape China's develop-mental challenges and possibilities. The geographic endowment provides the foundation upon which economic and social development proceed and cer-tainly cannot be escaped. But at the same time, that environment is continu-ously being rebuilt through ceaseless economic activity.

BIBLIOGRAPHY

Suggestions for Further Reading

Van Slyke (1988) is a lively introduction to Chinese geography through the perspective of the Yangtze River. Chi (1963 [1936]) is still an excellent account of different regions.

There are several excellent atlases of China now available in English, but perhaps the most beautiful is Institute of Geography (2000).

Sources for Data and Figures

Figure 1.1: Based on Sun Jingzhi (1988).

Figure 1.2: Based on Leeming (1984) and Institute of Geography (2000).

Figure 1.3: Based on Institute of Geography (2000).

Figure 1.4: Based on Fairbank and Goldman (1998).

Table 1.1: World Bank, World Development Indicators, http://devdata.worldbank.org/dataonline.

Data on Chinese landforms in this chapter come primarily from Zhao Ji (1990); with additional material from Zhao Songqiao (1994) and Li Ruluan (1984). CIA (1971, 52–53) has interesting maps that explicitly show the analogies between the United States and China.

The macroregion approach was created by Skinner (1977), though the map reproduced in Figure 1.4 is from Fairbank and Goldman (1998). Statistics on macroregions are drawn from Li Ruluan, updated from *SYC*.

Details on the links between specific groups of Chinese overseas and their source areas in China are given in Zhang Xianghan et al. (1990).

Coal and petroleum reserves come from British Petroleum. Chinese verified reserves of different minerals are in *SYC* 2005, 10–12.

References

BP (2005). British Petroleum. *Statistical Review of World Energy*, June. Accessed at http://www.bp.com/statisticalreview.

Chi, Ch'ao-ting (1963 [1936]). *Key Economic Areas in Chinese History: As Revealed in the Development of Public Works for Water Control*. New York: Paragon Book Reprint Corporation.

CIA [Central Intelligence Agency] (1971). *People's Republic of China: Atlas*. Washington, DC: U.S. Government Printing Office. Most of these maps can be accessed at http://www.lib.utexas.edu/maps/china.

Fairbank, John King, and Merle Goldman (1998). *China: A New History*, enl. ed. Cambridge, MA: Belknap Press of Harvard University Press. Accessed at http://www.history.ubc.ca/lshin/teaching/311/week1/m_region.htm.

Institute of Geography, Chinese Academy of Sciences, and China Population and Environment Society, eds. (2000). *The Atlas of Population, Environment and Sustainable Development in China*. New York: Science Press.

Leeming, F. (1984). *Selected China Maps*. Leeds: Department of Geography, University of Leeds.

Li Ruluan, ed. (1984). *Ziran Dili Tongji Ziliao* [Natural Geography Statistical Materials], new ed. Beijing: Shangwu Yinshuguan.

Liu Changming (1998). "Environmental Issues and the South-North Water Transfer Scheme." *China Quarterly*, no. 156 (December), 899–910.

Skinner, G. William (1977). "Regional Urbanization in Nineteenth-Century China." In Skinner, ed., *The City in Late Imperial China*. Stanford, CA: Stanford University Press.

Sun Jingzhi (1988). *The Economic Geography of China,* Hong Kong: Oxford University Press.

SYC (Annual). *Zhongguo Tongji Nianjian* [Statistical Yearbook of China]. Beijing: Zhongguo Tongji.

Van Slyke, Lyman P. (1988). *Yangtze: Nature, History and the River.* Reading, MA: Addison-Wesley.

Zhang Xianghan et al. (1990). *Huaqiao Huaren Daguan,* 11–18. Guangzhou: Jinan Daxue.

Zhao Ji, ed. (1990). *The Natural History of China.* New York: McGraw-Hill.

Zhao Songqiao (1994). *Geography of China: Environment, Resources, Population and Development.* New York: Wiley.

2 The Chinese Economy Before 1949

The year 1949 appears at first to be a great divide in Chinese history. The government is radically different after 1949, and even more dramatic is the growth performance. Before 1949, China never launched into rapid, modern economic growth; since 1949, China's economy has always grown rapidly, despite sometimes disastrous policies imposed during Maoist times: For more than a century—from the early nineteenth to the middle of the twentieth century—China's economic performance was mediocre at best. Moreover, under pressure from the West, China disintegrated politically. The most common interpretation has been that China's economy failed in the nineteenth and early twentieth centuries and that 1949, therefore, was a real turning point. After all, the differences are so great that something fundamental must have changed.

This traditional view has been challenged by a group of economists who see the Chinese economy in the early twentieth century as having been largely successful (T. Rawski 1989; Brandt 1987, 1990; Myers 1980). Thomas Rawski (1989) presented revised estimates of aggregate output that imply slow but steady growth in per capita output after the late nineteenth century. Perhaps more important is the philosophical basis of this group's argument. They see the traditional Chinese economy as having been well suited to support economic development. There was indeed some governmental failure during the beginnings of development, but governmental failure was not significant enough to destroy the robust potential of the traditional economy. Moreover, economic development is a long-term process that consists of the accumulation of human and physical capital, together with the evolution of institutions appropriate to a modern economy. Thus this group stresses continuity between the features of the traditional economy and the rapid growth experience that became so obvious after 1949. Implicitly, China would have grown rapidly under any economic system and, lacking a socialist revolution, could have been expected to engage in development along capitalist lines.

The traditional view of Chinese society pre-1949 is strongly defended by another group of scholars, mainly historians (Eastman 1988; Esherick 1991; Richardson 1999 reviews the debate). This group stresses such societal features as the increased pressure on living standards from population growth, the absence of qualitative change in agricultural technology, the continuing pressure of class division and extraction of rents and other surpluses from the poorest farmers, and the risk of famine and disease that threatened the majority of the population. To this group, the turning point at 1949 is the result of a social as well as economic revolution. They see the traditional society as being crippled by unfair distribution of control over land and other income-producing assets. In their view, corrupt political power prevented the emergence of economic growth that could provide benefits to a broad spectrum of the population. Unable to solve its problems, the society was at the mercy of increased population pressure on limited resources. Revolution provided a way to solve some of these problems and unleashed a rapid acceleration of economic growth.

One side (composed primarily of economists) stresses economic continuity—the presence of favorable economic conditions on either side of a divide. In their view, the acceleration of economic growth after 1949 could only have occurred if many favorable conditions were already in place. An even more dramatical acceleration of growth in Hong Kong and Taiwan after the 1950s supports the idea that conditions were favorable for capitalist growth. The other side (composed primarily of historians) stresses the social discontinuity—the presence of radically different social conditions on either side of the 1949 divide. In that view, the sudden acceleration of growth indicates that some new set of conditions was in place that enabled a "takeoff" to occur. Did the Chinese economy "fail" before 1949, and if so, why? Was the Chinese traditional economy well suited to economic development? If so, why was the actual response to the Western challenge so feeble? Was a basis laid, in the pre-1949 era, for the vigorous growth after 1949? To begin to address these questions, we first examine the traditional Chinese economy during three broad time periods, then evaluate the legacy of the traditional economy.

2.1 THE TRADITIONAL ECONOMY, 1127–1911

2.1.1 High-Productivity Traditional Agriculture

Chinese traditional society was overwhelmingly rural, with over 90% of the population living in the countryside. Farmers employed a sophisticated agricultural technology to wrest high crop yields per unit of land cultivated (King

1911). These yields depended on the massive application of human labor to small plots of farmland. A complex and highly productive agricultural technology developed, based not on modern science, but on the trial and error of generations of farmers. A "traditional triad" of farm technology consisted of three key elements: selected seed varieties, organic fertilizer, and irrigation. Early ripening rice was adapted from Southeast Asia as early as the Southern Song dynasty (AD 1127–1279). Its short growing season allowed farmers to plant two or more crops of grain annually on a single plot of land. Organic fertilizers were applied to fields to maintain soil fertility. Every available nutrient was recycled into the soil: Most important was manure from humans ("night soil") and animals, but farmers also added pond mud, lime, and green algae to the soil—even the clay bricks used to make chimneys were crushed and spread on fields after they had absorbed enough smoke to build up organic compounds. Finally, sophisticated irrigation systems allowed farmers to precisely control the water on their fields and take full advantage of better crop varieties and fertilizer. Rice shoots were sprouted in seedbeds, then transplanted to flooded fields. As the rice plants matured, fields were drained and the ripe plants were harvested. The productivity of each element was enhanced by the presence of the other elements of the triad.

This highly productive traditional agricultural system could function only with the massive and intensive application of labor. Preparing fields and irrigation canals, hauling fertilizer, and transplanting seedlings were all backbreaking work. The average product per unit of land was high, but the average product per unit of labor input was low. Many farmers barely produced enough to feed their families. But farmers were always able to find some work for an additional hand: the marginal product of labor was even lower than the average product, but it did not drop quickly to zero as more laborers were added. A growing population was supported, but incomes and consumption standards remained low. One of the most striking characteristics of this agricultural system—in contrast to that which evolved in Europe over the same period—is the limited role of animals in farm work and human diet. Meat was a luxury for most Chinese, protein consumption was inadequate, and almost all calories and protein came from grain.

The intensive application of human labor to small plots of land reminded early Western visitors to China of gardening rather than of farming as they knew it, but these observers were also uniformly impressed by the high yields and the intense utilization of resources they observed. The persistent recycling of wastes changed the composition of soils and served to maintain productivity. "Owing to many centuries of cultivation, there were no natural soils left [by the nineteenth century in China]. All soils were man-made in varying degrees" (Vermeer, 1988, 224). The high-productivity system was created first in the Lower Yangtze, then spread to lowland and riverside areas where irrigation was feasible. Population growth pushed farmers higher up the slopes of hilly country. The introduction of New World crops—especially corn (maize) and potatoes—allowed farmers to spread onto new lands less suited to traditional crops.

This agricultural system supported a growing population for 400 years. Population quintupled between 1400 and 1820: from an estimated 72 million in 1400, at the beginning of the Ming dynasty (1368–1644), population grew to around 381 million in 1820. China's population grew at a rate of 0.4% per year over this long period, quite fast for a premodern population (Chapter 7). By 1820, China accounted for an estimated 36% of total world population (Maddison 1998; Wang 1999). Moreover, it appears that living standards in China were stable until the early 1800s—there is no evidence of large increases or decreases—and close to average world living standards. China thus accounted for about a third of world GDP in 1820.

2.1.2 The Commercialized Countryside

The densely populated countryside supported a thick network of markets. In areas that were suitable to the building of canals—particularly the Lower Yangtze and Pearl River deltas—regions were tied together by a highly developed system of water transport. The major rivers, particularly the Yangtze, provided links among regions, while the Grand Canal linked the food-surplus Lower Yangtze with the food-deficit North China Plain. For places on the water transport network, even heavy and bulky commodities could enter into trade. Local markets were joined into channels for interregional trade. Dense population and transport networks supported a highly commercialized premodern economy, including sophisticated institutions, competitive markets, and a small-scale "bottom-heavy" economy (Zelin 1991; Brandt 1990; Naquin and E. Rawski 1987).

2.1.2.1 Sophisticated Institutions

Institutional support for the economy included the following:

• Widespread use of money. Paper money was one-third or more of total money in circulation as of 1820.

• Familiarity with large formal organizations. Clan or lineage organizations had extensive economic functions. Sometimes formal shares were issued to regulate an individual's membership in a corporate-lineage or local-place association.

• Advanced commercial procedures. Written contracts were ubiquitous. Contracts extended beyond business transactions to regulate obligations to family, the gods, and the afterlife. As early as the first century AD, "tomb contracts" proving the right of the dead to occupy a given plot of ground were buried with the dead. The use of middlemen in personal and commercial transactions was nearly universal.

• Legal and customary institutions that supported the economy. Courts existed and were used for lawsuits. Interregional trade was often regulated by local-place and merchants' associations that helped resolve disputes and created support networks.

• Traditional banks that allowed merchants to transfer funds nationwide.

2.1.2.2   Competitive Markets

• Highly competitive markets for most products. Recent studies of such markets as coal and iron, textiles, and tea confirm that each of these was characterized by numerous suppliers, easy entry, and frequent exit.

• Competitive and efficient markets for land and labor.

• Substantial social mobility. There was no aristocracy or castes defined by birth. Individuals frequently migrated in search of economic opportunity. There were few socially imposed barriers to mobility. While inequality was significant, potential social mobility was real.

2.1.2.3   Small-Scale, "Bottom-Heavy" Economy

Agriculture was based on individual, small-scale households. There were no plantations or large landed estates. Most nonagricultural production was also small-scale and done by rural households. Textiles, leather goods, and iron tools—as well as food products such as wine, tea, sugar, noodles, and edible oils—were all produced by microenterprises in the countryside. Many households farmed, manufactured handicrafts, and marketed their own output. Thus the Chinese traditional economy was a vigorous, household-based economy.

Households were also directly linked to a number of different markets. In many cases the consecutive stages of a production chain were handled by separate specialized households connected by markets. For instance, this kind of vertical segmentation characterized the manufacture of silk cloth. The raising of silkworms, care of silkworm cocoons, spinning of raw silk thread, and weaving of silk cloth were all carried out separately by specialized households or small firms that dealt with each other on the marketplace. Thus chains of small processors and middlemen linked household producers, merchants, and consumers.

One of the first successes of a "globalizing" China was the rapid growth of the tea export industry after 1880. At its peak more than a million households, mainly in Fujian Province, participated in the tea industry. The average farm household produced a couple of hundred pounds of tea per year, which was in turn processed by hundreds of small tea factories. This export industry grew rapidly around the turn of the twentieth century. But the Chinese system did not cope well with the rise of competition from Japan and India after the twentieth century began. Competitiveness required standardization and reliable high quality, which China's small-scale and dispersed producers were not organized to provide. As a result, Chinese exporters in the 1920s were pushed out of a world market they had created. As the export industry declined, households exited tea production as rapidly as they had entered it.

This was an economy with a fluid and flexible allocation of resources. On the positive side, resources and labor moved efficiently to the use with the highest rate of return, and exited such activities just as rapidly when returns fell. On the other hand, economic activity was fragmented into small-scale businesses with little capital. For example, cotton fabric was woven in three quarters of China's counties, but large-scale textile mills, the foundation of the industrial revolution elsewhere, did not emerge in China until the twentieth century. Accumulation of capital into large enterprises was either very difficult or else inefficient compared with dispersed household-based production. Indeed, this fluidity may have been partially the result of a need to avoid risk, a need to prevent wealth from being too obvious to potential predators or rapacious officials. Nevertheless, it is impossible not to be impressed by the sophistication of the traditional Chinese economy. We would have expected the traditional Chinese economy to respond well to new challenges and opportunities presented by the impact of the West. And yet, as we shall see, this was not to be the case.

2.1.3   Crisis of the Traditional Economy?

Despite its enormous strengths, there are signs that the Chinese traditional economy was running up against increasingly severe limitations during the course of the nineteenth century. Inexorable population growth was placing an increased burden on resources that were, at least for the time being, relatively fixed. By the end of the eighteenth century, virtually all the potentially cultivated land in China was being farmed, except for a final frontier in Manchuria, in the Northeast. Elvin (1973) argued that China was in a "high level equilibrium trap." Traditional technologies permitted high levels of output, but the opportunity for new investments to further increase output was gone. Riskin (1975) has shown that there was ample elite income available to be invested, so the explanation must be that the productive potential of the traditional technologies was approaching exhaustion, or that institutions did not support productive investment.

During the peak of its capabilities in the eighteenth century, the Qing dynasty had been able to provide the main public goods needed to maintain economic stability. But by the end of the eighteenth century, the Qing dynasty had clearly entered a period of dynastic decline. The reserves of food in public granaries began to decline after the 1790s. Maintenance of large-scale irrigation networks, crucial to high agricultural productivity, began to deteriorate (Elvin and Liu 1998; Will and Wong 1991). Farmers encroached on wetlands and lakes that were essential parts of the complex river ecologies. As population continued to grow, the rural population became increasingly vulnerable to any breakdown in the rural system, with the result that floods or droughts could cause terrible famines. For example, the Wei River Valley, site of the ancient city of Xi'an, had practiced sophisticated irrigation for over 2,000 years. But by the nineteenth century, this infrastructure had broken down and left the population vulnerable to droughts. Subsequently (1928–1931), two million perished in a catastrophic famine after three years of consecutive drought. Even at its best, the Chinese imperial government was always a thin layer upon a vast population. Imperial government revenues were never more than 2%–3% of national income. Around 1800 there was only one government worker per 32,000 people in China, compared with one for every 600 to 800 in Europe at the same time (Perkins 1967). The government was incapable of mobilizing the funding or manpower needed to support the economy as the population grew and public infrastructure deteriorated.

The impact of these social stresses fell disproportionately upon the poor. The fact that this was a fluid, competitive, market-based economy should not allow us to forget the grinding poverty that weighed upon the vast majority of Chinese. Income inequality was significant. Imperial degree–holding "gentry," who amounted to much less than 1% of the population, received about 20% of total national income (Zhang Zhongli 1955). Land distribution was not extremely unequal: given the importance of labor inputs, small farms were an efficient organizational form. But there were significant disparities in income that were crucial for an economy at such a low standard of living. Tenancy was much more common in the wet rice lands of the south, particularly in the richest delta lands of the lower Yangtze and Guangdong. In the north, tenancy was uncommon, and the main problem was fragmentation into farms too small to support a family because the marginal product of labor was very low. By the time data are available—from large-scale rural surveys carried out during the 1920s and 1930s—they show substantial tenancy. According to a 1931–1936 survey conducted by the National Agricultural Research Bureau of the Republic of China, 46% of rural households were owners, 24% owner-tenants, and 30% tenants. Rents were high—about 45% of total output. Many farmers were in debt—various estimates collected by Feuerwerker (1969, 87) suggest that 40%–55% of households were in debt, paying annual interest rates of 20%–40%. For heavily indebted tenant farmers—indeed, for owners of small plots struggling to survive—life was very difficult indeed. Many poor farmers were unable to marry or sustain households and helplessly experienced the extinguishing of their lineage, which was the most serious offense against parents and ancestors. Sophisticated traditional agriculture allowed the growth of a huge population, but that population was highly vulnerable to any breakdown in the agricultural system that supported it. As Tawney (1964) put it in the 1930s, "The Chinese peasant is like a man standing on tiptoe up to his nose in water—the slightest ripple is enough to drown him."

It appears that China was pressing up against the limits of economic possibility given traditional technologies—creating severe crisis—just at the time when a massive challenge was developing from the West. It is clear that ecological exhaustion deprived the economy of readily available materials, such as lumber and metal, and that environmental problems were becoming more severe. The Chinese government was not only unable to develop a coherent response to the external challenge; it was even unable to maintain its own most basic functions. During the 1860s southern China erupted in the Taiping Rebellion, which lasted a decade and ultimately devastated much of the lower Yangtze valley. Thus China entered a century-long period of decline just as the European countries were entering an unprecedented period of economic and population growth.

2.1.4   The Failed Response to the West and Japan

During the nineteenth century foreign powers began to have an increasingly severe political, military, and economic impact on China. Potentially, the economic stimulus from this contact could have been positive, but in fact China during the nineteenth century tumbled into profound social crisis. This crisis was certainly aggravated by the political and military challenge from the West, even though it goes beyond anything we can explain by the direct Western impact. Foreign encroachment on China began during a period of dynastic weakness, and it began with an economic crisis. For many centuries China had run an export surplus with the outside world, including Europe. Imported silver paid for traditional Chinese exports of silk, tea, and porcelain. Steady silver inflow expanded the money supply and contributed to economic expansion until the 1820s. But in the early 1800s, Britain was the dominant world power, and British merchants were unhappy with the steady drain of silver into China. They searched for a commodity that would appeal to Chinese consumers and that could be imported into China and redress the trade imbalance. They finally located such a commodity in opium. Chests of opium—grown in India—were imported by British merchants through Hong Kong into China. By the 1830s, China was importing more than it was exporting. China now faced both an economic problem—a slowdown caused by slow adjustment to a shrinking supply of monetary metals—and a new social problem, opium addiction.

Chinese attempts to stop the inflow of opium led to the Opium War with Britain in 1839. The British crushed the hopelessly outmoded Chinese defenses, and in the Treaty of Nanking (1842) forced China to cede Hong Kong to British rule and open the first five Treaty Ports to foreign control. Through 1895, China fought four more wars against foreign encroachment and lost each one of them. After each loss, China was forced to pay reparations to the victors and open more Chinese cities to foreign residence and control. The Qing government, already enfeebled, was buffeted by internal and external crises, and never developed an effective response. Internally, the Taiping Rebellion of the 1860s and the Boxer Rebellion of the 1890s were the most notable sources of disruption. Externally, a range of foreign powers attempted to carve out separate spheres of influence in China, so the Chinese government had to cope with multiple adversaries.

Economically, politically, and militarily, Japan gradually took over from the Britain the role of the main foreign power encroaching on China, beginning with the Sino-Japanese War of 1895, which led to the seizure of Taiwan and its incorporation into the Japanese empire. One reason for China's relatively feeble response to foreign pressure may have been that it was under steady pressure for more than a century from a series of different adversaries and never had a "breathing space." In the wake of the antiforeign Boxer Rebellion, an allied force from eight countries (six European plus the United States and Japan) occupied Beijing and forced the Qing government to sign the 1901 Boxer Protocol. Essentially, the imperial government was placed under house arrest, and control over tariffs and other tax revenues was ceded to the foreign powers to guarantee payment of a huge indemnity. It is hardly surprising that the Qing government collapsed 10 years later, in 1911.

China's historical opening to the outside world thus coincided with a prolonged period of national humiliation. National weakness tempted foreign aggression, and foreign conquest further enfeebled China. Foreign investment was not allowed in China before the 1895 Treaty of Shimonoseki, which ended the Sino-Japanese War and provided for China to accept foreign investment. The beginnings of modern industry in China date from shortly after the signing of this treaty. Foreign investment was overwhelmingly concentrated in Treaty Ports, which were governed by foreign powers and not subject to Chinese jurisdiction. At their peak, there were more than 80 Treaty Ports, of which Shanghai was the most important. Extraterritoriality (foreign exemption from domestic law) and foreign control of Treaty Ports and customs revenues were politically controversial until their abolition in the mid-twentieth century. Because of this association between foreign contact and national humiliation, policies of economic and political "opening" to foreigners have remained a sensitive issue through the present day.

The Chinese response to the foreign challenge contrasted sharply with that of Japan. Under foreign threat, Japan was able to strengthen the national government and stave off direct foreign intervention. The Japanese state was strengthened by a radical land reform that redistributed as much as 10% of GNP to the government and to a rising class of entrepreneurial landowners. The government then rapidly initiated a state-sponsored program of industrialization, technology transfer, and manpower training. The Chinese government was incapable of mounting such a response. Some progressive Chinese officials understood the type of measures required to meet the foreign challenge. In the late 1800s these officials did sponsor some industrial projects, including most notably an iron and steel mill in Wuhan and shipyards and armories in the Shanghai area. These projects were called "official supervision and merchant management" (*guandu shangban*), because the projects were government sponsored but with management delegated to experienced merchants. Some of these projects were simply too ambitious to succeed. Poor management and quality problems plagued the Wuhan steel mill; and even with a government guaranteed monopoly as supplier of rails for the first railroad, demand was weak. The Wuhan mill, like most of the other projects, ultimately failed.

Maddison (1998) has compiled some long-run estimates of world population and GDP. The estimates are very rough, but they provide some idea of the relative changes that were occurring during this period. By 1913, after recovering from the Taiping catastrophes, the population of China was about 437 million. Population growth since 1820 had dropped off dramatically, and China had fallen from one-third to one-quarter of total world population. More critically, in 1820, China's overall GDP had accounted for 32% of world GDP; but by 1913, it had declined dramatically to only 9% of world GDP. Estimated per capita GDP had been 90% of the world average in 1820; and although China's per capita GDP declined only slightly between then and 1913, in relative terms it sank to less than 40% of the world average, since this was the period when the economies of Europe and the United States surged ahead. Because of the choice of years and population estimates, these figures might slightly overstate China's relative decline, but the general picture is surely correct. From being one of the centers of the civilized world, China had descended to a position of obvious underdevelopment and backwardness. Given the collapse in relative position, the aggressive and predatory attitude of Western colonialism, and the complete failure of the Chinese government to develop a coherent response to the West, it is understandable that the impact of the West turned out to be highly traumatic.

2.2   THE BEGINNINGS OF INDUSTRIALIZATION, 1912–1937

After the collapse of the Qing dynasty and the 1911 Revolution, China entered a new phase in which political and economic change became evident to all. Modern industrial development began, and modern transportation and communication links opened up new possibilities for other sectors. Immediately after 1911 came warlord domination, political fragmentation, and civil war, but in 1927 the Nationalist (Guomindang) Party unified the nation. For 10 years, until the Japanese invasion in 1937, China enjoyed relative peace, and the Nationalist government was able to begin building the institutional framework for development. This period is often called the "Nanjing decade" after the capital of the Nationalist government, during which the government began, tentatively, to invest in such things as education and agricultural extension services. A national surveying project led to an inventory of national resources, and national development plans were drawn up. Few of these activities came to fruition during this period, but groundwork was laid for the future. Skilled individuals were trained, and new technologies were developed, such as the creation of new crop strains. Metaphorically and literally, some seeds of future growth were sown.

2.2.1   Industry

From a tiny base, modern factory production grew at 8%–9% annually between 1912 and 1936, quite a rapid pace of industrialization at this time (John Chang 1969). In 1933 modern factories produced 2% of GDP and employed a million workers, although this was only 0.4% of China's labor force. Two distinct patterns are apparent in this initial industrial growth: "Treaty Port industrialization" and "Manchurian industrialization."

Modern industry began in enclaves in the Treaty Ports during the early twentieth century. This was the dominant pattern of industrialization in China proper (i.e., China "inside the Great Wall," excluding Manchuria). Foreigners began to operate factories around the turn of the century, and Chinese quickly followed suit. Early enclave industrialization was concentrated in light, consumer-goods industries, that is to say, in industries at the downstream end of the value chain (see Chapter 3 for further discussion). According to the 1933 census of industry in China proper, textiles made up 42% of total output, and food products (including tobacco) a further 26%. Modern industry was concentrated in a few treaty ports. For example, 70% of textiles were produced in the three cities of Shanghai, Tianjin, and Qingdao. Shanghai alone accounted for 40% of industrial output in 1933. Output from modern textile mills grew rapidly, replacing imports. By the 1930s, China had basically stopped importing textiles and was instead importing significant quantities of raw cotton to feed its own mills.

Enclave industrialization was started by foreigners and grew under the impetus of foreign example and competition. However, native Chinese capitalists quickly became major actors in this process. By the 1930s some 78% of the value of factory output came from Chinese-owned firms, and they were gaining market share. It is clear that the skills necessary for modern industry diffused quickly. Successful Chinese industrialists often had some kind of foreign experience or contact with foreign businesses that provided their initial entry into modern industry. These skills spread rapidly, though, and helped form a basis for further industrialization, particularly in Shanghai. One example was the Shanghai Dalong Machinery Company. Initially set up as a ship repair station, it gradually diversified into repair of machinery for the textile industry. By the late 1920s it began to produce its own models of textile machinery. Spillover of modern industrial skills had clearly begun in some parts of China. Another example is the prominent Rong family of native capitalists, headed by Rong Zongjing, who established the first modern flour mill in Wuxi (outside Shanghai) in 1904. By the 1930s, Rong family enterprises were producing almost a quarter of the cotton textiles and a third of the factory-milled flour produced by Chinese-owned factories.

A very different pattern of industrialization emerged in Manchuria (the Northeast; Table 2.1). Investment in Manchuria was carried out primarily by the Japanese government and by quasi-official affiliates of the Japanese government such as the Southern Manchurian Railroad. Japanese government-sponsored industrialization of Manchuria was carried out to meet a mixture of economic and strategic objectives. Development was focused on heavy industries and railroads. The Japanese developed a dense network of railroads

Table 2.1
Two patterns of industrialization

	China proper	Manchuria
Market	Domestic China	Japanese industry
Ownership	Chinese, foreign	Foreign
Structure	Light, consumer goods	Heavy, mining, producer goods
Skill formation	Steady accumulation	Little transfer of skills
Linkages	Backward	Few or none

and actively exploited the rich deposits of coal and iron ore in the region. For example, the Japanese developed a huge steel mill at Anshan, which is still today one of China's largest producers of steel. Construction began in 1917, and the Japanese poured investment into the mill for 15 years—funded by the Southern Manchurian Railroad—before production was stabilized and profits began. Nowhere in China proper would we have been able to find an investor capable of sustaining an industrial project that required so much capital.

Japanese-sponsored industry in Manchuria was expected to be profitable if possible, but strategic considerations were very important. Most Manchurian industries produced raw materials for Japanese domestic industries. Japan was the most important market. Machinery to operate the factories was imported from Japan. Managers were discouraged from subcontracting with small Chinese firms for inputs or for maintenance and repairs. Moreover, skilled positions within industry were intentionally reserved for Japanese nationals. Thus there were few linkages and spillover effects from vigorous industrialization in Manchuria. In 1933, Manchurian industry accounted for only 14% of total output. However, the Manchurian share of value added was nearly twice this, because of the greater importance of heavy industries with a higher ratio of net to gross output. Moreover, Manchurian industry was poised for dramatic expansion during the subsequent period.

2.2.2   Evaluation: How Broad Was Development in the 1912–1937 Period?

There is wide agreement that a small but significant modern sector grew in China during the 1920s and 1930s. Less clear is the impact that this modern sector had on traditional sectors. Rawski (1989) in particular stresses the potential positive impact on traditional sectors of growing demand from modern sectors, growing cities, and increasing trade. Ingeniously extracting information from limited data, Rawski estimates that agriculture, handicrafts, and traditional transport all had positive growth between 1914 and 1936. Combined with rapid growth of the small modern sector, this finding leads him to conclude that GDP per capita rose modestly but significantly over the period. The complexity of the relationship between modern and traditional sectors can be seen by examining the single most important industrial sector, cotton textiles, on which extensive research has been done (Richardson 1999, 58). The textile industry has two main segments, spinning and weaving, and the impact of growing factory production was very different on the traditional hand-spinning and hand-weaving industries. Factory spinning is much more efficient than hand spinning, so factories took over most of the growing market. Household spinning declined by more than a third through the 1930s, causing significant hardship in regions where farm households had specialized in spinning. Factory weaving also grew rapidly, taking a third of the market by the 1930s, but in this case the total market increased by more than enough to accommodate a significant increase in hand-weaving output as well. Hand weaving, it turns out, produces a warm and durable product much prized by rural people. Cheaper machine-spun yarn made it possible to produce a lower-cost blended fabric with greater durability and a larger market than traditional homespun.

The cotton textile industry thus exemplifies the complexity of the impact of modern technologies. Some areas benefited, stimulated by new technologies and new sources of foreign and domestic demand. Other areas lost out, as their products were unable to compete with new products. In agriculture, increased commercialization allowed intensification to continue without a technological revolution. Growing cities in eastern China increased the local demand for urban-oriented products, in particular cotton, peanuts, vegetables, fruit, rapeseed, and tung oil. In suburban areas there were also increased opportunities for off-farm employment. Was the introduction of new crops and the attendant commercialization sufficiently widespread to keep rural incomes from declining, or even lead to an increase? Clearly, there were a handful of regions that benefited from increased opportunities, particularly those around growing coastal cities. Most farmers, and especially those in the interior regions, continued to operate on the margin of subsistence as they had for centuries, and they probably noticed little impact. Industrialization had clearly made a start; a foundation had been laid for future progress; but industrialization had not begun to fundamentally change the overall structure of the Chinese economy.

In a broader sense, this was a vibrant society laying the basis for future development. Literacy gradually began to increase. Beginning with individuals born after 1920, there is a gradual but steady improvement in literacy rates that even the subsequent war does not interrupt. Moreover, China was quite open to foreign influence during this period. Some 100,000 Chinese students went abroad for long-term study. The largest number went to Japan, and significant groups went to the United States and Europe as well. As of 1936, 370,000 foreigners were resident in China. This large interchange created substantial flows of technology, as well as creating an open and stimulating intellectual and cultural environment. Shanghai became the center of a vigorous hybrid modern culture. Although society was divided by sharp political and social fissures, it seemed to be moving forward rapidly.

2.3   WAR AND CIVIL WAR, 1937–1949

A steadily increasing Japanese presence loomed over the successes of the interwar period. Japan had already gained a toehold in Manchuria when it seized the Liaodong Peninsula from Russia in 1905. Moreover, Japan received the former German concessions in Shandong after World War I. In 1931, Japan established the puppet state of Manchukuo, effectively extending control to all of Manchuria. And in 1937 the Marco Polo Bridge incident outside Beijing marked the beginning of the Japanese invasion of China proper. For China, this initiated a nearly unbroken period of warfare that lasted more than a decade, until the Communist victory of 1949.

War brought mass suffering to the population and serious damage to the economy. The disruption of war created conditions that allowed China's civil war between Nationalists and Communists to fester. The Japanese invasion weakened the Nationalist government, and Communist guerrilas were able to gain a new legitimacy by fighting the Japanese. The end of the Pacific war in 1945 merely laid the stage for a final showdown between Nationalist and Communist armies. The fog of war also obscures our understanding of the important changes that occurred during this decade. The wartime economy is often omitted from descriptions of China's development. In fact, however, several important changes occurred in this 12-year period.

2.3.1   The Rise and Fall of a Japan-Centered East Asian Economy

Rapid military industrialization in Manchuria under Japanese sponsorship serves to throw light on a more general phenomenon of East Asian development through the 1940s. During this period, a Japan-centered East Asian economic system was coming into existence. Fostered in part by the explicit imperialist calculations of the Japanese government and in part by the intrinsic economic dynamism of East Asia, the Japan-centered economic system had a distinct structure. In some respects, patterns of economic development in

China are easier to perceive if we ask how the different regions of China were related to the Japanese economic system (Ho 1984).

At the core of that system was Japan itself. Most manufacturing and services, as well as government, were reserved for Japan. Next came an inner circle of food producers, primarily Taiwan and Korea. These were incorporated into the empire; and although political repression was intense, the Japanese managed these "assets" carefully, since they were seen as part of the permanent inner circle of the Japanese empire. In both Taiwan and Korea, the Japanese carried out land surveys and strengthened the tax base. They built a good transportation infrastructure and improved education, agricultural extension, and health care. Mortality declined in both colonies, and literacy—defined as ability to read and write Japanese!—increased.

Next came a middle circle of raw-material and semiprocessed-goods suppliers. Manchuria was the primary example (Korea also produced some industrial materials). Manchuria produced both agricultural materials (soybeans and soy-cake fertilizers) for Japan and also crucial industrial materials. Ironically, there was also petroleum in Manchuria, but the Japanese did not discover it. Japanese policy toward Manchuria was more frankly exploitative than toward Taiwan. There were few efforts to foster broad-based economic growth or to spread the benefits of growth to the population. Finally, an outer circle, including most of China proper, was composed of regions with potential markets and sites for investment and future expansion. By the mid-1930s, Japan had surpassed Britain to become the largest foreign investor in Shanghai (at a time when two-thirds of foreign investment in China proper was in Shanghai). The various regions of the Japanese economic empire interacted in a reasonably well functioning economic system. With the Japanese defeat in the Pacific war, this system collapsed. After 1949, China withdrew from the East Asian economy, and East Asian economic integration did not reemerge until many decades later.

2.3.2 The Rise of Manchuria

Even though the Japanese imperial project ultimately collapsed, its contribution to building the industrial economy of Manchuria turned out to be long lasting. Manchurian industrialization actually accelerated during the early war years, growing at least 14% annually between 1936 and 1942. By contrast, industrial output in Shanghai and the rest of China proper peaked in 1936 and never regained prewar output levels until after 1949. By 1942, Manchuria produced the bulk of China's electric power, iron, and cement, and more than half of industrial output value. By the end of the war, the *majority* of China's industrial capacity was in Manchuria.

2.3.3   Increased State Intervention

During the war the Nationalist government retreated into the interior of China, setting up a temporary capital at Chongqing in Sichuan (Kirby 1990, 1992). Wartime pressures, as is always the case, led to an increase in state intervention in the economy. Before the war there had been no significant public sector in Chinese industry. In order to move industry inland from Shanghai and build new inland military industrial capacity, the Guomindang government turned to a kind of planning commission, called the Natural Resources Commission (NRC), to run government-sponsored development. Originally focused on mineral development, the NRC was staffed primarily by engineers and gained a reputation as a relatively efficient and honest department of the government. By the early 1940s the NRC was running factories with about 160,000 workers (compared with the one million total factory workers in 1933). Of all industry in unoccupied China, state-run firms accounted for 70% of the capital and 32% of the labor.

Meanwhile, in occupied Shanghai, the Japanese authorities were restructuring industry to support their war aims. Many Shanghai firms were converted to military production, and output of machinery and armaments increased while consumer-goods output dropped. By the end of the war a large part of Shanghai industry was being run by the Japanese military authorities. Already the largest foreign investor in Shanghai, Japan confiscated many factories during the war and forced some Chinese capitalists into collaboration. All these firms were taken over by the Guomindang in 1945. The combination of NRC-developed industries and confiscated Japanese and collaborator factories gave the Nationalist government a large industrial stake in the late 1940s, with the government controlling about two-thirds of modern industrial capital. By 1947 the Chinese government controlled 90% of iron and steel output, two-thirds of electricity, and 45% of cement output. In addition, most major banks and transportation companies were government controlled. This state-run economy in embryo was taken over by the Communist government after 1949.

2.3.4   Inflation

Attempting to pay for the war, yet separated from its economic base in the lower Yangtze, the Nationalist government turned to printing money to finance operations. The result was accelerating inflation, and ultimately hyperinflation. As the government collapsed, inflation became worse. If the Shanghai prewar price level is taken as 100, the price level in 1948 was 660 million. Severe macroeconomic imbalances threatened to cripple the economy.

2.4 LEGACIES OF THE PRE–1949 ECONOMY

2.4.1 Legacy for the Socialist Era (1949–1978)

The immediate legacy of the war years was extreme disruption and serious damage to the economic infrastructure. Destruction of industrial capital and deterioration of agricultural infrastructure (particularly irrigation networks) were serious, and they crippled the economy. At the same time, financial chaos, manifested in hyperinflation, required immediate remedial action that inevitably detracted from short-run economic development. Moreover, war had disrupted whatever economic growth had begun in the 1920s and 1930s, so China was still very poor, probably slightly behind India at this time (Table 2.2).

Several of the adverse economic experiences pre-1949 may have contributed, ironically, to the relatively smooth adoption of socialist institutions after 1949. The Chinese experience with foreign aggression from 1839 through 1945—from the Opium War through the Anti-Japanese War—naturally caused China to be deeply suspicious of Western institutions and world views. China developed a strong aversion to foreign dominance that led to support for closed-door socialist development strategies. Moreover, the reputation of the Nationalist government—the primary opponent of the Communists—was seriously compromised by hyperinflation and by its inability to manage the economy between 1945 and 1949. More generally, the chaos, damage, and suffering of more than a decade of war made the Chinese population willing to accept even a repressive government if it could credibly promise peace and a degree of economic security.

More concretely, wartime changes in the economy aided the Communist government in the execution of its socialist industrialization strategy. The

Table 2.2
A benchmark comparison: China 1952 and India 1950

	China 1952	India 1950
GNP per capita (1952$)	50	60
Population (million)	573	358
Rice yields (ton/acre)	2.5	1.3
Wheat yields (ton/acre)	1.1	0.7
Industrial output per capita		
Coal (kg)	96	97
Steel (kg)	2	4
Electricity (kW)	0.005	0.04
Cotton spindles	0.01	0.03
Railroads (km; 1936)	20,746	72,000

Japanese had begun the task of developing a core of heavy industry in Manchuria. Subsequently, those industries were seized by the Soviet Army, then passed ultimately into Chinese government hands. In China proper the combination of NRC-developed industries and companies confiscated by Japanese authorities created a foundation for the victorious Chinese Communist Party (CCP) to establish direct control over the industrial sector. In fact, the Nationalist government had even created the nucleus of a planning apparatus, and many skilled officials from the Nationalist Natural Resource Commission even stayed on to work under the new People's Republic of China. Thus the infant Communist government did not have to start from scratch, nor did it have to engage in politically sensitive nationalizations of industry for the first several years.

By 1949, China was still very poor, but development had nevertheless begun. China had a relatively good endowment of human capital. Literacy rates were reasonably high and had already begun increasing. A small university system had been created, and skilled individuals had been trained abroad. Some modern industrial and transport capital had been created that could serve as a nucleus for further development. The socialist development strategy followed between 1949 and 1978 turned its back on the vitality of the traditional economy, but ironically, the fruits of past success dropped into the lap of the new government, which received something like a mandate for its new approach to development.

2.4.2 Legacy for the Post–1978 Market Economy

Important as the legacy of the traditional economy was to the socialist era, it was arguably even more important to the post-1978 market economy. As China began to open up, familiarity with the traditional household-based economic system provided a robust potential to adapt to new economic opportunities. Everywhere in China after 1978, we saw the return of the traditional. Most important, small-scale household businesses sprang up throughout China to meet the market needs that had been neglected under socialism. Under the general rubric of "township and village enterprises," rural businesses grew rapidly in many areas and many different organizational forms, but nowhere more vigorously than in those parts of China where the densely populated, highly commercialized countryside had flourished (Chapter 10). Traditional economic centers suddenly revived with astonishing speed. The Lower Yangtze macroregion began to reclaim its traditional economic primacy, while the Northeast (heartland of the planned economy) receded in importance. There was even a revival of traditional market-based organizational forms, in which large numbers of very-small-scale specialized firms coordinated through markets with upstream and downstream producers. This pattern was exemplified by the intense entrepreneurial development of private business in Wenzhou, along the southeastern coast. Indeed, that China has been able to grow so rapidly after 1978 is due in no small part precisely to the entrepreneurial and competitive behaviors that had been nourished by the traditional economy.

Traditional links with parts of "maritime China" outside the People's Republic of China also revived quickly. The Special Economic Zones (SEZs) established early in the reform era reflected the importance Chinese leaders placed on reestablishing ties across boundaries (Chapter 1). Indeed, the rapid economic growth of Hong Kong and Taiwan during the 1960s and 1970s could in itself be considered a continuation and vindication of the traditional economy. After all, these were regions within the traditional Chinese economy that had followed a path of evolutionary growth from traditional beginnings and had relied primarily on small firms to jump-start economic development. After 1978 the capabilities that firms in Hong Kong and Taiwan had developed were reintegrated with the labor and other resources within the People's Republic, creating explosive growth of foreign trade. In this respect, as well, the traditional economy laid down a highly positive legacy for development after 1978.

Finally, the traditional economy may have left a complex legacy shaping the nature of the transition from plan to market. Foreign intrusion into China was still a sensitive issue in the late 1970s. SEZs were promoted by Deng Xiaoping to jump-start the process of economic opening. The SEZs limited the scope of foreign incursion, but simultaneously demonstrated that policymakers were willing to overcome their traditional aversion to foreign domination. The resulting policy echoed some features of the Treaty Ports forced on China in the nineteenth century, but this time under Chinese sovereignty. These early experiments with SEZs may have contributed to the distinctive "dual track" approach that became a defining feature of Chinese institutional transformation (Chapter 4). The SEZs allowed a new set of market friendly rules to operate in the interstices of the planned economy, foreshadowing the broader transformation of the Chinese economy. Indeed China's approach to the transition overall, including a fiercely independent resolve to pursue a reform program with "Chinese characteristics," may plausibly be linked to the traumatic 100 years of encounter with the West.

In this and many other respects, China's contemporary economy includes a rediscovery of the traditional. Did China's traditional economy fail? It would be more accurate to say that the positive potential and achievements of China's traditional economy were repressed for years. War, civil war, and socialism seemed to make the traditional economy inadequate and irrelevant. From our contemporary standpoint, however, the traditional economy has rebounded. Commercial and entrepreneurial networks and behaviors, rooted in the past, have a new-found relevance and provide a positive legacy for the future.

BIBLIOGRAPHY

Suggestions for Further Reading

The historical literature on China is vast and extremely accessible. For a perspective on China's recent economic history similar to that adopted here, see Richardson (1999). An interesting anthology that brings together related themes from different periods of China's modern history is Kallgren et al. (1991). For a broad overview of Chinese history that is also eminently readable, see Spence (1999). Jung Chang's *Wild Swans* (1991) manages to capture an enormous sweep of Chinese history through a purely personal family memoir.

Sources for Data and Figures

Table 2.2: Kumar (1992). Length of Chinese Railroads from Rawski (1989, 208–09).

References

Brandt, Loren (1990). *Commercialization and Agricultural Development: Central and Eastern China, 1870–1937*. Cambridge: Cambridge University Press.

Brandt, Loren (1987). "Farm Household Behavior, Factor Markets, and the Distributive Consequences of Commercialization in Early Twentieth-Century China." *Journal of Economic History*, 47, no. 3 (September): 711–37.

Chang, John K. (1969). *Industrial Development in Pre-Communist China: A Quantitative Analysis*. Chicago: Aldine.

Chang, Jung (1991). *Wild Swans: Three Daughters of China*. New York: Simon & Schuster.

Eastman, Lloyd (1988). *Family, Fields, and Ancestors: Constancy and Change in China's Social and Economic History, 1550–1949*. New York: Oxford University Press.

Elvin, Mark (1973). *The Pattern of the Chinese Past*. Stanford, CA: Stanford University Press.

Elvin, Mark, and Liu Ts'ui-jung, eds. (1988). *Sediments of Time: Environment and Society in Chinese History*. New York: Cambridge University Press.

Esherick, Joseph (1991). "Review of Loren Brandt, *Commercialization and Agricultural Development: Central and Eastern China*." *Journal of Economic History*. 51, no. 2 (June): 501–03.

Feuerwerker, Albert (1969). *The Chinese Economy, ca. 1870–1911*. Ann Arbor: Center for Chinese Studies, University of Michigan.

Ho, Samuel P. S. (1984). "Colonization and Development: Korea, Taiwan and Kwantung. In Ramon Myers and Mark Peattie, eds., *The Japanese Colonial Empire, 1845–1945*, 347–98. Princeton, NJ: Princeton University Press.

Kallgren, Joyce, K. Lieberthal, R. MacFarquhar, and F. Wakeman, eds. (1991). *Perspectives on Modern China: Four Anniversaries*. Armonk, NY: M. E. Sharpe.

King, Frank H. (1911). *Farmers of Forty Centuries*. Emmaus, PA: Rodale Press.

Kirby, William C. (1990). "Continuity and Change in Modern China: Economic Planning on the Mainland and on Taiwan, 1943–1958." *Australian Journal of Chinese Affairs* 24:121–41.

Kirby, William C. (1992). "The Chinese War Economy." In James C. Hsiung and Steven I. Levine, eds., *China's Bitter Victory: The War with Japan, 1937–1945*, 185–212. Armonk, NY: M. E. Sharpe.

Kumar, Dharma (1992). "The Chinese and Indian Economies from ca. 1914–1949." *STICERD Research Program on the Chinese Economy*, CP no. 22, May, London School of Economics.

Maddison, Angus (1998). *Chinese Economic Performance in the Long Run*. Paris: Development Centre of the Organisation for Economic Co-operation and Development.

Myers, Ramon (1980). *The Chinese Economy, Past and Present*. Belmont, CA: Wadsworth.

Naquin, Susan, and Evelyn Rawski (1987). *Chinese Society in the Eighteenth Century*. New Haven, CT: Yale University Press.

Perkins, Dwight (1967). "Government as an Obstacle to Industrialization: The Case of Nineteenth-Century China." *Journal of Economic History*, 27(4):478–92.

Rawski, Thomas (1989). *Economic Growth in Prewar China*. Berkeley: University of California Press.

Richardson, Philip (1999). *Economic Change in China, c. 1800–1950*. Cambridge: Cambridge University Press.

Riskin, Carl (1975). "Surplus and Stagnation in Modern China." In Dwight Perkins, ed., *China's Modern Economy in Historical Perspective*, 49–84. Stanford: Stanford University Press.

Spence, Jonathan D. (1999). *The Search for Modern China*, 2nd ed. New York: W. W. Norton.

Tawney, R. H. (1964). *Land and Labour in China*. New York: Octagon Books.

Vermeer, Eduard (1988). *Economic Development in Provincial China: The Central Shaanxi since 1930*. Cambridge: Cambridge University Press.

Wang, Gabe T. (1999). *China's Population: Problems, Thoughts and Policies*, 6, 28–29, 38–39. Aldershot: Ashgate.

Will, Pierre-Etienne, and R. Bin Wong (1991). *Nourish the People: The State Civilian Granary System in China, 1650–1850*. Ann Arbor: Center for Chinese Studies, University of Michigan.

Zelin, Madeleine (1991). "The Structure of the Chinese Economy During the Qing Period." In J. Kallgren et al., eds., *Perspectives on Modern China: Four Anniversaries*. Armonk, NY: M. E. Sharpe.

Zhang, Zhongli (1955). *The Chinese Gentry: Studies on Their Role in Nineteenth-Century Chinese Society*. Seattle: University of Washington Press.

3 The Socialist Era, 1949–1978: Big Push Industrialization and Policy Instability

After the People's Republic of China (PRC) was established in October 1949, the Chinese economy was wrenched out of its traditional framework and completely reoriented. China's new leaders turned their backs on China's traditional household-based, "bottom-heavy" economy, and set out to develop a massive socialist industrial complex through direct government control. Planners neglected labor-intensive sectors suitable to China's vast population, and instead poured resources into capital-intensive factories producing metals, machinery, and chemicals. The early achievements of coastal enclave industrialization oriented to the Pacific were discarded, and a new inward-directed strategy was adopted. China turned to the Soviet Union as its primary model, as well as its chief trading partner and source of technology.

For 30 years, China pursued this vision of socialism. We label this development strategy "Big Push industrialization," because it gave overwhelming priority to channeling the maximum feasible investment into heavy industry. This development strategy, in turn, shaped virtually every aspect of the Chinese economy. The first section of this chapter covers the "Big Push" economic strategy, which describes the overall pattern in which resources are allocated. To implement this strategy, a planned economic system was phased in between 1949 and 1956 (and then phased out after 1979). The term "economic system" describes the institutions that govern specific resource-allocation decisions: this is covered in the second section of this chapter. The type of system China adopted is often called a "command economy," because market forces were severely curtailed and government planners allocated resources directly through their own "commands," which were the crucial signals in the economy. The command economy was a very effective way to subordinate individual economic decision-making to the overall national development strategy.

Even though the general framework of Big Push strategy and command economic system covered China's pursuit of socialist development throughout this period, the framework was interpreted differently over the years, and policy shifted in ways that were unpredictable and disruptive to the economy. Indeed, economic instability and a pattern of policy oscillations marked the years through 1978. This chapter uses the framework of policy instability to describe some of the most important episodes during China's socialist period. A few distinctive and successful Chinese adaptations were made to the Big Push/command economy model, and some catastrophic and misguided policies were followed. The GLF stands out as the most peculiar, and the most terrible, of all these episodes, overshadowing even the Cultural Revolution. Since 1979, China has gradually dismantled virtually all the institutions of the command economy. Nevertheless, the legacy to China's contemporary economy from the period of the socialist planned economy is large and complex. Indeed, no area of the contemporary economy completely escapes the aftereffects of the command economy. We conclude with a brief assessment of the socialist period and its legacy.

3.1   THE BIG PUSH DEVELOPMENT STRATEGY

After 1949 the PRC followed a socialist heavy-industry-priority development strategy, or Big Push strategy. Consumption was squeezed, as rapid industrialization was given highest priority. The government controlled the bulk of the economy directly and used its control to pump resources into the construction of new factories. Investment, virtually all of which was government investment, increased rapidly to over a quarter of national income. Investment rates worldwide have risen since the 1950s, but even today poor countries on average invest 20% of GDP. China, by 1954, at a time when it was still a very poor country, had pushed its investment rate up to 26% of GDP. (See Figure 3.1, which shows gross capital formation—the sum of new investment in physical assets, replacement investment, and accumulation of inventories—as a share of GDP.) Investment soared further during the GLF, but then crashed in the catastrophic aftermath of the Leap. Over the long term, as Figure 3.1 shows, China's investment rates have been high and rising, though sometimes unstable.

Most investment went to industry, and of industrial investment, more than 80% was in heavy industry. With planners pouring resources into industry, rapid industrial growth was not surprising: Between 1952 and 1978 industrial output grew at an average annual rate of 11.5%. Moreover, industry's share of total GDP climbed steadily over the same period from 18% to 44%, while agriculture's share declined from 51% to 28% (measured at current prices; see Chapter 6 for further discussion). Entire new industries were created—for

Figure 3.1
Investment as a share of GDP

example, those producing electric generating equipment, chemical fertilizer, and motor vehicles. Most important, economic growth was jump-started, after the stagnation and disruption of the depression and war years. The Chinese economy took off during the 1950s, and the Big Push strategy seemed to be working. The new government was able to mobilize the fiscal and other resources to finance a sustained investment effort.

The PRC was not the only part of East Asia where growth accelerated in the 1950s. Hong Kong and Taiwan underwent rapid industrialization, and they did so largely by following the strategy of development that the PRC had abandoned. A direct comparison of strategies can provide further insight into growth in all these regions (Table 3.1). It is possible to view the entire industrial economy as a series of "value chains" or streams that connect many different activities. At the top of the stream is natural resource extraction and materials industries; these feed in to refining, processed-materials, and machinery industries; and ultimately at the bottom of the stream are final products for businesses and consumers. China, with its heavy-industry–priority strategy, focused on industries in the upper and middle stages of the industrial economy. These industries can be considered "strategic," in the sense that they have the most linkages with other industries. For example, an industry such as steel has important linkages "downstream," because if it supplies high-quality, low-cost steel to machinery and equipment makers, it will lower their costs and

Table 3.1
Two contrasting industrialization strategies

	Heavy-industry–priority, PRC	Light-industry–priority, Taiwan, Hong Kong
Basic strategy	Strategic industries with most upstream and downstream linkages	Begin with downstream consumer goods industries; gradually work upstream
Saving done by	Government, state-owned enterprises	Households, private business, government
Investment decisions	Government	Private business, government infrastructure
Source of demand growth	Domestic industries, government investment projects	Foreign and domestic consumer-goods markets
Household income	Slow growing	Moderate to fast growing
Coordination by	Plan	Market, with some government "steerage"
Openness to world	Low	High

stimulate their development. But steel also has important linkages "upstream," because its growth increases demand for coal, iron ore, and specialized machinery, stimulating the growth of those industries as well. (An input-output [I-O] table is a tool that shows all the direct supply relationships between sectors, and it can be used to quickly compute the full direct plus indirect implications of any change in output or demand.) Growth based on heavy investment in strategic sectors tends to create a self-reinforcing, but also self-contained, process. Heavy industrial sectors are developed that supply each other's demands, based on the government's investment decisions, but there are limited spillovers to market development. Such an approach goes easily with a strategy of national self-reliance and limited openness to the outside world.

Hong Kong and Taiwan, by contrast, specialized first in textiles, food products, and other light consumer goods. In other words, they concentrated on the "downstream" end of the industrial value chains. These are also the "early industries" in which most developing countries begin their industrialization process. Not accidentally, they were also the most important sectors in China's "enclave industrialization" during the 1920s and 1930s. Indeed, in some cases, it was the same people running the factories: many Shanghai textile entrepreneurs moved to Hong Kong in the 1950s, and other Shanghai businessmen went to Taiwan. The markets for these industries were primarily abroad, particularly in developed countries. Openness to trade meant that industrialists could obtain their inputs—raw materials and equipment—on the world market. Only later, after successful light-industry development, did Taiwan and Hong Kong move "upstream," developing industries that were more technologically demanding and capital-intensive, sometimes with government help. It is striking that Hong Kong, Taiwan, Korea, and Singapore all made a relatively smooth transition from their early light-consumer manufacturing to more technologically demanding sectors, and economic growth accelerated in all four of these economies in the 1960s and 1970s. In other words, despite the absence of domestic interindustry linkages in the initial phases of industrialization, Taiwan and Hong Kong were able to more than compensate through other advantages of openness. Cheaper production because of access to lowest-cost inputs from the world market, faster absorption of world technology, and faster learning about export markets led to more rapid growth of living standards, and ultimately to a more rapid convergence to world best practice. Thus, although growth accelerated in the PRC under the impetus of the Big Push, growth accelerated even more in other parts of East Asia at the same time. By 1978, Taiwan and Hong Kong were far ahead of the PRC and served an important demonstration effect in convincing Chinese leaders to reform and open up the economy. When, after 1979, the PRC finally reoriented its development strategy and modified the Big Push strategy, it discovered that there were many unexploited opportunities in light manufacturing and export markets. China returned to those neglected opportunities, often in collaboration with businesses from Hong Kong or Taiwan. (See Chapters 16 and 17 for a description of the interaction among the economies of the PRC, Hong Kong, and Taiwan in the contemporary period.)

3.2   THE COMMAND ECONOMIC SYSTEM IN CHINA

How did planners manage to channel resources into their Big Push industrialization strategy? What were the key institutions that shaped the way decisions were made? China adopted the "command economy" system from the Soviet Union, and it had the following fundamental characteristics:

• The government owned all large factories and transportation and communication enterprises. In the countryside, agricultural collectives took over ownership of the land and management of the farm economy.

• Planners issued commands that assigned production targets to firms and directly allocated resources and goods among different producers. Prices lost their significance as the primary signal that directed resource allocation in the economy. Finances were used to audit and monitor performance, not to drive investment decisions.

• While the government neglected the microeconomic allocation role of prices, it nevertheless controlled the price system and set relative prices to channel resources into government hands and into Big Push industrialization.

• The government and Communist Party reinforced their control of the economy through a hierarchical personnel system, in which the Communist Party controlled managerial career paths.

These were the characteristic institutions of the system created initially in the Soviet Union under Stalin. China copied them during the 1950s. As we shall discuss, during the 1960s and 1970s, China altered these institutions to fit with Maoist ideology and to accommodate an economy that was much poorer than its Soviet mentor.

The government owned the factories and controlled the price system, and not surprisingly, factory products were expensive and farm products were cheap. That is, the socialist state intentionally assigned prices to the products of industry (owned by the government) that were relatively high, and assigned prices to the products of agriculture (owned by peasant collectives) that were relatively low. The socialist state maintained terms of trade between the state-enterprise sector and the household sector that were highly favorable to state enterprises. In 1953 (even before agricultural collectives were formed) the Chinese government established compulsory procurement of grain from farmers, creating a government monopoly over key agricultural goods that lasted more than 30 years. Farmers were forced to meet procurement quotas established by the state grain monopoly, at low fixed prices. With cheap farm products, the "markup" on manufactured consumer goods was high (on cotton cloth, for example), while wages were kept low and stable. Given these systematic biases in price setting, agriculture seemed to be a "low-return" activity, while manufacturing appeared to be highly profitable. But not wanting too many farmers to leave the farm, the government imposed restrictions on mobility (see Chapter 5).

The surpluses of government-controlled firms made up the main source of government revenue. The distorted price system meant that state-owned industrial enterprises were extremely profitable—even when they were not very efficient—and they served as a "cash cow" for the government and for the economy as a whole. This system is what gave the Chinese government the fiscal capacity to mobilize resources for Big Push industrialization and its other priorities. A modern tax system was not necessary: Already by the mid-1950s, government could raise more than a quarter of GDP as budgetary revenues, an impressive level for such a poor country and far higher than anything achieved by the Nationalist government before the war.

After establishing the essential prerequisite of government control over the economy, specific decisions were implemented through the planning system. "Material balance planning" was the main technique used to actually run the economy. The term "material balance" refers to the computation of sources and uses of an individual commodity that a planner "balances" in allocating all supplies. Planners simply assigned "quantities" and ignored "prices." There were output plans for individual producers and supply plans that transferred resources among producers. In theory, a planner could use an input-output table to compute the interdependent needs of the whole economy. In practice, though, China was too big and its producers too diverse for planners ever to have been able to coordinate the economy through a single technical device. Instead, planners divided blocks of resources among different stakeholders, drew up their own wish lists of priority projects and the resources they needed, and then allocated anything left over to the numerous unmet needs. The foreign sector could be used as a last resort to make up for scarcities and sell surpluses.

Other types of control were used to reinforce control over materials. Control over personnel was exercised through the *nomenklatura* system. The *nomenklatura* is a list of urban jobs that are controlled by the Communist Party, which thereby manages personnel throughout the public sector. The Communist Party set up a strict hierarchy, in which each level supervises the performance and appointment of personnel at the next lower level. As a result, control of career paths, and thus of the ultimate incentive structure, rests with the Communist Party. Finally, control over financial flows and credit was also exerted from the top, typically through a state monopoly banking system (or "monobank") that audited compliance with state directives. Prices, profits, money, and banking all existed in this system, but the financial system was "passive." That is, financial flows were assigned to accommodate the plan (which was drawn up in terms of physical quantities), rather than to independently influence resource allocation flows. The only exception was for household budgets: households could decide how to allocate their incomes among a limited supply of consumer goods.

With all the plans, commands, and controls, the typical state-owned enterprise had very little authority. It could not adjust its labor force, did not retain any of its profits, and could do little other than scramble to find additional inputs and increase production. Yet at the same time, the core planning system in China was much less centralized and much less tightly controlled than it was in the Soviet Union. Small firms were more important in China's industrial structure than in the Soviet Union. Transportation and communication were less developed, so it is not surprising that central control was exercised less effectively. For example, central planners in Beijing allocated a maximum of 600 different varieties of industrial product, while the Soviet Union by the 1970s had allocated 60,000 separate commodities. In other ways, too, China's system was less centralized, especially in the 1970s, after financial decentralization reinforced decentralization of the planning system, providing local governments with substantial leeway in making economic development decisions. Arguably, there was less decision-making authority at the top (central government) and bottom (enterprise) of the Chinese industrial economy. More authority, however, could be exercised by those in the middle, typically local government officials.

But in one respect, China was substantially more controlled than the Soviet Union: ideological and social control was especially tight. Politics was "in command" during the Maoist years, and the Communist Party rigorously controlled speech, and even thought. China maintained very strict controls over labor, including restrictions on movement and on remuneration. Migration to urban areas was tightly restricted, and during the Cultural Revolution, 17 million urban school-leavers were sent out to the countryside (see Chapter 5). Employees in state enterprises stayed in a given enterprise for life, sometimes even passing jobs on to their children. Labor mobility was virtually nonexistent. It was illegal in principle and impossible in practice for firms to fire workers, and quits were also almost unknown. Despite decentralization, the system in many respects was extremely rigid.

3.3 POLICY INSTABILITY

China's history since 1949 has been a stormy one. Even after the 1949 revolution, sharp turns in policy—including economic policy—marked nearly every period of China's development. Changes, and even reversals, of direction were common in many areas of economic policy. As a result, the legacy of the socialist period is especially complicated. In some periods the policy emphasis was so distinctive that it has been described as a unique Chinese or Maoist "model" of development. At other times policy stayed closer to an orthodox Soviet model or was driven by short-run pragmatism. These different periods had very different economic outcomes, ranging from highly successful to catastrophic.

Shifts in economic policy often came with sharp political conflict. Mao Zedong himself repeatedly changed economic policies in accordance with his own revolutionary ideals or personal wishes. He often portrayed the resulting policy changes as part of his own personal struggle against political opponents.

The Communist Party has consistently monopolized political power since 1949, so major policy issues have often played out as internal power struggles dividing the party. Winners in factional fighting have used policy advocacy to prevail over their opponents, and have imposed policies they favored once they won power. For all these reasons, the twists and turns in policy in Maoist China are generally narrated from a political point of view. While acknowledging the importance of politics, this section provides a brief narrative of the 1949–1978 period in which the emphasis is on economic changes and political factors are downplayed. This approach allows us to present a compact narrative while also capturing the diversity and instability of policy orientations.

One approach to this topic is provided by the data shown in Figure 3.2. The figure shows the percentage growth of investment in each year (using the same underlying data as Figure 3.1). The data show clearly the successive periods of rapid investment growth, followed by slower growth or even decline. Figure 3.3 gives labels to five successive waves of rapid investment growth. Each time the growth of investment in a single year surpasses 20%, it signals a "leap forward." Each "leap" is a phase of more rapid investment growth, but also corresponds with a period of political mobilization and institutional transformation. "Leaps" tend to be radical, or leftist, phases of maximum social change. Five cycles of political and economic mobilization are evident in the Chinese

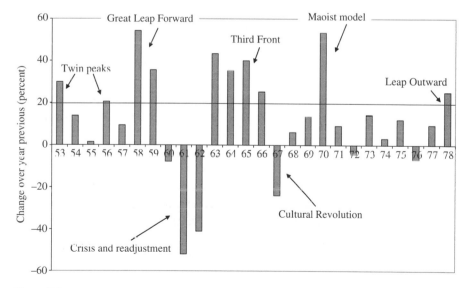

Figure 3.2
Growth of investment

data. Typically, each leap was followed by a phase of retrenchment, consolidation, and slower investment growth. Often, these retrenchment phases were characterized by a more moderate political climate as well (although the early Cultural Revolution, 1967–1968, is an important exception). Thus investment cycles correspond to policy cycles and recurrent policy conflict. Policy swings like a pendulum from left to right and back again, driving and in turn being driven by economic developments. This approach can provide a simple framework to organize the complex history of socialist China, and it allows us to divide the era into subperiods that are quite different from those used by the Chinese government.

3.3.1 Economic Recovery, 1949–1952

The new leaders of China came to power in 1949 committed to building socialism in China, a commitment which, to them, meant that they would recreate in China a version of the Soviet economic model. After all, they were a Communist Party, and there is no evidence during the early years of a fundamental debate or disagreement among the leadership over the desirability of adopting the Soviet model. However, it was by no means certain how rapidly China should (or could) build a Soviet-style system, nor the extent to which China would seek to precisely emulate Soviet practices. China faced immediate economic problems. Wartime damage to industry and agriculture had been substantial, and hyperinflation was raging. The invasion of South Korea by North Korea in June 1950 greatly intensified the hostility the capitalist powers felt toward the new Communist Party government. A trade boycott against China was instituted, as Chinese intervention turned the Korean War into a protracted stalemate. These events pushed China into an especially close embrace with the Soviet Union, while also keeping Chinese policymakers focused on the need to be prudent and careful. In fact, the government was able to move rapidly to restore the domestic economy and experienced a remarkable run of successes in the first few years. Tight control of the budget and money supply brought inflation under control by the end of 1950. At the same time, industry and agriculture were both rehabilitated fairly smoothly. By 1952 both industry and agriculture surpassed their highest prerevolutionary levels, and the stage was set for a new phase of development. The signing of an armistice in Korea in the summer of 1953 cleared the path for a new era.

What is particularly striking during these early years is how effectively the new government adapted its ideology to the economic and political challenges of the day. In the countryside, the party pushed through a radical land reform. Communist party workers descended on rural areas throughout the country to distribute land to poor peasant households. Between 1950 and 1952—while the Korean War was raging—42% of China's arable land was redistributed, much of it in the south where Communist guerrillas had not previously carried out land reforms. At this stage, land was still owned privately by households, but ownership of land was largely equalized. In this way the Communist Party consolidated support among average and poor farmers and destroyed the economic and political power of landlords. At the same time they deferred until later the question of how rapidly farmers would be organized into agricultural collectives.

In urban areas the new government took over many factories, including those expropriated from the Japanese after the war and those belonging to the Guomindang or to capitalists who fled China after the revolution. But policy was generally welcoming to other social groups. Under the rubric of "New Democracy," the Communist Party welcomed those non-Communists who were willing to work with the new government. Capitalists who were willing to stay in China—and there were many—were encouraged to expand production at their factories. Quite a few of the planners who had worked for the NRC in the Nationalist government were willing to continue working for the Communist government in the same capacity. Many intellectuals and scientists were convinced to contribute their skills to the construction of the new China. By putting skilled entrepreneurs and technicians to work, the government was able to revive industry surprisingly quickly. The government's own investment was focused on the Northeast, which was critical to the Big Push development strategy, since it contained the largest and most important heavy industries. Ironically, these factories had initially been created by Japanese investment as part of Japan's own state-sponsored industrialization program, and had been taken over by the Russians at the end of World War II. Now, the factories passed into Chinese government hands and were rehabilitated fairly quickly with Soviet aid. The heavy industries of the Northeast became a testing ground, where the institutions of the command economy were introduced for the first time. By the end of 1952, economic recovery and rehabilitation had become a resounding success. This was the signal that the time had come to launch socialist industrialization nationwide.

3.3.2   1953 and 1956: The Twin Peaks of the First Five-Year Plan

The five years from 1953 through 1957 are described by Chinese official media as the period of the First Five-Year Plan. In fact, it was a period of nearly constant policy change and adjustment. While the basic Soviet model was not in question, there were serious policy issues concerning the pace of transformation, the degree of centralization that was appropriate for China, and the appropriate policies on wages and incentives in urban areas, among other issues. Soviet-style institutions were put in place, especially during two periods of mobilization and rapid change that were followed by periods of retrenchment and consolidation. Ironically, even though the direction of change was consistently toward a Soviet system, the reality on the ground was one of a mixed and diverse economy through most of the period, because the Soviet model had not yet been imposed in monolithic form. This point is important because the period was one of dramatic economic success.

During the 1950s every aspect of Chinese society was subject to massive influence from the Soviet Union. The Soviet Big Push strategy and the command economy system were copied wholesale. At the same time, Soviet industrial technology and organizational design were transplanted into China. The "twin peaks" of especially rapid change came in 1953 and 1956. In the first peak (1953), investment was ramped up quickly as part of the beginning of nationwide investment planning on the Soviet model. Compulsory agricultural procurement was adopted. The very first Five-Year Plan, nominally covering 1953 through 1957, was drawn up "half in Moscow, half in Peking." At the heart of the plan was the construction of 156 large industrial projects, all of them imported from the Soviet Union or from Eastern Europe. Virtually all these projects were built in inland regions or in the Northeast. Thus the beginning of planning in China also meant the beginning of regional distribution and the attempt to move the industrial center of gravity away from the coastal enclaves. The Russian machinery embodied fairly advanced industrial technology, and blueprints and technical specifications were generally provided as well. The Soviet Union provided massive training and technical assistance across the board. Nearly every field was shaped by Soviet advice and training, ranging from architecture and sports training, to industrial engineering, to the organization of scientific research and educational institutions. Some 6,000 Soviet advisers came to China, typically for periods of a year or two; and more than 10,000 Chinese students studied in the USSR. While China paid most of the ordinary costs of supporting advisers, there was a substantial aid component to this assistance, and it would have been extremely difficult for a regime that had no experience with nationwide comprehensive planning to roll out a successful investment plan without assistance.

The initial investment surge of 1953 almost immediately threatened to reignite inflation and was curtailed. Moderate economic conditions prevailed in 1954–1955, and China was still a mixed economy. Household farms dominated agriculture, although the government had already established a monopoly over grain purchases and farmers were being encouraged to join cooperatives. In the cities, private businessmen were allowed to run factories and shops, although most capitalists were being pressured into signing contracts with the state-run wholesalers. But this balance was about to change.

During the second peak of transformation, the "High Tide of Socialism," in 1955–1956, the transformation to public ownership was abruptly pushed through. It began in mid-1955, as Mao Zedong criticized the slow pace at which farmers were joining agricultural cooperatives and accused the officials in charge of rural policy of timidity, likening them to old women "hobbling with bound feet." Mao's criticism touched off a mass campaign to push farmers into producers' cooperatives, a campaign that raged through the winter of 1955–1956. Mao's personal intervention at this time was of crucial importance. The shift of policy led immediately to the organization of virtually all peasants into agricultural cooperatives. At the end of 1954, only 2% of farm households had been enrolled in cooperatives or collectives; by 1955, 14% were enrolled; and by the end of 1956, 98%. Attention then turned to the cities, where during early 1956 private factories and shops were turned into cooperatives or else "joint public-private" factories with substantial control exercised by the state. Private ownership, having survived and grown for six years since the establishment of the PRC, was virtually extinguished during six months in late 1955 and early 1956. Investment growth accelerated to a new peak, as the government pumped resources into the newly established socialist organizations. Two waves of mobilization had produced dramatic social and economic change. The Soviet model was in place, and the year 1956 was thus the first year that China operated a fully "socialist" economy.

3.3.3   Retrenchment: The "Hundred Flowers" of 1956–1957

At the moment when China had just created the key features of the command economy, replicating those that Stalin had created in the Soviet Union, Nikita Khrushchev stood before the 20th Congress of the Soviet Communist Party and on February 25, 1956, denounced Stalin and revealed the crimes of Stalinism. Khrushchev set off global shock waves by declaring that all socialist countries had the right to determine their own path to build socialism. In China, leaders responded by relaxing the political environment while coping with increasingly serious economic problems, caused by the stresses and strains associated with the overly rapid pace of change and industrial growth in 1955–1956. Nearly five million workers had been absorbed into the state sector in 1956, and while about half were urban dwellers previously employed in private businesses, the other half were rural dwellers migrating to the cities. Average wages had grown rapidly, and a flood of new bank credit was extended in rural areas to finance the infant agricultural cooperatives. At the same time, agricultural output stagnated. While rapid collectivization did not cause a dramatic decline in output—as it had in the Soviet Union in the 1930s—the countryside was buffeted by institutional change, and supplies completely failed to keep pace with the increase in demand. Both economic and international political factors were soon pressuring the Chinese leadership to moderate the pace of change.

By mid-1956, Chinese policy pronouncements had swung 180° from those of a year earlier, stressing the importance of careful, gradual change, and criticizing the earlier policy as "reckless advance." In September 1956 the Communist Party convened its Eighth Congress—actually the first such meeting since 1949—which charted a program of economic moderation. Following the Eighth Congress, programs of economic reform were openly discussed that envisioned an economic system with a significant, though subsidiary, role for the market mechanism, and which even contemplated the revival and coexistence of different forms of ownership. This party congress thus touched off a period of liberalism that was later to find echoes in many of the programs advanced after 1978. Economic liberalism spread gradually into the political domain, and by early 1957 party leaders were calling for open political discussion, a movement labeled the "Hundred Flowers." To some, these policies suggested an alternative path to a distinctive Chinese socialism, more moderate and market oriented than the Soviet model. However, the actual outcome of this complex period was far different from what anyone anticipated.

The Hundred Flowers seemed to promise an important new departure for China. Even though the shift to the Hundred Flowers was rooted in the stresses and strains of the overheating of the previous year, it seemed to promise a new era of self-confidence and social flexibility. In fact, such a shift would have made perfect sense, because overall China was looking back at a record of remarkable success. Extraordinarily rapid economic growth had taken place, and industrial production expanded 17% annually between 1952 and 1957. Virtually every sector of the economy was rehabilitated, and the groundwork for sustained future growth was laid by massive investments in education and training. It was a period of rapid social mobility, as farmers moved into the city and young people entered college. It was a period of dramatic progress now looked back upon with nostalgia by many of those in China old enough to remember it. Having accumulated experience in its own economic construction, China now seemed well on the way to defining its own brand of socialism, one that was more flexible and market responsive than the Soviet model. But it was not to be. Within months Mao Zedong had taken the spirit of change so evident in 1957 and turned it in a dramatically new and ominous direction. From unprecedented success, China was about to plunge into unprecedented disaster. The GLF was taking shape.

3.3.4 The Great Leap Forward, 1958–1960

The GLF was the most dramatic, peculiar, and ultimately tragic period in the history of the PRC. The turning point that signaled the emergence of the Leap actually came in mid-1957, when Mao suddenly attacked liberal critics who had spoken out in the Hundred Flowers. Within weeks Mao initiated a broad "Anti-Rightist Campaign" that targeted nonparty intellectuals and anyone with an independent mind. Over the next few months some 800,000 intellectuals and others who had spoken out during the Hundred Flowers period were condemned, removed from their jobs, and, in many cases, sent to labor camps. The political atmosphere changed overnight. When economic-system reforms that decentralized power were finally readied in November 1957, they were implemented in a political atmosphere of renewed radicalism. Mao turned China in a new direction, shifted gears, and accelerated, straight into a brick wall.

The GLF itself was dominated by a highly politicized intoxication with growth that envisaged a bold leap toward a fully communistic society within a few years. The Leap is often seen as the period when China under Mao first developed a vision of socialism that was distinct from the Soviet model. Indeed, widespread enthusiasm for the Leap in its early years was fueled by dissatisfaction with the huge factories and bureaucratic organizations that had been implanted in China as part of the Soviet-style system. But at the same time, the Leap was also a simple intensification of the Big Push strategy. In fact, the most basic economic outcome of the GLF was a massive increase in the rate at which resources were transferred from agriculture to industry. The GLF was the product of a "vision, rather than a plan" (Schurmann 1966, 74), and logical consistency was not always maintained. Indeed, the essence of the GLF was the attempt to resolve contradictions by doing everything simultaneously, regardless of real resource constraints. Nevertheless, there were indeed a number of innovative elements:

1. "Communes" were established in the countryside. A commune was a large-scale (bigger than any collective) combination of governmental and economic functions. It was used to mobilize labor for construction projects, provide social services, and develop rural small-scale industries.

2. Material incentives and monetary rewards were rejected. Bonuses were eliminated in state industry, and free markets in the countryside were shut down.

3. Control over economic decision-making was decentralized.

4. A "walking on two legs" technology policy was established, in which simple technologies (appropriate to a poor nation) were to be combined with advanced industrial technology.

Throughout 1958 the ideological atmosphere became steadily more extreme, and at the same time the leadership began to receive more and more good news about the economy. A spectacular autumn harvest in 1958 comfortably surpassed those of the previous two years. Output of steel increased rapidly. Growth was real, but these reports were also inflated: in the overheated ideological environment, party officials competed to report ever more remarkable successes, with the result that the statistical reporting system became more and more inflated, and ultimately collapsed. The leaders became convinced that unprecedented political mobilization had enabled the Chinese economy to break through the resource constraints that had seemed so overwhelming at the beginning of 1957. Blinded by their own ideological fervor and the breakdown of their statistical "eyes and ears," the top leaders made two fateful decisions. First, they reduced the supply of production resources (labor and even land) available for agriculture, and especially for food production. Second, they increased the procurement of grain, the compulsory deliveries of food to the state. The first decision implied that there would be less food produced in the countryside; the second that the state would take more out.

At first, the impact of these policy measures was obscured by an apparently inexhaustible growth surge. Nearly 30 million new workers were absorbed into the state sector during 1958. In rural China more millions of able-bodied workers were drawn out of agriculture to work in rural factories, including highly publicized "backyard steel mills." Those workers remaining in agriculture were instructed to reduce the acreage sown to grain after the 1958 harvest. Top leaders had allowed themselves to be convinced by crackpot science, which claimed that deep plowing and superdense compact planting of seedlings could double or triple crop yields. This would allow farmers to allocate more land to commercial crops, particularly cotton, needed to feed industry's voracious appetite. Laborers at all levels were pushed to work overtime, seven days a week, in a frenzied attempt to do everything at once. In industry, large- and small-scale factories grew simultaneously ("Walking on two legs"); educational and cultural enterprises expanded almost as rapidly as industrial enterprises. In the communes, new social services, including communal dining halls and child-care facilities, were initiated on a large scale; mass poetry-writing sessions were held. Industrial output targets were repeatedly revised upward, especially the target for steel production. Workers were exhorted to surpass Britain within three years and to catch up with America. In fact, industry grew rapidly. While much of the output was unusable junk, the fundamental problem was not the poor quality of industrial output, but rather the drain of resources and manpower away from agriculture that was entirely unsustainable.

The insanity of the Leap would not have been possible if the party had not silenced critical voices during the Anti-Rightist Campaign or if peasant voices could have been heard warning of disaster. For a brief period it seemed as if the party itself might see the dangers and correct its policies. In the summer of 1959 the party convened a work conference at Lushan to decide on measures to address serious imbalances that were already emerging, including local food shortages. But after several days of discussion, Mao Zedong suddenly seized on the comments of the minister of defense, Peng Dehuai, to launch a bitter attack on the critics of the GLF. A new Anti-Rightist campaign was launched, this time targeting those within the Communist Party and government who had dared to make realistic criticisms of the Leap. Both core policies of GLF were resumed: state-sector employment surged again during 1960, and grain procurement reached new heights. But by this time there were few reserves of food or human energy for the system to draw on. Harvests were declining, and food stocks were being exhausted. As the system careened into 1960, local food shortages were ballooning into regional shortages, and China was facing a massive subsistence crisis.

External factors exacerbated the situation during 1960, but it is clear that the fundamental problem was the willful blindness of China's leaders, beginning with Mao Zedong. Relatively poor weather in 1960 exacerbated the food crisis, but did not cause it. In the summer of 1960, Nikita Khrushchev, alarmed by the increasingly erratic and dangerous tilt to Chinese policy, suddenly recalled all Soviet advisers from China. The move was doubtless intended to pressure China to abandon its profoundly misguided policies, but the result was a permanent rift between the two countries. In 1960 full-blown famine burst upon China. The famine was fundamentally rural, and most severe in inland provinces. Several inland provinces were absolutely devastated. Cumulative excess mortality reached 11% of the population of Sichuan, and nearly 6% of the populations of Guizhou and Anhui (Figure 3.3). Throughout the worst times, the state continued to extract grain from the countryside and supply urban areas, maintaining an appearance of normality in the main coastal cities.

Chinese official population data fully reflect the magnitude. There are different ways to use the data to compute the full extent of the catastrophe, but

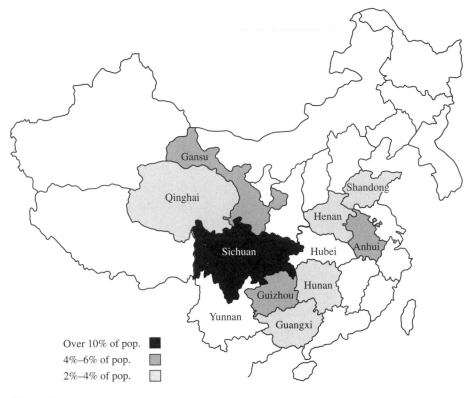

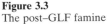

Figure 3.3
The post–GLF famine

they agree that through the end of 1961, about 25–30 million excess deaths occurred due to the great Chinese famine. In addition, another roughly 30 million births were postponed due to malnutrition and shortage. The worst effects of the famine began to recede during 1962, although mortality remained significantly above normal. By the end of 1962 the worst of this immense catastrophe was over. It was the largest famine of the twentieth century, anywhere in the world. Though the catastrophe is acknowledged officially in China, there are no photographs, nor memorials to the dead.

3.3.5   Retrenchment: Crisis and "Readjustment," 1961–1963

Finally, in early 1961, the Chinese leadership recognized the necessity of drastic action. A new set of policies were rammed through at the beginning of the year. Investment was chopped back, and some 20 million workers were sent back to the countryside. Within the rural sector, the communes were drastically restructured, to place responsibility for agricultural production on smaller groups of households. Bonuses and other material incentives in industry were revived. Nationwide, small factories were shut down by the thousands as an attempt was made to concentrate production in a smaller number of relatively efficient plants; rural industry in particular was cut back. Control over the economy was recentralized in an attempt to restore order. Virtually all basic necessities were rationed in an attempt to minimize the impact of shortages. Existing production was reoriented, to the extent possible, to provide greater inputs into agriculture. China, which had been exporting food during the 1950s, entered the world grain market for the first time and became a net importer of food.

Crisis control policies continued and were extended through 1964. Free markets—closed during the Leap—were reopened to provide an additional channel for peasants to supply food to cities and soak up purchasing power. Imports of consumer goods and market liberalization gradually stabilized prices at a new, higher level. During 1963 attention shifted from crisis management to the elaboration of a new set of long-term policies. Initial drafts of a new Five-Year Plan implied a turn away from Big Push policies and an attempt to restore living standards. These policies seemed no more than common sense at the time. Agriculture had been seriously weakened by misguided policies that had destroyed valuable land in an attempt to build water-control projects, build mines and factories, and cut down forests. Living standards in both cities and the countryside had been eroded by shortages and inflation. And China could no longer rely on assistance from the Soviet Union. The new draft plans envisaged rehabilitating existing industrial bases in the coastal regions and concentrating new investment in industries (especially chemical industries) that could support and bypass agriculture by producing fertilizer and chemical fibers.

3.3.6   Launch of the Third Front, 1964–1966: A New Expansion Hijacked by Radicalism

The moderate policies developed between 1961 and 1964 were not continued. Alarmed by China's isolation in the world and threatened by the increasing American involvement in Vietnam, Mao Zedong shifted China's development strategy again during 1964. As the worst of the post-Leap crisis ended, Mao pushed for the construction of the "Third Front." The Third Front was a massive construction program focused on China's inland provinces (Figure 3.4). The objective was to create an entire industrial base that would provide China with strategic independence. By building factories in remote and mountainous interior regions, Mao hoped to ensure that China's industrial base would not be vulnerable to American or Soviet military pressure. Beginning

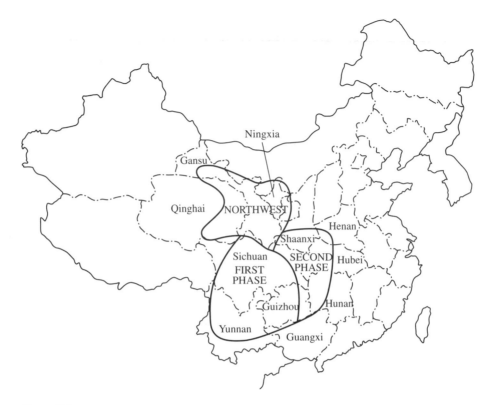

Figure 3.4
The Third Front, 1964–1975

in late 1964 a new "high tide" of production was begun that focused on the construction of factories and railroad lines in China's southwestern provinces, particularly Sichuan and Guizhou. With this program the Big Push strategy was firmly reestablished as the basis of China's development policy, this time with a militarized and regionally redistributive cast. During 1965 and 1966 investment and industrial production surged as the first stages of inland construction were completed. The Third Front dominated economic construction from late 1964 onward. However, the rapid expansion of which it was a part was brought to an abrupt halt by the eruption of the Cultural Revolution.

3.3.7   Retrenchment: The Cultural Revolution, 1967–1969

In August 1966, Mao launched the so-called Cultural Revolution. The Cultural Revolution has many definitions and even more explanations. The term "Cultural Revolution Era" is often used in China to refer to the entire 10-year period between 1966 and Mao's death in 1976, a usage in which it becomes synonymous with an entire era dominated by a particular kind of leftist political rhetoric. A more accurate approach, however, is to use the term to describe a shorter period of political disruption and unrest that lasted between 1966 and 1969. During this period, Mao encouraged groups of students, called Red Guards, to overthrow the entrenched Communist Party leadership, except for Mao himself. The Communist leaders of China, including Deng Xiaoping, were suddenly subject to criticism, dismissal, and sometimes worse, at the hands of gangs of students and "revolutionary workers." The Cultural Revolution is far too complex and peculiar a phenomenon to be dealt with here: it is usually seen either as an attempt by Mao to use young people to revive the revolutionary spirit and cleanse China of bureaucratic tendencies, or else as a Machiavellian plot by Mao to purge his own opponents in the power structure. In either case, the result was substantial disruption and a gradual descent into unrestrained factional conflict.

From an economic standpoint, the Cultural Revolution (in the narrower definition) was, surprisingly, not a particularly important event. The Cultural Revolution produced a lot of dramatic new political imagery but had relatively little effect on the economy. This result clearly occurred because of the unusual coincidence between a phase of radical politics and a phase of economic retrenchment. In contrast to the GLF, the disruption of the Cultural Revolution was "managed" quite effectively: investment was curtailed in a relatively orderly fashion; agricultural production was only slightly affected; and while industrial production declined, the fall was moderate, and production of vital necessities and priority projects continued. The guiding economic policies before the Cultural Revolution were quickly reinstated after the worst disruption was over, beginning in 1969. As in 1965–1966, the focus of economic construction continued to be the Third Front. One difference was that by 1969 the threat from the United States in Southeast Asia was deemed to have decreased, while relations between China and the Soviet Union had continued to deteriorate and had reached the point of open military clashes at disputed points on the border and ominous Soviet saber rattling.

3.3.8 The Maoist Model: A New Leap in 1970

Between 1969 and 1971, as China emerged from the "narrow" Cultural Revolution, a new "leap forward," focused on the Third Front, unfolded. This time there was no massive diversion of resources from agriculture, but investment surged and consumption was restrained as all efforts went to industrial construction. During this period China was operating under something approaching martial law. The army had been called in to quell the factional fighting into which the Cultural Revolution had deteriorated, and the direct involvement of the army in civil affairs was now reinforced by the perception of a military threat from the Soviet Union. Along with militarization of society came a systematic attempt to revive some of the ideals of the GLF. Once again, material incentives were criticized and bonuses eliminated; once again, control over economic decision-making was decentralized; once again, an attempt was made to develop rural and urban industry simultaneously. The difference from the Leap was that austerity was built into the program from the beginning. Rather than trying to do everything simultaneously, the Chinese people were urged to tighten their belts and give everything for construction. For a while these policies seemed to bear fruit, and production quickly surpassed pre–Cultural Revolution peaks.

In what way was this Maoist model a distinctive variant of the overall Soviet system? We can identify five elements:

1. Pervasive militarization of the economy. Priority was given to the national defense–related investment program of the Third Front. In addition, the People's Liberation Army had been called in to resolve Cultural Revolution factionalism. As a result, uniformed army officers were often managing production facilities. Austerity was encouraged.

2. Decentralized operation of the economy. Rural industries were encouraged, particularly the "Five Small Industries" that directly served agriculture (see Chapter 10).

3. Relative autarky was practiced. Economic links with the outside world were minimized, and regions within China were expected to achieve as much self-sufficiency as possible.

4. There was an almost complete absence of material incentives (bonuses or piece rates). There were few markets of any kind for farmers, and no market for grain.

5. Market-driven labor mobility virtually ceased. Urban school-leavers were sent to the countryside, and the government directed manpower and resources to remote inland areas, but migration and urbanization halted.

3.3.9   Retrenchment: Consolidation and Drift, 1972–1976

During 1971 economic problems began to emerge once again. In spite of the general mood of austerity, industrial growth was once again outpacing agricultural growth by too wide a margin. The steadily swelling ranks of industrial workers were putting pressure on the food supply. In the decentralized and generally disorganized process of investment, too many new projects had been started that could not be expected to begin producing for many years. An increasingly large amount of manpower and other resources was being tied up in construction, while the output necessary to support these people and projects was not forthcoming. Economic pressures were suddenly reinforced by dramatic political events. In late 1971, Lin Biao, a key Cultural Revolution leader and the head of the military, was suddenly purged, and almost immediately thereafter a rapprochement was engineered between China and the United States, marked by the visit to China of President Richard M. Nixon in 1972. With the sudden relaxation of the international environment and the purge of China's most powerful military figure, the leadership was in a position to address the emerging economic problems.

The premier, Zhou Enlai, took the lead in introducing a new, more moderate course. Investment was cut back, and the priority given to the Third Front was dramatically reduced. Some investment was shifted to coastal regions where it could be completed more efficiently. Economic relations with the capitalist world were reestablished, and a decision was made to spend US$4.3 billion to import industrial equipment. One of the largest items was a set of 11 very-large-scale fertilizer plants from a U.S.–Dutch consortium. During 1972–1973 a major restructuring of Chinese economic policy in a more moderate direction was emerging. As Zhou Enlai's health deteriorated, Mao brought the moderate Deng Xiaoping, a prominent victim of the Cultural Revolution, back to power at the end of 1974. During 1975, Deng presided over a "rectification" of policy, trying to overcome some of the worst of the Cultural Revolution problems, but these dizzying political changes would not cease, and Deng was again ejected from power in 1976.

Political struggles prevented a thorough reorientation of Chinese policy. Figure 3.2 shows the annual pattern of fluctuating investment: It was impossible to get follow-through on any systematic economic policy. The aging Mao refused to allow any criticism of policies associated with the Cultural Revolution and encouraged a group of radicals (subsequently dubbed the "Gang of Four") to obstruct trends toward economic rationalization. While the radicals succeeded in radicalizing culture and ideology, they never had control of economic policy-making. Nevertheless, their political power led to a period of deadlock in the top leadership, which increasingly turned into an open power struggle as it became clear that the succession to Mao was near. Between 1974 and 1976 economic policy-making was paralyzed.

3.3.10   The Leap Outward: 1978 and the End of Maoism

This deadlock was finally broken by the death of Mao Zedong in September 1976. Within days a new leadership threw the Gang of Four in prison and quickly turned its attention to economic matters. Through 1977, conscious of the chaos that had come to dominate economic administration, the post-Mao leadership concentrated on a series of rectification and data-collection exercises. Investment was maintained at modest levels while a program of moderate recentralization was carried out. Systematic rehabilitation of key sectors such as railroads was carried out. While rehabilitating the economy, the leadership was making big plans. The new leader, Hua Guofeng, staked his prestige on a massive investment push, framed as a 10-year plan for the 1975–1985 period. This plan envisaged the creation of 120 major projects, all large in scale and most in heavy industry. Ten huge integrated steel mills were envisioned, as well as 10 new oil fields, 30 large power plants, and 5 new ports. Lying behind this grandiose plan was a belief that the Chinese economy was capable of rapid growth: If only China could purge leftist politicians, focus attention on economics, and rebuild economic institutions, it could experience a major economic takeoff.

Yet it was not to be, for China was not yet ready for economic acceleration. The plan was based on specific calculations that were faulty. Between the early 1960s and 1977, China's petroleum production had grown by 15% annually, and Hua Guofeng's 10-Year Plan was based on the idea that China would use petroleum earnings to pay for high-quality industrial capital goods embodying the latest Western technology: for this reason it was dubbed in Chinese a "great leap outward." Given the decimation of the planning apparatus during the Cultural Revolution years, planners were in no position to address the difficult problems of absorption of new technologies and massive resource flows, selection of sites and detailed project planning, and coordination of multiple new projects. Instead, the "leap outward" collapsed of its own weight, for two reasons. First, in an unrealistic environment, investment plans at all levels kept being raised, just as they had been in the GLF, 20 years earlier. Given permission to import foreign technology, numerous Chinese agencies began signing large contracts with foreign suppliers. By late 1978 serious discussions were proceeding on at least US$40 billion worth of projects, and about US$7 billion worth of contracts were actually signed. This would have been a massive commitment for an economy only barely open to the outside world. Second, China's effort to develop its oil fields to increase exports was running into unexpected obstacles. In fact, half of China's oil production all along had come from the single field of Daqing in Manchuria, and this field was showing signs of depletion. During 1977 and 1978, China drilled nearly 15 million meters of new oil wells (which would have cost several billion dollars in the West) and struck oil only once, at a remote site in Xinjiang. It became clear that China did not have the oil to pay for these expensive contracts. The entire leap-outward strategy collapsed, as it became apparent to all that it was infeasible.

3.3.11 A Final Turning Point: The Third Plenum and the Beginning of Economic Reform

Finally, at the end of 1978, political factors came together in a way that allowed a fundamental departure from the economic and other policies of the Cultural Revolution era. The December 1978 "Third Plenum" initiated a new era in the Chinese economy and in Chinese politics. The third "plenum" (i.e., meeting of all members) of the 11th Central Committee marked an unmistakable break with the past. Politically, the plenum marked the return of Deng Xiaoping to the position of paramount leader, in alliance with other veteran CCP leaders, such as Chen Yun and Li Xiannian. Ideologically, the way was opened to free discussion of a number of previously taboo topics. In the economic realm, a host of new policies were adopted. From 1979 onward, the discussion of specific economic policies belongs with the contemporary period of economic reform (Chapter 4), rather than with the legacies of the command economy.

3.4 LEGACIES OF THE SOCIALIST PERIOD

3.4.1 The Legacy of Policy Instability

The details of the political conflicts that repeatedly split Maoist China are exhausting, sometimes bewildering, and ultimately dispiriting. By the end, the aged Mao was an enormous obstacle to China's development, confusing his own personal power and self-justifications with China's realities and needs. Yet from the economic standpoint, a rather simple picture emerges. Here was a system that set all the strategic and systemic settings to maximize the flow of resources into industrialization. It concentrated discretionary power at the top, so that leaders could throw resources at whatever their priorities were. The system, in other words, was set up to maximize the potential to "leap." But every time the system really began to accelerate, it ran into fundamental problems. The economy would overshoot and hit its head on the ceiling. What was this "ceiling"? The ceiling was the inability of agriculture to rapidly generate adequate food surpluses, combined with the weak capacity of the system to generate productive employment for its abundant labor.

This legacy had some important consequences after 1978. First, it generated profound dissatisfaction with the standard socialist system, even among

CCP leaders. While there was no fundamental rejection of the socialist system in the late 1970s, there was a remarkably deep willingness to experiment and revise, founded on deep misgivings about the socialist system. Second, the sharp political divisions meant that CCP leaders could disassociate themselves from the failures of the past by blaming mistakes on Mao, who, after all, richly deserved the blame. Finally, China's leaders could find in the past, in periods of experimentation or economic recovery, policy models that might be appropriate in an era of economic transition. The most significant sources of inspiration were the 1956–1957 Hundred Flowers, at least the economic-policy components, and the agricultural-policy experiments in the early 1960s, immediately after the GLF famine. Indeed, the policy of contracting farm output to households, which was the critical reform breakthrough in the early 1980s, actually had its roots in Anhui Province in 1962–1963. Even the decentralization of the early 1970s had some demonstration value to reformers in the 1980s. Finally, reformers at the end of the 1970s had learned how deep-rooted the problems of the planned economy were, and they were aware of potential alternatives.

3.4.2   The Shortcomings of the Development Strategy

There were a number of adverse factors associated with the socialist development strategy. First, the single-minded pursuit of industrial development meant that consumption was neglected. During the entire 1952 through 1978 period, gross capital formation grew at an average annual rate of 10.4%, and it was 13 times as large in 1978 as in 1952; but household consumption grew at only a 4.3% rate and was triple the 1952 level by 1978. After allowing for population growth, per capita household consumption grew only 2.3% annually, by official statistics, which somewhat overstate real growth. Moreover, the urban–rural differential was significant: urban growth at 3% was significantly above rural growth of 1.8%. Thus by 1978 per capita consumption in urban areas had slightly more than doubled, but rural per capita consumption was only 58% higher than in 1952. Consumption growth of this magnitude would be perceptible, but slow, and certainly not exceptional by comparative standards.

Growth in services was neglected. Normally, as an economy develops, agriculture shrinks in relative importance while industry and services expand (this relationship is discussed in more detail in Chapter 6). However, this generalization was not true for China between 1952 and 1978. Services actually *declined* from 29% of GDP to 24% of GDP over this period, mostly because of a declining contribution from commerce. The government was hostile toward the marketplace and independent businessmen: In 1952 there was one retail salesperson for 81 people, but by 1978 there was one for 214 people. There was one restaurant for every 676 people in 1952, but only one for 8,189 people in 1978. Social services like science, education, and health altogether increased their share of GDP, but by less than one percentage point.

The relative shrinkage of the retail sector reflected the fact that there was no real competition on consumer markets, and there was thus little quality improvement and few new products introduced. Moreover, pricing policy further discriminated against consumption. Any consumer good that could vaguely be considered a "luxury" was priced with a high markup, satisfying egalitarian impulses and also conveniently soaking up excess purchasing power. Such goods—including relatively mundane items such as wristwatches and electric fans—were often not affordable by average households, even when available. Indeed, even given slow income growth and high prices for luxuries, rationing was imposed to limit demand and distribute goods in scarce supply. From 1955 until well into the 1980s, ration coupons were required for the purchase of grain and cotton cloth. While the scope of rationing fluctuated with the degree of shortage, as of 1978 there were some kinds of ration restrictions in place for more than 20 items, including, besides grain and cloth, such items as soap, tofu, and good-quality bicycles. The degree of shortage of basic consumer goods was much greater than in the Soviet Union, which abolished most rationing after World War II.

A second major shortcoming of the development strategy was that employment creation was relatively slow. Because most industry was capital-intensive and services were neglected, new labor requirements were modest. Between 1952 and 1978 the total labor force grew by 191 million (from 207 to 398 million), but growth of the modern industrial and service sectors only absorbed 37% of the *increase* in the labor force! The agricultural workforce grew by 2% per year over the entire period. By 1978 the agricultural labor force was 70% larger than it had been in 1952, notwithstanding a virtually zero increase in cultivated land and rapid ongoing industrialization. As a result, underemployment, particularly in rural areas, remained a serious problem.

Third, much of the industrial investment was not only capital-intensive, but also relatively demanding technologically. Plants were often large, complex, multistage commitments that took years, even decades, to construct and put in operation. This fact had immediate implications: the economic return was often low, in the sense that capital was tied up for many years without producing output. Indeed, there were numerous cases of Chinese factories that never fully ramped up mass production of complex processes, steel mills, for example, that encountered problems with difficult ores and complex processes.

Perhaps as a result, the industrial growth rate showed a tendency to decelerate: growth was highest during the 1950s (17% per year between 1952 and 1957) and slowed to 8% per year during the 1970 to 1979 period. In a sense, Chinese industrialization strategy was overambitious. By concentrating on capital- and technology-intensive heavy industries and neglecting labor-intensive consumer goods industries, the Chinese were pouring scarce resources into difficult undertakings while ignoring opportunities to exploit relatively "easy" projects. The strategy created an important heavy industrial base, but those assets were being used at very low efficiency.

3.4.3 Human Capital Base

One area where it is possible to have a positive appraisal of China's socialist policies is the investment in basic human capital. The flow of resources into basic health and education was fairly substantial throughout the socialist period, and Chinese people were healthier and better educated at the end of the Socialist era. While individual consumption growth was restrained, "socialized" consumption such as education and health grew rapidly. Moreover, these outlays were often made in ways that benefited lower-income members of society. Thus, even though the Cultural Revolution shut down the university system for years, primary education spread significantly during the same period, and illiteracy declined rapidly. Strong entry-level health care institutions in the countryside were built up during the same period. The result was that life expectancy at birth climbed to 60 for the overall period 1964–1982, according to our best estimates. This was quite high for a country at China's income level, and up from about 50 in 1957 and perhaps as low as 30 in the early years of the twentieth century (Banister and Hill 2004). According to the 1982 census, two-thirds of the population was literate, again a fairly good comparative performance. Basic industrial skills were widespread in the population.

One is tempted to claim that the socialist system did a fairly good job of providing for basic needs and putting a subsistence floor under its poorest citizens. The problem is that the terrible famine of 1959–1961 makes a mockery of this statement. What good does it do to provide for your citizens basic needs for 27 years if you force on them policies of starvation in the other three years? In effect, the irrationalities of the system were so profound that they destroyed what could and should have been its proudest achievement. After December 1978, Chinese leaders struggled to transform a system that they themselves had built over the preceding 30 years. As a result of the twists and turns of the preceding decades, the system they confronted was more decentralized, more contested, and less entrenched than that of the Soviet Union. Chinese leaders perceived more options and flexibility, and they were determined not to be left behind by their dynamic East Asian neighbors.

BIBLIOGRAPHY

Suggestions for Further Reading

For good overviews and discussion of the socialist era, see Riskin (1991), Lardy (1987), and Lin, Cai, and Li (1996). There is now an extensive literature on the GLF and the subsequent famine. Becker (1996) is a moving account. The data were first seriously analyzed by Ashton et al. (1984). Since then, important contributions have been made by Chang and Wen (1997), Peng (1987), Lin and Yang (2000), and many others. Joseph, Wong, and Zweig (1991) is a good reassessment of the Cultural Revolution period.

Sources for Data and Figures

Figure 3.1: NBS (1999, 6–7); *SYC* (various years).

Figure 3.2: NBS (1999, 6–7); *SYC* (various years).

Figure 3.3: Lin and Yang (2000); NBS (1999).

Figure 3.4: Naughton (1988).

References

Ashton, Basil, Kenneth Hill, Alan Piazza, and Robin Zeitz (1984). "Famine in China, 1958–61." *Population and Development Review* 10 (December): 613–45.

Banister, Judith, and Kenneth Hill (2004). "Mortality in China 1964–2000," *Population Studies* 58:1, 55–75.

Becker, Jasper (1996). *Hungry Ghosts: Mao's Secret Famine.* New York: Free Press.

Chang, Gene Hsin, and Guanzhong James Wen (1997). "Communal Dining and the Chinese Famine of 1958–1961." *Economic Development and Cultural Change* 46 (October): 1–34.

Joseph, William, Christine Wong, and David Zweig, eds. (1991). *New Perspectives on the Cultural Revolution.* Cambridge, MA: Harvard University Press. Includes reassessments of rural industry, the Third Front, and central-local relations during the Cultural Revolution.

Lardy, Nicholas (1987). "The First Five Year Plan, 1953–1957," and "The Great Leap Forward and After," in Roderick MacFarquhar and John K. Fairbank, eds., *The Cambridge History of China,* vol. 14: *The People's Republic,* Part 1: *The Emergence of Revolutionary China, 1949–1965.* New York: Cambridge University Press.

Lin, Justin Yifu, Fang Cai, and Zhou Li (1996). *The China Miracle: Development Strategy and Economic Reform.* Hong Kong: Chinese University Press. The section on the socialist development strategy is especially good.

Lin, Justin Yifu, and Dennis Tao Yang (2000). "Food Availability, Entitlements and the Chinese Famine of 1959–61." *Economic Journal* 110 (January), 136–58.

NBS [National Bureau of Statistics, Department of Comprehensive Statistics] (1999). *Xiandai Zhongguo 50 Nian Tongji Ziliao Huibian* [Comprehensive Statistical Data and Materials on 50 Years of New China]. Beijing: China Statistics Press. Easily accessible source of official data, with headings in Chinese and English.

Naughton, Barry (1988). "The Third Front: Defense Industrialization in the Chinese Interior." *China Quarterly* 115 (Autumn): 351–86.

Peng, Xizhe (1987). "Demographic Consequences of the Great Leap Forward in China's Provinces." *Population and Development Review* 13 (December): 639–70.

Riskin, Carl (1991). *China's Political Economy: The Quest for Development since 1949.* New York: Oxford University Press.

Schurmann, Franz (1966). *Ideology and Organization in Communist China.* Berkeley: University of California Press.

SYC (Annual). *Zhongguo Tongji Nianjian* [Statistical Yearbook of China]. Beijing: Zhongguo Tongji.

Market Transition: Strategy and Process

Since China launched economic reforms at the end of 1978, market transition has extended over almost 30 years. Indeed, today China has already spent as long a period building a market economy as under Maoist socialism. China's economy has been transformed by successive waves of economic reform. Over the years the content of the reform process has adapted to new challenges and circumstances, and has been continuously reformulated. There have been failures and reverses on occasion, but what is most remarkable is simply how far China has come toward a market economy and how the reform process has maintained its relevance as the challenges the economy faces have changed. By at least the mid-1990s, China had successfully moved away from the command economy and adopted a functioning market economy. Nevertheless, even today, the process of market transition in China is far from complete. Many of the institutions necessary for a market economy are rudimentary, and further market building and institutionalization are necessary. The broad issues of transition extend into every aspect of the economy today. In this chapter, the focus is on the overall process of market transition. Subsequently, Chapters 5 through 20 focus on specific sectors or aspects of the contemporary economy, covering the years since 1978, with each sector viewed within the context of China's transitional economy.

This chapter begins by examining some of the assumptions and objectives that China's reformers brought to the transition process. These assumptions led to a distinctive approach to market transition that differentiated China from other formerly socialist economics, ultimately coalescing into a strategy of gradual transformation. The breakthrough in rural China is stressed at the beginning because it was the key early success that drove reforms onward and allowed Chinese reformers to grapple with successively more fundamental issues of transformation. The chapter then lays out a basic framework for China's transition process, interpreting the overall reform process as consisting of two main phases. The first phase of gradualist, dual-track, decentralizing reforms developed directly out of the rural successes. The basic purpose of this phase was to begin the dismantling of the command economy while maintaining economic growth, an objective that was substantially achieved. Markets were introduced into nearly every area, ownership was diversified, and competition created, all within the framework of the existing institutions. During the second phase, after about 1993, the emphasis of reform shifted as it became more fundamental and thorough. The main accomplishments of this phase have been the remaking of the institutional setup to make it compatible with a market economy, the dramatic shrinkage of the state sector, and the creation of conditions enabling fair competition among all market participants. The second stage is still ongoing. While both phases of reform can be seen to have produced substantial successes, Chinese policymakers still struggle to improve the functioning of the market economy, while coping with the social problems created by transition thus far.

4.1   THE CHINESE APPROACH TO TRANSITION

China's approach to economic transition was quite different from that of most of the other socialist countries. China's leaders viewed China, quite correctly, as a low-income developing country, and the imperative of economic development was constantly on their minds. It was never conceivable to Chinese policy-makers that their economy would postpone economic development until after an interlude of system transformation. It was always assumed that system transformation would have to take place concurrently with economic development, and indeed that the process of economic development would drive market transition forward and guarantee its eventual success. Individual reform policies were frequently judged on the basis of their contribution to economic growth (rather than to transition as such). In the beginning, this approach was followed because reformers literally did not know where they were going: they were reforming "without a blueprint" and merely seeking ways to ameliorate the obvious serious problems of the planned economy. But even after the goal of a market economy gradually gained ascendance in the minds of reformers, it was not anticipated that market transition would be completed until the economy reached at least middle-income status. And in fact, that is exactly what eventually happened.

The approach to transition was starkly different in Eastern Europe and Boris Yeltsin's Russia. In those countries, the predominant objective of committed reformers was to move as rapidly as feasible to a modern market economy. Reformers had a model to aim for—neighboring Western European economies—and wanted to shed the legacy of Communism as quickly as possible to begin a rapid convergence to this model. Reformers did not believe that their governments could correct distortions in their economy. There were too many distortions, too deeply interrelated. Moreover, those reformers had come to power through the democratic process and had a profound distrust of the Communist Party leaders they had replaced. How could they even be sure that party bureaucrats and planners would follow the instructions of the new governments? It was better to smash the entire edifice, eliminating as many distortions and privileges and the resulting rent-seeking opportunities as possible, and start all over from the bottom up. If in the process there was some short-term loss of output, so be it. This strategy was often called the "big bang." For these reformers, it was of critical importance to free prices as quickly as possible, to let the price system begin to work. It was seen as better to undergo the costs early, in order to lay the foundation for healthy long-term growth later. Subsequent experience, however, showed that those costs were much greater than anticipated.

In contrast, Chinese reformers saw unmet needs everywhere in their economies. Some needs were unmet because China was poor and underdeveloped, and others were unmet because the command economy was wasteful: reformers did not make a fundamental distinction between these two types. The command economy had lavished resources on expensive industrial projects while neglecting simple and easily satisfied demands of consumers. Chinese reformers, in essence, decreed that individuals and organizations should be allowed to satisfy unmet needs and earn some additional income, and if, in the process, this new activity tended to erode the command economy and had to be exempted from some of its rules, so be it. Chinese reformers lowered barriers and gradually opened up their system, giving individuals and groups the opportunity to act entrepreneurially and meet market demands. Early reforms created pockets of unregulated and lightly taxed activity within the system. Reformers allowed such pockets to open up because they were seen as contributing to developmental objectives. For example, rural communities were allowed to run township and village enterprises outside the plan because doing so would contribute to local investment and economic growth. Foreign businesses were allowed to operate freely in special economic zones because that approach would increase investment in China and might convince foreign corporations to transfer technology to China. Such policies were seen as contributing to growth while not initially threatening the overall ability of the government to manage and direct the economy.

As a result, early reforms almost never reduced or eliminated distortions; instead they loosened control over resources so that those distortions

encouraged resources (people, money, initiative) to flow into these less regulated "pockets." Individuals or communities saw "niches" available that they
could exploit. First movers made high profits. Only rarely did one see a "level
playing field." But this process set up an economic dynamic leading to intensified competition. Gradually, the process of attracting new entrants into
"pockets" in the planned economy went far enough that the overall balance
between plan and market began to shift. The plan, from having been the solid
material out of which a few pockets were excavated by pioneering entrepreneurs, became more like a sponge floating in a sea of predominantly market
activity. From this point, achieved by the mid-1990s in most sectors, a new
phase of economic reform could begin. The focus of reforms shifted toward
dissolving the compulsory plan and creating uniform rules and tax rates for
all sectors of the economy. The dual-track plan and market system was phased
out, and most prices were unified at market prices. Astonishingly, there was
never any "big bang." The process was achieved with a minimum of economic
disruption and relative social stability. The contrast is striking to the protracted
economic downturn and social upheaval that followed transition in Eastern
Europe and Russia.

4.2   HOW DID REFORMS START? THE INITIAL BREAKTHROUGH IN THE COUNTRYSIDE

China's market transition began at the end of 1978 with a wide-ranging
reassessment of nearly every aspect of the command economy. Indeed, there
was at this time a broad social relaxation after the storms of the Cultural Revolution: political prisoners were freed, millions of sent-down youth returned
to the cities, and discussions were relatively free and wide-ranging. In this environment, the extent of the possible was not known, and experimental reforms
were launched in nearly every sector of the economy. However, it was in the
countryside that reforms succeeded first, and it was the dramatic success of
rural reforms that cleared the way for continuing and progressively more profound change (Chapter 10).

The rural reforms began with a simple policy decision: the government
should reduce the pressure under which farmers had operated for the previous 30 years. For years, China had been locked into a losing cycle with its
farmers: pressured to collect more grain from farmers, procurement targets
had been kept high and procurement prices low. But farmers had resisted this
unattractive bargain: grain production had grown slowly; farmer marketing
had increased slowly; and farmers were unenthusiastic about investing more

time and money in agriculture. At the end of 1978—indeed, at the landmark Third Plenum itself—China's leaders made a decision to ease the terms of trade with agriculture and "give farmers a chance to catch their breath." Procurement targets were stabilized and slightly reduced; procurement prices were raised; and, most importantly, prices for farm deliveries above the procurement target were raised dramatically. These decisions were not easy to make, for they involved substantial trade-offs: in order to pay for the policies, planners in 1979 had to reduce investment, double grain imports in three years, and chop back the ambitious technology import program of the "leap outward" (Chapter 3). The only thing that made these choices palatable to China's leaders was their conviction that the rural economy needed an opportunity for profound restructuring and rehabilitation.

At first, reformers had no clear idea how that restructuring of the farm economy would take place. All farmers were compulsory members of agricultural collectives, and reformers did not initially envision a change in that arrangement, but they were willing to give farmers more breathing space. Reformers at this time were emphasizing the necessity to give enterprises in other sectors expanded decision-making autonomy and better incentives, and the same offer was made to agricultural collectives. Collectives were allowed to experiment with different payment systems for farmers and better ways of organizing and marketing output. Collectives adopted a wide range of innovative approaches, but eventually they began to gravitate toward a radical solution: contracting individual pieces of land to farm households. Farm households took over management of the agricultural production cycle on a specific plot of land, subject to a contractual agreement that they turn over a certain amount of procurement (low price) and tax (zero price) grain after the harvest. This policy essentially recreated the traditional farm household economy, with the collective reduced to being little more than a landlord. Because it implied such a dramatic reduction in the role of the collectives—everything short of abolition—this policy was extremely controversial. But Chinese leaders decided not to block it, and after 1980 they gradually shifted and gave it de facto support.

What happened next was quite astonishing. The institution of contracting land to households spread rapidly throughout rural China and became nearly universal by the end of 1983. Agricultural production began to surge. Helped along by higher prices and the increased availability of modern inputs such as chemical fertilizer, production climbed rapidly through 1984 (see Chapter 11). By 1984 grain output had surged to 407 million metric tons, more than one-third higher than in 1978. There was enough grain for everybody in China. The decades in which China's industrialization had been repeatedly held back by agricultural weakness seemed suddenly to be over, and the centuries of a China fundamentally short of food were over as well.

In fact, the increase in grain output was only half the story. Freed to allocate their own labor in the way they wanted, farmers increased grain output while actually *reducing* the number of days spent in the grain fields. Instead, they sharply increased their labor input into nongrain crops and nonagricultural businesses. The number of workers in township and village enterprises (TVEs)—locally run factories—increased rapidly, and output from this sector surged as well (see Chapter 12). These TVEs were not incorporated into state plans, so their output either went to meet heretofore unmet market demands or else created new competition for the existing state-owned enterprises. In either case, TVE activity was disruptive and set off profound changes. Successful farm and TVE reforms emboldened reformers, giving them confidence to persist in the reform project. With this background, reformers were prepared to push forward in other sectors where initial efforts had not met with immediate success. Moreover, rural incomes increased rapidly, and reforms gained the support of the bulk of the rural population.

4.3   A TWO-PHASE FRAMEWORK OF ECONOMIC REFORM

Successful rural reforms also reinforced a certain approach to the reform process. Rural reforms had been achieved with little economic or social disruption, largely because a type of dual-track system had been adopted. When farmers contracted for their land, they agreed to turn over a certain amount of grain to the government: the rest was released to the market. Reformers saw in this experience a model of using contracts to stabilize some crucial pieces of the existing economic system while freeing up other pieces. The contracts built in vested interests—in this case, the government and its need to ensure access to grain—while also providing powerful new incentives to farmers, since they kept 100% of the harvest above the contracted deliveries. Reformers sought to extend this approach to industrial and commercial reforms, and in so doing they created a pattern of economic reform that strongly characterized the period from 1978 through about 1993. Reform overall was decentralizing, shifting power and resources from the hands of central planners to local actors, while core interests were protected, often through contracts. This process allowed entry barriers to be reduced and market forces to grow. By 1993, though, this particular pattern of reform had largely run its course. The market sphere had expanded sufficiently that the economy had "grown out of the plan." The focus of policy-makers shifted, as it became increasingly necessary to build a firmer institutional basis for the market economy that was developing. Table 4.1 shows

Table 4.1
Contrasting styles of economic reform

1980s reform	1990s reform
Zhao Ziyang: cautious, consensual decision-making	Zhu Rongji: Rapid, personalized decision-making
Introduce markets where feasible; focus on agriculture and industry	Strengthen institutions of market economy, focus on finance and regulation
Dual-track strategy	Market unification, unite dual tracks
Particularistic contracts with powerful incentives	Uniform rules: "level playing field"
Competition created by entry; no privatization	State-sector downsizing; beginnings of privatization
Decentralize authority and resources	Recentralize resources, macroeconomic control
Inflationary economy with shortages	Price stability, goods in surplus
"Reform without losers"	Reform with losers

the main elements of reform strategy in the two periods, laid out to highlight the contrasts between them.

4.4   ELEMENTS OF CHINA'S TRANSITION THROUGH 1992

In discussing the 1980s (more broadly 1979–1992), the character of China's gradualist transition can be summarized in nine key features, described in the following subsections, which contributed most directly to the period's success. Also, it may not be coincidental that through most of this period the key policy-maker was Zhao Ziyang, premier from 1980 until 1987 and then first party secretary until the Tiananmen Square demonstrations in 1989. Although Zhao was always subordinate to Deng Xiaoping, it was Zhao himself who was responsible for the day-to-day policy-making that steered the Chinese transition through this first period. Zhao had to defer not only to Deng Xiaoping, but also to other senior revolutionary leaders, most important of whom was Chen Yun. Partially because of this political environment, Zhao's policy-making was cautious and gradual, and he had to be able to create at least a passive consensus behind each policy he wished to push forward. Zhao's key challenge was to extricate the economy from the grip of command-economy institutions, which he was able to do. China avoided a Soviet-style collapse by disentangling itself gradually from the institutions of the planned economy.

4.4.1   Dual-Track System

Perhaps the most characteristic feature of China's initial departure from the planned economy was the dual-track system. The Chinese term *shuangguizhi* refers to the coexistence of a traditional plan and a market channel for the allocation of a given good. Rather than dismantling the plan, reformers acquiesced to a continuing role for the plan in order to ensure stability and guarantee the attainment of some key government priorities (in the Chinese case, primarily investment in energy and infrastructure). The dual track implied a two-tier pricing system for most goods: a single commodity had both a (typically low) state-set planned price and a (typically higher) market price.

It is important to stress that the dual track refers to the coexistence of two coordination mechanisms (plan and market) and not to the coexistence of two ownership systems. By the mid-1980s, most state-owned firms were still being assigned a compulsory plan for some output but had additional capacity available for production of above-plan, market goods. Thus the dual-track strategy was one that operated within the state sector—indeed, within each state-run factory—as well as in the industrial economy at large. This fact was essential because it meant that virtually all factories, including state-run factories, were introduced to the market and began the process of adaptation to market processes. The dual-track system allowed state firms to transact and cooperate with nonstate firms, allowing valuable flexibility. But the growing importance of collective, private, and foreign-invested firms should be considered apart from the dual-track system strictly defined, since most of these firms were predominantly market oriented from the beginning (Wong 1986).

4.4.2   Growing Out of the Plan

The mere existence of the dual-track system is not in itself sufficient to propel an economy in transition to a market economy. In a sense, all planned economies had some kind of dual-track system, because they all had various black and "gray" markets outside the formal planning system. But China planners in 1984 made a broad commitment to keep the overall size of the central-government materials-allocation plan fixed in absolute terms. Since the economy was growing, this commitment implied a gradual process in which the plan would become proportionately less and less important until the economy grew out of the plan. Figure 4.1 shows this process at work with respect to sales and allocation of finished steel, arguably the single commodity most characteristic of the planned economy. Up until 1984 the quantity of steel allocated by central government planners increased in step with production. Unusually in a planned economy, there was also a substantial share of total output allocated by local government planners, which also seems to have been increasing over time. A tiny share of output was sold inde-

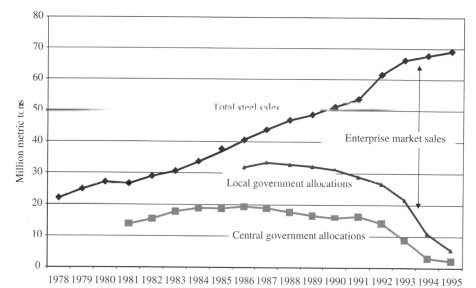

Figure 4.1
Steel production and planned allocation

pendently by enterprises. After 1984, though, the quantity allocated by the central government leveled off, and nearly all the increment in output was channeled onto the market, that is, left to the control of enterprises to sell at the best price they could obtain. In the early 1990s quantities allocated began to decline in absolute terms, and then dropped precipitously around 1993. After that point, the economy had grown out of the plan. A generally credible commitment to freeze the compulsory plan set in motion a dynamic process that gradually increased the share of nonplan, market transactions in the economy and made the dual-track system into an unabashed transitional device.

The commitment to grow out of the plan crucially altered incentives at the level of the individual enterprise. With their plans essentially fixed, enterprises faced "market prices on the margin" (Byrd 1991). Even those firms with compulsory plans covering, say, 90% of capacity, were in a position such that future growth and development of profitable opportunities would take place at market prices. The plan served as a kind of lump-sum tax on (or subsidy to) the enterprise. So long as the commitment not to change it was credible, it really had no impact on any of the enterprise's decision-making. Current decision-making would be based on market prices, and so would profit maximization. In that sense, the plan became irrelevant.

4.4.3   Particularistic Contracts

In order to make the dual-track system work, planners signed individual contracts with every state-owned enterprise. These contracts specified tax payments and contributions to the material-balance plan (somewhat on the model
of the rural household contracting system). In practice, this policy meant there
was no regular tax system—the de facto tax rate was specific to an individual
enterprise. Each contract was drawn up on the basis of the firm's performance
in a previous base year, so that each existing enterprise was grandfathered into
the transitional system (see Chapter 13).

4.4.4   Entry

The central government's monopoly over industry was relaxed. In China the
protected industrial sector was effectively opened to new entrants beginning
in 1979. Large numbers of start-up firms, especially rural industries, rushed to
take advantage of large potential profits in the industrial sector, and their entry
sharply increased competition and changed overall market conditions in the
industrial sector. Most of these firms were collectively owned, and some were
private or foreign owned. The crucial factor is that the central government sur-
rendered in practice its ability to maintain high barriers to entry around most
of the lucrative manufacturing sectors. This lowering of entry barriers was
greatly facilitated in China by the nation's huge size and diversity, as well as
the relatively large role that local governments played in economic management even before reform. Large size and diversity meant there was scope for
competition among firms in the "public sector," even if each of these firms
remained tied to government at some level.

4.4.5   Prices Equating Supply and Demand

Flexible prices that equated supply and demand quickly came to play an
important role in the Chinese economy. Beginning in the early 1980s a significant proportion of transactions began to occur at market prices, and in 1985
market prices were given legal sanction for exchange of producer goods
outside the plan. Consequently, state firms were legally operating at market
prices, since virtually all state firms had some portion of above-plan production. Gradual decontrol of consumer goods prices—initially cautious—steadily
brought most consumer goods under market-price regimes. An important
benefit of the legitimacy given to market prices was that transactions between
the state and nonstate sectors were permitted, and they developed into a
remarkable variety of forms. Simple trade was accompanied by various kinds
of joint ventures and cooperative arrangements, as profit-seeking state-run

enterprises looked for ways to reduce costs by subcontracting with rural non-state firms with lower labor and land costs.

4.4.6 Incremental Managerial Reforms Instead of Privatization

State-sector managerial reforms were carried out as an alternative to a more radical policy, privatization. As state firms faced increasing competitive pressures, government officials experimented with ways to improve incentives and management capabilities within the state sector. This experimental process focused on a steady shift in emphasis away from plan fulfillment and toward profitability as the most important indicator of enterprise performance (Chapter 13). There is substantial evidence that the combination of increased competition, improved incentives, and more effective monitoring of performance did improve state-enterprise performance over the 1980s. Logically there is no reason why privatization could not be combined with a dual-track transitional strategy, but practically there are obvious reasons why there would be alternatives. Urgent privatization tends to follow from a belief that state-sector performance cannot be improved, and often leads to a short-run "abandonment of the enterprise" as the attention of reformers shifts away from short-run performance and to the difficult task of privatization. Conversely, the sense that privatization is not imminent lends urgency to the attempt to improve monitoring, control, and incentives in the state sector. Clearly, the Chinese approach worked adequately during the early stages of transition. But debate continues about whether the moderate performance improvements in the state sector that were achieved were large enough to be judged successful.

4.4.7 Disarticulation

Along with measures to reform the core of the planned economy, Chinese reforms also advanced by identifying economic activities that were the least tightly integrated into the planning mechanism and pushing reform in these limited areas. Early reforms followed a strategy of "disarticulation," in which successive sections of the economy were separated from the planned core. This was clearly not an intentional strategy, but rather one that emerged from the nature of the policy process and from the concern of Chinese policy-makers not to disrupt the core economy. The early establishment of special economic zones is the most obvious example of such policies—export-oriented enclaves were created that had, initially, almost no links to the remainder of the economy (see Chapter 17). This approach is also one of the reasons that reforms succeeded first in the countryside. Policy-makers realized that it was not necessary that all the countryside be integrated into the planned economy.

Beginning with the poorest areas, some regions were allowed to detach from the planned economy. So long as the state could purchase sufficient grain to keep its storehouses full, it could afford to let the organizational form in the countryside devolve back to household farming. Caution led to a strategy of disarticulation.

4.4.8   Initial Macroeconomic Stabilization Achieved Through the Plan

When China's reformers faced serious macroeconomic imbalances in 1979–1981, they used the institutions of the planned economy to cut back investment and relieve pressure on the economy. Rather than combining stabilization and reform into a single rapid but traumatic episode—as in a "big bang" transition—the Chinese used the instruments of the planned economy to shift resources toward the household sector and relieve macroeconomic stresses at the very beginning of reform. This dramatic shift in development strategy created favorable conditions for the gradual development of markets. Inflationary pressures were vented off as supplies grew, rather than being resolved in a quick transition from suppressed to open inflation. In a related fashion, the planning structure was used to provide an initial impetus away from the capital-intensive Big Push strategy and toward more sustainable labor-intensive sectors. This initial shift toward a more labor-intensive strategy was given urgency by the need to provide jobs for a large group of unemployed young people, including many who had returned to the cities from the countryside. Clearly, planning would be an unwieldy and ineffective instrument to carry through such a shift over the long term. But the temporary use of this instrument to lower unemployment tended to preserve stability and solidify support for the reform orientation.

4.4.9   Continued High Saving and Investment

Continued high saving and investment were made possible by a gradual takeover of national saving from government by households (Chapter 18), made possible by macroeconomic stability. The Chinese government intentionally reduced its share of GDP during the early stages of reform in order to allow rural and urban households more resources and better incentives. Fortunately the steady increases in household income and the increasing opportunities in the economic environment led to a rapid increase in household saving. The fact that households were willing to rapidly increase their voluntary saving was a side benefit to the relatively stable economic environment reformers purchased through gradualist reforms. Rapidly increasing household saving indicates that households believed their assets would be reasonably secure. In turn, household behavior contributed to macroeconomic stability because it offset the reduction in government saving that took place at the same time. Reduced government saving was due to a steady erosion in government revenues, which itself was ultimately traceable to the dissolution of the government industrial monopoly. Total national saving remained high, thereby sustaining high levels of investment and growth. An indirect consequence was a vastly enhanced role for the banking system, serving as an intermediary channeling household saving to the enterprise sector. While this process was relatively smooth, it was difficult for the government to acquiesce in and to manage the decline in its resources, and macroeconomic policy-making became more complex and more difficult.

4.4.10   Conclusion of First-Phase Reforms

On balance, and in retrospect, the policies described here can be seen to have a clear coherence and to have been overwhelmingly successful. Reduction of the state's monopoly led to rapid entry of new firms. Entry of new firms combined with adoption of market prices on the margin led to enhanced competition and began to get state-sector managers accustomed to responding to the marketplace. Gradual price decontrol was essential. Competition eroded initially high profit margins for state firms and induced the government, as owner of the firms, to become more concerned with profitability. The government experimented with better incentive and monitoring devices, and this experimentation improved state-sector performance. Nonetheless, the state sector grew more slowly than the nonstate firms that were entering new markets. The economy gradually grew out of the plan, as both the plan itself and the state sector as a whole became less dominant elements in the economy. Yet this growth occurred with economic continuity that was attributable to the maintenance of a small planned sector as a kind of stabilizer, as well as to robust saving and investment that powered continued economic growth.

However, the ultimate success of the first-phase reform process was not always self-evident while it was ongoing. On the contrary, reform was always contested, and the achievements of reform were constantly subjected to harsh scrutiny from conservatives who were skeptical of reform. One result of this policy competition was a pattern of "two steps forward, one step back." Reforms seemed to advanced strongly in certain years (1979, 1984, 1987–1988) and retreat in other years (1981 1982, 1986, 1989). Relating to these policy cycles, macroeconomic cycles also persisted throughout the reform process. Bold reform measures tended to be implemented after stabilization had achieved some success. Reform measures then contributed to renewed macroeconomic imbalances, eventually leading to a new period of macroeconomic austerity. As a result, the outcome of macroeconomic policies was frequently fundamental in determining the success or failure of specific reform initiatives (see Chapter 18). Oddly, this pattern of "political business cycles" mirrors the experience in the socialist economy; after 1978, however, the expansionary phases were phases of accelerated reform, rather than phases of political mobilization.

At times, these macroeconomic cycles yielded a side benefit. Planners were unable to keep up with rapidly changing cycles and were buffeted by rapid changes in economic conditions. The almost intractable task of planning an economy can only be carried out in conditions of artificially imposed stability; without that stability, the inadequacy of attempts to plan the economy became increasingly evident. But individual cycles also imposed very substantial costs on the economy, as well as undermining political support for reformist politicians. Indeed, by far the most serious challenge to the reform process came in the wake of just such a cycle, when deteriorating cyclical economic conditions in 1989 fed an upsurge of urban discontent.

4.5   THE TIANANMEN INTERLUDE

During 1988–1989 one of the severe cycles of macroeconomic imbalance described in the previous section led to a serious political crisis. Urban discontent in 1989 was fueled by a number of factors: rising inflation that eroded real incomes, anger at corruption and arbitrary privilege, and rising expectations about political and economic change. All these feelings were powerful motivating factors to students who poured into Tiananmen Square in central Beijing to mourn the unexpected death of Hu Yaobang, who had been an important reformist leader. Hu, in fact, had been particularly respected because of his willingness to fully rehabilitate more than a million Chinese who had been scapegoated and persecuted by either the Anti-Rightist Campaign or the Cultural Revolution, or both. A volatile mixture of expectations and grievances fueled extravagant hopes and massive disillusionment, and led to months of demonstrations in China's main square. Reformist leader Zhao Ziyang refused to order the military to clear the square by force. Ultimately, Zhao was ousted, and conservative leaders ordered the military into the square. Hundreds were killed, many of the most influential reformists in the government were sidelined or exiled, and the course of China's reform was forever altered.

However, the process of market transition resumed after about two years of backsliding. Economic reforms were able to survive because of the broader dynamics of the process. Certainly, economic causes were an important part of the social crisis leading up to the Tiananmen debacle. Soaring inflation during 1988–1989 ate away at real urban incomes that had been protected for most of the 1980s. A sense that the government was failing to honor a kind of implicit social compact with urban residents fueled discontent. At the same time, the measures that had been taken to curb inflation were already starting to bite into economic growth and cause expectations of the future to be revised downward. In this difficult short-term environment, the sense that political promises had been betrayed and political reforms were running off the tracks fueled a powerful sense of disillusionment and protest.

Yet from a long-term perspective, it is more striking that it was very rare for a major social group to suffer significant economic losses during the 1980s. In particular, the position of workers in state-owned enterprises (SOEs) was protected during the course of reform. The resulting pattern has been labeled "reform without losers" (Lau, Qian, and Roland 2000). Rural residents gained from the dissolution of collectives, improved agricultural prices, and the rapid growth of nonagricultural production in the countryside. Urban residents gained either because they were able to exploit new niches in the economy or because their economic position was protected by continuing government support for state enterprises. The broad enjoyment of the benefits of reform—and the absence of a group clearly disadvantaged by reform—meant that reform was still widely popular, despite the debacle at Tiananmen Square.

After the Tiananmen Square political crisis, a period of conservative ascendancy followed, between 1989 and 1991. The conservative attempts to roll back reforms were completely without success, however, and are often forgotten. Urban inflation, which had seemed so corrosive in 1988, was in fact quickly controlled, and market forces corrected other imbalances in the economy with a speed that surprised conservatives and left planners far behind. As it became clear that the conservatives had no viable program, their support among the Communist Party elite began to crumble.

It was in this situation, as the pendulum was swinging back toward renewed reform, that Deng Xiaoping himself emerged to give that pendulum a forceful push. In early 1992, Deng took a "Southern Tour" that had him visit the SEZs he himself had authorized more than a decade earlier. Deng gave a ringing endorsement to the concept and reality of the SEZs, a traditional bellwether of Chinese Communist elite opinion. Deng reemphasized the need for accelerated economic reform and specifically reaffirmed a nonideological, pragmatic approach to experimentation. "Development is the only hard truth," Deng declared, "It doesn't matter if policies are labeled socialist or capitalist, so long as they foster development." Deng's pronouncements were about principles, not practical policies, but they were sufficient to restore the government's commitment to economic reform and tip the balance of political power in Beijing. In October 1992 the 14th Congress of the Communist Party convened and endorsed a "socialist market economy," making clear that markets must extend to all main sectors of the economy. This was one of Deng Xiaoping's last decisive personal interventions in Chinese policy-making. Of course, while Deng's advocacy was sufficient to reignite economic reform, Deng was unwilling and perhaps unable to resume progress in political reform. As a result, Deng's legacy ultimately included an unbalanced combination of vigorous economic reforms and relative political stagnation.

4.6 THE SECOND PHASE OF REFORM, 1993–PRESENT

The post–Deng Xiaoping leadership was associated with a new phase of economic reform, but one that developed organically out of the earlier phase. In economic policy the figure of Zhu Rongji quickly emerged as the most important voice. Zhu established himself as the dominant voice in policy-making in mid-1993, while he was still vice premier, and was then formally elevated to premier in early 1998. Zhu's policy-making was rather different from that of his most important predecessor, Zhao Ziyang. Zhu had a strong, decisive personality and often made quick, personal decisions. Zhu presided over much of the second period of economic reform, until he stepped down as premier in 2003.

The contrasts between this period and the preceding one were shown schematically in Table 4.1. Key features of the second phase of reform can also be conceptualized in terms of prerequisites, regulatory changes, and outcomes. Three policy measures were essential prerequisites to the overall package: ending the dual-track system, recentralization of fiscal resources, and macroeconomic austerity. Having established a firm macroeconomic policy base, reformists shifted to a focus on regulatory and administrative restructuring in the key market sectors: the banking system, the tax system, the system of corporate governance, and the external sector, through membership in the WTO. The outcomes of this policy regime were a shift from inflation to price stability, a dramatic downsizing of the state-enterprise sector, the acceptance of a moderate amount of privatization, and the emergence of a "reform with losers." Zhu Rongji's policies were consistently associated with stronger, more authoritative government institutions and more decisive policy-making.

4.6.1   Prerequisites

4.6.1.1   Market Reunification

By the early 1990s the dual-track system had served its function. Figure 4.1 shows that after 1991 allocation of materials (in this case, steel), after having been kept constant for several years, dropped off rapidly. By the end of 1993, material-balance planning was abolished altogether. The orthodox planning system disappeared with barely a whimper, scarcely noticed. Particularistic contracts with individual enterprises were also allowed to lapse. One side of those contracts had become obsolete (delivery of within-plan output), while the financial side was in conflict with impending fiscal and tax reforms, which were high on the reform agenda.

4.6.1.2   Recentralization

It seems paradoxical that centralization could be a main tenet of reform in the second reform era, when decentralization had been a key part of the first era of reform. In fact, though, it was essential that further economic reforms develop a more appropriate division of responsibilities between central and local. During the first period of reform, the motivating force behind decentralization had been the need to introduce markets and incentives into the system. During the second period, management responsibilities were more clearly divided between center and local, but in a way that tended on balance to be recentralizing in terms of the ultimate control of resources. The central government needed to strengthen its regulatory and macroeconomic management functions. In order to do so, it also needed to establish an adequate and reliable source of finance revenues, which it was able to do. Figure 4.2 shows the outcome, a fundamental turning point in 1995. During the course of more than 15 years of reform, China's fiscal position had eroded significantly, dropping from 33.8% of GDP in 1978 to only 10.8% at the low point in 1995. The decline of budgetary revenues was driven primarily by the inexorable erosion of the old system in which state enterprises raised revenues from their monopoly position. More generally, fiscal decline was also the logical result of a transition strategy that stressed decentralization of authority and benefits, along with releasing resources from government control to the marketplace. Despite the successes achieved in transition, by the early 1990s it was widely perceived that China had a serious fiscal crisis. Key fiscal reforms—discussed in Chapter 18—provided a new, broader tax base for the economy and led to a steady revival of government budgetary collections. From 1995 onward, a modern tax system was gradually built up.

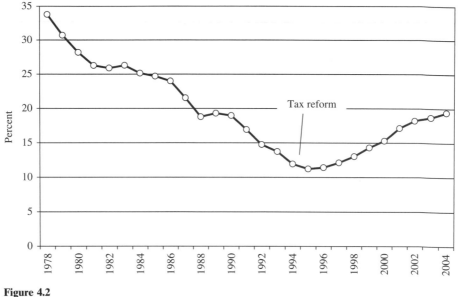

Figure 4.2
Budgetary revenue share of GDP

4.6.1.3 Macroeconomic Austerity

Macroeconomic austerity was both a short-term and a long-term necessity. In the wake of Deng Xiaoping's Southern Tour a gold rush mentality of speculation and financial excess quickly led to a surge of bank credit and accelerating inflation. Zhu Rongji made his mark by initiating a tough period of macroeconomic austerity in mid-1993. A financial crackdown was clearly necessary, but it turned out that this crackdown signaled the beginning of a new macroeconomic policy regime, which delivered much less cheap credit to state-owned enterprises and a slower growth of money and prices. By 1997 at the latest, it was clear that Chinese policy had shifted to a long-term policy of macroeconomic conservatism and had managed to deliver a significant degree of macroeconomic stability (see Chapter 18). This shift was an essential prerequisite to making public enterprises responsible for their own profits and losses, providing them with a "hard" budget constraint. Tough macroeconomic policies created conditions under which further enterprise restructuring was driven primarily by market forces.

4.6.2 Regulatory Approach and Administrative Restructuring

Zhu Rongji also presided over a new, more regulatory approach to economic reform. The new reforms were regulatory in the sense that they introduced new rules (and new prices) that at least in principle applied equally to all economic actors. There was more focus on creating and regulating competition as a force for economic change and less on direct government action in managing productive enterprises. By the 1990s, with the economy having "grown out of the plan," the most important tasks were to improve the legal and regulatory environment, create a "level playing field," and reduce some of the most obvious distortions in the economy. Regulatory and administrative reforms in the four most important sectors of the economy are described in the following sections. The commitment to this new direction was strongly signaled early on, when three crucial measures—a new fiscal system, a new foreign trade system, and the new Company Law—were made effective on January 1, 1994.

4.6.2.1   Fiscal and Tax System

Fiscal reforms in 1994 were designed to arrest the slide in budgetary revenues, but also to transition to a broader tax base by implementing a 17% value-added tax and other business taxes. These taxes had relatively low rates, compared to the old system, but they were uniform and applied to all economic actors. The strong performance of tax revenues after 1995 showed that broadening the tax base was successful. Fiscal reforms were also designed to put central-local government fiscal relations on a sounder and more stable basis. They did so by increasing the share of total taxes initially collected by the center and establishing a set of rules for sharing revenues between central and provincial governments (see Chapter 18).

4.6.2.2   Banking and Financial System

The banking system underwent fundamental restructuring during the second half of the 1990s. The People's Bank of China (PBC) had been nominally established as a central bank in 1983, but at that time it remained beholden to government officials at both central and provincial levels. The bank was finally given a workable organizational structure in late 1998, when a restructuring plan abolished the provincial-level branches and set up nine regional branches along the lines of the U.S. Federal Reserve Board. Combined with a renewed mandate to conduct monetary policy, and with a monetary policy board established as a governance and advisory body, the central bank began to play an active role in determining and implementing monetary policy. This administrative restructuring took place in tandem with the adoption of macroeconomic austerity: state-run commercial banks soon found themselves facing a much harder budget constraint, as their access to easy government money was curtailed. In turn, they began to pass tougher standards on to their clients in state-owned enterprises.

Shortly after the constitution of a central bank system, banking authorities began to tackle the enormous problem of lax financial supervision and non-performing loans in all the state banks. In 1999 four asset management corporations were established to take over some of the nonperforming loans of the four big state commercial banks and begin to liquidate them for as much residual value as possible. Clearly, these are essential steps on the long and difficult road to a stable banking system. Eventually, in April 2003, the PBC supervisory functions were spun off to the newly created China Bank Regulatory Commission (see Chapter 19).

4.6.2.3 Corporate Governance

A large-scale effort to restructure the state-owned corporate sector was begun with the passage of the Company Law at the end of 1993. The Company Law contained provisions for all state-owned enterprises to gradually reorganize as limited-liability corporations with clarified corporate governance institutions. These provisions have been only gradually implemented but have slowly transformed the organizational structure of the Chinese public sector (see Chapter 13). The systematic restructuring of corporate governance was combined with selective listing of state-owned companies on China's newly opened stock markets, which grew significantly during the late 1990s (Chapter 19). Together these measures changed the structure of China's large state-owned companies and created a demand for government regulation that had not previously been evident. With implementation of a securities law in July 1999, the China Securities Regulatory Commission's (CSRC) branches became operational nationwide, thus forming a centralized and unified network of securities supervisors. At the same time, a host of new central government agencies were established to deal with other types of regulatory oversight, including, for example, the State Intellectual Property Office and the State Administration of Technical and Quality Supervision. China began to make progress toward a regulatory state.

4.6.2.4 External Sector: Membership in the World Trade Organization

Extensive foreign-trade reforms were passed at the end of 1993 that unified China's foreign exchange regime, devalued the currency, and established current-account convertibility. These were important steps forward that Chinese authorities expected to clear the way for membership in the WTO. As it turned out, an arduous process of negotiation and compromise was required before China finally acceded to the WTO in December 2001. Accession involved Chinese acceptance of an extraordinarily broad range of regulatory undertakings, designed to allow China to harmonize with international standards. At the same time, and even more fundamentally, WTO accession implied an important further step in the degree of openness of the Chinese economy and in the extent to which foreign goods and companies could compete in China.

4.6.3   Outcomes

4.6.3.1   From Inflation to Price Stability

After 1996, Chinese inflation was tamed. Although cycles were not completely eliminated—another expansionary phase emerged after 2002—the overall macroeconomic context swung sharply toward price stability. The context of price stability and increased competition greatly intensified the product market pressure on Chinese firms, especially public enterprises.

4.6.3.2   State Enterprise Restructuring and Downsizing

From the mid-1990s, Chinese authorities began to cut the formerly close ties that bound government and state-owned enterprise. Public firms faced increased product market competition and pressure, on the one hand, and reduced access to funding from government banks, on the other. Gradually state-owned enterprises moved toward a significant restructuring and down-sizing, encouraged by the government. State-enterprise restructuring has meant converting vaguely defined public ownership into more explicit, legally defined ownership categories, sometimes involving privatization. Following the 15th Communist Party Congress in September 1997, local government officials were given an almost free hand to proceed with state-sector reforms that included bankruptcy, sales and auctions, and mergers and acquisitions. Throughout the 15 years of economic reform, between 1978 and about 1993, although the state sector had shrunk in relative importance, it had continued to grow in absolute terms, both in output and in employment. As Figure 4.3 shows, since the mid-1990s state-enterprise employment has declined dramat-ically. While some of these workers are in firms that remain government con-trolled (but no longer traditional state-owned), the overall size of public enterprise employment dropped by more than 40%.

Given the decentralized nature of the Chinese economy, the progress of state-owned-enterprise restructuring depended on the incentives facing local governments, which "owned" the majority of SOEs. In fact, SOEs had already ceased to be "cash cows" on which local government officials could draw: Industrial SOE profits were 15% of GDP in 1978, but fell below 2% of GDP in 1996–1997. Local governments began to rethink the value of possessing

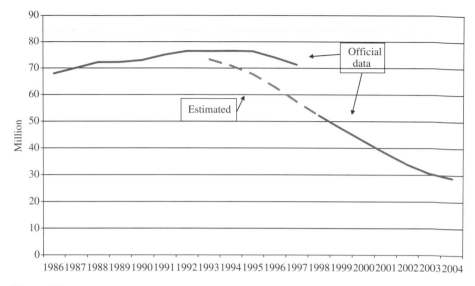

Figure 4.3
SOE workers

their own SOEs and increasingly concluded that they derived few advantages
from local state ownership that could not be achieved just as well from a generally prosperous local economy.

4.6.3.3   Privatization

The Chinese government has never unambiguously embraced privatization
and continues to avoid the term in favor of vague circumlocutions such as
"restructuring." However, privatization, often in the form of management
buyouts, became common in the TVE, collective, and SOE sectors after the
mid-1990s. More generally, private businesses have been given gradually
increasing recognition and legitimacy. Indeed, the rise of private business is
perhaps an inevitable consequence of a policy shift toward a level playing field.
By the end of 2004 the urban private sector, without counting foreign-invested
firms, employed about twice as many workers as the traditional state sector:
55 million, compared with less than 30 million in SOEs.

4.6.3.4   Reform with Losers

The momentous changes in transition strategy have broken sharply with one
of the key characteristics of reform in the early period. Reform after 1993
clearly imposed significant losses on substantial social groups. Most directly
affected were state-enterprise workers, who had been a relatively privileged

group in the past. Millions have been laid off, and further millions have abandoned failing firms (see Chapter 8). Subject to employment uncertainty for the first time since the establishment of the PRC, some state workers suffered precipitous losses in income and social standing. In general, groups and individuals are less sheltered from competition than in the past. Thus, while transition has continued to move ahead, the benefits of transition are now far more unequally spread among the Chinese population than was the case in the 1980s.

4.7 CONTEMPORARY CHALLENGES

The shift in transition strategy around 1992–1993 means that China's approach to transition is now somewhat less distinctive than it was previously. Economic policy-making in China now more closely resembles that in other transitional economies, such as Poland and the Czech Republic, and there is no longer a polar opposition between "big bang" and "gradualist" transitions. Reformers in both groups of transition economies now focus on maintaining stable and consistent fiscal and financial policies, and both are engaged in building a regulatory environment that can reduce corruption, support an advanced market economy, and protect fair and equal competition. The qualitative responses to the challenges of transition are now more similar.

Nevertheless, the Chinese experience has many valuable lessons to teach. These lessons come from a broad view of China's transition, however, and not from specific policies that should be transplanted to other economies. After all, the Chinese policy-making process has been extremely complex, and produced dramatically different outcomes in different periods of "gradualist" transition. Discussions of China's transition have often failed to make this clear. Sachs and Woo (1994), for example, argue that the successes of China's early reforms were actually due to the advantages of underdevelopment, which gave China a relatively large, flexible, rural economy that served as a seed-bed of reform. However, underdevelopment surely has costs as well as benefits, and is unlikely to be make reforms unambiguously easier. The early reforms were successful precisely because they were effectively adapted to the specific challenges and opportunities provided by China's situation at that time. Second-stage reforms were then dramatically recast and adapted to a whole new set of challenges and opportunities. As McMillan (2004) points out, the lesson is not that a specific set of circumstances provides intrinsic advantages, but rather that careful policy-making, firmly grounded in local conditions, has a much better chance of success than prepackaged policy prescriptions. Moreover, policies that give weight to development of social and economic capabilities will be more successful than policies that overemphasize institutional changes. As Deng Xiaoping said in the midst of China's transition process, "development is the only hard truth."

Despite the remarkably successful record of transition thus far, there is no guarantee of continued success in the future. In 2003, a new administration took over in China. Hu Jintao became the top Communist Party official and government leader. Wen Jiabao succeeded Zhu Rongji as premier, and continuing the transition-era division of responsibility, immediately became the predominant economic policy decision-maker. Under Wen, the style of policy-making has changed rather dramatically, becoming more consultative and deliberate than under Zhu Rongji. The fundamental policy direction has not significantly changed, although the policy agenda has broadened. It has become clear that policy-makers today face the dual challenge of advancing the transition process while also cushioning the impact of changes that have increased inequality and reduced economic security. On the one hand, the transition process is far from complete; on the other hand, problems created during the second phase of transition urgently require remedial action.

The second phase of transition was far more profound and thorough than the first phase, but in many areas the institutions created are still far from adequate. The financial system (Chapter 19) remains dominated by state-owned banks and subject to influence by government and well-connected insider groups. Weak legal accountability finds its reflection in the financial system in a trail of nonperforming loans and bad assets, followed by government bailouts. The tax system has been reconstructed but fiscal relations between central and local governments are still weakly specified, and local fiscal capacity gravely underdeveloped (Chapter 18). Chinese corporations have been given a coherent legal charter, but most are far from developing world-class standards of corporate governance and the ability to compete in the global marketplace (Chapter 13). Chinese regulatory agencies have been created, but they are still not fully independent from the government management bodies from which they were originally "hived off." This list could be extended but the key challenges and focus of reform remain strengthening the financial, fiscal, and regulatory apparatus and building the institutions of a sophisticated market economy.

The specific challenges are changing and becoming, in a sense, more "political." China is struggling to develop a broader and sounder system of ownership, with a stronger, and more transparent system of property rights. The need to develop a legal and regulatory system is increasingly urgent, and the demand for legal rights and regulatory fairness is increasingly widespread in the population. But thus far, progress in developing a regulatory apparatus has been limited by the fact that transparency, accountability, and oversight run into limits when they touch on the ultimate structure of political power. China's reformers have made numerous efforts to strengthen checks and oversight within the system, but they all ultimately rely on a kind of self-policing by the CCP. The economy is still politicized, and powerful interest groups frequently involve the cooperation of political and economic elites. Under these circumstances, corruption is inevitably a serious problem, both in its own right and because of the way it obstructs resolution of other problems. A true "level playing field" remains to be created.

A different set of challenges face China's reformers as they struggle to cushion the impact of economic changes on vulnerable sectors of the population. Inequality has increased sharply (Chapter 9), and economic life has become much more uncertain. In the rural sector, incomes have increased but have lagged stubbornly behind urban incomes. Chinese policy-makers used the first phase of transition very effectively to build support for further reforms. As mentioned previously, reform in the 1980s was a kind of "reform without losers," making some better off without significantly harming any major group. But this set of benign social outcomes was sacrificed after the mid-1990s. Unable to indefinitely protect SOEs from competition, reformers shrank the state sector quickly. Not surprisingly, once policy-makers made up their minds to "smash the iron rice bowl" and downsize the state-sector, marketization leapt ahead, even though pension and health-insurance programs were far from complete. As a result, significant segments of society, in both urban and rural areas, feel left out of the prosperity they see developing around them. Reformers need to carry out remedial work, repairing some of the holes that have developed in the urban social safety network, and bringing some basic social security protections to rural workers. More broadly, reformers need to ensure that reforms bring as many economic benefits as possible to a large majority of the population, protecting the more vulnerable sections of the population while also, incidentally, reinforcing the pro-reform sentiments that developed during the 1980s.

Indeed, the post-2003 Hu Jintao–Wen Jiabao administration immediately shifted the rhetorical emphasis of the government toward greater solicitude, toward rural areas, and toward regions and individuals left behind in the development process. Expressions of good intentions have been followed by significant policy changes that, for example, have reduced the tax rate in rural areas, and eliminated some of the unreasonable extra burdens that rural-to-urban migrants experience in cities. Still, these shifts in orientation need to be reinforced by effective policies that bring the benefits of growth more inclusively to a broader swath of the population. This will not be easy. Current policies lock in the growth of an increasingly competitive and open economy. The commitments to the WTO, of which China became a member in December 2001, limit China's ability to protect large sections of the economy from international competition. This will inevitably accelerate the pace at which the market discriminates between successful and unsuccessful market competitors. While this process is driving the creation of a more productive and competitive economy, it also increases the urgency for China to provide effective policies to ease the transition of millions out of obsolete, low-productivity jobs, and speed their finding of productive roles in the emerging economy. Only if the benefits of reform are broadly spread will China be able to make the next step to a highly functioning market economy.

BIBLIOGRAPHY

Suggestions for Further Reading

Wu (2005) has the best comprehensive coverage of China's transition. For a quick introduction to the contending perspectives on China's gradualist approach versus the Russian and Polish "big bang," see McMillan (2004) and Havrylshyn (2004). Some key works that discuss transition in Eastern Europe and in China include World Bank (1996), Sachs and Woo (1994) and McMillan and Naughton (1992).

Lau, Qian, and Roland (2000) introduced the analytic concept of "reform without losers," which serves as the basis for the two periods of reform used in this text. Qian (2003) is also an absorbing account. Naughton (1995) covers the period through 1993 in more detail. Qian and Wu (2003) adopt a similar two-period interpretation.

Sources for Data and Figures

Figure 4.1: Naughton (1995): 224.

Figure 4.2: *SYC* (2005, 271, and preceding years). Official data have been adjusted to make the categories consistent over time and comparable with international conventions. Official data treat subsidies to loss-making state enterprises as a negative revenue item; these subsidies have been added to both revenues and expenditures.

Figure 4.3: *SYC* (various years) and statistics published by the Ministry and Labor and Social Security (various years). See Chapter 8 for discussion.

References

Byrd, William (1991). *The Market Mechanism and Economic Reforms in China*. New York: M. E. Sharpe.

Havrylshyn, Oleh (2004). "Avoid Hubris but Acknowledge Successes: Lessons from the Postcommunist Transition." *Finance and Development*, September, pp. 38–41, in "Point/Counterpoint—Reform: What Pace Works Best?"

Lau, Lawrence, Yingyi Qian, and Gérard Roland (2000). "Reform Without Losers: An Interpretation of China's Dual-Track Approach to Transition." *Journal of Political Economy*, 108(1), February, 120–43.

McMillan, John (2004). "Avoid Hubris, and Other Lessons for Reformers." *Finance and Development*, September, pp. 34–37, in "Point/Counterpoint—Reform: What Pace Works Best?"

McMillan, John, and Barry Naughton (1992). "How to Reform a Planned Economy: Lessons from China." *Oxford Review of Economic Policy* 8(1), 130–43.

Naughton, Barry (1995). *Growing out of the Plan: Chinese Economic Reform, 1978–1993*. New York: Cambridge University Press.

Qian, Yingyi (2003). "How Reform Worked in China." In Dani Rodrik (ed.), *In Search of Prosperity: Analytic Narratives on Economic Growth*, 297–333. Princeton, NJ: Princeton University Press.

Qian, Yingyi, and Jinglian, Wu (2003). "China's Transition to a Market Economy: How Far Across the River?" In Nicholas C. Hope, Dennis Tao Yang, and Mu Yang Li, *How Far Across the River?*, 31–64. Stanford, CA: Stanford University Press.

Sachs, Jeffrey, and Wing Thye Woo (1994). "Structural Factors in the Economic Reforms of China, Eastern Europe, and the Former Soviet Union." *Economic Policy*, 9(18), April, 101–45.

SYC (Annual). *Zhongguo Tongji Nianjian* [Statistical Yearbook of China]. Beijing: Zhongguo Tongji.

Wong, Christine (1986). "Ownership and Control in Chinese Industry: The Maoist Legacy and Prospects for the 1980s." In Joint Economic Committee, U.S. Congress, *China's Economy Looks Toward the Year 2000*, 571–603. Washington, DC: U.S. Government Printing Office.

World Bank (1996). *From Plan to Market: World Development Report 1996*. Oxford University Press.

Wu, Jinglian (2005). *Understanding and Interpreting Chinese Economic Reform*. Singapore: Thomson.

5 The Urban–Rural Divide

The difference between urban and rural society is especially pronounced in China. While some urban–rural gap is inevitable in a developing economy, the urban-rural gap in China is unusually large. Extensive administrative barriers were set in place during the 1950s as part of the command economy. For 50 years urban and rural areas have had different governance structures and different systems of property rights. Most important, because of the systemic differences, China has what amounts to two different forms of *citizenship,* one rural and one urban. Rural dwellers have fewer privileges than urban dwellers and rarely attain the entitlements of urban citizenship. In China city and countryside often seem like two different worlds, running on different technologies, organized in different ways, and having a different standard of living. These differences have been maintained by strict controls on mobility. From the 1960s into the 1990s, it was extremely difficult for rural people to move to the city. In the past several years, mass rural-to-urban migration has begun, and the invisible walls separating urban and rural society have begun to break down. But while migration has begun reshaping Chinese society, the gap between urban and rural will take many years to disappear.

This chapter first describes the origin and nature of the separate organizational structures and property-rights regimes that characterize the rural and urban economies. These help explain the depth of the divide between urban and rural society, and also serve to introduce the peculiar Chinese property-rights regime. Property rights shape the structure of incentives in any economy, and thus shape economic development as well as market transition. The Chinese property-rights and governance regimes are unusual and differ substantially between urban and rural society. Barriers to mobility and different kinds of citizenship complete the institutional divide. Section 5.2 discusses the process of urbanization. Urbanization is a normal part of economic development, but here again China's extreme policies produced a highly distorted and extremely unusual pattern of urban development. During the Cultural

Revolution rural-urban migration was virtually nonexistent, and cities did not grow for 20 years. After these policies were relaxed at the end of the 1970s, the urbanization process restarted and then accelerated in the 1990s. Section 5.3 discusses migration, which, since its reemergence in the 1990s, has increased rapidly. Finally, the chapter discusses the economic consequences of the urban-rural divide. Chinese policy-making is characterized by substantial "urban bias," and this is associated with a large urban-rural income gap. In recent years most of the institutional features dividing urban and rural have been relaxed, and there is now significant movement from rural to urban. Despite these changes, the urban–rural income gap has not yet shrunk, and it is unlikely to do so in the next few years.

5.1   A DUALISTIC SYSTEM: THE DIVISION BETWEEN URBAN AND RURAL

5.1.1   Origins of the Urban–Rural Divide

Today's large urban–rural gap has its roots in the socialist period, for there were few barriers between urban and rural society in traditional China. As described in Chapter 3, during the 1950s every Chinese citizen was connected through his or her workplace to the socialist state. Virtually every business and productive enterprise was converted to public ownership and became subject to direct or indirect government control. These institutions were implemented in systematically different ways in urban and rural areas. Urban residents were organized by their place of employment, that is, by their "work unit," or *danwei*. Almost all urban work units were nationalized, that is, converted to state ownership. As a result, state ownership became the predominant form of ownership in urban areas, with two consequences. First, urban work units were knit into a formal hierarchy, subject to direct government planning, command, and control. Second, the work units gradually built up a system of social benefits and entitlements, which was extended more or less uniformly to all urban workers. Urban residents became a relatively privileged group in Chinese society, and the work unit became the basic building block of urban society.

Rural institutions were quite different. Private property in land was eliminated in 1955, and the land in every village was pooled together and became the property of the village as a whole, of the "collective." Collective ownership became the predominant form of ownership. Village residents automatically became members of the new agricultural collectives, and access to land was equalized within the collective. However, there was no mechanism to redistribute resources across collectives, and there were no standards or entitlements that applied to all rural residents. Collectives were encouraged to support social services out of their own local resources, but they had no claim on national resources. The agricultural collective's primary function was to sell agricultural produce and earn revenue, and they could provide social-services and public-goods only if they generated a surplus from the sale of agricultural produce. As a result, the level of benefits and public goods provided was much lower than in the city. Rural residents were poorer than urban residents, and they had a cheaper and less comprehensive set of social institutions to serve them as well.

The different urban and rural administrative systems were tools to carry out the socialist Big Push strategy. The two systems were used to carry out two drastically different functions: The rural system was used to extract low-cost food and fibers from the farmers. The collectives were supposed to manage agricultural labor and deliver grain to the government. In the urban areas, the work units themselves received government investment, and urban workers were considered to be the vanguard of socialism. Thus the roots of the dualistic system lay in the government's strategy to extract resources for industrialization, as discussed in Chapter 3. The Chinese government used its control to purchase low-cost farm products, a policy which enabled the government to keep wages low and state-owned factories profitable. A key element of the system was grain rationing, introduced in 1955. Ration coupons were delivered to urban residents through work units: At first seen as a short-run expedient, grain rationing in fact lasted for more than 30 years. The whole dualistic system worked as an implicit tax on farmers, who had lower incomes because they were compelled to sell grain to the government at artificially low prices. The result was that farming—and especially growing grain—became an even lower-return occupation than it had always been.

To keep the system functioning farmers had to be tied to the land. Controls intensified and the dualistic system gradually hardened into something much more pervasive, rigid, and insidious. At first, many farmers migrated to the cities to take up better-paying factory jobs, and social mobility was significant through the first years of the GLF (1958–1960). But when the GLF collapsed, everything changed. The government kept extracting food from the country side, long after it became clear there was no more to take, while urban dwellers continued to receive at least some of their grain rations. Suddenly it became a huge privilege to be an urban dweller: Famine emerged and spread in the countryside, devastating predominantly rural provinces, such as Sichuan and Anhui (1960–1962), but urban dwellers were spared the worst. An urban household registration had become a meal ticket, while rural people had only a license to starve.

As the magnitude of the post–GLF catastrophe became apparent, China's leaders began to drastically limit their obligations to city dwellers. The government continued to provide food rations to all registered urban dwellers but severely restricted the number of eligible beneficiaries. Six million urban residents, mostly recently arrived from the countryside, were cajoled into returning to their native villages in 1961–1962. Most were never allowed to return to the city. The system of household registration had initially been meant to monitor population movements, not control them, but as new, restrictions on rural-to-urban migration began to be strictly enforced, household registration became a fundamental determinant of a family's life prospects. Without an urban residence permit, or *hukou*, a farmer could not go to work in the city, and it became almost impossible for a rural household to get an urban *hukou* after the early 1960s. Rural-to-urban migration dwindled practically to zero. From the mid-1960s onward, the system hardened into a kind of caste system, with dramatically different entitlements and privileges to urban and rural people. The rigidity of the system grew directly out of the trauma of the GLF (Cheng and Selden 1994).

Only much later, after successful rural reforms in the early 1980s, did China begin to soften this rigid institutional dualism. Successful rural reforms eased concern over basic food supplies and increased the availability of grain in free markets. Grain rationing was gradually phased out, and an urban residence permit was no longer required to eat. The government began to ease restrictions on migration to the cities, at first for smaller cities and for temporary migrants. Broad economic changes have increased opportunities for rural workers in the city and have resulted in very substantial migration flows, as we will discuss in this chapter. However, the urban residence permit still exists, and possession of an urban *hukou* still marks a fundamental divide in Chinese society. For the average farmer, it has not actually become much easier to obtain an urban residence permit, although it has become much easier to live in a city without one. Without an urban residence permit, though, a rural migrant still has little or no access to the benefits that urban dwellers enjoy, including health care, social security, and education for accompanying children. Administrative regulations still divide urban and rural people into two classes of citizens.

5.1.2   The Urban Economic System

5.1.2.1   The *Danwei*

Through the mid-1990s, urban life in China was defined by the privileges associated with a *hukou* and by membership in a *danwei*. The urban residence permit was a form of entitlement that guaranteed the holder membership in a *danwei* and thus, of course, a job. When a city dweller graduated from middle school—or university, if smart and lucky—he or she was assigned employment as a matter of course. Thereafter, the work unit became responsible for providing services and benefits to the urban resident. During the peak period of the urban *danwei*, from the mid–1960s until well into the 1990s, urban residence conveyed the following benefits:

• Job security

• Guaranteed low-price access to food grains, as well as other scarce commodities

• Health care (about 40% of all general hospital beds were in the state-owned industrial system)

• A pension and other benefits, including health care, upon retirement

• Primary and middle school education for their children (70% of state enterprises ran schools of some kind)

• Low-cost housing, supplied by the work unit

These extensive subsidies added up to significant privilege. They also implied that the urban price system was extremely distorted, since many important services and staple foods were provided at prices well below cost. A distinctive feature of the Chinese system was permanent employment. After the restrictions on rural-to-urban migration were put in place in the mid–1960s, job mobility between urban work units disappeared as well. In this sense—as discussed in Chapter 8—the Chinese work unit was quite different from the Soviet model from which it otherwise derived. Once a worker entered the *danwei*, he or she expected to remain a member of that *danwei* for life (Lü and Perry 1997).

The most common type of urban work unit was the SOE, which produced goods and services and earned revenues and profits. However, a work unit could also be a nonprofit public-service unit (PSU, still owned by the government), or it could be a government department. Despite their different primary functions, the different types of work units had many features in common. First, each was integrated into a national administrative hierarchy, with managers appointed by the Communist Party. Furthermore, the benefits each work unit provided to its workers were explicitly defined as entitlements, specified by statute or regulation. The benefits were thus part of an implicit urban social compact, which the government has consistently recognized and tried to protect (though not always successfully, as discussed in this chapter and in Chapter 8). Finally, in addition to its primary function, each unit had responsibility for social and cultural activities, and even for political coordination. The work unit was the fundamental building block, or cell, of urban society. Many work units even had the physical form of a cell, with a perimeter brick wall enclosing a nucleus of productive activity. The *danwei* was a microcosm of urban society, into which individuals were born and in which they lived, worked, and died.

5.1.2.2 Urban Property Rights

Just as urban work units and workers were incorporated into a single national administrative hierarchy, so, in similar fashion, all urban property was incorporated into a national, hierarchical system of state ownership. All urban land was nationalized during the 1950s. All large-scale urban businesses were state owned. Municipal government budgets were treated as subdivisions of the national budget. Thus municipal receipts and expenditures were incorporated each year into the integrated national budget. In effect, therefore, the government assumed responsibility for water, sewage, transportation, police protection, and schools—the entire panoply of ordinary services. As Judith Banister (1987, 328) described the classic system: "Urban areas are essentially owned and administered by the state."

Most of the enterprises that were nominally "state-owned" were not actually managed by the national government. Especially after China embraced the development of small-scale enterprises, it was impossible for the national government to exercise effective oversight of its far-flung assets. Inevitably, the authority to manage state firms was delegated to local governments, even while nominal ownership remained with the national government. Successive rounds of decentralization, especially in the early 1970s, created de facto property rights for local governments. With day-to-day control over decision-making, local government leaders had significant authority over both cash flow and decisions about use of land and other assets. But these rights were always seen as delegated to the local government by the national government, and local officials were formally agents of the central government and the Communist Party, part of a chain of authority leading to the highest political officials in Beijing. As a result, economic reforms after the 1980s consisted of repeated, careful renegotiations of the lines of authority within the state-run hierarchy.

Urban land markets developed in this hierarchical context. All urban land is owned by the state, at least in theory, even today. But a system has evolved in which rights to use land for up to 50 years are bought and sold. A market for transferable urban leaseholds emerged during the 1990s. Under this system, the use rights of existing occupants are usually, but not always, recognized—there are "squatter's rights"—and with the permission of local government they can be bought and sold. Urban land has become an important source of wealth, both for state-run enterprises and for the individuals who control the land conversion process. Land transactions are taxed, but most of the value is captured by the occupying enterprise, the local government, or private parties.

5.1.3   The Rural Economic System

5.1.3.1   Rural Collectives

No attempt was ever made to integrate rural areas into the hierarchical system of national state ownership that prevailed in the cities. There is of course a government hierarchy in the countryside. This hierarchy extends down to the level of the county, and today below that to the township level. However, the bulk of rural life is outside this governmental system, and the agricultural collectives were never part of this formal government hierarchy. Even today, villages, which have their own village councils and elect village leaders, are not formally part of the government hierarchy. Rather, they are theoretically autonomous organizations. (In practice, important decisions must be approved by government and party officials at the township and country levels.) Thus, even during the period of agricultural collectives, from 1955 through about 1982, most rural residents were organized into local bodies with a primarily economic function. The organization was all-encompassing and subject to political control, but it was still relatively looser than organization in the city. This organization is described further in Chapter 10. Agricultural collectives were thus "low-power" organizations, and membership did not convey any entitlements to government services. Rural collectives simply did not have the financial resources to subsidize a large range of goods and services, so rural residents were much more likely to pay full cost for the public services they received.

5.1.3.2   Rural Property Rights

Just as rural collectives were never incorporated into the national administrative hierarchy, so, in similar fashion, rural property, including land, was never integrated into the system of national state ownership. The agricultural collective in principle owned the land, as well as nonagricultural rural enterprises. Thus ownership rights in the countryside were never as centralized—as concentrated in the hands of bureaucrats—as was the case with urban state ownership. Rural households always had access to the land. Households retained their own houses (and the land the houses were on, of course) and had access to farmland through the village collective.

During the rural reforms of 1978–1984, collective farming ended in almost all of China, and family farms returned as the dominant agricultural form. Each collective divided up the land among its individual household members, according to formulas negotiated within the collectives. Historical ownership (before collectives) was ignored in favor of formulas based on the number of workers and the number of mouths to feed in a household. By all accounts this process went smoothly, and it has been called, with reason, "the most egalitarian land reform in history" (Walder 2000). But even after dividing up the land, the land system did not change over to a simple private property system. Although land is *worked* by individual households, the formal ownership still remains with the "collective." A complete formal system of private property of rural land does not exist. Instead, farmers sign contracts with the collective giving them land-use rights for periods that have gradually been lengthened, and now often extend up to 50 years. Even today peasants do not own the land free and clear. This system has a number of unusual side effects:

• Collectives in many areas of China can and do redistribute land periodically. According to one large-scale study, farmland has been redistributed at least once in 66% of the surveyed villages, and three or more times in 25% of the villages (Rozelle and Li 1998). Usually, redistribution is carried out in order to accommodate natural population growth. Thus, although private households have use rights and cash-flow rights, these are not absolute.

• As a result of this system, there is very little landlessness. With almost all peasants having access to some land, there is little of the crushing poverty caused by absolute landlessness found in many developing economies. Indeed, a rough guarantee of access to land is the most important form of social insurance in the countryside. In some poor and remote areas collectives disappeared after the land was first distributed. In these areas peasant households have de facto ownership, and landlessness could eventually develop.

• The lack of completely secure land tenure affects farmer incentives. The rewards for investment in the land's long-term productivity are diluted (since there is a possibility land may be redistributed). Land cannot be used as collateral for borrowing, and land use-right markets have been slow to develop. Moreover, there is an additional cost to permanent out-migration. Families that migrate away permanently may have to surrender their land to the collective; such a move is costly, and as a result, few make it. Instead, the system encourages families to leave some family members on the land while sending others out for temporary, but sometimes long-term, jobs outside agriculture.

5.1.3.3 "Fuzzy" Property Rights and Land-Use Disputes

In rural areas, then, property rights have remained complex and locally negotiated. There is no national land registry where property rights are inscribed. Instead, each individual village holds records of the land-use rights that have been distributed by village action. As the Chinese economy has developed, land has become much more valuable. Cities have sprawled out beyond their original limits, and industrial and commercial uses of land have exploded. But rural land is officially "collective" property, and the use rights were granted to farm households for the purpose of farming. As a result, when there is an opportunity to convert land to industrial or commercial use, or lease land to an outsider, village heads and township officials frequently take those business decisions upon themselves. As the representative of the collective that owns the land, the village head argues that it is up to him to decide how to manage that land. Officials negotiate the sales price, and arrange compensation or relocation for displaced farmers. In the course of these transactions, many officials also find ways to enrich themselves.

Yet, for most farmers, access to the land is their lifeline, and (unlike urban residents) farmers have had guaranteed access to the land for the last 50 years. When the land is sold or leased out from under them, rural people react with anger, particularly when compensation is unfair. The largest cause of social conflict in China today is almost certainly disputes over land deals (Cai 2003; Yu Jianrong 2005). Corrupt land transactions have repeatedly caused mass protests at the local level. The central government has responded by passing, in 2003, a new law on rural land contracts that guarantees farmers' property rights and provides guidelines for fair compensation. However, the law has not prevented disputes which seem, if anything, to be increasing in frequency. China's rural residents appear to demand more secure property rights in land than the current system provides them.

Complex and sometimes "fuzzy" property rights have also affected the trajectory of rural nonagricultural enterprises, the so-called "commune and brigade" enterprises that grew up during the 1970s. After 1982, these became the TVEs and played an enormous role in the Chinese economy (Chapter 12 is devoted to the TVE phenomenon). Many of these firms were "collectively owned," in the sense that theoretical ownership rested with the collectives, either as a legacy of earlier sponsorship, or because township and village governments took the lead in establishing new TVEs after the break-up of the agricultural collectives. Analogous to the land system, ultimate ownership stayed with the collective, while use rights were delegated, often to highly entrepreneurial firm managers. The precise distribution of property rights over

TVEs was negotiated in a local, face-to-face process. The complexity of these arrangements has led some to describe TVE property rights as "fuzzy." In fact, the property rights were able to accommodate numerous stakeholders flexibly, adapt to an enormous range of situations, and often produce effective and entrepreneurial organizations. It is ironic that publicly owned entities, the TVEs, played a crucial role in opening up the Chinese system to market competition and further economic reform.

5.1.4   The Evolution of the Rural and Urban Systems During Market Transition

In the complex process of market transition since 1978 both the rural and urban systems have been fundamentally transformed. Those changes have eliminated the agricultural collectives, eliminated the system of permanent employment in the city, and sharply diminished the importance of the urban *danwei*. Those broad changes are considered in more detail in subsequent chapters, especially Chapter 8 on urban labor markets and Chapter 10 on rural organization. Here we note simply that the dynamics of change were very different in rural and urban areas. The rural system was more loosely organized and thus, in some sense, easier to change. Much of the economic activity in the countryside was outside the scope of national government control. But correspondingly, when the agricultural collectives dissolved, the supply of rural public goods simply collapsed. The national government, accustomed to the principle of self-reliance for collectives, did not step in to replace the services that collectives had provided in previous years. By contrast, the urban system was harder to change because social services were not only provided through the work unit, but also guaranteed by an explicit system of entitlements. Precisely for this reason, though, the national government has felt compelled to defend at least some parts of the urban social contract. In the cities enterprise reforms tried as much as possible to strip out the social functions from SOEs and change them into profit-oriented businesses (Chapter 13). But these services were not removed from the urban *danwei* until there was some kind of rudimentary socialized program set up to take over those functions. Thus, although the "social safety net" in urban China is tattered and has some large holes, the government still attempts to provide social services to urban dwellers. The government has invested extensive policy-making resources into trying to redesign the urban social safety network and provides extensive financial support for health care and social security, both directly through the government budget and indirectly through the provisions of the social insurance system.

The result of this differential evolution is especially clear in the health care system. Rural dwellers by and large pay a much larger share "out of pocket" for health care services than do urban residents, notwithstanding their lower incomes. The World Health Organization (2000, 190–192) ranked 191 countries on a variety of measures relating to health and the effectiveness of the health delivery system. Overall, China performed reasonably well, except for the measure of "fairness of financial contribution to health care provision." On that scale, China ranked 188th out of 191 countries. The explanation is evident: most urban dwellers, with higher incomes, pay little for their health care, while most rural residents pay out of pocket for health services as delivered or pay regular premiums for minimal insurance coverage. Two other countries that ranked with China at the bottom of the list—Brazil and Vietnam—also have large rural populations without health insurance and urban dwellers who benefit from extensive welfare provisions. To be sure, reforms have not always worked to the benefit of urban workers. Workers now must pay a portion of their wages for health insurance, and there are co-pays for many services. More troubling, there are gaps in coverage that can leave urban workers exposed to catastrophic illness. But overall, urban workers remain far better off than rural residents, who are more or less on their own.

Another area in which dramatic change clearly favored urban residents was housing. Beginning in the mid-1990s, most urban work units began to sell their housing to the occupants, and the pattern of housing ownership in urban China completely changed. During a period of several years through 1999, 48% of all urban households purchased their apartments from their work units. By 2005 the proportion of urban housing units owned by the occupants had surpassed 80%, including new and existing private housing as well as privatized work-unit housing. Urban residents who purchased their residences from their work units did so on quite favorable terms. Workers and retirees with greater seniority paid lower prices. The average price paid for a converted apartment was 19,000 *renminbi* (RMB), about $2,300, or roughly the average urban household's annual income. Workers were generally able to pay for the apartment over 10 years with low or zero interest charged. Housing privatization has marked a tremendous change in the nature of urban society, tending to push it toward a middle-class society. Widespread urban home ownership has supported a booming market in consumer durables and home improvements. City dwellers were allowed to sell distributed housing after a waiting period of up to five years, and urban property markets grew rapidly after 2000.

The experience with urban housing reveals a fundamental characteristic of China's reform process. Urban residents benefited greatly from the privatization and marketization of urban housing. Even though the dissolution of the *danwei* system deprived urban workers of many of the old social protections, reforms were still devised in such ways that urban residents benefited disproportionately. In that sense, the urban–rural gap continues to exist in China, not just as an administrative divide, but also as an influence on contemporary policy-making.

5.1.5   Invisible Walls: Administrative Barriers Today

The most important barrier separating urban and rural in China is the system of household registration. Every household in China is required to be registered in their permanent home. A key feature of the system, however, is that registration is both for a specific *location* and for a specific *status*, either urban or rural. That status is nearly impossible for an individual to change, and it is passed on from generation to generation. Indeed, through 1998 a child automatically inherited the household status of his or her mother. As a result, a rural woman was unable to change the status of her children by marrying an urban resident. Given traditional patrilocal marriage in China, in which women typically moved in with their husband's family after marriage, this rule blocked what would otherwise have been an important channel of mobility and caused the household registration system to harden into an almost caste-like system of segmentation. Permitting inheritance of status through either parent was one strand of a liberalization package adopted around this turn of this century.

Even today, only those with urban residence permits—popularly called urban *hukou*—have the right to live permanently in cities. Since the 1980s, access to the *hukou* has been substantially liberalized, but the *hukou* still exists, and its possession still makes a difference. Chinese citizens now have more ways to obtain urban household residences. It is fairly easy to obtain a *hukou* in a town or small city. A migrant must simply find a job and be gainfully employed for a year or more. But migrants have many fewer options if they wish to obtain a *hukou* in a large city, and it is especially difficult to relocate to Shanghai or Beijing. Recent graduates from good colleges can move their *hukou* without much difficulty, given the desire of many Chinese cities to foster knowledge-intensive industries. Wealthy individuals can procure a "blue-stamp" *hukou*, either by outright purchase or by bringing a substantial new investment or new business to the city. In fact, a 1994 study estimated that three million urban *hukou* had been purchased through 1993 at an average price of 8,000 RMB ($1,000, well over the annual urban wage). Yet these programs for the wealthy or highly educated have not made an urban *hukou* substantially easier to obtain for the majority of Chinese citizens (Wu and Treiman 2004).

For the average migrant a more important consideration is that it has become much easier to stay and work in urban areas for extended periods without a formal urban *hukou*. From the mid–1990s, the Chinese government began to seriously reconsider its policy toward migrant workers. Booming regional centers, led by export-oriented cities in Guangdong Province, demanded more factory labor. Policy-makers in Beijing became increasingly receptive to the plight of migrant workers and of the rural communities from which they came. The official attitude toward migrant workers has shifted from discomfort and hostility to recognition of the need for migration and officially expressed compassion for the plight of many migrant workers. In 2005 the central government acknowledged that migrants had a right to live and work in the city, and that they "ought to" have access to the social services available in the city. Most cities now have provisions for temporary registration and employment of migrants.

Actual reform of the *hukou* system, though, is a slow process. Local city governments have been hesitant to fully embrace migrants. When downsizing of state enterprises left city governments struggling with serious unemployment problems, many responded by trying to keep immigrants out in order to protect the jobs of local residents. Urban public services are expensive to provide, and city governments are not eager to extend access to education and health services to migrants and their children. Migrants also face discrimination and exploitation. Factory managers and construction foremen are eager to keep migrants in a weak bargaining position and earning low wages. Indeed, in a startling number of cases, employers simply do not pay migrants at all. The Beijing Youth Center for Legal Aid and Research conducted a survey of more than 8,000 rural-to-urban migrants in eight provinces in December 2003. They found that 48% of these migrants had experienced nonpayment of wages they had earned. Moreover, such workers had little recourse, since pressing a case for nonpayment took several thousand RMB of lost work time and administrative fees. The National Trade Union estimated a total of 100 billion RMB ($12 billion) in unpaid wages in China. In response to these revelations, a program was launched to force employers to pay up, but it is unlikely to have eliminated the abuses.

Toward the end of 2004 several provinces—including Hubei, Shandong, and Zhejiang—announced that they would adopt within the next year a new household registration system that would finally do away with the distinction between urban and rural permits (Shandong 2004; Zhejiang 2004). Not only is *hukou* reform difficult because powerful interests are at stake, but also, because of the dramatic difference between urban and rural systems, reform raises questions of entitlements. At what point will a migrant be entitled to social security in the city and education for his children? At what point will that migrant lose his entitlement to land in the countryside?

5.2   URBANIZATION

Urbanization is a vital part of the development process. As development occurs, workers move out of agriculture and into industrial and service jobs that can be performed much more efficiently when they are concentrated in cities rather than dispersed in the countryside. China is now in the middle of a period of rapid urbanization. At the end of 2005, China's population was 43% urban. China is no longer a predominantly agricultural economy, and agriculture accounted for only 13% of GDP in 2004. Still, the majority of China's people live in the countryside, and when rural industry and services are included, they still produce 48% of China's GDP (CASS Rural 2005, 36, 42). China's urbanization rate today is within the normal range for a developing country, but China reached its present stage through a trajectory that is utterly unique, and even bizarre. In most developing countries the pace of urbanization is determined by the decision-making of millions of separate individuals, who assess their own life chances and decide to leave the countryside and go to the city. But China's past process of urbanization was determined primarily by government policies that, until recently, tightly constrained the scope for individual choice.

The data that describe the process of urbanization in China are shown in Figure 5.1. The series in shaded circles shows the percentages of Chinese citizens classified as "nonagricultural," that is, those with urban residence permits. These numbers correspond to the discussion of the urban *hukou* earlier in this chapter and are unique to China. The series in dark squares shows the proportion of the Chinese population resident in urban settlements of a minimum size. These numbers are conceptually consistent with definitions of urbanization in other countries, and they can be used to make comparisons. Together, the series reveal China's bizarre history of urbanization. Between the end of the 1950s and 1978, China de-urbanized. According to either series, the urban share of the population declined by more than two percentage points. From 1964—a relatively normal year, and one with a population census—the urban share declined by a percentage point. This de-urbanization has no real parallel in any other country. Since the rest of the world was steadily urbanizing, China became more and more unusual through the late 1970s. In 1964, China's urbanization rate was 18.4%, compared with 26% for all developing countries (World Bank WDI). By 1978, China's urbanization rate was only 17.9%, but

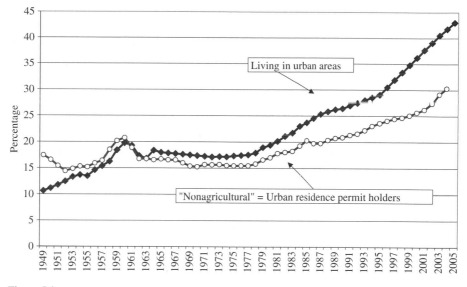

Figure 5.1
Urban share of total population

now compared with a developing country average of 31%. Since 1978, China has begun to urbanize very rapidly: indeed, China's 2005 urbanization rate had grown to equal the developing country average of 43% (2003 data). China has caught up and become a normal urbanized country.

In the pre–1978 period, the numbers clearly show the impact of China's draconian restrictions on population movement. The early peak of urbanization, during the GLF in 1960, was of course unsustainable. But what is most remarkable is the tight control exercised over urbanization between 1964 and 1978, a period in which the size of the urban economy tripled. During this entire period, access to urban residence permits was jealously guarded, and almost no farmers were allowed to move to the city. Indeed, there was even forced out-migration from urban areas. From the mid–1960s to the mid–1970s, millions of urban dwellers were sent out to the countryside. The largest group, around 17 million, consisted of young middle school graduates who were "sent down" to the countryside in the wake of the Cultural Revolution. "Sent-down" youth remained in the countryside for periods ranging from two years to a lifetime, instructed to learn the realities of work from the poor and middle peasants. Workers were also mobilized to leave big cities to build factories in western China. Between 1955 and 1976, China's largest city, Shanghai, experienced a net out-migration of 1.86 million people, and its total population did not grow at all. That such unusual population dynamics could occur is a testament to the extreme degree of political control and mobilization in Maoist China. As Ma Hong said, "Every time there was a political movement, one of the aftereffects was another big batch of urban people sent to the countryside" (Zhang Shanyu 2003, 362, 367, 376).

The broad social relaxation that accompanied the beginnings of reform in 1978 ended the most extreme forms of population control. "Sent-down" youth began to return to the cities, signaling the beginning of a process of gradual relaxation of controls on mobility and the resumption of urbanization. At first, government officials were extremely cautious, trying to restrict population growth to the smaller cities and preventing the growth of megacities. It was not until the 1990s that planners began to grudgingly accept the fact that the largest cities also need to grow and in the long run might even increase their share of the total urban population. Eventually, an estimated 60% of the out-migrants from Shanghai returned to that city, returning home and participating in its current economic growth.

Urbanization in China over the past 30 years has been extremely broad-based. Migration to the large cities has resumed, cities have sprawled into the countryside, and new urban settlements have grown up in formerly rural areas. In 1982 there were only 2,660 small towns with established urban management systems (*jianzhi zhen*); by 2001 the number had grown to 20,374 (Zhang Shanyu 2003, 321). Perhaps the most remarkable urban transformation has occurred in the Pearl River Delta in Guangdong Province. On the eastern side of the Pearl River a 120-kilometer stretch of land changed from entirely rural to predominantly urban in 25 years. Between Hong Kong and the provincial capital of Guangzhou, two entirely new cities have grown up—Shenzhen and Dongguan—creating a chain of four large cities of over six million population each. In the Yangtze Delta urbanization took off about a decade later than in the Pearl River Delta, but the same pattern of "urbanized countryside" seems to be emerging. In the north, Beijing has sprawled outward from its center, building out now beyond a fifth ring road. These transformations mean that urbanization statistics are not always entirely precise, but they also reflect a genuine change: the boundaries of urban and rural, which were easily discernable 20 years ago, have blurred and become less distinct as urban and rural interpenetrate.

Figure 5.1 also shows that, as described previously, urban residence permit holders have increased much more slowly than total urban residents. By 2003 more than 10% of China's population was resident in an urban area but without an urban residence permit. By 2020, 60% percent of the population is expected to inhabit urban areas, and another 100–200 million rural residents will move into the urban workforce. How China handles this ongoing wave of urbanization, in terms of density, transportation, and concentration in large cities, will shape many aspects of China's evolving society. Moreover, the pattern of continuing rapid urbanization will depend crucially on how effectively China moves in reducing the differences between urban and rural citizens.

5.3 RURAL–URBAN MIGRATION

Rural-to-urban migration has grown rapidly in China since the 1990s, but migrants still face discrimination and limitations on their ability to integrate into urban society. Most migrants remain on the fringes of urban society, sleeping in substandard housing, typically on the outskirts of the city, working long hours, and planning a return to the countryside. Indeed, in many respects Chinese rural migrants in the city resemble undocumented Mexican migrants working in U.S. cities. By migrating they substantially increase their income-generating potential and begin to work their way upward. Moreover, they contribute both to the economy in which they are working and to that of their home villages, largely by remitting funds home. But they remain in a kind of twilight status, subject to discrimination and mistreatment. Migrants need more effective channels to integrate into urban society. Inevitably, this process of integration requires access to the education, housing, and social services that go with full urban citizenship.

5.3.1 Overview of Migration

How large is migration in China today? The sudden emergence and growth of large-scale migration in China produced much initial confusion about the nature and magnitude of the phenomenon. In its broad outlines, migration in China—and especially rural-to-urban migration—is similar to migration in many other developing countries. But Chinese migrants had become unfamiliar visitors in China's cities during the long period of population immobility. Their reappearance evoked complex and sometimes negative reactions from city dwellers. The Chinese term *liudong renkou* ("floating population") has a number of different definitions that can produce widely varying estimates of total numbers. Data from the 2000 census can trace a more precise picture (Liang and Ma 2004). The census counts individuals who have been living for at least six months in a place other than that in which their household is registered. Using this precise definition of the long-term "floating population," it comprised a total 144 million individuals, nearly 12% of China's population. Almost half, 65 million, were local, individuals living away from their official residence but within the same county. The other 79 million are the long-distance, long-term "floating population." They can be further divided into within-province (but cross-county) migrants, who amounted to 36 million, and interprovincial migrants, who amounted to 42 million. The long-distance "floating population" can be compared with the count in the previous censuses of 1990 and 1982, and these data are shown in Figure 5.2. China's long-distance "floating population" has increased dramatically, soaring from 7 million in 1982, to 22 million in 1990, to 79 million in 2000, 6% of the total population. Interprovincial migration has increased especially rapidly.

Migrants have especially been attracted to the booming southern coastal regions. Overall in 2000, 53.5% of the floating population was living in the southern coastal provinces, which had a quarter of the country's people. By far the most important destination is Guangdong Province, which recorded 21 million "floating population" in the 2000 census, making up 25% of the total provincial population. Large-scale migration to the three Lower Yangtze provinces of Shanghai, Jiangsu, and Zhejiang started later than that to Guangdong but has also grown rapidly. These three provinces had 15 million floating population in 2000, amounting to 11% of their total population. In addition to the "floating population," migrants include the 20 million individuals who have succeeded in having their household registrations permanently transferred in the five years preceding the 2000 census. These "permanent"

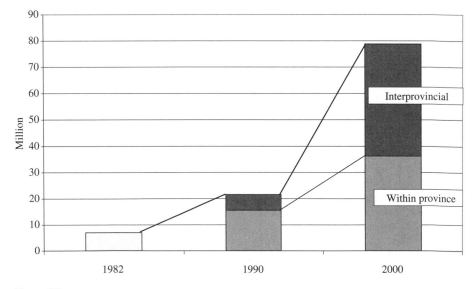

Figure 5.2
The long-distance "floating population" in China's censuses

migrants have a very different profile from the "floating population." They are much more highly educated and predominantly urban in origin, and the most important reason for changing their household registration is education.

5.3.2   Characteristics of Migrants

As administrative controls weaken, migration in China appears to be increasingly similar to migration in most other developing countries, which are also undergoing extensive rural-to-urban migration and urbanization. A common framework used around the world is to explain migration in terms of pull and push factors. Pull factors basically refer to the attraction of higher-income jobs in cities, while push factors reflect the absence of economic opportunity in the source location. Research in China has consistently found that migrants are attracted to regions with higher wages and greater job opportunities. People move in search of economic opportunity. Push factors are probably weaker in China, because, as noted earlier, there is little landlessness in China, although there are certainly areas of extreme rural poverty.

More broadly, migrating to the city is only one of several options open to Chinese rural residents as they seek economic opportunity outside of agriculture. The choices involved and the determinants of migration are discussed more fully in Chapter 8. However, certain characteristics of migrants are distinctive. Rural residents are much more likely to migrate if they are young and male. The probability of migration is by far the highest for those aged 16–20 and declines by about half for every 10 years of age thereafter. In the 1990s a male was three times as likely to migrate as a female with the same characteristics. However, female participation in migration has been rising more rapidly than males, and the differential is shrinking. Export-oriented, light-industry factories in southeast coastal areas prefer to hire female workers, and these act as magnets for female migration. Male migrants are more broadly scattered across the construction sites, factories, and businesses of urban China.

5.4   ECONOMIC CONSEQUENCES OF THE URBAN–RURAL DIVIDE

As mentioned previously, urban–rural gaps inevitably open up during the development process. Industrialization begins in cities during the early stages of development, and at first virtually all of the modern economy is located in cities. In comparison with urban residents, rural people have lower educational levels, are equipped with less capital, and suffer the economic impact of remoteness and incomplete markets for many needed resources. Not surprisingly, participants in the modern economy, namely urban residents, earn higher incomes, while rural dwellers, remaining within the traditional economy, have much lower incomes for a long time. The following section attempts to chart some of the impact on incomes and living standards of the urban–rural divide.

5.4.1   Living Standards and Restrictions on Mobility

When Chinese planners essentially stopped rural-to-urban migration during the 1960s and 1970s, they also imposed a wage freeze on urban residents. Indeed, average real wages (which measure the purchasing power of wages corrected for price changes) drifted downward for 20 years, largely because of the greater numbers of younger workers at the bottom of the wage scale. Despite this wage freeze, the urban–rural income gap actually increased during this period. The main reason for this increase is that urban employment expanded to incorporate virtually all young women. As female labor-force participation became nearly universal, almost all urban households came to have more than one breadwinner. Moreover, strict birth control policies, implemented first in the big cities, reduced the number of dependent children. The result was that the urban dependency ratio (total population/employed population) decreased steadily. Because of these demographic effects, per capita urban incomes continued to rise, even though wages stagnated. Between 1957 and 1977 real wages declined, but the average dependency ratio declined from 3.4 to only 2.0, so urban per capita incomes continued to rise. Rural incomes, by contrast, stagnated. With increased population bottled up in the countryside, the marginal physical product of workers fell. Since government agricultural procurement prices remained roughly unchanged, the marginal value product fell as well.

In order to understand the evolution of the urban–rural gap in recent years, we can use the ratio between per capita money incomes for urban households and those of rural households, shown in Figure 5.3. This information is recorded in the large sample household surveys that are conducted by the Chinese National Bureau of Statistics. Of course, this ratio cannot adequately reflect the full gap between urban and rural residents. As described earlier, urban dwellers not only have higher money incomes than rural dwellers, but they also enjoy a range of subsidies that they receive in addition to their higher money incomes. However, it is difficult to quantify the monetary value of these subsidies, and this can only be done for a few benchmark years. (This topic is covered further in Chapter 9.) The fact that consumer prices are higher in the city partially offsets subsidies. Moreover, changes in the extent to which subsidies are implicit or explicitly included in income will affect the urban–rural

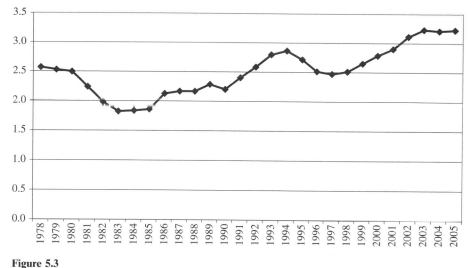

Figure 5.3
Ratio of urban-to-rural household income

comparison. Thus these figures provide only partial information. The data show that when China launched its reform initiative in 1978, the urban–rural divide was already rather wide: the per capita income of the urban resident was 2.6 times higher than that of the rural resident. In the early years of reform, the urban–rural gap shrank, as the success of rural reforms sharply boosted the farmers' income. Starting from 1984, however, the gap began to widen again. Nevertheless, until 1992 the gap was still somewhat smaller than that of 1978. Rapid urban-centered economic growth in the 1990s led to renewed polarization. For a brief period 1995–1997, the gap shrank again, largely because of a sharp increase in agricultural market prices. But high prices were not sustained, and between 1998 and 2003 the urban–rural gap again widened dramatically. The urban–rural divide today is significantly wider that it was in 1978.

Even as restrictions on mobility ease, economic pressures on Chinese farmers are likely to continue. China's entry into the WTO in 2001 has been followed by a gradual phase-in of import liberalization measures that affect farm prices. In essence, the WTO agreement places an upper limit on Chinese farm prices, preventing them from rising significantly above world prices. According to calculations of the Chinese Development Research Center, WTO membership will mean the loss of about 13 million jobs in wheat, cotton, and rice production (compared with an alternative scenario in which China did not adopt import liberalization). These job losses will be offset by the gain of 2.5 million jobs in other agricultural occupations, plus 10 million jobs in textiles and apparel, commerce, and construction. In essence, further integration into the global economy will speed the movement of Chinese resources into sectors in which China has comparative advantage (labor-intensive manufacturing) and out of sectors in which China has comparative disadvantage (especially grain production that intensively uses scarce land). For this shift to take place, rural residents will have to migrate. The shift in relative prices caused by trade liberalization can be expected to put downward pressure on rural incomes. The urban–rural gap will thus continue to be a feature of the Chinese economy.

5.4.2   Addressing the Urban–Rural Divide

In recent years the widening of the urban–rural income gap and the expected impact of WTO membership on farmer income have combined to focus the attention of Chinese policy-makers on rural incomes. The result has been, since 2003, the systematic adoption of policies designed to improve rural incomes and prevent the urban–rural income gap from widening further. Central State Council Document No. 1 of 2003 outlined the policy objective, and practical policy measures have followed systematically. By the end of 2005 the government had abolished the agriculture tax, thus substantially easing the tax burden on farmers. Moreover, a program of direct subsidies has been established for grain growers. These policies are designed to protect rural incomes, not to discourage rural-to-urban migration. Indeed, 2003 also saw the roll out of the "Sunshine Policy," designed to provide prospective migrants with rudimentary job training and information about conditions in destination cities. For perhaps the first time in the history of the PRC, central government policy after 2003 began to systematically correct for past urban bias and tilt toward helping farmers (see Chapter 18 for further details). Yet to be truly effective, these policies will have to be combined with policies at the local level that protect the rights of rural farmers and migrants, and seek to fully integrate migrants into urban society.

5.5   CONCLUSION

The administrative barriers dividing urban and rural areas have economic origins and economic consequences. As socialist China underwent development, economic policies were created that affected the mobility of labor as well as the compensation structure in urban and rural areas. The most important economic consequence is that workers in the urban economy enjoy relatively generous wages and benefits while rural labor remains penned up within the rural economy. The result is an extensive misallocation of labor combined with excessive inequality. Rural workers earn below their marginal product, while urban workers may earn above their marginal product; and the income gap between the categories is larger than it would normally be. Economic reforms began a process of dismantling, or at least lowering, barriers between the urban and rural economies. This dismantling of barriers has been slow but important, and it accelerated after the mid-1990s. Today these barriers have lost some of their earlier importance, but they still remain fundamental in understanding the functioning of the Chinese economy, as well as in determining the different life outcomes of Chinese households.

BIBLIOGRAPHY

Suggestions for Further Reading

Knight and Song (1999) combines microeconomic analysis based on survey data with a broad structural view. Solinger (1999) brings the subjective and objective experience of peasant migrants to the city into sharp focus.

Sources for Data and Figures

Figure 5.1: NBS Department of Comprehensive Statistics (1999: 1) for series by residence permit; updated from SAC, various years; and Population Statistics Yearbook 2005: 265. SYC for standard urbanization series, updated from Annual Economic Report (2006).

Figure 5.2: Liang and Ma 2004.

Figure 5.3: SAC 2005: 102. Updated from Annual Economic Report (2006).

Urbanization Rate: Average of all low and middle income countries is from World Bank, World Development Indicators (average includes China). China data is from SYC and Annual Economic Report (2006), which differ slightly from World Bank reported data for China. The exact standard for judging an urban settlement differs significantly across countries, so cross-national comparisons of urbanization are not precise. Moreover, the Chinese data have been revised several times by Chinese statisticians, most recently in the wake of the 2000 census. The post-2000 definition includes people in settlements larger than 3,000, plus those under urban management (defined according to administrative criteria). Chinese statisticians have revised earlier data in an attempt to make them consistent and comparable across time, but some comparability problems remain. Zhang Shanyu (2003: 289–291) has a good discussion.

References

Annual Economic Report (2006). National Bureau of Statistics. "Zhonghua Renmin Gongheguo 2005 nian guomin jingji he shehui fazhan tongji gongbao [National economic and social development statistical report of the People's Republic of China]" February 27, 2006, accessed at www.stats.gov.cn/tjgb/ndtjgb/qgndtjgb/t20060227_402307796.htm

Banister, Judith (1987). *China's Changing Population*. Stanford: Stanford University Press.

Cai, Yongshun (2003). "Collective Ownership or Cadres' Ownership? The Nonagricultural Use of Farmland in China." *China Quarterly*, no. 175, September, 662–80.

CASS Rural Development Research Institute and NSB Rural Society and Economy Investigation Team (2005). *Nongcun Jingji Lupishu, 2004–2005 Nian: Zhongguo Nongcun Jingji Xingshi*

Fenxi yu Yuce [Rural Economy Green Book 2004–2005: Analysis and Projection of China Rural Economy]. Beijing: Shehui Kexue Wenxian.

Cheng, Tiejun, and Mark Selden (1994). "The Origins and Social Consequences of China's Hukou System." *China Quarterly*, no. 139, September, 644–68.

Knight, John, and Lina Song (1999). *The Rural-Urban Divide: Economic Disparities and Interactions in China*. Oxford: Oxford University Press.

Liang, Zai, and Zhongdong Ma (2004). "China's Floating Population: New Evidence from the 2000 Census." *Population and Development Review*, 30(3), September, 467–88.

Lü, Xiaobo, and Elizabeth Perry, eds. (1997). *Danwei: The Changing Chinese Workplace in Historical and Comparative Perspective*, 169–94. Armonk, NY: M. E. Sharpe.

National Bureau of Statistics, Department of Comprehensive Statistics (1999). *Xiandai Zhongguo 50 Nian Tongji Ziliao Huibian* [Comprehensive Statistical Data and Materials on 50 Years of New China]. Beijing: China Statistics Press.

Population Statistics Yearbook (various years). National Bureau of Statistics, Department of Population and Employment Statistics, ed., *Zhongguo Renkou Tongji Nianjian* [Population Statistics Yearbook of China]. Beijing: Zhongguo Tongji.

Rozelle, Scott, and Guo Li (1998). "Village Leaders and Land-Rights Formation in China." *American Economic Review (Papers and Proceedings)*, 88(2), May, 433–38.

SAC (Annual). *Zhongguo Tongji Zhaiyao* [Statistical Abstract of China]. Beijing: Zhongguo Tongji.

Shandong (2004). "Shandong Is Eliminating the Distinction Between City and Rural Registration." *Huasheng Bao*, August 20, http://www.people.com.cn/GB/shizheng/14562/2726307.html.

Solinger, Dorothy (1999). *Contesting Citizenship in Urban China: Peasant Migrants, the State, and the Logic of the Market*. Berkeley: University of California Press.

SYC (Annual). *Zhongguo Tongji Nianjian* [Statistical Yearbook of China]. Beijing: Zhongguo Tongji.

Walder, Andrew (2000). "Chinese Society." Public Lecture. Institute for International Studies Conference, "China at the Crossroads." Stanford University, May 19, 2000.

World Bank (various years). World Development Indicators. Washington, D.C.: World Bank. http://devdata.worldbank.org/dataonline/.

World Health Organization (2000). *World Health Report 2000*. Geneva: World Health Organization. http://www.who.int/whr/2000/en/whr00_annex_en.pdf.

Wu, Xiaogang, and Donald J. Treiman (2004). "The Household Registration System and Social Stratification in China: 1955–1996." *Demography*, 41(2), May, 363–84.

Yu Jianrong (2005). "Social Conflict in Rural China Today: Observations and Analysis on Farmers' Struggles to Safeguard Their Rights." *Social Sciences in China*, March, 125–36.

Zhang Shanyu (2003). *Zhongguo Renkou Dili* [China Population Geography]. Beijing: Kexue Publishing House.

Zhejiang (2004). "Zhejiang Will Implement a Unified Country-City Household Registration System Next Year." *Xiandai Jinbao*, December 27, http://www.china.org.cn/chinese/zhuanti/jrfwc/739294.htm.

II PATTERNS OF GROWTH AND DEVELOPMENT

Beijing 1985: The form and scale of cities reshaped by structural change.

6 Growth and Structural Change

Economic growth, in the simplest meaning of the term, can be visualized as an increase in the total amount of goods and services available. This is measured by the growth of GDP, which is the total of all the value added in an economy. Adjusting for population growth gives the total amount of goods and services available per individual, that is, GDP per capita. The development process is a gradual but steady and sustained increase in output per capita. Output increases because society accumulates physical capital to equip workers to become more productive and because households boost the productivity of their family members by investing more into human capital, especially health and education. Technology becomes more sophisticated as better-educated, better-equipped workers become more adept at their work. In addition, many structural changes occur in regular patterns as the economy is reshaped by the actions of many individuals.

The previous chapter began the discussion of structural change with one of the most important aspects of structural change, the shift from a rural to an urban society. In this chapter the discussion of structural change is broadened to take a comparative perspective on growth, labor, and the changing distribution of GDP. China's economic development has followed a process that shares many common features of structural change with other developing countries. One purpose of this chapter is to provide benchmarks that show how far China has come along a common development path, as well as to discuss problems with Chinese data. At the same time, by drawing out the common features, this chapter also highlights the ways in which the Chinese pattern was unusual and distinctive. The emphasis in the preceding chapter was on the unique institutions that impeded structural change in the case of the urban–rural divide; the emphasis in this chapter is on the common processes that drive structural change and growth in all economies.

The comparative and structural perspective illuminates several aspects of China's economy. First, although China's development processes resemble those in other economies, China is also unusual in three respects: China invests more than other economies, concentrates more on manufacturing than other economies, and has grown more rapidly than other economies. Second, the structural perspective helps explain why China is growing so rapidly. High investment accounts for a great deal of China's rapid growth. In addition, China is at the stage of economic development where very rapid structural change provides an impetus for high-speed growth. Third, a structural perspective provides a basis for projecting China's future development. Because structural change occurs in regular patterns, we can expect that China will repeat many of the changes undergone by earlier-developing East Asian economies. In particular, we should expect China's rapid growth to continue for another decade and then begin to moderate as labor force growth slows and rural-to-urban shifts wind down. Structural change is associated with social change: As industry and modern services grow, new urban social groups emerge that have higher incomes and new skills. New markets and new social possibilities emerge along with those groups.

6.1 GROWTH

China grew fast between 1949 and 1978, but growth really took off after the beginning of reform in 1978. Moreover, the acceleration of economic growth coincided with the slowing of population growth, so per capita growth accelerated even more dramatically. According to official data, shown in Table 6.1, average annual GDP growth accelerated from 6% in the pre–1978 period to 9.6% in the 1978–2005 period. At the same time, population growth decelerated from 1.9% per year before 1978 to only 1.1% after 1978. As a result, per capita GDP growth more than doubled, jumping from 4.1% to 8.5% annually. China's post–1978 growth experience has been extraordinary by any standard.

6.1.1 Data and the Measurement of Growth

The data shown in Table 6.1, and indeed used throughout this text, are official Chinese data. How reliable are these data? First, they are the most reliable

Table 6.1
Growth of per capita GDP (average annual growth rates, percentage)

	GDP	Population	GDP per capita
1952–1978	6.0	1.9	4.1
1978–2005	9.6	1.1	8.5

data we have. That is, there is no plausible alternative set of data for China, and no one has ever demonstrated that the extensive Chinese numbers published are mutually contradictory or inconsistent with externally verifiable facts. So the truth is that we have no choice but to use official data. And after all, the official data are the product of a data-collection network systematically analyzed by a large group of conscientious government statisticians. Having said this, there are many reasons to emphasize that the data are neither as precise nor as reliable as we would like. China is both a transition economy and a developing country. GDP data from most developing countries are prone to substantial errors, and statistical accuracy is a problem in transitional economies because the magnitude of change is so large.

Especially troubling is that China made a transition to a new data-collection system in 1998 that was in some respects a failure. Attempting to adjust data-collection procedures to an economy with many more small-scale businesses, the National Bureau of Statistics (NBS) shifted to sample survey estimates of the size of small-scale industry and services. The resulting GDP numbers were not only arguably less reliable than before, but were also difficult to corroborate with consistent pastime series. Indeed, during 2005 the NBS revised GDP upward by 16% to reflect a more inclusive count of small-scale service providers primarily in transport, retailing, and restaurants. (These new estimates are used through this textbook.) Moreover, the 1998 changeover to the new system happened to coincide with a period of exceptionally rapid change in the real economy, and so our picture of the 1998–1999 period is especially indistinct. As discussed in Chapter 14, the problem is particularly acute with respect to energy data, which completely breaks down at that time. Unfortunately, Chinese data are not necessarily becoming more accurate.

Three sets of problems afflict Chinese data: prices, coverage, and politics. First, official statistics do not adequately correct for the effects of inflation. The GDP deflator, the measure of inflation that is used by official government statisticians to convert nominal (current-price) GDP growth to real (constant-price) growth, grows more slowly than almost every other measure of inflation. Ren (1997) and Young (2003) present good accounts of the data, together with convincing arguments for the use of alternative price indexes. Using different price indexes lowers the overall GDP growth rate by 1.6 percentage points annually for the period Young examines (1978–1998). This problem is most acute for the 1980s, when inflation was rampant. Since 1996, prices have been stable, and this problem has become less serious. Second, statisticians have a very hard time accounting for the expanding scope of the economy. Twenty-five years ago, China did not produce color televisions, to say nothing of computers. Chinese statisticians tend to count fast-growing items like computers by valuing them at their early, very high, prices, which overweights them and therefore overstates growth. But there are also fast-growing items that had very low prices at the beginning of the era, such as health care and housing. Many of these were rationed at the beginning of the period but are now readily available at market prices. Counting these items at their beginning-of-period prices creates another source of inaccuracy, but one that tends to understate growth. The net effect is unclear.

Third, and finally, data collection is intertwined with politics in China in a way that reduces the accuracy of statistics. The NBS has a monopoly on statistical collection, so the benefits of a competitive market place have not reached the data field yet. Many crucial data series—including GDP—are used as success indicators for local officials, who therefore have incentives to inflate or otherwise distort the numbers that are reported. Moreover, the Communist Party monopoly over the press affects the way economic news is reported. For example, when revisions are made to GDP data, they are almost never used to revise growth rates downward, even when doing so would seem to be logically appropriate. These are serious problems, and they tell us to use caution with Chinese data and accept the data only within a fairly large margin of error.

6.1.2 Growth in Comparative Perspective

The problems discussed in the preceding section do not indicate, however, that Chinese economic growth is somehow illusory. Quite the contrary: some key elements of the economy are fully verifiable; for example, exports have grown much more rapidly than GDP and are fully corroborated by the independent statistics of importing countries. If China's GDP were actually growing significantly more slowly than official figures indicate, exports would have increased their share of GDP even more dramatically, and it would be difficult to explain how exports had grown so much more rapidly than GDP. China's dramatic export boom only makes sense in the context of a rapidly growing GDP. There are a number of similar cases of readily verified series (fiscal revenues, for example). As noted before, no alternate procedure for assessing China's growth meets basic consistency checks; and finally, rapid growth and transformation correspond to the commonsense evidence of personal experience. Overall, then, there is likely to be some upward bias to the official recorded growth rates, but it will not change the fundamental picture of rapid growth. Allowing for inadequate deflation during the 1980s and early 1990s, and perhaps for an undercount of GDP in 1978, we might well adjust Chinese GDP growth by lowering it one to two percentage points per year. Such an adjustment would put China's per capita GDP growth at around 7% per year for the entire 1978–2005 period. This is still the most sustained period of rapid economic growth in human history.

Growth of per capita GDP above 6% for a prolonged period of time is not unprecedented, but worldwide it has only happened in three episodes, all of them in East Asia. First, Japan led the way with growth of GDP per capita slightly above 8% per year for 18 years, from 1955 to 1973. After 1973, Japanese growth moderated, but it remained healthy until the end of the 1980s. Second, during the 14-year period from 1982 through 1996, several East Asian economies grew at very high rates. During this period, annual growth of GDP per capita in Korea was 7.4%; in Taiwan 7.1%; and in Thailand 6.8%. However, these economies experienced a fairly dramatic economic shrinkage after 1996 and slower growth thereafter, suggesting that some part of the rapid growth before 1996 might have been unsustainable. The third episode is China since 1978. China's contemporary growth thus represents the third major East Asian growth surge. After correction for statistical overstatement, China's growth is probably not more rapid than the other two. However, China's growth is still unique: it affects many more people than the two previous episodes; and China's growth surge is still going strong after 27 years, far longer than the other two episodes.

6.1.3   Instability in Growth

Figure 6.1 shows that there has been a pronounced cyclical pattern to GDP growth post–1978. There have been four periods of especially rapid growth, close to or surpassing 10% per year. Peaks are evident in 1978, 1984–1985, 1992–1994, and 2003–2005. Each peak growth period produced serious strains on the economy, including inflation and sectoral bottlenecks, and was followed by a phase of retrenchment and slower growth. Long-term growth is clearly a good thing, but it does not follow that maximum growth in a short time period is always desirable. Growth must be sustainable to deliver its benefits. Although China exhibits significant macroeconomic instability, so far each retrenchment has been followed by a renewed growth cycle, and there is no obvious reason why rapid Chinese growth cannot be sustained for another decade.

6.2   INVESTMENT

Closely related to China's rapid growth is the enormous investment effort China has made over the past 25 years. Ironically, since China has abandoned the Big Push socialist development strategy, its investment rate has actually

Figure 6.1
Annual GDP growth, 1978–2005

risen. Indeed, the most immediate explanation for China's rapid growth has been the very high rate of investment China has sustained. The basic facts are shown in Figure 6.2, which shows total capital formation and its two components, fixed capital formation and inventory accumulation. We are most interested in fixed capital formation (shown in a solid line), which corresponds to new factories, roads, and housing and which is fundamental to economic growth. Gross fixed capital formation was already around 30% of GDP at the end of the 1970s, and it stayed in that range through most of the 1980s. During the 1990s, however, fixed capital formation increased to about 35% of GDP, before taking another jump upward to 40% of GDP in 2004. Fixed capital formation surpassed 40% of GDP in 2005. China's investment rate is not only high, but also rising. Some part of the most recent increase in investment may well be unsustainable, part of a macroeconomic phase of overheating, but the long-term trend to an increased fixed investment ratio is clear.

Have we ever seen investment rates this high before? Yes, but only in exceptional circumstances. Again, the two previous episodes of rapid growth in East Asia were also characterized by high investment, although not quite as high as China today. Japan invested 35%–37% of GDP in gross fixed capital formation during 1970–1973 at the very end of its long boom. Korea sustained a very high fixed investment rate from 1990–1997, peaking at 39% in 1991.

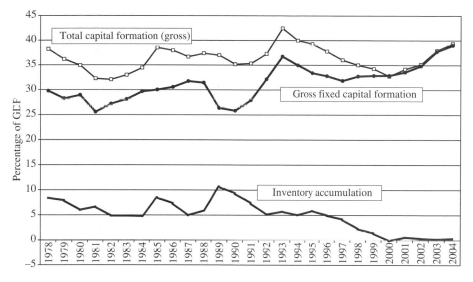

Figure 6.2
Gross capital formation

For brief periods in the mid-1990s, Thailand and Malaysia invested over 40% of their GDPs in fixed capital (1993–1996 and 1995, respectively). Thailand and Malaysia achieved their very high investment rates to a significant extent by relying on inflows of foreign direct investment, which equaled 5%–6% of GDP. Japan and Korea, however, did not rely on foreign investment to any significant degree at all.

China certainly hosts a significant amount of foreign investment, amounting to about 4% of GDP over the last decade. However, unlike Thailand and Malaysia, China has not run a current account deficit in recent years and thus is not dependent on foreign capital inflows to finance its domestic investment. On balance, Chinese investment is fully financed through Chinese domestic saving. Thus Chinese domestic saving rates are also very high, as they must be to finance the prodigious investment effort. Of course, foreign investment still plays an important role in the Chinese economy. In essence, China uses the opportunities and skills that foreign direct investment brings to identify and develop productive investment projects. The increased return created by these more productive projects contributes to keeping the overall investment rate high.

High investment is a major explanatory factor and precondition for rapid growth in China, as it has been in previous episodes of rapid East Asian growth. Clearly, a big part of the answer to the question "Why is China growing so fast?" is simply "Because it invests so much." We can better understand China's experience—and in turn use the Chinese example to shed light on global economic growth—by looking at some of the basic relationships between investment and growth. Particularly during the 1940s through the 1960s, economists examining development and growth tended to see investment as the key to growth. Development economists argued that the first task of development was to increase investment from, say, 5% of national income to 15% or more. (Today most economies already invest more than 15% of national income, and China, obviously, invests much more than this.) The simplest possible growth model, called a Harrod-Domar model, is one that includes only fixed capital as a source of growth: this simple model can make sense only if labor is so abundant that labor to work the new capital is always available at insignificant cost. In that case, a model can be structured by defining a constant capital/output ratio. That is, set a parameter, $k = K/Y$, where small k represents the number of units of capital (K) required to produce each unit of GDP or income (Y). In a reasonably well functioning economy we might expect this capital/output ratio to be a number between roughly 3 and 6. Assume that in a given economy, such as China, this ratio is fixed in the short term and equal to 4. The output (GDP) is given by the capital stock:

$$Y = 1/k \times K$$

And growth is given by the increment in the capital stock:

$$dY = 1/k \times dK$$
$$dY/Y = 1/k \times dK/Y$$

Since, if we ignore depreciation, dk/Y = Investment/Y; then call the growth rate g and the investment rate i, so that growth is a linear function of investment:

$$g = i/k$$

In China's case, as the investment rate is pushed up to 40% of GDP, the growth rate of the economy as a whole approaches 10% (10% = 40%/4). Clearly, this simple relationship captures something important about the Chinese growth experience.

While illuminating, this perspective is too limited. In the first place, international experience shows that the relationship between investment and growth is not so straightforward and that it cannot explain very much of the variation in the growth experience across countries. A significant investment effort is a prerequisite to growth, but today virtually all economies invest more than 15% of GDP, and yet some are growing robustly while others are not growing at all. In fact, even for a single economy, the investment rate tends to be relatively persistent over the long term, but countries' growth rates can fluctuate dramatically, as indeed China's experience also demonstrates. While there is definitely an association between investment and growth, the relationship is neither as strong as we might expect, nor the causality as clear as predicted (Blomstrom, Lipsey, and Zejan 1996; Easterly and Levine 2001). The East Asian growth experiences clearly depend on a significant investment effort, but not necessarily on the extremely high investment rates that characterize China or Korea. The economy of Taiwan, for example, has achieved very rapid growth, but fixed capital formation was only occasionally pushed above 30% (and the last time was in 1980). Even if investment fuels growth, investment is costly. Resources are diverted from consumption, so investment involves "belt tightening." The challenge over the long run is to understand how economies achieve sustained increases in the productivity with which labor and capital are used.

In a standard economic viewpoint we would expect to see that continuous increases in capital gradually run into diminishing returns. The rate of investment is thus ultimately determined by the rate of return on investment: investors will continue to put money into investment until the marginal returns fall to their cost of capital. Even in the standard "neoclassical" view of growth, then, while the investment rate is an immediate determinant of growth, it is still necessary to understand the productivity of investment to explain the rate of investment. In another view of the growth process, the key factor in growth is technology change, which responds to different factors than just investment. In this view, "idea gaps" are more important than differences in fixed capital endowments in explaining performance. Because technology transfer can lead to jumps in the productivity of an economy, it is the most fundamental determinant of growth. In this view, the ability to absorb technology is determined endogenously by an economy's education, institutions, and policy. Investment does not necessarily run into diminishing returns—since technology is "nonrival" and can be shared without cost—but investment is no longer the decisive factor in explaining growth, either. These alternative views apply to the case of China.

China is an unusual case precisely because the investment rate has remained high under dramatically different economic systems and regimes. During the Big Push period the investment rate stayed high regardless of the productivity of investment because of government's direct role. China's transition to a market economy was unique in that gross fixed capital formation never dropped below 25% of GDP, even in the lowest years (1981 and 1989–1990). This is dramatically different from other transitional economies, where investment was similarly high under the command economy but collapsed during the transition. Further, China only gradually reduced that part of investment that is basically waste. Figure 6.2 shows that *total* capital formation is composed of both fixed capital formation and inventory accumulation. While some inventory accumulation—buildup of stockpiles in factories and stores—is a necessary part of economic growth, market economies typically spend less than 1% of GDP on inventory accumulation, except during unanticipated recessions. China, like other command economies, consistently spent over 5% of GDP on inventory accumulation, largely because of the buildup of worthless, low-quality or unsuitable product. These levels of inventory accumulation can serve as an indicator of the persistence of command-economy-type inefficiency in the system. China displayed this inefficiency through the mid-1990s but still managed to keep investment high. Then, after the second phase of reform in the late 1990s, inventory accumulation fell to essentially nothing. The economy could have adapted by increasing consumption's share in GDP; instead, investors responded to the improved productivity of the economy by stepping up investment. Total investment rose past its previous heights. Because none of this was inventory accumulation, total fixed investment soared well past its previous heights.

A key element of the Chinese experience, then, is one of consistently high investment that appears to be sustained by a gradual increase in the productivity performance of the economy. This interpretation is supported by the fact that inflows of foreign direct investment have remained strong, indicating that foreign businesses continue to find profitable projects in which to invest. High investment rates "cause" economic growth, in a mechanical sense, but are also themselves a symptom of productivity improvements that are the ultimate source of economic growth. Explaining these improvements, though, is challenging. At a minimum, skill, institutions, and policies have to be adequate to support productive investments, and national actors have to be willing to defer consumption, maintain their own saving rates, and plow resources back into investment. These topics are covered elsewhere in this book.

6.3   STRUCTURAL CHANGE: COMMON PATTERNS

The sustained increase in output per capita that comes from the development process is caused by accumulation of new physical and human capital, and by improvements in productivity. Productivity increases because existing jobs are upgraded and, equally important, because workers leave existing jobs in the traditional sector and move into modern sectors, where productivity and the potential for future growth are higher. Thus the long-term growth of output is inevitably associated with important structural changes. These can be traced both through the labor force and through GDP.

All countries begin development predominantly agricultural. In the early stages of development, farmers make up the bulk of the labor force, and most value added is in agriculture. As development proceeds, certain common patterns of structural change are observed that are associated with the growth away from a predominantly agricultural economy and to an industrialized and diversified economy. The simplest way to track these changes relies on classifying all economic activity into three sectors: primary (agriculture, including fisheries, forestry, and animal husbandry); secondary (including mining, manufacturing, construction, and utilities); and tertiary or service (including transportation, communications, household and business services, social services, and technology and education).

The first obvious change during the development process is that the share of the labor force in the primary sector declines. As economies begin to move out of low-income status and into the ranks of middle-income economies, the absolute number (and not just the share) of workers in agriculture begins to decline. The remaining farm laborers boost their productivity and are able to feed the entire country. This process continues indefinitely: a high-income country like the United States has only 3% of its labor force in agriculture. Rozelle (2004, 60) calls the decline in agriculture's share the "iron law of development." It may seem initially that agriculture plays an entirely passive role, shrinking steadily as the economy modernizes. In fact, successful developing economies typically experience modernization of the agricultural sector as an early and integral part of overall development. As will be discussed in Chapter 11, agricultural development "feeds" the broader process of economic growth in a number of fundamental ways: providing food at low cost, which keeps wages economy-wide at reasonable levels; releasing workers for growing modern sectors; and providing a source of finance and markets for modern growing sectors. Healthy agricultural development leads to more rapid development overall.

The process of industrialization, starting from a small base, gradually changes the structure of the economy. The secondary sector grows through the initial stages of development, increasing the number and share of workers and the share of GDP. Industry does not grow forever, though. At a certain point the industrial share of GDP levels off. Moreover, as industrial productivity continues to rise, the share of workforce in industry declines. There is no iron law for industry-sector development; country experience is diverse and reflects individual specialization and endowment. However, an "average" pattern is that the industrial share of GDP tends to increase until a country reaches an income level of around $10,000 GDP per capita, evaluated at purchasing power parities (PPP; Box 6.1), and then levels off, and may even decline. Manufacturing—the most important part of the secondary sector—typically peaks at about 20%–25% of GDP, but there is considerable variation.

The tertiary, or service, sector displays even more diversity. During the early phase of development the share of the service (tertiary) sector does not necessarily change by a large proportion. Many underdeveloped economies have large proportions of their labor force engaged in services. However, these are predominantly low-value jobs: small-scale retail and repair, hauling goods, and personal services. Early development in these economies may result in a declining agricultural share and an increasing industrial share without a large change in tertiary employment. However, above the threshold that we can set roughly at $10,000 per capita PPP GDP, the service sector's share inevitably increases, since both primary and secondary sectors are declining. As an economy like that of the United States reaches a GDP per capita of $40,000,

Box 6.1
Purchasing Power Parities (PPP)

GDP for each country is initially calculated on the basis of that country's currency, so China's GDP is calculated first in RMB. However, in order to make comparisons among countries, we need to convert GDP or GDP per capita into some common benchmark currency, most often the U.S. dollar. The simplest way to do so is simply to use the prevailing exchange rate. However, conversion using exchange rates is often unsatisfactory, because the price structures of different countries can be extremely different, varying according to relative scarcities, and exchange rates can sometimes fluctuate dramatically. An alternative is to calculate PPPs. For China, this means first calculating how many RMB it takes to purchase a given basket of goods and services, and then comparing this figure to the U.S. dollar cost of an equivalent basket in the U.S. economy. This ratio is then used to value the "purchasing power" of the RMB, which allows us to express Chinese GDP per capita in comparable PPP-adjusted dollars. This procedure is especially useful for evaluating living standards or the incidence of poverty, and we will use it in Chapter 9 when we discuss those topics.

In addition, when a PPP calculation is done for many different countries, it gives us a common benchmark to evaluate the development process. The computation is difficult because the bundles of goods and services produced and consumed in different economies vary quite significantly. PPP calculations require a great deal of data, and no two calculations will be exactly the same. However, a number of large comparison projects (including one by the World Bank) have produced PPP estimates according to a consistent methodology for a large number of economies. The discussion of common patterns of structural change in the text is based on World Bank series of PPP-adjusted GDP per capita. According to the World Bank, China's PPP-adjusted GDP per capita was almost $5,000, in constant 2000 dollars, in the year 2004.

it has 70% of its employment in services. Let us now see how well these patterns apply to China.

6.4 STRUCTURAL CHANGE IN CHINA: LABOR

China's labor force is huge: the economically active population was 740 million according to the 2000 census. A very high, and increasing, share of the population is of working age, and a very large share of the working-age population does in fact participate in the labor force. These facts are discussed more fully in the following two chapters, but they are introduced here to provide background for the process of structure change in the labor force. Labor-force structural change takes place in the context of unrelenting pressure on the employment-generating capability of the economy. The ability of the growing modern sector to absorb labor is a key determinant of the economy's ability to transform itself.

As Figure 6.3 shows, at the end of the planned economy era in 1978 the Chinese labor force reflected both the fact of underdevelopment and the distortions imposed by the administrative regime that divided urban and rural. At that time the remarkably high figure of 71% of the workforce was engaged in agriculture. (The overall rural share of the labor force, including rural

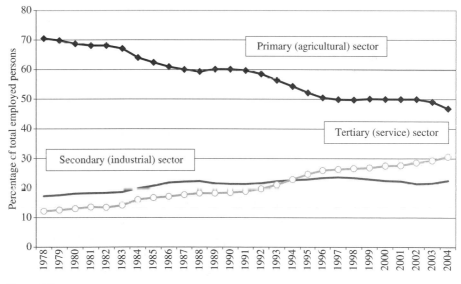

Figure 6.3
Structural change in employment

industry and service along with agriculture, was 76% at this time.) Following common patterns of structural change, the share of the labor force in agriculture has declined significantly since 1978, and it fell significantly below 50% for the first time in 2004. Especially rapid bursts of structural change took place in three periods: from 1983 through 1987, from 1991 through 1996, and after 2003. The first burst shows the early success of rural reforms: as collectives were disbanded and farm output surged in the early 1980s, millions of farmers left to take up new nonagricultural jobs, especially those in TVEs (Chapter 12). The second burst occurred in the early 1990s, as economic growth surged and restrictions on rural-to-urban migration were significantly reduced. The third burst corresponded with the 2003 investment-driven acceleration of the economy. Periods of more rapid economic growth are also periods of expanding opportunity for rural workers and of accelerating structural transformation. The absolute number of agricultural workers reached a peak of 391 million in 1991, and it has since started its long, steady decline. By the end of 2004 the number of agricultural workers reached 353 million, for a cumulative decline of about 10%. China no longer has a clear majority of its workers in agriculture; China is thus no longer a predominantly agricultural economy. But with half of its workers still in agriculture, China remains on the doorstep of a modern economy, with much transformation still ahead.

Particularly noteworthy is the very slow pace of structural change between 1996 and 2002. The exodus of workers from agriculture slowed dramatically after 1996 because of the impact of state-sector restructuring. State enterprise downsizing led to mass layoffs in state-run factories (Chapter 8). The urban unemployment rate increased sharply and created a much more difficult urban job market for potential rural-to-urban migrants. Indeed, the proportion of the labor force in industry has been a little above 20% since the late 1980s, while industrial output has continued to grow as a share of GDP. This is consistent with a view of Chinese industry as characterized by many underemployed workers through the mid-1990s, many of whom were subsequently let go. The release of surplus workers caused the structural transformation of the labor force to stall out temporarily at the turn of the century, resuming only after 2003.

Figure 6.3 also shows the gradual growth of China's late-developing service sector. The share of workers in services in 1978—merely 12%—is astonishingly low. There is some undercount involved here, since statisticians are unlikely to have captured all the employees of urban industrial work units who were actually providing services to other work-unit employees. But it is undoubtedly true that, as noted in Chapter 3, socialist development involved a neglect of investment in the service sector, as well as discrimination against individual service providers. Given that background, it would be expected that market transition should create a dramatic expansion in service-sector employment. Figure 6.3 certainly shows vigorous service-sector growth, as its share of the work force has climbed steadily to more than 30% in 2004. Nevertheless, given the depth of suppression of the service sector pre–1978, one could have expected an even more impressive growth. Moreover, many middle-income developing countries have 40% or more of their labor force in services. China's low figure may reflect an undercount of small-scale service businesses. But even adjusting for under-reporting, it appears that reforms have had a slow and relatively weak impact on increasing the employment of service sectors. This may be due to the fact that while market opening and diversification have proceeded strongly in goods-producing sectors (primary and secondary sectors), the government has maintained near monopoly controls over a number of higher-skill service sectors, including those relating to finance. Since the late 1990s, as industrial restructuring has caused a reduction in manufacturing employment, service employment has begun to grow somewhat more rapidly and has taken up some of the workers displaced from industry. This is a favorable sign, and it indicates that the economy has the potential to generate more service-sector employment, thereby providing new jobs for underemployed and low-productivity workers in agriculture and industry.

6.5   STRUCTURAL CHANGE IN CHINA: GDP

Structural change can be viewed through the changing shares of total GDP produced by the primary, secondary, and tertiary sectors. Unlike in the case of labor, which we could measure simply by counting bodies, GDP must be measured in value. Therefore, we must choose an appropriate price standard for comparison and properly treat changing prices over time. These issues are particularly important in the case of China because the Big Push socialist development strategy imposed distortions both on the price system and on the true structure of the economy. As discussed in preceding chapters, the priority placed on industrial development, together with the need to ensure a source of budgetary revenues, led the socialist government to follow a high-price policy for industrial output, leading to an overstatement of industry's contribution to GDP. Prices of agricultural products and services were, in relative terms, undervalued. At the same time, however, planners followed a development strategy that gave priority to industry, leading to a precocious real development of industry.

The result of these factors is that China's GDP in 1978, measured in the prices of that year (1978), was dominated by industry. The secondary sector produced 48% of total output, agriculture only 28%, and the service sector a tiny 24%. Working for the distorted prices set by the government, an industrial worker was over seven times as productive as an agricultural worker. During the post–1978 reforms, many of the distortions imposed on the price system by the government pre–1978 were eliminated. The gradual opening of the economy to competition and international trade, along with the elimination of government price controls, drove down the relative price of manufactured goods, compared with services and agricultural products. Industry displayed the lowest rate of inflation, while at the same time enjoying the highest real growth rate in the economy. Price changes and real growth rates were thus negatively correlated in China. This is a common phenomenon observed in growing economies, but the effect is especially large in China because the initial-period price distortions were very big and growth has been especially rapid.

The negative correlation between price and real growth means that the output of the three sectors in China has grown at roughly similar rates when valued at current prices (since higher growth tends to offset lower price inflation, and vice versa). As a result, measured at current prices, the sectoral composition of GDP in China seems to display no consistent trend. For example, the share of industry in current price GDP has never surpassed the 48% recorded in 1978, and even in 2004 that share was only 46%. The constantly shifting price base of current prices cannot give a true measure of structural change. The best alternative is to use constant prices from a relatively recent year, since we have good reason to believe that recent prices are closer to world prices and since we know that earlier prices were highly distorted. When we do so, using the implicit sectoral GDP deflators to revalue sectoral output to a constant-price basis, the long-run pattern of structural change emerges clearly. Figure 6.4 uses prices from 2004 to measure structure and structural changes through 2005. It also provides another look at the structure of the economy in 1978 by looking at shares of GDP measured in 2004 prices. Using this price base, agriculture produced 42% of GDP, while industry produced 29% in 1978. This more moderate number means that China in 1978 did not display such an unusually high level of industrialization early on as initially appears. Moreover, when 1978 output is revalued according to the more realistic prices of 2004, an industrial worker is not quite three times as productive as a farmer (instead of seven times as productive). A productivity differential of this magnitude would be similar to that reported in other developing countries, and reflects reasonably well the better education and equipment that industrial workers have compared to farmers. In both these respects, China

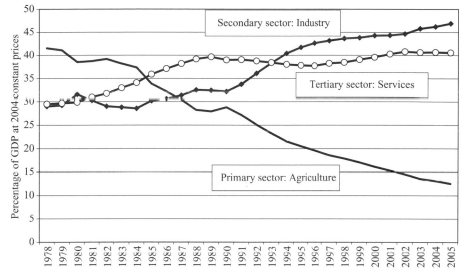

Figure 6.4
Composition of GDP

turns out to be a less extreme outlier than one would have concluded just by looking at current price data.

Figure 6.4 displays a clear picture of structural change since 1978. Two periods can be discerned. During the first period, from 1978–1990, structural change was moderate and marked by complex trends. Agriculture's share declined, slowly at first, as reformers gave renewed priority to agriculture in the six years through 1985. The service sector grew rapidly, reflecting its strong recovery from the highly repressed conditions of the command economy era. By contrast, the industrial share increased relatively slowly, growing by only three percentage points through 1990. However, with the renewal of economic reform and rapid growth after 1991, structural change resumed with renewed intensity. Rapid industrial growth dominated the process. The share of GDP originating in industry jumped from 32% in 1990 to 42% in 1995, and then continued to trend upward, surpassing 46% in 2004. Indeed, the industrial boom has been so overwhelming that the share of services, which we would normally expect to be increasing in a rapidly growing economy at China's income level, has leveled off around 40% of GDP since 1990 (even after incorporating higher estimates of service sector value-added revised to correct an undercount of small-scale service providers). During this industrial boom, agriculture's share of GDP has resumed its rapid decline, sliding from 29% of GDP in 1990 to 13% in 2004 (measured in constant 2004 prices). China is leaving behind its history as a predominantly agricultural economy as it undergoes rapid industrialization, but its service sector still lags behind the explosively growing manufacturing economy.

6.6 STRUCTURAL CHANGE AND GLOBALIZATION

China's industrial share in 2004 was extremely high. Industry includes mining, petroleum extraction, and utilities, which of course vary substantially across countries and which are not particularly large in China. For international comparative purposes, it is most useful to compare the share of GDP that is produced in manufacturing. In China, manufacturing makes up three quarters of the overall secondary sector (which includes construction as well as industry). Thus, manufacturing value-added accounted for 35% of China's GDP in 2004. This a very high share of manufacturing in GDP for a large country. A few countries have concentrated 35% of GDP in manufacturing (Brazil in 1982 and Thailand in 2003; Malaysian manufacturing accounted for 33% of GDP in 2000), but none of these countries has quite reached China's extreme levels of concentration or sustained it as long. Clearly, China's high manufacturing share is related to China's high investment rate, which keeps the demand for materials and machinery high, and to government policies that foster industrial growth. It is thus ironic that since China abandoned the Big Push strategy, both its investment rate and its manufacturing share have risen to unprecedented highs.

However, it is also clear that China's high manufacturing share is closely related to its emergence as "the world's factory." Globalization changes some of the patterns of structural change. As China emerges as a favored site for certain types of manufacturing worldwide, and as it clusters certain stages of Asia-wide manufacturing networks, it clearly can continue to expand its manufacturing sector for a longer period than if it were not so integrated into world industry (Chapter 16). An instructive contrast, touching on globalization and also on economic development patterns, is with India. The pattern of structural change in India is shown in Figure 6.5. Like China, India shows a steady decline in the share of agriculture in its overall GDP. But the relationship between change in industry and services is reversed in the two economies. In India, industry's share has remained roughly constant, while services have climbed to more than 50% of GDP. Each country has established a comparative advantage in one broad sector, then developed along a path of steady growth in the comparative-advantage sector. In that sense, globalization and international trade create additional opportunities for specialization and apparently "unbalanced growth" that would not exist in an economy less integrated with the world.

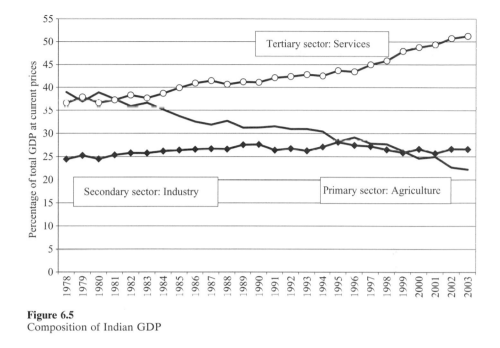

Figure 6.5
Composition of Indian GDP

6.7   CONCLUSION

Economic growth has been intertwined with structural changes throughout China's economic development process. By examining the benchmarks of structural change, we have been able to identify where China has forged its own unique path in a process of dynamic development. China's command economy and Big Push industrialization strategy included policies restricting labor mobility and controlloing prices, as well as neglecting agriculture and services. These policies all had ramifications for China's growth and structural changes that caused a divergence from the development-process benchmark. Yet, despite these divergences, China has followed general patterns of development found throughout the world. Today China is a vast diverse nation with an unusually large manufacturing sector, highly developed urban centers, a lagging service sector, and underdeveloped rural areas. The process of structural change is well under way, but continued restructuring is on the horizon. In the next chapter, we turn to a discussion of China's demographic structure and the unique benefits and challenges it poses to China's further economic and social development.

BIBLIOGRAPHY

Suggestions for Further Reading

For a good discussion of the regularities of structural change in development, see Perkins et al. (2001). World Bank (1997) has a very accessible discussion of structural change and productivity growth in China. The literature on Chinese growth is very large: Holz (2005) lays out the main considerations in an approachable form, with an emphasis on labor quality.

Sources for Data and Figures

Figure 6.1: *SYC*, post–1993 revised according to NBS (2006).

Figure 6.2: *SYC* (2005, 64). An approximation based on GDP expenditure side data, revised post–1993 on the assumption that fixed investment and inventory accumulation remain the same as in earlier data, but total GDP revised as in NBS (2006).

Figure 6.3: *SYC* (2005, 118).

Figure 6.4: *SYC* (2005, 51, 53); post–1993 revised according to NBS (2006).

Figure 6.5: World Bank, World Development Indicators.

Table 6.1: National Accounts Division (1997); *SYC* (2005, 51, 53); post–1993 revised according to NBS (2006).

The discussion in the text, as well as the data presented in Figures 6.1, 6.2, and 6.4 are based on the revisions of GDP data after 1993 presented by NBS (2006). These revisions increased 2004 GDP by 16.8%, primarily because of a 48.7% upward revision in the value of tertiary sector output, better covering small-scale businesses. A number of unresolved questions have required compromises: Data have been presented here in a way that is the *least* favorable to the chapter's arguments. For example, Figure 6.2 is created with investment taken from the earlier unrevised expenditure accounts (thus, assumed unchanged), but normalized by the larger postrevision GDP figure.

The weakest parts of the national accounts data are the implicit price deflators. Young (2003) estimated that GDP growth in the 1978–1998 period was 8.1%, instead of the officially recorded 9.7%, based primarily on alternative price indexes. Even more troubling, the NBS has several times revised nominal values without changing constant price growth rates, thus in effect using changes in implicit deflators to make up the difference. For example, TVE industrial output was revised downward after the 1995 industrial census, but industrial and GDP growth rates were never lowered. In the most recent revisions, industrial output in 2004 was found to be higher than previously recorded, but industrial growth rates were not revised upward (though service sector growth was). The new official GDP growth rate, incorporated into Table 6.1, is higher than the previous rate, but lower than it should have been had industrial output growth been revised upward. I owe this point to Carsten Holz.

Comparative data on investment rates, growth rates, and structure are from World Bank, World Development Indicators.

Taiwan data are from Taiwan CEPD (2005).

References

Blomstrom, Magnus, R. Lipsey, and M. Zejan (1996). "Is Fixed Investment the Key to Economic Growth?" *Quarterly Journal of Economics*, 111(1): 269–76.

Easterly, William, and Ross Levine (2001). "It's Not Factor Accumulation: Stylized Facts and Growth Models." *World Bank Economic Review*, 15(2): 177–219.

Holz, Carsten (2005). "China's Economic Growth 1978–2025: What We Know Today about China's Economic Growth Tomorrow." Hong Kong University of Science and Technology, Center on China's Transnational Relations, Working Paper No. 8. http://www.cctr.ust.hk/articles/pdf/WorkingPaper8.pdf.

National Accounts Division, National Bureau of Statistics (1997). *Zhongguo Guonei Shengchan Zongzhi Hesuan Lishi Ziliao* [The Gross Domestic Product of China, Historical Materials], *1952–1995*. Dalian: Dongbei Caijing Daxue.

NBS (2006). National Bureau of Statistics. "Woguo Guoneishengchan Zongzhi Lishi Shuju Xiuding Jieguo" [The Results of Revision of China's Historical GDP Figures]. January 9, 2006, at http://www.stats.gov.cn/tjdt/zygg/t20060109_402300176.htm.

Perkins, Dwight, Steven Radelet, Donald Snodgrass, Malcolm Gillis, and Michael Roemer (2001). *Economic Development*, 5th ed., 85–87, 652–53. New York. W. W. Norton.

Ren Ruoen (1997). *China's Economic Performance in an International Perspective*. Development Centre of the Organization for Economic Co-operation and Development. Paris: OECD.

Rozelle, Scott (2004). "The Rural Economy" and Discussion in Hearing before the US-China Economic and Security Review Commission, *China as an Emerging Regional and Technology Power: Implications for US Economic and Security Interests*, 36–61. Washington, DC: U.S. Government Printing Office.

SYC (Annual). *Zhongguo Tongji Nianjian* [Statistical Yearbook of China]. Beijing: Zhongguo Tongji.

Taiwan CEPD (2005). Council for Economic Planning and Development Republic of China. Taiwan Statistical Data Book, http://www.cepd.gov.tw/upload/statis/TSDB/2005DataBook@ 774477.875041538@pdf.

World Bank (1997). *China 2020: Development Challenges in the New Century*. Washington, DC: World Bank.

World Bank. *World Development Indicators* (Washington, DC: World Bank. http://devdata. worldbank.org/dataonline/.

Young, Alwyn (2003). "Gold into Base Metals: Productivity Growth in the People's Republic of China During the Reform Period." *Journal of Political Economy*, 111(6): 1220–61.

China is the world's most populous nation. About 20% of world population is Chinese, down from 30% in the 1950s. Global population trends depend, to a significant extent, on China's demographic trajectory, and the slowdown in China's population has contributed significantly to global demographic deceleration. It is not only because of its size that China's population is of interest. China's recent population history contains two of the most remarkable episodes ever observed in a human population. The first of these was the famine that followed the GLF: the largest famine of the post–World War II era, anywhere in the world; the biggest population disaster of our time. The second episode was the extraordinarily rapid reduction in birth rates during the 1970s, engineered by strict government birth control policies, that was faster and more complete than any similar fertility decline elsewhere in the world. In addition to their intrinsic interest, these two episodes have implications for the present and future of China's economy. Past demographic trends have resulted in a population today that is young and has a remarkably low dependency rate, which is favorable for growth. Those same trends dictate that in the future China will face particularly rapid population aging, which will create a significant social burden at a time when China's income is still comparatively low.

7.1 THE DEMOGRAPHIC TRANSITION

In traditional societies population growth rates are typically low. As noted in Chapter 2, China's premodern population grew for over 400 years at about 0.4% per year, and China was already the most populous country in the world by a large margin in the 1800s. In fact, this long-term growth rate appears to be near the maximum of what premodern societies can sustain. Despite the fact that birth rates are high in traditional societies, population growth is slow

Box 7.1
Birth rates and total fertility rates

There are two rates most often used to describe reproductive rates. The first and simplest is the birth rate, which expresses the number of births as a percent of the total population (sometimes called the crude birth rate). This statistic has the advantage that is easy to obtain and provides information about current population growth. Population growth equals the crude birth rate minus the crude death rate. However, birth rates are sensitive to the age composition of the population; for example, the birth rate will be temporarily higher when there is a larger proportion of women at childbearing ages. The second rate is the TFR, which is calculated in order to describe the underlying behavior of the population and understand long-run trends. The total fertility rate is computed by first calculating the age-specific birth rate for women in a given year. That is, the birth rate is calculated separately for 18-year-old women, 19-year-old women, and so on. These age-specific rates are then aggregated to form a total birth, or fertility, rate of a representative woman as if she were passing through the successive years of her life according to the average pattern of all women in that year. Alternately stated, the total fertility rate expresses the number of children a woman would have during the course of her life if her fertility in each year of her life were equal to the average fertility of all the women in the population of that age during the reference year. Total fertility rates are not affected by the age structure of the population, but they are affected by changes in the timing of births. If, on average, women begin to delay births, the total fertility rate will be temporarily lowered for a period. When the total fertility rate falls below 2.1, fertility is below the replacement level, and population growth will eventually fall to zero.

because death rates are also high. It is common for traditional societies to have birth rates in the range of 30 to 40 per 1,000 and death rates fluctuating from 20 to more than 40 per 1,000.[1] Population is in a precarious balance. When harvests are poor or diseases strike, population shrinks. Although each adult woman has many children, many die in infancy. The total fertility rate (TFR), a measure of the total number of children a typical woman bears during her lifetime, typically hovers around 6 (Box 7.1). China remained in a premodern demographic pattern until after 1949. Death rates were high, and disease, crop failure, and civil war undoubtedly caused population to decline in the worst years. Between 1850 and 1950 estimated population growth was 0.3% per year, which, because of the social and economic setbacks China experienced, was even lower than the preceding four centuries. Population growth resumed after 1949, and China's first modern census, in 1953, counted 594 million people.

During the modernization process, population vital rates change in fairly regular ways. First, nutrition and sanitation improve, and as a result

---

1. Demographers commonly express population changes as a ratio to 1,000. A birth rate of 40 per 1,000 and a death rate of 20 per 1,000 imply a population growth rate of 20 per 1,000, or 2%.

population health increases. As a result of improved health, death rates decline. Infant mortality rates drop fairly quickly, as simple improvements in maternal care and nutrition take place and a handful of deadly communicable diseases are controlled. Initially, this decline in death rates takes place without any corresponding change in birth rates. Birth rates stay high, and might even increase at first, because better fed, healthier women are more fertile. As a result, population growth accelerates. Many babies are born to each woman, and the majority now survive into adulthood and have children of their own. Population growth rates accelerate from under 10 per 1,000 to as high as 30 per 1,000 or more, resulting in a population explosion. This type of population explosion occurred in Europe during the nineteenth century. In most parts of the developing world, however, declining death rates and the associated population explosion did not occur until after World War II. In China death rates began to decline soon after the Communist government took control in 1949. In the early 1950s rapid improvements in sanitation, more equal distribution of available food, and control of the most important communicable diseases began to drive death rates down. Birth rates remained high, and by the mid-1950s the population was growing more than 2% per year: China began its own population explosion.

The population explosion does not continue indefinitely. Birth rates begin to decline gradually in nearly all populations we observe. What causes birth rates to decline? One factor is that families require fewer births to reach their preferred number of children, or "target family size," because infant survival rates increase and because birth control technology improves. But the more important factor is that social changes associated with modernization lead families to prefer smaller families, and this preference translates into a smaller target family size. Social changes redefine the costs and benefits of children to the parents. As families move to cities and as women enter the (paid) labor force, the opportunity cost of the mother's time becomes greater. The mother can contribute more to the family's income by working outside the home, rendering it more expensive to have her stay home and take care of children. Additionally, families leaving agriculture have less use for child labor. An especially important role in declining birth rates is played by increasing levels of education, both for the mother and the children. As the child's education becomes more highly valued, families increase their target levels of education for their children. Families begin to think of children as beings that need to be supported in school, at first for five or six years, and then, later in the development process, for 10 or even 20 years. As a result, the costs of supporting children through the end of the educational process become much greater. Families decide to have fewer, "more expensive" children, and invest more resources in each child. An increase in the mother's level of education has a major impact, because it affects fertility through a number of different channels simultaneously. Better educated mothers have a higher outside wage, and the opportunity cost of their time is higher. But better educated mothers also value the child's education more and have a better understanding of health and contraceptive issues. For all these reasons, as development proceeds families tend to have fewer children, and then try to invest more scarce time and resources in each individual child. Some say they trade "quantity" for "quality."

As a result of falling birth rates, population growth slows down, but this process can take a long time. In the European countries that experienced clearly falling death rates by the second half of the nineteenth century, birth rates fell slowly but steadily for about a century. By the late 1970s total fertility rates had fallen well below the replacement rate in many developed countries, such as Germany and Japan. Their populations continued to grow, though slowly, due to the combined effects of age structure and immigration. In 2005, Japanese population declined for the first time. This process—from low through high to low population growth—is called the demographic transition. While the demographic transition took about a century in Europe, it has proceeded more rapidly in other countries since World War II. In East Asia the demographic transition has been particularly fast. Japan and Taiwan, for example, have already completed a rapid transition to a low-birth-and-death-rate, low-population-growth equilibrium. China has also made the demographic transition under unusual circumstances and in less than 20 years.

7.2 CHINA'S DEMOGRAPHIC TRANSITION

China's demographic experience is shown graphically in Figure 7.1. The solid line shows births, per 1,000, and the shaded line shows deaths. The vertical difference between the two lines is the annual population growth rate (per 1,000). Before we can direct our attention to the long-range trends shown by the figure, we must consider the extraordinary event shown in the figure. The most striking thing is undoubtedly the demographic crisis that peaked in 1960, the final year of the GLF. The graph shows clearly the surge in deaths in 1960 (above the otherwise clear trend of a declining death rate) and the collapse in births. As death rates soared and birth rates plummeted, China's population declined (see Chapter 3 for description). Demographers estimate the excess deaths from the GLF by first inter-polating a normal mortality curve, in which death rates would have declined smoothly between 1957 and 1962 in line with

Figure 7.1
Vital rates

long-term trends. Excess deaths equal the area under the actual mortality curve and above the normal one: by this estimate, the crisis caused about 30 million excess deaths from starvation or aggravated disease conditions. In addition, many millions of births were deferred because of the famine conditions. The enormous quantities of demographic data published by the Chinese government since the 1982 census all clearly show the immense impact of the GLF.

We must set to one side the GLF catastrophe in order to consider the long-run trends depicted. First, the sustained decline in death rates, aside from the GLF surge of mortality, is quite impressive. This is not the only case of such a rapid sustained reduction in death rates in the world, but it is unusual because it occurred in such a large population that was still at a relatively low level of income. The causes were typical of sustained improvements in population health anywhere in the world: improved sanitation, water supplies, and pest control and vaccination programs, combined with improved nutrition, particularly for the poorest groups. In the Chinese case, the governmental emphasis on public health and preventive medicine, combined with a large network of basic-level health care workers—that is, midwives and "barefoot doctors"—made possible this substantial achievement. Estimates of life expectancy at birth increased substantially, from an estimated 41 years in the early 1950s to an official figure of 71 in the 2000 census (Zhang Shanyu 2003, 92; Banister and Hill 2004 adjust the official 2000 figure to 70 to account for underreporting of infant mortality).

Birth rates stayed high from the early 1950s through 1970, fluctuating in the range of 35 to 45 per 1,000 (again, leaving aside the plunge from 1959–1961). Indeed, birth rates were at their highest in 1963. This peak reflects the phenomenon of "replacement births," wherein households that had been postponing births or had lost family members during the famine years now had an unusually large number of births as conditions improved. Overall, through 1970, China resembled most developing countries during that period. Consistently high birth rates combined with steadily declining death rates meant that the population was growing extremely rapidly. Population growth peaked in the mid–1960s at nearly 3% per year.

Up until 1970 the trends that China experienced with respect to vital rates were rather typical. But there are few precedents for the extremely rapid decline in birth rates after 1970. Between 1970 and 1977, China's birth rate decreased by 50%. Total fertility rates dropped even more rapidly, declining from 5.8 in 1970 to 2.7 in 1978 (Table 7.1). We can recognize this decline as the ordinary process of the demographic transition, except that it occurred at a compressed and accelerated rate. The decline has been sustained through the 1990s, as total fertility rates appear to have declined well below the replacement rate. According to official Chinese data, the total fertility rate in 2000 was only 1.22, but this number has been rejected as too low by most observers (for reasons that will be discussed later). Table 7.1 shows (as China B) some alternative estimates by Retherford et al. (2005), which may still be biased downward. Regardless, there is little doubt that Chinese fertility has fallen rapidly and is now probably below replacement level.

Table 7.1
Fertility decline in East Asia (total fertility rate)

Year	China A	China B	Korea	Thailand	Taiwan	Hong Kong
1950–1955	6.2		5.2	6.6	6.7	4.4
1955–1960	5.4		6.1	6.4	6.0	4.7
1960–1965	5.9		5.4	6.4	5.1	5.3
1965–1970	6.0		4.5	6.1	4.2	4.0
1970–1975	4.8		4.1	5.0	3.4	2.9
1975–1980	2.9	3.1	2.8	4.3	2.7	2.3
1980–1985	2.5	2.4	2.4	3.0	2.2	1.8
1985–1990	2.4	2.3	1.7	2.6	1.7	1.4
1990–1995		1.6				
1995–2000		1.4				

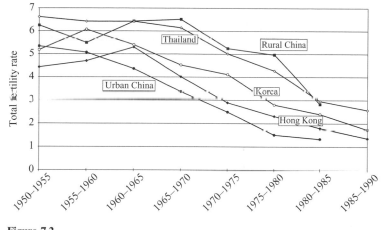

Figure 7.2
Comparative fertility decline

Figure 7.2 shows the comparative fertility data from Table 7.1 but combines them with separate fertility rates for urban and rural China. These data show that the Chinese experience is less extraordinary than one might suppose when placed in the East Asian context. Chinese urban fertility, to be sure, drops fastest and stays lowest of the series shown, but Chinese rural fertility is the highest. The two extremes of Chinese society thus bracket the other East Asian economies. Here again, the big gap between urban and rural society (Chapter 5) is particularly salient in China. Urban society in China has many features that are associated with smaller target family size. For a low-income country, urban China displays high female labor force participation, high female educational attainment, high educational aspiration for children, good access to health and contraceptive services, and a relatively good social security system. By contrast, rural China displays none of these features. Thus social and institutional features strongly accentuate the basic urban–rural difference in target family size: in a rural setting, children can contribute to agricultural household income at quite a young age. Farm children care for pigs, goats, and chickens as young as six or seven, and start to earn their keep. Rural households have higher target family sizes, and it is not surprising to see large differences in fertility dynamics in Chinese cities and countryside.

7.3 THE ROLE OF GOVERNMENT POLICY

Shortly after China's first modern census in 1953, the government initiated family planning, reflecting some alarm among population officials who began to confront the magnitude of China's population problem. This early program was modest in scope, providing contraceptive information and services on a voluntary basis. Even this small program was abandoned in the late 1950s, though, after the personal intervention of Mao Zedong. Mao argued that China's big population was an advantage and that human labor and creativity would allow people to wrest a living—and create a better society—despite limited resources. However, the disaster following the GLF convinced many in China's leadership that there was a place for family-planning policies, and Mao eventually allowed such policies to go forward. During 1962–1966 pilot programs of urban family planning were put in place to provide information about birth control.

Encouraged by the results of voluntary programs, the Chinese government launched its first all-out family planning initiative in 1971. This policy was known as *wan-xi-shao,* or later-longer-fewer, meaning "later marriages, longer spacing between children, and fewer children in total." The legal minimum age of marriage was increased, and couples were urged to wait before having a second or third child. The policy lasted through 1978, and it was directed at both urban and rural couples. In many respects, this policy was highly successful. Total fertility rates were cut in half, from 5.8 in 1970 to 2.7 in 1978. Virtually all the reduction in fertility was the result of fewer births of third and higher order. Through 1979 the probability of a couple having a second child, given that they had already given birth to a first child, was 95% (Feeney and Yu 1987). This could be characterized as a "Two-Child, but Wait, Policy."

The success of the later-longer-fewer policy was not sufficient to allay fears of a population crisis. Even with reduced fertility rates, population growth was set to accelerate as China's "baby boomers" reached marriage age. China's baby boomers were the large cohorts born during the 1962–1971 period (including "replacement births" after the GLF), and they were set to enter their childbearing years during the 1980s and early 1990s. China's leaders worried that continued population growth would outstrip the nation's population carrying capacity and obstruct economic development. Population "hawks" argued that it was necessary to reduce fertility rates below replacement levels, at least temporarily, in order to prevent another wave of births. Only tough measures, they argued, could break the inexorable momentum of continued population growth. Policy tightened, and in September 1980 the government formally adopted the "One-Child Policy" and a target population of 1.2 billion in the year 2000.

The One-Child Policy seeks to convince Chinese families that the most desirable number of children is one, and it provides an array of sanctions and penalties for women who have two or (especially) more than two children.

The One-Child policy was immediately controversial, particularly since the implementation was extraordinarily strict through the first five years or so. In 1983, for example, policy called for mandatory insertion of intra-uterine devices (IUDs) for women with one child, sterilization for couples with two or more children, and abortion for unauthorized conceptions. By 1984 domestic resistance and international controversy led the Chinese government to a substantial relaxation of the policy, which could be more aptly described as a "One-and-a-Half-Child Policy" after 1984. The government officially renounced forced sterilization and forced abortion. Provincial governments developed implementing legislation that allowed second children to couples if their first child was a girl and or if hardship factors were involved. The result was a significant liberalization of the policy nationwide. Since 1990 there have been further fluctuations in the strictness with which the policy is promoted nationwide.

Implementation of the One-Child Policy has been delegated to local government, and officials at the provincial level and below are evaluated, in part, on their success in lowering population growth rates in their locality. As a result, local officials are under substantial top-down pressure to control births, and they sometimes resort to actions that contravene declared central government policy, such as coercive sterilization or abortion. On the other side, local implementation has allowed significant regional variations in the One-Child Policy. In order to avoid charges that China was seeking to control the populations of non-Han ethnic minorities, the One-Child Policy was not applied to minority groups; in fact, birth rates for ethnic minorities are about double the rate of Han Chinese.

The One-Child Policy subjects all Chinese households to monitoring of fertility and births. This monitoring is much more intense in urban areas, where work units routinely track their female workers' fertility cycles, but it also exists in rural areas. In urban areas, work units may be assigned birth quotas, and couples may sometimes have to "wait their turn" before being allowed to have even their first child. Couples who pledge to have a single child receive a "one-child certificate" that entitles them to various privileges, including preferential access to day care and schooling. After the permitted first child, couples come under various forms of pressure to limit future births.

In most rural areas, if the first child is a girl, couples are allowed to have a second child without much interference; in other areas, the original one-child principle continues to be pressed with the original urgency. If a couple becomes pregnant after their allotted one or two children, they will first be subject to pressure from local family planning workers to abort the fetus. Family-planning workers will visit the couple repeatedly, perhaps daily, trying to persuade them to submit to an abortion. If the couple go ahead with an unauthorized birth, they will be subject to various penalties. In most provinces substantial financial penalties, equal to a household's annual income or even more, are levied on families that have a third or fourth child. If families are unable to pay, their belongings may be confiscated, or their house might even be knocked down. At the same time, peasants in many areas resist the One-Child Policy. Births are sometimes hidden, and newborn children spirited away to be raised by relatives.

7.4 CONSEQUENCES OF THE ONE-CHILD POLICY

The One-Child Policy has been controversial since its inception. Proponents described it as a necessary emergency response to an immediate surge in the population at peak childbearing ages. Critics argued that the policy was neither necessary nor appropriate, and they claimed that the unanticipated consequences of the policy were too severe. Despite the strictness of the One-Child Policy, it has never been fully successful. Even during 1983, the year of maximum strictness, 19% of total births were third order and above, and in other years of the 1980s about half of all births were first children, and half were second or higher order births. Partially for this reason, China's population exceeded the original target of 1.2 billion in 2000, reaching 1.266 billion in the census that year. Some demographers have argued that a more moderate policy might actually have been more effective, by continuing to provide positive incentives for families to delay births and increasing overall compliance (Bongaarts and Greenhalgh 1985).

The One-Child Policy involves a substantial level of coercion applied by the government against the Chinese population. Yet the level of coercion varies substantially from region to region. In large cities the average voluntary target family size has probably dropped below the birth limits set by government policy. Chinese demographers have computed an implied policy total fertility rate for each province, which tells us what the TFR would be in that province if there were perfect compliance with policy. The lowest is Shanghai (1.28), and the highest is Xinjiang (2.4). However, 13 provinces have actual TFRs significantly below the policy TFR, and the difference is largest in those urban and coastal areas where the policy is most strict. The biggest difference is Shanghai, which had an actual 2000 TFR of only 0.68 (Zhang Shanyu 2003, 68–71). Thus there are significant parts of China where little coercion is required to implement the policy and other areas where there is substantial resistance. In other provinces—especially poor, rural provinces like Guizhou

Table 7.2
Sex ratio (males per 100 females)

Year	At birth	Population aged 0–4
1953	104.9	107.3
1964	103.8	106.5
1982	107.6	107.0
1990	111.8	109.8
1995	116.6	118.8
2000	117.8	120.8
2003		121.2

and Jiangxi—fertility is significantly above what is theoretically permitted by policy.

The most important side effects of the One-Child policy derive from the Chinese preference for sons. The traditional cultural preference for boys is sustained by the marriage system. Girls "marry out," leaving their home village, while boys remain in the village and often stay in the family homestead. Boys are thus more likely to contribute to the household's income and support the parents in old age. Girls, while they may be willing to help, are at the very least some distance away, bound to a new family, and with fewer resources and less ability to assist aged parents. Thus boys are culturally and materially more valuable to many peasant households than girls. When this preference for boys collides with government-enforced birth limitation in China, the result is an extremely unbalanced sex ratio.

In most populations, more boys than girls are born. The average ratio is 106 boys for every 100 girls, with some normal variation, such that anything between 103 and 110 might be considered within the normal range).[2] In traditional China female infanticide dramatically skewed this ratio. In the late 1930s there were more than 120 boys for every 100 girls. Economic and social progress after 1949 brought this imbalance steadily down, so that during the 1960s and 1970s there were around 108 boys for every 100 girls at young ages (Table 7.2; see Coale and Banister 1994). However, since the early 1980s the sex ratio has again risen. Moreover, as Table 7.2 shows, the sex ratio has climbed steadily and significantly. In the 2000 census, the relative number of boys per 100 girls in the 0–4 age group was 120.8, clearly outside the normal range. These numbers imply that, given the number of boys, more than 12 million girls were "missing" in the 2000 census.

2. In most populations boys experience slightly higher mortality rates than girls, such that the sex ratio tends to equalize as groups reach reproductive ages. In old age women outnumber men in China as in other societies.

Where are the missing girls? In some remote areas, female infanticide may persist, but most observers feel that this is not a major cause of the imbalance. Many baby girls are simply unregistered with the authorities, and not reported to census takers either. Given the penalties incurred for unauthorized births—primarily by the family, but also by local officials who are responsible for meeting birth control targets—families choose not to report births or to delay reporting as long as possible. Indeed, 12% *more* 10-year-olds were recorded in the 2000 census than newborns in the 1990 census, implying that families successfully hid children—most of whom were girls—from census takers in 1990. If a similar rate of underreporting prevailed in 2000, it could account for as much as one-third of the missing girls (Cai and Lavely 2003). If China's increasingly mobile population has led to a higher rate of successful underreporting, the number of missing girls accounted for could even be greater.[3]

However, underreporting cannot fully explain unbalanced sex ratios, which have risen consistently, not only in rural areas, but also in cities where surveillance is much tighter (Zhang Yi 2004). Instead, the most important factor probably is the availability of sex-selective abortion. Since the early 1980s ultrasound machines, which can determine the sex of the baby in utero, have become widely available throughout China, including the countryside. While it is technically illegal for ultrasound technicians to reveal the gender of the fetus, such regulations are easily evaded. Indeed, diffusion of ultrasound machines has been associated with worsening gender imbalances in many Asian societies. Under pressure to limit the total number of births per family, many Chinese families appear to make the choice to limit those births to more highly valued male children. Adding to the problem is the fact that mortality rates for girls are higher than those for boys, a pattern that is again in sharp contrast to that normally observed in other societies. The skewing of sex ratios is a problem in itself; it also has severe implications for China's social development. The future scarcity of females relative to males may cause a "bachelor problem," placing a premium on brides and adding to the frustration of the rural poor who may be unable to find mates.

7.5 CHANGING AGE STRUCTURE OF THE POPULATION

The current age structure provides a window of opportunity for China's economy: China has the advantage of a young population with low dependency

---

3. Underreporting also implies that China's population, population growth rates, and fertility rates are all higher than official figures. Demographers in China and internationally have devoted substantial efforts to correcting official data in light of this underreporting.

rates. That is, both young and old dependents represent a relatively small share of the population. In 2000 just over 70% of the population was between the ages of 15 and 64 (compared with an average of 61.5% for all middle-income countries). Assuming consistent fertility and mortality rates, population trends can be extrapolated into the future. Figure 7.3 shows the dependent population (the sum of children and seniors) expressed as a percentage of the population of working age (15–64), that is, as a "dependency rate," between 1990 and 2050. China's dependency rate had already declined to just below 50% in 2000, and it dropped further to 40% in 2005. China today—from 2005 through 2015—is in a trough of its dependency rate. This trough exists because China's baby boomers, born in the 1960s, and even the following "baby-boom echo," born in the late 1980s, are now mainly in the workforce. The dependency rate of the young is now dropping sharply, because of the effect of the draconian birth control policies described in this chapter. At the same time, older dependents (65 and up) are not yet a large segment of the population, because China has emerged from poverty so recently and the decline in death rates that began in the 1950s is only now leading to an increased share of the elderly.

An age structure of this sort has both tangible and intangible benefits. Recently much attention has been given to the possibility of a "demographic dividend" caused by declining dependency rates during the high-speed phase

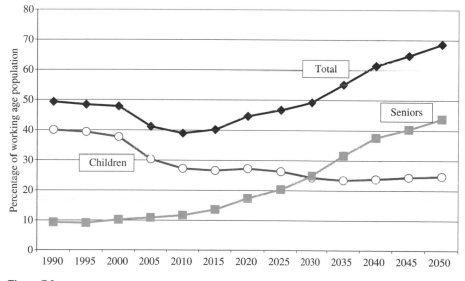

Figure 7.3
Dependency rates

of economic development in a number of East Asian economies (Mason and Kinugasa 2005). Declining dependency rates imply that the working-age population is growing more rapidly than the population as a whole, a fact which will lead to more rapid growth of per capita GDP for any given increase in productivity per worker. More generally, lower dependency rates imply higher material living standards for any given level of worker productivity. In China declining dependency rates can help explain a portion of the rapid growth in per capita GDP over the past two decades. In addition, it is plausible that a society with low dependency rates will save more and thus have more to invest. This possibility exists because, if much of household saving may be explained by "life-cycle" motives, today's workers will set aside resources for their old age, while today's elderly will draw down balances accumulated earlier. Thus China's extremely high domestic saving and investment rates in recent years (Chapters 6 and 18) can be plausibly linked to the low dependency rate. Finally, less tangibly, a young population is more adaptable and able to accept the rapid social changes that have accompanied the shift to a market economy.

The persistence of fertility and mortality rates combines with the existing structure of the population to produce predictable patterns of change of the labor force. During the 1980s and 1990s the working-age population grew extremely rapidly, and of course significantly more rapidly than the population as a whole. During the 1980s the working-age population grew 2.5% annually. Moreover, population growth combined with rural-to-urban migration to fuel an even more rapid growth of the urban labor force, which has grown at above 4% per year since the 1980s.[4] However, as Table 7.3 shows, the growth of the labor force is now beginning to slow substantially. The labor market is just now absorbing the last huge birth cohort (the "baby-boom echo" born in the late 1980s), and future cohorts of young people entering the labor force will be those born since the 1990s, when birth control policies had fully taken hold and the size of birth cohorts was much smaller. Given the existing age structure and assuming that age-specific fertility rates remain constant, growth of the working-age population will drop off quickly and reach zero growth after 2015. Once labor-force growth drops to zero, the only source of growth of the modern labor force will be migration from agricultural employment. Table 7.3 is constructed with the assumption that rates of rural-to-urban migration will remain constant. Under this assumption, the rural labor force

---

4. Changes in the definition of employment adopted in 1990, as well as in the definition of urban and rural labor forces, make it extremely difficult to precisely track changes in employment in the 1980s.

Table 7.3
Growth of working-age population (average annual rates, percent)

Year	National	Rural	Urban
1982–1990	2.5		
1990–1995	1.7		
1995–2000	1.4		
2000–2005	1.0	−0.1	4.1
2005–2010	1.0	−0.9	3.2
2010–2015	0.5	−1.6	2.5
2015–2020	−0.1	−2.4	1.6
2020–2025	0.0	−2.3	1.5
2025–2030	−0.2	−2.8	1.1
2030–2035	−0.7	−3.8	0.6
2035–2040	−0.8	−3.9	0.3
2040–2045	−0.5	−3.5	0.3
2045–2050	−0.6	−3.6	0.0

will begin to shrink in size rapidly, while the urban labor force will maintain slower growth for another two decades. Slower urban labor-force growth may reduce some of the pressure on urban employment, while still allowing a robust process of structural transformation to continue at least until 2020 or so. Slower growth of the urban labor force will almost surely be associated with slower overall GDP growth as well. If growth of the urban labor force drops by three percentage points between 2005 and 2025, GDP growth might also be expected to slow by a roughly similar magnitude.

Demographically, the years from 1990–2025 represent a window of opportunity, which is extremely favorable for China's economic growth. Later on, an aging population will create substantial strains on China's social system. Particularly after 2015, rapid aging will require an effective response as the age structure of the country will place greater burdens on those currently employed. It is estimated that the number of Chinese over 60 years old will increase from 128 million in 2000 to 350 million in 2030. This increase means that in 2030 the senior dependency rate will reach 25% and surpass the child dependency rate. As Figure 7.3 shows, dependency rates will continue to increase for a long time after 2030. Rapid population aging essentially echoes the earlier declines in fertility and mortality. In China's case, the impact of the rapid decline in fertility is amplified by the mandatory retirement (beginning at age 60 in many sectors) of the oldest baby boomers, which will begin around 2015.

In rural areas, the elderly rely primarily on their children for financial support (Table 7.4), Males are much less likely to be dependent on their children than are females, but this is mainly because they are forced to continue working as long as they are able. By contrast, most city dwellers are already

Table 7.4
Primary source of support for population 60 and over, 2004

	Working	Pension or insurance	Children
Urban men	8%	80%	12%
Urban women	4%	59%	38%
Rural men	43%	12%	46%
Rural women	23%	4%	73%

out of the workforce and receiving pensions after 60 years of age. Whether or not the elderly are financially dependent on their children, most live in the same household with them. In rural areas only 9% of those aged 60 and over do *not* live in multigenerational households, while in urban areas 26% live independently. Indeed, children are legally obligated to care for their parents in their old age. This traditional reliance on children will face severe strains as a result of China's declining birth rate. By 2030 the average 65-year-old urban dweller will have only one child, and the average rural resident of that age only 2.3 living children.

Rural and urban areas both face difficult challenges in dealing with future aging. Rural areas are arguably at a disadvantage. Rural elders are usually not covered by the pension plans that are commonplace in urban areas, have a lower overall income, and will have higher dependency rates caused by the outflow of working-age youths to urban areas. These three factors result in the rural elderly being more dependent than urban elderly on their own income and financial transfers from their children. In the cities, however, most workers enjoy some kind of promised pension after they retire. However, until the early 1990s all of China's pension liabilities were unfunded, meaning that the pensions of currently retired persons were paid from the tax payments of current workers, and nothing had been set aside for future retirees. Since the 1990s the Chinese government has struggled to set up a functioning and funded pension system, and reforming the pension system has become an important issue (covered in Chapter 8). In this respect, China resembles many other countries that are struggling with the implications of population aging for social security and pension programs. But there is one important difference. Most of these other countries are developed countries that grew rich first, and then grew old. China will grow old before it has had the opportunity to grow rich.

7.6   CONCLUSION

The One-Child Policy has shaped China in many important ways and has had important impacts on its economic development. The One-Child Policy forced China through the demographic transition at an accelerated pace and created an exceptional demographic window of opportunity for growth during the reform era. At the same time, the One-Child Policy is responsible for the exceptional severity of problems that will challenge policy-makers in the immediate future. The One-Child Policy will cause the number of retirees and the future elderly dependent ratio to increase particularly quickly, exacerbating future demographic strains. The One-Child Policy has led to serious gender imbalances that may ultimately lead to discontent and further problems. In addition, the One-Child Policy has led to "the collapse of a credible government birth reporting system" (Wang Feng 2005).

The increasing burdens associated with the One-Child Policy have led to a new wave of criticism of the policy (Peng Xizhe 2005). From the beginning, critics argued that less coercive alternatives to the One-Child Policy could be equally effective in the long run, particularly given the rapid reduction in fertility already observed during the 1970s (Bongaarts and Greenhalgh 1985). Indeed, the high tide of the "demographic crisis" that the One-Child Policy was designed to avert has already ebbed, as the number of women at peak childbearing age has been declining since the early 1990s. If the One-Child Policy were to be relaxed some time in the next 10 to 20 years, a modest increase in the birth rate would help to ameliorate the trend toward an aging population. Even today, new families in urban China are frequently being created from the marriage of two "only children," and these families have the right to have two children under existing rules. A rapidly urbanizing and developing Chinese society perhaps no longer requires the extreme measures of the One-Child Policy.

BIBLIOGRAPHY

Suggestions for Further Reading

Peng Xizhe (2004) and Wang Feng (2005) are two short and outstandingly clear discussions of the issues relating to the One-Child Policy today. Many articles in *Population and Development Review* contain accessible discussions of Chinese demography; see especially Johnson (1994) and Coale and Banister (1994).

Sources for Data and Figures

Figure 7.1: Banister (1987), updated from U.S. Bureau of the Census.

Figure 7.2: Johnson (1994).

Figure 7.3: U.S. Census Bureau, International Division.

Table 7.1: Johnson (1994), Retherford et al. (2005) for China B.

Table 7.2: Population Census Office, as reported in Cai and Lavely (2003, 15), except 2003 reported in Zhang Yi (2004). 1995 and 2003 from One Percent Sample Survey.

Table 7.3: Through 2000, *SYC* (2005, 188); projections by U.S. Census Bureau, International Division.

Table 7.4: Population Statistics Yearbook 2005: 106–113.

Age structure: World Development Report (1994, 210). The 1996 Projections of the Chinese population are from U.S. Bureau of the Census, International Data Base. I am indebted to Loraine West for providing the data and taking the time to explain it thoroughly.

References

Banister, Judith (1987). *China's Changing Population*. Stanford, CA: Stanford University Press.

Banister, Judith, and Kenneth Hill (2004). "Mortality in China 1964–2000." *Population Studies*, 58(1), March, 55–75.

Bongaarts, J., and S. Greenhalgh (1985). "An Alternative to the One-Child Policy in China." Center for Policy Studies, Working Papers. New York: Population Council.

Cai, Yong, and William Lavely (2003). "China's Missing Girls: Numerical Estimates and Effects on Population Growth." *China Review*, 3(2), Fall, 13–29.

Coale, A. J., and J. Banister (1994). "Five Decades of Missing Females in China." *Demography*, 31(3): 459–79.

Feeney, G., and Jingyuan Yu (1987). Period Parity Progression Measures of Fertility in China. *Population Studies*, 41(1): 77–102.

Johnson, D. Gale (1994). "Effects of Institutions and Policies on Rural Population Growth with Application to China." *Population and Development Review*, 20(3), September, 503–31.

Mason, Andrew, and Tomoko Kinugasa (2005). "East Asian Economic Development: Two Demographic Dividends." *East-West Center Working Papers: Economics Series*, No. 83, Honolulu, June.

Peng Xizhe (2005). "Is It Time to Change China's Population Policy?" *China: An International Journal*, 2(1), March, 135–49.

Population Statistics Yearbook (various years). Department of Population and Employment Statistics, National Bureau of Statistics. *Zhongguo Renkou Tongji Nianjian* [*Population Statistics Yearbook of China*]. Beijing: Zhongguo Tongji.

Retherford, Robert D., Minja Kim Choe, Jiajian Chen, Li Xiru, and Cui Hongyan (2005). "How Far Has Fertility in China Really Declined?" *Population and Development Review* 31(1), March, 57–84.

SYC (Annual). *Zhongguo Tongji Nianjian* [Statistical Yearbook of China]. Beijing: Zhongguo Tongji.

Wang Feng (2005). "Can China Afford to Continue Its One-Child Policy?" *AsiaPacific Issues*, No. 77, March. Honolulu: East-West Center.

Zhang Shanyu (2003). *Zhongguo Renkou Dili* [China Population Geography]. Beijing: Kexue Publishing House.

Zhang Yi (2004). "Woguo Renkou Chusheng Xingbiebi de Shehen ji Jijiang Zaocheng de Shida Wenti" [China's Unbalanced Population Sex Ratio and Ten Problems That It Will Create]. Chinese Academy of Social Sciences, Population and Labor Economics Research Institute, November. http://www.sociology.cass.net.cn/shxw/zxwz/t20041117_3459.htm.

8

Labor and Human Capital

Under the command economy there were no labor markets in China. Each worker was a lifetime member of one of the two vast systems of public employment, urban and rural. This system was slow to change, especially in the cities: employment in SOEs continued to grow well into the 1990s, nearly 20 years after the beginning of reform. But then, beginning in the mid–1990s, China laid off almost 50 million workers, 40% of the public-enterprise workforce. Today the entire system of government-controlled employment has dissolved, and active labor markets have developed nationwide. Well-functioning labor markets can create the foundation for a skilled and prosperous economy. However, China still faces many challenges. The old system had provided a job for everyone; when it broke down, unemployment surged, and it remains a serious chronic problem. How can China upgrade the quality of its labor force? Are workers adequately rewarded for extraordinary skills and talent? How can China support the rapidly aging population as retirements increase? These challenges have grown, even as labor market changes have contributed to the overall growth of China's economy.

Many who visit China for the first time are surprised at the predominance of physical labor in China. It is still common to see human labor used for tasks that could easily be accomplished by machines. Human labor power is used to break up rocks, dig ditches, and carry heavy objects. In the southern countryside it is not unusual to see men and women with bamboo staves slung over their shoulders carrying 70- or 80-pound loads up and down steep hillsides. The human counterpart to a low GDP per capita is a life of backbreaking toil. In a low-income economy there are few realistic choices. For the worker, work is difficult and exhausting; for the business, labor is cheap, and there is little incentive to substitute machine power for human labor. If labor markets work well, however, they play a central role in the development process and in the transformation of labor. Working labor markets create jobs that require and reward specific skills and education. Workers have an incentive to get training and education, and businesses have an incentive to seek out and reward the worker with greater talent or training. China's labor force is in the middle of this transformation: from predominantly low-skill, hard physical labor to a middle-income economy where education and skill begin to transform the nature of work for many workers.

Section 8.1 examines the institutional changes in the labor system over the past decades, beginning with snapshots of employment in 1978 and in 2003. That examination leads into a discussion of the transformation of the urban state sector during 1995–2000, during which mass layoffs led to the emergence of both labor mobility and significant open unemployment. The discussion turns to the formal and informal sectors in the urban economy today, and then to rural labor markets. Section 8.2 examines the functioning of labor markets. How well do labor markets reward productive attributes like education and experience? Recent work examining returns to human capital and migration is discussed. Progress in raising educational standards in the labor force is considered. The migration decision is examined in the context of changing labor markets. Section 8.3 looks at the social security system. An organized system of social security is one of the differentiating factors between formal and informal sectors of the urban labor market. Since the successful operation of a social security system depends on the age composition of the population, China faces a particularly acute challenge in crafting a viable social security system that will survive coming rapid aging. These complex market and institutional factors are reshaping the position of workers in China's contemporary economy.

8.1 THE INSTITUTIONAL TRANSFORMATION OF CHINESE LABOR

8.1.1 The Labor Force

The number of employed persons in China was 752 million at the end of 2004. Even relative to China's huge population, this is an enormous number. As discussed in the previous chapter, because of the age structure of the population, a relatively large proportion of the population—just over 70% in the 2000 census—is of working age. Moreover, labor-force participation (the proportion of the working-age population actually working or actively looking for work) is also very high, primarily due to very high female labor-force participation. Chinese women work, and nearly all young urban women are currently employed. Labor participation was measured at 86% in the 1990 census, and has drifted down since, because of increased college enrollments and early retirement (SYC 2005, 120–121; Populations Statistics Yearbook 2003, 264).

As a result of these factors, China has an exceptionally young and economically active population, which is quite favorable to economic development and perhaps to economic reform as well. China is extremely well placed to take advantage of the "demographic dividend" discussed in the previous chapter. The average age of employed people (urban and rural together) has been increasing but remains low; from an average age of 31 in 1978 it increased to 37 in 2000. Productivity probably improves as the work force ages slightly, certainly through the 30s. Moreover, this relatively young work force has shown enormous adaptability to the changes brought by economic transition.

8.1.2   Employment: Ownership and Labor Mobility

In the final years of the command economy system 99% of China's workers were in publicly owned undertakings, two-thirds of whom were in agriculture and one-third in everything else (Figure 8.1). In 1978 in the countryside, most workers farmed the land as members of agricultural collectives, and another 6% of the total labor force worked in publicly owned TVEs (called commune and brigade enterprises at that time). Only 2% of the labor force worked outside this system, in tiny "team enterprises," set up under the village collectives or occasionally as individual traders or haulers. In urban areas the entire labor force was organized either into state-run units or into urban collectives. A tiny handful of private businesses (150,000), mostly elderly traders or repairmen, had somehow managed to stay independent through 30 years of socialist mobilization.

There was virtually no labor mobility in this system. Chapter 5 described how tight controls had been placed on rural-to-urban migration in the 1960s after the collapse of the GLF and how urban residence had become a privileged status. Mobility of all kinds, including job mobility, declined sharply. The government assumed direct control over all urban hiring: From the early 1960s onward, the government assigned 95% of high school or college graduates to work and took the authority to hire and fire away from individual enterprises (Bian 1994). Voluntary job mobility *within* urban areas disappeared, while workers gained protection from being fired. By 1978 voluntary quits and fires had become virtually nonexistent: in that year 37,000 workers in all of urban China quit or were fired, about one-twentieth of one percent of all permanent workers. A worker was 10 times more likely to retire and four times more likely to die on the job than to quit or be fired. The state decided your job, and a job was for life. This complete absence of labor markets was an extraordinary feature of the Chinese command economy. In the Soviet Union, workers were rarely fired but they were free to quit. In fact, in 1978, in the Russian Republic,

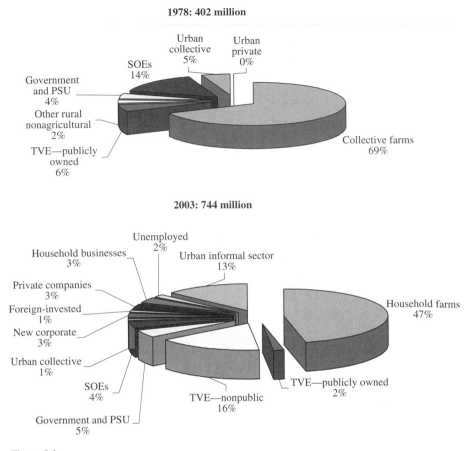

Figure 8.1
Employment by ownership

16% of all industrial manual workers quit their jobs during the year (Granick 1987, 109). Voluntary job turnover was hundreds of times more common in the Soviet Union than in China. The extra rigidity of labor markets in China clearly grew out of the effort to control population movement and employment after the GLF. When the process of market transition began, after 1978, urban labor market rigidity was a severe handicap that slowed progress in the gradualist transition and hampered the efforts of reformers to introduce market forces.

Thus, even though change came fast in rural areas, reformers were extremely cautious in introducing labor markets in the cities. During the first era of reform (Chapter 4) the dissolution of the agricultural collectives created hundreds of millions of household farm businesses. It became much easier to start a business, in both rural and urban areas, and entry of new businesses led to a much more diverse ownership structure. But for almost 20 years, from 1978 until about 1996, change in the urban employment system was confined within strict boundaries.

• Private businesses faced official discrimination. Small-scale businesses like restaurants and small workshops were acceptable, but it was almost impossible to run a large, capital-intensive business as a strictly private concern.

• Publicly owned enterprises were not allowed to lay off workers for many years. Reformers were concerned that guaranteed employment was the foundation of an implicit urban social compact, and during the first era of reform they did not challenge this important vested interest.

Instead, labor reformers began to build in some flexibility on the margins of the system. New workers were hired for five-year contracts after 1986, with contracts renewed only when both sides were satisfied. Young contract workers were much more likely to quit or be fired when their contracts expired than were old-style permanent workers. Some tiny cracks appeared in the facade of the labor system.

Thus state ownership still loomed large in the overall employment picture through the mid–1990s. Indeed, total employment in SOEs actually *increased* from 58 million in 1978 to 75 million in 1996. In 1996, *18 years* after reforms began, state employment still accounted for the bulk of urban employment. Moreover the three types of publicly owned enterprises—SOEs, urban collectives, and TVEs—still accounted for 24% of total employment, down only a fraction from 25% in 1978! Through the mid–1990s, then, the features of the first phase of China's gradualist transition strategy were very much in evidence: publicly owned enterprises generated much of the increased employment and output in the economy; reform was "without losers," as state jobs were protected; and marketization began with product markets and only slowly extended to labor markets.

But then in the mid-1990s this whole institutional setup changed dramatically. SOEs, under increasing competitive pressure, began laying off redundant workers. Figure 4.4 showed the dramatic decline in state enterprise workers after 1996. In fact, beginning around 1993, more than 30 million SOE workers were laid off, 38% of the entire labor force, and almost 50 million urban workers of all kinds. The proportion of urban collective workers laid off was even higher than that of SOE workers. With this huge shift in policy (discussed further in section 8.1.3) public employment shrank dramatically. Shortly thereafter, from the late 1990s, the Chinese government began to give greater legitimacy and legal protection to private enterprise. Together these changes had a huge impact on the ownership composition of employment, which had taken another major step in the direction of a diversified market economy by 2003. All the major publicly owned enterprise forms shrank significantly after the late 1990s. Employment in SOEs dropped to 4% of the labor force; urban collectives dropped even more dramatically, to 1.3%; and collectively run TVEs declined precipitously to 1.7% of total employment. The share of these three public enterprise forms together collapsed from 24% of the labor force in 1996 to only 7% in 2003. (A more inclusive definition of publicly owned firms would include the 2% of the labor force employed in government-controlled new corporations [Chapter 13], still a huge drop to 9% of the labor force in 2003.) The scale of change was enormous: if anything in China's transition counts as a "big bang," this is it. Labor mobility increased dramatically, as did unemployment. People now change jobs regularly, and migrate in search of economic opportunity. The increase in job mobility was driven by the rapid increase in involuntary layoffs from state firms.

As of 2003, almost 5% of the Chinese labor force works for the government or for government-run PSUs. This sector has grown slightly as a share of total employment, largely because of an increase in government-paid teachers. Deducting government and public enterprise workers, more than 80% of China's workers now work for the private sector. The largest share of the private sector workforce is the household farmers who make up 47% of total labor, but even the urban labor force is now predominantly private. Combining companies registered in urban areas, and TVE records, private companies now account for 8.6% of total employment; registered "self-employed" or household businesses for 7.2%; other corporate forms, not directly government controlled, for 2.7%; and foreign companies, 2.1%. Together, this gives a registered, nonfarm private sector that employs 20.7% of China's workers. As Figure 8.1 shows, a very large informal sector is an extremely important part of labor markets, both in urban and rural areas. This small-scale and frequently unregistered sector is not very accurately captured in our statistics, but there is no doubt that it is large. It accounts for almost 20% of total employment (including most, but not all, rural nonagricultural employment outside collective TVEs). Unemployment—including both traditional registered unemployment and workers laidoff from SOEs—accounted for 2% of the total workforce. Change has indeed been dramatic, and the most dramatic change has been the most recent. China has now created a flexible, diversified employment system, but one without the certainty and guarantees of the old system.

8.1.3   Employment, Unemployment, and State-Sector Downsizing

*Under*employment has always been a serious problem in China. Under socialism jobs were provided for all, but work was often meaningless and poorly paid. Workers bottled up in the rural sector at times had little to do. A brief episode of open unemployment emerged in China at the beginning of the reform era (1978–1979) when millions of the "sent-down" youth returned to the city and had to find work. But Chinese urban work units created make-work jobs for their sons and daughters during that episode. Afterward, open unemployment was kept below 3% through most of the 1980s and 1990s by the cautious labor policies described earlier. In turn, those cautious policies were partly a response to the pressure of numbers, brought about by the rapid growth of population and labor force during the 1980s (the same bulge that elicited the One-Child Policy). Policy-makers were loath to cut state employment as long as the labor force was growing so rapidly, at an average 2.5% per year through the 1980s. Policy-makers constantly pointed to China's surplus labor as a burden that forced them to proceed cautiously in economic reform, continue to tolerate (and even create) make-work jobs, and rule out more dramatic reform measures that might increase productivity rapidly at the cost of sharp short-run increases in unemployment. Only after the mid–1990s did reformers gain enough confidence in the flexibility of the urban economy that they were willing to reverse this stance.

During the mid–1990s the dramatic acceleration of labor reforms began with the determination to tackle the problem of overmanning in SOEs. At first, new categories of workers were created within the enterprise: the "surplus worker" and, subsequently, the "off-post" or "laid-off" (*xiagang*) worker. Enterprises were told to identify surplus workers, organize them into new activities, and "optimize" the employment structure within their work unit. Then, in the mid–1990s, these workers began to be discharged from the work unit, and a massive group of "laid-off" workers was created. During the course of a decade, from 1993 through 2003, an official count of 28.18 million state-enterprise workers were laid off. In fact, this number is a lower bound, because it was not until 1998 that the diverse local data and procedures were unified into a logically consistent category of laid-off workers (*Labor and Social Security Yearbook* 2004, 478). After 1998 the Chinese government created the new Ministry of Labor and Social Security and launched a massive effort to collect data, systematize procedures, and channel workers laid off from their enterprises into Reemployment Centers (RECs). The RECs were designed to provide retraining and job-search assistance. Perhaps more crucially, the REC took over the worker's affiliation from the enterprise, paid into the worker's social security and welfare funds, and typically provided a stipend to the worker. Workers were supposed to remain affiliated with the Reemployment Center for a maximum of three years, or less if they could find a new job more quickly. In a prosperous city like Shanghai or Beijing, this system meant that a redundant worker could receive as much as five years of transitional assistance and support as he or she was gradually eased out of state employment. Less prosperous cities, however, were not usually able to maintain such a high standard of support. The Chinese government thus made an effort to buffer the shock of a massive and traumatic change.

Figure 8.2 lays out the broad patterns of change that led to almost 50 million people losing jobs in state enterprises, urban collective enterprises, other types of enterprise, and government and PSUs. The vertical bars show the number of enterprise workers (not including employees of government and PSUs) newly laid off in the course of each year (these numbers are official data from 1997; estimated data through 1996). Layoffs surged in 1995 and 1996, and for four years (1996–1999) on average more than seven million workers were laid off annually.

The solid areas depict the stock of unemployed and laid-off workers, not yet reemployed, at year-end. The bottom region shows registered unemployed, and the top region the laid-off (*xiagang*) workers, who are never included in unemployed as long as they retain their designation as "laid-off" and maintain their affiliation with the RECs. The sum of these two categories, then, represents the official total of urban residents without gainful employment. In 1993 there were some seven million in this broad category of unemployment, with many of the three million laid-off workers still associated with their work unit. By 1996–1997, this total had soared to 15 million, nearly all of them separated from the work unit. Thus total unemployment more than doubled in the course of three years. Nevertheless, the government forged ahead, laying off six million in 1997, more than seven million in 1998, and almost eight million in

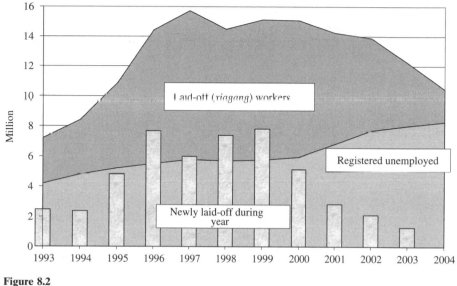

Figure 8.2
Laid-off and unemployed workers

1999. The number of new layoffs only began to taper off after 2000, and by then the system of permanent employment was shattered forever.

What happened to these laid-off workers? The official Chinese claim is that three-quarters found new jobs. That may be true, but since, as we shall see, the number of formal-sector urban jobs declined significantly over this period, most of the new jobs must have been in the informal sector. Many workers took early retirement, which was commonly made available to male workers as young as 50 and female workers as young as 40. Some workers, after three years in the REC, made a further transition to registered unemployment. Thus Figure 8.2 shows that official unemployment increased after 2000 while the stock of unemployed laid-off workers declined. This change occurred because laid-off workers began to "graduate" from the RECs into the ranks of the unemployed. Total unemployment (the sum of the two) peaked in 1997, but then stayed very high through 2002 with more than 14 million unemployed. Thus the unemployment rate peaked at 8%–10%, much higher than the 3% registered unemployment rate the government was headlining at the time.[1]

---

1. This discussion attempts to adjust the official unemployment statistics to make them logically consistent. It does not attempt to make them internationally comparable, or find the "true" unemployment rate. The numbers are somewhat misleading in that they consider only workers with their household registration in urban areas, so that migrants are not considered either in the numerator (unemployed) or the denominator (urban labor force).

After 2002, China's economic boom finally began to bring down the number of unemployed substantially. At year-end 2004 there were still 10 million unemployed in urban China, including 8.3 million registered unemployed and over two million laid-off workers.

The handling of the large number of laid-off SOE workers was a massive attempt at social engineering. Substantial cost and effort were expended to buffer SOE workers from the immediate shock of unemployment, yet laid-off workers still experienced dramatic reductions in their income and standard of living (Appleton et al. 2002; Giles, Park and Cai 2006). Laid-off workers searched for new employment while retaining some income and some benefits (especially housing and health insurance) provided through their work unit. The actual impact on laid-off workers varied enormously from place to place, both because local economic conditions vary substantially and because local governments were responsible for policies toward labor markets. City governments were responsible for juggling almost contradictory objectives: shrinking state enterprises, improving the efficiency of labor markets, keeping unemployment low, and protecting local citizens' interests (Solinger 2004). Local officials decided how much transitional support to give laid-off workers.

Shanghai, for example, pioneered a program of maximum feasible transitional support given to laid-off workers. Shanghai established its first REC in July 1996, initially for laid-off workers from the textile and instrument sectors, which had undergone early consolidation. Shanghai's RECs, like those that came later elsewhere, were funded by the SOE, the SOE's supervising government agency, and the municipal government in approximately equal parts. The SOE benefited, since it paid only one-third of the worker's support instead of being responsible for all of it, as it had been previously. Shanghai's program was extraordinarily expensive, supporting 250,000 workers at an annual cost of one billion RMB. Moreover, by encouraging early retirement as a major channel for laid-off workers, the city acquired additional ongoing pension liabilities of over one billion RMB annually (Urban Labor 1998). In essence, Shanghai, a growing and relatively wealthy jurisdiction, was able to provide massive subsidies to SOEs and laid-off workers, protecting their standard of living while easing their exit from the state sector.

The polar opposite from Shanghai was the far northeastern province of Heilongjiang, struggling with a stagnant economy and huge, uncompetitive heavy industrial plants. Laid-off workers in Heilongjiang received stipends from their RECs equal to only 6% of the average SOE wage in 1997, compared with 43% in Shanghai. Far from being able to provide additional billions for early retirements, Heilongjiang was not even able to meet its existing pension obligations and was in arrears of its pension obligations by over one billion RMB in 1997, with half a million SOE retirees going unpaid (Mo Rong 1998). Not surprisingly, large-scale and occasionally violent protests erupted in Heilongjiang, and eventually the central government was forced to step in and assume some of Heilongjiang's pension obligations. Most cities in China were in between the Shanghai and Heilongjiang extremes.

Though the massive open unemployment associated with state enterprise downsizing has receded somewhat with the economic boom of 2003–2005, China will have a serious, chronic unemployment problem until at least 2015. The urban sector must absorb millions of new workers annually over the next decade and more. However, as Chapter 6 noted, China has still not fully exploited the employment-generating possibilities in the services, and rapid development of service employment could ease the challenge. If the economy does manage to absorb most of the available labor over the next decade, the seriousness of the unemployment problem will then begin to ease as the combination of slower labor-force growth and completion of structural transformation take effect.

8.1.4   The Informal Sector: Emerging Dualism Within Urban Labor Markets

A large proportion of laid-off workers eventually found work in the urban informal sector. The informal sector refers to the generally small-scale, unlicensed businesses that are an important part of urban economies in most of the developing world. China under the planned economy had virtually no informal sector, except for farmers selling goods on short trips to urban markets. However, in recent years the combination of rural-to-urban migration and mass layoffs from publicly owned urban enterprises has led to rapid growth of the urban informal sector. Thus, as state firms shrink and restructure, the old identity between public worker and urban resident has disappeared. Instead, there is now a division within the urban labor force that, to some extent, mirrors and replaces the old division between urban and rural workers. The overall contours of this development can be seen from the aggregate numbers on urban employment. Although those numbers are not very accurate in their coverage of the informal sector, they still provide a clear picture of the emerging reality.

Figure 8.3 shows the evolution of urban employment according to official data. Quite a few striking trends emerge: The absolute number of government employees and workers in PSUs (*shiye danwei*) has changed little in 20 years. State and collective enterprises shrank dramatically, while a group here labeled "new corporate" has increased. These new corporate forms include limited-liability and joint-stock companies, some of which are still

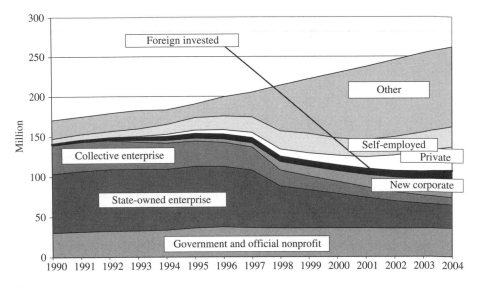

Figure 8.3
Urban labor force

government controlled. As a first approximation, it makes sense to group all these new corporate forms, along with state and collective enterprises, government employees, and urban foreign invested firms into the urban formal sector.

The urban formal sector, in this definition, has declined from 152 million in 1996 to only 105.5 million in 2003 (then began to grow again, reaching 106.7 million in 2004). The bulk of the growth in the urban labor market—which expanded from 200 million to 265 million between 1996 and 2004—has occurred in the private, self-employed, and "other" categories. Some private firms, to be sure, are large, formally organized firms, but not many, because if they were organized as limited-liability firms they would be included in "new corporate" employment. "Other" employment simply represents workers known to exist because surveys and census investigations reveal the size of the overall urban workforce, but who are not enumerated in any of the registered organizational forms. The "other" category picks up most of the migrants and unregistered businesses. The informal sector, broadly defined to include private, self-employed, and "other," has grown from 48 million to almost 160 million and is now considerably larger than the formal sector.

Migrants and urban dwellers now compete in at least some labor markets that are part of this rapidly growing small-scale informal sector. Migrants dominate certain job sectors—such as construction and textile mills—where labor is particularly tiring or boring and urban workers lack interest. Urban residents receive preferential treatment in some sectors, including government or local service trades. Thus a segmented labor market has emerged in cities. However, in certain sectors, such as retailing, restaurants, and petty trade, migrants and city dwellers compete head to head. During the 1990s laid-off workers had a strong incentive to maintain their ties to work units or RECs but work in informal gray markets at the same time. In these markets they encountered rural immigrants offering similar labor services. At the same time, intensified competition began to pressure existing SOEs to ignore regulations and hire rural migrants, who are much cheaper and have a reputation as harder workers (Urban Labor 1998). The existence of labor-market competition does not mean that the division between urban and rural residents has disappeared, nor that competition takes place on a level playing field. Not only do urban administrations side with urban residents in many regulatory matters, but also permanent urban residents often continue to receive various kinds of subsidies. Thus, even when they earn the same wages as rural migrants, their total incomes are typically higher.

8.1.5   Rural Labor Markets

Rural labor markets are also changing rapidly. Of course, the majority of rural workers continue to be employed on family farms. However, China's rural labor markets showed a dramatic expansion in nonagricultural employment through the 1990s. According to one large survey (de Brauw et al. 2002), the proportion of individuals having some off-farm employment increased dramatically, rising from 15% of the labor force in 1982 to 32% in 1995, and further to 43% in 2000. These trends are changing China's countryside. Most dramatically, by 2000, 76% of the 16–20 age group had some kind of off-farm work, and less than a quarter of those working off-farm had spent any time in agriculture at all. A generation of rural residents is leaving the land, and the process appears to be accelerating in the decade after 2000.

There is a wide variety of off-farm job choices available to rural residents today. In some regions farmers may create a nonagricultural business while living at home or commute to a job in a rural enterprise in a nearby town. To simplify, we can group rural worker choices into three categories: continue to farm, leave the farm and undertake local nonagricultural labor (perform wage labor or start a business), or migrate away from the locality. Both these latter two options have increased in popularity. Indeed, the share of off-farm workers who were migrants out of the village began to increase rapidly around 1990, and by 2000 about as many off-farm workers were migrants as were local, with slightly over 20% of the total rural labor force falling into each category.

Even among the long-distance migrants enumerated in the census (Chapter 5), almost a quarter had relocated to other rural areas, to work either in agriculture or in rural enterprises. Diverse rural labor markets provide an alternative to urban migration.

8.2   HOW WELL DO LABOR MARKETS FUNCTION IN CHINA TODAY?

Given the rapid, but still incomplete, changes in labor-market institutions in China, it is worthwhile to ask how well these labor markets work. We would like to know if the most productive workers are rewarded for their productivity. Ideally we would hope to find that productivity is rewarded and that factors irrelevant to productivity, such as rural or urban status, have no impact on rewards. In practice it is impossible for us to directly measure the productivity of individual workers. Instead, we can examine the impact on worker income of attributes that we expect to have an impact on productivity. The most important of these is education, a measure of human capital, which we expect to have a positive impact on productivity (Box 8.1). In section 8.2.1 we examine the evidence with respect to returns to education, and then in section 8.2.2 we look at China's changing human capital endowment. In section 8.2.3 we briefly examine three other attributes that might be related to worker productivity: experience, Communist Party membership, and gender. These are not less important than education, but the interpretation of existing results is more complex, and we simply touch on a few incomplete observations. In section 8.2.4, we examine the interaction between individual characteristics and the migration choice.

8.2.1   Returns to Education

The socialist system did a fairly good job of providing basic education to the population as a whole. Public support for education and training in China spread literacy and basic industrial skills very broadly in the population. But the socialist system did a very poor job of rewarding individuals who had attained higher levels of skill or education. When researchers began to study the determinants of urban incomes in China at the end of the planned-economy period (in the late 1970s and early 1980s), they found that incomes were not consistently higher among individuals with more education. Other correlates of higher income were significant: Communist Party membership, being male, and having more seniority on the job were all associated with higher incomes. But education did not significantly increase income. The private return to education was very close to zero.

Box 8.1
Human capital and the return to education

Economists have paid increasing attention recently to the role of human capital in the development process. Human capital is the resource that is created by investment in knowledge. Like physical capital, human capital is a factor of production, that is, a basic resource that is used, but not used up, in the production process.

Like physical capital, human capital is produced by prior activities. Education is the most important producer of human capital, but human capital can also be created by on-the-job experience, by investing in good health, or through other investments. Human capital is different from physical capital because it is not tangible: you cannot see it or touch it. But note that human capital does have an owner. An individual "owns" the human capital that is created by his or her education. The higher income that is created by a better-educated worker belongs to the worker.

The return to human capital is sometimes referred to as the "knowledge premium." The knowledge premium refers to the additional earning power a better-educated worker commands. In the United States there is substantial evidence of an increased knowledge premium—referring to the return to a university education—since the early 1980s. This trend may be a result of the impact of technological change on the production process or a result of the globalization of the world economy.

The most common approach to assessing the value of the knowledge premium is to estimate the Mincerian return to education, an approach named for the economist Jacob Mincer who pioneered it. The Mincerian return to education is the coefficient on the years of education when wages are regressed on a set of explanatory variables. Interpretation of the coefficient depends on a range of restrictive assumptions. Moreover, since educational attainment can often signal for unobservable individual characteristics, interpretation of the coefficient value depends on the manner in which difficult issues of selection bias and labor-market signaling are handled. Most of these issues are beyond the scope of the discussion in this chapter. In China the changes in magnitude of the knowledge premium as measured by the Mincerian return to education are sufficiently large that the technique can give us substantial insight into the evolution of labor markets.

This result revealed how inconsistent China's system was at that time with a fully functioning market economy. Perhaps the most fundamental requirement of a well-functioning market economy is that an individual is able to feel secure that she will be able to reap the income created by an investment she makes, so long as that investment succeeds in creating new output and income. Investment in education—in human capital—increases the overall productivity of the economy. For a market economy to function, an investment that increases social productivity must also provide a reward to the individual. Only in that case will individuals have the incentives to make socially productive investments. Since education is expensive, it is unlikely that the government could bear the whole cost, even if it wanted to; individual households will inevitably bear a substantial part of the cost of education. Thus a positive and significant private return to education is essential for the continued healthy investment necessary for a more productive economy. The return to education is also a good index of the extent to which labor markets have developed and are able to provide adequate rewards to those who invest in human capital. It is impossible to envisage a healthy market transition in China without a substantial increase in the return to education.

An extensive literature has examined the changing returns to education in urban China. A remarkably consistent result has emerged from this literature showing that the rate of return to education began to climb in the early 1990s and sustained an important increase through the next decade. Zhang Junsen et al. (2005) trace the return to education in urban China from 1988 through 2001, using annual data (Figure 8.4). They show that in the late 1980s and early 1990s an urban worker would improve his income by 4%–5% per year for each additional year of schooling he completed. This was far below the world average of 9.7%, and even farther below the low-income country average of 10.9% (Psacharopoulos and Patrinos 2002). However, the rate of return climbed during the 1990s, and in 1999–2001 the measured rate of return was around 10%, quite close to the world and low-income country averages. Zhou Xueguang (2000) uses recollected income data to examine the return to education over an even longer time frame: he finds that returns to education approximately doubled in the 1987–1993 period, compared with earlier periods. Appleton, Song, and Xia (2005) exploit an especially rich data set that covers urban incomes in four benchmark years from 1988 to 2002. They find

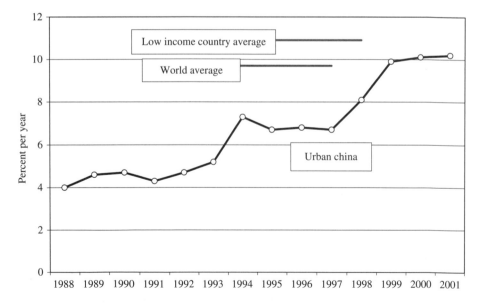

Figure 8.4
Return to an additional year of schooling

that the return to education estimated in cross section increased from 3.6% in 1988 to 7.5% in 2002, roughly consistent with the results of Zhang Junsen et al. With their (panel) data set they are able to control for unobserved individual attributes (fixed effects) and occupational effects. As expected, this adjustment lowers the measured return to education, but the pattern of increasing returns to education over the entire period is even stronger.

Such figures do not prove that Chinese labor markets are functioning efficiently, but the results are consistent with increasingly competitive labor markets. They show Chinese labor markets overcoming an obvious distortion in their functioning that was bequeathed to them by the planned-economy era. How did this dramatic change take place? During the 1990s market forces reshaped the way that workers were rewarded. Not only were more incentives available to those who performed or produced more productively, but structural changes in the demand for labor changed the determinants of income. Among existing workers, less-educated workers were significantly more likely to be laid off: by one recent empirical result, each year of education reduced the likelihood of being laid off by one percentage point (Appleton et al. 2002). Thus layoffs put downward pressure on the income of less-educated workers. Conversely, it is widely accepted that foreign-invested firms are bidding up the wages of educated urban workers. A wide range of skills—including management and English language—are considered valuable to foreign-invested firms, and their bids put upward pressure on the wages of more educated workers. Appleton et al. (2002) found that an additional year of education increased the income of both "never-laid-off" urban workers *and* rural-to-urban migrants by about 7%. Laid-off workers reported a much smaller income response to education (just below 4% for one year of education), a result the authors attribute to the newness of the markets, which means that laid-off workers are unable to smoothly translate their education or experience into income. Overall, the increase in the return to education provides some reassurance that individuals will invest in their own human capital and contribute substantially to the accumulation of skills necessary to drive China forward into an increasingly skill-intensive economy.

8.2.2 Human Capital and Educational Attainment

What then is the evidence on the accumulation of human capital in China? Despite China's rapid progress, average levels of educational attainment are still low. According to the 2000 census, only 20% of China's working-age population has a high school education. Table 8.1 shows the data on educational attainment in benchmark years. However, the categories shown in the table are defined in an inclusive manner that tends to overstate overall educational

Table 8.1
Educational attainment of population (percent)

Population, 15 and above	1982	1990	1995	2000	2004
Tertiary (above grade 12)	0.9	1.7	2.3	4.7	6.7
Upper middle (up to grade 12)	10.0	9.4	9.4	14.4	15.6
Lower middle (up to grade 9)	23.8	27.2	31.0	39.1	—
Primary (up to grade 6)	30.8	43.2	43.6	32.9	—
No formal schooling	34.5	18.5	13.6	9.0	—

attainment. Each category includes partial attainment, so attendance for a year or two is sufficient to be placed in a category: graduation is not required. Moreover, a large part of tertiary education consists of three-year junior colleges and technical schools; China also has extensive degree-granting adult education programs that are included. With these qualifications in mind, it can be seen that the gap with developed countries is still very large. For example, in 2002 in the United States, 84% of the population above 25 years old has graduated from high school, and 52% have some college. Graduates of four-year colleges make up 26.7% of this group (U.S. Census Bureau).

However, educational attainment in China has been increasing very rapidly, particularly in higher education. When China emerged from the Cultural Revolution, the pattern of educational attainment was very unusual. The 1982 census, conducted at the beginning of the reform era (see column 1 of Table 8.1), showed that basic education was fairly widespread for a low-income country, with two-thirds of the adult population having received formal schooling. While one-third of the population was illiterate or semiliterate, this was significantly less than India, for example, where more than half the population at this time was illiterate. However, less than 1% of the Chinese population had any college education at all. India at this time had three times as many college graduates per capita as China.

After the reform era began—and in reaction to the perceived excess of egalitarianism of the Cultural Revolution—educational resources were concentrated on building up higher education. Moreover, progress in this area accelerated after the mid–1990s. After years of investing in, and restructuring, the system of higher education, the number of graduates began to increase especially rapidly in 2001. From 2001 through 2005, the total number graduating college *tripled*, increasing from one million to slightly over three million (see Chapter 15). The results have been impressive, as Table 8.1 documents. By 2004, 6.7% of those 15 and above have some education at the university or junior college level, more than seven times the proportion of 20 years ago. This is an astonishingly rapid growth rate, and China has caught up with India, even though India's college enrollments have also been growing rapidly through this period.

The emphasis on higher education has led to some neglect of primary education, particularly in rural areas. Nevertheless, Table 8.1 shows that progress continued to be made at the bottom of the educational pyramid. The share of illiteracy declined rapidly, as large cohorts of relatively well-educated young students tipped the balance of population. By 2003, only 2.4% of the 15–45 year age group was illiterate. Besides age, gender and residence are important determinants of literacy: 19% of rural females over 15 are illiterate, compared with 8% of rural males. In the cities, only 7% of females and 2% of males are illiterate. The average years of schooling of the population (age six and above) has increased steadily, reaching eight in 2004 (Population Statistics Yearbook 2004: 302; 2005: 54–57, 320). By comparison, the adult population averages seven years of education in Mexico, 10 in Korea and 12 in the United States.

Moreover, from the mid–1990s, the government began to place more emphasis on basic education. A program was adopted to make nine years of education compulsory, and to eliminate illiteracy among young people, initially in those counties with sufficient economic development and budgetary resources to support the effort on their own. The program has been steadily expanded since that time, and as of 2004, the Chinese government claimed that 2,774 county-level jurisdictions, accounting for 94% of China's population, had programs of some kind in place (Ministry of Education 2005). This is an impressive effort, but the ultimate outcome is not yet clear. The problem is money. The bulk of education funding comes from local level governments. In rural areas, local finances have been squeezed by changes in the fiscal system that reduce their revenues (Chapter 19), as well as recent limitations on their ability to collect informal fees from the population. The result is that total outlays for education in China were at 3% of GDP consistently through the 1990s, considerably lower than other comparable economies. Thus while local governments are under political pressure to show and report action in spreading universal education, they have not been given adequate resources to follow through in practice. The gap in teacher preparation and quality of facilities between rural and urban areas is enormous.

Ambitious plans have been announced to address these problems. Scholarships are to be expanded to all needy students by 2007; a system of free primary school education is to be in place in all rural areas by 2010; and free universal primary education is to be implemented by 2015 (Ministry of Education 2005). Following through on this plan will require a substantial sustained commitment of funds from the central government. In recent years,

China has advocated policies of "putting people first," fostering technological creativity, and adopting a "scientific approach to development." A recent government planning document pointed out that "Accelerating the development of education is the basic path to converting the enormous pressure of population in our country into the comparative advantage of abundant human resources." (Eleventh Plan Suggestions [2005], Section 30). If these statements are to be anything more than empty slogans, the government will have to take over funding of universal primary education.

Despite recent improvement, China's educational structure overall is very much that of a developing country. Underinvestment in girls' education persists. While illiteracy is far lower among the young, the gender imbalance remains: more than twice as many girls as boys do not go to school. Another strikingly vulnerable group is the children of migrants to the city. These children are charged fees, which can often be prohibitive, to attend local public schools. In response, special privately run "migrant schools" have sprung up to provide a bare minimum of education at a reasonable price. The government has promised to address this problem, but progress so far has been slow. Even with an activist role for government, households will likely bear a large part of the cost of higher education. The improvement in the returns to education documented in the preceding section explains some of the rapid increase in educational attainment over the past 10 years. Although higher education has become more expensive for Chinese households, those with the means have generally been willing to pay, because of the positive returns to investing in education. However, in order to ensure the continued rapid spread of higher education, the government will have to do more to ensure access for all of China's population.

8.2.3   Other Attributes

While education is prima facie productive, the impact of other worker characteristics is more ambiguous. Work experience—virtually identical to age in China—was amply rewarded in socialist China, in what was essentially a seniority wage system. During the reform era the returns to experience have declined moderately, but they have not disappeared (Appleton, Song, and Xia, 2005; Zhang Junsen et al. 2005; Zhou Xueguang 2000). This change seems consistent with greater market competition: on the one hand, skills acquired by young people have become more valuable, and some of the on-the-job experience of older people has become obsolete; on the other hand, expertise and productivity still increase with years on the job. Finally, these studies show that the variation in returns to education by ownership type and sector have tended to narrow over the years. At least among urban residents, barriers among workers are being reduced. Unfortunately, we do not have good enough data to track the differences in returns between urban residents and rural–urban migrants. Presumably this difference is still large and significant.

In socialist China membership in the Communist Party was rewarded with a significant income differential. Just as it was natural to anticipate that marketization would bring an increase in the return to education, it also seemed natural to most analysts that marketization would bring about a decrease in the return to Communist Party membership. In fact, this has not happened. Both Appleton, Song, and Xia (2005) and Zhou Xueguang (2000) find that returns to party membership actually increased during the reform era. According to Appleton, Song, and Xia, the premium increased from 7% to 20% of income between 1988 and 1999, before falling back slightly in 2002. Does this result indicate that Communist Party members have all along had knowledge and skills that have become more valuable during the era of marketization? Or does it reflect increasing opportunities for Communist Party members to intervene in, and profit from, the operation of the market? In either case, it shows that membership in China's Communist Party has economic benefits for individuals and that these benefits have continued or increased during reform.

During the socialist period gender gaps in wages were relatively modest. Although women were not strongly represented in the ranks of top management, the system was one of "equal pay for equal work." Appleton, Song, and Xia find that the gender gap—the difference of male and female wages for comparable levels of experience and education—increased from 12% in 1988 to 22% in 1999 before falling back to 19% in 2002. They consider this a moderate level, comparing it to a gender gap of 25% in the United States in 2000. To the extent that the gender gap results from discrimination, it represents a failure of the competitive marketplace. Women were more likely than men to be laid off from state firms during their restructuring, a fact which may also reflect discrimination but which certainly indicates a change in the selection process by which women remain in the labor force. More analysis is needed to understand these important changes.

8.2.4   The Migration Decision

Having examined the return to different worker characteristics or attributes, we are now in a position to return to the phenomenon of rural-to-urban migration, described in Chapter 5, and examine the individual decision-making process more closely. Migrants move in search of opportunity. Thus we expect migration to be driven by an income differential, as migrants seek higher incomes. The best studies of Chinese migration have interpreted it through the framework of household decision-making. The basic premise is that the decision to migrate is made by households rather than individuals. Migration is initially costly, and households must subsidize the initial costs of out-migration, typically of a young adult household member. They do so because they expect that migration will bring long-run benefits to the household. Thus, although the individual income gap between the urban wage and the return to farming is the right starting point for understanding rural-to-urban migration, it is only the beginning. For example, Taylor, Rozelle, and de Brauw (2003) find that an additional family worker increased the chance an individual would migrate in the 1990s by 28%, because a larger family is able to support the migrant's initial costs and can more easily sustain agricultural production.

Unique institutional features in China also shape the migration decision. At the place of origin, ties to the land continue to be strong because land ownership is to some degree contingent on farmers using the land. Migrants may fear losing their land-use rights, since the collective has the authority and incentive to redistribute scarce land to those with more stay-at-home workers. At the place of destination, the household registration system in China raises the costs (and risks) of living in the city, making it much more expensive to settle down. Moreover, as discussed earlier, the urban labor market is strongly segmented, and some occupations are still not open to migrants. For these reasons, we might expect Chinese migration to take the form of "sojourning," of medium-term residence in the city, followed by a return to the native place. In fact, migration everywhere is characterized by a significant share of sojourning. But if this phenomenon turns out to be even more important in China, it may have a significant impact on rural development patterns.

In fact, we observe that migrants often return to their place of origin, in part to fulfill long-term life goals, such as marriage and raising children (Hare 1999; Roberts et al. 2004). How should we understand these returned migrants? Do they represent those who have failed in the city and now retreat to their native place? Or do they represent relatively well educated residents who return with new experiences and entrepreneurial ideas, and who can provide benefit to their places of origin? Zhao Yaohui (2002) studied return migrants in six provinces. She found that older and married persons were more likely to return, and that the probability of return declined as the migrant's stay in an urban location lengthened. Perhaps surprisingly, more education significantly raised the probability a migrant would return. These features seem to suggest that returnees may be those who have positive skills and experiences they can bring to bear in their place of origin.

The interaction between education and out-migration is particularly worth attention. In most studies of migration, education is found to encourage migration. Indeed, a large part of the economic value of education in rural areas comes precisely from the fact that it increases the chance that a worker will relocate and find a higher income outside his place of origin. However, several of the initial studies of migration in China found a very weak relationship between education and migration. Zhao (1999) studied a large sample in Sichuan province and found that although schooling raised the probability an individual would take a nonagricultural job in his or her place of origin, it had an insignificant effect on raising the probability of out-migration. Hare (1999) found similar results in an intensive study of Xiayi County in Henan Province. De Brauw and Giles (2005) studied the interaction between rural high school and migration, and found that high school does little to increase the income of migrants, and that, perhaps as a result, out-migration is an alternative to attending high school. These studies suggest that the positive benefit of migration might be limited by the institutional rigidities of China's system. If education does not increase the benefits of migration, it may be that the full range of opportunities potentially created by migration is still limited in the Chinese context.

However, de Brauw et al. (2002) found that the migrant labor force has been getting younger and that formal education has been increasingly rewarded. In fact, in their study they found that each year of education increased the likelihood of migration by 17% in the 1990s, up dramatically from the 6% increase they found in the 1980s (through recollected data). This finding may be related to the rapid increase in the proportion of young people in the migration stream. Younger workers are increasingly specializing in off-farm work, either through migration or local nonfarm employment, and this trend may be changing the migration calculus. Many of these younger workers have little or no direct experience with farming. They are more likely to stay in the city over the long term, and they have generally foreclosed the option of farming in their place of origin. The share of female migrants, while still below that of males, has also been increasing rapidly. This finding suggests a shift in the pattern of migration in China away from the temporary sojourning of the previous generation and toward a new mass movement as young people leave the land. For this shift to be sustained, though, China's urban labor markets must prove capable of absorbing the increased inflows and expanding the opportunities available to migrants.

8.2.5   Labor Markets Concluded

Labor markets in China appear to be increasingly competitive and more effective at rewarding the productive characteristics of workers. In both urban and rural areas there is evidence that the returns to education are increasing.

Nevertheless, China's labor markets are still distorted by institutional barriers and incomplete markets. The initial absolute separation between urban and rural work has been eliminated, but it has been replaced by a segmented urban labor market, with rural migrants overwhelmingly working in the informal sector. A deepening of labor-market integration can be expected to significantly improve the productivity of the Chinese economy.

8.3 SOCIAL SECURITY

Social security is one of the defining characteristics of the formal sector of the urban labor market. It is also a critical issue for China's future, an issue in which many of the distinctive characteristics of the Chinese economy play a role, sometimes unexpected. Under the old system urban workers routinely enjoyed social security as part of their employment under the "work-unit" system: work units paid pensions to their own retirees out of their own profits. The number of retirees was not large, and since the enterprises were not profit maximizers or competitive firms, the funds were not at issue. But as China has moved toward a market economy, it has been essential to move the entire social security system out of the work unit's control and shift it to a national social program administered by government agencies. Important beginnings have been made in this direction: indeed, the downsizing of the state sector documented at the beginning of this chapter was delayed until some rudimentary social insurance mechanisms were in place to take over responsibility for laid-off workers. But at the same time, progress in this area has been uneven, and the problem of creating a viable social insurance network is particularly great in China for the following reasons:

• Urban workers are accustomed to a pension system and feel a sense of entitlement; social security must reach a minimum level to match expectations and succeed politically.

• Enterprises operate in a competitive market and cannot disproportionately bear the burden of paying out pensions. Older firms with many retirees would be enormously burdened. Pension funds must absorb the payment obligation.

• China will face population aging with unprecedented speed and at an unusually low level of per capita income (Chapter 7). After 2020 the elderly population will grow very rapidly.

• The financial base of the traditional social security system—the SOE and government employers—has been shrinking very rapidly, and the growing sectors of the urban economy are often outside the scope of existing social security mechanisms. The formal sector, with social security provisions, is a declining share of total urban employment.

• Finally, the downsizing of state firms created a large number of relatively young retired people, state workers in their 50s who were allowed to retire because there was no more work available for them.

This combination of early retirement, generous pensions, and increasing elderly dependency rates will create serious economic challenges for China in the coming years. All the rapid demographic and institutional changes in China over the past 20 years come together to intensify the problem of social security.

As the nature of the employment relationship changes in China, new institutions are being crafted to take up some of the burden previously assumed by the work unit. The recent pension reform began with modest efforts to pool the risks of the existing SOE pension system. Reflecting the patterns of gradualism and bottom-up organization that have characterized much of the reform process, pension funds and medical insurance programs have been established at the local government level. However, thus far China has no unified national system. Currently only urban residents (generally employees of government agencies or SOEs) are offered public pension benefits. The majority of the population in the rural areas is not covered by the public pension system, with a few exceptions in rich areas where local governments offer pension benefits to the elderly. Pensions for government employees are paid from the government budget. As such, the pension system is an amalgam of hundreds of separate pension systems with different contribution rates, coverage levels, and benefit calculations, all of which causes further complications in the creation of a unified system for Chinese retirees.

However, the national government gradually has attempted to unify provincial programs into a national social security program and to expand coverage to all urban workers. After several years of experiments in various regions and enterprises, the State Council in March 1995 issued "The Directive on Further Reform of the Enterprise Pension System." The objective of this directive was to establish a multipillar pension system involving funds contributed by the state, employers, and individuals. This system consists of three elements: a basic public pension funded on a pay-as-you-go basis, a fully funded pension funded by mandatory contributions, and voluntary personal savings. The first two of these three elements are funded by contributions from the enterprises and the employees; the size of the contribution ranges from 10% to 20% of the employees' total wages, depending on the region. Of this 10%–20%, employees contribute about 2%–5%, and the rest of the premiums are borne by the enterprises (West 1999).

The first of the three pillars, the public pension, provides only minimum levels of old-age security (with a target replacement of about 50% of wages). The hope is that the partially funded nature of this system will enable the government to avoid the old-age crisis that is being experienced by many industrialized countries, a crisis that will otherwise loom for China 20 years from now. Outside the basic public pension, the Singapore model of treating old-age social security as mainly a financial-sector issue (with mandatory contributions and market-based operations) is attractive to Chinese policy-makers. The first attempts to create fully funded pensions had limited success. However, it seems that the Chinese government is making a serious attempt not to overburden fiscal authorities with a huge public pension system, which makes sense given the immaturity of China's financial markets (see Chapter 19).

In September 2000, China's State Council established a national social security fund, directly under the administration of the State Council. It manages the funds allocated by the central government and those raised through selling state-owned assets. Other important tasks include selecting professional asset-management companies and entrusting the fund's operation to them. The fund has also been allowed to invest some of its money in the stock market through selected asset-management companies. Previously pension funds could only be invested in bank deposits and government bonds, a requirement which meant losses would occur during periods of low interest rates. Thus the creation of pension funds should have lasting repercussions on the broadening of the financial markets.

Table 8.2 shows that the social security system has already become fairly large. In 2003 there were already 45 million retirees, one for every 2.7 workers covered by the basic program. The total number of covered workers was 116 million in 2003, compared with 105.5 million workers in the urban formal sector, as calculated earlier. Thus the government has made some progress in

Table 8.2
Social security system

Year	Total retirees (million)	Ratio employed to total retirees	Total urban pensions (billion RMB)	Total pensions share GDP (percent)
1980	8.2	12.8	5.0	1.1
1990	23.0	6.1	39.6	2.1
2000	38.8	3.5	273.3	2.8
2003	45.2	2.7	414.9	3.1
2004	46.7		451.1	2.8

extending coverage through the formal sector and has also including some private and rural firms. Notwithstanding the fact that some new firms (including foreign-invested firms) with young workforces and low retirement burdens would prefer not to participate in the program, coverage of the formal sector is now close to complete. Nevertheless, an increasing share of urban workers are in the informal sector, and most have no social security coverage at all. Despite the incomplete coverage, the sums involved are large and are growing rapidly. In fact, the average pensioner in 2000 received approximately 75% of the average state wage that year, similar to the replacement rates over the past 20 years. Moreover, these funds, although increasingly resembling a national social security program, have thus far been consolidated at the provincial level only in most cases.

In fact, despite the progress made, the social security system remains very much a work in progress. Because the demands on the system have been so much larger than anticipated, and local control of funds an obstacle, progress has been slow. Pension outlays have not yet been incorporated into budgetary figures, except for the direct fiscal payments government has had to make to keep the system solvent. In 2003 government had to kick in about 15% of total funds to subsidize deficit regions, accounting for about 6% of central government outlays. Pension funds have been troubled by scandals, as local government officials have diverted balances in the funds to their own priorities. Funding shortfalls have been caused by the inability (and unwillingness) of enterprises to pay into their accounts, combined with the generous retirement benefits that have been extended to younger retirees. The initial reform design of having individual retirement accounts designated from the worker's individual contributions failed, because there was not enough money to actually fund them. A new push to establish such accounts was evident after 2004. Pension funds in the Northeast are known to be especially troubled, and there have been public demonstrations and protests over failures to pay pensions on time. One of the main provisions of the Northeast Revitalization Program rolled out after 2003 was to have the central government guarantee the pension programs in the Northeast. In the face of such issues, the pension programs have not provided sufficient funds to cover current pension outlays, much less provide a secure financial basis for future outlays. This failure presents a challenge to policy-makers in terms of future social stability.

The pension system is just one pillar of the overall social insurance system. Health insurance has also been dramatically transformed in recent years. Widespread implementation of health reform did not begin until 2000, but by 2004 the system already covered 90 million workers (*SYC* 2005, 798). Health insurance reform clearly involves a lesser degree of coverage for urban workers than the former system provided. Not only do workers now have to contribute a portion of their paycheck for health insurance, but in addition there are gaps in coverage for certain kinds of catastrophic illness (Duckett 2004). According to the 2002 household survey (Chapter 9), 32% of urban workers (formal and informal) have no health insurance at all. While health insurance reform has succeeded in stripping out one social function from the business enterprise, it has reduced income security and is extremely unpopular among urban residents.

8.4   CONCLUSION

Dramatic changes have reshaped nearly every aspect of China's labor economy. These changes have eliminated the privileged social status that state-enterprise workers had occupied under the command economy. At the same time, changes have opened up new sources of mobility, both for rural workers seeking urban employment and for urban workers with higher levels of skill and training. Overall, urban incomes have increased dramatically. But at the same time these institutional changes have led to increasing income diversity within urban areas. For those workers who have been laid off, the reduction in income has been exacerbated by the need to adapt to continuing job insecurity and the recognition that social insurance provisions are far less complete and reliable than they were before. The increasing bifurcation of urban areas into a formal and informal sector creates new social challenges for China.

BIBLIOGRAPHY

Suggestions for Further Reading

Brooks and Tao (2003) is a recent overview. De Brauw et al. (2002) on rural labor markets is essential reading. Knight and Song (2005) is a good overview with several indepth chapters. Li Shi and Sato (2006) collects a number of important papers.

Sources for Data and Figures

Figure 8.1: *Labor Yearbook* (1994); *SYC* (2004, 122–23, 132, 177).

Figure 8.2: *Labor Yearbook* (1996, 409; 1997, 213, 405; 1998, 431–31; 1999, 441; 2000, 409–10; 2001, 401–02; 2002, 109–10; 2003, 135; 2004, 146); *Labor and Social Security Yearbook* (2004, 478); Yang Yiyong (1997); Mo Rong (1998); 2004 stock of laid-off workers from Annual Economic Report (2005), with state workers estimated as 70% of total. Data on 2004 newly laid-off workers not yet published.

Figure 8.3: *SYC* (2005, 120–21).

Figure 8.4: Zhang Junsen et al. (2005, 739).

Table 8.1. 1982 from 1982 Census Summary (1985), pp. 360–61. 1990, 1995, and 2000 from Population Statistics Yearbook (1996: 5, 154–55; 2002: 287). 2004 from SYC (2005), pp. 105–07.

Table 8.2. *Labor Yearbook* (various years); SYC (2005): 795–800.

Labor data: The primary sources of official data on labor are the *Labor Yearbooks* published by the Ministry of Labor and Social Security (sometimes in collaboration with the National Bureau of Statistics), the *Labour and Social Security Yearbooks* from the same ministry, and the statistical reports posted on the ministry's Web site, http://www.molss.gov.cn/index_tongji.htm.

In 1978 there was some additional job movement, because the state reassigned workers to new enterprises—including those in distant cities—in accordance with the state's needs and development strategies. The numbers discussed do not cover workers changing jobs within the state sector either through voluntary choice or job reassignment. An additional category of "discharge and suspension" was generally for political or criminal offences. In addition, there were 11 million short-term workers in the state sector who did not have lifetime employment (*Labor Yearbook* 1993, 318).

References

1982 Census Summary (1985). Population Census Office, State Council. *Zhongguo 1982 Nian Renkou Pucha Ziliao (Dianzi Jisuanji Huizong) [1982 Population Census of China (Results of Computer Tabulation)]*. Beijing: Zhongguo Tongji.

Annual Economic Report (2005). National Bureau of Statistics. "Zhonghua Renmin Gongheguo 2004 nian guomin jingji he shehui fazhan tongji gongbao [National economic and social development statistical report of the People's Republic of China for 2004]" February 28, 2005, accessed at www.stats.gov.cn/tjgb/ndtjgb/qgndtjgb/t20050228_402231854.htm.

Appleton, Simon, John Knight, Lina Song, and Qingjie Xia (2002). "Labour Retrenchment in China: Determinants and Consequences." *China Economic Review*, 13(2–3): 252–76.

Appleton, Simon, Lina Song, and Qingjie Xia (2005). "Has China Crossed the River? The Evolution of Wage Structure in Urban China During Reform and Retrenchment." *Journal of Comparative Economics* 33: 644–63.

Bian, Yanjie (1994). "*Guanxi* and the Allocation of Urban Jobs in China." *China Quarterly*, no. 140, December, 973.

Brooks, Ray, and Ran Tao (2003). "China's Labor Market Performance and Challenges." IMF Working Paper (Asia and Pacific Department) WP/03/210, November. Washington, DC: International Monetary Fund.

de Brauw, Alan, and John Giles (2005). "Migrant Opportunity and the Educational Attainment of Youth in Rural China," July 6. Available at http://www.msu.edu/~gilesj/adjg1final.pdf.

de Brauw, Alan, Jikun Huang, Scott Rozelle, Linxiu Zhang, and Yigang Zhang (2002). "The Evolution of China's Rural Labor Markets During the Reforms." *Journal of Comparative Economics* 30: 329–353.

Duckett, Jane (2004). "State, Collectivism and Worker Privilege: A Study of Urban Health Insurance Reform." *China Quarterly*, no. 177, March, 174–89.

Eleventh Plan Suggestions (2005). Chinese Communist Party Central Committee. "CP Center Suggestions on Setting the 11th Five-Year Plan for National Economic and Social Development," October 11. Accessed from October 18, report at news.xinhuanet.com/politics/2005-10/18/content_3640318.htm.

Giles, John, Albert Park and Fang Cai (2006). "How has Economic Restructuring Affected China's Urban Workers," *China Quarterly*, no. 185 (March), 61–95.

Granick, David (1987). "The Industrial Environment in China and the CMEA Countries." In Gene Tidrick and Chen Jiyuan, eds., *China's Industrial Reform*. New York: Oxford University Press.

Hare, Denise (1999). " 'Push' and 'Pull' Factors in Migration Outflows and Returns: Determinants of Migration Status and Spell Duration among China's Rural Population." *Journal of Development Studies*, 35(3): 45–72.

Knight, John and Lina Song (2005). *Towards a Labour Market in China*. Oxford: Oxford University Press.

Labor Yearbook (various years). National Bureau of Statistics, Department of Population, Social, and Science and Technology Statistics, and Ministry of Labor and Social Security, Department of

Planning and Finance, ed., *Zhongguo Laodong Tongji Nianjian* [Yearbook of Labor Statistics of China]. Beijing: Zhongguo Laodong.

Labor and Social Security Yearbook (various years). Ministry of Labor and Social Security, ed., *Zhongguo Laodong he Shehui Baozhan Nianjian*. Beijing: Zhongguo Laodong Shehui Baozhang.

Li Shi and Hiroshi Sato, eds. (2006). *Unemployment, Inequality, and Poverty in Urban China*. New York: Routledge.

Ministry of Education (2005). "China Universal Education Report [*Zhongguo Quanmin Jiaoyu Guojia Baogao*]," November 10. At http://www.edu.cn/20051110/3159881.html.

Mo Rong (1998). *Jiuye: Zhongguo de Shiji Nanti* [Employment: China's Problem of the Century], 20, 28–9. Beijing: Jingji Kexue.

NBS [National Bureau of Statistics] (2004). *Annual Report*.

OECD (2005). *Governance in China*. Paris: Organization for Economic Cooperation and Development. Chapters 1–2 on government employees, civil service, and PSUs. Available at http://www.sourceoecd.org/governance/926400842X.

Population Statistics Yearbook (various years). National Bureau of Statistics, Department of Population and Employment Statistics, ed., Zhongguo Renkou Tongji Nianjian *[Population Statistics Yearbook of China]*. Beijing: Zhongguo Tongji.

Psacharopoulos, George, and Harry Anthony Patrinos (2002). "Returns to Investment in Education: A Further Update." World Bank Policy Research Working Paper No. 2881, September.

Roberts, Kenneth B. (2002). "Female Labor Migrants to Shanghai: Temporary Floaters or Potential Settlers." *International Migration Review*, 36(2), Summer, 492–519.

Roberts, Kenneth D, Rachel Connelly, Zhenzhen Zheng, and Zhenming Xie (2004). "Patterns of Temporary Migration of Women from Anhui and Sichuan Provinces of China." *China Review*, 52.

Solinger, Dorothy (2004). "Policy Consistency in the Midst of the Asian Crisis: Managing the Furloughed and the Farmers in Three Cities." In Barry Naughton and Dali Yang, eds., *Holding China Together: Diversity and National Integration in the Post-Deng Era*. New York: Cambridge University Press.

SYC (Annual). *Zhongguo Tongji Nianjian* [Statistical Yearbook of China]. Beijing: Zhongguo Tongji.

Taylor, J. Edward, Scott Rozelle, and Alan de Brauw (2003). "Migration and Incomes in Source Communities: A New Economics of Migration Perspective from China." *Economic Development and Cultural Changes*, 52(1), October, 75–101.

Urban Labor (1998). Urban Labor Market Research Group, China Economy Research Center, Beijing University. "Shanghai: Stratification and Integration of Urban and Rural Workers." *Gaige*, 4:99–110.

U.S. Census Bureau. U.S. educational attainment available at http://www.census.gov/population/socdemo/education/tabA-2.pdf.

West, Loraine A. (1999). "Pension Reform in China: Preparing for the Future." *Journal of Development Studies*, 35(3), February, 153–83.

Yang Yiyong (1997). "China's Unemployment Problem: Current Conditions, Trends, and Appropriate Measures." In Liu Guoguang, Wang Luolin, and Li Jingwen, eds., *1998 Nian Zhongguo Jingji Xingshi Fenxi yu Yuce: Jingji Lanpi Shu* [1998 China Economic Conditions, Analysis and Projections: Economic Blue Book]. Beijing: Shehui Kexue Wenxian.

Zhang Junsen, Zhao Yaohui, Albert Park, and Xiaoqing Song (2005). "Economic Returns to Schooling in Urban China, 1988 to 2001." *Journal of Comparative Economics*, 33:730–52.

Zhao Yaohui (1999). "Labor Migration and Earnings Differences: The Case of Rural China." *Economic Development and Cultural Change*, 47(4):767–82.

Zhao Yaohui (2002). "Causes and Consequences of Return Migration: Recent Evidence from China." *Journal of Comparative Economics*, 30:376–96.

Zhou Xueguang (2000). "Economic Transformation and Income Inequality in Urban China: Evidence from Panel Data." *American Journal of Sociology*, 105(4), January, 1135–74.

9

Living Standards: Incomes, Inequality, and Poverty

Income has grown rapidly in China, but inequality has also increased dramatically. Income growth has provided China the ability to reduce poverty and risk, and increase consumption and leisure. But growth has not spread these benefits equally through the population. Instead, China exemplifies the complex possible relationship among income growth, inequality, and poverty. Household income growth has indeed been rapid in China since 1978, and individual Chinese are clearly much better off than they were 25 or 30 years ago. Moreover, the number of people in extreme poverty has declined dramatically. But over the same period the distribution of income has become *much* more unequal. Income growth has been fastest among the best-positioned urban households in coastal regions and slowest among rural households in the western and northern regions. Thus Chinese society has become much better off, much less poor, but much more unequal. The deterioration in income equality implies that tens of millions of low-income households have lagged behind, improving their living standards less than better-positioned households. Within China an increasingly widespread perception holds that society is less equal than it used to be and less fair than it should be.

The basic trends in Chinese income, described in the previous paragraph, emerge clearly from nearly all the data available from China. There is no debate about these basic trends. However, more precise—and more fundamental—characterization of household income in China is challenging, and some topics are highly debated. The data needed to accurately measure poverty, inequality, and well-being are hard to collect in any country. Moreover, distinctive features of the Chinese economy—the large urban–rural gap, peculiarities in the nature of income, and changes in the composition of household income over the reform period—present challenges in both the collection and interpretation of data. This chapter begins with the income data and then discusses poverty and inequality. The discussion is then broadened to include alternative measures of the population's well-being, including health and literacy. These gauges are placed in a comparative framework to determine how well Chinese people have reaped the benefits of economic growth.

9.1 INCOME GROWTH

Household income has grown rapidly in China. The repeat visitor to China can see with her own eyes the striking evidence of improved standards of clothing, eating, and housing. The best source of statistical data on this dramatic transformation comes from a large household survey that Chinese statisticians have carried out annually since the late 1970s. Statisticians survey two separate large samples, one rural and one urban (defined as those holding urban residence permits, as discussed in Chapter 5). This chapter begins with an overview of what this source tells us about the growth of household income, because this is the basis for much of what we know, and do not know, about Chinese income trends. Table 9.1 shows data from the urban and rural household income series, converted into 2004 constant prices with the (official) consumer price index. According to these data, both rural and urban household incomes have grown extremely rapidly: both more than quintupled between 1978 and 2004. The general picture of rapid income growth in both rural and urban areas is surely accurate.

However, when we examine the data more closely, we see three rather different periods. We look at the data in reverse chronological order, taking the most recent period first. This is because the data are most reliable for the most recent period.

• From 1991 through 2004 urban household income grew at the extremely rapid rate of 7.7% per year sustained over 13 years. During this period, rural

Table 9.1
Growth of real per capita household income

	Rural net household income	Urban disposable income
Income in constant 2004 prices (RMB)		
1978	(About 500)	1,701
1985	1,343	2,728
1991	1,585	3,612
2004	2,936	9,422
Average annual growth rate (percent)		
1978–1985	(About 15)	7.0
1985–1991	2.8	4.8
1991–2004	4.9	7.7

In 2004, one RMB was worth $0.12 at the official exchange rate, or $0.55 at PPP.

growth was also respectable, but not as spectacular as that in urban areas, running at 4.9% per year.

• The immediately previous period, from 1985 through 1991, was a period of significantly slower growth for both sectors, but the relative position of urban and rural households was about the same. Urban income growth had chugged along at the respectable rate of 4.8% per year, but rural incomes had grown at the comparatively slow rate of 2.8% annually.

Thus the urban–rural gap has been widening for about 20 years, from its minimum in the mid–1980s. This finding corresponds with the discussion in Chapter 5, and it is clearly evident in the data. Moreover, these data are fairly reliable back through 1985 because they are based on reasonable calculation of consumer prices in the two sectors and on broad-based data collection. Unfortunately, the data on the 1978–1985 period are much less reliable.

• Officially, the data show that rural incomes soared between 1978 and 1985, in the wake of rural reforms, growing 15% per year (as shown in Table 9.1). Urban household incomes also increased robustly, at 7% per year. But during this period, the urban–rural gap narrowed significantly, and it reached its lowest point ever in the mid–1980s.

Unfortunately, these calculations of real income growth simply cannot be accepted. The problem is that they are based on shoddy calculations of the rural consumer price index, which can be shown to be inaccurate. The real growth of rural incomes in this early period is clearly overstated. This inaccuracy is very unfortunate because it is virtually certain that rural incomes *did* grow extremely rapidly during this period, and almost certainly faster than urban incomes. For now, we cannot reliably estimate the rate of growth. Therefore, the long-run growth of rural incomes is also somewhat overstated. Unless the National Bureau of Statistics goes back and recalculates a reliable rural consumer price index, we will not know the actual magnitude.

There are other limitations to the official data. The household survey covers only rural residents and urban people with residence permits, so migrants and others with intermediate status are not covered at all. There are also significant differences between urban and rural in the way income is measured, as well as differences over time in how in-kind incomes are evaluated. These problems limit comparability, overstate the growth rate of rural incomes in the earlier period, and may also somewhat overstate the growth of urban and rural incomes in other periods (for data discussion see Bramall 2001; Gibson,

Huang, and Rozelle 2003; Park and Wang 2001; and Ravallion and Chen 1999). Yet despite these shortcomings, the picture of rapid income growth is robust. Moreover, the household surveys provide an extremely rich body of data that can be used to support further analysis and diverse efforts to go beyond the simple headline number of average income growth. In the following, two efforts that further develop the data from the household survey will be discussed in the course of examining trends in poverty and inequality.

9.2   POVERTY

9.2.1   Rural Poverty

Growth reduces poverty, and one of the great successes of China's economic reform has been a dramatic reduction in the number of people living in poverty, especially in the early years of reform.

9.2.1.1   Official Poverty Line

Chinese official data present a picture of extraordinary poverty alleviation, with the 250 million rural residents who lived in poverty in 1978 reduced to 26 million in 2004. Poverty reduction was most rapid at the beginning of the reform era, as poverty numbers were cut in half by 1985. Possibly never before in history have such a large number of people climbed out of absolute poverty in such a short time. Poverty reduction slowed dramatically after the mid–1980s, but over time sustained economic growth has continued to lower the number, and proportion, of people in absolute poverty. The Chinese official data for 2004 show just 2.8% of the rural population with incomes less than the official poverty threshold. Using the official poverty line, virtually no urban dwellers are in poverty, so poverty is fundamentally a rural phenomenon. However, the Chinese official poverty line is very low, equal to 627 RMB per person per year in 2002, considerably lower than the internationally comparable poverty line used by the World Bank, which we will discuss later. It is understandable, though, that a poorer country would set a lower standard for poverty; indeed, this is a regular international pattern. The incidence of rural poverty according to the Chinese official poverty line is shown as the lower line in Figure 9.1.

9.2.1.2   World Bank Internationally Comparable Poverty Line

Ravallion and Chen (2004) make a broad revision of Chinese data to correct problems and make Chinese measures comparable to international standards.

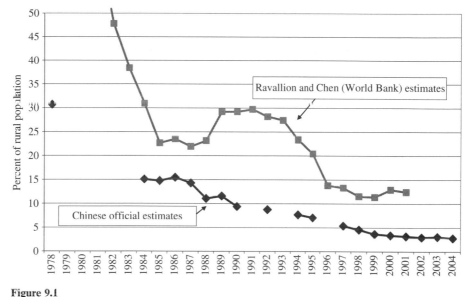

Figure 9.1
Incidence of rural poverty in China

In the first place, the World Bank's standard is equal to the in-country equivalent of one U.S. dollar per day, evaluated at PPP (see Box 6.1 for discussion). According to Ravallion and Chen's calculations, this internationally comparable poverty standard equaled 850 RMB per person in the Chinese countryside in 2002. The difference with the Chinese standard of 627 RMB might not at first seem to be large: converting at exchange rates, it increases the threshold from $76 to only $103. However, it makes a huge difference in the evaluation of poverty today because there are a very large number of people in the Chinese countryside very near those poverty thresholds. With the higher threshold, the percentage of rural residents in poverty jumps from 3.2% by the Chinese standard to 12.5%, and the total number jumps from 29 million to 114 million. Poverty is a much more serious and persistent problem in China today than one might suspect by using only the Chinese poverty standard. Moreover, the World Bank poverty line is drawn in order to capture the number of people who do not have enough food to provide adequate nutrition for their families. After adjustment for differences in local prices (the PPP calculation), those under the poverty line are unable to achieve an adequate caloric intake even when they spend half their income on food. Thus, those households falling between the Chinese official poverty line and the World Bank poverty line likely suffer from chronic malnutrition. Furthermore, the vulnerability of low-income households has increased substantially over the reform period, as greater economic insecurity and reduced access to health care have made the position of the poor more precarious.

However, Ravallion and Chen's recalculations do not detract from the Chinese record in poverty reduction; rather, according to their standard, the total number of poor people is larger in all periods, and the number escaping from poverty is also larger. According to Ravallion and Chen's data, a large majority of Chinese farmers were below the $1 per day poverty standard in the early 1980s, and more than 400 million Chinese rural residents graduated from poverty, double the 220 million the Chinese claim officially.[1] Ravallion and Chen's calculations are most accurate for the most recent periods, though, and they enable us to track the progress of poverty alleviation more closely. They show clearly that after the mid–1980s poverty alleviation stalled and that the proportion in poverty actually increased through 1991. During the 1993–1996 period there was again dramatic progress. Since 1996 poverty alleviation has been much slower, and progress more limited. The Chinese official data, by contrast, show a suspiciously smooth process of poverty reduction, and the specific subperiods do not emerge clearly from the data.

9.2.1.3   Explaining Poverty Trends

What economic causes explain these patterns with respect to rural poverty alleviation? The spectacular decline in rural poverty in the early 1980s reflected the dramatic coming together of a number of one-time factors. The terms of trade of agriculture improved dramatically, as ultralow procurement prices that had discriminated severely against farmers were raised, the supply of modern inputs to farmers increased dramatically, and the dissolution of collectives allowed farmers to work harder and allocate inputs into agriculture more efficiently. Land was initially distributed to households on a highly

---

1. In fact, Ravallion and Chen overestimate Chinese poverty in the late 1970s because they use the official price deflators, which, as discussed previously, are inadequate for rural areas before 1985. Even the official Chinese poverty measure implicitly rejects the official deflators. The official poverty measure for 1978 could have been calculated in a logically consistent manner by adjusting today's poverty line downward by the intervening inflation rate (this is what Ravallion and Chen do). However, that adjustment would lead them to conclude that the poverty line in 1978 was 180 RMB per year. (Because the official deflators say there was not much inflation, it would only be necessary to reduce the poverty threshold a modest amount.) But that approach would lead to the calculation of a huge volume of poverty in 1978, nearly universal poverty. However, these statisticians experienced the Chinese countryside in 1978, and they recall that not everyone was impoverished, and that 180 RMB was in fact easily enough for an adequate consumption standard. Instead, they use an ad hoc but reasonable poverty line of 100 RMB per person in 1978. This results in a much smaller calculation of total poverty in 1978, and therefore smaller total numbers of those emerging from poverty in the early 1980s.

egalitarian basis, and virtually everyone got a share. Periodic redistribution of land in many areas of China means that there is a floor for intravillage poverty, and there are few landless laborers. Moreover, because poverty had been so pervasive in the prereform countryside, general economic growth was quite efficient in reducing poverty. The huge reduction in poverty in this initial period serves as an indirect measure of the extent of policy-created poverty under the previous economic policy regime. Most of these factors were exhausted by the mid–1980s, and the speed with which poverty was reduced slowed.

After the mid–1980s poverty alleviation became much more difficult. The Chinese government recognized the problem and set up a special Leading Group for Poverty Reduction in 1986, directly under the State Council. The main achievement of this Leading Group was to designate a total of 328 impoverished counties that were eligible for special assistance. (The number of designated counties was increased to 592, or about 20% of all counties, in 1993.) Geographic targeting of designated poor counties has been the focus of China's antipoverty strategy ever since. Appraisals of this program are mixed. Government funding was initially generous, but then stagnated until the late 1990s. Targeting is not particularly precise, because many of the residents of poor counties are not poor and there are significant numbers of poor people outside poor counties. Nevertheless, rigorous evaluation indicates that the designation does raise economic growth in poor counties by around 1% annually (Park, Wang, and Wu 2002). Inflation in the late 1980s eroded the agricultural terms of trade and reduced access to market goods by the poor. A second dramatic reduction in poverty came during the 1993–1996 period. Again, broad economic forces coincided to produce a significant impact on rural poverty. Agricultural terms of trade improved again, as marketization of rural procurement surged ahead and government began to provide support prices for farmers. Most important, nonfarm rural employment and migration surged during this period, opening up many new opportunities.

Why then has poverty reduction been relatively slow since 1996? Particularly in the late 1990s, growth was highly concentrated in urban coastal areas. As a result, remote areas, particularly those having few resources and suffering from environmental degradation, have been little affected by growth. China's poor counties are especially common in a belt around the Aihui–Tengchong line (see Chapter 1), where dense population runs up against the limit of environmental sustainability. Market forces have so far frustrated the Chinese government's effort to raise farm prices and thus improve the terms of trade of agriculture. In fact, farm prices fell in the late 1990s in the wake of market liberalization. Urban reforms reduced the overmanning of urban enterprises, creating urban unemployment and increasing labor-market competition, thereby restricting the opportunities for impoverished rural households to send migrants to new jobs. Overall, China's fiscal system does a poor job of providing fiscal resources to poor regions (see Chapter 18), so government funds are not redistributed in a progressive pattern and are inadequate to improve living conditions of the rural poor. Continuing restrictions on migration limit the "way out" for residents of persistent-poverty locales. Since 2000 the Chinese government has devoted substantial resources to broader geographic development initiatives, particularly the Western Development Program. Those initiatives are multistranded: most of their funding goes to support expanded infrastructure investment, which may help poor people in the long run but does little in the short run. However, the program does increase fiscal resources in poor western regions and helps many poor villages afford schoolteachers and social services. Overall, powerful economic forces limit the "trickle-down" impact of economic growth, and government policies have limited effectiveness in helping the poor.

9.2.2   Urban Poverty

Unlike most of the developing world, poverty in China has been largely a rural phenomenon. In the past, policy kept urban population low by restricting immigration, and then guaranteed everyone a public sector job (see Chapters 5 and 8). Since China's opening, most economic growth has occurred in the cities. Traditionally, urban inhabitants enjoyed stable social welfare conditions and extensive government subsidies of basic needs. Today, while this cushion of assured benefits is eroding, there are still very few permanent urban residents (those with urban residence permits) with incomes below the poverty line. Ravallion and Chen find that in 2002 the cost of living in the city was 41% higher than in the countryside; based on this calculation they adopt a poverty line of 1,200 yuan per person per year in the city. Even with this higher threshold, they find that only 0.5% of the urban population was in poverty in 2001. While cities are becoming less equal and unemployment and disability can result in serious economic hardship, very few permanent urban residents are in absolute poverty. However, it should be remembered that this finding reflects their sample, which covered permanent urban residents only; migrants are not included. We will return to discuss this problem in a following section.

9.2.3   Overall Poverty

Using separate urban and rural poverty lines, and combining the two samples, Ravallion and Chen find that 8% of China's total population was in poverty in 2001, down from 22% in 1991. The decline was mainly due to the decline in rural poverty, which accounted for almost 11 percentage points of the total 14% decline. About 3% was due to urbanization, and less than 0.5% to the reduction in poverty in urban areas.

9.3 INEQUALITY

Under the socialist economy Chinese society was dualistic but egalitarian. That is, although the gap between urban and rural residents was large (society was "dualistic"), incomes were fairly equal within each of the urban and rural sectors ("egalitarian"). At first, rural reforms in the late 1970s and early 1980s narrowed the urban–rural gap. The result was that China became less dualistic at a time when it was still highly egalitarian in both its urban and rural sectors. As a consequence, around 1983–1984, China was probably the most equal that it has ever been, even more equal than under socialism.

Economists often use the Gini coefficient as a summary measure of income distribution. The Gini coefficient ranges in value between 0 and 1. A Gini coefficient of zero would signify that income was perfectly equally distributed, while a Gini coefficient of one would indicate that all income was concentrated in the hands of a single individual. In the real world, low values of Gini coefficients are observed for the relatively equal economies of Sweden, 0.25, Japan, 0.25 and Germany, 0.28. High values are recorded for economies with high inequality such as Brazil, 0.59, or Mexico, 0.55 (UNDP 2005, 270–272). As Figure 9.2 shows, China's overall Gini coefficient in 1983, measured on income, was 0.28, which made China one of the most equal countries in the world. China's urban society was especially equal, with an intraurban Gini of only 0.166.

It is worth emphasizing how unusual it was that China at that time had a low Gini coefficient. Generally speaking, big countries have higher Gini coefficients (since they contain a greater diversity of natural endowments), and China is certainly big. Moreover, lower- and middle-income economies typically have higher Gini coefficients than developed, high income countries, and China was certainly a lower-income economy in 1983. Comparable levels of equality are seen in the small former socialist states, but most of those are very small and have much higher income than China in 1983. For a big, developing country, China had an exceptionally equal society. The figure for urban China was especially unusual, since in most developing countries cities are more unequal than the countryside.

Since the early 1980s, though, inequality in China has increased steadily and inexorably. As Figure 9.2 shows, inequality has climbed steadily within both

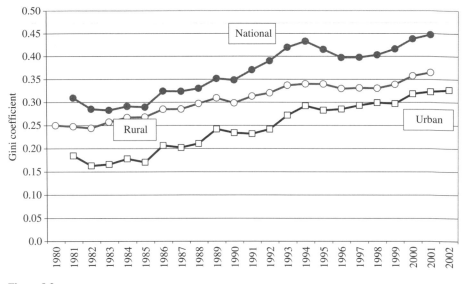

Figure 9.2
Evolution of Gini coefficient

rural and urban areas. Total national inequality is higher than either rural or urban inequality in every year because the urban-rural gap is large. Moreover, total inequality has increased even more than urban or rural inequality, because the urban-rural gap has increased since 1983. By 2001, China's overall Gini coefficient had increased to 0.447. China's increase in inequality is unprecedented. China is now more unequal than the average middle-income country, and about as unequal as the average low-income country. China does not yet approach the extreme inequality typical of the large Latin American economies, but China is now significantly more unequal than most Asian developing countries. For example, India's Gini is 0.325; Indonesia's is 0.34; and Korea, at significantly higher levels of income, is 0.32. China is now similar to the most unequal Asian developing countries, such as Thailand, 0.43, or the Philippines, 0.46. Current Chinese levels of inequality, as measured by the Gini coefficient, are near the middle of the range of developing economies, if assessed in light of China's size and geographical diversity. But this is a dramatic change from China's past record, and there may be no other case where a society's income distribution has deteriorated so much, so fast. As a side note, China's Gini coefficient has surpassed that of the United States, which has also been rising and which equaled 0.408 in 2000. Thus in the course of two decades China has gone from being one of the most egalitarian societies, about as equal as Japan, to being more unequal than the United States.

What economic causes lay behind this dramatic change in income distribution in China? Many factors contribute. The most important single factor in Chinese inequality is the urban–rural gap. As we saw in Chapter 5, socialist institutions reinforced the urban–rural divide and in this respect contributed to inequality. Market reforms at first shrank this gap because they benefited rural residents first. But ultimately market reforms contributed to inequality because they led to the acceleration of urban economic growth. It is sometimes argued that the economic development process inevitably leads to a medium-term increase in inequality. Simon Kuznets (1955), a pioneering scholar of economic development, argued that inequality would increase during the initial stage of development but decrease in subsequent stages. Kuznets' logic was that pockets of modern economic growth would first generate high incomes in a few limited areas while income remained low in most of the traditional economy, but that later growth would ripple out to most of the economy. The first phase of this prediction certainly seems to be true in China, amplified by three factors: China's huge size and geographic diversity, which limits spillovers; the catalytic role played by foreign trade and investment, which naturally concentrates in coastal cities; and the legacy of socialist institutions. The result has been increased inequality as high incomes are concentrated in fast-growing coastal cities.

Inequality has also increased within each of the urban and rural sectors. In the urban economy returns to various kinds of capital have increased dramatically. Before reform, nobody possessed any income-generating capital, so equality was high. After reform, urban residents have increasingly been differentiated between those who possess the capital, skills, and opportunities to benefit from the new economy and those who do not possess the requisite capital and skills. Returns to human capital, as discussed in Chapter 8, have increased substantially, and human capital is relatively unequally distributed. Moreover, some urban residents have been stuck in declining segments of the economy and have experienced reductions in income. The ability of well positioned individuals to take advantage of opportunities generated by market distortions, including corruption and privileged access to opportunities, must also contribute to urban inequality. Within rural areas, the most disequalizing part of income has been the wage and profit opportunities created by TVEs and by individual entrepreneurship. These new income sources have been highly concentrated in suburban areas (Chapter 10) and thus made the overall countryside more unequal.

Will Chinese society continue to become more unequal? Or will market forces begin to reduce inequality as growth spreads and distortions and barriers are reduced? Will the development process ultimately lead to a reduction of the urban–rural gap, as the countryside is transformed by technological change and out-migration? Will political and legal reforms make China more fair and more predictable and, by reducing special privileges, ultimately make China more equal? These trends have the potential to halt, or even to reverse, the hitherto inexorable increase in the Gini coefficient. If reinforced by a reorientation of government social policy, broad development trends could lead to a more equal Chinese society.

9.3.1   Accounting for All Income Sources

The discussion of income inequality in the preceding section still suffers from some important limitations. Urban dwellers receive additional income as benefits or subsidized services that are not well captured by the existing measures of (mostly cash) income. Rural residents also receive noncash income, but the forms of this income are completely different from those in urban areas, and both were different under the planned economy than we would expect in a market economy. An ambitious collaboration between academics and the Chinese Academy of Social Sciences and National Statistical Bureau has made an effort, over many years, to account more broadly for all important sources of income for urban and rural residents. This international team carried out a series of supplemental surveys, in conjunction with the normal household survey, in three benchmark years—1988, 1995, and 2002—in a large and fairly representative subsample of China's provinces. The results from this important analysis show China moving along a rather different transition path. Remarkably, however, the end point is completely consistent with that produced by the other methodology. This method produces a Gini coefficient of 0.45 in 2002, which is identical to the Gini calculated by Chen and Ravallion for 2001 (Khan et al. 1993; Khan and Riskin 1998, 2005).

In the analysis of Khan and Riskin (KR), China started out in the 1980s considerably less egalitarian than portrayed by the conventional statistics, primarily because urban dwellers received substantial benefits. Complete accounting for urban incomes raised them by 55%. Urban dwellers enjoyed large subsidy income, especially for the implicit value of ration coupons that were provided them free of charge. They also benefited from significant housing subsidies, since most paid extremely low rents while living in work-unit-supplied housing. Surprisingly, though, a complete accounting of rural incomes raised them, too, by almost 40%, mostly because of the imputed value of owner-occupied housing, as well as because of the re-evaluation of homegrown food at market prices (instead of procurement prices). KR computed an overall national Gini coefficient of 0.38 in 1988, significantly above the Chen and Ravallion (CR) estimate of 0.33.

Subsequently, however, KR's national Gini climbed less quickly than CR's Gini through 1995, and then leveled off while the CR Gini continue to climb. By 2002 the two calculations were identical. What accounts for this difference in trends? The difference is that KR found that most hidden urban subsidies had by 1995 either been eliminated or converted into explicit form. Ration coupons had been abolished, and subsidized housing had been privatized. By 2002 urban comprehensive income was now just 29% higher than money income, while the estimate for rural households was that comprehensive income was now 33% above money income. Since the difference between urban and rural is practically unchanged by the inclusion of noncash income, KR's method of calculation now yields a result very similar to CR's most standard computation. The two methods end up with very similar pictures of China's condition as of 2002.

KR's analysis is extremely useful. It is true that in most countries imputed income from owner-occupied housing, for example, is not included in calculations of income distribution. CR's results are perhaps more appropriate to use in cross-national comparisons. However, KR's results give us a better sense of the overall evolution of all the different components of income. KR's results provide grounds for a slightly more optimistic portrayal of Chinese income distribution, in which inequality may have reached a peak in the mid–1990s and leveled off since (though this would need much more corroboration before it could be widely accepted). Moreover, KR remind us that accounting for income growth in China is tricky because such a large part of comprehensive income was once received as subsidies, in noncash form, especially in cities. Failing to account for these subsidies causes us to overstate the growth of income.

9.4   PHYSICAL QUALITY OF LIFE INDICATORS

Given some of the complexities with the income data discussed in this chapter, it is worthwhile to look at other indicators of living standards, in particular those that directly reflect the health, physical security, and well-being of the population. So-called physical quality of life indicators (PQLI) provide another look at living standards and a way to compare China with other countries. Economic growth, particularly in the early stages of development, is strongly correlated with improvement in PQLI. Moreover, PQLI arguably provide a more direct measure of improvements in the quality of life.

9.4.1   Life Expectancy at Birth

Of the various constituents of PQLI, perhaps the most important is life expectancy at birth. Life expectancy summarizes the impact of health and nutrition on the human organism. Life expectancy provides information about the net impact of environmental hazards (usually by-products of an industrializing society) compared with other kinds of health hazards more characteristic of underdevelopment.[2] China's life expectancy is relatively high. According to the United Nations, life expectancy in 2002 was 70.9 years, a level that puts China right in the middle of middle-income countries. It is about the same as Latin America as a whole, which has a much higher income per capita, but less than developed countries where life expectancy averages 78 (UNDP 2005; Banister and Hill 2004). As in developed countries, life expectancy is higher for women (73 years) than for men (69). Life expectancy has continued to increase during the reform period, inching steadily upward from an average 67.8 in 1980 to 68.5 in 1990. During that period life expectancy increased more for women than for men (by about 2 years).

The steady improvement in life expectancy is encouraging because during the period of rapid economic growth over the past 20 years there has been an erosion of institutions supporting health, nutrition of the poorest, and the social role of women. The life-expectancy statistics indicate that, on balance, the positive impact of economic growth has been larger than the negative effect of eroding social security institutions. Nonetheless, improvement of life expectancy has been much less rapid than income growth. Life spans have grown virtually everywhere in the world—except in the countries affected most severely by AIDS—and China's performance is not exceptional. Indeed, 25 years ago China had unusually impressive life expectancy data compared to its low income. More recently income "caught up" with life expectancy, and China now looks more like a normal country, albeit one that still has a relatively good life expectancy.

9.4.2   Other Health-Related Indicators

Closely related to life expectancy are other health-related indicators. Infant mortality (death of child during first year of life) is low in China, at 30 per 1,000 in 2003. That figure equals the middle-income-country average, about the same as Brazil, but not as good as Mexico's 23. China's infant

---

2. Moreover, in the calculation of an *average* life expectancy, each individual counts equally as a single unit. When we track changes in income, using them as a proxy for changes in well-being, the welfare of high-income individuals is implicitly being counted more than that of low-income individuals.

mortality rate may also be understated by the omission of some birth reports. However, the percentage of infants with low birthweight is reported as only 6%, which would be near developed-country levels and which supports the picture of a relatively healthy birth environment. Also important are changes in the nature of mortality. In the early stages of development, infectious diseases take a heavy toll on children and adults alike, and account for the majority of deaths. However, these sources of mortality can be *relatively* easily reduced by moderate investments in sanitation and preventive health care. China has already passed this initial hurdle: 85% of children are immunized against the main childhood diseases. Today China faces challenges relating to the "second health revolution." The primary causes of death are similar to those in developed countries. The most important are heart disease, cancer, and lung diseases. These are not simple communicable diseases, but are instead often chronic diseases related to population aging and lifestyle issues. Environmental pollution plays a role, as does cigarette smoking. Sexually transmitted diseases, including AIDS, have emerged as significant health-care problems. Obesity, once virtually unheard of, has been an unwelcome companion of higher incomes.

9.4.3 Education

Another important PQLI is education. Literacy rates in China are quite high, calculated at 91% of the adult population in 2003. This figure is slightly above the middle-income-country average of 90% and compares favorably with Brazil's 88%. Rates of illiteracy are significantly related to age: while 12% is the average rate of illiteracy, more than 70% of those over age 68 are illiterate, while only 5% of those 21–25 years old are illiterate. Even at these rates, there are 145 million illiterate adults in China. As discussed in Chapter 8, progress in raising literacy rates in China came early. For three decades under the socialist system, China followed a development strategy that included substantial attention to so-called "basic needs." Stress was placed on provision of basic health and education services to the population. That legacy remains, even though recent progress has not been particularly impressive. Literacy and basic education are widespread in the population.

9.4.4 Human Development Index

One important effort to summarize a large number of PQLI indicators is represented by the Human Development Index (HDI) of the United Nations Development Program (UNDP). The HDI has been computed for a large number of countries; it is the simple average of indices for life expectancy, literacy and school enrollment, and price-adjusted PPP GDP per capita. The UNDP has also sponsored a series of *China Human Development Reports*, and the 2005 report is especially good (UNDP and China Development Research Foundation 2005). The report gives the HDI for each of China's provinces, which provides a convenient way to compare China's provinces, with each other and also with other developing countries. What emerges first from this exercise is that there is significant variation among China's provinces (Table 9.2). The most well-off province is the municipality of Shanghai, while the least well-off is Tibet, with Guizhou the least well-off within the populous eastern half of China. Of course, much of the ranking reflects the urban–rural gap (see Chapter 5) and the relative proportion of urban residents in each province. However, we can see that Shanghai's overall HDI is comparable to Hong

Table 9.2
Comparison of Human Development Index, 2003

Chinese provinces		Nations	
High human development			
		Norway	0.96
Shanghai	0.91	Hong Kong	0.92
Beijing	0.88	Korea	0.90
Tianjin	0.86	Argentina	0.86
Guangdong, Liaoning, Zhejiang, Jiangsu	0.81–0.82	Mexico	0.81
Medium human development			
Heilongjiang, Fujian	0.79	Brazil, Malaysia, Colombia	0.79
Shandong, Hebei, Jilin	0.77–0.78	Thailand	0.78
Hainan, Xinjiang, Hubei, Shanxi,	0.75–0.76	Philippines	0.76
Hunan, Chongqing		**China 2003**	**0.75**
		Turkey	0.75
Henan, Inner Mongolia	0.74		
		China 1999	**0.72**
Jiangxi, Guangxi, Shaanxi,	0.73		
Sichuan, Anhui			
Ningxia	0.71		
		Indonesia, Vietnam	0.70
Qinghai, Gansu	0.68		
		Guatemala, Honduras	0.67
Yunnan	0.66	Egypt	0.66
Guizhou	0.64		
		China 1990	**0.63**
		India	0.60
Tibet	0.59		
		Myanmar	0.58
		China 1980	**0.56**
		Pakistan	0.53
Low human development			

Kong's, Korea's, or Argentina's; and several coastal provinces have, like Mexico, inched into the "high" human development category. There are a number of predominantly rural provinces just below the all-China average with HDI approximately the same as the Philippines or Turkey; while several western provinces, such as Gansu, Yunnan, and Guizhou are below Indonesia and Vietnam, and comparable to Honduras or Egypt. From these comparisons, it is plainly evident that China faces continuing severe developmental challenges. At the same time, China's HDI ranking has improved substantially during the past 23 years, as one would expect in a rapidly growing economy. Today China is just below the middle-income economies of Brazil, Thailand, and Columbia.

9.5 INCOME, GDP PER CAPITA, AND PURCHASING POWER PARITY ONCE AGAIN

How does China compare with other developing countries? At this point it makes sense to return to per capita GDP and the calculation of price-adjusted (PPP) GDP per capita. We have already used PPP methodology to apply an internationally comparable poverty line to China and assess some aspects of structural change in Chapter 6. Moreover, PPP GDP per capita is also one component of the HDI discussed in the previous section. Here we return to examine PPP GDP per capita and ordinary GDP per capita, measured at exchange rates, in a comparative context. Table 9.3 gives some comparisons with respect to GDP and PPP GDP. China's GDP per capita at exchange rates was US$1,274 in 2003. The first six countries shown in Table 9.3 are the large, semi-industrialized economies that were shown in Table 9.2 to have HDI levels similar to China. All of these economies have achieved a level of GDP per capita—evaluated at exchange rates—that is considerably higher than that of China. Brazil and Thailand have twice China's per capita GDP, and Turkey and Malaysia three times.

The distance between China and these large middle-income economies narrows when we compare GDP per capita evaluated at PPP. As discussed in Box 6.1, a PPP calculation is superior for assessing real living standards. Table 9.3 illustrates the general rule that the PPP-calculated income of poor countries is much higher than the exchange-rate (ordinary) calculation of income. This rule holds because services and nontraded goods in poor countries embody a great deal of unskilled labor, which is the abundant (and thus cheap) factor in those countries. As a result, goods and services that do not enter into trade are much cheaper (relative to developed-country prices) than those that

Table 9.3
Gross domestic product per capita, 2003

Country	PPP (current US dollars)	Exchange rate (current US dollars)	Ratio PPP/exchange rate
Malaysia	9,512	4,187	2.3
Mexico	9,168	6,121	1.5
Brazil	7,790	2,788	2.8
Thailand	7,595	2,305	3.3
Turkey	6,772	3,399	2.0
Colombia	6,702	1,764	3.8
China	**5,788**	**1,274**	**4.5**
Philippines	4,321	989	4.4
Guatemala	4,148	2,009	2.1
Indonesia	3,361	970	3.5
India	2,892	564	5.1
Vietnam	2,490	482	5.2

do enter into trade. PPP calculations give full weight to goods and services that do not enter into international trade, while exchange rate-based comparisons are implicitly based on only those goods and services that do enter international trade (and which therefore influence the exchange rate). China follows this general rule: its PPP-adjusted income per capita is much higher than its exchange-rate-calculated income per capita. But for China the difference between the two calculations is even larger than we might have expected. This result is due to the fact that there are a large number of nontraded goods in China that have especially low prices, such as urban housing, health care, and basic food products. These push down the cost of living in China and imply that PPP-adjusted incomes are higher than we would otherwise expect. Table 9.3 shows that comparisons based on PPP calculations can significantly alter the relative position of countries, compared to ordinary exchange rate GDP per capita. In the comparisons, China tends to improve its relative performance. In addition to closing some of the gap with Turkey, Thailand, and Brazil, China trades rank with Guatemala, for example, which has a higher exchange rate GDP per capita than China. However, using PPP does not change the comparison with India, which like China has an especially large multiple of PPP GDP to exchange rate GDP.

9.6 CONCLUSION

No single indicator can tell us how much economic growth in China has contributed to well-being. However, the combination of many indicators allows us to draw a reasonably accurate picture and to place China in the context of other developing countries. China's GDP per capita (at exchange rates) ranks China as an economy just moving from a lower-income to a middle-income country. In fact, measures of well-being in China look considerably better than we would expect from such a characterization. Some part of this adjustment is due to the impact of China's price system and exchange rate: a shift to PPP-evaluated GDP per capita reduces some of the gap between GDP per capita and the other outcomes, such as those captured by the HDI.

Even after the shift to PPP-adjusted GDP per capita, China's performance looks relatively good. China's HDI is similar to middle-income countries—Turkey and Brazil—that have higher PPP GDP levels. Undoubtedly, some of this difference reflects the legacy of China's relatively egalitarian, socialist past. Basic health and education diffused through the countryside 30 years ago have a continuing impact on population well-being today. Trends in inequality over the past 20 years, though, tell us that China will no longer reap benefits from these past policies. Moreover, increased inequality tears at the social fabric in other respects as well. Future improvements in the quality of life will depend on the way in which growth policies are crafted to spread the benefits of growth as widely as possible to the whole society. This is true not only because a more inclusive growth model will spread the ultimate benefits of growth more broadly among the population, but also because a healthier, better fed, and better educated population will better sustain the next phase of future economic growth.

BIBLIOGRAPHY

Suggestions for Further Reading

The 2005 volume of the *China Human Development Report* is excellent, and easily available online (UNDP and China Development Research Foundation 2005). Yao, Zhang, and Hanmer (2004) take the discussion the next step forward.

Sources for Data and Figures

Figure 9.1: *SAC* (2005, 104); Ravallion and Chen (2004).

Figure 9.2: Ravallion and Chen (2004); cf. Bramall (2001).

Table 9.1: *SAC* (2005, 101); *SYC* (2004, 347).

Table 9.2: UNDP and China Development Research Foundation (2005, 154); UNDP (2005, 219–23).

Table 9.3: UNDP (2005, 266–69). Chinese data have been revised upward 15.7% to accord with NSB's revisions of national income accounts. See Chapter 6.

Life expectancy: UNDP, *Human Development Report* (2005, 219–22). Chinese official data (*SYC* 2004, 98) are slightly higher (71.4 years in 2000), but appear to overstate life expectancy because of an undercount of infant mortality. Despite suspicions about Chinese data reporting, recent work indicates that a life expectancy figure above 70 survives most consistency checks, see Banister and Hill (2004).

All Gini coefficients from UNDP (2005, 270–72).

References

Banister, Judith, and Kenneth Hill (2004). "Mortality in China, 1964–2000." *Population Studies*, 58(1), March, 55–75.

Bramall, Chris (2001). "The Quality of China's Household Income Survey." *China Quarterly*, no. 167, 689–705.

Gibson, John, Jikun Huang, and Scott Rozelle (2003). "Improving Estimates of Inequality and Poverty from China's Household Income and Expenditure Survey." *Review of Income and Wealth*, 49(1), March, 53–68.

Khan, Azizur, Keith Griffin, Carl Riskin, and Zhao Renwei (1993). "Sources of Income Inequality in Post-Reform China." *China Economic Review*, 4(1), Spring, 19–36.

Khan, Azizur, and Carl Riskin (1998). "Income and Inequality in China: Composition, Distribution and Growth of Household Income, 1988 to 1995." *China Quarterly*, no. 154, June, 221–53.

Khan, Azizur, and Carl Riskin (2005). "China's Household Income and Its Distribution, 1995 and 2002." *China Quarterly*, no. 182, 356–84.

Kuznets, Simon (1955). "Economic Growth and Income Inequality." *American Economic Review*, 45(1), 1–28.

Park, Albert, and Sangui Wang (2001). "China's Poverty Statistics." *China Economic Review*, 12:384–98.

Park, Albert, Sangui Wang, and Guobao Wu (2002). "Regional Poverty Targeting in China." *Journal of Public Economics*. vol. 86, issue 1 (October), pp. 123–53.

Ravallion, Martin, and Shaohua Chen (1999). "When Economic Reform Is Faster Than Statistical Reform: Measuring and Explaining Income Inequality in Rural China." *Oxford Bulletin of Economics and Statistics*, 61 (February):75–102.

Ravallion, Martin, and Shaohua Chen (2004). "China's (Uneven) Progress Against Poverty." World Bank Policy Research Working Paper 3408, September.

SAC (Annual). *Zhongguo Tongji Zhaiyao* [Statistical Abstract of China]. Beijing: Zhongguo Tongji.

Stockholm Environment Institute in collaboration with United Nations Development Programme (UNDP) China (2002). *China Human Development Report 2002: Making Green Development a Choice*. New York: Oxford University Press.

SYC (Annual). *Zhongguo Tongji Nianjian* [Statistical Yearbook of China]. Beijing: Zhongguo Tongji.

UNDP (2005). *Human Development Report 2005: International Cooperation at a Crossroads*. New York: Oxford University Press. http://hdr.undp.org/reports/global/2005/.

UNDP and China Development Research Foundation (2005). *China Human Development Report 2005*. http://www.undp.org.cn/downloads/nhdr2005/NHDR2005_complete.pdf.

Yao, Shujie, Zongyi Zhang, and Lucia Hanmer (2004). "Growing Inequality and Poverty in China." *China Economic Review*, 15:145–63.

III THE RURAL ECONOMY

The contemporary Chinese countryside, Yangshuo 2005. (Courtesy of Chuck Morrow.)

10 Rural Organization

The village is the fundamental unit of rural society today, as it has been for centuries. However, the Chinese village was swept by two dramatic revolutions during the second half of the twentieth century. The first, during the 1950s, converted every village into an agricultural collective and mobilized hundreds of millions of farmers to build a socialist countryside. The second revolution, just as dramatic and consequential as the first, dissolved the collectives and vaulted much of the countryside into a modernizing and marketizing economy after 1979. Both these revolutions imprinted their features on the Chinese countryside—superimposed on the traditional village—and both left pervasive legacies that shape the Chinese rural environment today.

In this chapter, we examine the dramatic changes in rural organization that have helped make the Chinese countryside what it is today. We examine, in section 10.1, the traditional, organic organization of Chinese rural life. Section 10.2 looks at the rural collectives: the nature and distinctive features of the collectives; the process of organizational change; and their dissolution. Section 10.3 examines the second revolution in the Chinese countryside. It stresses the fact that the impact on agricultural production has been unambiguously positive, but the impact on other aspects of rural life has been much more mixed. The failure to find an alternative to some of the social functions of the collectives presents China with ongoing challenges. Section 10.4 examines the emergence of rural land markets. Although factor markets developed very slowly in the wake of the dissolution of collectives, they are emerging strongly in the decade of the 2000s.

10.1 THE CHINESE VILLAGE

Nearly every Chinese farmer lives in a village, which has been the dominant form of rural organization for as long as records exist. By one count there are

3.8 million villages and hamlets in China. In the developed areas around large cities, especially along the coast, what were originally separate villages now merge into a dense landscape of suburban industrialization and urban sprawl. In remote areas, village size dwindles, settlements may consist of only five or six houses, and there are a few areas where farmers live in individual farmsteads. Especially in the south, some villages, known as single-lineage villages, are composed entirely of households with the same surname. The national government promotes the idea of the administrative village, which should have a "village committee" to serve as a rudimentary institution of self-governance and to carry on some of the functions of the agricultural collectives that were dismantled in the early 1980s. At year-end 2004 there were 632,000 of these administrative villages. Administrative villages may incorporate several natural villages or hamlets, and there are also villages where no village committees function.

Villages vary enormously in their level of modernization and connection to the outside world (Ministry of Agriculture 2004, 5, 275–76). In the most prosperous areas, houses of reinforced concrete, usually two stories high, have become the norm over the past decade. In most areas, houses are predominantly wood and brick, and about a quarter of rural housing is still built of clay or rammed earth. The countryside is being connected rapidly to modern communications networks. As of 2003, 619,000 villages had a telephone, double the number of 10 years earlier, and motor vehicle access was available to 642,000. However, outside the prosperous coastal deltas, most villages have little modern infrastructure. Only 349,000 villages had running water in 2003. About 20% of rural households have access to improved household cooking facilities (gas or electric stoves). The remaining 80% cook either with coal or with straw or twigs gathered from the fields or forests. Interiors are dark and smoky, and indoor air is polluted. Chinese farmers continue to rely on traditional technologies for many aspects of life and work, even though every part of rural China has been affected, and is being more deeply affected, by the impact of modern technologies and the modernizing Chinese state.

The dominant activity in nearly all villages is farming. When villagers need to carry out other tasks, they generally go to a nearby "market town," which hosts a regular periodic rural market. Once or twice a week, or perhaps every 10 days, farmers come from surrounding villages to sell produce, buy and sell livestock, and purchase other producer or consumer goods. The market town is the most likely place in which a teahouse, retail shop, or credit organization would set up operation. In an influential article, Skinner (1964–1965) suggested that we interpret the entire Chinese countryside as being loosely organized into "standard market areas." Each standard market area consists of a market town and the surrounding villages from which that town is easily accessible within a day's walk. The market town is the primary locus of interaction between the villager and the larger economic and cultural worlds. The standard market area thus roughly corresponds to the boundaries of the world that an average villager would experience on a regular basis. Occasional trips to larger towns or cities notwithstanding, virtually all the individuals with whom the villager has regular face-to-face contact would be within the standard market area. A traditional hierarchy of places exists, organized by primarily economic forces into households, villages, market towns, and higher-order urban settlements. This hierarchy of places (and economic functions) has existed for hundreds of years, and it exists today as well.

10.2 AGRICULTURAL COLLECTIVES

After 1949 the government of the People's Republic gradually superimposed a new organizational structure on the traditional base. The socialist organizations did not do away with the traditional rural organizations, but the existing institutions were forced into new molds and given new functions by the Chinese state. The most fundamental change was the organization of farmers into collectives, which took over responsibility for agricultural production from individual households. From the mid–1950s to the early 1980s, the collectives were the dominant rural institution. The state adopted an intrusive and transformative approach to rural institutions. The collectives were disbanded in the early 1980s, and the Chinese government has since then been less aggressive in imposing a specific organizational form on the countryside. However, institutional experimentation continues, as the Chinese government tries to reinvent and restructure rural institutions.

During the heyday of the socialist economy, planners used socialist rural institutions to procure a steady supply of agricultural produce at a low relative price. The entire socialist development strategy was predicated on the state's ability to mobilize resources for industrial investment. In order for the state to control those resources, it had to be able to extract resources from the countryside. The state imposed a direct agricultural tax on cropland, but much more important was the implicit tax the state imposed in the form of compulsory delivery of agricultural produce, especially grain, at low, state-set prices. In the early 1950s the state had already established systems of compulsory sales of grain and cotton, the two most important marketed crops. The rural collectives that developed subsequently were designed to smooth the extraction of agricultural surpluses from the countryside.

At the same time, the entire Chinese leadership, from Mao Zedong down, was committed to using rural organizations to transform the nature of rural life. Mao famously said that Chinese peasants were "poor and blank," meaning that they could be remade into exemplary socialist citizens. Rural collectives were seen as a cheap and effective way to remake the countryside, while providing new social services and improved production inputs. Thus the rural institutions created by collectivization were multifunctional. Their primary role was always to organize agricultural production, but collectives were also organizations for the delivery of services and goods that had previously not been available in the Chinese countryside, as well as the organizational starting point for new kinds of activity. In addition, they were inevitably instruments for the extension of state political control into the countryside. After 1970 the government started birth-limitation policies and extended some control over reproductive behavior as well. Collectives helped the government maintain tabs on rural residents and provided a convenient conduit for economic and political innovations that the government was promoting in the countryside.

10.2.1   Features of the Agricultural Collectives

Despite the transformative role of the collectives, their primary function was agricultural production. There were three basic definitional characteristics of the collectives:

1. The land was pooled and worked in common. Collectives differed from farmers' co-ops in other economies because of this basic characteristic: Cooperation was not restricted to marketing or service delivery, but rather included farming itself. Ownership of the land was transferred to "the collective," meaning the residents of a given village. Individual farm households kept ownership of their homes and a few farm animals, and they also retained control of "private plots" (which ranged from 3% to 10% of cultivated area). All other productive assets were owned by the collective.

2. The collective served as the basic accounting unit. The collective itself purchased agricultural inputs (often on credit), coordinated farm tasks, and sold output after the harvest. Each able-bodied worker was assigned a daily job by the collective, and labor was coordinated. With the income derived from sale of the harvest, the collective paid off debts incurred to buy inputs and set aside money in a number of collectively controlled funds. Only after these costs were paid and set-asides were deducted did the collective calculate the net income that was available to be distributed to households. Households received income both in kind (primarily as food grain) and in cash. The most important collective funds that were set aside were the accumulation (or investment) fund and the public welfare fund.

The size of this basic accounting unit fluctuated over time, as the collectives were gradually adapted to the traditional social structures of the Chinese countryside. The earliest accounting unit was the agricultural producers cooperative (APC), which was about the size of a large village, on average. During the GLF, in 1958, the size of the accounting unit jumped as many APCs were merged into a single giant commune, which often had 5,000 or more households (Table 10.1). This huge and unwieldy organization helped lead the countryside to disaster, and in the immediate wake of the GLF three important changes were made. First, the commune itself was made smaller so that it typically corresponded with a market town and a standard marketing area. Second, the accounting unit was dropped all the way back down to a smaller group than even the old APCs had been. This was the "team," a relatively small group of about 30–40 households that corresponded to a small village or hamlet, or to a neighborhood of a larger village. The team became the primary accounting unit between 1962 and 1981. Finally, the whole structure was organized into a three-level hierarchy, consisting of commune, brigade (large village), and team. The commune and the brigade managed most nonagricultural activity, including industrial development and governmental functions such as health and welfare, education, and public safety. This basic configuration lasted until the early 1980s.

3. Net income was distributed to households on the basis of work points. Individuals earned "work points" that were entered into ledgers over the course of the year as the work was done. At the end of the year, after the harvest was

Table 10.1
Changes in the organization of agriculture

Natural units	1956–1958	1958–1959	1962–1981	1982–present
Standard marketing area—market town		Commune* (over 5,000 households)	Commune (2,000 households)	Township (3,000 households) government and economic corporation
Large village	Agricultural producers Cooperative* (100–250 households)		Brigade (200 households)	Village
Small village or neighborhood	Team		Team* (c. 30 households)	
Household	Household	Household	Household	Household*

*Basic accounting unit.

in, the total net income of the collective was computed and divided by the total number of work points earned during the year. Only then did the collective members learn the value of a work point. In 1978, according to household surveys, average distributed collective income amounted to 88.5 yuan per person (a little over $50 at the prevailing exchange rate). However, most of this was received in the form of distributed grain; only 25.5 RMB ($15), less than a third of the total, was in cash. Besides collective distributed income, households also earned income from their private plots. In 1978 private activity generated 36 RMB (mostly in cash), primarily from the sale of crops and animals raised on private plots. In addition, households received an average 9 RMB in mostly cash "other" income, including remittances from relatives. Thus, even under the collectives, households received most of their money income from household activities but relied on the collectives for their supplies of staple foods.

The work-point system gave the collective enormous control over the distribution of income. There was, however, substantial experimentation with different methods of assigning work points, searching for methods that would effectively motivate workers, minimize monitoring costs, and yet be consistent with socialist ideals. During the Cultural Revolution collectives were pressured to use the "*Dazhai* system," under which each worker evaluated his own work contribution in front of village meetings and then invited public comment and criticism. In most places most of the time, though, work points were assigned more routinely for tasks completed or days of labor. Most collectives were too close to subsistence levels and too aware of their economic vulnerability to be willing to indulge in much utopian experimentation. Perhaps more important, the work-point system gave the collective the ability to tax itself to finance various activities that were not directly productive. By assigning work points to the local teacher and paramedic, for example, the collective could ensure that they received a share of the community's income.

10.2.2 Discussion of Collectives

In principle, the collectives could have been market-oriented cooperatives, responding to price and other economic signals. In practice, though, the practical decision-making autonomy of the collectives was severely restricted, in part because government leaders could not resist the temptation to use the collectives to impose their own broad agenda on farmers. Collectives were an attractive instrument for attaining government goals, and government officials could never successfully commit to a hands-off policy. Collectives were used to attain three types of objectives: economic, social, and political.

The primary economic objective, not surprisingly, was organizing agricultural production. In this task it is clear that the collectives failed. The collectives created incentives for farmers to show up for work every morning (otherwise no work points would be received), but it was more difficult to motivate farmers to work hard throughout the day. It was difficult for collectives to coordinate tasks among 40 or 50 households, especially since tasks were spatially separate and had to be expertly timed through the seasons. Long-term, face-to-face relations could ensure that the most important tasks got done in a reasonably effective way, but they could not provide the most efficient forms of work organization. There are no economies of scale in most types of agricultural production in China, so collectives were unable to improve efficiency by organizing larger units.

However, the collectives were able to mobilize resources and so increase the total inputs available for production. In the early years traditional graves that had taken up farmland were plowed under, and scattered fields were consolidated. In this way the collectives augmented the effective land supply. The collectives mobilized and rewarded labor during the agricultural off-season. Construction projects, large and small, were undertaken during the winter. During the 1970s, 100 million workers (30% of the rural labor force) were mobilized for a few weeks of slack-season construction each year, primarily building and repairing irrigation systems. During the 1920s the average farmer had actually worked only 160 days per year, but by the late 1970s the average farmer was working 200 to 275 days per year (Vermeer 1988, 157). A huge effort was invested in China's irrigation system.

Collectives were also a convenient way to organize nonagricultural activities. Productive services were provided by rural credit cooperatives (RCCs) and supply and marketing cooperatives (SMCs), which were nominally independent but integrated into the collective organization in the countryside. The RCCs collected household savings and provided liquidity to agricultural trade. The SMCs supplied most of the modern agricultural inputs that were required as agriculture developed and purchased most of the farmers' marketed surplus. Even more important was the role of collectives in developing rural industries, especially after 1970 (Chapter 12). The social functions of the collectives included the provision of social services—especially education and health—as well as insurance against risk. The work-point system made it extremely convenient for the collective to tax its own members to provide social services. All that was required was a decision to award work points to the local teacher or medic. By the mid–1970s such a system had created a network of rudimentary social services (discussed later in this section). The system paid for 1.2 million rural teachers, for example, and pushed the number of children in schools up to unprecedented levels.

The collectives were also a mechanism to buffer risk. Within a given collective households were less subject to risk, because the collective guaranteed access to land and provided modest welfare payments in the event of extreme need. In 1979 some 15 million households received some kind of relief, either from the state or the collective, although the collective contribution only averaged 3 RMB per household (NBS 1985, 129, 132). Many other households "owed" the collective for staple foods distributed, and many poor collectives were in arrears to the government. A basic safety net had been created.

Finally, the collectives inevitably had political functions as well. The collectives were a channel for education and indoctrination. Collective registration was used to control migration and prevent population movements that were not approved by the government. After 1970 the collective system was used to implement controls on fertility and restrict births in the countryside. Although it was primarily part of the three-level collective structure, the commune functioned part-time as the lowest level of government in the countryside.

The collectives were not an efficient system for organizing agricultural production. However, they were a surprisingly adequate system for organizing much of the rest of rural social and economic life. Particularly after the harsh lessons of the GLF, the rural collective system between about 1962 and 1982 settled down into a reasonably stable configuration. As Table 10.1 showed, the three-level collective system of commune, brigade, and team adapted reasonably well to traditional forms. The commune headquarters was built in the market town, and the commune corresponded roughly to the standard marketing area. The brigade corresponded to the large village. Meanwhile, the team was adapted to a subvillage unit. As such, it was of moderate size, consisting of individuals who knew each other well and interacted on a face-to-face basis. In 1978 the average team had 167 men, women, and children. This basic accounting unit was much smaller than, for example, a Soviet collective farm, and it probably did an adequate job of maintaining farm production. The team specialized in agriculture; most of the nonagricultural functions—both economic and noneconomic—were taken over by the brigade and commune. Thus the three-level collective system also represented a reasonably effective division of labor among organizational forms. It persisted in this form for about 20 years, until the dramatic changes of the early 1980s.

10.2.3   The Agricultural Policy Environment of the Collectives: "Grain First"

In practice, agricultural collectives were rarely, if ever, given sufficient autonomy to respond to market incentives. Collectives were generally forced to
respond to pressures to give priority to grain production. "Grain First" policies were exemplified by the slogan "Take grain as the key link" (*yiliang
weigang*), which characterized policy during most of the collective period, but
especially during the Cultural Revolution. The emphasis on grain production
can be seen as a consequence of the overall development strategy. Strategy
emphasized compulsory procurement of grain from the peasantry at a low
price. The state-set low price of grain, combined with compulsory targets for
delivery of grain, served as an implicit tax, making the peasantry indirectly pay
much of the cost of the industrialization drive. However, precisely because
grain prices were low, peasants had few economic incentives to grow grain for
sale. Once their own subsistence needs were met, peasant households would
have preferred to pursue more lucrative undertakings (economic crops or
household sideline activities) on which the state did not impose such onerous
hidden taxes. But the Chinese government was unwilling to allow such a diversion of peasant energies, at least until their need for grain supplies for the cities
had been met. As a result, the collective system was used to apply extraeconomic pressure on peasant households to meet or exceed their grain-
procurement targets. The effect of this pressure in retarding agricultural
growth was significant, and the costs great (Lardy 1983).

• The emphasis on quantitative targets instead of on prices and markets meant
that peasant households were unable to devise their own maximization strategies, shifting resources among competing alternative uses, particularly when
acreage targets were used to reinforce procurement quotas. The collectives had
little autonomy to decide how much land would be used for various kinds of
crops.

• The emphasis on output quantity meant that many collectives were forced
to maximize grain output even when doing so did not increase income. Areas
that were well suited for grain were pressured to grow more than was consistent with income maximization. For example, in the rich Yangtze Delta collectives were forced to grow three crops of rice per year, employing more and
more labor-intensive production strategies, transplanting seedlings, and
increasing fertilizer and irrigation inputs. The additional inputs cost more than
the value of the additional grain produced (Wiens 1982).

• Grain First policies stressed grain self-sufficiency everywhere, especially
during the Cultural Revolution. Areas that were not well suited to grain were

pressured to grow grain anyway. The result was a loss of opportunities for regional specialization and a decline in interregional shipments of grain.

Grain First policies implemented through the collectives did succeed in increasing grain output, but often at the expense of other products. Total grain output grew at 2.2% annually between 1955–1957 and 1977–1979 (averaging over three years to reduce the impact of weather). That increase was slightly faster than population growth, so output per capita increased 0.2% per year. Grain availability increased somewhat more because grain imports began after the GLF, lowering the procurement burden on China's peasants and allowing them to retain and consume more grain. However, growth of cotton and oilseed output—the two most important crops after grain—was considerably slower. Cotton output grew 1.5%, and oilseed output only 0.5% annually over this period, both less than population growth. Per capita production of oilseeds was 28% lower in 1977–1979 than in 1955–1957. Rural household per capita consumption of poultry, eggs, and fish also declined, although higher meat consumption may have compensated.

A paradoxical result of the Grain First policy was that a uniform national policy led to a wide range of local outcomes. Some regions did well, particularly if they fell into the group well suited for grain production that were designated "high and stable yield areas." These areas accounted for a large share of grain procurements, and they received priority access to modern inputs such as fertilizer, machinery, and electricity. These areas were able to reap the benefits of the agricultural "green revolution" (discussed in Chapter 11) and experienced substantially improved living standards. Other areas, which did not have a comparative advantage in grain production, were forced to strive for grain self-sufficiency. By the time they produced enough to be self-sufficient, little or no land was left over for other crops, so they grew only grain. Regions that initially had a comparative advantage in grain production, in contrast, were able to expand production with green revolution techniques and then divert some of their land to cash crops to raise incomes. These effects sometimes produced perverse "reverse specialization" under which localities were growing more of the crops in which they had the least comparative advantage.

10.3   THE SECOND REVOLUTION IN THE COUNTRYSIDE: RURAL REFORMS, 1979–1984

After 1978 the relaxation of policy in the countryside led to explosive changes, described in Chapter 4. The Third Plenum in December 1978 made relatively modest adjustments in rural policy that touched off major changes in rural society. Indeed, only two new policies were adopted at first: (1) an across-the-board increase in agricultural procurement prices and (2) a reaffirmation of the right to self-management of collectives. Individual farming was explicitly condemned. With higher grain-procurement prices, it became less necessary to coerce grain surpluses out of the peasantry with extraeconomic means. Policy-makers gradually reduced their emphasis on the Grain First policy, even stepping up grain imports for a few years in order to allow new patterns of specialization to emerge in the countryside. With higher prices and less extraeconomic compulsion, decision-making autonomy for the collectives came closer to being a reality.

An unanticipated consequence of the expanded autonomy of collectives soon emerged, however. In some areas, collectives began experimenting with more radical reforms in the way that work points were allocated. Instead of allocating work points for inputs (for labor days, reputation, or effort), some collectives began allocating work points for output, linking the remuneration of a given work group or household to the output of a specific plot of land. Some went even further and simply contracted pieces of collective land to individual households to cultivate. Such experiments clearly tested the limits of the collective system as it had been practiced up to that time. During 1978 and 1979 peasant experiments with individual household agriculture were tolerated and protected in the provinces of Sichuan and Anhui. These were provinces that had suffered greatly during the GLF, and by the late 1970s they were governed by close associates of Deng Xiaoping—Zhao Ziyang and Wan Li, respectively. After successful experiments, the provincial leader Zhao Ziyang was promoted to national premier and, not surprisingly, expanded the boundaries of permissible local policy and experimentation. The most radical policies were initially limited to relatively poor and remote areas, and grain-surplus areas were kept on a tight leash to stabilize all-important government procurements. As success emerged in poor areas, the scope of permissive policies was steadily increased.

By 1981–1982 a nationally defined program of contracting land to households, known as "household contracting" or the "household responsibility system" emerged as the clearly preferred organizational system. By the end of 1982 more than 90% of China's agricultural households had returned to some form of household farming. Initially land was contracted to households for one year, or even for a single harvest cycle. Quickly, however, it was seen that contracts should be longer to be most effective, and most collectives moved to 3-year contracts. These were soon succeeded by 5, 15, and then, in many areas, 50-year contracts to the land. What happened next was quite dramatic.

10.3.1 Production Surges in the Wake of Rural Organizational Change

The growth of grain production accelerated dramatically. This increase was particularly striking, since the stress on grain had been relaxed in order to give households some slack to find a more efficient mix of output. Despite the reduced emphasis, grain output growth between 1977–1979 and 1983–1985 jumped to 4.1% annually, from the previous 2.2%. From previous peaks of just over 300 million tons per year, the annual harvest surged to the tremendous bumper harvest in 1984 of 407 million tons. For the first time in years there was enough grain to go around, and China was even a net grain exporter in 1985 for the first time since the GLF.

The acceleration of grain output growth was the key, given the centrality of grain to the Chinese diet at this time. Nevertheless, output growth was actually greater in virtually every other sector of agriculture. Cotton and oilseed production grew at 15% and 16% per year, respectively. Meat production surged, growing at just below 10% per year. Still more remarkably, these gains occurred in the context of a shift toward a less labor-intensive agriculture. Left to themselves, farm households showed that they valued their labor time more highly than collective planners had. With greater freedom to allocate labor, farmers worked harder, but shorter hours, and shifted cultivation toward crops with lower labor requirements, even though those sometimes had lower value per unit of land. Sorghum, millet, and sugar beets all showed large increases in relative share: these are all slow-growing, relatively low-value crops that require modest labor inputs. Labor inputs to the main staple crops declined as well, after having increased steadily for 20 years under the collectives (Table 10.2). Moreover, as discussed in the chapters on structural change and TVEs, substantial labor was freed to move into nonagricultural activities. Rural reforms had shown that it was possible to produce more with less input, once the incentive and policy environment was set right.

Rural change was rapid because the household responsibility system was adopted quickly. But other aspects of the rural system changed more slowly. The state continued to procure most of the grain crop. There was a movement

Table 10.2
Labor days per hectare

Crop	1953	1978	1985
Rice	250	421	328
Cotton	300	908	643
Wheat	120	461	218

toward use of multitier prices, with the state paying a near-market-price premium for procurements above the minimum compulsory quota. Meanwhile, free markets grew outside the state apparatus. Gradually, government marketing restrictions were eliminated in most crops and sideline products. But the government maintained systematic control over key elements of the marketing system, particularly over cotton, staple grains, and fertilizer, well into the 1990s. In fact, it was not until 2000 that the government finally freed up the price of cotton and allowed textile mills to purchase cotton directly from farmers. While property rights concerning land changed rapidly by the early 1980s, the market system for agricultural output only developed gradually over more than two decades.

10.3.2   The Side Effect of Reform: Rural Public Services Decline

A side effect of successful reform has been reduced efficacy of rural institutions in providing nonagricultural outputs. The success of reforms in agricultural production demonstrated conclusively that rural collectives were less efficient in agriculture than household farms. But in the provision of social services, the collapse of collectives left a void in the countryside. Rural collectives were important in health care and education, and after their elimination the supply of both declined. Here we concentrate on the rural health care system, but the process was similar, though less dire, with respect to primary education.

The rural collectives were key components in the creation of an impressive system of base-level health care delivery in rural areas. The successes in improving life expectancy and basic health conditions, described in Chapter 9, were made possible by an unprecedented system of organizations that provided basic health services to most of China's villages. The level of care provided was, of course, primitive, but it had a large impact on overall health. This improvement occurred because the system provided three critical components: first, it provided an efficient way to invest in preventive (as opposed to curative) health care; second, it provided basic services for the most easily treated diseases and injuries; third, it provided, at least in some regions, a system of referrals to higher level medical services. Thus basic health care was brought to most villages for the first time. Simple as those services were, they were effective in providing elementary sanitation and protection against the most prevalent infectious diseases. In addition, the ability to mobilize large numbers of people was used in campaigns against public health threats as well; for example, a campaign was waged against the snails that invested flooded rice fields and carried the debilitating disease schistosomiasis.

In addition, in June 1965, Mao Zedong proclaimed that "the focus of health care work should shift to rural areas." This was one of the few areas where Maoist ideology had genuine positive effects and did not consist merely of empty slogans. Government health care resources were shifted to rural areas after the mid–1960s. Previously only some 25% of China's hospital beds were in the countryside, but by the mid–1970s more than 60% of the much larger total number of beds was in the countryside. By the mid–1970s a network of medical services had been created in the countryside. A nationwide system of paramedics was developed. These paramedics were part-time medical workers who continued to farm as well. Brigade-level "barefoot doctors" typically participated in a six-week training course at the county town, their only medical training: There were 1.5 million barefoot doctors in China by the mid–1970s. Even more lightly trained team para-medics, who might have only taken a simple first aid and sanitation course, numbered another 3.3 million. With a total army of rural paramedics of 4.8 million, each of China's million or so villages had access to four or five part-time paramedics.

These paramedics, at both the brigade and team levels, were paid in work points. In practice, therefore, they were compensated by a tax on the output of the local community, since assigning work points to paramedics meant that the value of the work points assigned for farm work was reduced. In turn, their services were generally provided free to community residents. Most Chinese farmers were thus covered by a rudimentary system of medical insurance, called "cooperative health services." For simple complaints they could turn to their local paramedic. If the ailment was more serious, they could be referred to the hospital in the commune or county town. By rough estimates, some 70%–80% of the rural population was covered by cooperative health services at the end of the 1970s.

With decollectivization in the 1980s, the flow of resources into this system collapsed. The production teams were no longer assigning work points, so there was no method at hand for compensating health workers. Some communities wrote land contracts in which households paid "rent" to the community to support social services, and communities with profitable TVEs could fund health services out of those revenues. But the proportion of communities that could fund health services out of the public purse declined dramatically. The number of paramedics dropped dramatically. The original "barefoot doctors" disappeared, of course, but the government introduced a program under which former barefoot doctors (and others) could be examined and certified as "village doctors." By 1992, 800,000 paramedics had been certified as village doctors, and of course many uncertified doctors took up practice. But the total number of active rural paramedics declined to less than a quarter of the 1970s peak. The total number of rural hospital beds stagnated, with the result that the number of hospital beds per thousand rural residents, after reaching a peak of 1.5 in 1985, began a long, steady decline to 0.72 in 2003 (Zhang and Kanbur 2005; NBS Rural Survey 2004, 215). Because of the drop in public financing, the total health-related resources available in the countryside declined substantially.

Without resources the insurance system of "cooperative health services" collapsed as well. From coverage of 70%–80% of the rural population, cooperative insurance dropped to cover less than 10% of the population by the mid–1980s. The Ministry of Health has carried out a large-scale survey of health care availability every five years since 1993. All three surveys show essentially the same result: about 80% of rural people have no health insurance whatsoever. Less than 10% have cooperative health services, and these are almost all in relatively developed areas close to coastal cities. In the minority of cases where health insurance is available, it is funded primarily by individual premiums (accounting for about two-thirds of funding), with the village contributing about one-sixth and township governments and enterprises accounting for the other sixth (CASS Institute of Finance and Trade Economics 2004, 155–164). Several times during the 1980s and 1990s the central government talked of rebuilding the system of rural cooperative health care, but policies were not well designed, efforts were inconsistent, and funding was inadequate. The problems with rural health care were obvious enough, but no good solution was at hand.

In 2003 a previously unknown, highly infectious, and often fatal disease—severe acute respiratory syndrome, or SARS—spread rapidly out of Guangdong Province. The disease quickly leapt to most of China's largest cities, including Beijing, causing near panic. Rural migrants fled the cities: during the first 10 days of May 2003, 4.5 million migrants returned to their rural homes, in some cases bringing the disease with them (Population Commission 2003). As these fleeing migrants melted back into their home villages, China's leaders—and the world—faced a terrifying reality: there was no rural health care system that could take care of the bulk of these rural returnees. There were no health care facilities available to track their progress, quarantine them if necessary, or respond to further spread of the infection. If the disease were to take root and spread in the Chinese countryside, there was nothing the Chinese government could do to stop it. As it turned out, the epidemic did not spread. For unknown reasons the new disease suddenly lost potency in the summer season and faded away as quickly as it had come. China sidestepped a catastrophe through good luck.

The magnitude of what almost happened drove home the inadequacy of the Chinese rural health care system. Chinese leaders strengthened their commitment to building a "new kind" of cooperative rural health care system, one that provided coverage for serious or catastrophic diseases and that would be subsidized by upper levels of government (local in the case of Eastern China, national in the case of Western China). Trial implementation began in 2003 and was scheduled to expand to 40% of China's counties in 2006. The central government (or provincial governments in more prosperous areas) was slated to contribute 20 RMB for each participant in the program. Still, as of 2003, only 14% of China's rural residents participated in cooperative health care, and again the bulk of these were in the most prosperous areas (77% in Shanghai and 30% in Guangdong), In some large rural provinces such as Hebei, Shaanxi, and Gansu, only 2%–3% of the population participated (NBS Rural Survey 2004, passim; Jin Renqing 2005; World Bank 2005). New insurance programs therefore have a long way to go.

Today, when rural residents need health care, they pay out of pocket. In the comprehensive survey of health coverage launched by the Ministry of Health in 1998, it was revealed that rural residents paid for 87% of their health care expenses themselves. This figure contrasts sharply with the experience of urban residents, who paid for 44% of their own health care expenses (Zhang and Kanbur 2005, 193). Most urban residents continue to be covered by some form of health insurance, although coverage is declining in cities as well. Moreover, the prices charged for hospital stays increased by six times during the 1990s, and clinic fees increased by eight times (CASS Institute of Finance and Trade Economics 2004, 158). As a result, 46% of rural residents responding to a recent survey reported that they had not sought medical care in a recent case of need because of the cost. Their only option was to wait and hope. These institutional failings, if not corrected, will make it difficult to build on China's past record in basic health.

10.4   THE EMERGENCE OF RURAL LAND MARKETS

Transition to a market economy in rural China ultimately means that a full complement of well-functioning markets with supporting institutions must be created. The gradualist approach to reform in rural areas, as well as the "fuzziness" of land property rights described in Chapter 5, resulted in the very slow growth of rural land markets. As late as the early 1990s a detailed survey of North China villages revealed that only 3% of land was rented in or out by farmers (Benjamin and Brandt 2002). Short-term labor markets also developed slowly, perhaps because virtually all potential laborers had access to their own land. It appeared that a variety of factors were contributing to low transactions volume on land markets. Most important was simple uncertainty as to whether the national government approved of such transactions and would provide property-rights protection in case of disputes. Perhaps equally significant was that local government and party cadres had a vested interest in maintaining some kind of collective ownership stake in the land, including the option of redistributing land on occasion. Farmers might hesitate to challenge cadre interests by renting land in or out on a large scale. Finally, there were no formal land registries to support complex transactions.

During the late 1990s, as Chinese government policy swung to become more favorable to migration and to comprehensive marketization, policy-makers began to be concerned with improving the efficiency and volume of land markets. This concern culminated in the adoption of the Rural Land Contracting Law in 2003. The basic purpose of the law was to make rural land property rights more clear and absolute, in order to facilitate the development of land markets. Villages were instructed to sign new land contracts with 30-year lease terms. The boundaries of lands were to be demarcated more precisely, and the process of rebuilding land registries to be accelerated. Several basic forms of land-use rights transfer, including sale, lease, and subcontract, were given sanction and specific legal form. To implement these changes, the government set off a "second round of land contracting," which was under way in nearly all Chinese villages by the end of 2003.

These changes have coincided with substantial increase in the speed at which land markets are developing. A 1998 survey of six large farm provinces found that 5.3% of land was rented out and that 9.8% of rural households leased out some of their land. In 2001, Sichuan reported that 5.6% of its land was rented out. In developed coastal areas, this proportion is typically much higher. In three highly commercialized Zhejiang counties, between 25% and 33% of land was already rented out in 2001. In Zhejiang province as a whole, a larger survey reported the proportion of land rented out increased from 11.5% in March 2001 to 22.8% at the end of 2003. In the Pearl River Delta, 19% of land is rented out (CASS Rural 2004, 90–93). These numbers indicate that land markets are now developing rapidly in commercialized coastal areas. Poorer inland areas lag behind, of course: In Shaanxi even in 2002 only 3% of land was rented out. However, this pattern corresponds to the one that prevailed in China's traditional economy. Tenancy and multiple layers of land rights were much more highly developed in the dense, commercialized, wet-rice culture of southeast China. Individual owner-farmed plots predominated in poorer northern dry-wheat areas. Consolidation of plots will certainly be required in pursuit of economies of scale, as more of the young people leave the land, and as farmers specialize in particular market crops. The explicit government legal support of land rights and transactions makes property rights more secure, thereby facilitating labor movement and land reallocation.

Overall, the development of land markets follows a principle shaping much of China's transition strategy. Reforms have unfolded at different rates in different markets. Rural reforms began with a change in farmers' use rights in land. Reforms then spread slowly to product markets, only gradually working down to the more fundamental, and more sensitive, development of markets for land, labor, capital, and finance. In China's countryside the transition to competitive product markets is essentially complete, but the development of a healthy and thriving land market has really just begun since the turn of the millennium. This incipient reform promises a new stage of rural change and reconstruction. Dramatic changes in rural land property rights, combined with large-scale out-migration, portend a third wave of rapid, even revolutionary, change and restructuring in the Chinese countryside.

BIBLIOGRAPHY

Suggestions for Further Reading

Chan, Madsen, and Unger (1984) is an excellent account of a village in Guangdong through the years of Maoism, combining readability with a scholarly approach. Zhou (1996) is a stirring account of rural reform. Skinner (1964–1965) is a highly readable discussion of the relationship between spontaneous economic organization and political organization in the Chinese countryside, which also contains the classic account of how communes conformed to traditional patterns in the countryside. Cao Jinqing (2000) combines firsthand observation of China's countryside today with analysis that is firmly grounded in China's modern history. World Bank (2005) is a good introduction to the rural health challenges.

Sources for Data and Figures

Table 10.2: Taylor (1988), pp. 740, 747.

A useful source of data on the rural economy is Ministry of Agriculture (2004, 5, 275–76) for data on villages; *SYC* (2004, 392–93) for housing; *SAC* (2005, 115) for administrative villages.

References

Benjamin, Dwayne, and Loren Brandt (2002). "Property Rights, Labour Markets, and Efficiency in a Transition Economy: The Case of Rural China." *Canadian Journal of Economics*, 35(4), November, 689–716.

Cao Jinqing (2000). *China along the Yellow River,* trans. Nicky Harman and Huang Ruhua. London and New York: RoutledgeCurzon.

CASS Institute of Finance and Trade Economics, ed. (2004). *Zhongguo Caizheng Zhengce Baogao 2004/2005. Kexue Fazhanguan: Yinling Zhongguo Caizheng Zhengce Xin Xilu [China Fiscal Policy Report 2004/2005. The Scientific Development Concept: Guiding New Train of Thoughts on China's Fiscal Policy].* Beijing: Zhongguo Caizheng Jingji, 2004.

CASS Rural (2004). CASS Rural Development Research Institute, with National Bureau of Statistics Rural Survey Group, *Nongcun Jingji Lanpishu, 2003–2004 Nian: Zhongguo nongcun jingji xingshi fenxi yu yuce [Green Book of China's Rural Economy: 2003–2004 Analysis and Forecast on China's Rural Economy]*. Beijing: Shehui Kexue Wenxian.

Chan, Anita, Richard Madsen, and Jonathan Unger (1984). *Chen Village: The Recent History of a Peasant Community in Mao's China*. Berkeley: University of California Press.

Jin Renqing (2005). "Address to the National Fiscal Work Conference," December 19, 2005. Accessed at http://www.mof.gov.cn/news/20051221_2205_11287.htm.

Lardy, Nicholas (1983). *Agriculture in China's Modern Economic Development*. New York: Cambridge University Press.

Ministry of Agriculture (2004). *Zhongguo Nongye Tongji Ziliao 2003*. Beijing: Zhongguo Nongye.

NBS [National Bureau of Statistics] (1985). *Zhongguo Shehui Tongji Ziliao* [China Society Statistical Materials]. Beijing: Zhongguo Tongji.

NBS Rural Survey (2004). Nongcun Shehui Jingji Diaocha Zongdui, ed. *2004 Nongcun Xiaokang Lanpishu [The 2004 Blue Book on Achievement of Well-Being in Rural Areas]*. Beijing: Zhongguo Tongji, 2004.

Population Commission (2003). China Population and Birth Planning Commission. "First Dynamic Statistics Done on Rural Population Movements in Order to Combat SARS" [in Chinese]. May 21, 2003, at www.poultryinfo.org/sars/200352374577.htm.

SAC (Annual). *Zhongguo Tongji Zhaiyao* [Statistical Abstract of China]. Beijing: Zhongguo Tongji.

Skinner, G. W. (1964–1965). "Marketing and Social Structure in Rural China," 3 parts. *Journal of Asian Studies*, 24:3–43, 195–228, 363–99.

SYC (Annual). *Zhongguo Tongji Nianjian* [Statistical Yearbook of China]. Beijing: Zhongguo Tongji.

Taylor, Jeffrey. (1988). "Rural Employment Trends and the Legacy of Surplus Labour, 1978–86." *China Quarterly*, No. 116. (December). pp. 736–66.

Vermeer, Eduard (1988). *Economic Development in Provincial China: The Central Shaanxi since 1930*. Cambridge: Cambridge University Press.

Wiens, Thomas (1982). "The Limits to Agricultural Intensification: The Suzhou Experience." In U.S. Congress Joint Economic Committee, ed., *China under the Four Modernizations*, 462–74. Washington, DC: U.S. Government Printing Office.

World Bank (2005). "Meeting China's Rural Health Challenges." http://www.worldbank.org.cn/English/content/314y63381193.shtml.

Zhang, Xiaobo, and Ravi Kanbur (2005). "Spatial Inequality in Education and Health Care in China." *China Economic Review*, 16:189–204. See the sources cited therein as well.

Zhou, Kate Xiao (1996). *How the Farmers Changed China: Power of the People*. Boulder, CO: Westview Press.

For years, food availability was the gravest challenge that faced China. From the failure of the GLF into the 1980s, the basic question of whether Chinese agriculture would be able to feed China's growing population remained unsettled. Today that question has been answered: In the last 25 years, China's agriculture has displayed the productivity and resilience necessary to feed China, and even to run a modest agricultural trade surplus in most years. Using as an indicator total output of grain—by far the most important product of Chinese agriculture—production in 1956 and 1957 (after recovery from war and revolution) was near 200 million metric tons. Since then it has increased to a peak of 512 million tons in 1998 before leveling off. How did Chinese agriculture achieve this sustained growth? One simple fact that will emerge from this chapter is that the Chinese countryside has undergone a technical revolution, beginning in the 1970s. Before 1970 the technology of agricultural production was basically prescientific, in that it relied on traditional techniques (albeit refined through centuries of experimentation) without significant application of modern inputs. During the 1970s this picture began to change as new technologies and modern inputs began to flow to the Chinese countryside in significant quantities for the first time. During the 1980s and 1990s the technological transformation of Chinese agriculture accelerated, and output began to rely on massive application of modern inputs. This ongoing revolution has established the basis for further increases in agricultural supply going forward.

On the demand side, China's agriculture faces new challenges. As incomes rise in China, demands for improved diet are dramatically reshaping markets for food. Traditionally almost totally dependent on grain, China's consumers are increasingly demanding a diverse diet, which puts greater and different demands on the agricultural system. How successful will China be in increasing and diversifying food production in the future? Much of the answer is rooted in technical change. Technical change in agriculture requires research and investment. Research produces better plant varieties, new fertilizers, and improved cropping systems, while investment in land can improve land quality and control of water. This chapter will focus on technical change in Chinese agriculture, emphasizing changes in the package of inputs for agriculture, made up of land, labor, seeds, water, fertilizer, and machinery, and examining the resulting changes in output. There will be brief discussions of a theory of how innovation takes place in agriculture, of Chinese agroecology, and of the agricultural research system itself. After reviewing the past record, the chapter examines three forces reshaping Chinese agriculture today. A new round of investment in agricultural support industries will be required to provide fresh produce and higher quality foods. A new wave of technological innovation, based on genetic engineering, will provide increased supply of some foods. Finally, the current wave of globalization, following China's WTO membership in 2001, opens up new possibilities for agricultural specialization, while also creating new competitive challenges for China's farmers.

11.1   OVERVIEW OF POST–1949 AGRICULTURE

During the 1950s, agricultural output grew mainly due to the rehabilitation of traditional agricultural systems and the mobilization of labor through agricultural collectives. Modern technologies with the potential to transform China's agricultural system began to appear in the 1960s. Beginning in the 1970s a Chinese green revolution began to transform agriculture. Surprisingly, the key elements of the green revolution—improved seeds, fertilizer, and irrigation— were the same three elements on which the traditional system was based (Chapter 2). However, the green revolution elements were produced through the systematic application of scientific research and the use of industrial methods to produce improved inputs.

After 1949, newly formed agricultural collectives, discussed in the previous chapter, were used to accelerate the pace at which agricultural inputs were created, based on traditional agricultural technology. This acceleration was most evident in rapid expansion of the area under irrigation and in the increase in the number of days farmers put into land improvement. Per capita grain production recovered, and it was running about 300 kilograms by the 1955–1957 period (Figure 11.1). This was (barely) enough to feed the population adequately, given the highly equitable food distribution that China had at the time. But this level was not to be sustained. The folly of the GLF pushed production per head to below subsistence levels (not shown in Figure 11.1) and led to the famine described in previous chapters. Perhaps surprising is the fact that in the

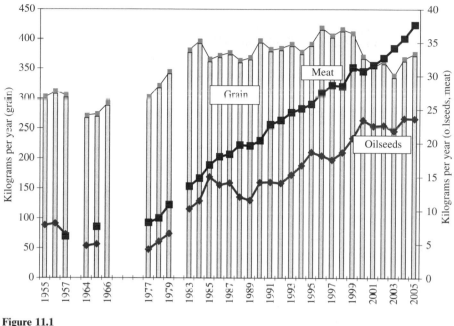

Figure 11.1
Per capita agricultural output

mid–1960s, even after the recovery from the worst of the post-Leap famine, per capita output was still well below the 1955–1957 level, implying that millions were still on the margins of subsistence. It was not until the late 1970s that per capita output had clearly returned to 1950s levels, only slowly creeping back up to the 300-kilogram level. After rural reforms per capita output initially soared toward 400 kilograms in 1984. Subsequently growth slowed, but the 400-kilogram-per-capita benchmark was again surpassed in 1996–1998.

What lay behind the steady increase in production from the mid–1960s through the 1980s? Beginning in the 1960s, Chinese scientists began to produce green revolution technologies that were able to push agricultural production up to qualitatively higher levels. Green revolution technologies were pioneered in the West, but Chinese scientists, working independently, created parallel achievements and, in one or two areas, made independent breakthroughs that surpassed what was done in the West. A particularly striking fact is that the green revolution, while based on modern science and technology, is based on the same triad of modernized varieties, large-scale fertilizer application, and precise water control on which Chinese traditional agriculture was also founded. During the later 1960s and 1970s, China's agriculture grew from the process of intensification of land use—now with modern science used to accelerate the application of nutrients to the soil. New patterns of grain crop-ping evolved, including triple cropping and intercropping of different varieties, to facilitate this intensification.

While producing an adequate increase in grain output, the agricultural poli-cies adopted through the 1970s neglected potential gains from diversification and commercialization. Indeed, the increased output of grain was achieved in part through the Grain First agricultural policy (Chapter 10) that stressed grain to the exclusion of many other crops. This policy succeeded in main-taining growth in per capita grain output, but it resulted in harmful reductions in per capita output of a number of important nongrain crops. For example, as Figure 11.1 shows, production of oilseeds per capita was significantly lower in the 1970s than in the 1950s. Average availability was less than a tablespoon of vegetable oil per day, and oil was strictly rationed. Considering that Chinese cuisine is dependent on vegetable oil for deep-frying and stir-frying, and that a tablespoon of oil is hardly adequate for a single dish, one can see that Chinese households were limited to a monotonous and austere diet, even when there were adequate calories. Beginning in 1979 policy shifted drasti-cally and output surged. Even more striking than the increase in grain is the remarkable increase in nongrain products, such as oilseeds and meat. Peasants were given much greater control over their own economic activity, and this resulted in very large one-time-only gains as peasants responded to better incentives, to work harder but also to meet market demands more effectively. This produced a better geographical output mix, in which products were better suited to the varieties demanded and the location of production was better suited to natural conditions.

11.2   TECHNOLOGY CHOICE AND TECHNICAL INNOVATION IN AGRICULTURE

Agriculture in China, as anywhere else, adapts to the availability of produc-tion factors, such as land and labor. Farmer use of inputs and their relative proportions in the agricultural production process are determined by relative resource scarcity and hence the relative input prices. Figure 11.2 shows the standard way that economists analyze the choice of technology in agricultural production (or any kind of production, for that matter). The horizontal axis shows the quantity of land, and the vertical axis shows the quantity of labor used in the production process. The curved line is an isoquant: At any point on the isoquant, a given output, x, can be produced with the use of the quan-

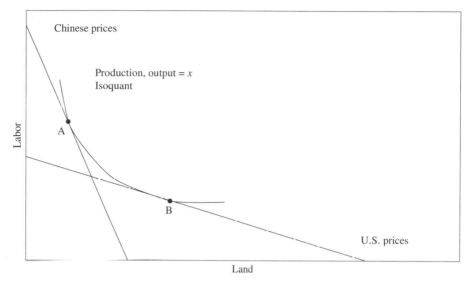

Figure 11.2
Choice of technology

tities of land and labor corresponding to that point on the graph. Different points on the isoquant display varying factor (input) proportions: the isoquant shows the range of input combinations that are technologically capable of producing output = x. In a land-abundant, labor-scarce economy like the United States, the shallow straight line expresses U.S. relative prices: one worker's wage equals the rental value of a large area of land. Any point on this line shows an equal cost outlay for production in the United States. Minimizing cost, a U.S. farmer will produce output = x at point B. In China's labor-abundant, land-scarce economy, the much steeper straight line displays Chinese relative prices: a small plot of land has a rental value equal to one worker's wage, and any point on the steep line is an equal cost outlay for production in China. Minimizing cost, a Chinese farmer will produce output = x at point A. A Chinese farmer will use a labor-intensive production process, applying large amounts of labor to a small amount of land, relative to, for example, a U.S. farmer. This much is a straightforward application of relative prices and cost minimization.

This simple analysis can be extended to the more challenging area of technological change. The "induced-innovation" hypothesis states that technical change is also derived from the demands of cost-minimizing agents to save on relatively scarce resources and to use relatively plentiful ones. Chinese farmers will especially value new technologies that allow them to economize on land—

that is, to use the existing land resources more intensively. They will thus seek out and adopt new technologies that allow them to apply more of (relatively cheap) labor to their land. Hayami and Ruttan (1985) originally demonstrated this process for the cases of agricultural development in the United States and Japan over the period from 1880 to 1980. The growth paths of the two countries differ greatly. In the United States, with plentiful land and relatively scarce labor, power machinery was developed to substitute for relatively scarce labor. In Japan, with plentiful labor and relatively scarce land, a package of high-yielding seeds, fertilizer, and water control was developed to substitute for relatively scarce land. While the paths of development were different, the rates of growth and levels of output were commensurate. The different paths implied by this East Asian experience and North American experience are shown in Figure 11.3 (note that the axes are different from Figure 11.2). China, like Japan, followed a process of technical advance in agriculture in which the fundamental achievement was the improvement in yields per unit of land. We might label the two paths "tractorization" versus "chemicalization."

In the following, we trace how this process of intensification took place in practice in China. Agricultural production, arguably, is distinctive precisely because of the way it must always be adapted to concrete conditions. For

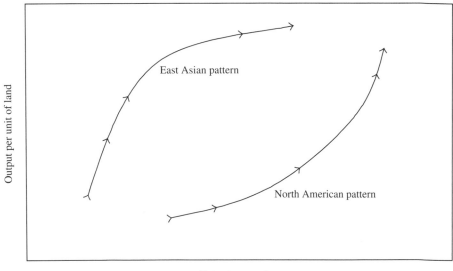

Figure 11.3
Induced-innovation paths

example, plants require time to grow, and certain operations must be carried out at certain times. It may be possible to shorten the time required for a crop to mature, and it is possible to substitute one type of input for another, but time—and waiting—are essential ingredients. Different climatic regions, or agroecological zones, will be better for certain crops than others. China is traditionally divided into rice- and wheat growing regions, and then into a larger number of subregions. The dividing line between the rice and wheat is about 33° north latitude, between the Yangtze and Huai rivers (see Figure 1.2). The rice region has abundant water and a longer growing season, and it has long had significant irrigation networks. The green revolution was easily adapted to these conditions. The wheat region tends to be short of water, and has a shorter growing season. Nevertheless, irrigation networks were rare until very recently, so farmers were dependent on seasonal rainfall. The innovations of the green revolution could not be applied to the wheat region until substantial infrastructure construction and technology adaptation had taken place.

To support growth in agricultural output in all regions, a sophisticated network of agricultural research stations was developed. According to the induced-innovation hypothesis, in most of China, with abundant labor and relatively scarce land, we expect to see technology that is land saving—or land augmenting—and labor using, as in the Japanese case. Expanding the land available for cropping is not much of an option in China, since nearly all land that is economical to cultivate is under cultivation. Since such an extensive form of development is not possible, intensification of land use is necessary. This has often required land improvement, which may entail land leveling such as terracing, where small flat plots are carved into hilly or mountainous topography. Sowing cultivated land more than once each year, or multicropping, has grown significantly since the 1950s, with substantial regional variation. In Zhejiang Province the multicropping index is sometimes above two, indicating that, on average, farmland in that province is sown more than twice in a given year. Multiple cropping includes rotation, intercropping, and relay cropping. Crop rotation is the sequential planting of crops one after another. It entails sowing, cultivating, and harvesting one crop followed by another crop. Rotation patterns are diverse and can be quite complicated, ranging up to intensive three- to seven-year patterns of crop succession. When compared to monoculture (growing the same crop repeatedly in succession), such great diversity in the crops grown has positive effects on soil fertility and disease prevention, in addition to increased output in the short run. Intercropping is the cultivation of two crops at the same time in the same field in alternating rows. There may be physical advantages to such a practice, such as one tall crop requiring direct sunlight shading a shorter, more shade-tolerant crop. Growing conditions for one are improved while conditions for the other remain unchanged. Relay cropping is intermediate between rotation and inter-cropping. One crop is planted, and before it is harvested another is planted in the same field. This technique gives the second crop a head start on growth with no appreciable effects on the first crop.

11.3 THE GREEN REVOLUTION

"Green revolution" technology updates and improves the traditional input package of seeds, fertilizer, and water. It allows great intensification of agri-cultural production. High-quality water control and delivery, manufactured agricultural chemicals, especially fertilizers, and water- and fertilizer-responsive varieties of seeds are the components of the system. China has invested much money, human capital, and time in developing appropriate systems of high-yielding modern varieties adapted to specific local conditions. A crucial feature of the green revolution technologies is that they form a com-plementary package of techniques: the productivity of each specific technol-ogy is significantly enhanced by the presence of the other technologies. There is thus a triad of green revolution techniques that must be implemented together in order to achieve maximum efficiency. A simple way to display this complementarity is to look at the output response of different crop varieties to fertilizer application. Figure 11.4 shows that traditional crop varieties increase yields, up to a point, with application of chemical fertilizers. Green revolution crops—so-called high-yield varieties, or HYVs—are superior not so much because they produce more in the absence of fertilizer, but rather because HYVs make it possible to continue to apply fertilizer and continue to get a significant positive output response with much larger total fertilizer application.

11.3.1 Irrigation

The first part of the green revolution triad to be developed in China was quality irrigation and drainage throughout the country. Starting in the early 1950s, irrigation projects were built and technical capacity increased. Figure 11.5 shows the development of irrigated area. Construction of irrigation proj-ects was carried out by labor from the collective farms, mobilized during the winter slack season. Irrigated area grew rapidly, as shown in Figure 11.5, through the collective period until the late 1970s. During the 1980s irrigated area stagnated, and even declined slightly. This pause was related to the decline

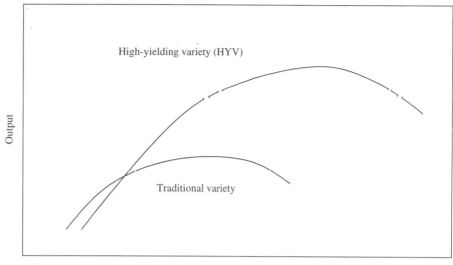

Figure 11.4
The green revolution: fertilizer responsiveness

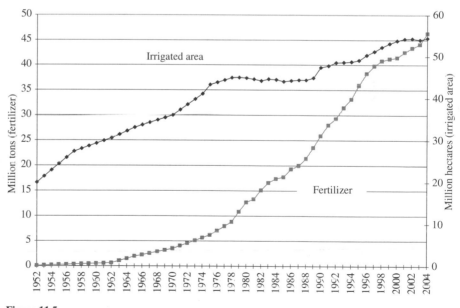

Figure 11.5
Fertilizer and irrigated area

in public-good provision that marked the dissolution of the collectives. It was not until new organizational forms were worked out for irrigation districts in the 1990s that expansion of irrigated area resumed.

Power machinery has been introduced to improve the efficiency of water control. In the 1950s water was lifted by human power or animal traction. Today two-thirds of the irrigated area is serviced by machine pumping, facilitating the more precise water control necessary to support production of HYVs. There were 50 million power-driven pumps in the Chinese countryside in 2004. More and larger power equipment has been brought to bear on the problem of providing water to crops. Another technical advance is the development of tube wells to provide water on the North China Plain. As Chapter 1 recounted, the whole Yellow River area is chronically short of water, with much competition between urban, industrial, and agricultural water users. Lack of water has been a key constraint to expanding production in this area with rich soil and abundant sun. Many areas of the North China Plain have a high saline water supply; as a result, salt builds up on otherwise productive land when water evaporates (salinization). This means that introducing irrigation water from surface sources without additional drainage capacity is not technically feasible. Many aquifers underlie the North China Plain, but this rich water resource was unavailable to Chinese farmers until a submersible pump that could develop sufficient head to deliver fresh water from 30 meters below the surface was in mass production. During the 1970s literally millions of pumps permitted much more intense exploitation of aquifers and rapid expansion of wheat production. Thirty years later, however, overexploitation of aquifers may be leading to a water crisis and, eventually, to the curtailment of wheat production on the North China Plain (Chapter 20).

11.3.2 Agricultural Chemicals

The second leg of the green revolution tripod is agricultural chemicals, including chemical fertilizer and pesticides. In the traditional agricultural input system used in China, large amounts of organic fertilizer, up to six tons per hectare, were used. Organic fertilizer provides sufficient nutrients for traditional varieties, but it is very labor intensive to use, is unpleasant to handle, and does not give the boost in yield that modern HYVs require. Initially meant to augment the labor-intensive organic fertilizers, chemical fertilizer production at first developed slowly (see Figure 11.5). In the 1960s and the early 1970s small-scale local factories produced nitrogen fertilizers of low quality. In 1973–1974 the central government made a huge commitment to the development of a modern domestic nitrogen fertilizer industry by purchasing 13 large synthetic ammonia and urea factories from abroad. It was initially planned to reverse engineer and duplicate these plants in each province, but the huge and sophisticated plants proved more daunting than expected. Instead, additional imports were arranged, and a fairly large domestic fertilizer industry was gradually built up.

As Figure 11.5 shows, fertilizer supply really took off between 1978 and 1996, during which time supplies quadrupled from an already substantial base. Domestic capacity alone was insufficient to meet the demand, so China has resorted to the international market over the past 25 years. China has preferred to import fertilizer, augmenting domestic food output, rather than importing food. During the mid–1970s there was certainly latent, unsatisfied demand for fertilizer, and the reforms that followed gave farmers new stronger incentives. Fertilizer has been a key part of the emerging modern triad.

11.3.3 Seeds

The third leg of the green revolution tripod is improved seeds. Improvement and molding of the genetic characteristics of germplasm requires investment in research capacity. The outcomes of that investment are demonstrated in the higher yields of improved crops made more responsive to high fertilizer applications and timely irrigation. Research capacity in agriculture has been developed strongly but unevenly since 1949 (Pardey, Roseboom, and Anderson 1991, 226–234). Even before 1949 the Republic of China, during the Nanjing decade, launched an initial research and development effort. During the 1950s the People's Republic founded a multilevel research system with the Chinese Academy of Agricultural Sciences (CAAS) at the apex. Along with provincial-level academies and an agricultural extension service in every county, China built a seed production and distribution system that is today the largest in the world. The disruption of the GLF and Cultural Revolution caused great problems for agricultural researchers. But even in the middle of the Cultural Revolution, there was some progress, as agricultural technology, research, and extension organizations were created at the county, commune, and brigade levels (see Table 10.1). The focus was put on adaptation of cultivars to local conditions and dissemination of new varieties. Little attention was paid to basic agricultural science, but practical and adaptive work advanced. After 1979 research institutes were reconstituted, and basic research was begun again. Provincial-level and lower-level institutes focus research more on local conditions, and the overall system is unusually decentralized compared to other countries.

This national agricultural research system produces and disseminates the technologies that make the green revolution possible. The most important among the outputs is improved seeds for HYVs. Plant-breeding programs include components of conventional plant breeding like selection and hybridization as well as a gradual move into advanced genetic engineering techniques. During the 1950s the stock of plant material was augmented by seeds imported from abroad, including wheat, cotton, and maize and new material from domestic sources. Chinese scientists developed the first true high-yielding dwarf variety of rice in 1964. This was two years before the International Rice Research Institute in the Philippines released its own revolutionary high-yielding dwarf, IR-8, an event that is frequently taken as the beginning of the global green revolution. Dwarf varieties were a critical breakthrough in the green revolution. Dwarf varieties can absorb enormous amounts of nutrients from fertilizer, since they channel more of the plant's energy into the grain and less to the (short and stubby) stalk. This development solved the problem of lodging—plants toppling over because of weak, spindly stalks—that had bedeviled early research efforts. Following their own breakthroughs, Chinese scientists established contact with the international agricultural research system during the 1960s that led to the exchange of germplasm with the collections at the various international crop institutes. These helped Chinese scientists advance during the travails of the Cultural Revolution.

Another successful experience was the introduction and extension of hybrid varieties of various crops. Hybrid maize was introduced in 1961, and by 1990 about 90% of sown area was sown with the hybrid variety. Hybrid rice was introduced in 1976, and by 1990 it was sown to more than 40% of rice-sown area. Hybrid varieties produce an increased yield, but their output cannot be used as seed for the next generation of crop. China was able to disseminate hybrid varieties largely because the agricultural extension service was quite reliable in supplying new generations of seed to farmers. Here is an example of institutional infrastructure created during the socialist period—indeed, strengthened during the Cultural Revolution—that contributed to rapid technological change and robust output growth later during the market reforms. The green revolution technologies are complements: However, in China, it was not until the 1980s that all three legs of the tripod were available to stand on. There were, therefore, latent technological gains that could only be realized when all three elements were present simultaneously. In fact, the completion of this technological revolution took place at almost exactly the same time as the institutional revolution led by rural reforms. Some observers argue that tehnological change was the most important cause of increased agricultural productivity improvement in the early 1980s. They stress the complementarity of fertilizer, the last leg of the green revolution triad to arrive (Stone 1990), and the adoption of improved seed varieties, especially hybrid rice (Huang and Rozelle 1996). This view contrasts with the mainstream interpretation, which holds that the incentive properties of rural reforms deserve most of the credit for productivity increase (McMillan, Whalley, and Zhu 1989; Lin 1992). In either case, we should recognize the crucial role of both incentives and technological change, and also how recent the technological revolution in China's countryside has been. Indeed, it is a transformation that has occurred since the 1980s. The picture of recent technological transformation is further strengthened when we look at motive power in the countryside.

11.4   MOTIVE POWER IN THE COUNTRYSIDE

In the traditional cultivation system animal traction and human muscle were the sources of power. Figure 11.6 shows the evolution of motive power in the countryside. Until the early 1970s mechanical power was relatively insignificant. Human labor was augmented primarily by beasts of burden, with draft animals pulling the plow and doing the heavy hauling. Draft animals—oxen, horses, mules, and camels—were attractive in the 1950s because animals not only provided power cultivation, but also provided organic fertilizers, could be used for transportation, and provided some food security. The recovery of the

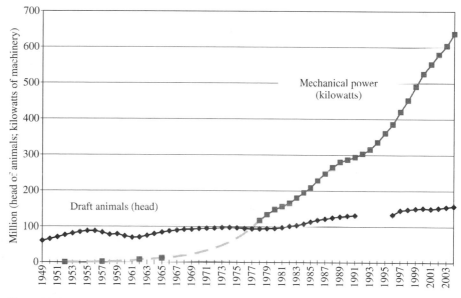

Figure 11.6
Rural motive power

rural economy in the first half of the 1950s is reflected in the substantial increase in the number of draft animals. However, the peak year was 1955, and after collectivization the number of draft animals first stagnated and then, after the GLF, plunged. Clearly, peasant households were not enthusiastic about seeing the collectives take control of their household animals. There was not a catastrophic collapse in the number of draft animals, as there had been in the Soviet Union, but the 21% decline in total draft animals between the 1955 peak and the 1961 trough dealt a heavy blow to farm productivity. The stock of draft animals recovered through the early 1970s, only to stagnate again in the period just before rural reforms kicked in at the end of the 1970s.

Mechanical power began to be significant in the countryside in the 1970s. (Note that in Figure 11.6 the scales for draft animals and mechanical power are roughly comparable. A kilowatt of mechanical power capacity is equivalent to 0.736 horsepower. Thus the relative position of the two lines roughly reflects the aggregate importance of animal and mechanical power in the countryside: Total machine power surpassed animal power only in the late 1970s.) Labor-augmenting technology, particularly mechanization, is a traditional feature of the "Big Push" industrialization strategy that China initially borrowed from the Soviet Union. As our preceding discussion of induced innovation indicated, it was not likely to be appropriate in China, given Chinese factor endowments. Despite this obvious mismatch, Chinese agricultural planners under socialism invested large sums of capital in developing agricultural machines such as large tractors that were poorly suited to China's conditions. Farmers resisted adopting them, of course, using big tractors as miniature trucks to haul bricks and fertilizer around the countryside. However, some farm machinery, such as the small electric pumps discussed earlier, made crucial contributions to the modern input package, permitting a rapid extension of irrigation through drilling of wells and expansion of irrigation networks over complex terrain.

Machine power in agriculture developed slowly, first in irrigation and then in cultivation. After reforms peasant households shifted away from large tractors toward trucks (for hauling) and small tractors for tilling. The number of small-scale tractors grew dramatically. Starting at 1.4 million in 1978, the number grew to 14.5 million in 2004 (SYC 2005, 449). These small tractors are maneuverable, affordable, and more suited to the scale of production in Chinese agriculture. Indeed, the overall composition of mechanical power is quite different from what it would be in a land-using agricultural economy like the United States, where most of the mechanical power would be in tractors and harvester-combines. In China, of the total machine power in 1995, 22%

was in hydraulic machinery (pumps, etc.), 22% consisted of small tractors, 17% was transport equipment, and 13% was agricultural processing equipment. The Chinese countryside is being transformed by the widespread application of mechanical power to the rural economy, and this transformation is extremely recent.

11.5   OUTPUT AND YIELDS: THE CHALLENGE OF INTENSIFICATION

By the end of the 1990s, then, Chinese agriculture had successfully united modern science-based inputs with a steady intensification of the agricultural production process. Total grain yields have tripled in the 50 years since 1952. Grain still makes up about two-thirds of the sown area. Rice is the most important grain crop, by a significant margin, and yields are more than double what they were, thanks largely to the improved seeds. Wheat yields have increased dramatically. Maize has become the second-largest crop, surpassing wheat, because of its importance as animal feed. The most important nonfood crop by far is cotton, which accounts for 3%–4% of sown area.

Table 11.1 shows that by the end of the twentieth century China had achieved yields in rice and wheat that were well above world averages and, in the case of wheat, above U.S. yields. These results were achieved by employing almost four times as many workers per hectare as the world average, and 150 times as many workers per hectare in the United States. A high proportion of total land is irrigated, but Chinese farmers use few tractors. Most striking is the fact that Chinese fertilizer consumption per hectare is almost three times world averages and more than twice that of the United States. Figures for pesticides, if conveniently available, would certainly show that China applies more than world or U.S. averages.

Table 11.1
Comparison of yields and inputs per hectare of cropland, 1997

	Unit	China	World	United States
Production per hectare				
Rice, paddy	Tons	6.2	3.9	7.0
Wheat	Tons	3.7	2.7	2.8
Corn	Tons	4.6	4.3	8.6
Soybeans	Tons	1.7	2.2	2.6
Fertilizer consumption per hectare	Kilograms	271	94	111
Farm workers per 100 hectares	Number	310	82	2
Land irrigated	Percent	40	18	13
Tractors per 1,000 hectares	Number	6	18	27

It is not clear that intensification of agriculture in China can be pursued much further than it already has been. The Chinese and nearby coastal environment is overburdened by the excessive amounts of nutrients from chemical fertilizer in the water. Toxic pesticides are hurting bird and animal life. Groundwater and surface water sources are both showing signs of severe overexploitation. Groundwater levels in some places in Hebei Province are falling more than 1 meter per year (Lohmar et al 2003). Moreover, the workers are beginning to leave agriculture: as Chapter 6 pointed out, since 1991 the agricultural labor force has declined by about 10%. Fortunately, it will probably not be necessary to follow the path of continual intensification. Three forces are now redirecting Chinese agriculture onto a new, uncertain, but hopeful path: change in the structure of demand caused by rapid income growth, a burst of technological potential caused by genetic modification technologies, and a change in patterns of specialization caused by globalization. We shall discuss these three in turn.

11.6   DIVERSIFICATION AND THE CHALLENGE OF THE FUTURE

The future development of Chinese agriculture will be driven by the imperative of dietary improvement. Until recently the Chinese diet has been dominated by grain consumption. As recently as 1981, 94% of the calories in the average Chinese diet came from plant products (87% from grain). Even more surprising is that *protein* came 90% from plant products (83% from grain) and only 10% from all animal products. Recently demand pressures have been concentrated on food products with high-income elasticities in the middle-income range relevant to today's China: these include meat, fresh fruit and vegetables, poultry, and eggs. A dietary transition shifts consumption from carbohydrates to higher levels of protein, fat, and sugar. This transition happens in virtually all countries as they move to middle- and upper-income status. Not coincidentally, problems with obesity begin to become serious at the time of this transition, and this is the case in China as well.

Dietary improvement places new demands on the agricultural system. It does not necessarily reduce the pressure on grain production, because, ironically, increased consumption of meat usually requires still higher levels of grain production. The reason is that meat production is a relatively inefficient way of conveying calories to the human consumer. Animals convert vegetable calories into a more highly valued food, but through a relatively "expensive" conversion process. In general, China's grain production should continue to increase, but different varieties of grain will be grown, and most of the increment will be converted into meat. A new animal-feed industry is developing that mixes grain with oilseed meal (especially from soybeans) and vitamin and protein supplements. New systems of feedlots, slaughterhouses, and marketing networks also develop alongside new feeding systems. These developments are all occurring in China, but they are happening at a surprisingly slow pace. China's traditional "bottom-heavy" economy is reasserting itself. By far the largest source of animal protein in China is pig farming, and China raises more than half of the world's pigs. But remarkably, 80% of those pigs are still raised by traditional household producers, raising several pigs in the barnyard. These producers can compete because they feed their pigs largely on farmyard by-products and waste, as well as green roughage, including leaves and stalks, tubers, and pumpkins. Improved feed grain accounts for only 36% of their feed needs. This remarkably efficient small-scale economy runs by recycling everything the farmstead produces (Iowa State 1998). The evolution of this sector will have a big impact on, for example, world soybean trade.

Chinese producers are moving out of traditional grain crops and into higher-value crops, especially horticultural products. These can produce much higher returns, but they depend crucially on a more sophisticated infrastructure. A crucial link is cold-chain facilities for warehousing and transporting high-value frozen and perishable foods. Most urban households have refrigerators and spend an increasing share of their food money at supermarkets. For the farm sector to truly take advantage of this shift, however, requires a more sophisticated transport and storage system.

11.7   GENETICALLY MODIFIED ORGANISMS

China is making a major research and development effort in biotechnology, especially in genetic modification. Moreover, Chinese genetically modified organisms (GMOs) have moved rapidly into the field and produced some substantial successes. Perhaps the most dramatic is the development of genetically modified Bt Cotton, which has an inserted gene that makes the plant less susceptible to insect pests. Cotton is not only an important crop in its own right, but it is also the plant that receives the heaviest dose of pesticides. Insect pests have developed resistance to many pesticides, with the result that Chinese cotton farmers in the late 1990s were applying a toxic cocktail of several kinds of pesticides (even including illegal DDT) to their fields. Bt Cotton was developed by the CAAS in the mid–1990s and released in 1997. (Monsanto also developed a Bt cotton strain about this time.) Bt Cotton gives farmers an 8%–10% yield increase, but the biggest payoff is that it enables an almost two-thirds reduction in the amount of pesticides applied to cotton. Bt Cotton has revitalized the North China cotton crop, which had been reeling during the early 1990s (Pray et al. 2002; Huang et al. 2003).

China is making a broad effort in biotechnology that will likely see important applications in other crops. In contrast to most countries, most of China's effort comes from publicly funded, governmental research institutes, such as CAAS. Since the late 1990s government funding for this effort has begun to increase rapidly. Already in 1999, China's government invested $112 million in plant biotechnology, comparable to the funding levels of governments even in developed countries (although still less than the largest private agribusiness companies). Many different types of output are foreseeable from this effort, but none is more important than genetically modified rice. Chinese researchers are especially strong in building insect and disease resistance into crops. In the case of rice, though, we will also see strains with added vitamins and protein emerging from the pipeline soon. A new wave of technological change will reshape Chinese agriculture.

11.8 GLOBALIZATION

China's entry into the WTO is having an important impact on agricultural development in China. Membership in the WTO imposes limits on how much China can protect its agriculture. Competition from food imports will keep a cap on how high China can push up farm prices, if it chooses to do so. Thus, in that sense, globalization limits some of China's policy options in the rural sector. Yet what is most striking is that in the last decade China has not emerged as a large net food importer. Instead, it has steadily altered policy in the direction of supporting agriculture. Beginning in 2004 a new round of subsidies and tax reductions promised to put the national government in the position of providing net support for agriculture for the first time since 1949. More positive government policies have been met with a strong output response from Chinese agriculture. Total net grain imports have been modest. China is surprisingly self-sufficient in food. In fact, China imports bulk, land-intensive products, such as wheat (the most important), corn, cotton, and soybeans. The one bulk product that it exports is rice. However, China has rapidly expanded its exports of labor-intensive horticultural products. Vegetables, flowers, fruits, and canned and processed foods have been exported in increasing volumes. Clearly, international trade is highly advantageous to the

Chinese economy as it makes use of the differential between its own factor endowments and those of developed countries, even within the agricultural sector.

Since China is the largest agricultural producer in the world, it is crucial that productivity continue to increase. Were China to enter international grain markets to the extent that, say, Japan and Taiwan have, considerable upset would be caused by dramatic price increases. People used to worry that China's need for food might put a heavy, even insupportable, burden on world grain markets (Brown 1995). This worry has receded significantly in the past several years. China's surprising self-sufficiency in food looks set to continue for the foreseeable future. Moreover, China today clearly has enough foreign exchange to consistently meet its food needs on the world market, and the rest of the world clearly has enough land to supply more food if higher prices warrant. The question for the future is: to what extent will China's policies adapt further to the opportunities of globalization, in particular through accepting greater dependence on world markets for grain? Deep integration in the world economy in that sense would open up new sources of productivity growth and benefit for economies around the world.

BIBLIOGRAPHY

Suggestions for Further Reading

Nyberg and Rozelle (1999) and USDA (2002) are both good overviews of the rural economy, touching on virtually the entire range of issues. Lin (1992) is a classic article that is an eminently clear and effective argument based on estimation of the agricultural production function.

Sources for Data and Figures

Figure 11.1: SYC 1991, 357; 1996, 378; 2005, 462–69. Meat production is carcass weight, total production of pork, mutton, and beef. Official meat production data are adjusted downward in accord with the procedures in Ma, Huang, and Rozelle (2004).

Figure 11.3: Derived from Hayami and Ruttan (1985).

Figure 11.5: *SYC* (1991, 323, 331, 356; 2005, 451).

Figure 11.6: *SYC* (1991, 323, 331, 356; 2005, 449, 467).

Table 11.1: Gale (2002, 8).

References

Brown, Lester (1995). *Who Will Feed China? Wake-up Call for a Small Planet.* New York: W. W. Norton.

Gale, Fred (2002). "China at a Glance: A Statistical Overview of China's Food and Agriculture." In USDA (2002, 5–46).

Hayami, Yujiro, and Vernon W. Ruttan (1985). *Agricultural Development: An International Perspective.* Baltimore: Johns Hopkins University Press.

Huang, Jikun, and Scott Rozelle (1996). "Technological Change: Rediscovering the Engine of Productivity Growth in China's Rural Economy." *Journal of Development Economics*, 49:337–69.

Huang, Jikun, Ruifa Hu, Carl Pray, Fangbin Qiao, and Scott Rozelle (2003). "Biotechnology as an Alternative to Chemical Pesticides: A Case Study of Bt Cotton in China." *Agricultural Economics*, 29:55–67.

Iowa State Food and Agriculture Extension (1998). "Pigs in China: Impacts of Chinese Swine Feeding Practices on Future Chinese Feed Grain and Livestock Trade." Available at http://www.fapri.iastate.edu/bulletin/nov98/chineseSwine.htm.

Lin, Justin Y. (1992). "Rural Reform and Agricultural Growth in China." *American Economic Review*, 82:34–51.

Liu, Yunhua, and Xiaobing Wang (2005). "Technological Progress and Chinese Agricultural Growth in the 1990s." *China Economic Review*, 16:419–40.

Lohmar, Brian, Jinxia Wang, Scott Rozelle, Jikun Huang, and David Dawe. (2003). *China's Agricultural Water Policy Reforms: Increasing Investment, Resolving Conflicts, and Revising Incentives*, Agriculture Information Bulletin No. 782, Washington, D.C.: U.S. Department of Agriculture, Economic Research Service, http://www.ers.usda.gov/publications/aib782.

Ma, Hengyun, Jikun Huang, and Scott Rozelle (2004). "Reassessing China's Livestock Statistics: An Analysis of Discrepancies and the Creation of New Data Series." *Economic Development and Cultural Change*, 55(2), January, 445–73.

McMillan, John, John Whalley, Lijing Zhu (1989). "The Impact of China's Economic Reforms on Agricultural Productivity Growth." *Journal of Political Economy*, 97(4), August, 781–807.

Nyberg, Albert, and Scott Rozelle (1999). *Accelerating China's Rural Transformation*. Washington, DC: World Bank.

Pardey, P. G., J. Roseboom, and J. Anderson (1991). *Agricultural Research Policy: International Quantitative Perspectives*. New York: Cambridge University Press.

Pray, Carl, Jikun Huang, Ruifa Hu, and Scott Rozelle (2002). "Five years of Bt Cotton in China: The Benefits Continue." *Plant Journal*, 31(4): 423–30.

Stone, Bruce (1990). "Evolution and Diffusion of Agricultural Technology in China." In Neil G. Kotler, ed., *Sharing Innovation: Global Perspectives on Food, Agriculture and Rural Development*, 35–93. Washington, DC: Smithsonian Institution.

SYC (Annual). *Zhongguo Tongji Nianjian* [Statistical Yearbook of China]. Beijing: Zhongguo Tongji.

USDA (2002). U.S. Department of Agriculture, Economic Research Service. *China's Food and Agriculture: Issues for the 21st Century*. Washington, DC: USDA.

Rural industry has been an important part of China's economy for centuries, but it played an especially important role during the golden age of TVEs, from 1978 through 1996. During this period TVEs played the catalytic role in transforming the Chinese economy from a command economy to a market economy. Springing up in the rural areas, which were much less rigidly controlled than the cities, the entry of TVEs provided competition to state-run industrial enterprises and drove the process of marketization forward in the entire economy. TVEs increased rural incomes, absorbed rural labor released from farms, and helped narrow the urban–rural gap.

TVEs had a special distinction during this period because of their unusual ownership and corporate governance setup. Originating under the rural communes, most TVEs were collectively owned: TVEs thus presented the unusual spectacle of publicly owned enterprises growing rapidly and providing the competitive challenge that dissolved the monopoly previously held by public (state-run) enterprises. A diverse set of TVE models adapted to a range of different conditions and ended up fundamentally changing nearly every part of the Chinese economy.

TVEs underwent a further dramatic transformation after 1995–1996. Most obviously, TVEs privatized. A range of different local approaches were used, but the result was that by the new millennium, TVEs had undergone a dramatic conversion to a mostly privately run ownership structure. The ownership transformation is best understood in the context of large changes in the overall economic environment in which TVEs operated. After the mid–1990s, TVEs were forced to undergo substantial restructuring. Product market competition intensified, and credit became scarcer and more expensive. Newly private TVEs responded to these pressures, but some firms went out of business, and the collectively owned TVE sector shrank. Overall, the ability of the sector to absorb rural labor declined. TVEs today face significant challenges, but TVEs overall have continued to grow and evolve and take on new roles in China's economy. Rural industries today are less tied to their local government and community, and are rapidly taking new forms and roles.

12.1   ORIGINS OF THE TVEs

As described in Chapter 2, rural household businesses were very important in China's traditional economy, leading it to be called "bottom heavy" because of the preponderance of small, household-based, flexible, and market-oriented production units. Rural households spun and wove cotton, raised silkworms, and reeled silk thread; they cured tobacco, milled grain, and made noodles. Households made mud bricks and hewed timber, carted goods to market, and ran shops and businesses. Most of China's rural areas were knit into a dense web of markets and sideline occupations. The most important nonagricultural undertakings were handicraft operations processing agricultural goods and converting them into market goods.

The organic link between growing and processing agricultural product in the countryside was broken under the command economy. When the state established its monopoly control over agricultural goods—during the 1950s, as described in Chapter 3—rural processing businesses were inevitably cut off from their supplies. Grain, cotton, silk, peanuts, and soybeans—the staple supplies of nonagricultural businesses—were taken by the state immediately after the harvest. In fact, during the 1950s the countryside became deindustrialized. As the rural population was organized into agricultural collectives, nonagricultural production declined, and the state itself took over virtually all manufacturing production (Fei Hsiao-t'ung 1989). Of course, these policies were an integral part of the creation of the command-economy system.

The harmful effects of this policy on the rural areas were soon evident. Household income declined in commercialized rural areas where a high proportion of income previously came from sideline activities. Some formerly prosperous, densely populated regions found they had difficulty supporting large populations on the tiny amount of agricultural land available per capita. Many specialized handicrafts fell into decay as state factories moved into mass production. One among the many strands of policy during the GLF was an effort to change the overwhelming dependence on agriculture in rural areas by creating Communes and encouraging them to engage in a wide range of nonagricultural undertakings. Under the new Communes, villages were encouraged to start factories and construction teams, as well as service undertakings of all kinds. But as described in Chapter 3, the drain of manpower from agriculture proved to be disastrous, especially in the less developed provinces. Virtually all these Commune-sponsored enterprises were shut down during the terrible post-Leap crisis in 1961–1962.

A second attempt to develop rural industry occurred during the Cultural Revolution era. After 1970, during the Maoist "new leap forward," the government encouraged a new wave of state-sponsored rural industrialization under the rubric of "commune and brigade enterprises."[1] This time, care was taken to avoid the problems that crippled the GLF. Movement of workers out of agriculture was carefully controlled; rural industries were tied to the agricultural collectives; and rural industries were constantly exhorted to "serve agriculture." The communes and brigades that had been organized during the GLF served as platforms for industrial development, and rural industry began to revive rapidly during the 1970s under Cultural Revolution era policies.

This 1970s rural industrialization was very different from traditional rural industry, which had primarily processed agricultural products. The new exhortation to "serve agriculture" was interpreted narrowly to mean supplying producers' goods to agriculture. Policy during the 1970s stressed the "Five Small Industries," rural industries that included iron and steel, cement, chemical fertilizer, hydroelectric power, and farm implements. Rural industries were expected to replicate the heavy-industry–based Big Push development strategy: the factories were small relative to urban factories but large compared to rural workshops and factories in most countries. The Five Small Industries were all capital-intensive industries usually thought to be characterized by significant economies of scale (Wong 1982). They did not employ very many workers, relative to the expensive investment required, and government subsidies were important in some sectors. As a result, through 1978, rural industries did not absorb a significant part of the rural labor force, which was still overwhelmingly engaged in agriculture: 90% of the rural labor force was engaged primarily in agriculture in 1978.

Rural industries in the 1970s were a peculiar product of the command economy. If it had been feasible to integrate rural industries at that time into the command-economic system, they would have been, but since most industries were low-tech firms serving a few local customers, it was much more practical to leave them outside the plan. At the same time, rural enterprises were

---

1. After 1982 the communes were renamed townships, and brigades returned to being villages, so commune and brigade enterprises became township and village enterprises. For consistency, I will refer to them as township and village enterprises, or TVEs, throughout.

firmly ensconced in the existing collective structures in the countryside, as their very name—commune and brigade enterprises—indicated. Workers in rural industry sometimes got paid in work points, and rural-industry profits were sometimes used to raise the value of work points for the collective as a whole. Revenues earned from rural enterprises were regularly channeled by community governments to public works and aid-to-agriculture projects (Wong 1988, 18–21). In a sense, rural collectives were being allowed to share in some of the income-earning potential created by the state's monopoly over industry. Maoist China was well-known for its promotion of rural industry, but the type of industry fostered was a curious offshoot of the command economy. As of 1978, China still lacked the dense network of small-scale, nonagricultural activities that characterize prosperous countrysides in Asia, but which China had suppressed in the 1950s.

12.2 THE GOLDEN AGE OF TVE DEVELOPMENT

During 1979 the central government shifted its policy toward rural enterprises in important respects. The general liberalization of that time included a relaxation of the state monopoly on purchase of agricultural products, allowing more to remain on rural markets and thus available to rural enterprises for processing. The new policy was "Whenever it is economically rational for agricultural products to be processed in rural areas, rural enterprises should gradually take over the processing work" (System Reform Commission 1984, 97–104). TVEs, since they were collective firms, were still ideologically safe: urban firms were encouraged to subcontract work to TVEs. Once rural industries were allowed to perform agricultural processing, they were essentially free to engage in whatever activity they could find a market for. The highly restrictive Cultural Revolution model of rural industrialization was relaxed, and rural industrialization was permitted in response to multiple market opportunities. Of course, state firms and state procurement monopolies fought to maintain their monopolies, and there were policy twists and turns and slow progress in the sensitive areas. Nevertheless, local government officials quickly recognized the economic implications of TVE development, and became vigorous advocates and defenders of TVEs. Indeed, for many localities, TVEs were the only available path out of poverty.

Between 1978 and the mid–1990s, TVEs were clearly the most dynamic part of the Chinese economy. TVE employment grew from 28 million in 1978 to a peak of 135 million in 1996, a 9% annual growth rate. TVE value added, which accounted for less than 6% of GDP in 1978, increased to 26% of GDP in 1996, notwithstanding the fact that GDP itself was growing very rapidly during this period. The growth of nonagricultural income raised rural incomes and made a contribution to shrinking the urban–rural gap. Not only has TVE growth been rapid, but that growth has also played an important role in the transformation of the Chinese economy, as TVEs have created competition for existing SOEs and served as a "motor" for the entire transition process. In industry TVEs presented mounting competition for SOEs throughout the 1980s and early 1990s. SOE monopoly profits were competed away as aggressive TVEs drove price relationships into line with underlying costs. SOEs had to implement new incentive programs and improve efficiency in order to survive in the face of the TVE competitive onslaught. In the foreign trade area TVEs provided opportunities for Chinese exporters to move into new labor-intensive manufactures. In the end TVEs transformed virtually every aspect of the Chinese economy.

12.3   CAUSES OF RAPID GROWTH

Why were rural industries able to grow so rapidly? There is no single answer; rather, a confluence of five favorable factors contributed to rural industrial success: favorable fundamentals, ability to tap into monopoly rents, favorable institutional environment, revival of traditional locational patterns, and organizational flexibility.

1. TVEs faced factor-price ratios that reflected China's true factor endowment. China's basic economic endowment is that it possesses abundant labor, limited land, and scarce capital. One of the greatest irrationalities of the Big Push strategy was that it gave priority to capital-intensive industries. Urban factories faced an incentive environment created by planners of the Big Push strategy: Labor was expensive, since total worker compensation was quite generous (Chapters 5 and 8), while capital was cheap, because it was often allocated without charge or provided at highly subsidized interest rates. TVEs, by contrast, faced factor prices much more in line with China's real factor endowment. Through the 1980s rural-enterprise worker salaries were less than 60% those of state enterprise workers, and total compensation was much less than half that of urban workers. Once TVEs were cut loose from the Maoist Five Small Industries straitjacket, they adapted quickly to the underlying availability of production factors. TVEs rarely had access to subsidized capital. The bulk of TVE capital was provided at near-market interest rates or came from internally generated funds with a high opportunity cost. As a result, the ratio of labor to fixed capital in TVEs was nine times that of state-run industry

(Findlay and Watson 1992). Figure 12.1 shows that TVEs (in this case village firms) were specialized in those sectors with low capital-labor ratios, where the competitive advantage of their low wages was biggest. Facing realistic factor-price relationships, TVEs faced the right incentives to find lines of profitable business that were most appropriate in the Chinese economy and that, over the long run, gave them an advantageous competitive position. Economic fundamentals were on the side of the TVEs.

2. TVEs were able to share in the monopoly rents created for state firms; rural industries were extremely profitable. Rural enterprises were remarkably profitable in 1978: the *average* rate of profit on capital was 32%. If we include tax—because TVEs were often created by local governments who could claim a share of the tax revenues generated—the total rate of profit and tax per unit of capital was 40% (capital is here defined as the value of depreciated fixed capital plus all inventories). The high rate of profitability was not merely the result of better and more realistic use of production factors and consequent lower costs, described in the previous paragraph. Indeed, in subsequent years, even as TVEs developed a broader network of supporting services and many TVEs began to achieve economies of scale, profitability declined steadily and precipitously.

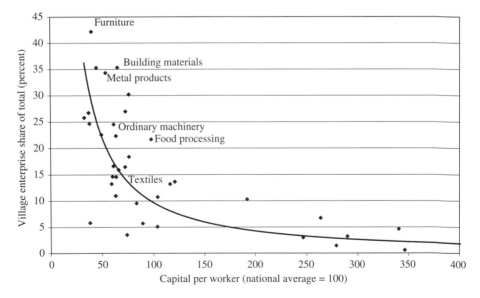

Figure 12.1
Village-enterprise share of total output × capital intensity, 1995

What can explain this pattern of rapid growth combined with steadily declining profitability? Early TVEs were in a position to benefit from the protected market created for state-run factories. By easing the state monopoly over industry, the Chinese government allowed TVEs to enter this previously protected market and share in a portion of the monopoly profits. First-mover advantages were large big enough to repay early entrants with windfall profits. In this situation continued entry only gradually created competition. State firms scarcely noticed the competition at first, because they were protected by a cushion of high profits. As long as they could gain access to low-price raw materials, they were indifferent to a few TVEs producing similar products. But gradually, as entry continued, competition among TVEs and between TVEs and state firms began to compete away monopoly profits and erode profit margins.

The existence of empty niches also contributed to this pattern of high initial profits followed by steadily declining profitability. Empty niches existed for two reasons. Certain commodities—particularly miscellaneous consumer goods—had simply not been provided by the inefficient command economy, and TVEs jumped in to meet needs until then largely unmet. For example, this response explains much of the early success of the Wenzhou region, where small-scale rural firms specialized in such items as buttons, ribbons, and elastic bands in a variety of colors and specifications; producing these items for a market of one billion led to explosive growth. In addition, a whole series of new markets were created by the sudden growth of rural incomes and the relaxation of rural economic policy. For example, rural housing construction took off, and new rural industries developed to supply building materials to this new market. In both situations, early entrants could expect windfall gains, and the presence of potential windfalls naturally induced extremely rapid entry. Gradually entrants created competition that eroded the exceptional profits available early on.

3. The institutional framework surrounding TVEs was favorable to development. Local governments became enthusiastic partisans of TVE development. At first, local governments were also the de facto owners of many TVEs. Although TVEs were nominally "collectives," it was almost never the case that the "collective" referred to was limited to the workers and managers in the TVE itself. Rather, the TVEs were owned by the rural collectivity as a whole (Chapter 5), which in practice was usually represented by the local village or township government. Later, from the 1980s onward, the ownership of TVEs diversified away from local government ownership, but local officials still had powerful incentives to develop TVEs. TVEs provided employment and money to local economies, and they were often the only realistic source of both. Local government support contributed to the formation of a favorable environment for TVEs in at least three ways:

a. Formal taxes were low on rural industry, so money stayed local. Rural enterprises enjoyed very low tax rates, and particularly low tax rates on profit. By contrast, state-run industrial firms benefited from government price policy, but they also paid the price in a very high tax rate—sometimes 100%—on profits. Rural enterprises enjoyed the benefits of price policy without the corresponding high tax burden. This unbalanced treatment seems peculiar unless we recall that during the early phase of reform China's leaders conceived of rural enterprises primarily as a device to increase the resources available to agriculture. The average rate of profit tax collected from TVEs remained very low: in 1978 this was only 8%, and by 1980 it had declined to 6%. It then gradually climbed to around 20% by 1986, where it has remained since. While formal tax rates are low, profits paid to local government "owners" were often substantial. In the early 1980s firms at the township and village levels paid about 30% of their total profits to local governments to "support agriculture" and social services, as well as additional funds for "management fees." Local governments were especially happy to have these funds because they were classified as "extrabudgetary" and therefore did not have to be shared with higher-level governments (as was the case with budgetary revenues). In turn, most local governments recycled this money back into new and expanded TVEs, since they perceived a high return for their funds in these investments.

b. Local governments acted as guarantors for TVEs, so bank capital was available. The sponsorship of China's TVEs by local governments greatly enhanced the access to capital of these new businesses. By contrast, the experience of other transforming socialist economies has been that new start-up businesses proliferate, but that such businesses have difficulty getting access to capital and as a result remain small, undercapitalized, and dependant on informal capital markets. Local government officials acted as intermediaries and guarantors, reassuring local agents of the banking system that their loans would ultimately be repaid. Indeed, in some cases, local government officials actively pressured local branches of the banking system to provide funds to their firms.

Despite local government actions supporting and serving as guarantors to TVEs those TVEs had mostly, but not completely, hard budget constraints (see Box 13.2). Government sponsorship served to spread the risks incurred by these new start-ups, essentially by having the entire local community absorb the cost of failure. Soft budget constraints—implying no responsibility for failed or misguided investments—would have been disastrous in China's rural economy. But it is unlikely that perfectly hard budget constraints for start-up businesses would have been optimal, either—a certain amount of "insurance" provided to startups by local governments almost certainly enhanced welfare. By underwriting a portion of the risk of entry, local governments enabled start-up firms to enter production with a larger size, to start with some mechanization, and to exploit the economies of scale that came from moving away from the smallest form of household production.

c. Existing credit institutions were easily adapted to support TVEs. With local governments facilitating the flow of capital to rural enterprises, those firms were able to take advantage of China's relatively abundant household saving. Chinese traditional credit clubs and other forms of informal credit markets were put to good use. As Chinese rural household saving skyrocketed during the 1980s, the supply of funds to the local rural credit cooperatives (RCCs) expanded drastically. The RCCs, nominally independent, locally controlled financial co-ops, had in fact been used before reform primarily to transfer the modest rural savings to urban uses. With the onset of reform the RCCs had much more money, and they also were allowed to lend a much greater proportion of it locally. The result was that the RCCs emerged as the main source of financial resources for the TVEs. Thus RCC loans to TVEs increased because RCC deposits increased, because they were allowed to lend more local deposits in the local areas, and because they increased the share of their local loans that went to TVEs. Local money stayed local, and so those areas that enjoyed successful TVE development early, when profits were high, were able to "snowball" rapidly into significant production scale.

4. Revival of traditional economic ties meant that proximity to urban areas fostered rural industry growth. The growth of China's rural industries has occurred primarily in regions that might more properly be termed suburban, or at least, in areas that are part of the immediate hinterland of cities. Rural industries are also highly concentrated regionally, with coastal areas containing a disproportionate share of rural industries. In 1988, three coastal provinces—Jiangsu, Zhejiang, and Shandong—accounted for 17% of China's rural population, but 43% of total rural industry, and exactly half of all township-and village-level industrial output. Such geographical concentration is entirely natural. These areas were better located to begin with, having more of the locational assets required for city growth; in turn, because cities had developed, they could also provide transport networks, communications, markets, technology, and other conditions that boost productivity throughout the cities' hinterlands, as well as in the cities themselves. Therefore, it is not surprising to find that "rural" enterprises are more likely to thrive in regions where they can benefit from the spillover effects of the urban economies.

Rather, what is striking is that these organic linkages between city and countryside had been so thoroughly cut off during the command economy. As a result, even a modest recovery of urban–rural linkages, beginning in the 1970s, resulted in rapid growth of suburban industry, given the low base from which it was starting. The growth of rural enterprises in periurban areas was facilitated by direct cooperation between urban state-run firms and rural factories, primarily in the form of subcontracting. In the three province-level municipalities of Beijing, Shanghai, and Tianjin an estimated 60%–80% of rural industrial output was produced by firms subcontracting with large urban factories. The proportions were only slightly lower in nearby provinces: linkages with Shanghai firms "played a decisive role in the development of TVEs in southern Jiangsu" (Tao Youzhi 1988, 100). Such arrangements were facilitated by family relations; rural people who had migrated to the cities and urban youth sent from Shanghai to the countryside during the Cultural Revolution helped rural firms get started. Later on, rural firms purchased talent from the cities, especially by paying high salaries to technicians and retired urban workers. Urban SOEs were willing to cooperate: as state firms gained a greater interest in profit they sought to reduce costs, and subcontracting operations to rural enterprises became increasingly attractive (particularly in the garment industry). Such relationships also allowed urban firms to escape from some of the tight constraints of the state-run industrial system. By entering into relations with rural firms, state firms could gain access to the resources they needed (particularly land and labor) in an environment in which accounting standards and supervision were somewhat less strict than in the state sector. TVEs gave state-firm managers a certain amount of flexibility to escape the rigid controls of the state sector.

5. Organizational diversity accommodated growth. A simple but important aspect of TVE development was that there was no single organizational model that TVEs had to follow. In fact, TVEs were sometimes government run, but often and increasingly they were private. Over time a group of true worker cooperatives emerged, as well as employee-owned corporations. TVEs were sometimes bureaucratic, but often highly adaptable. In this respect they were very different from SOEs, which were compelled to adopt a uniform organizational form. As a result of this flexibility, TVEs were able to adapt to a broad range of opportunities. As we will see in section 12.4, a variety of different regional "models" of rural industrialization grew up, each plausibly suited to a different set of economic conditions.

A steadily increasing share of TVEs was privately run. During the course of the 1980s new small-scale firms were started by entrepreneurs, and many firms started under collective auspices became de facto private firms. Sometimes these firms continued to register enterprises as collectives, because this practice was safe politically. Local officials formed alliances with entrepreneurs—sometimes for mutual benefit, sometimes more predatory in nature—as rural industrialization spread. There was a complex mixture of costs and benefits from this interaction between public and private. After the late 1990s the stigma on private business dissipated, and TVEs became predominantly private. In all periods, because TVEs were not constrained to a single organizational form, localities were able to adapt as the advantages and disadvantages of various options became evident.

6. Conclusion: Causes of rapid growth. Rural enterprises grew up in the interstices of the command economy system. It should be clear that their successful growth cannot be understood in isolation from that system. The command economy, having destroyed the traditional diversified rural economy in the 1950s, then created the distinctive conditions for the emergence of a new diversified rural economy during the 1980s. The influence of the command economy is particularly clear in the profitability of early rural enterprises, the differential tax treatment accorded rural enterprises, and the close links between emerging rural enterprises and the existing state-run urban economy. Moreover, the unique semipublic character of rural enterprises assisted in the supply of capital to these firms. These "artificial" conditions were the most powerful proximate causes of the explosive growth of rural industry in the 1980s.

Yet rural enterprise growth would not have taken root had it not been favored by additional, more fundamental considerations. Of these, the basic fit between rural enterprises and China's underlying factor endowment is the most important. Next in importance is the fact that the rural sector became a fertile ground for organizational experimentation in which the entrepreneurial energies of the Chinese population were given ample expression. Finally, China's huge size may have played a crucial role. The simple fact that China has some 2,000 counties, over 40,000 townships, and more than a million villages was crucial to the success of rural industry. Even when townships tried to operate miniature command economies, the fact was that ultimately they were subject to competition from thousands of other townships and villages. When firms could not make money, there was no one from outside the village to bail them out, and they had little choice but to go bankrupt. In this fundamentally competitive environment, each township or village found that it faced a relatively hard budget constraint and had to make its own enterprise economically successful. Rural enterprises created competition for state firms, and they were themselves shaped by the competitive process. Ultimately, this competitive climate may have been adequate to overcome some of the disadvantages under which rural enterprises labored due to local government control and the distortions of the economic system as a whole.

12.4 DIVERSE REGIONAL MODELS OF TVE DEVELOPMENT

Responding to different regional conditions, TVEs developed in different patterns in different parts of China. Each pattern or model provides information about the forces shaping Chinese rural development.

12.4.1 The Southern Jiangsu (Sunan) Model

Southern Jiangsu, or "Sunan" for short, is the relatively prosperous and developed area of the Yangtze Delta around Shanghai, an area that has been among the most economically advanced regions of China for centuries. Here the dominant model of TVE development was one in which the township and village governments and collective ownership maintained the leading role. This model developed in areas of southern Jiangsu where TVEs flourished early, beginning in the early 1970s. TVEs began developing while the collective system was still firmly in place in the countryside. As TVEs expanded, the collectives maintained control, even when the collective system declined elsewhere. Because of the longer history and greater capital resources in these areas, TVEs tend to be much bigger, more capital-intensive, and more technologically sophisticated than TVEs in other parts of the country.

Elements of the southern Jiangsu model appeared wherever TVEs grew up early, close to cities. "Suburban" areas with locational advantages and entrepreneurial village leaderships developed TVEs early under the collectives, and village leaders subsequently tended to maintain control for a decade or more. Subcontracting and technical assistance ties with urban SOEs were often important. Conversely, once this model developed, the collective structure remained sturdy because the TVEs generated profits that could support local government. These villages tended to develop a kind of "corporate village" in which village leaders ran an entire business complex. At the same time, such corporate villages maintained government social services and sometimes even provided welfare benefits to village residents. These "corporate villages" were sometimes suspicious of outsiders, since they wished to protect the lucrative jobs, benefits, and opportunities of locals. These localities were the most likely to directly subsidize agriculture with TVE profits, so that local farmers could join in the general prosperity.

12.4.2 The Wenzhou Model

The town of Wenzhou is only about 300 kilometers south of southern Jiangsu, on the coast of the neighboring province of Zhejiang, but it has a very different geographical setting, and it evolved a very different model of TVE development. Rugged and fairly remote—despite its coastal location—Wenzhou was quite removed from the urban influences so important in southern Jiangsu. From the beginning of its explosive growth, Wenzhou's economy has been based on private ownership. Firms in Wenzhou were initially tiny, based on individual households, and specializing in modest articles of daily use. Wenzhou businesses first flourished selling buttons, ribbons, plastic ID card holders, and other ordinary items. Wenzhou peddlers then took these items throughout China, filling a market need for diverse, inexpensive items that state firms had filled either very poorly or not at all.

Wenzhou is a very special place, with a long cultural tradition of entrepreneurship and spectacular economic growth in the past 25 years. But elements of the Wenzhou model appeared in any place where farmers were willing to seize entrepreneurial opportunities but did not have advantageous suburban locations. In these areas the collectives never successfully developed TVEs into moneymaking propositions. As a result, the collectives were weak and often disappeared early in the reform process. Individually owned firms sprang up in response to opportunity, and they naturally tended toward labor-intensive activities oriented toward the market. Indeed, perhaps the most striking feature of this model in Wenzhou itself is the intense reliance on the market to coordinate all aspects of production. The Wenzhou button industry, for example, developed around individual households that specialized in individual stages of the button-production process. Households that milled plastic blocks into button rounds sold these rounds, in a specialized marketplace, to households that drilled holes in the rounds and finished the buttons. In turn, a different group of households that specialized in mounting buttons on button cards would purchase the finished buttons at another specialized marketplace. Button cards would be sold to peddlers at still another market. In this fashion, production chains linked by markets sprang into existence. This pattern appeared repeatedly for different commodities. Many private businesses— even private banks—developed in this Wenzhou model.

12.4.3   The Pearl River Delta Model

In the Pearl River Delta—the region between Hong Kong and Guangzhou that is the core of the Southeast Coast macroregion—TVEs developed rapidly under the stimulus of foreign investment. This model was pioneered by Hong Kong businessmen who had grown up in the delta and returned to their home villages to start cooperative businesses. In these transactions, village leaders acted as managers of village assets, leasing land, signing contracts for export processing, and coordinating labor and social issues. As in the southern Jiangsu model, nearby urban (Hong Kong) businesses and local governments both played an important role. Production grew rapidly in large factories. In the Pearl River Delta, however, factories were usually export-oriented manufacturers of light, labor-intensive products.

The big difference between the Pearl River Delta model and the southern Jiangsu model is that the Pearl River Delta model is so much more open both domestically and internationally. Of course, the prosperity of the model depends on openness to foreign trade and investment. The TVEs themselves were often partly foreign owned (Hong Kong owned). But these villages also tend to be quite open to workers from other parts of China as well. While the southern Jiangsu corporate villages tended to protect from outsiders the good jobs their own locals held, the Pearl River Delta needed workers for their large labor-intensive export factories. The Pearl River Delta became by far the largest destination in China for migrant workers. Villagers in the Pearl River Delta earned locational "rents" by being open to both foreign and domestic agents.

12.4.4   Failed or Absent TVE Development

As item 4 of section 12.3 indicated, TVE development was highly concentrated in areas with strong economic potential. Conversely, there are many areas of China where TVE development was weak or nonexistent. A survey of the diversity of forms of TVE development must acknowledge that large swaths of rural China have little in the way of TVE development. In remote areas, where transportation is costly and difficult, there are few business opportunities available to TVEs. Without TVEs to contribute to the local economy, incomes are much lower, village governments are weaker (and may even have collapsed), and there are few options available to provide essential services to residents. In these areas out-migration has become one of the few options for increasing income.

12.5   THE TRANSFORMATION OF TVEs IN THE NEW CENTURY

The entire TVE sector underwent further dramatic transformation after the mid–1990s. First, TVEs faced a more challenging external environment, and their overall growth rate slowed significantly. Second, faced with this external pressure, TVEs restructured and transformed into predominantly privately owned businesses. Finally, new forms of economic cooperation and competition grew up as TVEs adapted to the new challenges and opportunities.

12.5.1   The Changing Economic Environment of TVEs

During the mid–1990s fundamental changes occurred in the economic environment in China. These changes were associated with a shift in economic reform strategy, discussed in Chapter 4. National government policy shifted toward building markets and regulatory institutions. At the same time, macroeconomic policy shifted to a more restrained stance, designed to control inflation, and an emphasis was put on greater financial independence and accountability for banks. All these changes translated into a tougher competitive environment for TVEs. At first many TVEs had trouble responding, and the very rapid growth of TVEs came to an abrupt end.

Figure 12.2 shows employment of all TVEs. In the 1980s and early 1990s, TVEs created millions of new jobs for rural residents. As the data presented in Figure 12.2 show, the pace of TVE job creation dropped off abruptly after 1996. TVE employment only significantly surpassed the 1996 peak of 135 million workers in 2004, when the total inched up to 139 million. This slowdown primarily reflects a change in macroeconomic conditions. Urban firms also had to cope with a more competitive market economy, and they responded either by closing up shop or by developing more effective market responses. Urban firms were forced to expand into market niches previously left empty and to develop nationwide marketing strategies, putting them into head-to-head competition with TVEs. The market for consumer goods shifted from one in which shortages were predictable parts of daily life to one in which virtually all goods were regularly available.

With increased market integration and competition, TVEs lost their protected position. There were few, if any, empty niches for TVEs to exploit. Moreover, as incomes, especially urban incomes, rose, consumers increasingly demanded higher quality products than traditional TVEs, with their outdated technologies, could provide. TVEs seemed to lose their special role in the economy. It is not coincidental that overall structural change in the economy also slowed down after 1996, as shown in Chapter 6. With TVEs less able to

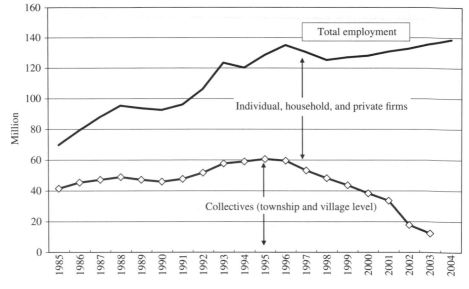

Figure 12.2
TVE employment

absorb workers from agriculture, the agricultural share of total employment stagnated for several years. It was not until well into the decade of the 2000s that structural transformation resumed and TVEs resumed absorbing labor.

In fact, TVEs continued to grow after 1996, albeit at rates closer to overall GDP growth than in the past. TVE value added as a share of GDP increased from 26% in 1996 to 30% in 1999, and then leveled off through 2004. TVEs, under pressure, appear to have raised labor efficiency, producing more output without adding workers and thereby, of course, becoming less labor-intensive. TVEs in general have become less special, but they have led the rest of the economy in becoming more private.

12.5.2 TVE Restructuring: The Great Privatization

Figure 12.2 shows the dramatic change in the ownership composition of TVEs. Collectively owned TVEs at one time dominated the entire TVE sector. After the 1980s, even though private firms grew rapidly, collective TVE employment continued to increase through 1995, at which time collectives still accounted for almost half of TVE employment. But the situation has changed dramatically in the 10 years since, and collective firms today represent less than 10% of total TVE employment. Ownership figures are not precise. Certainly in the past there were private firms that operated under the polite fiction of being collectives. As national policy has accepted private business, these firms have come out of the closet and acknowledged their true identity. On the other hand, figures for collectively owned TVEs (see Table 12.2) include only firms 100% owned by the township or village and thus excludes firms where the local government may continue to have a significant, or even controlling, stake. Still, more precise numbers would not change the basic picture. TVEs began as an offshoot of the rural collectives, but today they are predominantly private businesses.

The unique position of TVEs as publicly owned enterprises was thus a defining characteristic of the "golden age," from 1978–1996. In no other transitional economy did public enterprises play the pivotal role that TVEs played in China (not even in Vietnam, which had no publicly owned TVEs despite having a similarly large rural economy). A broad spectrum of interpretation has been put forward to explain public ownership of TVEs. At one extreme, public ownership of TVEs has been interpreted as the result of a uniquely cooperative Chinese culture, which enabled local actors to resolve incentive problems without explicit contracts (Weitzman and Xu 1994). Such an explanation is most plausible in the early phase of TVE development, when the absence of population mobility meant that local actors were forced to deal with each other repeatedly, and face-to-face. At the other extreme, publicly owned TVEs are seen, at best, as adequate adaptations to the political constraints and insecure private property rights that the central government imposed (Chang and Wang 1994). Between these extremes, some argued that in an environment in which many markets are missing or underdeveloped, local governments were able to leverage their access to credit, land, and relationships in the service of local economic development. Local governments could operate like diversified corporations with relatively hard budget constraints at the community level, combined with operational flexibility at the firm level. Qian and Jin (1998) explain the variation in public ownership across provinces by variations in the level of product and credit market development. Publicly owned TVEs are sometimes also seen as striking the right balance in motivating local government officials. Public ownership protected local interests against expropriation by higher-level government, while local government officials were given strong incentives and hard budget constraints (Che and Qian 1998; Rozelle and Boisvert 1994).

What seems clear is that changes in the economic environment gradually reduced the benefits of public ownership, and increased its costs. As market competition and population mobility increased, the local government owners adopted more powerful incentive systems to reward TVE managers (Chen 2000; Chang, McCall, and Wang 2003). Latent shortcomings of public ownership became more evident. As markets developed, public officials were not as necessary as a market replacement. Privatization was the increasingly widespread response of local governments to these changing conditions (Li and Rozelle 2003; Dong, Bowles, and Ho 2002). At the same time, national ideological constraints were being relaxed. Many external factors thus changed simultaneously.

12.5.2.1 National Policy and Local Models

National policy toward private ownership began to shift around 1995, and the taboos against private business were gradually lifted. Restrictions on the ability of local governments to privatize their public firms were eased at the same time. This shift in national government policy was a necessary prerequisite to the wave of TVE privatization. However, the specific means and pace of privatization were invariably locally determined. As a result, we can track a process of experimentation with incentive mechanisms that culminates in privatization, and observe a broad range of privatization outcomes and mechanisms.

12.5.2.2 Market Conditions and Privatization

In section 12.5.1 the general argument was made that an intensification of market competition was an important driver of institutional change in the TVE sector after 1996. Specific links with privatization include the following:

Need to Restructure: Laying Off Workers   Although TVEs had never had the kind of lifetime employment system that SOEs adopted, public ownership was often associated with local government efforts to keep local employment as high as possible. TVEs did not try to minimize wage costs, sometimes following policies of "two workers for each job" in an attempt to increase local nonagricultural employment. Moreover, publicly owned firms can find it difficult to lay off workers in times of adversity. Almost certainly, the slowing of labor absorption by TVEs is related to the transition to increased private owners.

Capital Availability: Changing Interests of Banks   After the Asian Financial Crisis in 1997–1998, China's leaders paid much more attention to the soundness of the Chinese banking system. Banks were given incentives to focus on risk and profitability, leading them to vet lending projects more carefully and discriminate among types of firms. At about the same time, the ability of local governments to provide credit guarantees for their local publicly owned TVEs declined. Profitability of TVEs declined steadily from the heights in the 1980s, so local governments had fewer financial resources to redistribute and weaker incentives to provide financial bailouts for loss-making firms. Under these conditions, banks no longer had such a strong preference for lending to firms backed by local governments. In fact, some banks even prefer to lend to private firms, which have collateral that can be seized if necessary (seizure of assets from public firms is significantly more difficult). A more "businesslike" banking sector eroded some of the benefits of public ownership and tended to push TVEs in the direction of privatization.

Managerial Labor Markets   As the Chinese economy became increasingly private and market oriented, managers of TVEs saw dramatic changes in their opportunity costs. Managers of publicly owned TVEs had typically enjoyed high incomes and significant privileges from their jobs, but the manager's point of comparison was within the local community: most managers did not become personally wealthy. Today TVE managers have abundant evidence of private managers who have become rich and powerful. Lists of the richest private businesspeople in China are a common and popular feature in the business press. It is likely that the best managers were unwilling to settle for the moderate compensation offered by public firms, and without a privatization option, they would have left the TVE sector altogether.

These channels of influence through various types of markets combined with the most fundamental channel, through the intensification of punishing product-market competition. Driven both by judgments about the relative efficiency of different ownership types and by market pressures, local governments have been increasingly "voting" for private ownership and converting their TVEs. Village leaders today are being asked to concentrate on government policy issues. In the new economic environment it simply is not possible for managers to wear two or three hats and successfully run a business while also managing the village's political affairs.

12.5.2.3 Insider Privatization

Because TVE privatization has been locally initiated and managed, the forms of privatization have varied from place to place. Still, one common observation of many different case studies is that "insider privatization" has been a common form of privatization, probably the most common. That is, TVE privatization has generally ended up with incumbent managers or closely related

Table 12.1
Distribution of shares in privatized TVEs (three sites in Shandong and Jiangsu, 2000)

Shareholders	Percent
Managers	53
Other board members	25
Workers (nonmanagerial)	18
Local government	3
Others	2

government officials owning significant shares of the privatized firms. Table 12.1 shows the results from one careful study of three sites in Shandong and Jiangsu. This level of insider privatization is unusual in government-managed privatization processes. In most such privatization processes, insider privatization is discouraged, and there is an attempt to attract outside bidders in the hopes of driving up the price of the firm. Insiders have a great deal of local knowledge about the firm. They probably have a better idea about the value of the firm than the government officials who are selling it have. But incumbent managers are also in a position to manipulate the preprivatization performance of the firm and, in particular, to make the firm look worse so that it can be purchased at a lower price. Because of the difficulty in monitoring the price at which privatization takes place, insider privatization presents many opportunities for corruption and plundering of public assets.

Privatization to insiders certainly has advantages as well. Incumbent managers are experienced, and their familiarity with the firm should give them advantages in running it after privatization. TVE managers, even under collective ownership, were often observed to have exceptionally close and enduring relationships with the firm. Many managers were in fact the entrepreneurs who started the firms, under collective auspices. In those cases, managers may have a legitimate claim to own part of the privatized firm. There is a significant question, however, as to whether there has been sufficient transparency and oversight over the privatization process. Ironically, the fact that China has never officially embraced "privatization" as such, preferring imprecise euphemisms like "restructuring," may have hindered the development of an open and transparent privatization process. At the same time, TVEs have always been a local phenomenon, embedded in the ongoing face-to-face relationships among members of a rural community. In that sense, TVE management and privatization are everybody's business. Whether or not that fact results in sufficient oversight, it has certainly led to significant local variation in the process of privatization and restructuring.

12.5.2.4 Local Variation in the Privatization Process

Local control of TVE privatization has resulted in a natural laboratory of experimentation with incentive mechanisms. Three experiments are worth mentioning.

• Some public TVEs, especially in Zhucheng, Shandong Province, were converted into worker-owned joint-stock companies, usually called joint-stock cooperatives. Workers were allocated purchase rights for shares. Allocations were not equal: managers could receive allocations as much as 20 times as large as an ordinary worker, although the average was around four times. A single share cost about 5,000 RMB, roughly a worker's annual wage, but time payment and favorable financing were available. After one year workers could sell their shares to other workers. The objective was to enfranchise workers while also creating the unambiguous property-rights structure of a joint-stock company. As Table 12.2 shows, there were 3.7 million workers in joint-stock cooperatives at the end of 2003.

• In many localities the government has retained a stake in the firm, essentially trying to operate a joint venture with the new private manager. (In these cases the local government retains a much larger stake than that shown in Table 12.1 for three locales.) Indeed, it can be hard to determine what constitutes a privatized firm today among China's TVEs: local governments may retain stakes ranging from 20% to 50%.

• "Privatization with a tail" is a common practice. In many places, local governments have confronted incumbent managers with a choice. Purchase the TVE free and clear at a "high price" (above book value), or purchase it at a

Table 12.2
TVE employment by ownership, 2003

	Million	Percent
Domestic capital enterprises	128.4	94.6
Private firms	38.7	28.5
Other	31.0	22.8
Individually run	29.9	22.0
Collective	12.4	9.1
Limited liability	10.3	7.6
Stock cooperatives	3.7	2.7
Joint stock	1.8	1.3
Jointly operated	0.7	0.5
Hong Kong/Taiwan invested	4.9	3.6
Foreign invested	2.4	1.8
Total	135.7	100.0

"low price" (at or below book value) and agree to pay the local government a share of profits over the next five to 10 years. In this case the "tail" is the future profit share. This is essentially an information-elicitation device. If managers believe the firm will increase profits, it will be in their interest to offer a higher price today; if they are genuinely skeptical about the firms future prospects, they would prefer to pay a lower price today. Such a mechanism can help overcome the problems of insider knowledge that we would expect to be severe in the Chinese context (Li and Rozelle 2003).

Despite these local variations, Table 12.2 makes abundantly clear that straightforward private ownership is now the dominant form of China's TVEs. One striking result of recent case studies is that privatization has proceeded rapidly even in those areas, such as southern Jiangsu, where collective ownership was formerly dominant. That developed region is still distinctive in many ways, but it may be losing its distinctive Sunan model of TVE development under collective ownership.

12.6 EMERGENCE OF NEW FORMS OF RURAL INDUSTRY IN THE TWENTY-FIRST CENTURY

The transformation of the TVE sector in the new century has not been limited to a conversion to private ownership. TVEs have adapted to a more open, competitive environment, and the ties that link TVEs to local governments have become weaker. TVE markets are increasingly interregional. Moreover, many of the seedbed areas of TVE growth have themselves been transformed, from rural regions in proximity to cities, to something like cities themselves, or at least to a densely populated "urbanized countryside" that is knit together with new highway networks.

One of the most striking developments has been the emergence of highly competitive "industrial clusters" in rural and suburban areas. The key feature of a cluster is the large number of firms that contribute to a single specialized product. Typical industrial clusters include scores—perhaps hundreds—of small firms that compete with each other but cooperate to form a link in a relatively complete industrial chain. Clusters may have three or four large firms cooperating with scores of small firms. Typical, though, is an exceptionally fine division of labor among different stages of the production process. Small, competitive firms specialize in extremely narrow activities. Relationships between firms can be quite complex, but they are generally mediated by efficient markets, in which a balance is struck between flexibility and long-term cooperation. Clusters generally produce light consumer goods. Examples include sock industry cluster in Zhuji municipality which is estimated to produce 35% of *world* sock production, and Liushi Township, which produces low-voltage electrical equipment. Both of these are in Zhejiang Province, which can be considered the center of industrial cluster development, with at least 519 recognized industrial clusters (Qian 2003).

Industrial clusters are phenomena that have emerged in many places around the world. The shoe industry in Brazil and the garment and luxury-goods industries in Italy display many of the same characteristics. Yet we can also identify in this phenomenon in China some typically Chinese elements that we observed already in the traditional Chinese economy, as well as in the early Wenzhou model of TVE development. The clustering of numerous small producers, linked to a larger marketplace by a series of smaller intermediate-good markets, is a form of industrial organization with a long tradition in China. Today, there are a number of industries where a resurgence of this type of organization has been accompanied by a surge in the competitiveness of Chinese goods on the world marketplace. Indeed, TVE export orientation has remained strong, and it has even increased in recent years. In this sense and many others, the "TVE sector" is again in a period of rapid change and restructuring.

BIBLIOGRAPHY

Suggestions for Further Reading

The literature on TVEs is especially rich. First, there is a rich body of descriptive and case-study material that provides a good introduction to the topic. For example, Byrd and Lin (1990) assemble a team of Chinese and international scholars for mixed case-study and analytic work. Second, there is a stimulating literature on the institutional underpinnings of the TVE phenomenon. Chang and Wang (1994), Che and Qian (1998), Weitzman and Xu (1994), and, in a somewhat different vein, Rozelle and Boisvert (1994) are important milestones in this literature.

Sources for Data and Figures

Figure 12.1: Third Census Office (1997, 5, 46–197, 198–233) provides village level and total national capital and labor, respectively.

Figure 12.2: TVE Bureau (2003); *TVE Yearbook* (2004, 102, and earlier volumes), *SAC* (2005, 44).

Table 12.1: Dong, Bowles and Ho (2002, 421).

Table 12.2: *TVE Yearbook* (2004, 102).

References

Byrd, William, and Qingsong Lin, eds. (1990). *China's Rural Industry: Structure, Development and Reform*. New York: Oxford University Press.

Che, J., and Qian Yingyi (1998). "Insecure Property Rights and Government Ownership of Firms." *Quarterly Journal of Economics*, 113(2), May, 467–96(30).

Chen, Hongyi (2000). *The Institutional Transition of China's Township and Village Enterprises: Market Liberalization, Contractual Form Innovation and Privatization*. Aldershot: Ashgate.

Chang, Chun, and Yijiang Wang (1994). The Nature of Township-Village Enterprises. *Journal of Comparative Economics*, 19(3):434–52.

Chang, Chun, Brian P. McCall, and Yijiang Wang (2003). "Incentive Contracting Versus Ownership Reforms: Evidence from China's Township and Village Enterprises." *Journal of Comparative Economics*, 31:414–28.

Dong, Xiao-yuan, Paul Bowles, and Samuel P. S. Ho (2002). "The Determinants of Employee Ownership in China's Privatized Rural Industry: Evidence from Jiangsu and Shandong." *Journal of Comparative Economics*, 30:415–37.

Fei Hsiao-t'ung (1989). *Rural Development in China: Prospect and Retrospect*. Chicago: University of Chicago Press.

Findlay, Christopher, and Andrew Watson (1992). "Surrounding the cities from the countryside," in Ross Garnaut and Guogang Liu, eds., *Economic Reform and Internationalisation: China and the Pacific Region*. St. Leonards, N.S.W.: Allen and Unwin. pp. 49–78.

Li, Hongbin, and Scott Rozelle (2003). "Privatizing Rural China: Insider Privatization, Innovative Contracts and the Performance of Township Enterprises." *China Quarterly*, No. 176 (December). pp. 981–1005.

Qian, Pingfan (2003). "Development of China's Industrial Clusters: Features and Problems." *China Development Review* 5:4 (November), pp. 44–51.

Qian, Yingyi, and Hehui Jin (1998). "Public Versus Private Ownership of Firms: Evidence from Rural China." *Quarterly Journal of Economics*, 113(3), August, 773–808.

Rozelle, Scott, and R. N. Boisvert (1994). "Quantifying Chinese Village Leaders' Multiple Objectives." *Journal of Comparative Economics*, 18, February, 25–45.

SAC (Annual). *Zhongguo Tongji Zhaiyao* [Statistical Abstract of China]. Beijing: Zhongguo Tongji.

System Reform Commission (1984). *Jingji Tizhi Gaige Wenjian Huibian 1977–1983* [Collected Economic System Reform Documents 1977–1983] Beijing: Zhongguo Caizheng Jingji.

Tao Youzhi (1988). *Sunan Moshi yu Zhifu zhi Dao* [The Southern Jiangsu model and the Road to Prosperity]. Shanghai: Shanghai Shehui Kexue Yuan.

Third Census Office (1997). Disanci Quanguo Gongye Pucha Bangongshi, ed., *Zhonghua Renming Gongheguo 1995 Nian Disancia Quanguo Gongye Pucha Ziliao Huibian* [The Data of the Third National Industrial Census of the People's Republic of China in 1995]. Beijing: Zhongguo Tongji. Zonghe, Hangyezhuan [Volume 1: Overall, Sectoral].

TVE Bureau (2003). TVE Bureau, Ministry of Agriculture, *Zhongguo Xiangzhen Qiye Tongji Ziliao 1978–2002* [China Township and Village Enterprise Statistical Materials, 1978–2002]. Beijing: Zhongguo Nongye.

TVE Yearbook (Annual). Zhongguo Xiangzhen Qiye Nianjian Biaji Weiyuanhui [China Township and Village Enterprise Yearbook Editorial Commission], ed., *Zhongguo Xiangzhen Qiye Nianjian* [China Township and Village Enterprise Yearbook]. Beijing: Zhongguo Nongye.

Weitzman, Martin, and Chenggang Xu (1994). "Chinese Township-Village Enterprises as Vaguely Defined Cooperatives." *Journal of Comparative Economics*, 18(2):121–45.

Wong, Christine (1982). "Rural Industrialization in the People's Republic of China: Lessons from the Cultural Revolution Decade." In Joint Economic Committee, U.S. Congress, *China under the Four Modernizations*, 394–418. Washington, DC: U.S. Government Printing Office.

Wong, Christine (1988). "Interpreting Rural Industrial Growth in the Post-Mao Period." *Modern China*, 14(1):3–30.

IV THE URBAN ECONOMY

Urban commercial exuberance: red lanterns in Shanghai's Ganghui Mall. (Courtesy of Micah Fisher-Kirshner.)

13

Industry: Ownership and Governance

Since 1978, China has gone through an industrial revolution. Nearly every aspect of the technological and institutional foundations of Chinese industry has been transformed. China's industry has grown at a real annual rate of around 15% since 1980. By the end of the century industrial output was ten times what it had been in 1978. Whole new industries have been created; structural change has been enormous, and China has emerged as the industrial workshop of the world. This chapter addresses the institutional changes that lie behind this dramatic transformation. Chapter 14 will examine structural change, that is, the changes in the composition of industrial output.

Institutional change in industry was central to the transition from a planned to a market economy. State-owned industry was the core of the command economy, the area where government control was the most pervasive and where the most compelling national objectives and vested interests were in evidence. The transformation of China's industrial system is discussed here in four sections. Section 13.1 presents a broad-brush description of change in the ownership of Chinese industry. Section 13.2 briefly discusses changes in industrial finance. Those two sections then set the stage for a more detailed discussion of institutions of corporate governance in Chinese state-owned industry. Section 13.4 covers privatization and hybrid-ownership forms.

This approach allows us to first sketch the impact of the most important external factor that drove institutional change in Chinese industry: the entry of new firms that steadily created an intensely competitive product market. A competitive product market is one of the most important external forces that discipline a firm and force it to become more efficient. In China the entry of new firms and the emergence of a competitive product market were intimately related to the emergence of TVEs, discussed in Chapter 12. Later, private and foreign-invested firms, contributed to a diverse ownership structure. The loss of protected markets in turn deprived SOEs of the high markups and surplus earnings they had once enjoyed, and caused dramatic changes in the system of industrial finance and in the financial position of industrial firms.

Having described the external forces driving institutional change, the chapter then discusses and analyzes corporate governance in the industrial sector. The partial and incremental reforms adopted within the state sector beginning in the 1980s are described as an experiment in incentive mechanisms. China did not privatize significant numbers of state firms during the 1980s; indeed, it did not even systematically separate SOEs out from the hierarchical state bureaucracy in which they were embedded. But China did fundamentally strengthen the incentives that motivated SOE managers and shifted their orientation toward profitability. Subsequently, under pressure from changing competitive and financial conditions, China launched a second wave of industrial reforms during the second phase of transition, after the mid–1990s. This new wave centered on corporatizing SOEs and improving their governance mechanisms. As section 13.4 covers, significant privatization and downsizing of the public enterprise sector also began at this time. These efforts have continued, with varying degrees of emphasis, through the present. Substantial changes have occurred in corporate governance in both large-scale firms and small and medium-sized enterprises. Today Chinese firms face intensifying competition from global firms, particularly after entry into the WTO. It is still not clear whether China's corporations have established governance institutions of sufficient quality to enable them to continue improving productivity and meet global competition.

13.1 OWNERSHIP CHANGE: A DIVERSE INDUSTRIAL BASE

During the early phase of China's industrial transition (1978–1993), privatization of state firms played almost no role. Instead, entry of new firms was the dominant force that drove a realignment of the ownership composition of Chinese industry. The TVEs, described in the previous chapter, played the main role in this process early on. It was not until the decade of the 2000s that privatization of state firms began to occur in really significant numbers. A variety of ownership forms began to develop in Chinese industry during the 1980s, and only gradually was the diverse ownership structure that we see today created (Box 13.1). Thus, while the scale of change has been enormous, there has also been continuity, most strikingly in the continued role of SOEs. Even today, large state enterprises play an important role in the Chinese economy. The following section traces the

Box 13.1
Ownership and Governance

> Ownership consists of two main components: the right to income and the right to control. The owner of an asset has the right to the income produced by that asset, after paying out the part of income that has been contractually promised to outside parties. The income right is thus the right to the residual income. A joint-stock company must first pay off banks and bond-holders to whom it owes money, and the owners—the shareholders—then receive the net income. The owner bears the risk of loss and enjoys higher income if profits increase. The right of physical control is also residual, in the sense that control of the asset may be limited by contract or public regulation, but the owner has the right to decide what happens to an asset after all the contractual obligations are fulfilled. Ownership rights are residual rights.
>
> Because control and income rights do not always coincide, there is a need for mechanisms of corporate governance to coordinate the interests of different parties. Except in the smallest private companies, physical control of assets is typically delegated to managers and employees who do not own the property and thus do not enjoy residual income rights. Even when managers own a share of the company, their actual physical control of the company's assets is typically much greater than their share of income rights. Owners need mechanisms to oversee and motivate managers in their interest, or else they would not be able to earn a return for investment in the firm. Relatedly, minority shareholders need protection of their rights against controlling shareholders. Otherwise, controlling shareholders might use their control to extract resources from the firm to the detriment of minority shareholders (a process known as "tunneling.")
>
> Corporate governance refers to the set of mechanisms that induce individuals with de facto control over assets to make decisions that maximize the value of the company to the owners. These mechanisms are designed to minimize the potential conflict of interest between those with control and those with income rights. They include institutions that specify the distribution of decision-making rights and responsibilities among different participants in the corporation, paying special attention to the way that shareholders delegate responsibility to managers. The corporate governance system provides the structure through which company objectives are established, and the means to monitor performance and attain those objectives (OECD 2004).

evolution of ownership through the two periods of Chinese transition that were described in Chapter 4.

13.1.1 Ownership Change in the First Period of Transition

On the eve of economic transition, in 1978, China's industry was made up of thousands of similar, publicly owned organizations. The traditional SOE—the "work unit" integrated into the government bureaucracy—dominated the scene, as it had since the 1950s. SOEs produced 77% of industrial output. "Collective enterprises" were factories that (like the agricultural collectives) were nominally owned by the workers in the enterprise but were actually controlled by local governments or other state bodies. Urban collectives produced 14% of output, and rural TVEs produced the remaining 9%. Most industry was urban and middle-sized. Very small firms were practically nonexistent (less than 5% of output), and multiplant corporations did not exist. The dominant SOEs carried many burdens. As the prototypical urban work unit (*danwei*), SOEs were responsible for the welfare, health, and political indoctrination of their workers. Managers had little flexibility and low rewards, and they were required to fulfill plan targets and carry out numerous other commands given by various parts of the bureaucracy. There was little accountability or risk.

The new entrants, the TVEs, came into the reform era largely unburdened by these external obligations. Once allowed into the industrial marketplace, they were poised to expand rapidly. We can best see the process of change by fast-forwarding to 1996 (Table 13.1; this is the same benchmark year used for urban employment in Chapter 8). Although 1996 was a few years after the policy changes of 1993, it represents the high-water mark of the trends that characterized the entire first era of transition. Over the 18 years 1978–1996, TVEs—collectively owned firms in the countryside—increased their share of total output from 9% to 28%. Overall collective firms, urban and rural, reached their maximum share of output value in 1996, accounting for 36% of the total as Table 13.1 shows. The SOE share of total industrial output declined steadily, from 77% in 1978 to only 33% in 1996. Foreign-invested enterprises (FIEs) began to achieve significant mass after about 1990. From 1978 through 1996, the industrial economy became less state-run, but it was still dominated by publicly owned firms. Publicly owned TVEs were consistently the most rapidly growing sector and the most dynamic factor in industrial transformation.

Private firms also sprang up, primarily in the small-scale sector. China had very few small firms under the planned economy, and the potential was huge. Chinese authorities were content to let the small-scale sector revive with relatively little interference. However, property-rights protection was minimal in this early phase: Private firms faced significant obstacles if they sought to grow big. The Chinese state showed benign neglect toward private firms only as long as they remained small. Indeed, continued discrimination against private firms

Table 13.1
Ownership composition of industrial output (percent of current-price output)

	1978	1996
State-owned enterprises	77	33
Collective enterprises	23	36
(of which: TVEs)	(9)	(28)
Private and household	0	19
Foreign invested	0	12
(of which, foreign nationals invest)		(7)
(of which, Hong Kong and Taiwan)		(5)

was one of the reasons that collective firms grew so rapidly. By 1996, then, China had developed a kind of tripod industrial structure, in which state, collective, and private (domestic and foreign) firms each produced about one-third of total output. Gradualist transition, in its first phase, produced dramatic growth of markets and an impressive diversification of ownership, while maintaining a large state role in the economy.

13.1.2   Ownership Change from 1996 Through the Present

A new wave of industrial reforms began in the mid–1990s, and, as discussed in Chapter 4, reform strategies underwent an important change. A milestone was the adoption of the Company Law in 1994. The Company Law provided a uniform legal framework into which different ownership forms fit. The Company Law provided a framework for "corporatizing" SOEs, that is, converting traditional SOEs into the legal form of the corporation, more appropriate to a market economy. Once an SOE was converted into a corporation, it had the option of diversifying its ownership by selling off some of the shares of the corporation. The corporate form also facilitated eventual privatization and provided an option for new hybrid ownership forms. In a sense, adoption of the Company Law signaled the intent of policy-makers to create a common legal framework in which any ownership form could operate, potentially creating a level playing field for competition. As a result of these changes, the distinct boundaries between ownership forms that are the basis of the classification shown in Table 13.1 began to blur after the mid–1990s. The adoption of the Company Law signaled the beginning of a new round of institutional change, the effects of which were felt only gradually (Lin and Zhu 2001). Indeed, they are still being worked out today.

At first, the impact of gradual reorganization of SOEs was overshadowed by the massive downsizing of the state sector that was described in Chapter 8. Tens of thousands of SOEs and urban collective firms were shut down. Laid-off workers totaled 40% of the SOE workforce, and the urban collective workforce shrank by more than two-thirds. The changing ownership composition of industry was also shaped by a policy adopted at the 15th Communist Party Congress (September 1997) called "grasping the large, and letting the small go." In "grasping the large," policy-makers sought to focus their attention on the largest, typically centrally controlled firms, reorganize them into even larger and hopefully more competitive enterprise groups, and restructure and refinance them, while keeping them under state control. In "letting the small go," policy-makers were giving local governments much greater authority to restructure their own firms and, in particular, to privatize or close down some of them. Underlying the differentiation between central and local policies was the dramatically different ways the central and local state industrial sectors had evolved over the reform era. After 20 years of reform, the central government industry was increasingly concentrated on energy, natural resources, and a few sectors with substantial economies of scale. These sectors were often protected by high barriers to entry, real or regulatory, and they had remained profitable. As a result, the central government tried to keep control of these firms. By contrast, local governments in the 1990s still ran factories across the gamut of industrial sectors. As a consequence, local government-run factories were not only much smaller than those of the central government, but also much more exposed to competitive pressures and consequently much less profitable. In fact, in the mid–1990s all the state-owned small and medium enterprises put together were losing money. Local governments were motivated to get rid of loss-making enterprises, and they also were confident that they could privatize firms in competitive sectors without many problems.

Complex forces of restructuring, competition, and privatization thus began to reshape Chinese industry after the mid–1990s. The statistical system began to change as well. Starting in 1998 statisticians began to collect complete information only on "above-scale" firms, that is, state-owned firms and nonstate firms with an annual output value of more than 5 million RMB ($600,000). The state ownership share of this above-scale industrial sector continued to decline, but, as Table 13.2 shows, relatively slowly. The most dramatic change was the increase in the share of joint-stock companies, which surged to 42.1%. However, the category of joint-stock companies (row 2 of Table 13.2) overlaps with that of state ownership (row 1): As SOEs converted to joint-stock corporations under the Company Law, those corporations in which the state maintained a controlling interest are included in row 1 of Table 13.2. The very largest state firms—for example, big oil firms like Petrochina and Sinopec—became joint-stock corporations, sold shares to the public, and listed on the Shanghai Stock Exchange, but they remained state controlled. In the above-scale sector, then, the share of output produced by state-controlled firms has only drifted down gradually. The share of collective firms, however, dropped dramatically. After reaching a peak of importance in 1996, collective firms are now rapidly privatizing and becoming less distinctive. Foreign-invested firms, finally, continue to gain in importance, but at a moderate pace.

Among the above-scale and state-controlled firms shown in Table 13.2, an important subcategory is the group of large firms controlled by the central government. In June 2003, control of those firms was transferred to a new organization, the State Asset Supervision and Administration Commission

Table 13.2
Ownership composition of industrial output (above-scale industry), percent

	1998	2004
SOEs and corporations controlled by the state	49.6	38.0
Joint-stock corporations	6.4	42.1
Foreign-invested enterprises	24.7	30.8
Collective enterprises	19.6	5.3

Table 13.3
Central government share of state-run industry, 2002

	Workers (million)	Assets (billion RMB)
All state-controlled firms	24.9	8,972
Central government	5.9	4,336
Percent	23.7	48.3

(SASAC), which was designated as the agency responsible for exercising the central government's rights of ownership of nonfinancial firms. Subsequently, during 2004 and 2005, local SASACs were set up at the provincial and munici-pal level as well. Central SASAC did not hold on to very many firms, but, as Table 13.3 shows, those firms were the largest and most highly capitalized firms in the state sector. The most important sectors under central SASAC's control were petroleum and refining, metallurgy, electricity, and military industry, plus telecommunications. Together, these five sectors accounted for two-thirds of central SASAC's workers and three-quarters of the value of its assets. The per-sistence of the large-scale, heavily capitalized and concentrated, centrally con-trolled state sector provides a significant element of continuity in the Chinese industrial ownership structure.

Small-scale industry is extremely important, but trends in the small-scale sector since the mid–1990s are not entirely clear. The last year that the National Statistics Bureau officially reported data on the output of the small-scale sector was 1999. Those data indicated that small firms, producing less than 5 million RMB output, accounted for 42% of total output. In the years since, small-scale industry has been subject to conflicting pressures. Privatiza-tion and liberalization have expanded the space in which small private firms can maneuver. But there was a "shakeout" of Chinese firms around the turn of the millennium. More intense market competition after 1997 exposed the vulnerability of small, undercapitalized firms with backward technology, and many small firms shut down. As Chapter 12 showed, TVE employment growth slowed dramatically around this time. These factors may have reversed the trend of increasing small firm market share that had been a feature of market transition up until 1996. An economic census conducted at the end of 2004 turned up contradictory indicators. On one hand, the census counted 5.3 million unincorporated family businesses engaged in industrial production, along with 947,000 private companies. Together these businesses employed a staggering 59 million workers, and both the number of businesses and the number of workers were considerably higher than earlier estimates. However, the estimate of total industrial sales from the census, compared with earlier figures on sales of the above-scale sector, implied that only 23% of industrial sales come from the small-scale sector (Economic Census 2005; SYC 2005, 488, 491). This difference indicates a considerable decline in the share of small firms, or else an acknowledgement that the 1999 figures for small-scale industry were inflated to begin with. The apparent trend toward larger industrial enterprises may reflect the fact that many private firms have now "graduated" to above-scale size. However, it also indicates that the decline in the state share of output has been much more gradual than the decline in state employment. As state ownership has become increasingly concentrated in large, capital-intensive firms—and as demand for energy and raw materials has pushed prices up for those firms—state-controlled companies have sustained only a small decline in their share of total output, measured in current prices. In 2004, state-controlled firms accounted for roughly 29% of industrial sales, since they accounted for 38% of above-scale output (see Table 13.2), which according to the Economic Census was about 77% of total industrial sales.

13.2 INDUSTRIAL FINANCE

Under the planned economy, industrial finance was not a pressing issue. In the protected markets in which SOEs operated, margins were high and SOEs generated ample profits. These profits were transferred to the state budget, which plowed them back into the firms as part of the Big Push industrial investments. Figure 13.1 shows that in 1978, at the beginning of reforms, SOE profits were huge, totaling 14% of GDP. Entry of new firms (especially TVEs) created increased competition, and the excess profits of SOEs were gradually competed away. By 1996 profits were almost zero. At this point, policy-makers faced crisis: SOEs could no longer depend upon protected prices to generate surpluses, and there was little choice other than accelerating reforms. The downsizing of SOEs, the layoffs and ending of lifetime employment in SOEs, described in Chapter 8, can be seen as an ultimately inescapable response to the impact of market competition on SOEs. Figure 13.1 also shows that SOE

Figure 13.1
State industrial enterprise profit

restructuring achieved some success after 2000. A smaller, revamped state sector, concentrated in fewer larger firms, was able to increase profits, and the state sector hooked into the booming economy in 2003–2005 to push profits up to almost 4% of GDP.

The decline in protected monopoly profits inevitably affected every aspect of industrial finance. As SOEs turned over less money to the government, so the government provided much less money to SOEs for investment. In 1978 the government budget funded 62% of all fixed investment in state-owned units, most of it going to industry. But budgetary grants declined to less than 3% of industrial investment by 1997. The decline in budgetary finance forced SOEs to exploit new sources of financing in order to maintain investment and growth. Increasingly SOEs turned to the banking system. Banks had not financed any long-term investment under the command economy. Banks had only provided trade credit—short-term financing for inventories—and this primarily to the commercial sector. During reform, policy-makers gradually shifted over to rely on bank loans to finance the industrial sector, a decision that had important consequences economy-wide. It was consistent with the macroeconomic changes taking place during the reform period, as government saving declined while households rapidly increased their saving rates, and it was associated with a major change in the role of banks in the economy (Chapters 18 and 19). The opening up of bank financing for industry eased the transition process, but it also contributed to later problems in the banking system with nonperforming loans. Within the industrial sector, firms increasingly had recourse to indirect finance (loans from banks), displacing the earlier system of direct finance (funds from the owner, that is, from the government).

Bank lending to finance long-term investment in the industrial sector began just when managers were first given incentives to increase enterprise profitability. This shift to bank lending was consistent with basic incentive principles: If SOEs had to repay their investments with interest, it was thought they would surely pay more attention to the profitability and risk of their investments than if they were investing nonrepayable government grants. But in fact SOEs turned increasingly to bank credit without much concern about their future ability to repay, and the indebtedness of SOEs steadily increased. One commonly used measure of the relationship between firms and banks is the ratio of total bank debt to shareholder equity, or the debt-equity ratio (sometimes called a leverage ratio). Equity is the residual value of the firm after contractual obligations to repay banks and other creditors have been deducted. For China, we can calculate a debt-equity indicator by first approximating equity as the value of total assets minus total debt. It is thus an imputed ownership stake, approximating the state's interest in the firm.[1] Table 13.4 shows trends in Chinese industrial SOE debt-equity ratios, along with international comparisons. Under the command economy, the debt-equity ratio was of course very low, at 12%. "As the government gradually abandoned its direct financing of industrial activity through the budget," Holz (2003, 140) points out, "the ratio had nowhere to go but up." By 1994 the debt-equity ratio had climbed steadily and reached a peak of 211%. Comparatively speaking, this is a high ratio, as Table 13.4 shows, similar to that of Japan or Thailand, economies which are well known for the dominant role banks play in financing industry. Although China's 1994 ratio was not as high as that of the highly leveraged Korean firms, the rapid sustained increase and the comparatively high level, in conjunction with low profits, were enough to alarm Chinese policy-makers. By the mid–1990s, Chinese firms had gone from being nearly debt free to being among the more indebted firms in the world in less than 20

---

1. The equity figure calculated in this way is very close to the data on "shareholder net equity" that is provided for some years by Chinese statistical sources. The debt-equity ratio is also equal to the liability/asset ratio ÷ (1 − the liability/asset ratio). As Holz (2003) explains, these indicators can only give a rough basis for comparison over time and internationally, because assets are accounted for on a cost-minus-depreciation basis, rather than on a market-valuation basis, and because the scope of accounting for assets has changed over time. SOE assets now include significant urban land-use rights, as well as nontangible assets such as trademarks and copyrights. See Holz for discussion.

Table 13.4
Debt-equity ratios, percent

China, state-owned industry	
1978	12
1994	211
1998	181
2001	147
2004	146
Comparison economies, 1988–1996 average	
Korea	347
Japan	230
Thailand	201
Indonesia	195
Germany	151
United States	103
Malaysia	91
Taiwan	82

years. Bank credit was being used to keep nonviable "zombie" firms afloat. The steady increase in debt indicated that firms were still subject to soft budget constraints and could rely on state-owned banks to provide credit as needed to keep them afloat. Combined with the trends displayed in Figure 13.1, the table shows the difficult state into which China's SOEs had fallen by the mid–1990s. With cash flow evaporating and debt accumulating, China's SOEs were virtually insolvent (Lardy 1998). The Asian financial crisis, which erupted in 1997, hit especially hard those economies such as Korea and Thailand where corporations were vulnerable because of high leverage ratios and meager cash flow; by contrast Taiwan's smaller companies with relatively low leverage ratios were much more resilient. Thus, after 1997, China's policy-makers faced serious challenges and also powerful lessons from neighboring economies. Both these factors helped convince the Chinese government to move beyond gradual marketization and step up the pace of industrial restructuring.

Since 1994, however, SOE debt levels have declined and stabilized. Debt-equity levels declined to 147% by 2001, and they were about the same in 2004. The decline in debt-equity ratios reflects both some improvement in financial health and a dramatic write-off of nonperforming bank loans. It is not possible to entirely disentangle the two causes. On the one hand, banks tightened their lending standards and began to behave more like commercial banks after the mid–1990s. This shift in bank behavior came during a period of macroeconomic austerity, and it coincided with the government's new willingness to let nonviable firms fail. As a result, many of the most highly indebted firms simply closed up during the mid–1990s, forcing banks to write off large amounts of unpaid debt. The government injected billions into the banking system to allow banks to write off bad loans and restructure debt for existing firms thought to be still viable. As part of restructuring, additional debt was sold back to the government by the banks and converted into new equity. In several rounds of recapitalization, the government injected a sum equal to at least 30% of GDP into the banks, allowing them to write off bad loans (Chapter 19). Obviously, these actions produced a substantial reduction in the leverage ratio of state-owned industry.

On the other hand, state-owned industry's overall financial position improved, in part because of the reduced interest burden in the wake of mass loan write-offs and in part because the worst-performing firms had been jettisoned. The large, centrally controlled state firms have regained profitability, in part due to their protected market positions. Debt-equity ratios in Chinese state-run industry are no longer unusually high. However, they are still significant, roughly equal to those in an economy such as Germany, where the bank role is very important. Debt-equity ratios are significantly higher than those in Taiwan or the United States. More importantly, most new finance of firms continues to be from banks, rather than through capital markets. As Chapter 19 discusses, more than 80% of enterprise funds in recent years have come from banks, with a small role for net fundraising from the stock market and an insignificant role for corporate bonds. Thus substantial reliance on bank credit continues to be an important characteristic of Chinese industrial SOEs, and there is no guarantee that debt-equity levels will not begin to climb again. Access to bank credit is an important determinant of a firm's ability to invest (or survive), and banks have large claims on the industrial sector. One of the challenges of corporate governance reform in China is to regulate the competing claims of banks and equity holders in industry. After all, one of the most basic requirements of a sound system of corporate governance is that it provides some assurance to those who provide finance to an enterprise that they will receive a return on their investment.

13.3 TRANSFORMING CORPORATE GOVERNANCE IN THE STATE SECTOR

A vast distance separates the enterprise under the planned economy from the modern, market-oriented corporation. Under the planned economy, what was called the "enterprise" was really a constituent part of an enormous bureaucracy. The enterprise was like a branch plant of the single vast undertaking that was Socialism, Incorporated. It did not possess any of the strategic planning, marketing, logistics, or personnel capabilities that we associate with a market business. Instead, as discussed in Chapter 5, the socialist enterprise served as a multifunctional social unit, the *danwei*. The government, through its hierarchically organized bureaucracy, exercised all the real powers of ownership. The government took all the enterprise's profit and made up its losses. Managers were kept busy fulfilling myriad different commands and tasks assigned by planners, in the name of the public, and were effectively hemmed in by a web of overlapping controls and restrictions. But none of the disciplines under which managers labored motivated them adequately to increase firm productivity or profitability. To transform a socialist enterprise into a profit-oriented company required change in multiple dimensions. At a minimum, the enterprise needed to change its organizational form, its objective function (the performance for which a manager is rewarded), and the prices or signals to which it responds, and it needed to face a "hard budget constraint"; that is, it needed to be responsible for its own financial performance and debts (Box 13.2). A schematic version of these elements is shown in Table 13.5.

Box 13.2
The Soft Budget Constraint

The term "soft budget constraint" was coined by Janos Kornai (1979, 1980) in his seminal studies of the socialist economy in his native Hungary. A soft budget constraint is said to exist whenever a loss-making company continues to receive financing. A perfectly hard budget constraint exists when a company has to cover all of its expenditures in a given period from its own income. The hard budget constraint is relaxed somewhat any time outside financing is available, for example, to fund investment or to tide a firm over temporary hard times. A completely soft budget constraint, then, refers to a situation where a firm can consistently lose money for a prolonged period and continue to receive financing or make a new investment without bearing any risk of failure. Varying degrees of soft budget constraint can be observed in any economy, but the soft budget constraint was especially prevalent in the socialist economy.

Kornai explained that the presence of a soft budget constraint fundamentally altered the incentive environment in which managers operated and changed the dynamics of the socialist economy. Without hard budget constraints, managers are free to pursue goals like expansion, prestige, and promotion without worrying about profitability. As a result, managers develop a virtually unlimited demand for new investment funds, phenomena Kornai labeled "investment hunger" and "expansion drive." Since demand for investment would expand indefinitely, Kornai argued that socialist economies would always be "resource constrained," in contrast to Keynesian, market economies that are "demand constrained."

In the transition process, it is inconceivable that the incentives of managers could be aligned with the requirements of a market economy without a substantial hardening of the budget constraint. Hard budget constraints mean subjecting firms to the discipline of the marketplace and limiting the politicization of the economy and the investment decision. At the same time, good firms need access to credit so that they can grow, so it is not optimal for budget constraints to be perfectly hard. In China we observe varying degrees of hardness of budget constraints. SOEs had almost completely soft budget constraints up until the late 1990s. TVEs by contrast, had significantly harder budget constraints, especially at the village or township level itself, although government officials would also intervene to slightly soften the budget constraints of individual firms. Private firms generally face hard budget constraints.

Table 13.5
Industrial enterprise transition: elements of analysis

	Pure plan	Transition A, 1979–1993	Transition B, 1996–current	Pure market
Organizational form	Element of hierarchical bureaucracy	"Incentivized" bureaucratic element	Reorganized into corporations	Multiform, strategic corporations
Managerial objective	Plan fulfillment; interests of danwei (work unit)	Profit by contract; interests of danwei (work unit)	Profit, but with qualifications	Profit; discounted present value of future profit stream
Price system	Planned prices	Dual-track prices	Market prices, with government intervention	Market prices, with regulation
Budget constraints	Soft	Soft	Hard, but with qualifications	Hard

In the different transition economies there have been two basic approaches to achieving this multidimensional transformation. The approach followed in Russia and many of the Eastern Europe economies was to break down as quickly as possible the hierarchical relationship in which enterprises were embedded. By stressing privatization, reformers advocated a quick, complete rupture with the hierarchy and a rapid conversion of ownership. Reformers accepted that price reform was a prerequisite for ownership reform, but as soon as prices could be liberalized, they advocated a rapid move to privatization. In this way, they hoped to set enterprises free from their bureaucratic supervisors quickly. Deprived of bureaucratic sponsors, firms would soon face hard budget constraints, and the new owners could be relied on restructure the organizational forms and managerial objectives through their own self-interest. That, anyway, was the theory: rapid privatization could be the driving force of realignment in all the elements of enterprise management. The Chinese approach in the initial phase of enterprise reform was nearly the opposite: it sought to make use of the hierarchical relationship in which enterprises were embedded, remaking incentives and organization, while simultaneously creating "dual-track" market prices. Reformers sought to make managers, as agents of the government, devote greater effort to improving enterprise productivity and profitability. They launched the package of incremental changes shown under "Transition A, 1979–1993" in Table 13.5.

13.3.1 Creating Corporate Governance: Transition A

During the initial period of Chinese industrial reform, the organizational form of the enterprise was only slightly altered, and the enterprise remained tied to the bureaucracy. Reformers were reluctant to disrupt the work unit that wrapped industrial workers in a cocoon of stability. Instead, reformers experimented with a variety of incentive devices, strongly increasing the rewards given to managers and tying incentives closely to profitability. Some of these incentive devices mimicked those that had succeeded in the agricultural sector; successful experiments from the rural sector were brought into the core of the planned economy, state-run industry. There was also a progression from "low-powered" to "higher-powered" incentives through the 1980s. At first, profit incentives simply consisted of modest bonus and investment funds, so *profit sharing* was a small percentage of total enterprise profit. Consequently, the *marginal* share of profit retained by the firm was small. Figure 13.2 shows typical marginal retention rates (the parameter *b*) during three successive periods of the 1980s. In the first pattern, enterprises were allowed to draw a specified percentage (usually less than 10%) from total profit if major targets were fulfilled. In the mid–1980s reformers moved to a pattern of *progressive profit sharing*, in which, in addition to a fixed base retention, the enterprise retained a specified percentage of the *increase* in profit (typically around 20%). In the third pattern, *profit contracting*, each firm would contract to remit a fixed amount of profit, and any profit earned above the contracted level—specified in advance between the enterprise and its supervising agency—was kept almost entirely by the enterprise. Thus the marginal retention rate was often 100% or close to it. There was a steady migration to higher marginal retention rates: as reward functions became steeper (that is, as *b* became larger), profit-oriented incentives became increasingly powerful at the margin.

Profit sharing (1979–1983)

$R = b \times \Pi$ $\quad\quad\quad\quad b < 0.10$

Progressive profit sharing (1983–1986)

$R = a + b\,(\Pi - \Pi_{t-1})$ $\quad 0.10 < b < 0.50$

Profit contracting (1986–1989)

$R = a + b\,(\Pi - \Pi_{contract})$ $\quad 0.50 < b < 1.0$

where *R* is retained profit or bonus, and Π is profit.

Figure 13.2
Creating high-powered incentives

For this approach to make sense, it had to be accompanied by the so-called "dual-track" pricing system. Firms, including SOEs, were allowed to buy and sell at market prices once they had fulfilled their plan responsibilities. Since the size of a typical firm's plan production was fixed, even SOEs faced market prices at the margin (Byrd 1991). With market prices and high-powered incentives at the margin, managers were motivated to expand market-oriented activity. The result was that an increasing share of transactions took place on the market. Gradually, the industrial economy grew into the market, and grew out of the plan. The "incentivization" approach helped to dismantle the bureaucratic economy and reorient firms to respond to market competition.

This approach had costs as well as benefits. The internal organization of most SOEs was basically unchanged, and the firm had to coordinate its activity not only with its immediate superior agency, but also with numerous other bureaucratic agencies, such as labor bureaus, local governments, and budgetary authorities. The most unproductive firms continued to be sheltered against the increasing tide of market competition. Moreover, the process of "incentivizing" the firm meant that managers were in some respects actually tied *more* closely to their bureaucratic superiors than they had been previously. Bureaucrats could now reward managers with substantial money and noncash rewards. Managers were negotiating profit contracts with their bureaucratic superiors, and the firm's retained funds were determined by how well it was able to meet the profit targets negotiated by the manager. Managers and their superiors worked closely together, understood each other well, and had broad scope for mutually beneficial deals. Each firm was special, and there was very little movement toward a "level playing field," a system of uniform treatment in which market forces would determine outcomes fairly and budget constraints would be hard.

Enterprise managers gained authority and autonomy. The focus on profit as the nexus of the relationship between manager and superior organ gave the manager more leeway to chart firm strategy on his own. Within the enterprise the "factory manager responsibility system" was widely adopted after 1984 to clarify the power of managers, rather than Communist Party officials, to make the key economic decisions in the firm. Managers found their position within the firm strengthened. Although managerial appointments were still decided by a higher level Communist Party committee and managers were still forced to form coalitions with workers, who could not be fired, managers increasingly wielded decision-making power within the firm. Profit was retained by the SOE as an entity, so while the manager had a large say in the disposition of profit, he also had to bring benefits to the workers. Most of China's enterprise-built housing, for example, was actually built during this period in the 1980s. The *danwei* system was in some respects strengthened.

The growing authority of enterprise managers, along with the growing marketization of the economy, began to create a new set of problems. Managers increasingly exercised the residual control rights over enterprise assets. Residual income rights still belonged in theory to the owner, the state, but managers controlled substantial retained funds. In the short run, profit contracting ameliorated some of the conflict of interest between manager and owner. But in the long run, managers, who had superior local, insider's knowledge of the enterprise's circumstances, could be expected to have decisive advantages in the negotiation process. Increasing managerial authority and declining government oversight of managers contributed to these problems. Managers bought and sold products at both planned and market prices, creating opportunities to pocket the margin between the two. Managers carved out significant flexibility to set up subsidiaries and cooperate with other types of firms, opening up new opportunities for complex related-party transactions. Moreover, as urban society became more affluent, aspirations increased, while it became much more difficult to monitor the manager's consumption. Increasingly, the need was perceived for a more fundamental restructuring of property rights and corporate governance, in order to create a better system of oversight over managerial discretion, a way to hold managers accountable for their actions in controlling public assets.

13.3.2   Creating Corporations: Transition B

In the mid–1990s a new program of enterprise reform was launched. The centerpiece of the new program was corporatization, but there was movement in many different areas simultaneously. Most important, Chinese reformers significantly hardened the budget constraints faced by enterprises. Chronic loss-making "zombie" enterprises were finally closed down or sold off on a large scale. The total number of industrial SOEs dropped from 120,000 in the mid–1990s to only 31,750 in 2004, including all state-controlled corporations. Some of the worst shuttered firms had been idle for years and were simply put out of their misery. Other firms were shut down when they failed to respond to the new macroeconomic conditions of the late 1990s. As described earlier, the financial position of SOEs was already deteriorating. As macroeconomic policy was significantly tightened in the middle of the decade, banks had less access to credit funds and they in turn passed on tougher lending standards and repayment provision to enterprises. Squeezed between more competitive product markets and tighter credit, many firms restructured and laid off redundant workers, or shut down altogether.

The new wave of enterprise reform was enabled by an economy-wide package of complementary institutional reforms.

• Tax reform at the end of 1994 finally eliminated profit sharing and the practice of profit contracting, instead shifting to a combined reliance on value-added tax and profit tax (Chapter 18). These changes increased the marginal tax rate for many firms, but led to lower overall taxes and a more equitable tax burden. Moreover, tax reform weakened the link between SOEs and their bureaucratic superiors.

• Banking reforms from 1995 created more professional and independent bankers (Chapter 19).

• Social security reforms in the mid–1990s, while not fully successful, did provide alternative funding for millions of workers and retirees in failing firms, protecting most pensions and providing some welfare and unemployment benefits (Chapter 8).

• Housing privatization began soon after enterprise reform, creating millions of new urban property owners (Chapter 5), some of whom were laid-off workers. Schools and clinics were gradually spun off into independent entities.

With these complementary reforms, reformers felt they had an alternate means of delivering social services, and could begin peeling the multiple noncore functions from the urban *danwei*. Leaders allowed enterprise reforms to go forward, gambling that the downsizing of SOEs and mass lay-offs could now take place at an acceptable political cost. These institutional changes combined with new initiatives to corporate governance within the state firm to form a distinct reform strategy, listed as Transition B in Table 13.5. The new reform package gained effectiveness from the complementarities among reform initiatives.

13.3.2.1 Corporatization and the Company Law: Objectives and Principles

The foundation of the policy of "corporatization" was the Chinese Company Law, part of the burst of reform measures in 1993–1994. We noted previously the importance of the Company Law in providing a vehicle for the diversification of ownership, including partial or complete privatization and the creation of a legal level playing field. Here we stress the other important function of the Company Law, which was to improve governance in SOEs. Under the Company Law, individual SOEs were to reorganize into corporations gradually, one by one. As Clarke (2003) explains, traditional state-owned enterprises (TSOEs) would essentially disappear as each was converted either into a joint-stock corporation (JSC) or a simpler limited liability company (LLC), intended for a smaller and more closely knit group of owners.[2] From the stand-

2. A special type of LLC was even provided for firms 100% owned by a single government agency.

point of state ownership, corporatization under the Company Law was designed not only to continue the trend of giving managers more authority, but also to establish a better system of oversight to ensure that managers pursued the same interests as their government owners.

Effective corporate governance aligns the interests of a firm's management with its owners. The crucial institution is the firm's board of directors, which the Company Law specifies is the supreme authority in the corporation. The state appoints the members of the board in its capacity as a shareholder in the firm. The board of directors then gives direction, oversees, and hires and fires managers. In this way, the state is to exercise its ownership rights by redefining its role as a pure shareholder. In principle, these organizational changes should produce three interrelated advantages:

• **Autonomy.** The organizational changes give the firm greater autonomy within a clear legal framework, since the firm's managers are now accountable to the board of directors, and only to the board of directors. The manager should no longer be obliged to take orders from multiple government agencies. Instead, government interests and objectives are supposed to be transmitted to the corporation through the board of directors appointed by government agencies and any other owners.

• **Depoliticization and profit maximization.** If several parties—including government agencies with diverse agendas—share ownership, the interests of the various parties are reduced to a common denominator, equity, and the new shareholders have only one way to voice their interests, shareholder voting. The shareholders now share a common interest—distributable profits—which encourages the owners to focus on the single target of profitability (Clarke 2003).

• **Encouraging specialized government oversight.** Some of the biggest problems with public ownership come from the lack of a specialized "ownership agency" designed to aggressively advocate the public interest. The firm is monitored by one or many agents of the state, but these have ill-defined and sometimes conflicting missions. Not one of these agents really has strong incentives to press the firm to achieve higher levels of efficiency, since none has a direct interest in profitability. Monitors may be negligent, or they may be captured by the interests they are supposed to monitor. Corporatization does not directly resolve this problem, but by clearly specifying ownership rights and responsibilities and linking these with the appointment power to the board of directors, the corporate form encourages the designation of an attentive government monitor with a strong derived interest in profitability.

How have these objectives been achieved in practice?

13.3.2.2   The Chinese System in Practice

Slow Implementation   Despite the fundamental importance of corporatization, actual implementation of the Company Law has been slow. Traditional SOEs are still far from extinct. Indeed, at the end of 2003 there were still 23,000 traditional industrial SOEs, producing one-third of state-sector output, while there were 11,000 state-controlled corporations (not TSOEs) producing two-thirds of state-sector output. Corporatized firms were four times the size of TSOEs, on average (*SYC* 2004, 513). Even those firms formally reorganized under the Company Law have not necessarily implemented the provisions effectively. The boards of directors have the central position in the legal structure outlined in the Company Law, but the majority of firms reorganized under the Company Law do not actually have functioning boards of directors. For example, all firms listed on the Chinese stock exchanges were supposed to have boards of directors with one-third independent directors by May 2003, but even among these firms, which we would expect to have by far the best corporate governance institutions, only 62% had boards by the deadline (Green 2004, 14). In response to a decade of slow implementation, there has been a renewed push since 2005 to encourage firms to formally constitute and empower boards of directors.

Forming Oversight Agencies   After government ownership is redefined as shareholding, the task remains to create an effective organization to actually exercise the government's ownership rights. After a number of unsuccessful experiments, China in June 2003 established the SASAC. SASAC's core mission is to carry out the government's functions as investor and owner of state assets, and thus separate these tasks from the government's role as public manager of society as a whole. Consistent with the principles of corporatization, SASAC's mission is much more clearly demarcated than previous agencies, in three important dimensions. First, SASAC exercises in principle all the responsibilities and benefits of ownership, and specifically is tasked to monitor enterprise operations in order to protect the rights of the government owner; to appoint members of boards of directors and establish procedures for appointing managers; and to approve major decisions in enterprise operation. Second, central government SASAC has authority over a specific list of non-financial enterprises—196 firms initially—and it exercises direct ownership only over those firms. Third, national SASAC's demarcation of authority freed local governments to set up their own local SASACs, which by the end of 2005 exercised ownership of state firms in every province. Thus for the first time the local ownership of state-run firms has a clear legal and regulatory framework, which frees local governments to proceed with the restructuring and privatization of their firms.

However, the demarcation of SASAC's authority is plagued with a number of difficulties. By far the most important is the inherent conflict with the Communist Party over appointment power. Arguably the most fundamental characteristic of the Chinese political system is that the Communist Party retains its traditional *nomenklatura* role, in which party committees make all the key personnel appointments in the state sector. Although the Communist Party has lost most of its ideological content and has become more meritocratic and development oriented, it obviously does not, and will not, appoint directors to companies solely on the basis of their ability to maximize profit and the value of the government's ownership stake. Indeed, since the Communist Party does not itself possess the ownership stake, it is not clear that party appointees have any interest in profit maximization as such at all. The Communist Party explicitly retained the direct appointment power for the top jobs of 53 of the 196 enterprises managed by central government SASAC and has delegated appointment powers for the other top jobs to the Communist Party Committee within SASAC (SASAC 2004, 99). The Communist Party holds on to its appointment power and thereby continues to shape the career paths and incentives of enterprise managers. Politicians and bureaucrats struggle to redefine these relationships in an economically rational way.

SASAC also does not directly collect the earnings to which its ownership stake entitles it. Most state firms gained the right to retain their after-tax profits during the earlier stages of reform. Some state firms do turn over profits or dividends but these go directly to parent firms or local governments (sometimes through local SASACs). Central SASAC is working hard to gain some budgeting authority but for now SASAC works very much as the agent of the Ministry of Finance. At the same time, SASAC's contol of revenues—and ownership authority—is limited by the powerful corporations directly *underneath* its oversight. Many of the 196 "enterprises" governed by central SASAC are in fact large holding corporations that evolved from the former government ministries. These corporations have hundreds of subordinate firms, control large sums of money, and exercise strategic control over decision-making. Moreover, these corporations typically retain their own revenues and remit only taxes (not profits) to the government. For example, SASAC exercises nominal ownership rights over the five large electricity conglomerates that produce virtually all of China's electricity, as well as the two primary electricity grid operators. These conglomerates in turn control hundreds of firms, including at least 10 listed corporations. These conglomerates are highly opaque, and in practice officials with political ties and little accountability exercise government ownership rights within the organization. There are numerous similar cases in the sprawling industrial empire overseen by SASAC. Thus SASAC has a long way to go before it can serve as a government holding company, exercising ownership rights in an unambiguous fashion, governed by law.

Oversight Based on Profit and Productivity   SASAC has, however, greatly stepped up the focus on profitability, especially maximization of asset value. SASAC has established ambitious goals for restructuring state assets, focusing on core capabilities, and maximizing (government) shareholder value. Indeed, central SASAC's approach has strong overtones of American business principles, including an instruction—borrowed from legendary General Electric CEO Jack Welch—that each SASAC firm should either rank 1, 2, or 3 in its respective markets or exit that market altogether. Firms under its purview have been consolidated—to 169 by mid–2005—and some noncore activities purged.

Despite consolidation, though, SASAC consistently argues for a large and ongoing role for government ownership at the central level. According to Li Rongrong, the head of SASAC, state ownership is appropriate in four sectors: national security, natural monopoly, important public goods or services, and important national resources. In addition, a few key enterprises in "pillar" (priority) industries, and high-tech sectors, should be maintained under state ownership. This rationale is consistent with the trends in the Chinese economy discussed earlier, because central government ownership is in fact concentrated in these sectors. The articulation of an explicit rationale for government ownership suggests a continuing gradual state withdrawal from competitive sectors where there is no compelling argument for a direct government role, but it also implies the persistence of a large central government-run industrial sector for the foreseeable future.

There is a deep underlying tension—and perhaps contradiction—between SASAC's effort to increase government shareholder value and its rationale for continuing government ownership. The argument is made in favor of government ownership in sectors characterized by market failures or an overriding public interest. Ideally, however, the public interest should be represented by separate, independent regulatory agencies. Before this can happen, however, China's embryonic regulatory agencies require administrative strengthening, stronger powers, rule of law, and greater transparency. Because this transformation cannot be achieved overnight, it is probably unavoidable that SASAC would combine regulatory and ownership authority in the early years of its mandate. But to the extent that SASAC itself takes on the responsibility to correct the market failure or represent the public interest, it diverts its attention from its core responsibility of maximizing state asset value. Moreover, because other bodies, such as the Communist Party, shape the managerial appointment process, there are additional pressures that divert managers from a focus on profit maximization. These multiple and inconsistent objectives, however, were precisely the inherent problems that plagued government ownership in the first place. If SASAC has to correct market failure and represent the public interest in every major corporate decision, it will be difficult for SASAC to motivate managers to maximize profit and hold them accountable for improving productivity.

13.3.2.3 Typology of Corporate Governance Systems

How is oversight of managers of publicly owned firms in China exercised? In order to answer this question, it is useful to review the main systems of corporate governance in use worldwide. How are managers motivated and overseen in other systems, when the owners themselves are not directly engaged in managing? Large corporations have long since institutionalized a substantial separation between ownership and managerial control. The two main methods through which managers' incentives are brought in line with the objectives of the owners, often classified into two systems, are discussed in this section.

The first method through which oversight of managers is exercised can be called *market based*. Primary reliance is placed on the stock market to implement effective corporate governance in what is also sometimes called the Anglo-American system. In the United States and United Kingdom shareholders are widely dispersed and do not generally have insider information about the individual company. As a result, these systems have relatively strong requirements for disclosure of public information and relatively strong emphasis on the protection of minority shareholders in law and regulation. The system exercises oversight over managers because the board of directors has unambiguous power to appoint and remove managers, and shareholders have clear authority over the board of directors. Dissatisfied "owners" exit the company by selling their shares, so share price is a sensitive indicator of performance, and low share price often leads to a replacement of management. In the extreme, low share prices may lead to a hostile takeover and the replacement of managers by a new group of investors. In this system, managers may also be shareholders, or they may earn options to buy shares, further aligning managerial interests with owners' interests.[3]

The second main method of oversight might be called *control based*. In practice, banks or founding families typically monitor managerial performance.

---

3. An additional strength of this system is that it has evolved to support complex chains of agency relationships. Intermediate institutions, such as pension funds and mutual funds, now hold the majority of shares, and because of their large stakes they monitor managers carefully. The system continues to work fairly well because most actors share a common focus on profit and stock market value.

This system is sometimes called the Continental or Japanese system, because in continental European and Japanese economies banks play a much more important role in monitoring corporate behavior. In this system oversight is exercised by groups that have access to insider information about the firm, either through the banking relationship or through supplier and customer relationships. The system accommodates the interests of a wider range of stakeholder groups than does the Anglo-American system. For example, worker interests are represented in the German supervisory boards, and *keiretsu* (related-company business group) interests have a voice in Japanese corporate decision-making; some of these interests are "insiders." The strength of this system may be its ability to accommodate the interests of many stakeholders in the elaboration of a long-run development program; the weakness is that the system may result in a lack of responsiveness and long delays in changing business strategy. Because of large strategic share-holdings by banks and related companies, ownership and control usually cannot be contested: hostile takeovers are extremely rare. Oversight is exercised by the bank and other related parties watching over the shoulders of managers. As long as management is effective and honest, there is little interference; if banks see problems begin to develop, based on their inside information, they step up their intervention and may even replace the management.

Chinese state ownership has many characteristics of a control-based system but there are also important differences. Certainly the state exercises oversight directly while also accommodating a range of stakeholders. Moreover, as Table 13.4 showed, China since the 1990s has had a relatively large reliance on banks as providers of capital, and the important banks are all state-run. But it would be a mistake to see the Chinese system as one in which corporate control is exercised through a combination of government and government-run banks. In most control-based systems, banks are privately owned, traditionally independent, powerful actors who vigorously enforce their interests. In China, however, banks have very few ways to enforce their interests; for example, legally they have low priority in repayment in the case of bankruptcy. Banks are not allowed to own stock directly. Most important, because of their long tradition of passively accommodating government lending policies, banks have neither the capability nor a clear mandate to aggressively monitor enterprise performance. In China, although the pattern of financing reveals the importance of banks, the system of corporate governance has no corresponding role for bank oversight. To the extent that China has a control-based system, the control is fragmented among state-owned industrial holding companies, SASACs at various levels, and government and Communist Party bodies. These agencies do not share consistent interests in firm performance or managerial incentives.

At the same time, China has clearly not created a market-based system of corporate governance. Stock market listings have been achieved for a large number of the biggest firms (1377 at the end of 2004), but they serve a very weak disciplinary role. In the majority of cases (79%), the listed firm has a parent company, and that parent generally has a controlling stake that cannot be challenged (Bai et al 2004). Measures have been taken to improve disclosure requirements and require independent directors on boards of directors. Independent financial journalism has begun to improve transparency, and some large scandals have been exposed. Nevertheless, these mechanisms are still immature and, because of the low contestability of control of most state-owned firms, the stock market cannot effectively discipline managers.

As a result of the weakness of both control-based and market-based system of managerial oversight, Chinese state firm managers have achieved an extraordinary degree of independence. One of the most persuasive pieces of evidence is the testimony of the managers themselves. The Shanghai Stock Exchange polled managers of listed firms and asked them to identify the most important internal and external constraints on their authority. The answers are shown in Table 13.6. Only 29% of managers chose the board of directors as their most important internal constraint, and remarkably, the second most common internal constraint, named by 25.8% of respondents, was "self-restraint," meaning that they perceive no significant internal restraints at all. Another 20% of respondents identified the Annual General Meeting as their most important internal restraint, a factor that is unlikely to wield much influence over managers during most of the year. The answers to external

Table 13.6

Most important constraints reported by CEOs of listed companies, 2000

Internal constraining factor	Percent	External constraining factor	Percent
Board of directors	29.2	Product markets	79.1
Self-constraint of managers	25.8	Stock markets	4.8
Annual general meeting	19.9	Managerial job markets	4.5
Bureaucratic superiors	13.2	Labor markets	4.0
Local government	5.4	Consumers	3.3
Supervisory board	3.4	Banks	2.7
Employees	1.7	Key suppliers	1.3
Enterprise party committee	1.3	News media	0.3
Trade union	0.1		
Total	100.0	Total	100.0

constraints were even more overwhelming: only product markets exercise a significant disciplinary influence over managers. By their own testimony, Chinese enterprise managers have achieved extraordinary discretion and autonomy.

Of course, this autonomy is not absolute. Managers must negotiate their authority with their controlling share-holders (Lee and Hahn 2004). As Tenev and Zhang (2002) point out, the boundaries between listed firms and their parent companies are new and arbitrary. Controlling shareholders sometimes exploit their firms for their own benefit to the disadvantage of other share-holders, the practice known as "tunneling." For example, parent companies sometimes extract direct payments from listed firms, borrow money on easy terms, use listed firms as guarantors for their own borrowing, or buy and sell goods and assets at unfair prices. Conversely, parent companies sometimes inject assets into listed firms for various reasons. Bai et al (2004) found that stock market valuations were lower as the controlling (state) shareholders had a larger stake and higher when minority shareholders held larger and more concentrated stakes. They interpret this to mean that more powerful minority shareholders provide some restraints on tunneling by controlling shareholders. When managers controlled the board of directors, valuations were lower. The danger is that a coalition of insiders is able to gain control of the firm without outside oversight or restraint.

An additional monitor of managerial performance is the Communist Party. The Party has the ability to remove, transfer, or promote managers, and managers are expected to follow Party instructions. The Party limits the manager's identification with a specific enterprise, in a way that may reduce the manager's incentive to maximize enterprise value and profit. But the Party also limits the manager's ability to divert enterprise resources for his own personal benefit. The party thus serves as one of the mechanisms of corporate governance, albeit one with as many costs as benefits. Indeed, Chang and Wong (2004) find that the accounting rates of return of listed firms were affected by the degree of influence exercised by the firm's Communist Party Committee. In their study, Party influence improved performance by reducing excess managerial authority but this was outweighed by reduced performance caused by Party interference with the Board of Directors.

Managerial Abuse: Asset Stripping and Related-Party Transactions   The extremely broad scope of managerial discretion inevitably leads to abuses in some cases. Although the penalties for corruption are severe, the overall institutional environment makes corruption relatively difficult to detect and punish unless it is particularly overt. Managers have wide discretion to establish subsidiaries and joint ventures. The scope for related-party transactions is wide. It is relatively easy to sell public resources for a price slightly under the true market price to a related party. It is relatively easy to set up a subsidiary, staffed by family members, that receives preference from the public enterprise in a range of business activities (Ding 2000). Such activities are believed to be prevalent in China, but there are no good data. The existence of these abuses does not mean that China is unusually corrupt. In fact, the Corruption Perception Index for 2005, published by the anticorruption watchdog group Transparency International, places China right in the middle of the countries surveyed (71st out of 146 countries). By this standard, China perhaps displays slightly less individual corruption than would be expected given its per capita income (perceptions of corruption decline as per capita GDP increases). The challenge to corporate governance in China is less individual corruption, and more the danger that large and interconnected groups of insiders will divert resources from the broader public interest to their collective and institutional interest. Thus far, institutions like the stock market may have improved the situation but have not yet brought transparency and external oversight fully into the state corporate sector.

13.4   PRIVATIZATION AND HYBRID OWNERSHIP

As mentioned previously, corporatization enables privatization, either complete privatization or diversification of ownership by selling off minority stakes to the public or to strategic investors. In fact, privatization has become very significant in China since the end of the 1990s. As in the TVE sector, the dominant form of privatization has been privatization to insiders—the existing managers and workers of the firm. Two policy precedents were crucial in setting off the current wave of privatization. The first was the development in the mid–1990s of a transitional ownership form, originally for TVEs, called joint-stock cooperatives. In these firms, all the shares of the originally publicly owned firms were sold to workers and managers at concessionary prices. After all the shares were sold, the firm converted into a joint-stock corporation, and workers could sell their shares after a year. In Zhucheng, in Shandong Province, 85% of the publicly owned firms (including 32 SOEs and 178 TVEs) were privatized in this way. The key innovation was that managers could take stakes that were 20 or more times larger than those of an ordinary worker (Huang and Huang 1988). The second precedent was established when the well-known Chinese computer company Lianxiang (now known as Lenovo internationally) converted to a corporation. In this case, the founding managerial team was clearly responsible for the success of the company, which they had created from scratch. After some hesitation, this group of managers was allowed to take a 20% stake in the company as founder's equity. The desire to foster China's high-tech industry and to emulate the intense entrepreneurial environment of Silicon Valley played a major role, and many new technology firms were allowed to distribute some equity to managers involved in start-up.

These two precedents opened the way for a gradual acceleration of restructuring, especially in small-scale industry. Privatization, especially insider privatization and managerial buyouts (MBOs), became a widespread phenomenon in China as the smaller firms were "let go." In addition, in many cases government retained some kind of minority stake in the firm, either directly or through subsidiary companies. Blended firms, especially in the technology industry, became common. In these cases the state's minority interest is typically passive, since the managerial group will have control of the firm through its combined management and equity positions. This newly emerging sector of Chinese industry—medium-size, predominantly private, but with hybrid ownership patterns—has emerged as a highly dynamic and rapidly growing sector. Without doubt, many of these firms are now run along purely commercial lines and have a strong focus on profitability. Much of the future of China's industry lies in the growth of this sector.

The actual privatization process, and particularly the prominence of MBOs, has proved to be highly controversial in China. Critics have argued that managers used the firm's assets to gain access to credit, which they then used to finance their personal purchase of the firm. Given the advantage that incumbent managers have in understanding and manipulating the firm, it is perhaps inevitable that the group will end up with a significant ownership stake in privatized firms. Moreover, the entire privatization process has been highly decentralized and run by local governments (and local SASACs after their establishment). Since there has never been a clearly articulated rationale for privatization—or even an announcement that privatization has been adopted as a policy—privatization has gone forward at a pace selected by local governments and, implicitly, firm managers. Locals do not have a rationale for holding on to public firms; they only have an instruction to maintain the state's interests. Privatization is delayed or accelerated according to local interests, and this fact inevitably opens up a wide scope for abuse.

As part of SASAC's mandate to protect the value of state assets, it has attempted to impose some limits on the process of insider privatization. SASAC has alternately banned insider privatization—while it developed new rules—and allowed it while attempting to impose greater rules and transparency. SASAC sets a lower limit for the price at which firms may be purchased: the net value of SOE assets. It also requires competitive bidding, encourages firms to be sold through regional property-rights exchanges, and limits the use of bank credit by managers to buy firms. These requirements are steps in the right direction, but they are still fairly easily evaded. The net-asset-price rule, in particular, since it is not a market-determined price but merely based on the purchase price of assets minus depreciation, creates distorted incentives. Ultimately, the high degree of discretionary control rights that managers have achieved, which was described earlier, inevitably translates into the privatization process. It is not surprising to see managers end up with a significant stake in privatized firms. Overall, because the process is extremely dispersed and nontransparent, we do not have a very detailed understanding of Chinese privatization.

13.5   CONCLUSION

Enterprise reform is arguably the central problem in the entire transition process. State-owned industrial enterprises were the core of the old command economy, and today the creation of effective, flexible, and efficient corporations is the crucial prerequisite to moving to a higher level of market economy, more productive and open to international competition. Yet so far China has produced only a handful of firms that approach international best practice in corporate governance. The firms on everyone's short list include Lenovo, the computer company; a few telecommunications equipment firms, Huawei and ZTE; and a few producers of consumer durables, such as Hai'er. These firms are well above the norm in Chinese industry and have developed impressive capabilities in a remarkably short time. But they are also a tiny minority, quite unrepresentative of Chinese industry overall.

Looking back on the transformation process, one is struck both by the huge successes and by the persistent failures. The first period of transformation must be judged an unambiguous success, despite the limits that circumscribed reform strategy during that period. The overall command structure was eroded and dismantled, without an abandonment of the state-run enterprise and without, perhaps as a result, a catastrophic economic decline. The second phase of transformation has gone far beyond the first stage, but in comparative terms the achievements are less impressive. Chinese privatization was delayed too long: there is no good reason for government to hang on to firms in ordinary competitive sectors, and privatization can improve performance (Megginson and Netter 2001). Even with the delay, Chinese privatization has been plagued by some of the same problems that afflicted the hasty privatization programs in Russia and Eastern Europe. Undoubtedly, the negative impact of China's insider privatization has been far less than of that in, say, Russia, since the privatized companies are much smaller and highly dispersed, and the largest companies have remained in state hands. But an opportunity to create a more broadly based system of private ownership has so far been lost, with negative consequences for the development of a harmonious society in China. Despite the enormous distance already traversed, China still has several steps to go in the creation of a high-functioning market economy.

BIBLIOGRAPHY

Suggestions for Further Reading

Qian (1995) lays out the main issues with exceptional clarity. Green (2004) and Tenev and Zhang (2002) provide good accounts of the current state of enterprise reform. Yusuf, Nabeshima, and Perkins (2006) provide current research results as well as an up-to-date review of the literature. For sources on SASAC and recent developments, see Naughton (2005). OECD (2005a, 2005b) are good discussions of governance and the corporate sector in China. For further analysis of reforms in the 1980s and 1990s, see Naughton (1995) and Wu (2005).

Sources for Data and Figures

Table 13.1: *SYC* (1997, 411); Naughton (1995, 329–33).

Table 13.2: *SYC* (2003, 461–63); *SAC* (2005, 135). Categories are not mutually exclusive.

Table 13.3: *SAC* (2003, 132); Lian Yuming (2004).

Table 13.4: *SYC* and *SAC*; after 1998 includes SOEs and state-controlled corporations; comparisons Claessens, Djankov, and Lang (1998, 141).

Table 13.6: Shanghai Stock Exchange (2003).

Figure 13.1: *SYC* (1994, 389; 1995, 395; 1996, 421; 1997, 431; 1998, 457; 2003, 476; 501, 506; 2004, Table XIV-15).

Figure 13.2: For discussion, see Naughton (1995).

Box 13.1: Definition based on OECD (2004).

References

Bai, Chong-En, Qiao Liu, Joe Lu, Frank M. Song and Junxi Zhang (2004). "Corporate Governance and Market Valuation in China." *Journal of Comparative Economics*, 32:599–616.

Byrd, William (1991). *The Market Mechanism and Economic Reforms in China*. New York: M. E. Sharpe.

Chang, Eric C., and Sonia M. L. Wong (2004). "Political Control and Performance in China's Listed Firms." *Journal of Comparative Economics*, 32:616–36.

Claessens, Stijn, Simeon Djankov, and Larry Lang (1998). "East Asian Corporations: Growth, Financing and Risks over the Last Decade." *Malaysian Journal of Economics*, Vol. XXXV 1&2 (June/December), 137–56.

Clarke, Donald (2003). "Corporate Governance in China: An Overview." *China Economic Review*, 14(4):494–507.

Ding, X. L. (2000). "The Illicit Asset Stripping of Chinese State Firms." *China Journal*, no. 43 (January), pp. 1–28.

Economic Census (2005). State Council First National Economic Census Leading Small Group Office and National Statistical Bureau. "Diyici quanguo jingji pucha zhuyao shuju gongbao yihao [Announcement of Main Numbers from the First National Economic Census, No. 1]," December 6, 2005, at http://www.stats.gov.cn/zgjjpc/cgfb/t20051214_402296016.htm

Green, Stephen (2004). *Enterprise Reform and Stock Market Development in Mainland China.* Frankfurt: Deutsche Bank Research, March 25.

Holz, Carsten A. (2003). *China's Industrial State-Owned Enterprises: Between Profitability and Bankruptcy*. Singapore: World Scientific.

Huang Sha'an and Huang Lijun (1988). "A Further Analysis of the 'Zhucheng Phenomenon.'" *Gaige*, no. 2, pp. 38–47.

Kornai, J. (1979). "Resource-Constrained Versus Demand-Constrained Systems," *Econometrica*, 47:801–19.

Kornai, J. (1980). *Economics of Shortage*. Amsterdam: North-Holland.

Lardy, Nicholas (1998). *China's Unfinished Economic Revolution*. Washington, DC: Brookings Institution Press.

Lee, Keun, and Donghoon Hahn (2004). "From Insider-Outsider Collusion to Insider Control in China's SOEs." *Issues and Studies*, 40(2), June, 1–45.

Lian Yuming (2004). "196 Jia Zhongyang Zhishu Qiye Zichan Zong'e da 6.9 Wanyiyuan" [The Total Assets of the 196 Directly Centrally Controlled Enterprises Has Reached 6.9 Trillion], pp. 525–27 of *Zhongguo Shuzi Baogao 2004* [China Report in Numbers 2004]. Beijing: Zhongguo Shidai Jingji.

Lin, Yi-min, and Tian Zhu (2001). "Ownership Restructuring in Chinese State Industry." *China Quarterly*, issue 166, pp. 305–41.

Megginson, William L., and Jeffrey M. Netter (2001). "From State to Market: A Survey of Empirical Studies on Privatization." *Journal of Economic Literature*, 39(2):321–89.

Naughton, Barry (1995). *Growing Out of the Plan: Chinese Economic Reform, 1978–1993*. New York: Cambridge University Press.

Naughton, Barry (2005). "SASAC Rising." *China Leadership Monitor*, issue 14, Spring. At www.chinaleadershipmonitor.org. See also issue 8 (Fall 2003), "The State Asset Commission: A Powerful New Government Body."

OECD (2004). Organization of Economic Cooperation and Development. "OECD Principles of Corporate Governance," at www.oecd.org/dataoecd/32/18/31557724.pdf.

OECD (2005a). *Governance in China*. Paris: Organization for Economic Cooperation and Development. Chapters 3, 10. Available at http://www.sourceoecd.org/governance/926400842X.

OECD (2005b). *OECD Economic Surveys: China*, issue 13. Chapter 2: "Improving the Productivity of the Business Sector," pp. 79–135 at http://hermia.sourceoecd.org/vl=2758661/cl=12/nw=1/rpsv/~3805/v2005n13/s1/p1l.

Qian, Yingyi (1995). "Reforming Corporate Governance in China." In Masahiko Aoki and Hyung-ki Kim, eds., *Corporate Governance in Transitional Economies: Insider Control and the Role of Banks*, 215–52. Washington, DC: World Bank.

SAC (Annual). *Zhongguo Tongji Zhaiyao* [Statistical Abstract of China]. Beijing: Zhongguo Tongji.

SASAC (2004). State Asset Supervision and Administration Commission. *Zhongguo Guoyou Zichan Jiandu Guanli Nianjian* [China State-owned Assets Supervision and Management Yearbook], 99. Beijing: Zhongguo Jingji.

Shanghai Stock Exchange (2003). *Corporate Governance Report*. Shanghai: Shanghai Stock Exchange.

SYC (Annual). *Zhongguo Tongji Nianjian* [Statistical Yearbook of China]. Beijing: Zhongguo Tongji.

Tenev, Stoyan, and Chunlin Zhang (2002), *Corporate Governance and Enterprise Reform in China.* Washington, DC: World Bank and IFC.

Transparency International (2005). *Global Corruption Report 2005.* Available at http://www.globalcorruptionreport.org/download.html.

Wu Jinglian (2005). *Understanding and Interpreting Chinese Economic Reform.* Singapore: Thomson.

Yusuf, Shahid, Karou Nabeshima, and Dwight Perkins (2006). *Under New Ownership: Privatizing China's State-Owned Enterprises.* Stanford, CA: Stanford University Press and World Bank.

14 Structural Change: Industry, Energy, and Infrastructure

Rapid growth of the Chinese economy in the last two decades has been led by the industrial sector. Fundamental structural changes associated with this growth have reshaped industry itself, as well as the relations between industry and other sectors. This chapter presents three selected topics relating to structural change. Section 14.1 presents an overview of changes within the industrial sector, focusing primarily on manufacturing. Section 14.2 looks at China's energy supply, considering both the composition of energy supply and the prospects for energy demand. Section 14.3 looks at infrastructure-dependent services, using telecommunications as an example.

China's rapid industrial growth has created significant new demands on world energy supplies and recently has triggered concerns about the adequacy of global energy resources. In fact, China has greatly improved the efficiency with which it uses energy. Chinese industrial growth patterns early in the reform period eased pressure on energy supplies, and only later did sustained economic growth renew pressure on energy availability. Market reforms and increased productivity gave a "breathing space" to the economy, but eventually high-speed development required increased energy supplies. The challenge is to sustain a healthy investment effort with continuing efficiency gains. These three topics sample the broad changes in the contemporary Chinese industrial economy and give insight into the practical problems involved in achieving this broader goal.

14.1 GROWTH AND STRUCTURAL CHANGE IN MANUFACTURING

Industrial growth was rapid throughout the post–1949 period. However, up until 1978, China's industrial development was concentrated on a few basic industrial materials. Between 1953 and 1978 per capita production of coal quintupled, that of steel increased by 11 times, and that of electricity increased by 16 times. But cloth production per capita only increased 30% over the entire 25 years, and many differentiated goods—and virtually all luxury goods—disappeared from the market altogether. Thirty-eight percent of total gross output was in the metals and machinery industry complex, yet the technological capacity of China's machinery output was extremely low, and low-quality standardized machinery was the primary product. We will be exaggerating only slightly if we say that Chinese industry in the late 1970s produced an iron pan and a bolt of blue cloth for each family, plus cement and machine tools for the state. Industry at this stage was hobbled by many shortcomings: It was extremely capital-intensive and, as we will see in section 14.2, extremely energy-intensive as well.

After 1978, China diversified into a range of relatively low-technology, labor-intensive consumer goods that had been neglected under the planned economy. There were opportunities to produce consumer goods that required little fixed capital investment; opportunities to produce niche goods that appealed to specialized markets, even relatively low-income ones, such as buttons and thread; and opportunities to generate new employment at relatively low cost. The pattern of structural change in industry that resulted can be analyzed using the vocabulary of value chains and intersectoral linkages that we introduced in Chapters 3 and 4. In a more standard industrialization pattern we would expect a country at China's income level to primarily be "moving upstream." That is, early development having focused on light, consumer-oriented manufacturing, especially textiles and food products, the current stage of industrialization would focus on producing the intermediate goods and production machinery needed to supply those downstream industries. This pattern (sometimes called "industrial deepening") emerged in Japan in the 1960s and Taiwan in the 1970s. But socialist China had emulated the Soviet Union and precociously developed a few strategic upstream industries. By 1978 light and textile industries had already declined to only 27% of total output, down from 64% in the 1950s, creating the illusion that China has already passed the early, labor-intensive phase of manufacturing development. But in fact that stage had barely begun.

As a result, structural change since 1978 has taken on an unusual character compared to developing market economies. Instead of observing movement upstream, we see a process of diversifying into previously neglected sectors. We might call this "makeup" or "payback" industrialization. Having practiced Soviet-style "catch-up" industrialization through the 1970s, China had the opportunity to carry out "makeup" industrialization during the 1980s. A whole range of labor-intensive, relatively low-technology sectors that had been neglected now presented excellent opportunities. As Table 14.1 shows, during the

Table 14.1
Real industrial growth rates, 1980–1995

Sector	Growth rate (percent)
Electronics and communication equip.	28.0
Furniture	21.9
Plastic products	20.8
Clay, stone, and other nonmetal mining	20.6
Wood and cane products	20.5
Synthetic fibers	20.4
Electric machinery	19.8
Pharmaceuticals	19.5
Leather and fur products	19.4
Metal products	19.4
Garments	19.2
Building materials	18.9
Machinery and instruments	16.9
Printing	15.9
Beverages	15.6
Paper	15.2
Ferrous metal mining	15.1
Toys, crafts, and misc.	13.7
Food proc. and products	13.3
Nonferrous metal mining	13.2
Rubber products	12.8
Tobacco products	12.8
Chemicals	12.5
Tap water	11.1
Textiles	10.2
Nonferrous metallurgy	10.2
Electricity and hot water	9.9
Ferrous metallurgy	9.3
Refining, coke, and coal gas	8.6
Coal	7.7
Oil and natural gas	4.4
Lumber	3.7

1980s and 1990s the fastest-growing sectors were typically light, labor-intensive manufacturing. Some of these previously neglected sectors were relatively high-technology, and others were decidedly "low-tech." Electronics, plastic products, and garments all grew 20% per year or faster. In a sense, then, China has been filling in the gaps in the industrial input–output matrix. The data in Tables 14.1 and 14.2 are taken from Chinese industrial censuses carried out in 1980, 1985, and 1995 that allow us to track changes in industry in detail. Overall industrial gross output grew at 14% annually between 1980 and 1995, when a consistent price base is used (compared with 15.7% reported in Chinese official data, using a shifting price base).

Table 14.2 summarizes one aspect of the data. The share of industrial output made up of differentiated final products—machinery and electronics, light

Table 14.2
Shares of total industrial output (percent)

Sector	1980	1995
Mining	12	6
Standardized products	33	26
Semistandardized	25	23
Differentiated manufactures	25	42
Utilities	5	3

Semistandardized products include chemicals, textiles, wood products, and building materials.

manufactures, plastic products, and so on—increased by about 17 percentage points. These are sectors in which it is much more possible to create value from product design and specifications tailored to consumer needs. Raw materials and intermediate goods—especially energy and metals—declined about 15 percentage points. These changes were directly related to transition strategy. Entry of new producers was most significant in light, labor-intensive manufactures, especially in very small-scale industry. Rapid opening to foreign trade also created new industrial opportunities, which especially up through 1995 were strongly concentrated in labor-intensive manufacturing.

This shift in industrial structure gave the Chinese economy a kind of breathing space. More highly fabricated, differentiated output was produced, giving industry the opportunity to create more value with given inputs of capital and energy. The most energy-intensive sectors—metallurgy, refining, electricity, and chemicals—grew more slowly than overall industry (although building materials, also energy-intensive, grew more rapidly). And in fact, the energy intensity of the economy declined substantially through the 1980s and 1990s, as we shall discuss later.

Since 1995 new patterns of structural change have emerged in Chinese industry. An economic census, taken at the end of 2004, presents a snapshot of some major changes. The detailed data for the census have not yet been published, so it is only possible to make a few preliminary observations based on current price output shares. First, the overall shift toward light, diversified manufactures clearly came to an end after 1995. Traditional light industry products typical of the early stage of industrialization declined dramatically as a share of China's industrial output between 1995 and 2004. Food products, textiles, garments, and leather goods dropped from 24% to 17% of total industrial sales. Instead, newly emerging industries with higher technological content grew robustly. Electronics and telecommunications equipment increased its share from 4.6% to 10.5% of total industrial sales. At the same time, there was evidence of industrial "deepening," as demand for materials and energy surged in the wake of ongoing industrialization and a sustained investment effort. Electricity increased its share from 4.4% to 7.1%, while ferrous and nonferrous metals increased from 9.2% to 10.8% of industrial sales. These data are only suggestive, since they are not adjusted for price changes and do not include unincorporated household businesses. However, they strongly indicate the onset of new patterns of structural change (Economic Census 2005). Moreover, several energy-intensive sectors are now growing more rapidly than industry overall.

14.1.1 Regional Growth Patterns

Structural change was strongly associated with differences in regional growth patterns. Regional change is not covered in depth in this book, but the relationship between regional and structural change should be noted. As is well known, coastal provinces grew much more rapidly than the national average. Coastal provinces were the best positioned to take advantage of the larger changes in industrial growth strategy. They were, of course, better positioned to take advantage of opportunities to engage in foreign trade, attract foreign investment, and absorb world technologies. In addition, coastal provinces were simply better endowed with skills and infrastructure. But coastal areas were also the areas in which traditional experience with labor-intensive manufacturing was widespread and where new firms entered the industrial arena most promptly. Coastal provinces benefited the most from the shift to a "lighter" industrial structure. An especially sharp contrast is with the three northeastern provinces, which exemplified the precocious development of heavy "upstream" industries in China. Disadvantaged by early specialization in energy production and heavy raw-material industries, the region suffered from obsolete factories and depleted resources. But the Northeast also benefited relatively little from the transition strategy of allowing entry of small-scale firms. As a result, the Northeast suffered a precipitous drop in its share of national industrial output from 16.1% in 1980 to only 8.6% in 2002.

14.2 ENERGY

China is an energy giant, but it is in many respects an immature giant. Problems relating to energy development have several times threatened to hold back China's economic development in the past. The energy crises of the past have been surmounted, but China continues to confront daunting energy challenges in the wake of rapid growth. Moreover, China's energy economy presents two huge challenges to the world as a whole: first, to integrate China's rapidly growing demand into the global energy economy; and second to mitigate the large environmental costs that China's inefficient energy industry imposes on China and the world. The stakes are high.

That China is an energy giant is easy to demonstrate. China is the number-two consumer of energy and generator of electricity (after the United States) and the number-three producer of energy (after the United States and Russia). China produced and burned 2.14 *billion* tons of coal in 2005, far more than any other country. Figure 14.1 shows trends in China's energy production since 1989. There are serious problems with the data between 1996 and 2003 (Box 14.1), for which we can only roughly correct, but long-run trends are clear. Between 1978 and 2005 total energy production grew at 4.5% per year, and energy consumption at 5.2% annually (Annual Report 2006). Filling the gap between domestic production and demand, China shifted from being a significant oil exporter to being a net importer in 1993. In 2005 coal made up 75% of China's domestic energy production, and the share of coal has shown no tendency to decline. In fact, if we ignore the data aberrations of the late 1990s, the share of coal in energy production has been creeping upward since the early 1980s. However, since China is importing an increasing volume of petroleum, energy consumption has become slightly less dependent on coal.

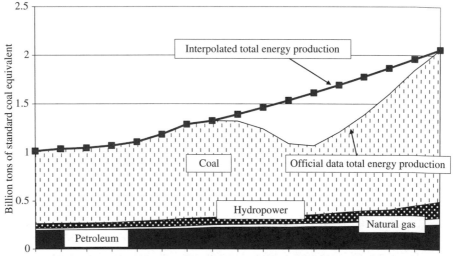

Figure 14.1
China energy production (official data and trend)

Box 14.1
Chinese Energy Statistics

There have been serious problems with Chinese energy data in recent years. According of official Chinese data, after decades of sustained growth total energy production began a sharp decline in 1996, and by 2000 it was 19.3% below the 1996 peak; the entire decline was accounted for by coal production, which supposedly declined 29%, while GDP officially grew 36%. These figures are preposterous. Of all the data problems mentioned in this text, this is the most flagrant and egregious case. In fact, this is an example of the breakdown of some aspects of statistical accuracy around 1998, along with the failure of the transition to a new statistical system in that year. In the case of energy, however, general problems were vastly aggravated by a special circumstance: during the industrial downsizing described in Chapter 8 and 13, Premier Zhu Rongji ordered that all small-scale, unlicensed coal mines be shut down. Since local economies were often dependent on local mines, local governments, rather than comply, simply reported, falsely, that their mines now had zero output. The official data also show a very rapid recovery growth of coal output from 2000 through 2005 (Annual Report 2006). This is equally implausible, and simply reflects a return to accurate reporting. In fact, reported 2005 coal output is consistent with a 5.1% annual growth from 1996, which would follow on a 4.6% annual growth from 1978 through 1996. The long-run growth rates, in conjunction with other evidence, lead us to tentatively conclude that statistical accuracy in the energy sector had recovered by 2005. These data problems must be addressed in order to select reliable benchmark years, and also because many international discussions of energy trends make use of the official data in inconsistent and misleading ways.[1]

Table 14.3 shows energy consumption and its composition in the world's top-10 energy users in 2004. China's heavy reliance on coal stands out in international comparison, making up 69% of consumption; only India, at 54%, is anywhere close. Petroleum now makes up 22% of consumption, and coal and petroleum together 91% of total consumption. Other large energy consumers have strikingly varying and diversified energy-consumption structures. The United States consumes a quarter of the world's energy, drawing large quantities of energy from all the major energy sources. France depends on nuclear power for almost 40% of its energy, while Russia draws on its huge reserves of natural gas for over 50% of its energy. The world excluding China depends much less on coal (only 21%) than China does. The biggest quantitative gap comes with natural gas, which made up just under 3% of China's energy use but 27% of world consumption. Gas and oil together make up only 25% of China's energy consumption but 66% of that in the world excluding China.

Thus China is overwhelmingly dependent on coal for primary energy generation, while the rest of the world is predominantly dependent on oil and gas.

1. For example, the World Bank's World Development Indicators partially, but only partially, correct for the implausible drop in Chinese energy output, then make comparisons based on compromise numbers.

Table 14.3
Top-10 world consumers of energy, 2004

	Total	Oil	Natural gas	Coal	Nuclear	Hydroelectric
	Million tons oil equivalent	Percent of total energy consumption				
United States	2,332	40	25	24	8	3
China	1,386	22	3	69	1	5
Russia	669	19	54	16	5	6
Japan	515	47	13	23	13	4
India	376	32	8	54	1	5
Germany	330	37	23	26	11	2
Canada	308	32	26	10	7	25
France	263	36	15	5	39	6
United Kingdom	227	36	39	17	8	1
Korea	217	48	13	24	14	1
World excluding China	8,838	39	27	21	7	6

Quite striking is the very small weight, in China, of the relatively "clean" technologies that the rest of the world uses to provide cheap energy with relatively few by-products: natural gas, nuclear, and hydropower. These sources represent 40% of world consumption but only 9% of Chinese consumption. China gets 5% of its total energy consumption from hydropower, which is substantial. China has begun to produce electric power from nuclear reactors, but this is still less than 1% of total energy consumption. China's dependence on coal begins to explain the relatively low efficiency of China's energy industry, as well as the severe environmental problems that result (see Chapter 20). The sheer technical efficiency of producing electricity from coal is inevitably lower than that from natural gas, for example, and the production of by-products is much larger. Moreover, as we will discuss, reliance on coal creates a large burden on the transportation system—since coal reserves are concentrated in the northern parts of the country—and the low technical efficiency of China's mining and power generation intensifies environmental problems. Thus the root of China's energy problems is its dependence on coal. It is also unfortunate that the world's two most rapidly growing economies, China and India, are both dependent on coal to power their growth.

14.2.1 Energy Efficiency of the Economy

The energy efficiency of the Chinese economy in 1978 was appallingly low; since then energy efficiency has increased substantially, but China is still a relatively inefficient user of energy. While energy consumption grew at 5.2% annually for the 27 years between 1978 and 2005, real GDP grew at almost

10%, so that China today produces 10 times the real GDP it produced in 1978 with three and a half times as much energy. Even allowing for some overstatement of real GDP growth, by any reasonable accounting China's economy has become more energy efficient. Given the flaws in China's energy data, comparisons of China's energy intensity with other economies are imprecise, but still worthwhile. The World Bank World Development Indicators compare the energy consumed to produce $1 of GDP across many countries, evaluated at purchasing power parities in 2000 prices. Adjusting China's data to correct both for the undercount of Chinese energy consumption in 2002 (using the interpolated 1995–2005 growth rate) and the revision of GDP data, it took China 0.24 kilograms of oil equivalent (koe) to produce $1 of GDP (evaluated at 999). That is a huge reduction from a staggering 0.92 kilograms back in 1978. This is similar to comparable developing countries. For example, Indonesia, Malaysia, and Korea are all at about 0.24 koe. However, Brazil and India are more efficient (at 0.15 and 0.20 koe, respectively). Developed countries are generally more efficient (Japan at 0.155 and the United Kingdom at 0.14, but the United States is at 0.23). Since the PPP adjustment for China is relatively large, a comparison of energy used per unit of GDP evaluated at exchange rates would be significantly more unfavorable to China, showing China using larger amounts of energy per unit of output than any of these comparison countries.

Three interrelated factors are shaping trends in China's energy efficiency and overall energy usage. The first is structural: industry is the biggest user of energy, and Chinese industry has been growing rapidly and makes up an unusually large share of GDP. While China gained some breathing space from the shift to a lighter, less energy-intensive output mix during the 1980s and early 1990s, such a shift cannot continue indefinitely, as long as investment remains high. Moreover, as modernization proceeds, the population increases its direct consumption of energy (in the form of lighting, electricity, and air-conditioning), as well as in automobile transport. These factors will tend to push up energy consumption per unit of GDP.

The second factor is institutional. Under the planned economy, there were many reasons why energy was used inefficiently. Energy prices were controlled at low levels; planners directed energy into wasteful and inefficient projects; and incentives to conserve energy were weak to nonexistent. As the economy has undergone reform, incentives to conserve energy have greatly improved, and energy conservation policies have been implemented. Price controls have been removed on most energy products, and in sectors where prices are still regulated (such as electricity) prices have been raised to adequately reflect resource costs. Profit-oriented producers have incentives to reduce energy consumption and seek new technological solutions. The third factor is technological. China's shift to openness has meant a sudden inflow of more-advanced technologies. Although those technologies have been selected primarily for their technological sophistication or low cost, many have had the side benefit of improving energy efficiency. The pace at which cleaner technologies are implemented will depend on government policy, as well as on the cost-benefit trade-off associated with specific technologies, some of which will be discussed later. For a period, China benefited from a uniquely positive combination of structural, institutional, and technological factors, and this allowed a sustained improvement in overall energy efficiency in the economy. However, we cannot assume that all three factors will continue to interact in such a benevolent fashion. Rapid growth will continue to create significant challenges for the energy sector, and it will take sustained successful policy-making to adequately manage those challenges.

14.2.2   The Three Main Energy Sectors

14.2.2.1   Coal

As China has searched for energy to feed the voracious appetite of its rapidly growing economy, it has not had the luxury of choosing among energy resources. China has been forced to rely on coal, in particular on small-scale coal mines, in order to maintain industrial growth. In that sense, China has continued to "walk on two legs," as the slogan from the GLF put it. While the national government was developing large coal mines, local governments and, increasingly, individuals have been authorized to develop small-scale coal mines, power plants, and factories. China's 1980s boom in TVEs was much in evidence in the coal sector. Exploitation of coal deposits by local village collectives and even individuals was allowed, notwithstanding the fact that resources were theoretically owned by the state. This trend combined with the highly dispersed character of China's coal resources to create a major boom in small-scale mining. Although China's large-scale coal reserves are concentrated in northern China, scattered reserves exist in much of the country. Indeed, as of 1995, coal mines were operating in 1,264 of China's 2,200 counties. After a slowdown in the late 1980s, small coal mines again began to grow rapidly in the 1990s. In 1995 there were 34,200 village-collective-run mines and 34,700 individually run mines, and these two small-scale types together accounted for 46% of total coal output, more than the big nationally run mines.

With the growth of small-scale mining, China's coal-mining sector has essentially undergone technological regression. Miners in these mines work under very poor conditions. Safety measures are practically nonexistent in most small mines, and accident rates are very high. There were 6,027 accidental deaths in coal mines in 2004, mostly in small mines; accident rates in large mines are much lower. Several large, deadly accidents were publicly acknowledged in 2005, and public concern mounted, but little change was perceptible. Because property rights are not well specified, conflicts are frequent, and the "owners" of mines have little incentive to invest in long-term upkeep or environmental maintenance. As a result, many coal-mining districts are dangerous, dirty, and disreputable. Moreover, although output has increased, this growth has come primarily from mines producing lower-quality output with much higher levels of impurities. This reduces the energy efficiency of downstream units that burn coal; moreover, since the coal they produce almost never undergoes benefici-ation, it cannot be used in clean-burning power plants. Instead, most of the coal is burned in small, inefficient industrial boilers or, worse, burnt directly in furnaces and cookstoves in Chinese homes.

All these considerations influenced Zhu Rongji's 1997 decision to attempt to close down mines that were out of compliance. However, his failure to do so highlights some harsh economic realities. Small mines have survived because they have adapted production technologies to fit China's real factor proportions: since labor is cheap and capital scarce, mines that use labor-intensive, low-capital production techniques are often cost effective. Since externalities are not priced into the mine owner's profit and loss state-ment, environmental costs are ignored, and small-scale mines are profitable. Dirty and dangerous small-scale coal mines are likely to be part of China's energy balance for the foreseeable future.

14.2.2.2   Oil and Gas

China is the sixth-largest oil producer in the world, just behind Mexico. In 2004, China produced 3.6 million barrels a day (175 million tons per year). However, China's oil reserves are not large, and the ratio between verified reserves and annual production is only 13.4, compared to 40 for the world as a whole. Therefore, China is exploiting its existing reserves at a much more rapid rate than most of the other major oil producers (although the United States' and Mexico's rates are similar to China's). China's oil industry was born with the discovery of the Daqing oil field, in northeastern Heilongjiang Province, in 1959. Oil production grew very rapidly for 20 years after the discovery of Daqing, but the growth rate dropped dramatically after 1978, and it was only 2% per year through 2004. Moreover, at the end of the century the Daqing field had begun a long, irreversible decline, but was still account-ing for nearly 40% of production. China was still relying on the same small handful of oil fields as before. China has had great difficulty locating other major fields, and the costs of extracting oil from Daqing and other mature oil fields are increasing steadily. Oil is being extracted from increasingly difficult, distant, and dispersed locales. Under these conditions, it is remarkable that China has managed to maintain a positive growth rate at all. Most of the increased output has come from offshore oil—which, after a disappointing start, began to contribute significant output in the late 1990s—or from new fields in the far Northwest, especially the Tarim Basin. Extraction and transportation costs for these fields are significantly higher than the old fields.

China's demand for petroleum is growing significantly more rapidly than its domestic supply. When China first emerged into the world economy in the late 1970s, it had significant oil surpluses to sell and exported a peak of 27 million tons (about 500,000 barrels a day) in 1985. But China's petroleum surplus has steadily declined as domestic demand has grown (Figure 14.2). China became a net petroleum importer in 1993, and imports have increased steadily since. Imports in 2004 were about 2.5 million barrels a day and rising. For comparison, Japan imports about 5 million barrels a day. China's imports are, however, set to continue a steady increase in the future. If present trends of very slow growing domestic production and rapidly rising domestic demand continue, China's imports would surpass 5 million barrels a day around 2015. With very high world oil prices in 2004–2005, concern about rising Chinese demand for oil was widespread. Such concerns should be kept in perspective. World oil

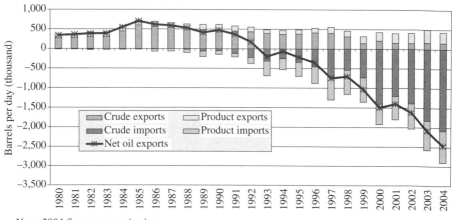

Note: 2004 figures are projections.

Figure 14.2
China's oil exports and imports, 1980–2004

markets transact 48 million barrels of oil a day; the United States takes 13 million barrels a day, more than a quarter. China's total imports in 2004 were about 5% of total world exports.

14.2.2.3   Electric Power

Electricity production has grown rapidly. Unusually, however, electricity production has grown less rapidly than overall industrial output, notwithstanding the conversion of many plants to electric power. Between 1980 and 1998 electricity generated grew 7.8% per year, a rate which seemed to be ample. Planners were caught by surprise, therefore, when rapid increases in demand for summer power, beginning in 2003, brought widespread brownouts and power limitations in many parts of China. However, both power generated and investment in the electricity sector increased rapidly in response. Electricity output increased 11% annually between 1998 and 2004. Lying behind these quantitative trends has been a large push to upgrade the power sector and reduce the share of small-scale, relatively inefficient coal-burning plants. Relatively large-size power plants, of 300 megawatts or above, have increased their share of total capacity from 17% in 1990, to 29% in 1996, to around 40% today. There has been a corresponding decrease in the amount of coal required to generate a kilowatt-hour of electricity, and some improvement in the volume of emissions. Nevertheless, there is a very long way to go in upgrading the quality of electricity-generating capacity.

The sheer quantitative challenge is also daunting. Electricity production has thus far generally kept pace with the economy's needs. However, per capita consumption of electricity is still in the range of a low to medium-income country. Chinese electricity consumption in 2003 was 1,464 kilowatt-hours per capita, about what it was in the United States in 1941, Japan in 1962, or Taiwan in 1975. Each of these three earlier-developing economies roughly quadrupled its per capita electricity use over about 25 years (slightly shorter in the case of Taiwan). This fact suggests that Chinese electricity output is also set to quadruple over the next 20 or so years. Given the extreme coal dependence of Chinese electricity generation today, even with significant productivity improvement a quadrupling of output almost certainly implies at least a doubling of coal production. It is not easy to envisage China mining and shipping something on the order of 4 billion tons of coal in the year 2030.

14.2.3   Energy Security, Diversification, and Imports

How will China address its energy challenges? It is quite clear that China will follow a conscious strategy of diversification of energy sources (Wu and Storey

2005). The domestic context of future energy strategy is the uneven geographic distribution of fossil fuel reserves within China. The northern half of China has about 90% of the gas and oil and 80% of the coal. Coal is particularly concentrated in a three-province region of north China, comprising Shanxi, northern Shaanxi, and western Inner Mongolia, which accounts for almost half of total reserves. Mountainous southwestern and western China have abundant potential hydropower resources, but these require massive long-term investments to be developed. The most rapidly growing part of China—the southeastern coastal area—has very few energy resources of any kind.

In the past this distribution problem meant that a large part of the country's transport system was tied up shipping coal from the north to the south. Coal shipments, at their peak, accounted for 60% of the total weight of long-distance rail shipments in China. Coal is also shipped eastward across northern China and loaded onto oceangoing ships, not only for export to foreign countries, but also for shipment down the coast to China's southeast. In the future the domestic distribution problem will be addressed in conjunction with China's energy-import policy, and China is now gearing up to become a large-scale energy importer over the long term.

The most promising areas for future onshore oil and gas production are in the northwest province of Xinjiang, in the Tarim and Ordos basins. These fields are a long way from the centers of demand, however, and require expensive new infrastructure. A new natural gas pipeline, built from Xinjiang all the way to Shanghai on the east coast, began delivering gas in 2005. Development of the Northwest can be tied in with increased import of oil and/or natural gas from China's continental neighbors. Construction began in 2004 on a pipeline to carry oil from Kazakhstan to the Chinese province of Xinjiang. A long-run objective is to gain access to Russian energy resources. (China currently imports small amounts of oil from Russia by railroad.) There are ambitious plans to build a pipeline from eastern Siberia, but the project has been stalled by Russian hesitation and competition between Japan and China to be the primary pipeline destination.

The southern coast will rely most on the newest and most expensive, but also cleanest, facilities. Nuclear power will be significant along the southern coast. As of 2005, China had nine nuclear power plants in operation and plans for up to 30 more, all of them near the coast. Import of liquefied natural gas (LNG) to specialized terminals on the south coast may play a significant role. Massive LNG terminals will go into operation in Guangdong and Fujian provinces. Of course, China will also import more oil on tankers. Today about 60% of China's imported oil comes from the Middle East, and this figure is not likely to decline dramatically. One big unknown is the amount of oil offshore in the Bohai Gulf and perhaps the East China Sea. Recently these fields have been exploited successfully, but they have not been fully explored, and disputes with Japan over mineral rights on the continental shelf are a serious problem. The emerging high degree of dependence on oil imports from the Middle East naturally pushes Chinese policy-makers to diversify supply as much as possible. China announced a strategic petroleum reserve in 2004 and aims to gradually create a stockpile equal to about one month worth of imports (compared to two months for the United States and five months for Japan). Exactly what combination of these strategies will ultimately emerge is still unclear. Given the needs and the uncertainties, China will continue to follow a multistranded approach, diversifying to reduce risk and exploiting as many different opportunities as possible.

14.3   TELECOMMUNICATIONS

China's telecommunications infrastructure is growing extremely rapidly, and it is rapidly approaching middle-income-country standards. This is a recent development: During the 1980s the Chinese economy was transformed by reforms and rapid growth, but telecommunications development lagged behind. Prices of telecommunications services remained tightly controlled, and the Ministry of Post and Telecommunications (MPT) maintained its monopoly status, serving both as the regulator and as the sole service provider. Home telephones were viewed as a luxury not generally affordable at China's income level, and most phones were in government offices or businesses. During the 1980s, MPT installed digital switching systems in major metropolitan areas and upgraded trunk lines, but overall investment remained low. China invested only 0.2% of GDP on telecommunications through most of the 1980s, far below the 1.0% of GDP that international experts were urging as a minimum effort required to substantially upgrade the telecommunications network. At the end of 1989, China still had only one telephone per 100 residents, and the number of independent paying subscribers was only half this.

The situation changed dramatically in the 1990s. Fundamental policies toward telecommunications shifted, as the government accepted the importance of telecommunications development for economic development in general and accepted the value of allowing individual households to possess their own phones. In 1993, MPT nominally split its telecom operations and regulatory functions, creating an entity called China Telecom to take over operations. A competing—but still state-owned—company, China United

Telecom, or Unicom for short, was created from outside the old MPT system. Unicom debuted officially on July 19, 1994, as a joint-stock company. Pricing policy changed, so that installation of telephones and provision of services became highly profitable. Waiting periods for phones dropped from several years to three to six months, and despite the high fees, demand for phones remained strong. Along with the increased installation fees, provincial post and telecom authorities (PTAs) were given increased financial flexibility, receiving accelerated depreciation allowances and, more importantly, permission to borrow investment funds. Investment in telecommunications soared, reaching 1.5% of GDP by 1993, and roughly sustaining that level subsequently. The telecom companies have been reorganized subsequently on several occasions, but the basic model was set: an oligopoly of centrally controlled, state-owned telecom companies that operated primarily on business principles. Telecom thus resembles the pattern of central government-owned industrial sectors described in Chapter 13.

The results have been extremely impressive. At the end of 2004, China had 312 million landline phone customers and 335 million mobile phone customers. These are the largest phone systems in the world, and the volume of newly added lines is largest by a very large margin. By the end of 2004 there were 51 telephones per 100 people, including mobile phones. This is an astonishing increase from the 1989 level, and China has vaulted ahead of middle-income comparison countries such as Brazil and Thailand. Moreover, China has steadily built an interprovincial fiber-optic cable network, totaling 645,000 kilometers by the end of 2004. Along with satellite transmission facilities, these cables provide the capability for high-volume transmission of voice and data. With the physical infrastructure increasingly available, China had 94 million Internet users in 2004. By the end of June 2005, China had 30.8 million broadband subscribers and is quickly reducing the gap with the United States' 38 million.

Rapidly rising incomes have fueled explosive growth in demand. Moreover, technological progress has dramatically reduced the cost of installing a modern telecommunications system. Most obviously, the availability of mobile telephones permits rapid adoption by those residents most willing to pay. The cost of installing digital switching and transmission facilities has declined rapidly. However, actually connecting the local telephone subscriber to the system—typically by laying down copper wire—remains costly and time-consuming. Most of the progress in increasing access to landline telephones has been in the cities: China's rural areas, with two-thirds of the population, have only one-third of the landline telephones. Technology has provided China an opportunity to "leapfrog" stages in the development of an advanced telecommunications infrastructure, and generally speaking China has been able to take advantage of the opportunity. However, to achieve this potential, China had to evolve an adequate institutional setup. First was an adequate business model in the telecom sector, with some degree of competition, but also enough monopoly power to reap significant profits. One of the surprising outcomes has been that China was able to build the telecom infrastructure without foreign financial or operational participation, to the surprise of many observers. China's WTO accession agreement commits China to allow minority foreign participation in some local telecom networks; as of the end of 2005 the legal framework was in place for such participation, but no actual ventures had been commenced.

14.4   COMMON FEATURES: INFRASTRUCTURE INVESTMENT

The essential common feature of energy and communications is that both these sectors require large-scale investment in physical infrastructure. An essential government function—particularly critical for developing economies—is ensuring the healthy growth of infrastructure investment. In the area of infrastructure there are two major requirements. The first is that the government provide financing for infrastructure investment, either directly or indirectly; this includes direct government finance as well as the creation of a regulatory and market environment that facilitates private investment in infrastructure provision. The second requirement is that the government provide a framework for infrastructure planning, in order to resolve land-use conflicts, ensure rational allocation of resources among alternative strategies, and provide guidance to private decision-makers. China's performance in infrastructure provision has generally been good, especially recently. Despite major changes in the structure of national saving and the organization of financial institutions (see Chapter 19), China has been able to maintain a robust level of investment in infrastructure.

Figure 14.3 displays the major trends in three major categories of physical infrastructure. Before 1993 the infrastructure investment effort was modest. Indeed, some development planners suggest, as a rule of thumb, that 6% of GDP needs to be invested in infrastructure to support rapid growth. By this standard, China during the 1980s was falling short, coasting on existing facilities. However, after 1993 investment in these three categories of physical infrastructure jumped to around 6% of GDP, and after 1998 infrastructure investment took another jump to a level around 8% of GDP. This is quite a substantial investment effort in comparative terms.

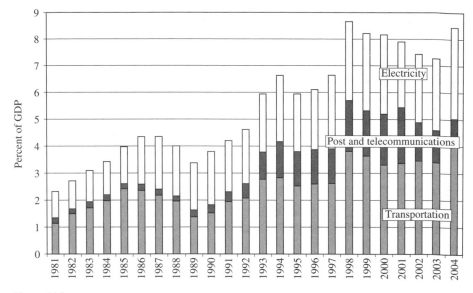

Figure 14.3
Physical infrastructure investment

The robust level of investment in electricity and telecommunications infrastructure, particularly after 1998, is consistent with the account given in the preceding sections. Transport investment has also been strong, particularly in highway construction. China is building a national network of express highways, which reached 34,300 kilometers in 2004 and is already the second-largest system after that of the United States. The extension of highways is of course racing against the growth in vehicle traffic, and it often seems that increasing congestion is a sign that the race is not being won. Transportation, like electricity, may well be a constraining factor on growth in particular regions and at particular times. However, from a broad overview, there is little evidence that development of these crucial supporting services is lagging behind the demands of the economy.

It is striking, however, that a similar institutional form has been adopted to manage development in these crucial infrastructure sectors. In electricity, telecom, and most long-distance transport (trucking is a partial exception), a small group of SOEs dominate the business. Those state firms have an explicit government mandate to support infrastructure development in their sector. They also have a significant degree of profit orientation and enough market power to be able to maintain healthy profitability. Much of the profit is plowed back into further investment. The situation with respect to petroleum development would of course be parallel. In all these cases, China has opted to maintain state ownership of companies as an alternative to creation of a stronger regulatory framework followed by privatization. This approach has dangers, because the companies under consideration have strong economic interests and significant market power while they are subject to only limited oversight. Yet in the short run this approach has turned out to be a viable and reasonably economical solution.

14.5   CONCLUSION

Even in the midst of rapid growth, China faces daunting challenges. As development proceeds, the structure of goods outputs changes in complex ways. The ability to move into labor- and skill-intensive final-goods manufacturing presents the economy with exceptional opportunities. At the same time, the need to invest heavily in infrastructure to overcome inherent limitations in energy, transport, and communication poses new challenges. China's ability to sustain rapid growth depends on the success with which these problems are confronted and overcome. The development of a market economy in China has shaped the economy in complex and sometimes apparently contradictory directions that are far different from what a central planner would ever have envisaged. Similarly, future development will be shaped by market forces in ways that are difficult to predict at present.

BIBLIOGRAPHY

Suggestions for Further Reading

A good introduction to China's energy options today is Sinton et al. (2005). The series of publications at the Web site of the China Energy Group at Lawrence Berkeley National Lab, available at china.lbl.gov/china_policy-cs.html, are worth a look. Barta (2005) is a good update.

Sources for Data and Figures

Accidents: State Administration of Work Safety (2005).

Coal mines: Coal Industry Yearbook 1996.

Japan and U.S. historical electricity consumption: Shealy (2004).

Telephone subscribers: *SYC* (2005; 584–85, 588).

Broadband connections: PointTopic (2005).

Table 14.1: Output data from Third Census Office (1997, 46–197); Industrial Census Office (1988, 88–121); TVE Yearbook (1996, 157–243). Sector-specific price deflators, derived from the state-owned sector only, have been used to convert sectoral output into 1995 prices. Price data from Third Census Office (1997, 30–45).

Table 14.2: Same as Table 14.1.

Table 14.3: BP (2005).

Figure 14.1: SYC (2005, 255). Updated with preliminary data from Annual Report (2006).

Figure 14.2: Wu and Storey (2005).

Figure 14.3: Fixed Investment (1997, 37–41); *SYC* (2005, 200–203).

References

Annual Report (2006). National Bureau of Statistics, "Zhonghuan Renmin Gongheguo 2005 Nian Guomin jingji he shehui fazhan tongji gongbao [PRC 2005 National Economy and Society Development Statistical Report]," February 28, 2006 at http://www.stats.gov.cn/tjgb/ndtjgb/qgndtjgb/t20060227_402307796.html

Barta, Patrick (2005). "China Continues To Fill Up on Oil, But Pace Slackens: Some Forces That Fueled Surge in Demand Dissipate as Local Bottlenecks Ease." *The Wall Street Journal* November 9, 2005; page A1.

BP (2005). British Petroleum. *Statistical Review of World Energy June 2005*. Access at http://www.bp.com/statisticalreview

Coal Industry Yearbook (1996). *Zhongguo Meitan Gongye Nianjian [China Coal Industry Yearbook]*. Beijing: Meitan Gongye.

Economic Census (2005). State Council First National Economic Census Leading Small Group Office and National Statistical Bureau. "Diyici quanguo jingji pucha zhuyao shuju gongbao yihao [Announcement of Main Numbers from the First National Economic Census, No. 1]," December 6, 2005, at http://www.stats.gov.cn/zgjjpc/cgfb/t20051214_402296016.htm

Energy Information Administration (EIA). www.eia.doe.gov/emeu/cabs/

Fixed Investment (1997). Fixed Investment Statistics Office, National Statistics Bureau. *Zhongguo Guding Zichan Touzi Tongji Nianjian 1950–1995* [China Fixed Investment Statistical Yearbook 1950–1995]. Beijing: Zhongguo Tongji.

Industrial Census Office (1998). State Council National Industrial Census Leading Small Group Office, ed., *Zhonghua Renmin Gongheguo 1985 Nian Gongye Pucha Ziliao* [People's Republic of China 1985 Industrial Census Materials]. Beijing: Zhongguo Tongji.

Point Topic Ltd, London, at www. dslforum.org/PressRoom/Q205DSLsubscribernumberspresentation.ppt

Shealy, Malcolm (2004). "Chinese Electric Demand." San Francisco: Unpublished discussion paper. July 13.

Sinton, Jonathan, Rachel Stern, Nathaniel Aden and Mark Levine (2005). "Evaluation of China's Energy Strategy Options." Berkeley: Lawrence Berkeley National Laboratory, China Sustainable Energy Probram (LBNL 56609), accessed at http://china.lbl.gov/publications/nesp.pdf

State Administration of Work Safety (2005). http://www.chinasafety.gov.cn/

SYC (Annual). *Zhongguo Tongji Nianjian [Statistical Yearbook of China]*. Beijing: Zhongguo Tongji.

Third Census Office (1997). Third National Industrial Census Office, ed., *Zhonghua Renming Gongheguo 1995 Nian Disanci Quanguo Gongye Pucha Ziliao Huibian* [The Data of the Third National Industrial Census of the People's Republic of China in 1995]. Beijing: Zhongguo Tongji. Zonghe, Hangyezhuan [Volume 1: Overall, Sectoral].

TVE Yearbook (Annual). Zhongguo Xiangzhen Qiye Nianjian Biaji Weiyuanhui [China Township and Village Enterprise yearbook Editorial Commission], ed., *Zhongguo Xiangzhen Qiye Nianjian* [China Township and Village Enterprise Yearbook]. Beijing: Zhongguo Nongye.

World Bank. *World Development Indicators*. Washington, DC: World Bank. http://devdata.worldband.org./dataonline/

Wu, Kang and Ian Storey (2005). "China's Energy Dependence, Security Policies, and Oil Diplomacy." Paper prepared for Second Conference on China's Capitalist Transition, East-West Center, Honolulu, Hawaii, August 10.

15 Technology Policy and the Knowledge-based Economy

What will China become during the twenty-first century? Previous chapters on the development process have shown that inputs into production in China are growing rapidly. China's manpower resources are vast and growing, and becoming healthier and better educated. The high saving and investment rates, combined with the rapid buildout in physical infrastructure, provide the physical capital needed for sustained growth. Economic policy has been well-crafted generally, enabling China to benefit from domestic market transition and international opening. By midcentury, then, there is no doubt that China will emerge as one of the largest economies in the world. Yet size is not the only important measure, nor does it define the limits of Chinese aspirations in assuming a global role in the coming decades. Will China become simply another middle income developing country, albeit one of enormous size? Will China remain in the foreseeable future what it is today: the world's factory, churning out massive quantities of laboriously produced goods? Or will China instead vault into the front ranks of world economics by contributing new products and procedures, innovative standards, and breakthrough ideas? Will China become a global center of innovation, joining the ranks of developed countries and the emerging East Asian centers of technological creativity?

These questions will be decided by the pace at which China adopts, adapts, and transforms the world's body of science and technology. Effective adaptation of technology will sustain rapid growth by increasing the productivity with which inputs are converted into output. Fast growth of inputs combined with a continuous increase in technology-driven productivity will be necessary if China is to sustain rapid growth over the coming decades. Moreover, it is not merely that the growth of output, in a mechanical sense, equals the growth of inputs plus the growth of productivity. In China today, there is a massive pool of talent and ingenuity that has only begun to be tapped. When the potential of this underutilized resource is finally realized there will be a global impact.

More economically effective utilization of knowledge is a step on the road to an increasingly creative and innovative society. Perhaps no issue more effectively unites policymakers, business leaders, and the public today in China than the desire to propel China into a high technology future.

China's technical capabilities today, however, are still quite mixed. Seki Mitsuhiro (1994) suggested that technological capabilities in general can be likened to a pyramid. The broad base of the pyramid consists of basic manufacturing capabilities such as forging, welding, and machining, exemplified by a simple machine shop. The intermediate zone represents complex manufacturing and assembly-line skills, exemplified by an automobile factory. The apex of the pyramid represents science and research capabilities, exemplified by a laboratory or a research institute. China, according to Seki, is unusual in that it emerged from the socialist era with a strong base, and also with surprisingly strong capabilities at the apex. Today basic industrial skills are widespread, and pockets of excellence in scientific and technological research are near the world frontier. But in the middle, China has been weak. The productivity of mass-production, assembly-line industries in China is still low, and China has very few first-class firms with significant leading-edge technologies. As a result of their weaknesses in these intermediate areas, China has been endeavoring to strengthen its industrial technology. China is trying to move its scientific capabilities "down" to the factory floor, while attempting to upgrade its existing factories to a higher level of skill.

One approach to analyzing technology in an economic context is to consider the triad of *technology effort* (reflecting the volume of resources thrown into research and development, or R&D, and the policy strategy that guides it), the *human resource base* (which defines the possible capabilities and reflects the long-run outcome of the technology effort), and the *institutions and incentives* that determine what ideas and technologies actually get applied to the production process (Cliff 1998; cf. Liu and White 2001). Both the technology effort and the growth of the human resource base contribute to accumulating knowledge, while institutions and incentives determine how much of the knowledge will be applied in the production arena. These two aspects—generating and applying knowledge—are two sides of the technology picture; the ability to apply knowledge is at least as important, in an economic context, as the technology effort or resource base, but more difficult to measure and assess. Section 15.1 examines the technology effort, starting with the size of the R&D commitment, and moving on to the strategic evolution of R&D policies. Section 15.2 examines the recent growth of the human capital base, while available evidence on the outcome of the technology effort is considered in section 15.3. The focus then shifts to the type and adequacy of the institutions that shape technology decisions today. The renewed commitment and consistency of the government's technology development policy that has emerged since the turn of the century is the focus of section 15.4. The other major factor determining technology upgrading is the nature of interactions between domestic firms and multinational corporations, which is the subject of section 15.5. It is these institutions—and particularly the interplay among government, foreign multinationals, and domestic high-technology firms—that will be crucial in determining whether China will make a rapid jump to a high-technology economy.

15.1   PURSUING CRITICAL TECHNOLOGIES: THE R&D EFFORT

Developing countries face immense technological challenges. Today's modern technologies come almost entirely from the rich countries, and developing countries are quite marginal in the global innovation process. The continuous stream of innovation emerging from the rich countries ensures that most of tomorrow's technologies will also come from developed economies. To be sure, this disproportion could potentially be a source of advantage for late developers. Since there is a substantial technology gap, there is an enormous backlog of modern technologies that developing countries could in principle adopt. Rather than expending resources on risky and uncertain research, developing countries could concentrate on transfer and adaptation of existing technologies. They ought to be able to pick and choose the "best" technologies, combining selected technologies with their inexpensive production factors to build competitive advantage for their companies.

But in fact, developing countries have enormous difficulties exploiting these potential advantages. It takes time and skills to be able to identify the technologies that are available and appropriate. When new technologies are purchased, it can take substantial effort and resources to actually get the technologies working on the factory floor, and productivity and profitability are typically low for a prolonged period as various bugs are worked out. Moreover, companies in developed countries increasingly view their technologies as income sources and fence off their intellectual property rights (IPR) with patents or secrecy. Developing economies have found it difficult to develop their technological capabilities and almost impossible to catch up with the technology leaders. Indeed, after Japan, only the East Asian economies of Korea, Taiwan, and Singapore stand out as unambiguous technology success stories. The success of Japan and Korea was particularly striking in that both sharply restricted direct investment by foreign companies.

In contrast to Japan and Korea in the 1970s, most developing countries today welcome foreign direct investment (FDI), largely because of their recognition of the difficulty of domestic technology development. The hope is that foreign investors will build sophisticated industries from which knowledge and technological capabilities will gradually spill over to the rest of the domestic economy. China fits into the general pattern of opening widely to FDI. Thus, although China runs an aggressive, sustained and multifaceted policy of promoting domestic technology, it does so in a context of economic openness. Chinese policy-makers are tempted to emulate past Japanese or Korean technology and industrial policies, but their policies and their effectiveness end up being quite different because of the different economic environment and different relationship with multinational technology companies. The greater openness to FDI is a characteristic of the global environment that China has fully embraced.

Whatever the global environment in which a country operates, it must invest resources in research and development in order to discover and adapt new, more productive technologies. R&D spending by successful developing countries follows a systematic pattern. Low- and lower-middle-income economies spend relatively little on R&D, typically less than 1% of GDP. Since it makes no sense for them to reinvent the wheel, they spend modest sums overall, and most is focused on the identification and adaptation of foreign technology. As economies approach middle-income status, their indigenous technology effort increases: They make more profound adaptations of existing technologies, absorb technologies that are closer to the developed economy frontier, and engage in some limited basic research. Expenditures on R&D begin to rise. For example, both Taiwan and South Korea pushed the R&D/GDP ratio above 1% in the early 1980s as they reached middle-income status and began to engage in much more challenging innovative activity. As economies reach developed-country income levels, the R&D/GDP ratio typically increases above 2%. For example, Korea crossed this frontier in 1992, and Taiwan in 1999. A handful of countries— Japan, Sweden, and Finland—had ratios above 3% by the end of the 1990s. They find that a technological effort of this magnitude is required to remain at the technological frontier. Some of the comparative figures are given in Table 15.1. China, with 1.1% of its GDP going to R&D in 2003, fits in this general pattern. With a technological effort, in proportional terms, somewhat ahead of comparable economies such as Brazil and India, but still well short of Taiwan or Korea, China is about where we would expect. By another measure—researchers per 1,000 employment—China is much further back, reflecting the still large labor force in the traditional agricultural and service

Table 15.1
Comparative indicators of R&D activity

	R&D outlays (percent of GNP)	Researchers per thousand total employment
China (2003)	1.1	1.2
Mexico (1999)	0.1	
Brazil (2000)	1.1	
India (2001)	0.9	
Taiwan (2003)	2.5	7.1
Korea (2003)	2.6	6.8
All OECD (2000)	2.2	6.6
France (2002)	2.2	7.5
United States (1999)	2.6	9.3
Japan (2003)	3.2	10.4
Sweden (2001)	4.3	10.6

sectors. Size matters: taking everything into account, China has the world's fourth-largest R&D effort, after the United States, Japan, and the European Union. Figure 15.1 graphically summarizes the data on proportional and absolute technological effort. China's importance will rise as the size of its overall economy grows and as the share of the economy going to R&D increases. The figure also shows the significance of Korea and Taiwan, important technology powers that carry substantial weight on the global technology stage.

15.1.1   The Trajectory of China's Technology Effort

Paradoxically, looking backward, the trajectory of China's technology effort does not follow the standard pattern of steadily increasing technology effort at all. From the 1950s through 1978, China, despite being a low-income country, pursued a high-technology-effort strategy. China mobilized available intellectual resources for defense purposes and created elite research institutions, particularly in the Chinese Academy of Sciences (CAS). Government outlays for science and technology–related purposes (the only R&D data available before 1989) actually peaked at 1.7% of GDP in 1964, the year China exploded its first atomic bomb, and averaged 1.4% of GDP from the late 1950s through 1978. Despite the apparent anti-intellectualism of the Cultural Revolution, China in fact mobilized substantial intellectual resources for its critical technologies effort. There were successes, especially military: atom and hydrogen bombs and intercontinental missiles. The big effort was completely consistent with the command economy and Big Push strategy described in Chapter 3.

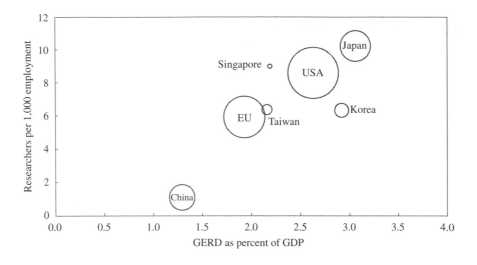

Figure 15.1
R&D efforts in selected economies, 2001. The size of the bubble represents the amount of R&D expenditure in current PPPs. GERD, gross expenditures or research and development.

The Soviet Union was China's technology patron during the 1950s. The Soviet Union transferred not only the technologies themselves—having a profound impact on every aspect of Chinese industrial and military technology—but also the key institutions that shape incentives to adopt technology. The organizational structure of the entire national system of research and innovation came from the Soviet model, beginning with the elite research institutes of the CAS. This was probably the largest coordinated transfer of technology across national borders ever known. Subsequently, when China and the Soviet Union abruptly split in the early 1960s, China was cut off from its technology source at a time when it had no alternative partners and very little market access to technology. Thus China approached a state of technology autarky for a decade from the mid–1960s through the mid–1970s. During this period China's strategy was to import a handful of factories that embodied specific industrial technologies, and then reverse engineer and replicate them domestically. A few key technologies in metallurgy and synthetic fibers were transferred in this way, and incremental improvements were made on some Soviet-legacy technologies, such as electricity generation, where equipment was scaled up to larger, more efficient units. But overall the gap between China and the world increased. Cut off from world technical progress, China had to fend for itself. In some cases China was unable to complete the ramp-up to efficient production levels of half-finished Soviet factories, including automobile plants. Isolated from the vital sources of science and technological progress, China fell further behind despite its massive technology effort. Anxiety over the widening technology gap was a major motivating force for China's opening.

During the reform era, China at first tried to keep government R&D outlays high, while beginning marketization in other areas. As Figure 15.2 shows, government budget outlays for science and technology stayed above 1% of GDP through 1986. But ultimately this level of government effort was not sustainable. With government SOE revenues eroding and the budget's share of GDP declining, China could not afford this technology effort. Moreover, the existing approach of often military-related R&D was under fire anyway for its low economic effectiveness. R&D was scaled back as policy-makers searched for a viable model. When the first R&D statistics become available, in 1989, they showed China investing only about 0.7% of GDP in R&D, and the effort slipped further to below 0.6% in 1994. By this time China was beginning to look like a "normal" country, with R&D outlays at or even below the level the standard pattern of R&D development would dictate. But Chinese policymakers had no desire to be merely normal: they actively sought to raise the R&D/GDP ratio above 1%. After 2000, R&D outlays in fact began to increase

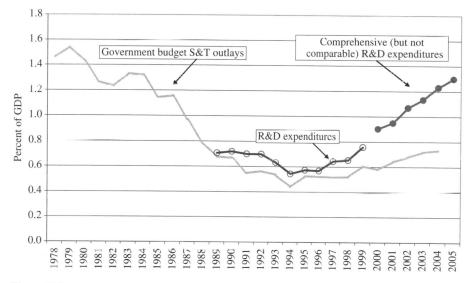

Figure 15.2
R&D expenditures (percent GDP)

through numerous channels. As Figure 15.2 shows, total R&D has climbed much more rapidly than government outlays for science and technology (S&T), and the R&D ratio reached 1.3% in 2005. This is a strong but appropriate R&D effort for a country at China's level of development. A more inclusive survey of business R&D was partly responsible for pushing up the overall rate of reported R&D, but this seems to have been a case of the statistical system belatedly catching up with a real trend, the diversification of research channels. The next section considers the way in which specific R&D strategies and policies interacted with the overall R&D effort.

15.1.2 Strategies of R&D Investment

Chinese policy-makers have maintained a high degree of consensus around the need to invest in new technology and improve China's technological standing. However, the means used to achieve this goal have varied substantially over the last 30 years. For convenience, the varying policies are grouped into seven approaches in the following subsections.

15.1.2.1 Do It Yourself

China's high R&D effort in the socialist period was in the classic "mission-push" mode of R&D. Leaders in China set a few key tasks, and planners then coordinated flexible multidisciplinary and multiskilled research groups—with plenty of money—to pursue those key goals. This worked well when there was broad agreement on priorities, and the objectives—two bombs and a missile—were achieved (Feigenbaum 1999). But this approach, in China as in the Soviet Union, was bad at transferring technology to the civilian economy. Security obsessions create secrecy barriers around the most talented scientists and engineers even today. When planners fund research with the avowed intent of aiding the civilian economy, they are not efficient at transferring technologies. Planners do not have the technical capabilities to evaluate the technology they have funded, so scientists are free to pursue theoretical research with very little effective oversight on the appropriateness of the undertaking. Scientists and engineers have no incentives to commercialize their discoveries, and factory managers have few incentives to seek out and implement innovations in the laboratories. High-prestige research institutes affiliated with the CAS were very good at producing, for example, *one* very sophisticated computer, but their achievement ended up as a single exemplar—as a "sample, display item, or gift"—rather than as a productive resource in the economy. Isolation from world science made these shortcomings particularly debilitating.

15.1.2.2   Buy It

At the beginning of China's opening (1978), massive purchases of industrial machinery from technology leaders seemed the quickest route out of China's scientific isolation. China seemed to be flush with revenues from anticipated oil exports. The first wave of contracts collapsed when China's oil revenues failed to materialize after 1978. Nevertheless, the government spent a lot for technology embodied in plants and equipment. During the 1980s, US$16.6 billion was spent on technology imports for existing plants, and another $30.2 billion on imports for new capital construction projects (Wang Huijiong 1996; Gu Yuefang 1996). Local governments were allowed to import equipment, but the response was often excessive and duplicative importation of the particular flavor of the day: More than 100 color TV assembly lines were imported in the early 1980s. Chinese policy-makers later gave poor marks to this policy because it was very expensive and ineffective in diffusing new technologies into the economy. As China's budgetary revenues skidded during the 1980s (see Chapter 18), China could no longer afford the luxury of prestige technology purchases. China today steers technology import toward "soft" technology licensing and away from the expensive purchase of "hard" assets that embody technology. In 2003, China signed technology import contracts worth US$13.45 billion, of which $9.5 billion was for intellectual property and only $3.9 for equipment embodying technology (NBS-MOST 2004, 359). International technology purchase is today one pillar of a multistranded technology development regime (Feinstein and Howe 1997).

15.1.2.3   Bargain for It

During the 1980s, China initiated complex negotiations with a number of large multinational corporations (MNCs). China sought MNC partners, who would be rewarded with privileged access to China's market in return for sharing technology. China ambitiously targeted world technology leaders. Negotiations between the two sides, each with some monopoly power, often dragged on for years. MNCs were not eager to give away their most advanced technologies, and China sought highly restrictive and comprehensive deals. Ultimately this approach led to protracted negotiations, delays in implementation, and later disputes over compliance. Very few projects produced the massive technology transfers that the Chinese side had anticipated.

There were individual successes, though. In a recent paper Mu and Lee (2005) argue that the joint venture Shanghai Bell Alcatel was a highly successful example of "trading market access for technology." First set up in 1984, as a joint venture with the Belgian Bell subsidiary of ITT, the venture had as its purpose the production of digital switches for telecommunications. The foreign partner was not a technology leader and was therefore willing to agree to very generous terms in order to achieve first-entrant rights to the Chinese market. The Bell Company agreed to transfer technology and to manufacture custom large-scale integrated (LSI) chips used in telecom in the Chinese facility. In subsequent years the joint venture enjoyed the patronage of the Ministry of Post and Telecom, which helped it to surmount numerous business difficulties. In return, many Chinese engineers were trained at or rotated through Shanghai Bell, and many were introduced to the concepts and technologies of digital telecom switches at that plant. According to Mu and Lee, this training was critical to developing the expertise that was later used in the development of domestic telecom equipment enterprises, including some very successful firms such as Huawei and ZTE Telecom (discussed in section 15.3). Today, this joint venture is still an important telecom supplier in China. France's Alcatel acquired the Belgian partner, and the Chinese ministry's stake was inherited by central government SASAC (see Chapter 13), making this one of the few Sino-foreign joint ventures that were under central government authority and that reflected its distinctive history.

Chinese policy-makers have moved away from this model of restrictive, bilateral monopoly bargaining over investment, technology, and market access. In most cases, they now prefer to let numerous investors compete in the marketplace. However, policy-makers continue to drive tough technology bargains that "trade market access for technology" when they think they have sufficient bargaining power to achieve results. For example, the Chinese government has recently been in negotiation with suppliers of nuclear power facilities, conditioning large-scale purchases on the agreement to transfer technology.

15.1.2.4   Seed It

As China scaled back direct government research in the 1980s, it developed a more sophisticated system of funding research. Budget allocations to research institutes were cut but partially replaced with a system of competitive grants. For basic science and research, institutes now prepare applications for specific funding purposes and submit them to funding agencies, the most important of which is the Natural Sciences Foundation. Government control of research agendas is increasingly exerted through the foundation. A new program to master, transfer, and diffuse key advanced civilian technologies, called the 86–3 Program, after the year and month of launch, designated 10 priority areas of high-technology development. Goal-dedicated research teams were encouraged and funded, although dispersion of funding sometimes limited effectiveness. The 86–3 Program has generally been judged a success, and it was succeeded 11 years later by a 97–3 Program.

In addition to basic technology development, a program of technology diffusion was also implemented, in various baskets. For example, the Torch program provides bank loans for technology adoption by enterprises, and the Spark plan funds technological upgrading for township and village enterprises. These programs by 2003 added up to 80 billion RMB, but most of the actual funding came from enterprises and bank lending. Thus the Chinese government has become more strategic and more effective in spreading its funds among research and technology diffusion measures.

15.1.2.5 Encourage Spin-offs

During the 1980s policy-makers tried to give research institutes stronger incentives to diffuse technologies into the civilian economy. Institutes and universities were allowed to contract with enterprises to provide technical services; they were also allowed to establish their own commercial subsidiaries. This permissive stance led to the creation of a number of new enterprises that became important in the development of China's high-technology industry. These firms operated in a hazy area of Chinese industrial organization: although they were "owned" by the state entity that spun them off, they were considered "civilian" (*minban*), in the sense that they had no direct bureaucratic supervisor. These firms therefore had significant operational freedom, and some grew into prominent computer and IT firms such as Beijing University's Founder or Qinghua University's Tongfang. The most successful of all these firms is one that we encountered already in Chapter 13, Lenovo (originally "Legend" [*Lianxiang*]) Computer. Lenovo was spun off from the Institute for Computer Technology of the Chinese Academy of Sciences in 1984, and it became an important presence in the burgeoning Zhongguancun high-technology district in northwest Beijing (Segal 2003; Xie and White 2004).

Lenovo followed an interesting trajectory: It initially developed as a commercial enterprise, acting as a distributor for foreign desktop computers. As Lenovo began to develop manufacturing capabilities, it specialized in relatively low-tech stages of the manufacturing process, notwithstanding the high-technology pedigree of its parent organization. Lenovo grew by transferring much of its manufacturing operation to Guangdong, which was much more open to international trade in the 1980s than was Beijing, and concentrating on labor-intensive production of motherboards and video cards. These processes required importing components, mounting them on boards, and reexporting, and Lenovo was successful enough to have achieved global market shares of 3% and 10%, respectively, by 1995. At the same time, the company became a major assembler of personal computers for the Chinese domestic market, holding a 28% market share by 2005. The company gained expertise imitating proven technologies and concentrating on assembly stages of production. The company today aspires to move into higher-technology manufacturing and to develop a stronger research component, and characterizes its strategy as "Commerce to Manufacturing to Technology." Lenovo's takeover of IBM's personal computer division in 2004 sent a strong signal about the company's potential significance. Not many spin-offs were as successful as Lenovo, but the creation of civilian spin-off firms marked a crucial stage of liberalization in China; it showed the extra latitude planners were willing to give high-technology firms, and it set the stage for more comprehensive liberalization in the late 1990s.

15.1.2.6 Open Up to Foreign Direct Investment

FDI into China exploded after 1992 (Chapter 17). Within a few years FDI had become the predominant source of technology inflows into China. Lying behind the change was a transformation in China's attitude toward foreign-owned firms. Rather than trying to craft a few individual technology bargains, limiting entrants in order to enhance their own bargaining power, planners accepted a more general approach in which a larger number of competitive technology suppliers would be allowed in the market. Chinese policy-makers continued to envisage a general trade of "market access for technology," but they reinterpreted the terms of the deal. The result was a flood of foreign investment, much of it in medium- to high-technology sectors. MNCs became increasingly important technology actors in China, not only through their attempts to access the domestic market, but also because of the speed with which they knit China into global production networks of high-technology items. In turn, China's policy toward foreign investment reflected growing awareness that government-sponsored technology development programs had not led to catching up with global best practices. As a result, Chinese economic bureaucrats and policy-makers became increasingly willing to provide market access and promises of protection of intellectual property rights to foreign multinationals if they were willing to transfer production to China. Accession to the WTO codified and made binding the promises that China was making to promote this type of technology transfer.

15.1.2.7 Support Domestic Entrepreneurship

The freedom given to domestic entrepreneurs lagged behind that accorded to foreign multinationals. It was not until 1999 that Chinese firms were given across-the-board support to enter high-technology fields as private firms and start-ups. In place of the earlier policy of only favoring large SOEs, the government now supports virtually all technologically advanced enterprises, including small, private start-ups and technology-intensive spin-offs from schools and research institutes. In an important shift, instead of seeing private firms as rivals with publicly owned enterprises, these firms are now viewed as "national" enterprises: nonstate firms can also be the national champions that represent China in the global market place. The nature of support for high tech firms has changed as well. Increasingly, the government provides a kind of across-the-board support for domestic enterprises designated "high technology." Tax breaks, access to low-interest credit lines, preference in procurement decisions, and other kinds of regulatory preference or relief are all used and are discussed further in section 15.4.1.

This brief review of seven approaches to technology acquisition has shown two things. First, there has been a restless ongoing search for institutions and policies that can effectively support China's ongoing drive to become a technology power. When a policy proves ineffective, it is dropped; new policies are constantly being tried. Second, the technology effort that China mounts today is extremely diverse and multistranded. "Do It Yourself" and "Buy It" have not disappeared but have been scaled back and mostly confined to national security areas. The other strands of China's research effort have become more important: broader and more inclusive technology bargains, massive interactions with multinational enterprises, strategic support for research, and across-the-board support for domestic high-technology entrepreneurs. The diversity and flexibility of China's R&D effort enhances its impact (Naughton and Segal 2002).

15.2 HUMAN CAPITAL RESOURCE BASE

Chapter 8 describes the general improvement in educational standards in China; this section focuses on technical personnel. Because of its enormous size, China has an impressive total of technical personnel, reporting a total of 1.16 million individuals engaged in R&D (full-time equivalent) in 2004, of whom 920,000 were scientists or engineers (*SAC* 2005, 183). These numbers have grown at 5% annually since 1995 (6.5% for scientists and engineers). At this rate, China will have more scientists and engineers engaged in research by about 2015 than any other country. The number of annual graduates of tertiary education (colleges and technical schools) has also been growing rapidly. In 1999, 858,000 college degrees were granted; in 2005, 3.07 million. Science and engineering majors make up about 45% of graduates, while economics, management, and law account for another 25%. Since 2004, then, China has been turning out a million graduates per year with science or engineering training (Figure 15.3). Thus it is not simply that China's human capital base is growing rapidly: it is also growing at an accelerating rate.

However, numbers like those in the previous paragraph must be used carefully. Three-year technical schools, which provide training roughly equivalent to the community college in the United States, accounted for 43% of graduates in 2004. These graduates have skills and training, but should not be classified as engineers. China's educational system includes many programs of adult and vocational training, so vast numbers of personnel are qualified with various kinds of technical credentials. Official statistics claim that 28 million out of 56 million state workers in SOEs and public service undertakings have some kind of certification including 12 million teachers (*SAC* 2005, 184). Some of these technical credentials are at a very low level, but they reinforce the picture of very large numbers of workers with some technical skills. This corresponds to the broad base of Seki's pyramid: the diffusion of these skills presents possibilities, for it suggests opportunities for technological upgrading in the workplace. China's factor endowments dictate that manpower is cheap but that the human capital inputs into training manpower are scarce and therefore expensive. The outcome is a large group of scientists and technicians, but one for which average standards are still relatively low.

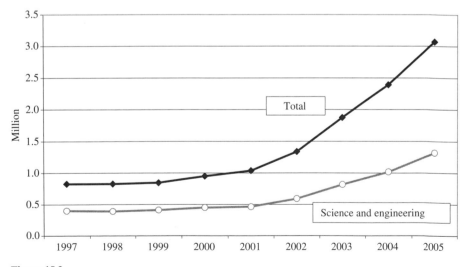

Figure 15.3
Graduates of college and technical school

At the top of the skills pyramid an important role is played by Chinese who have studied abroad. China in 2001 had 124,000 tertiary-level students abroad in OECD (developed) countries. Of these, 52,000 (42%) were in the United States, 26% in Japan, and 21% in the European Union. Official Chinese data indicate that more than 700,000 Chinese studied abroad from 1978 to 2003 and that 172,000 returned after graduation. By this account, about one in four of those who study abroad return to China. One independent study found that only 10% of Chinese PhD students in the United States intended to return after they received their PhD. Yet over the years training of Chinese scientists and engineers in advanced degrees overseas has contributed an enormous amount to the growth of China's human resource base. First, many do return, and some return with work experience in the United States or other foreign countries, which increases their value. Since about 1999, China's government has made strenuous efforts to encourage students to return voluntarily, and a booming economy has helped attract larger numbers home. Returnees have played a disproportionately large role in fostering new high-tech start-ups and upgrading educational institutions. Even when students do not return, they play a role in connecting domestic scientists and engineers to international networks of research and innovation (Schaaper 2004; *SYC* 2004, 781–82; "China Highlights" 2004; Zweig 2005).

Figure 15.1 showed the size of the total R&D effort converted at PPP rates. By this measure, China's aggregate R&D effort is substantially larger than that of Korea and approaches Japan's in total size. However, if we were to convert at official exchange rates, the value of the total Chinese R&D effort would be less than that of Korea and a small fraction of Japan's. Which is more appropriate? The PPP estimate picks up the much lower cost of skilled manpower in China, but the official exchange rate picks up the fact that most of the high-quality inputs needed in R&D must be imported and paid for at world prices. The truth thus lies somewhere in between. The Chinese effort is large, but it is less effective than in some other countries because of China's overall lower level of development.

15.3 THE OUTPUT OF THE R&D EFFORT

China's R&D effort was dominated by government research institutes for many years. Government research accounted for two-thirds of total R&D expenditure through the 1980s. The concentration of research in government institutes limited the economic effectiveness of R&D, while also making it difficult for us to assess that impact. This concentration of research in government facilities was in sharp contrast to market economies, where typically two-thirds of the researchers, as well as more than two-thirds of the R&D money, are in the business sector. In recent years, though, the share of R&D performed by Chinese enterprises has increased dramatically. An R&D census conducted in 2000, permits us to estimate shares of total R&D. The 2000 numbers found that 60% of total R&D activities were carried out in the enterprise sector, and this figure increased slightly to 62% in 2003. In terms of personnel, the enterprise sector had 50% of the R&D personnel in 2000 and 60% in 2003. Thus the data indicate that Chinese firms now account for about the same share of R&D outlays as their counterparts in market economies.

The increase in the share of total Chinese R&D undertaken by businesses may be somewhat less than the data indicate, though. In the first place, a large number of research institutes were converted into enterprises during 1999–2001. Some became stand-alone service providers, and many were amalgamated into the new industrial corporations that were being carved out of the state bureaucracy at this time. But many institutes have had difficulty redefining their mission to accord with a business perspective, and many institutes that were amalgamated subsequently declared independence and set up shop on their own (Hu Jiayuan 2005). Further, the Chinese government has recently rolled out an impressive array of tax incentives and support for R&D in the business sector: We should assume that enterprises have responded to these policies by classifying and reporting more activities than before as R&D, even before they actually increase R&D activities.

However, more detailed econometric work finds that Chinese enterprise-level R&D expenditures have a significant effect both on firm-level productivity and on the firm's ability to absorb technology. Hu, Jefferson, and Qian (2005) found that firm R&D outlays and foreign technology transfer are complements, and both are significant in explaining firm performance. Moreover, using the same data set, Fisher-Vanden and Jefferson (2005) found that firm-level R&D had a statistically significant effect in inducing firms to adapt existing technologies to shift toward more labor-intensive and capital- and energy-saving technologies. This finding presents strong evidence that businesses use R&D to develop production technologies that utilize China's abundant factors and economize on scarce factors, thus saving businesses money. In addition, there is no doubt that a few top information technology (IT) companies in China have begun to invest significantly in R&D. Huawei and ZTE, for example, the top telecom equipment firms referred to in section 15.1.2.3, report spending 14.7% and 7.6% of gross revenues, respectively, on R&D.

The pace of patenting in China has grown strongly and steadily. In 2003 more than 300,000 patent applications were submitted. This number, however, includes "utility models" and design patents, which are relatively modest adaptations of existing technologies. If we limit our scope to the 105,318 applications for new inventions, we find that almost half (48,549) of those applications were from foreigners and over half (56,769) were from Chinese citizens. Clearly the patent system is beginning to play a role in the strategies of foreign companies in China, which increasingly seek to protect intellectual property whatever the source. At the same time, Chinese inventors are beginning to find it worthwhile to start protecting their own intellectual property. Another piece of evidence comes from the changing behavior of MNC affiliates in China. Affiliates of U.S. multinationals in China have begun spending significant amounts on R&D. Affiliates of U.S. companies in China report spending 9.2% of their value added on R&D, significantly greater than the average rate of 3.3% for U.S. affiliates in all overseas locations (NSF 2004). This expenditure is very unusual, because it makes China the only developing country in which U.S. overseas affiliates conduct a significant amount of research and development.

The most apparent China differences in the distribution of R&D effort are outside the business sector. The share of government research institutes has declined, but in 2003 they still accounted for 19% of the personnel and 26% of the expenditures on R&D. Universities, however, account for 17.3% of the personnel and 10.5% of the expenditure. This is the reverse of the proportions of government and universities in most other countries. Government research typically accounts for around 10% of total R&D, and universities often account for 20% or more of total R&D. Thus China's R&D effort is characterized by relatively a strong government sector, a relatively weak university sector, and a still immature business R&D effort.

15.4   REDEFINING GOVERNMENT TECHNOLOGY POLICY IN THE TWENTY-FIRST CENTURY

Since the turn of the century, China's technological development has noticeably accelerated. Part of the acceleration may be due to the increase in R&D inputs attributable to government policy, and some part may also be due to the beginnings of a Chinese corporate sector with the ability to invest in R&D. Government policy shifts play an important role. For decades into market transition, China's government pursued various flavors of "industrial policy." Industrial policy targeted priority sectors, picked winners among firms (typically SOEs), and tried to compensate for distortions in the emerging market environment (Lu and Tang 1997; Marukawa 2000). Today, industrial policy has increasingly been subsumed into technology policy. The instruments have diversified, but the ultimate objective has become much more focused than in the past.

15.4.1   Aligning Incentives in Favor of High-Technology Development

Since 1999 technology policies have achieved a thorough alignment of incentives of government and corporate actors in support of the development of knowledge-intensive industry. A barrage of specific policies, some of them described here, have had a cumulative effect. While no individual policy has been overwhelmingly effective, together they ensure that actions taken in favor of the development of high-technology industry will meet with central government acceptance and will only rarely have negative consequences. First, post–1999 policies enable technological development because they abandoned much of the ideological baggage that had inhibited technological development up to that time. "National industry" was redefined to include foreign-invested firms and small private and hybrid start-ups, and national planners thereby removed many ideological obstacles to creative organizational approaches. Second, by greatly relaxing their effort to condition approvals of individual foreign investment projects on specific technology transfer, planners actually enabled much more rapid technology transfer. Thus, despite China's complicated and often contradictory mixture of centralized, decentralized, and quasi-federalist institutions, these enabling policies brought the incentives of many different levels of government into alignment. Localities were freed to do what they wanted to do anyway or exposed to heightened competition from other regions if they chose not to act.

Indeed, promotion of high-technology industry is arguably the central economic development policy of the Chinese government today. Technology development is the unifying thread that links together many aspects of economic policy in the Hu Jintao–Wen Jiabao administration (2002–). A newly emphatic stress on human resources as the foundation of development policy is clearly related, by way of the long-term development of the human capital base, to the promotion of technology industry. The top priority of foreign trade development has been placed firmly on the development of high-technology trade. Trade promotion policies stress that the key to upgrading exports is the promotion of high-tech exports, particularly those in which China has its own intellectual property, and it is taken for granted that government has a role in promoting such exports. In the sphere of corporate governance, as argued in Chapter 13, high-technology enterprises have been at the cutting edge of changes that give managers stakes in the firms they run. Finally, there is technology policy per se, in which an enormous range of subsidies and financial support packages are available to literally thousands of private, state-owned, and foreign-invested firms. The following points give the flavor of some of these provisions:

Tax Breaks. A whole range of amendments to the tax code have been made to make expenditure on R&D virtually costless for the enterprise: partial tax deduction for R&D expenditures; tax exemption for all income from the sale of new technologies and related consulting services; tax exemption for imports of equipment used in R&D and not available in China; and so on. The tax break that attracted the most attention, rolled out in State Council Document No. 18 of 1999, was a rebate that reduced value-added taxes from 17% to 3% for domestic software and integrated circuit producers. (This rebate was eliminated in 2005 after it was challenged by U.S. integrated-circuit companies as inconsistent with WTO rules.)

Subsidized Credit. Subsidized credit includes a domestic fund to support small and medium high-technology enterprises, interest subsidies for specific projects by large enterprises, and coverage of high tech exports by the Import-Export Bank.

Procurement Preference. Domestic high-tech firms are entitled to general preference in government procurement. In some cases, government procurement policies are specifically targeted to support domestic IT development, as in the case of smart ID cards with embedded chips.

Corporate Governance Provisions. Greatly influenced by the success of the U.S. "Silicon Valley model" of venture capital and start-up technology enterprises, Chinese policy-makers altered many aspects of their corporate governance procedures in order to accommodate venture-capital-assisted start-up businesses. Accounting regulations on the calculation of capital were changed to allow inventions and intellectual property to be counted as investment. High-technology firms were, in principle, allowed to set aside 35% of the net value of increased assets for stock options or other rewards for innovators and entrepreneurs. A small but lively venture capital industry was established, with most of the funds coming directly or indirectly from government agencies, but with a significant role for a few foreign venture capitalists as well. Provisions to allow listing of new high-tech companies on existing stock exchanges, as well as new listing venues, were rolled out in order to provide an exit option for venture capital.

Manipulation of Technical Standards. Having discovered that the Chinese domestic market could support a standard for video discs (VCD) that was separate from the global DVD standard, Chinese policy-makers became very interested in using Chinese technical standards to create competitive advantage for domestic firms. Efforts have been made with next-generation DVDs, third-generation digital telephony, and encryption, at least, to create advantage for Chinese firms (Linden 2004; Suttmeier and Yao 2004). Whether any of these efforts has produced any benefit is not certain.

These provisions were accompanied by a farrago of subsidies that also includes lower land prices, cooperative regulatory procedures, and patient and forgiving state-financed equity investors. The government has also invested substantial funds in projects such as the creation of an indigenous central processing unit (CPU) known as Godson. Prototypes of Godson 2 and 3 were released in 2005, with processing speeds up to 1 gHz. Together, these policies increase the flow of resources into knowledge-intensive industry and almost certainly, on balance, accelerate the development of high-technology industry. Like any industrial policy, these policy interventions draw resources away from other sectors that need resources (such as agriculture) and increase profits for businessmen who do not need additional profits. However, none of these policies dramatically distorts economy-wide market signals, and the overall costs are probably fairly modest, as well as being diffused through the entire economy.

Some of these policies may be successful, but they are unlikely to be the main determinants of China's future technological trajectory. They have costs and benefits, and it is unlikely that the benefit-cost trade-off for any specific policy is dramatically positive. But at the same time, the broad array of policies strongly signals local governments that virtually any action they take in support of high-technology industry and technological development will be acceptable. This approach insures that governmental actions at all levels are aligned in support of high-tech development.

15.5 DEEPER INTEGRATION INTO GLOBAL PRODUCTION NETWORKS

During the 1980s and 1990s, China rapidly integrated into global production networks, taking over low-tech, labor-intensive production stages from Taiwan, Hong Kong, and Korea (Chapter 17). Precisely because China specialized in the least technologically demanding stages of production, these linkages initially had few implications for technological development. Even when China was exporting finished goods that embodied high-technology components— such as laptop computers—the actual spillovers into indigenous technological capabilities were minimal. The global production networks involved in these high-tech commodities were largely closed, and Chinese domestic producers did not participate much, if at all. This history has spawned a realistic pessimistic literature about Chinese capabilities, based on the combination of observed concentration on low-technology stages of the value chain and observed weaknesses of Chinese corporations (Nolan 2002; Steinfeld 2004; Gilboy 2004; Cf. Rosen 2003).

The pessimistic literature highlights some of the real shortcomings of Chinese technological capabilities. However, very rapid changes in the configuration of global production networks make it unlikely that these backward-looking assessments will be very good guides to the future. In the first place, we already see a few selected industries where undeniably "high-tech" stages of production are moving to China. For example, the integrated circuit (IC) industry exemplifies nearly all the factors discussed in this chapter. For years, China attempted to nurture a domestic IC industry without succeeding in narrowing the technological gap behind world technology leaders. From 2001, though, China's more inclusive technology-promotion policies began to succeed in attracting joint-venture IC factories to the mainland. The most prominent of these firms, Semiconductor Manufacturing International Corporation (SMIC), rapidly shrank the gap with global technology leaders to less than two years, an impressive performance in this extremely dynamic industry. Without doubt, very substantial tax breaks and implicit subsidies were an important part of this process. Expertise from Taiwan and finance from diverse international sources were instrumental in the creation of what has become a flagship firm in China's "national industry." Despite the role of policy in encouraging a Chinese IC industry, it is clear that economic fundamentals had to be in place before the policies could bear fruit. China has already developed a huge demand for ICs as a result of the development of large telecommunications-equipment, personal-computer, and consumer-electronics industries. Indeed, even after robust recent development, China's domestic IC firms still supply a mere 16% of total domestic consumption. This robust demand enabled specific promotion policies to succeed.

The IC industry can also illustrate some of the more general changes occurring in the organization of global production networks. In the old days of the 1990s it was primarily low-technology stages of the manufacturing process that were "outsourced," because these were the only labor-intensive stages of the production process that could be easily relocated to labor-abundant locations such as China. However, today processes of vertical specialization, or "modularity," have progressed further than in the past and are beginning to transform manufacturing, services, and innovation in more profound ways. Some stages of production, services, or even research can be incorporated into modules that can be partitioned off from the rest of the value chain. The results of the work or innovation within the module can be summarized through a mutually accepted interface standard, so that downstream firms can use the results of the previous module without knowing what went on "inside" the module. This capability enables firms to pursue focused strategies that rely heavily on outsourcing across the value chain.

These changes have important implications for China's technological development. The same trends that led firms to slice up and relocate the manufacturing value chain are now increasingly coming to bear on the services embedded in the high-technology value chain, including research and development. Businesses are gaining more experience with international cooperation and offshoring; the cost of communications continues to fall. Meanwhile, manufacturing is a smaller part of the total value chain than it was before, and the increase in manufacturing sophistication has increased the demands on design and other capacities. As a result, there are many more opportunities to "outsource" knowledge-intensive services, such as software, engineering, and R&D. In the IC industry, improvements in semiconductor manufacturing productivity have been so rapid that they have exceeded the pace of technological progress in semiconductor design and related services. As semiconductor design becomes more of a bottleneck, the pressures to reduce its cost increase, and entrepreneurial businesses are more likely to find solutions that involve a China design component (Ernst 2004). Integrated-circuit design is now broken up into modules, and some of the work—initially the most routine and formalized—is outsourced to China. Design building blocks are modules that can be created and improved by one team, then assembled and reassembled in ever more complex packages by other teams of chip designers. Tiny IC design houses are thriving in China, and some MNCs locate design shops in China to take advantage of low-cost engineering talent. Modularization, in short, allows China to specialize in labor-intensive activities that also involve medium levels of engineering skill, which it has in abundance. These activities then provide a new pathway to technological upgrading, as design teams expand the scope of their competence. A similar process is at work in R&D centers: development tasks that can be routinized and formalized will ultimately be transplanted to China to a significant extent.

At the same time, Chinese domestic firms are utilizing international networks in their own ways. As Liu Xielin (2005) points out, many Chinese firms seek access to global technology at the cheapest cost, and combine it with their own capabilities to serve the Chinese market. Liu uses the mobile phone handset industry as an example: Chinese handset manufacturers purchase components that embody advanced technology (especially the ICs at the core of the phone's function) and assemble them into products adapted to the demands of the local market. This manufacturing is not initially a high tech process, but rather one closely adapted to market demand. However, Liu finds that as product design capabilities improve, the domestic industry has rapidly expanded its technological capacity as well. Lenovo Computer is another example: it is not a manufacturing powerhouse moving up with the IBM brand, as many have assumed. Instead, Lenovo is a strong domestic brand, with a diverse mix of manufacturing and technological development skills. In fact, in 2003, Lenovo outsourced 100% of its laptops, 70% of its personal digital assistants (PDAs), and 40% of its motherboards to Taiwan contract manufacturers, thus turning the "international subcontracting" model on its head (Jiang 2004). Increasingly complex business strategies are based on an increasingly fine division of the value chain; this process will create the most important points of contact at which advanced technology can spill over from world technology leaders to Chinese firms.

However, the re-creation of global value networks requires new cooperation around intellectual property. Close cooperation and trust are necessary. Again, this is exemplified by the IC industry. The production of any significant IC requires literally thousands of pieces of intellectual property. No developing country, including China, can ever hope either to "invent around" existing intellectual property or to license each essential piece of intellectual property at market rates. Indeed, no existing company, not even Intel, could produce without access to intellectual property owned by competitors. Typically the industry proceeds by various kinds of cross-licensing agreements. Various formulas—and sometimes significant hard bargaining—are used to work out the relative value of the intellectual property on each side, and a net financial flow from one company to the other is determined on that basis (Teece 2000). This situation presents China with two very large challenges. The first is to strengthen its protection of intellectual property rights so that it can become a full partner in cooperation with MNCs in high-technology industries. The second is to develop enough bargaining power such that Chinese firms have something to offer MNCs in exchange for their IPR. A few multinationals have begun to share their IPR with China's nascent IC firms, so a beginning has been made. Increasingly, the focus of Chinese government technology policy is on creating bargaining capital for China's high-tech industry, in order to improve China's standing in the exchange of technological information along global production networks. It is a process that has just begun, but it promises to transform China's technological capabilities.

15.6   CONCLUSION

The pace of technological change in China is likely to accelerate. As we have seen, China has now mounted a substantial technology effort that works through diverse channels. Policy-makers have been flexible and adaptive in their approaches. The human resource base is now growing rapidly, from a relatively low base, and this growth shows every sign of accelerating. The institutions and incentives that support technology adoption have changed very dramatically in just the last five or six years and now provide abundant rewards not only for technology pioneers, but also for those who implement improved technologies effectively. These changes are all occurring in a global context in which increasingly close cooperation and increasingly fine divisions of the value chain are rapidly leading to the relocation of technology-intensive services. These changes work strongly to China's advantage, and it appears that China has the human resource capacity and the institutional framework that will allow it to take advantage of the opportunity.

BIBLIOGRAPHY

Suggestions for Further Reading

There is vigorous discussion between optimists and pessimists about China's technological development, and this discussion is a good place to begin. Optimists focus on China's rapid improvement and on the creation of a coherent set of institutions to foster technological process. See, for example, Suttmeier and Yao (2004) and Liu Xielin and White (2001) for good analytic overviews with an optimistic tone. Pessimists (Gilboy 2004; Rosen 2004; Steinfeld 2004) focus on China's still low overall level and the limitations to the capabilities developed by Chinese firms. Fischer and von Zedtwitz (2004) put the discussion in temporal perspective. Liu Xielin (2005) is an interesting piece that puts forward a new paradigm of open cross-border networks. Book-length studies of specific industries include Lu (2000) on computers and Shen (1999) on telecom equipment.

Sources for Data and Figures

Figure 15.1: Schaaper (2004).

Figure 15.2: Technology Statistics Office (1990, 202–03); NBS-MOST (2004, 2); *SYC* (1998, 716); and NBS-MOST (Annual) and *SYC* (Annual).

Figure 15.3: *SYC* (2005, 697) and earlier volumes.

Annual Report (2006).

Table 15.1: OECD (2005, 18, 21, 57); NBS-MOST (2004). Recalculated with revised GDP data.

References

"China Highlights Achievements by Returned Overseas Chinese" (2004). *People's Daily* [English edition], March 2, at http://english.people.com.cn/200403/02/eng20040302_136322.shtml.

Chinese Academy of Sciences [Zhongguo Kexue Yuan]. (1998). *1997 Kexue Fazhan Baogao* [1997 Science Development Report]. Beijing: Kexue.

Cliff, Roger (1998). "China's Potential for Developing Advanced Military Technology," July 8. Santa Monica: RAND Corporation.

Ernst, Dieter (2004). "Internationalisation of Innovation: Why Is Chip Design Moving to Asia?" Economics Working Paper. Honolulu: East-West Center.

Feigenbaum, Evan (1999). "Soldiers, Weapons and Chinese Development Strategy: The Mao Era Military in China's Economic and Institutional Debate." *China Quarterly*, 158 (June), 285–313.

Feinstein, Charles, and Christopher Howe (1997). *Chinese Technology Transfer in the 1990s: Current Experience, Historical Problems and International Perspectives.* Cheltenham: Edward Elgar.

Fischer, William A., and Maximilian von Zedtwitz (2004). "Chinese R&D: Naissance, Renaissance or Mirage?" *R&D Management*, 34(4):349–65. Special issue on Chinese R&D.

Fisher-Vanden, Karen, and Gary Jefferson (2005). "Technology Diversity and Development: Evidence from China's Industrial Enterprises." Dartmouth College, manuscript, August 16.

Gilboy, George (2004). "The Myth Behind China's Miracle." *Foreign Affairs*, July/August. 33–49.

Gu Yuefang (1996). "On the position of technology import in the process of industrial development," In Jiao Xionghua, ed., *Zhongguo Jishu Yinjin de Jingyan yu Tansuo* [An Exploration of China's Technology Import Experience], Beijing: Zhongguo Biaozhun, pp. 8–45.

Hu, Albert, Gary Jefferson, and Jinchang Qian (2005). "R&D and Technology Transfer: Firm-Level Evidence from Chinese Industry." *Review of Economics and Statistics*, November, 87(4):780–786.

Hu Jiayuan (2005). "Why Is the Conversion of Government Research Institutes Running into So Many Obstacles?" [in Chinese]. *Zhongguo Jingyingbao*, July 19, available at http://www.sasac.gov.cn/gzyj2/200507190157.htm.

Jiang Xiaojuan (2004). "2003–2004: Zhongguo Liiyong Waizi de Fenxi yu Zhanwang [Analysis and Projection of China's Use of Foreign Capital," In Liu Guogong, Wang Luolin and Li Jingwen, eds., *Zhongguo Jingji Qianjing Fenxi 2004 Nian Chunji Baogao* [Blue Book of China's Economy (Spring 2004)]. Beijing: Shehui Kexue Wenxian, 2004, pp. 202–227.

Linden, Greg (2004). "China Standard Time: A Study in Strategic Industrial Policy." *Business and Politics*, 6(3), Article 4.

Liu Xielin (2005). "China's Development Model: An Alternative Strategy for Technological Catch-Up." Hitotsubashi University, Institute of Innovation Research Working Paper. March 22.

Liu Xielin and Steven White (2001). "Comparing Innovation Systems: A Framework and Application to China's transitional Context." *Research Policy*, 30:1091–114.

Lu Ding and Zhimin Tang (1997). *State Intervention and Business in China: The Role of Preferential Policies.* Cheltenham: Edward Elgar.

Lu, Qiwen (2000). *China's Leap into the Information Age: Innovation and Organization in the Computer Industry.* Oxford: Oxford University Press.

Marukawa, Tomoo, ed. (2000). *Iko-ki Chugoku no Sangyo Seiasaku* [China's Industrial Policy in Transition]. Chiba: Institute of Developing Economics.

MOFTEC (1999). *Zhongguo Duiwai Jingji Maoyi Baibishu* [White Book on China's Foreign Economics and Trade], 85–6, 131. Beijing: Jingji Kexue.

Mu, Qing, and Keun Lee (2005). "Knowledge Diffusion, Market Segmentation and Technological Catch-up: The Case of the Telecommunication Industry in China." *Research Policy*, 34(6):759–83.

NBS-MOST (Annual). National Bureau of Statistics and Ministry of Science and Technology, eds., *Zhongguo Keji Tongji Nianjian* [China Statistical Yearbook on Science and Technology]. Beijing: Zhongguo Tongji.

National Science Foundation, Division of Science Resources Statistics (2004). *U.S.-China R&D Linkages: Direct Investment and Industrial Alliances in the 1990s,* (NSF 04-306). Arlington, VA, February. Accessed at www.nsf.gov/sbe/srs/infbrief/nsf04306/start.htm.

Naughton, Barry, and Adam Segal (2002). "Technology Development in the New Millennium: China in Search of a Workable Model." In William Keller and Richard Samuels, eds., *Crisis and Innovation: Asian Technology after the Millennium.* 160–86. New York: Cambridge University Press.

Nolan, P. (2002) "China and the Global Business Revolution." *Cambridge Journal of Economics,* 26(1):119–37.

OECD (2005). *Main Science and Technology Indicators*, vol. 2005/1. Paris: OECD. http:// iris.sourceoecd.org/vl=917570/cl=32/nw=1/rpsv/cgi-bin/fulltextew.pl?prpsv=/ij/oecdjournals/ 1011792x/v2005n1/s1/p1l.idx.

Rosen, Dan (2003). "Low-Tech Bed, High-Tech Dreams." *China Economic Quarterly*, Q4, pp. 20–7.

SAC (Annual). *Zhongguo Tongji Zhaiyao* [Statistical Abstract of China]. Beijing: Zhongguo Tongji.

Schaaper, Martin (2004). *An Emerging Knowledge-Based Economy in China? Indicators from OECD Databases*. Paris: OECD, Directorate for Science, Technology and Industry, DSTI/DOC (2004)4, March 22.

Segal, Adam (2003). *Digital Dragon: High-Technology Enterprises in China*. Ithaca and London: Cornell University Press.

Seki Mitsuhiro (1994). *Beyond the Full-Set Industrial Structure: Japanese Industry in the New Age of East Asia*. Tokyo, Japan: LTCB International Library Foundation.

Shen, Xiaobai (1999). *The Chinese Road to High Technology*. New York: St. Martin's.

Steinfeld, Edward (2004). "Chinese Enterprise Development and the Challenge of Global Integration." In Shahid Yusuf, ed., *East Asian Networked Production*. Washington, DC: World Bank.

Suttmeier, Peter, and Yao Xiangkui (2004). "China's Post-WTO Technology Policy: Standards, Software, and the Changing Nature of Techno-Nationalism." NBR Special Report No. 7, May. At www.nbr.org/publications/specialreport/pdf/SR7.pdf.

SYC (Annual). *Zhongguo Tongji Nianjian* [Statistical Yearbook of China]. Beijing: Zhongguo Tongji.

SYC Annual Report (2006). National Bureau of Statistics, "Zhonghua Renmin Gongheguo 2005 Nian Guomin Jingji he Shehui Fazhan Tongji Gongbao [PRC 2005 National Economy and Society Development Statistical Report]," February 28, 2006 at http://www.stats.gov.cn/tjgb/ndtjgb/ qgndtjgb/t20060227_402307796.htm

Technology Statistics Office, NBS (1990). *Zhongguo Kexue Jishu Sishinian 1949–1989* [Statistics on Science and Technology of China 1949–1989]. Beijing: Zhongguo Tongji.

Teece, David (2000). *Managing Intellectual Capital: Organizational, Strategic, And Policy Dimensions.*; New York: Oxford University Press.

Xie, Wei, and Steven White (2004). "Sequential Learning in a Chinese Spin-off: The Case of Lenovo Group Limited." *R&D Management*, 34(4):407–22.

Wang Huijiong et al (1996). "The Mechanism of Technology Import," In Jiao Xionghua, ed., *Zhongguo Jishu Yinjin de Jingyan yu Tansuo* [An Exploration of China's Technology Import Experience], Beijing: Zhongguo Biaozhun, 1996, pp. 268–91.

Zweig, David (2005). "Learning to Compete: China's Strategies to Create a 'Reverse Brain Drain.'" HKUST Center on China's Transnational Relations, Working Paper No. 2, Hong Kong University of Science and Technology, January. Available at http://www.cctr.ust.hk/ articles/pdf/triggering.pdf.

Export goods for sale in the domestic economy, Wangfujing, Beijing 2006.

China has transformed into a global trade power. In 2005, China was the third-largest trading nation in the world (after the United States and Germany), and its trade is growing far more rapidly than that of any other large economy. China has now achieved a degree of openness that is exceptional for a large, continental economy. In 2005, China's total goods trade (exports plus imports) amounted to 64% of GDP, far more than other large, continental economies—such as the United States, Japan, India, and Brazil—which have trade/GDP ratios around 20%, the highest being Brazil's 25%. Trade liberalization has been an integral part of China's economic reform process since its beginning. The most recent phase of trade policy reform began with China's formal entry into the WTO, on December 11, 2001, which started the clock running on a series of liberalization commitments kicking in between 2001 and 2007. Besides marking a new phase of policy reform, WTO membership symbolizes China's coming of age as a participant in the global economic community.

China began trade liberalization with one of the most closed economies in the world. The institutional setup under the planned economy was designed to restrict trade to a handful of government monopolies, and actual trade was very small. Before 1979, China's total trade/GDP ratio never significantly exceeded 10%, and it reached a low point of only 5% in 1970–1971. What is particularly striking is that for almost 30 years China has undergone repeated waves of liberalization and trade promotion, and each wave has been followed by a surge of trade. In perhaps no other sector of the economy has the pattern of sustained incremental and cumulative reform been as obvious, and the outcomes so unambiguously positive for the Chinese economy, as in the foreign trade sector. Figure 16.1, which shows exports and imports as a share of GDP, shows how China's position has changed dramatically. In 1978, China's trade ratio was far below the world average. Between then and the early 1990s, China rapidly opened up and converged quickly to the world average, and the

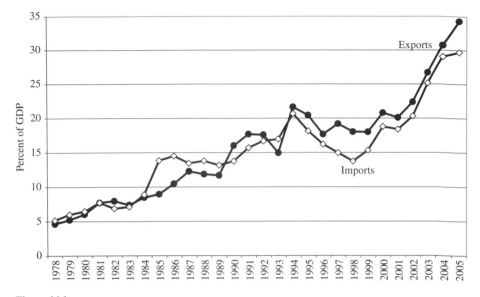

Figure 16.1
Exports and imports (share of GDP)

trade share stabilized through the late 1990s. Since 2002, trade openness has surged again. An enormous systemic transformation was necessary to convert China from one of the world's most economically isolated economies into a global economic player. International "opening" and domestic economic reform were complementary processes that are often paired in a single term to describe the post–1978 period: "Reform and Opening" (*gaige kaifang*). This institutional change is the first topic covered in this chapter.

In today's global economy, trade and investment are increasingly closely linked. In China as well, growth of trade has been driven by foreign investment that was itself part of East Asia–wide economic restructuring (see Chapter 17). The package and sequence of liberalization policies that China followed was adapted to the opportunities that China faced. A central element was a dualistic trade regime, which enabled China to adopt relatively liberal rules on export-processing trade while still protecting domestic markets. These rules enabled China to accommodate the wishes of foreign investors and helped bring China into increasingly integrated cross-border production networks. This topic will also serve as a bridge between the discussion of the institutional features shaping Chinese trade and the geographic and commodity composition of China's trade. The chapter concludes by emphasizing China's gains from trade. Its labor-rich and land-poor economy has gained much through exchange, particularly with resource- and capital-abundant economies.

16.1 BACKGROUND

Under the socialist economic system, before reforms, China was not always a closed economy. Indeed, in the early days of the People's Republic of China, from 1949 through 1960, China was quite open to trade and aid, which came almost entirely from the Soviet bloc. During the 1950s, China shut down most of the Pacific trade on which its economy had relied before the revolution and reoriented its trade toward the Soviet Union. More than two-thirds of China's trade between 1952 and 1960 was with Communist Party–led countries, and 48% was with the Soviet Union alone. Trade was a leading sector in China's economic transformation. China imported industrial materials such as steel and diesel fuel, as well as machinery, most crucially the complete industrial plants that were the centerpiece of China's first Five-Year Plan (1953 1957; see Chapter 3). China exported textiles and processed foods, and financed moderate trade deficits with the Soviet Union by borrowing. The GLF (1958–1960) at first encouraged further growth in trade with the socialist countries, as China's frenzied drive for investment increased its demand for imported machinery.

However, the economic crisis and famine that followed the collapse of the GLF led to dramatic changes, and China began a long, slow retreat into international economic isolation. Overall Chinese trade stagnated. Imports of industrial goods were curtailed sharply in the immediate post-Leap crisis, and scarce foreign exchange was diverted to desperately needed grain imports. Imports from the Soviet Union dropped sharply, and by 1970 trade with the Soviet Union accounted for only 1% of total Chinese trade, which did not grow at all between 1959 and 1970. The early 1970s were thus the low point of China's relations with the world economy, during the period of Maoist self reliance and strategic self-sufficiency. In 1970–1971 imports and exports together were only 5% of GDP. The food and light consumer products that China had previously exported were now in short supply domestically. Moreover, there were few foreign markets open for which China had any market intelligence: China's largest single export market was Hong Kong. China became a steady customer of Canadian, Australian, and Argentinean grain exports. Available foreign exchange had to be carefully husbanded to enable the import of a few critical industrial materials and technologies. Cut off from its supplies of Soviet technology, China made a few tentative purchases from new technology suppliers in Japan and Europe. A policy of extreme self-reliance was adopted, making a virtue out of necessity.

From the mid–1970s the economy began to recover from the worst of the Cultural Revolution, and supplies of light consumer manufactures (especially textiles) for export began to increase again. Around the same time, petroleum output from China's main field at Daqing began to increase rapidly, and some oil was available for export. As foreign-exchange earnings began to increase, China stepped up its technology purchases from the West and Japan. Fertilizer plants and steel mills were at the front of the queue of desperately needed technology items. These trading relationships seemed set to continue growing, and ambitious technology-import programs multiplied in 1977–1978. But when oil-field development programs fell through, it was unclear where the foreign currency needed to pay for the imports would come from. China for the first time was forced to confront the inherent problems created by its command-economy trading system.

16.2   THE PROCESS OF TRADE REFORM

The foreign-trade system that Chinese leaders sought to reform in the late 1970s was a typical Soviet-style command-economy model. The domestic economy was rigorously separated from the world economy by what we might term a "double air lock" that controlled flows of both goods and money. The first "air lock" was the centrally controlled foreign-trade monopoly. Twelve national foreign-trade companies (FTCs) exercised monopolies over both imports and exports. Only authorized goods were allowed to pass through this layer of control. A second "air lock" was the foreign-exchange system. The value of the Chinese currency (the *renminbi*, RMB, or yuan) was set arbitrarily, and it was not convertible. Individuals had no ability to exchange *renminbi* for foreign currency without special authorization, which was very difficult to get. Overlapping, redundant controls covered the flows of both goods and money. The only way to navigate this tangle of administrative controls was to be included in the foreign-trade plan.

The "double air lock" system was designed to insulate the domestic economy from the world economy while allowing a few key commodities to pass through the air locks. The FTCs bought and sold domestic commodities at planned prices, and world commodities at world prices. When imports passed through the air lock, they were repriced in accordance with domestic planned prices, and the FTCs regularly cross-subsidized money-losing products with revenues from profitable ones. The socialist price system was thus completely insulated from the influence of world prices. As discussed in Chapters 3 and 18, socialist prices were set so as to privilege the state-owned industrial system. Low-relative agricultural prices and high industrial prices were used to concentrate profits in state-owned factories, where they could be harvested for the government budget. If world market forces had been allowed to affect domestic prices, they would have gradually eroded the socialist price system and the government's traditional institutions for mobilizing resources. The socialist price system is an extreme version of the price relationships created by the common "import substitution industrialization" (ISI) development strategy. In ISI strategies, developing countries erect barriers against industrial imports, thereby protecting their new industries and (they hope) fostering industrialization. In China as well, one of the functions of the traditional foreign trade system was to protect state-owned industries.

Given this system of control, foreign trade served the interests of China's planners, who had simple preferences. The purpose of foreign trade was to import goods that could not be produced by Chinese firms and that would resolve domestic shortages or bottlenecks (food or raw materials) or bring in modern technology (embodied in industrial machinery). Exports were viewed as a sort of necessary evil, required because exporting was the only way to pay for imports. If goods were "not needed" for the domestic economy, they could be exported, but the cost of producing export goods was largely irrelevant, while the import of nonessential goods was severely restricted. As Chinese planners tried to step up the pace of technology imports in 1978–1979, though, they suddenly found themselves seriously short of foreign exchange and committed to imports that they could not pay for, since they were unable to increase oil exports. Foreign-exchange reserves, small to begin with, melted away at alarming speed. Foreign-trade reforms then began with an urgent attempt to increase and diversify sources of foreign exchange. China was already trading predominantly with market economies, a situation which was anomalous, given its state-monopoly trading system, and it was surrounded by dynamic export-oriented economies. This combination of motive and opportunity launched China on its program of economic opening, which culminated in dramatic changes to the world economy.

16.2.1   Initial Reform Steps

Rather than tackle the enormous task of transforming the whole foreign-trade system, Chinese policy-makers initially took modest but innovative steps to open up new trade channels in the southern provinces of Guangdong and Fujian in 1978–1979. The objective was to make use of the proximity of these provinces to Hong Kong and, to a lesser extent, Taiwan. At this time,

Guangdong Province was only a second-tier player in China's foreign trade, accounting for one-seventh of China's export revenues in 1978. Neighboring Hong Kong, however, was already a huge trading power. In fact, tiny Hong Kong exported as much as all of mainland China at this time. China's first step in opening came in 1978 when Hong Kong businesses were allowed to sign "export-processing" (EP) contracts with Chinese firms in the Pearl River Delta. A Hong Kong firm would ship (for example) fabric to a Chinese rural firm and have it sewn into shirts. The Chinese firm would be paid a processing fee, while the fabric and shirts would be owned by the Hong Kong firm at all times, so they did not have to pass through the foreign-trade system air locks. In this way, the export production network already created by Hong Kong could expand into China, but Chinese industrial firms were not exposed to import competition.

Shortly thereafter four SEZs were set up in Guangdong and Fujian. The SEZs—described more fully in Chapter 17—provided a secure footprint for the expansion of EP trade. Like other Export-Processing Zones (EPZs), the SEZs allowed imports in duty-free, as long as they were used in the zone to produce exports. As in other developing countries, policies like the SEZs and export processing allowed China to selectively promote exports, alongside what was still primarily a system of import substitution industrialization. The zones were enclaves that did not overly threaten the system of domestic protection. The provinces of Guangdong and Fujian were also given special powers within the existing foreign trade system. The provincial divisions of national FTCs were granted autonomy, as well as the right to retain foreign-exchange income they generated. Provincial authorities developed strong incentives to expand trade, and officials in both provinces became well known for their willingness to bend rules to facilitate trade. The special provisions, the incentives, and—above all—the proximity of Hong Kong fundamentally transformed Guangdong Province and made it into an export powerhouse. For the next 15 years, exports from Guangdong and Fujian grew twice as rapidly as those from the rest of China. Those provinces were fundamentally transformed from economic backwaters into crucial nodes in the global trade economy.

16.2.2 Liberalizing the Foreign-Trade System

By the mid–1980s, having created some initial breaches in the traditional system in Guangdong and Fujian, Chinese policy-makers began the task of liberalizing the main national trading system. A comprehensive liberalization package was adopted in 1984, but the results were alarming to policy-makers— imports surged more than 50% in 1985—and reformists scaled back many of the reforms. Despite setbacks, policy-makers maintained some flexibility, and within a few years they had transformed the rules for trade, largely dismantled the old foreign-trade monopoly, and created a framework for the subsequent growth of trade and investment. The main elements of the initial phases of trade reform included the following:

Devaluation. A realistic currency value is a prerequisite for successful trade reform. Before reform, China—like most socialist and import-substitution-industrialization economies—maintained an overvalued currency. In 1980 there were 1.5 Chinese yuan to the U.S. dollar, a rate at which it was generally unprofitable to export. By 1986 the value of the Chinese currency had declined to about 3.5 to the dollar, representing a real devaluation (after accounting for China's higher rate of inflation) of about 60%. In 1986 reformers also introduced a dual-exchange-rate regime, in which exporters outside the plan could sell their foreign-exchange earnings on a lightly regulated secondary market. In the market, dollars went for a higher price, thus contributing to a further, market-driven devaluation of the yuan. Exporting became profitable, and more expensive imports provided a check on import demand. The lower real value for the *renminbi* established by 1986 has been maintained ever since, at least through 2005, despite some short-term fluctuations.[1] China's devaluation in the 1980s coincided with a realignment of currency rates throughout East Asia. The Japanese yen appreciated markedly, followed by the new Taiwan dollar, setting the scene for a dramatic restructuring of output and trade.

Demonopolization of the Foreign-Trade Regime. The number of companies authorized to engage in foreign trade was allowed to expand dramatically. Industrial ministries were allowed to set up FTCs; the provincial branches of the former national foreign trade monopolies became independent; and many

1. In 1994 the official exchange rate was pegged at around 8.3 yuan per dollar; this devaluation was offset by domestic inflation within three years. Since that time domestic price stability and a fixed nominal rate have translated into a stable real rate. If the real value of the Chinese yuan is indexed at 100 in 2003, it was 250 in 1980, but it had already declined to 107 by 1986 and averaged 106 over the entire 1986–2003 period. The argument that the Chinese currency was undervalued in 2003 cannot be made based on past trends, but must stand or fall on the basis of improved Chinese capabilities and productivity after the turn of the century. Note that changes in the currency value affect the calculations of openness reported earlier in this chapter. Devaluation makes an economy appear more open because the value of the GDP denominator (measured in domestic currency units) declines relative to the trade numerator (measured in dollars). In China the average real exchange rate from 1957 through 1980 was 2.5 times the average real exchange rate in 1986 through 2003. If we use the later, more realistic exchange rate to calculate openness in 1970, total trade was 12.5% of (revalued) GDP. Though not as extreme as the values calculated using the contemporaneous exchange rates, this is still a comparatively low degree of openness.

local governments and SEZs set up trading companies. By 1988 there were 5,000 FTCs, every one of which was still state owned. Direct export and import rights were also granted to some 10,000 manufacturing enterprises. Exports were liberalized much more rapidly than imports: thousands of firms were competing to produce manufactured exports while domestic markets still remained sheltered from import competition. Equally importantly, there was a steady shift away from the trade plan and in the direction of financial incentives. The old export procurement plan was abandoned in 1988. Foreign-exchange targets and contracting systems similar to those used in industry were applied to FTCs (see Chapter 13). Provinces contracted to make fixed annual payments of foreign exchange to the central government and retained all foreign exchange earned above the contract.

Significant Changes in Pricing Principles. Profit retention and bonuses provided incentives, decentralization increased competition, and devaluation made exporting a potentially lucrative business. FTCs became much more cost sensitive: exporting predominantly on their own account, FTCs recontracted with domestic enterprises in a range of forms—industrial sub-contracting, enterprise groups, batch processing—in an effort to lower costs. FTCs sought out cheap producers of labor-intensive goods, which were often TVEs. The share of exports produced by TVEs increased rapidly, accounting for one-fifth of procurements by FTCs by the mid–1990s. On the import side, the system steadily adapted to transmit world price signals through to the domestic economy. Imports began to be priced according to the agency system, in which domestic prices equal the world price plus a commission paid to the importer, instead of assigning a domestic planned price equivalent. Stronger incentives pushed trading companies to adapt to opportunities that were increasingly shaped by world prices.

Creation of a System of Tariffs and Nontariff Barriers. Chinese policy-makers proceeded cautiously. They were wary of making mistakes, afraid of import surges, trade deficits, and hard currency debt. As reformers dismantled the planned trade system, they erected high tariff walls and substantial nontariff barriers to maintain protection of the domestic market. Under the old air lock system, tariffs had existed but had not been important at all, because the FTCs would carry out the trade plan and redistribute revenues and tax payments as necessary. In the early 1980s a new set of tariffs were promulgated that raised tariffs, which stayed high for the next decade. In 1992, according to the analysis in World Bank (1994, 56), China's tariffs were similar to other highly protected developing countries. The unweighted mean tariff was 43%, and the trade-weighted mean tariff was 32% (the same as Brazil at that time). Equally important were nontariff barriers (NTBs). The same World Bank study found that 51% of imports were subject to one or more of four different overlapping nontariff barriers. Indeed, NTBs and tariffs were "used in a complementary fashion to achieve the government's objectives" (p. 67).[2]

The most important NTB was the severely limited extension of trading rights. Direct domestic market access was reserved for FTCs, all of which were state owned. Manufacturing enterprises sometimes had limited trading rights but were authorized to import only for their own production needs. Moreover, FTCs were only chartered to engage in business within a particular product range ("business scope"), were often limited to a designated province, and were sometimes restricted to a specified category of customers. A number of the bigger central-government FTCs had monopolies on imports of sensitive commodities such as grain and fertilizer. The limits on trading rights kept most domestic firms from exploiting the relatively liberal provisions for EP contracts. Overall Chinese imports were regulated by a combination of tariffs, quotas, and administrative guidance exercised over state-owned trading companies.

Import Substitution and Export Promotion. By the mid–1980s, China had moved from a planned trading system to a system of high tariffs, multiple nontariff barriers, and abundant administrative discretion, a system that was in many ways typical of developing country ISI strategies. In fact, for China, this transformation had many advantages. The trading system, though still dominated by state-run organizations with significant market power, was increasingly oriented toward profits and revenue (in world prices). Steady reforms had created an essential minimum of flexibility that was a prerequisite for success in further reforms and that allowed the foreign-trade system to harmonize with changes in the domestic economic system. Finally, the changes that had been made corresponded to a process of "tariffication," in which trade barriers were first converted to tariff equivalents, so that China could negotiate reductions in order to join the WTO.

---

2. For example, nonessential consumer goods were not subject to NTBs but typically had prohibitively high tariffs. Commodities that the government viewed as essentials were subject to low tariffs but restrictive NTBs, typically being "canalized" to monopoly FTCs administered by the central government. For example, in 1992 grain, fertilizer, and steel were subject to tight quantitative controls, but they had tariffs under 20% and together accounted for a significant share (14%) of total imports. Finally, priority sectors such as automobiles and industrial machinery had overlapping high tariffs and NTBs.

But this partially reformed system was by no means liberal enough to create the dramatic Chinese export success that came later. The net impact of the system was to discourage exports, just as was the case in other ISI regimes. China therefore borrowed a page from the East Asian playbook and adopted selective measures of export promotion, designed to offset the antiexport bias for at least some products. A partial system of rebates of value-added taxes for exports was begun in 1985 and expanded in the 1990s. Banks provided preferential interest rates to exporters and lent generously to new investment projects designed to produce exports. Localities still had export targets to fulfill. But the most important such measure was the creation of an entirely separate export-processing trading regime, which allowed exporters to simply *bypass* the old centralized foreign-trade monopoly.

16.3   A DUALIST TRADE REGIME: THE EXPORT-PROCESSING SYSTEM

The early experiments with export-processing contracts that had begun in Guangdong Province as early as 1978 gradually grew into a fully blown export-processing regime. After 1986, recognizing the opportunities for China in the ongoing restructuring of Asian export production networks, Chinese policy-makers started supporting the "Coastal Development Strategy." All types of firms in the coastal provinces, including TVEs, were allowed to engage in these processing and assembly contracts. Foreign investors began to move into China's coastal provinces on a significant scale, and they were allowed to adopt a more flexible variant of export-processing contracts in which they took ownership of components and raw materials imported duty-free. By around 1987, China had established what were, in essence, two separate trading regimes. EP or export-promotion trade, responding to the extremely open regulations in which it developed, grew rapidly and soon surpassed trade through the original regime in size. That traditional, but now partially reformed, system of "ordinary trade" (OT) also grew, but much more slowly. The exemption from duties on imported inputs provided a significant cost advantage to those in the EP regime. More important was that under the EP regime exporters—predominantly FIEs—were allowed to sidestep the entire complex and unwieldy apparatus of import controls, canalization, and regulatory monopolies that restricted development of trade under the OT regime. Unlike virtually all domestic enterprises, FIEs were not required to go through state-run foreign-trade corporations (FTCs) to import. The association between the EP regime and FIEs meant that FIEs had a privileged status in the foreign trade system different from most domestic enterprises, especially when combined with special tax concessions made to attract foreign investment (Chapter 17).

None of the provisions of the Chinese EP regime were novel: All had their counterparts elsewhere in East Asia, and indeed, around the globe. What is unusual, however, is the sheer scale on which these provisions were introduced in China. In most countries such concessionary provisions are circumscribed within a designated and strictly policed EP zone. In essence, China created a gigantic EP zone throughout the entire coastal region. Although China's SEZs attracted a lot of attention, the boundaries of the export-processing regime actually extended far beyond the SEZs, to wherever an export-oriented FIE was located. These institutional provisions strongly reinforced advantages that FIEs had to begin with. As discussed in Chapter 17, most FIEs were from the neighboring economies of Hong Kong and Taiwan, and most had experience with export manufacturing and marketing. Chinese reforms accommodated their interests and allowed them to transplant this expertise to the mainland.

Figure 16.2 shows the enormous difference these factors made. The EP regime and foreign-invested enterprises together were the motor of China's export expansion. Figure 16.2 shows graphically the contribution of both these categories. EP trade climbed to 56% of total exports in 1996, then plateaud as the system began to move toward more comprehensive liberalization. FIEs have inexorably increased their share of total exports in every year, starting from only 1% in 1985 and reaching 58% in 2005. From a small base, FIEs gradually became important players in China's export growth; and then between 1992 and 2005 they accounted for fully 63% of incremental exports. The FIE share of the increment has shown no tendency to decline in recent years. Clearly, the liberalization of the environment for foreign investment has played a fundamental role in China's export success. The flip side of FIE growth has been the relatively less impressive performance of domestic firms. Domestic exporters, predominantly SOEs, have also greatly increased their exports, but have been less successful in gaining access to new world markets. Moreover, during the shakeout of the state sector (1995–1999), domestic firm exports stagnated for four years. Between 1985 and 2004 total exports increased 17.6% annually while domestic firm exports increased 12.5% annually, a respectable but far from miraculous performance.

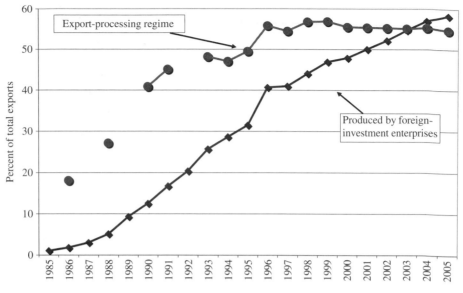

Figure 16.2
Share of exports from export-processing regime and foreign-investment enterprises

16.4   TOWARD AN OPEN ECONOMY

From the mid–1990s, building on the achievements in creating a functioning trading regime, China began to move in the direction of a genuinely open economy. Membership in the WTO was a powerful motivating factor. Reforms taken before WTO accession, in order to strengthen the case and prepare the economy for WTO membership, were just as important as those undertaken afterwards. A common theme linking these reforms is to reduce the degree of dualism in the trade regime and prepare the way for a more open economy. While mandated by WTO requirements, these reforms were also very much in accord with the objectives of reformists, who thus used the lure of WTO membership to help push through reforms that they favored in any case. The discussion of these changes first covers the currency reform of 1994, then the bundle of changes required by WTO membership. The impact of WTO-related liberalization is covered in section 16.4.3.

16.4.1   Currency Convertibility

On January 1, 1994, reformers abolished the secondary "swap" market for foreign exchange that had been one of the important transitional devices used for the previous eight years. The exchange rate was unified near the lower swap-market rate, and access to foreign currency was greatly liberalized: within 18 months, current-account convertibility was achieved. In effect, this means that any authorized importer of goods and services can purchase foreign exchange upon presentation of documentation of the trade flows. The 1994 foreign-exchange reforms were part of the coordinated package of fiscal, financial, and trade reforms that were rolled out simultaneously at the end of 1993 and beginning of 1994 (Chapter 4). One of the advantages of policy coordination was that the national taxation system was shifted to a much larger reliance on value-added taxes (VAT). The rules of the WTO permit exporters to rebate VAT on exports. Chinese policy-makers were thus quick to see the advantage of such rebates, and the 1994 reforms made the previously limited program of VAT rebates nearly universal. The 1994 reforms succeeded in moving China to a more integrated trading system with a minimum of disruption.

The 1994 success was only partial, however. Initially there had been high hopes that China would move quickly to full currency convertibility, including the capital account, and establish a "managed float" for the Chinese currency. A flexible exchange rate would adjust to long-run changes in supply and demand for foreign exchange but the Central Bank would still intervene in the foreign exchange market to stabilize the currency. Reformers were initially elated when demand for the currency stabilized at the level they chose, 8.3 *renminbi* to the dollar, nearly the old swap-market rate. The next step, however, did not go as they had hoped. Restrictions on the capital account proved difficult to eliminate in a period of macroeconomic turbulence. Following the Asian Financial Crisis of 1997–1998, all Asian currencies, including the *renminbi*, came under intense downward pressure, and policy-makers decided to hold the line and not allow the currency to depreciate. The managed float gradually became a de facto fixed exchange rate vis-à-vis the U.S. dollar, and the Hong Kong dollar, which was already pegged against the U.S. dollar. When Chinese exports started to grow rapidly after 2002, the fixed exchange rate, lack of capital account convertibility, and relatively low value of the *renminbi* became significant diplomatic and economic issues between China and the United States.

16.4.2   World Trade Organization Membership

When China formally applied to rejoin the GATT (General Agreement on Trade and Tariffs, the forerunner of the WTO) in 1986, it seemed that it might be a quick and relatively painless process. After all, China was at that time a pioneer of market reforms and was looked upon in the West at least as favorably as Poland and Hungary, which had entered the GATT in the 1960s and 1970s. But in fact it was not until 15 years later that China finally became the 143rd member of the WTO, on December 11, 2001. During those protracted negotiations, both China and the world trading institutions changed in fundamental ways.

One important reason for the lengthiness of the process, to be sure, was the shift in attitude toward China that occurred in the wake of the 1989 Tiananmen massacre and the dissolution of the Soviet Union the following January. After 1989 there was no longer a constituency for an "easy" entry by China into WTO. Even more important was the steady emergence of China as a serious export power. China was taken seriously as a competitive challenge, and antidumping actions against China had increased. At the same time, the frustrations of foreign companies dealing with China's relatively closed domestic market—one of the offshoots of the dualistic trading regime described earlier—had eroded support for giving China secure market access in developed-countries without a strict quid pro quo.

At the same time, the Uruguay Round negotiations that created the WTO in 1996 signaled a fundamental shift in the terms of global trade negotiations. Earlier agreements had been restricted to a clearly delineated "foreign-trade sector," but today are increasingly concerned with more fundamental systemic characteristics of the negotiating economies. In part, this shift came about because modern developed economies are now primarily service economies, and so international agreements understandably go beyond the former focus on internationally traded goods. Since services almost always involve some physical presence at the point of delivery, agreements about "trade in services" inevitably involve negotiations about regulation and investment conditions in the receiving, or importing, country. During the Uruguay Round itself, trade liberalization was achieved by a "Grand Bargain" between developing and developed countries: Developing countries got the promise of greater access for their light manufactures, especially textiles, and agricultural products in developed-country markets, while developed countries got the promise of improved access for, and protection of, their corporations operating in developing-country economies. With this "Grand Bargain," the way was cleared for the creation of the WTO and the extension of trade negotiations into new areas relating to services, investment, and intellectual property rights. This was exactly the bargain that China was required to make as a condition for WTO membership: granting broader and fairer access to its economy in exchange for greater access for its light manufactured exports to other countries. The terms of this complex bargain involved a vastly more complicated negotiating process than initially anticipated.

On the trade side, the most fundamental issue from the beginning was the requirement that China open up the OT regime and dramatically reduce the dualism of its trading regime. Most important was China's commitment to extend trading rights without restrictions, including giving trading rights to domestic and foreign private companies. Eventually, these new provisions were included in a foreign-trade law effective July 1, 2004. Under this law the Chinese government no longer restricts trade to a limited number of state-owned FTCs, except in a few agricultural commodities where state trading is still permitted. In those cases, China committed to a system of tariff-rate quotas (TRQs) for specific products, agreeing to lower tariffs up to a certain ceiling (after which higher tariffs kick in). The accession agreement specifically commits China to distribute a minimum share of the TRQ allocations to non-state traders. The commitment to a more accessible trade system was the most important component of WTO accession in the foreign-trade arena. Next most important were commitments to lower tariffs. In fact, China began lowering tariffs in preparation for WTO membership immediately after the foreign-exchange reforms of 1994, well before the actual agreements were finalized. The average nominal tariff was reduced in stages from 43% in 1992 to 17% in 1999, the year when the breakthrough in WTO negotiations finally came. In the actual agreement, China agreed to lower average industrial tariffs to 9.4% by 2005, and this rate was actually achieved in 2004. The agreement lowered average agricultural tariffs to 15%, which was also easily achieved.

16.4.3   Openness Revisited

This chapter began with a simple discussion of the openness of the Chinese economy, based on the ratio of total trade to GDP. Here we focus in the first instance on imports: after all, an economy's openness to imports is the most important dimension of its overall openness to trade, since it indexes both openness to competition and access to lowest-cost supplies. Figure 16.3 shows that imports as a share of GDP have climbed strongly, with a pullback between 1994 and 1998. Figure 16.3 further divides imports into two categories: ordinary trade (OT) imports on the bottom and EP and all other imports on the top. Recall that OT imports are sold on the domestic market, represent potential competition with domestic producers, and were the focus of tariff and nontariff barriers under the dualistic trade regime. It is striking that OT imports initially increased rapidly in the mid–1980s, reaching 12% of GDP in 1986, but then fell back to their starting point, below at 4.1% of GDP, by 1997. The import side supports the picture we sketched mainly from the export side: most of the trade growth came in the EP regime through the mid–1990s, and the OT regime was not liberalized significantly, and in some

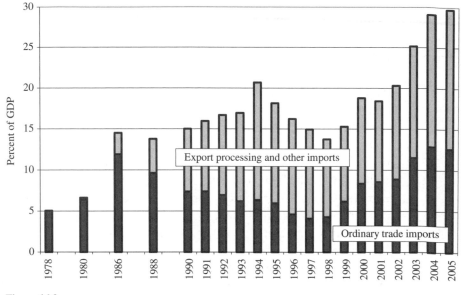

Figure 16.3
Openness measures of the Chinese economy

respects was even tightened. An early "false start" of trade liberalization through the OT regime was abandoned, and China shifted to it dualistic ISI regime.

From this baseline, we can see how dramatic the change associated with WTO membership has been. From its low point in 1997–1998, OT imports have surged as a share of GDP, surpassing previous highs, and reaching 13% in 2004. EP trade also grew rapidly, as new electronics sectors (especially laptop computers) grew rapidly and made extensive use of EP trade provisions. But it is the surge in OT trade imports that is most directly attributable to WTO-induced trade liberalization, and it is also the best index of the degree of openness. By the measure of OT imports/GDP ratio, China became more than three times as open to world trade in the six years from 1998 to 2004. The huge surge in China's foreign trade after 2002 can be directly associated with very recent liberalization of the import regime, driven by WTO membership.

16.5   OUTCOMES: RAPID GROWTH AND STRUCTURAL CHANGE

Each stage of the liberalization of China's foreign-trade system has been associated with a surge in exports and imports.

16.5.1 Exports

After 1979 exports grew rapidly as existing opportunities were exploited more fully and the need to earn foreign exchange was given priority. At first exports grew rather indiscriminately: As late as 1985 petroleum was China's largest single export, accounting for 20% of export earnings.

The really fundamental changes in the composition of China's exports date to 1985, when we begin to see the impact of the Coastal Development Strategy, the full-fledged rollout of the EP trading regime, and the increased participation of FIEs in export growth. Between 1985 and 1995, China's trade grew extremely rapidly. Moreover, there was a dramatic shift to labor-intensive commodities and a correspondingly large decline in natural-resource-based products. Indeed, it is one of the great paradoxes of China's foreign trade *before* liberalization that—despite China's obvious factor endowments—light, labor-intensive manufactures were a fairly modest proportion of China's exports. However, by 1995 all of China's top export commodities were labor-intensive manufactured goods.[3] Most striking up to that time was the sustained growth in textile and garment exports, and the rapid rise of sporting goods and miscellaneous manufactured goods.

Trade growth slowed in the 1996–2001 period. Trade as a share of GDP stabilized, though both were still growing at a healthy clip. The slowdown was partly due to the impact of external events (such as the Asian Financial Crisis), partly due to the 30% real appreciation in the RMB between 1994 and 1997, and partly due to the lack of dramatic progress in trade liberalization during that period. Chinese policy-makers seemed to accept that China's reliance on exports had reached a certain plateau and that future economic growth should be driven by the growth of domestic demand. The VAT rebate rate was reduced, and procedures for EP imports tightened, both actions being driven primarily by revenue considerations.

But the renewed liberalization of the trading regime signaled by WTO accession has led to a renewed surge in China's trade. After 2002 growth of both exports and imports surged above 20% per annum, and stayed high.

---

3. A number of studies have described the shift to labor-intensive manufactures in Chinese exports. According to the International Economic Databank (IEDB) maintained at the Australian National University, the share of labor-intensive products in China's exports increased from 37% in 1984 to 54% in 1994, while the share of agricultural and minerals intensive products together declined from 49% to 15%. In addition, according to the classification used by the IEDB, capital-intensive exports increased from 14% to 31% of total exports (again 1984–1994). The World Bank (1994, 9), using a different classification system based on U.S. factor proportions, found that between 1980 and 1990 labor-intensive manufactures went from 39% to 74% of total exports (with unskilled labor-intensive goods accounting for 29% and 51% of the total, respectively). See Naughton (1996) for discussion.

Significantly, this trade surge has been associated with a dramatic increase in the share of machinery and electronics items in China's exports, the share of which surpassed 50% of total exports in 2003. At the same time, growth of (now traditional) labor-intensive manufactures, particularly garments, has remained robust. Driven in part by anticipation of the end of textile import quotas at the end of 2004, production and exports have shifted to China, which has maintained its position as the lowest-cost producer. Overall, the composition of China's exports has shifted to much better reflect China's abundant labor endowment.

16.5.2   Imports

Table 16.1 shows that China primarily exports finished goods. Table 16.2 shows that these goods are mainly miscellaneous manufactured articles plus machinery and electronics. In the case of imports, it is the larger volume, rather than drastic changes in composition, that has increased China's gains from trade. Capital-intensive products have continued to account for about two-thirds of imports. In addition, closer inspection of those commodities indicates that many of them serve essentially as land substitutes, stretching China's limited land endowment. Examples include fertilizer, food grains, synthetic fiber materials, and iron ore, each of which is a major Chinese import. Capital-intensive commodities are often heavy, process-technology industries: steel, chemicals, synthetic fibers, plastic raw materials. Skill-intensive commodities include machinery, transport machinery, and electronics. China is a big net importer of these two commodity groups and a big net exporter of labor-intensive commodities. As a result, Chinese trade overwhelmingly corresponds to comparative-advantage principles and is likely of enormous benefit to the Chinese domestic economy. Another result is that China has substantial impact on world markets for a number of these commodity groups: copper, steel, fertilizer, and, increasingly, petroleum. These are areas where Chinese demand can move world markets.

Table 16.1 shows Chinese trade by stage of production, showing clearly how China imports raw materials and components, while exporting final goods. Indeed, two-thirds of China's imports are intermediates, and two-thirds of China's exports are final goods. What are the specific goods categories that correspond to these general aggregates? Table 16.2 shows a breakdown of China's imports and exports in 2003.

16.5.3   High Technology Trade

The rapid increase in China's export of electronics goods—and especially the export of laptop computers—is truly impressive. Does this trend mean that

Table 16.1
Trade by state of production, 2002

	Imports (percent)		Exports (percent)
Primary goods	10.3	Primary goods	2.9
Intermediate goods	63.3	Intermediate goods	37.1
Parts and components	27.5	Parts and components	15.5
Semifinished goods	35.9	Semifinished goods	21.6
Final goods	26.3	Final goods	60.0
Consumer goods	5.1	Consumer goods	40.3
Capital goods	21.2	Capital goods	19.7

Table 16.2
Composition of Chinese trade, 2003

	Imports (billion U.S. dollars)	Exports (billion U.S. dollars)	Imports (percent of total)	Exports (percent of total)
0–1. Food, beverages, tobacco	6.5	18.6	1.6	4.2
2–4. Crude materials, fuel, oils	66.3	16.3	16.1	3.7
33. Petroleum	26.7	5.8	6.5	1.3
5, 6. Chemicals and manufactured materials (excl. 65. textiles)	98.7	61.7	23.9	14.1
51. Organic chemicals	15.9	5.3	3.8	1.2
57. Plastics in primary forms	13.9	0.8	3.4	0.2
67. Iron and steel	22.0	4.8	5.3	1.1
7. Machinery and transport equipment	192.9	187.9	46.7	42.9
71–74. Industrial machinery	51.8	22.9	12.6	5.2
75–77. Electronic, telecom, and electrical machinery	123.5	150.0	29.9	34.2
8. Miscellaneous manufactured articles	33.0	126.1	8.0	28.8
82. Furniture	0.5	9.0	0.1	2.1
84. Clothing	1.4	52.1	0.3	11.9
85. Footwear	0.4	13.0	0.1	3.0
89. Miscellaneous	5.6	31.5	1.4	7.2
Total	412.8	438.4	100.0	100.0
NB: Specialized machinery, transport equipment, and instruments (71–74, 78, 79, 87)	89.6	44.1	21.7	10.1
NB: Textiles and garments (65, 84)	15.6	79.0	3.8	18.0
NB: Light manufactures (8, minus 87 instruments, plus 65 textiles)	27.0	146.0	6.5	33.5

China is becoming a technology power? While the answer to this question is complex, as discussed in Chapter 15, the immediate answer, based on the trade data, is "No, not yet." Virtually all of the high-tech electronics goods that China exports are produced under the EP trading regime. Indeed, in 2005, FIEs accounted for fully 88% of high-technology exports, nearly all under EP arrangements. Electronics production worldwide is carried out on the basis of global production networks, chains that link together production, research, and services that are carried out in many different countries. China is already an integral link in many of these production networks. But inspection of the actual products exported and the processes carried out in China reveals that China is overwhelmingly concentrated on the final assembly stage of production. This is a labor-intensive, medium-skilled activity, not a "high-tech" activity. Classification of China's exports by technological level can thus be extremely misleading. China has displayed a rapid increase in export of high-technology goods in recent years. However, the actual value added in China is generally not high-skilled activity, and these products are actually most usefully grouped with other labor-intensive products (such as garments and toys), the export of which has soared in recent years.

16.6   REGIONAL COMPOSITION OF TRADE WITHIN CHINA

Foreign trade understandably benefits the coastal regions of China, and the coastal provinces have grown significantly more rapidly than inland provinces on the strength of trade-related demand. Different coastal regions have, however, responded to the stimulus of trade opportunities in significantly different fashion. First, as can be expected, the trade policies that were followed provided an enormous stimulus to the southern coastal provinces of Guangdong and Fujian. Table 16.3 shows that the share of China's total exports produced by Guangdong, Fujian, and Hainan (which was spun off from Guangdong Province in 1988) rose dramatically from 16% in 1978 to 46% during the mid–1990s. These provinces benefited the most from preferential policies during the 1980s, and from the growth of foreign investment and EP trade. Guangdong, in particular, was encouraged to take "one step ahead" of the rest of the economy and become an economic showcase—perhaps even to become a "Fifth Tiger," following the "Four Tigers," the newly industrialized economies of Korea, Taiwan, Hong Kong, and Singapore.

During this initial period, the rise of the south coast eclipsed the growth of the region that had traditionally been China's richest and most sophisticated

Table 16.3
Regional shares of China's exports (percent)

	1978	1994–1998	2005
Southeast	16	46	36
Lower Yangtze	34	21	38
Northeast and North Coast	39	23	19
Rest of China	11	10	7

Southeast: Guangdong, Fujian, and Hainan.
Lower Yangtze: Shanghai, Jiangsu, and Zhejiang.
Northeast and North Coast: Liaoning, Jilin, and Heilongjiang; Beijing, Tianjin, Hebei, and Shandong.

economic macroregion, the Lower Yangtze (Chapter 1). The Lower Yangtze—grew robustly in the 1980s but was not oriented toward foreign trade in the same way as the south coast. The Lower Yangtze's share of China's exports dropped substantially, from 34% in 1978 to only 21% in the mid–1990s. However, since the mid–1990s, the Lower Yangtze has begun its own dramatic process of trade-related growth. Powered by significant inflows of foreign investment (see Chapter 17), the Lower Yangtze has seen its share of Chinese exports increase significantly, climbing back above its previous high to 38% in 2005. The Southeast, by contrast, has experienced its share declining to 36% in 2005, although its exports have continued to grow at a pace that would be considered quite healthy for most economies.

The northern regions have declined steadily in relative terms. Traditionally, the closely linked Northeast and North Coastal regions were a major force in China's trade. The northern regions exported a much more diversified set of goods, including heavy industrial products and, of course, oil. During the early 1980s, the share of this region at first increased as oil from the northeast, sold at historically high international prices, made a substantial contribution to China's foreign-exchange earnings. But since the 1980s the north has been in relative decline, falling below 20% of total exports in 2003. In particular, the share of the three Northeast provinces slipped below 5%, and the region was in danger of becoming economically marginalized.

Guangdong province is still the single largest exporting province, accounting for 31% of China's exports—and 38% of high technology exports—in 2005. Moreover, the trade/GDP ratio for Guandong is impressively high, at 178%, making it very similar to Malaysia, which has a trade/GDP ratio of 175%. The Lower Yangtze, rising rapidly, has trade/GDP around 90%, like the East Asia average (trade/GDP equals 81%). The "rest of China," with trade/GDP at 23%, is very similar to Brazil. There are dramatic differences in the degree of openness and of trade dependence among China's regions.

16.7 CONCLUSION

China has achieved trade success through a combination of domestic economic reform with an astute accommodation of the opportunities created by East Asian economic restructuring and foreign investment. It is an especially impressive achievement given how far China has come: From one of the most closed economies in the world, China has developed into the most open large economy in the world, and it has done so with a minimum of disruption and trade-related economic distress. How are we to understand a large, continental economy with "openness" sufficient to yield a trade-to-GDP ratio of 64%? First, we need to take account of the fact that trade is very unequally distributed within China. China is like an economic union of a very open coastal economy and a less integrated inland economy: like a union of Malaysia and Brazil, for example. Second, the very high trade/GDP ratios of economies like Malaysia or Thailand are achieved precisely because those countries are integral parts of cross-border global production networks (GPN), especially prominent in electronics. Those networks involve high-value items crossing borders, as trade, in order that relatively simple processing activities can be performed in different locations. Therefore, the value added in the export sector is actually quite small relative to the value of the trade flows. Of course, this is exactly the kind of activity that the Chinese dualistic trade regime was designed to encourage in the first place. But this outcome reminds us that the trade/GDP ratio is an index of openness, not a measure of the size of the traded-goods sector. In fact, actual Chinese value added in the export sector is a smaller share of total national value added than might have been guessed just by taking clues from the trade/GDP ratio.

China's trade growth has enormous momentum. WTO-related liberalization has lowered transaction costs as well as import costs, as access to trading opportunities has multiplied and been exploited. The abolition of textile quotas at the end of December 2004 is having a tremendous impact on China's exports. Continuing competitiveness in textiles and garments underlines the enduring impact of China's abundant labor endowment. The root of China's comparative advantage is still in labor-intensive manufacturing, where the highly elastic supply of cheap semiskilled labor will continue to work to China's benefit for at least a decade. In the years since WTO accession a more open and integrated trade regime has propelled China to the front ranks of world traders. Further stages of integration with the world economy will bring substantial benefits to China. Because China's factor endowments vary so significantly from those of the developed countries, China has a lot to gain from globalization. Its labor-rich, land-scarce, and capital-scarce economy benefits from exchange based on comparative advantage, while its dynamic and relatively well-educated labor force can quickly absorb technology and skills by observing and imitating global best practice. China has more to gain from globalization than any other economy in the world, except perhaps the United States.

BIBLIOGRAPHY

Suggestions for Further Reading

For a recent study that brings in China's trade development, investment, and technological absorption, see Gaulier, Lemoine, and Ünal-Kesenci (2005). Ng and Yeats (2002) trade some of the same underlying trends, but from a different, regionwide perspective. See Naughton (1997) for an earlier description of these international networks in formation. Fishman and Wei (2004) and Tong (2005) explicate, from different vantage points, the complex China–Hong Kong–United States trading relationship. In recent years, much of the literature on China's foreign trade has focused on the impact of China's accession to the WTO. Outstanding examples of this work are Lardy (2002) and the papers collected in the World Bank (2004). Lall and Albaladéjo (2004) consider the competitive aspect of China–East Asia trade relations.

Promptly updated data and some analytic papers are available on the Ministry of Commerce Web site: http://www.mofcom.gov.cn/tongjiziliao/tongjiziliao.html. The home page leads to significant English-language content, but coverage is inconsistent.

Sources for Data and Figures

Figure 16.1: *China Customs Statistics*, Annual, Issue No. 12. Updated from Ministry of Commerce Web site: http://www.mofcom.gov.cn/tongjiziliao/tongjiziliao.html. and http://gcs.mofcom.gov.cn/tongji2005.shtml.

Figure 16.2: Processing trade: *China Customs Statistics*, Annual, Issue No. 12. Updated from Ministry of Commerce Web site: http://www.mofcom.gov.cn/tongjiziliao/tongjiziliao.html. Exports from foreign-invested enterprises: *SYC*, Annual, updated from fdi.gov.cn/.

Figure 16.3: *China Customs Statistics*, Annual, Issue No. 12. Updated from Ministry of Commerce Web site: http://www.mofcom.gov.cn/tongjiziliao/tongjiziliao.html. and http://gcs.mofcom.gov.cn/tongji2005.shtml.

Table 16.1: Gaulier, Lemoine, and Ünal-Kesenci (2005, 24).

Table 16.2: *China Customs Statistics* (2003, 12).

Table 16.3: *SYC* (2005, 640–41, and earlier volumes).

References

Fisman, Raymond, and Shang-jin Wei (2004). "Tax Rates and Tax Evasion: Evidence from 'Missing Imports' in China." *Journal of Political Economy*, 112(2), April.

Gaulier, Guillaume, Françoise Lemoine, and Deniz Ünal-Kesenci (2005). *China's Integration in East Asia: Production Sharing, FDI and High-Tech Trade*. CEPPI Working Paper 2005-09. Paris: Centre d'Etudes Prospectives et d'Informations Internationales.

Lall, Sanjaya, and M. Albaladejo (2004). "China's Competitive Performance: A Threat to East Asian Manufactured Exports?" *World Development*, 32(9): 1441–66.

Lardy, Nicholas R. (2002). *Integrating China into the Global Economy*. Washington, DC: Brookings Institution Press.

Naughton, Barry (1996). "China's Emergence and prospects as a Trading Nation." *Brookings Papers on Economic Activity*, 2: 273–313.

Naughton, Barry (1997). *The China Circle: Economics and Technology in the PRC, Taiwan, and Hong Kong.* Washington, DC: Brookings Institution Press.

Ng, F., and A. Yeats (2002). " Major Trade Trends in East Asia: What Are Their Implications for Regional Cooperation and Growth?" Mimeo. World Bank.

SYC (Annual). *Zhongguo Tongji Nianjian* [Statistical Yearbook of China]. Beijing: Zhongguo Tongji.

Tong, Sarah Y. (2005). "The US-China Trade Imbalance: How Big Is It Really?" *China: An International Journal*, 3(1), March, 131–54, at http://muse.jhu.edu/journals/china/v003/3.1tong.pdf.

World Bank (1994). *China: Foreign Trade Reform.* Washington, DC: World Bank.

World Bank (2004). *China and the WTO: Accession, Policy Reform, and Poverty Reduction Strategies.* Washington, DC: World Bank.

For more than a decade China has been one of the world's most important destinations for FDI. Investment began to pour into China after 1992, and annual inflows have been over 40 billion dollars since 1996. Trending steadily upward, FDI inflows were at 63 billion dollars in both 2004 and 2005. These inflows are by far the largest of any developing country and have remained remarkably stable and robust despite substantial fluctuations in the Asian and global economies. China has accounted for about one-third of total developing-country FDI inflows in recent years. There is no doubt that the global manufacturing networks created by FDI in China will continue to play a critical role in the world economy.

Three distinctive characteristics have marked investment in China over the past decade. First, foreign direct investment has been the predominant form in which China has accessed global capital (as opposed to portfolio capital or bank loans). Second, an unusually large proportion of Chinese FDI inflows are in manufacturing industry, as opposed to services or resource extraction. Third, FDI inflows have predominantly come from other East Asian economies, especially Hong Kong and Taiwan. In each of these respects, China diverges from average world patterns. Each of these characteristics reflects the dominant role played by the cross-border restructuring of export-oriented production networks that originally developed in other, neighboring East Asian economies. These topics make up the first sections, and the main subject matter, of this chapter.

However, the distinctive characteristics of foreign investment in China thus far may not be a good guide to the future. The later sections of this chapter cover the new patterns that we can expect to see emerging. In the first place, the predominance of FDI reveals that China has not made much use of other forms of foreign investment. Thus China has considerable unexploited potential to tap world savings. Moreover, China's entry into the WTO, on December 11, 2001, began the process of liberalizing access to many service sectors that had previously been off-limits to foreign businesses. Finally, since late 2002 there has been evidence of the beginning of significant capital inflows to China outside of FDI. These inflows are surprising, however, in that they have come before the formal liberalization of the Chinese capital account. In section 17.6 we examine the Chinese balance of payments to trace the emerging patterns of capital inflows.

As pointed out in Chapter 16, investment and trade are closely linked, in China and in the global economy. This chapter delves into investment in greater detail, showing the concrete ways in which China has become integrated into the global economy. Section 17.1 sketches the importance of FDI in the Chinese economy. Section 17.2 focuses on SEZs in order to trace some of the key policy reforms that opened up the foreign investment regime. Section 17.3 discusses the investment regime today, tracing the inter-action among policy, regulation, and legal infrastructure, and moving to the impact of WTO membership. Section 17.4 outlines the particularities of China's investment regime: we examine the importance played by other East Asian economies in investment, and above all, in section 17.5 the three tightly linked "China Circle" economies: Hong Kong, Taiwan, and China. The final section looks at overall patterns of capital inflow. It shows the sectoral composition of FDI inflows and argues that the impact of WTO will be biggest precisely on FDI in the service sectors, such as finance, trade, and distribution. The chapter concludes with a brief look at China's balance of payments.

17.1 FDI IN THE CHINESE ECONOMY

China decided to accept foreign investment in 1978 and broke sharply with socialist orthodoxy in establishing SEZs in 1979 and 1980. Subsequently, through most of the 1980s, policy and institutional changes were more cautious, incremental, and geographically localized. Incoming FDI grew steadily through the 1980s and wrought important changes in the regional economies of Guangdong and Fujian. Nationwide the impact of FDI was moderate until the early 1990s. As Figure 17.1 shows, beginning in 1992–1993, the stream of incoming FDI turned into a flood. Investors from Hong Kong and Taiwan moved in first and became quantitatively most important. Developed-country investors followed close behind, and FDI inflows became large enough to fundamentally transform the Chinese economy.

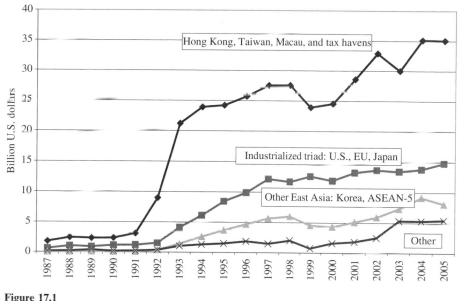

Figure 17.1
Main sources of FDI in China

What changed in 1992 to unleash a flood of foreign investment into China? Chinese policy shifts were signaled by a string of remarkable speeches Deng Xiaoping made during a famous "Southern Tour" in the spring of 1992. This was one of the last times that Deng placed his personal stamp on Chinese policy, hoping to rehabilitate the reform agenda and dissipate investor uncertainty created by economic retrenchment after the 1989 Tiananmen debacle. But grand policy pronouncements often have little impact on economic developments. Why was this one so momentous? Two factors made the difference. First, for more than a decade China had been gradually building credibility with foreign investors, gaining experience while liberalizing and building institutional infrastructure. However, the impact of these measures had been muted by concerns about China's future after the Tiananmen incident. When Deng succeeded in relieving the anxiety about China's overall policy direction, foreign investors responded quickly because the institutional foundations and FDI friendly policies had already been put in place. Second, up until that time China had largely confined incoming FDI to export manufacturing, and access to the Chinese market had been dribbled out to only a few selected foreign firms. From 1992, China began selectively opening its domestic marketplace to foreign investors. New sectors—especially real estate— were opened to foreign participation, and manufacturers were increasingly granted

Figure 17.2
Foreign direct investment as a share of GDP

rights to sell their output on the Chinese market. For the first time the huge potential size and rapid growth of the Chinese market played a direct role in attracting foreign investment.

Figure 17.2 shows foreign direct investment as a share of Chinese GDP. During the 1980s, FDI never exceeded 1% of GDP, but inflows crept steadily upward, finally exceeding 1% in 1991. FDI briefly exceeded 6% of GDP in 1994, but it then settled back to 5% of GDP and has grown more slowly than nominal GDP since then. Averaging 4% of GDP between 1996 and 2002, inflows slipped below 3% of GDP in 2005 for the first time since 1992.[1] These figures clearly place China in the category of countries that are relatively open to incoming FDI. They contrast sharply with the "Northeast Asian" pattern of China's development forerunners, Japan, Korea, and Taiwan. Incoming FDI was always considerably less than 1% of GDP in Japan and Korea during their periods of most rapid growth, and only slightly more in Taiwan. In recent years FDI inflows into Korea (especially) and Japan and Taiwan have increased. However, FDI inflows have never amounted to as much as 2% of GDP in

1. The FDI/GDP ratio is useful for international comparisons because we have normalized the value of FDI by dividing it by GDP. However, the ratio is also influenced by fluctuations in the valuation of GDP. The trends shown in Figure 17.2 are accentuated by devaluation of the official exchange rate in 1994 and real appreciation between 1994 and 1997.

Japan, Korea, or Taiwan. Instead, China's reliance on FDI has been of a similar magnitude to the developing Southeast Asian economies of Malaysia, Thailand, the Philippines, and Indonesia, where inflows around 4%–6% of GDP have been common. Some Southeast Asian countries have struggled to sustain FDI inflows of this level since the Asian financial crisis of 1997–1998. Generally speaking, though, China fits into a "Southeast Asian" pattern in which economies are quite open to FDI, particularly in export-oriented manufacturing, notwithstanding different degrees of protection in trade policy. Indeed, the similar levels of development and policy orientation have led many to perceive China and the Southeast Asian countries as being in competition for a limited total amount of FDI since 1998.

Some regions of China are in fact even more open to FDI than a "typical" Southeast Asian nation. Inflows into Guangdong and Fujian, scaled to GDP, were of course well above the Chinese national average. For the 11 years from 1993–2003 the average annual incoming FDI/GDP ratio was 13% for Guangdong and 11% for Fujian. Other open coastal areas were only a step behind Guangdong: Inflows to Shanghai averaged 9% of GDP, and those to Jiangsu and Beijing averaged 7%. These inflows were sufficiently large to transform these regional economies.

FDI's impact is multifaceted. First, FDI contributes to overall investment and structural change. The total amount of FDI is large: In 2004, the cumulative inflows of actually realized investment surpassed $500 billion. However, because China's own domestic saving rate is so high, China is less dependent on FDI for saving than many countries, in fact, less dependent than the average developing country. According to UN figures, all developing countries, excluding China, experienced incoming FDI equal to about 15% of their total gross fixed capital formation in 1999–2001. As Chapter 6 discussed, China's domestic saving and investment rate is extremely high, and gross domestic capital formation surpasses 40% of GDP. Thus incoming FDI in 1999–2001 accounted for 11% of total capital formation in China, less than the average. Moreover, China's GDP growth has been even more rapid than the growth of FDI inflows, so the share of FDI in GDP has been gradually drifting downward (see Figure 17.2).

However, FDI brings a bundle of management experience, marketing channels, and technology, along with the basic inflow of resources. Indeed, by definition, foreign direct investment includes some control over the production process, and thus some transfer of management expertise. FDI has become China's predominant source of technology transfer. As Chapter 15 described, China has run an activist program of technology development since the mid–1980s. Notwithstanding, the transfer of technology to production facilities in China by multinational corporations has clearly overshadowed all other forms of technology development since 1993. Moreover, Chapter 16 has described the central role that FIEs played in China's export expansion in the 1990s. After 1992, almost two thirds of the increment to China's exports came from foreign-invested firms. Thus, FDI has played an important role in industrial growth, technology transfer, and trade expansion.

17.2 "ZONES": THE GRADUAL LIBERALIZATION OF THE INVESTMENT REGIME

One of the peculiarities of China's FDI landscape is the proliferation of special investment zones of various kinds. The establishment of the first SEZs in China, in 1979, was a strikingly visible signal of commitment to economic opening. In subsequent years China has marked every major wave of liberalization with the establishment of a new batch of zones. Even today, although special zones are less special than before, much foreign investment is still located in zones of various kinds, and the rules of business are still subtly different inside the zones. Why does Chinese policy have this proclivity for special zones? The preference is consistent with the dualistic system that was such a prominent feature of the trading regime (Chapter 16). Zones permitted incremental progress within a rigid system.

Politicians in Guangdong began to lobby for a special zone during 1978, even before the adoption of national reform policies. Endorsement by Beijing in 1979, and, crucially, by Deng Xiaoping, meant that the SEZs became a symbol of the government's commitment to external liberalization. Zones permitting foreign businesses free operation in China were inevitably sensitive, because of China's history of foreign concessions (Chapter 2). Zones were easily portrayed by conservatives opposed to economic reforms as a derogation of China's sovereignty. Precisely for this reason, the establishment of the SEZs served as a powerful commitment device. By demonstrating to foreign businesses that China would maintain an open environment in a specific, easily monitored location, the SEZs enhanced the credibility of the reform process. At the same time, zones played a powerful symbolic role whenever the reform policies were contested: on two subsequent occasions (1984 and 1992), Deng Xiaoping traveled to the Shenzhen SEZ and endorsed its operation, as a prelude to a further wave of liberalization.

The initial SEZs were similar to the EPZs that had spread in Asia since the 1970s: they were regions in which foreign investment was encouraged by lower tax rates, fewer and simplified administrative and customs procedures, and, most crucially, duty-free import of components and supplies (Box 17.1). Thus

Box 17.1
How Chinese SEZs are Similar to Asian EPZs

China's special economic zones are a type of EPZ. The first EPZ in Asia was established at Kaohsiung in Taiwan in 1965. By the 1980s there were 35 EPZs in Asia, and most countries had them. A strikingly successful example has been the Penang Free Trade Zone in Malaysia, which initiated the development of Malaysia's substantial electronics industry. All Asian EPZs offer an essentially similar set of incentives for investors. First, components and raw materials can be imported duty-free and without administrative formalities, and exports leave the zone without export or sales taxes. Thus the zones are "outside" the country in which they are located, insofar as normal customs procedures are concerned. Second, company income tax holidays are typically granted for a period of three to 10 years. Third, the administrative procedures are streamlined, often through a "one-stop shop" coordination of permits, and usually through exemption of restrictions on foreign ownership and employment of foreign nationals that might apply in the rest of the economy. Fourth, the zone itself often operates as a commercial entity, building infrastructure and supplying utilities—often at a subsidized rate—to the foreign firms.

Asian EPZs offered a way to move toward export promotion without fundamentally overturning the structure of protection in place for domestic manufacturers. EPZs produced benefits in terms of employment created and foreign exchange earned, but at a cost of giving up significant tax revenues and forgoing potential linkages to the remainder of the domestic economy. Many EPZs started slowly and ended up costing more than initially envisaged, but the policies have typically been seen as ultimately successful in most of the countries that tried them. EPZs initially attract "footloose" investors in such sectors as garments and electronics assembly because of low wages and easy conditions for moving goods in and out. To varying degrees, some zones have been able to move beyond a few initial industries and contribute to broader-based process of industrialization. Chinese SEZs share all these fundamental characteristics with other Asian EPZs.

the SEZs were part of the early development of the export-processing regime described in Chapter 16. Yet the SEZs also went beyond the other Asian EPZs (Box 17.2). Because they also served as test beds for domestic economic reforms, they inevitably had a broader role to play in China's economic evolution. Wholly owned foreign subsidiaries were permitted in the SEZs long before they were allowed elsewhere. Moreover, since each of the four initial SEZs was intended to appeal to an economically significant group of overseas Chinese who were potential investors (Chapter 1), they served as important channels to outside groups. For all these symbolic and systemic reasons, the SEZs had great importance to China's economic reform. The SEZs also exemplified the pattern of Chinese policy-making during the first era of reform (as described in Chapter 4): dual-track, incremental reforms that started by creating a new system alongside, or in the interstices of, the existing one. The SEZs were not immediately successful. In relation to the high hopes they had inspired, the SEZs got off to a slow start. Foreign investment (especially high-tech investment) was initially disappointing, and infrastructure construction was expensive. The SEZs were attacked for facilitating smuggling and

Box 17.2
How Chinese SEZs are Different from Asian EPZs

Chinese SEZs were bound to be "more special" than other Asian EPZs (Chan, Chen and Chin 1986; Chu 1986). Other Asian EPZs were established in economies that were basically market economies, albeit sheltered from world markets and competition by ISI policies. Chinese SEZs were created in a planned, bureaucratic economic system, so the difference between the "rules of the game" in the SEZs and those in the domestic economy was bound to be large.

• The SEZs often served as "laboratories" for experiments with economic reforms. For example, Shenzhen SEZ was an early pioneer of both flexible wage systems (no limits to incentive payments) and tender bidding for construction projects. Experiments with development of land markets through leasehold, as well as equity markets, were significant innovations pioneered in Shenzhen during later phases of reform.

• The SEZs were governmental bodies with unusually high levels of autonomy compared to EPZs. During the early years SEZs were allowed to retain much of the tax, customs, and foreign-exchange revenues generated within the zones.

• The SEZs had multiple functions: They were seen as "windows" on the world, absorbing advanced experience in technology, administration, and business. Shenzhen in particular has been developed as a "comprehensive" site, including tourism, housing, and other services for Hong Kong people.

• Chinese domestic enterprises have also had a substantial incentive to invest in the SEZs. By setting up their own subsidiaries—even if they are not joint ventures with foreign businesses—Chinese domestic enterprises enjoy greater administrative flexibility, lower tax rates (15% income tax rather than 30%), and less complicated access to the outside world.

Reflecting their multiple roles and greater importance to the domestic economy, it is not surprising to find that China's SEZ are much bigger than other Asian EPZs, as the following table shows:

Size of China's SEZs and Asian EPZs (square kilometers)

	Initial 1980 Size	Size in 1990
Shenzhen	327.5	327.5
Zhuhai	6.8	121.0
Shantou	1.6	52.6
Xianmen	2.5	131.1
Kaohsiung, Taiwan		0.7
Penang, Malasia		1.2
Batam Island, Indonesia		36.6
Bataan, Philippines		3.4

corruption. At the same time, FDI quickly began to leak out into the surrounding countryside. The EP agreements being signed with small firms throughout the Pearl River Delta sometimes involved foreign businesses providing equipment and technology and being repaid with finished product (a type of FDI). Thus, early in the reform process, investment from Hong Kong began to find its way into many parts of Guangdong Province, beyond the SEZs. This was no less important for being composed of many small-scale transactions.

Reformers were not prepared to allow their standard-bearers to languish. When a second wave of liberalization began in 1984, it was signaled by a visit to Shenzhen SEZ by Deng Xiaoping, in which he proclaimed Shenzhen a successful experiment. Fourteen new "Open Cities"—including Shanghai—were designated along the coast, and all set up Economic and Technological Development Zones (ETDZs) that offered many of the same provisions as the SEZs. Moreover, they were authorized and encouraged to bargain aggressively with potential foreign investors to facilitate investment inflow. Shanghai quickly approved the application of the 3M corporation to set up a wholly owned subsidiary, even though there was no provision in Chinese law for foreign ownership outside the SEZs at that time. A dramatic proliferation of "zones" began. Hainan Island, in its entirety, was designated a SEZ, and the existing SEZs at Zhuhai, Shantou, and Xiamen were expanded enormously. Broad swaths of territory were declared open to foreign investment, including substantial rural areas. The Pearl River Delta in Guangdong, the Yangtze River Delta around Shanghai, and a swath of coastal Fujian near the Xiamen SEZ were opened to investment. A total population of 160 million was included among these newly open areas. Since the rural areas had few SOEs, the implication was that the foreign investors were encouraged to set up subsidiaries and joint ventures with rural collectives that would make use of low-cost rural labor outside the framework of the planned economy. Moreover, the opening of so many areas inevitably implied that local officials would be in competition to attract foreign investors and would offer competing packages of preferential policies.

At the beginning of the 1990s a third wave of opening of the Chinese economy was announced by . . . the creation of another SEZ. The Pudong (East Shanghai) special zone served as an advertisement, as well as a commitment device, by creating an SEZ in the heart of China's most developed region for the first time. Slightly larger than Shenzhen, the Pudong Development Zone possessed a population of 1.1 million even before development began. Moreover, 18 new ETDZs were approved in 1992–1993, as well as a new type of zone, the high-technology development zone. These

zones signaled both a commitment to reform and a shift in regional policy
because zones moved north and inland. Urban real estate was opened up to
foreign investment attracting massive inflows, especially from Hong
Kong. A central government document (1992, No. 4) allowed experiments in
retail and many other service sectors. Cumulatively, these measures sent a
strong message that investment was welcomed and that administrative restrictions were being reduced. They set the stage for the large role played by FDI
since 1993.

By 2003 there were well over 100 investment zones recognized by the
central government. There are six SEZs (the four original, Hainan, and
Pudong), 54 national-level ETDZs, 53 nationally recognized high-tech industrial zones, and 15 Bonded Zones (in which commodities can be legally parked
"outside" the country's customs borders). Some of these overlap, but in addition there are hundreds of zones run by local governments without central
support. Seventeen of the national ETDZs were established between 2000 and
2002 in the interior of China, as if to correct an oversight. By this time China
had launched the Western Development Program, so it was natural to extend
ETDZ privileges to the western interior provinces. Now, every province has
at least one zone. Bold, fragmented, open to outside investment, but with a
strong role for government: SEZs typify much of the Chinese transition
process.

17.3   THE INVESTMENT REGIME TODAY

China has a generally favorable regime for foreign investors today. Taxes are
moderate; investment protection agreements are in place with most countries,
and an apparatus for arbitration is available; and most legal provisions are
adequate in principle. The currency is convertible in the current account, and
there are few problems with repatriation of profit. The most striking features
of the investment regime are its relatively decentralized nature and the high
degree of discretion retained by government officials. While the formal
requirements are not onerous, every investment contract has to be approved
by some government level. In most other East Asian countries approval is also
required, but there is a single investment approval board that passes on all
proposed FDI projects in the country. In China, by contrast, approvals can be
granted by literally hundreds of local investment boards. Provinces and zones
(of various kinds) usually have the authority to approve projects valued at up
to $30 million, and even county governments are able to approve smaller proj-
ects (below $10 million).

In practice, this decentralized regime often favors the foreign investor. Foreign investors can play localities off against each other in search of a favorable package. Localities have strong incentives to attract foreign investors through lower taxes, even beyond the statutory concessions. Eager municipalities may provide concessionary terms on land-rental and utility rates. Sometimes local governments collude with investors to classify large projects as multiple small projects in order to evade central government monitoring. Foreign investors, in turn, have strong incentives to survey options in different localities and exploit the particularities of the investment system. For example, the statutory enterprise income tax rate in China is 33% (30% national plus 3% local). However, productive enterprises in SEZs and ETDZs are to be taxed at 15%, and coastal cities and provincially established zones may set the rate at 24%. In fact, these rates are merely baselines. Enterprises that export more than 70% of their output and enterprises designated as "high-technology" may enjoy further reductions, although not, in theory, below 10%. Moreover, within zones (but sometimes outside as well), a tax holiday is granted for the first two years an FIE is profitable, and tax rates are half the long-term rate for years three to five. Needless to say, these provisions provide enormous scope for bargaining about tax rates and other financial provisions.

While these multiple provisions may benefit the foreign investor, they also create difficulties. It is not always clear who has the ultimate power to approve a given set of tax rates or land-use agreements. Because regions compete, foreign investors may have to navigate surprisingly uncooperative and complex relationships between different regional or sectoral authorities. Moreover, the quality of local government services varies enormously. Some local governments display high levels of professionalism, while others are hobbled by corruption, lack of training, and lack of oversight and transparency. Problems with the enforcement of intellectual property rights (IPR) are also legion in China. National laws and regulations are reasonable, but local governments in many cases have no incentive to enforce national regulations, and they may have powerful incentives to violate them. Navigating the complex institutional environment can be costly for foreign investors.

The contractual forms in which FDI is embodied in China have evolved steadily toward modes that permit the foreign investor a higher level of control. In the early 1980s, FDI was dominated by contractual joint ventures (JVs) and joint development projects. Contractual JVs are flexible agreements of association that do not necessarily create an enduring legal entity, and they are particularly useful in situations in which investment is combined with some kind of service agreement, such as hotels. Profit can be divided among the

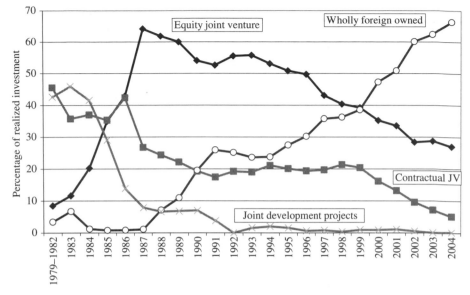

Figure 17.3
Modes of FDI in China

contracting parties in any form that is mutually acceptable. Joint development projects are a form of contractual joint venture tailored to oil exploitation. After the mid–1980s, China began to strongly encourage the use of equity joint ventures (EJVs), which became the dominant mode of investment. As Figure 17.3 shows, from 1987 through 1996 more than half of incoming FDI was in the form of EJVs. EJVs create a new legal entity in which the foreign and domestic firms have a stake. Their predominance during this period reflected the commonly held beliefs (on the foreign side) that long-term partnerships were necessary to operate in the Chinese environment and (on the Chinese side) that such partnerships would facilitate the sharing of information and technology. In practice, the "marriages" that made EJVs were often unhappy ones. Foreign investors found that their incentives were not always closely aligned with those of their Chinese partners, particularly when those partners were SOEs. While foreign managers were primarily concerned with earning profit or establishing market share, Chinese managers were often concerned with maintaining employment, building a larger firm, and accessing foreign technology. As China evolved toward a market economy, foreign investors increasingly felt they could operate independently, without the assistance of a Chinese partner and without the conflicting motives so often involved in an EJV. Foreign investors have increasingly prefered wholly owned subsidiaries. Chinese regulations—reflecting disappointment on the Chinese side as well with the success of these ventures—have evolved to accommodate these preferences. The share of FDI in the form of wholly owned subsidiaries of foreign companies has climbed steadily, and in 2004 it accounted for exactly two-thirds of total realized FDI inflows.

17.4 SOURCES OF INVESTMENT IN CHINA

As seen in Figure 17.1, FDI to China falls into four large fairly stable source groups. By far the largest is that made up of Hong Kong, Taiwan, Macau, and free ports or tax havens (which will be discussed later). The economic relationship among China, Hong Kong, and Taiwan is discussed further in the following section. Hong Kong is indisputably the biggest investor in China, accounting for 42% of the cumulative total in 1985–2005, according to official figures. These data show officially recorded inflows from Hong Kong and Taiwan easing off after 1998, but investment from various tax havens increased dramatically at the same time. In 2005, $12.3 billion in incoming FDI was from companies domiciled in the British Virgin Islands, Bermuda, the Cayman Islands, and other tax havens. From other sources we know that Taiwan businesses send substantial investment to the Cayman and virgin islands and other "free ports." Hong Kong businesses face their own political risks and motivations for transiting investment through a third location. In general, then, it is defensible to consider investment from these tax havens along with Taiwan and Hong Kong investment. When we do so—as in Figure 17.1—we see that investment remained fairly stable, around $25 billion, through 2001, before ticking up to $35 billion annually in 2004–2005. In the entire 1985–2005 period, Hong Kong, Taiwan, Macau, and all tax havens have accounted for 60% of total FDI in China. If half the tax haven investment originates with Hong Kong and half with Taiwan, they accounted for 47% and 12%, respectively, of cumulative investment in China, making them first and second.[2]

The developed-country triad of the United States and Canada, Japan, and the European Union (EU) accounted for 25% of the cumulative FDI in China in 1985–2005. This is an unusual feature of China's experience: worldwide, developed countries accounted for 92% of FDI in 1998–2002. The relative weight of each leg of the developed-economy triad regions is comparable at

---

2. Tax havens such as the Cayman and British Virgin islands are also popular choices for incorporation of high-technology start-up businesses in China itself. Creation of an offshore vehicle facilitates the financing of new ventures by both Chinese and offshore investors. Thus some portion of FDI from tax havens may reflect domestic Chinese investment. Since these high technology ventures are themselves often the protect of cross-national networks of entrepreneurs it is not certain how large the domestic component is compared to the investment from Taiwan and Hong Kong.

around 8% investment each (1985–2005). The United States was the third most important investor in China (after Hong Kong and Taiwan) through 2002, but U.S. investment has been on a downtrend since then. Judging by economic size and proximity, it is surprising that Japanese investment in China is not much larger than it is. Japan's GDP is six times as big as those of Korea, Taiwan, and Hong Kong put together, but Japanese investment in China is only one-eighth the total of those three. The prolonged Japanese economic stagnation during the 1990s is the main explanation for the limited amount of Japanese investment in China, combined with a relatively pessimistic appraisal of Chinese prospects that prevailed in Japanese commercial circles during the late 1990s. Since 2003 both the Japanese economy and the Japanese view of China have improved substantially. Despite political frictions between China and Japan, Japanese investment in China has surged. In 2005, Japan invested $6.5 billion in China, more than twice the $3 billion by the United States. The potential Japanese economic impact on China has only begun to be realized. In recent years, the EU has also been a somewhat larger investor in China than the United States, accounting for $5 billion in 2005.

Among other Asian investors, Korea and Singapore are by far the most important. Korean investment in China started late but it has grown extremely rapidly. In 2004 Korean investment soared $6.25 billion, vaulting past both the United States and Japan, before settling back to $5 billion in 2005. (Note the slightly bizarre result that, according to official data, the top three investors in China in 2004, in order, were Hong Kong, the British Virgin Islands, and Korea.) The more prominent role of both Japan and Korea in FDI in China may mark an important new stage of industrial restructuring. Both Japan and Korea invest heavily in northern provinces such as Shandong, Liaoning, and Jilin. This northward shift of economic dynamism could have a profound impact on the Chinese economy, potentially reversing the relative economic decline of the Northeast.

Hong Kong is not just the largest investor in China: Its role is special in almost every respect. In the first place, on July 1, 1997, the former British colony of Hong Kong became a Special Administrative Region (SAR) of China. Thus China's largest foreign investor is in fact not even foreign. However, there are abundant reasons to treat Hong Kong as "foreign," beyond habitual practice. Hong Kong has a dramatically different economic and administrative system from China; it has a much higher level of economic development that the rest of the mainland; the SAR government has decision-making authority over virtually all important economic decisions, including trade regulations; and, recognizing this fact, Hong Kong has long been an independent member of some international organizations, including the WTO. Given these factors, the classification of Hong Kong as a foreign investor in China is a welcome triumph of common sense.

From the 1950s through the 1970s, Hong Kong grew from a trade entrepôt to a manufacturing, finance, and trade center of formidable efficiency. As Hong Kong continued to grow in the 1980s, it was natural that manufacturing firms would seek additional space outside the crowded center city. But because Hong Kong itself is so small, urban growth inevitably meant relocation of firms a few miles away to China. When a Hong Kong factory moves to the suburbs, it creates "foreign" investment. Hong Kong's proximity to China also means its investors tend to have better information about policy changes inside China than do investors in other countries. Hong Kong businesses move quickly to take advantage of new opportunities in China when policy shifts. As a result, Hong Kong's share of incoming FDI is especially high immediately following new liberalization measures in China. Hong Kong was the source of more than 60% of China's incoming FDI after each of the three waves of liberalization described earlier: in 1979 (initial opening), 1987 (Coastal Development Strategy), and 1992, when it reached a phenomenal 68% share. Other foreign investors only gradually catch up to Hong Kong's inside information. The early mover advantages that Hong Kong businesses have seem likely to persist in the near future. On January 1, 2004, the Closer Economic Partnership went into effect between the PRC and the Hong Kong SAR. The partnership holds that Hong Kong firms—including Hong Kong subsidiaries of multinational corporations—will enjoy earlier access to some of the sectors being opened up in China as part of WTO accession (section 17.6.1).

Hong Kong is the home of many subsidiaries of corporations based elsewhere. There are about 1,000 foreign-company regional headquarters in Hong Kong (256 from the United States, 198 from Japan, and 106 from China). In some cases, investment originating elsewhere may be channeled through Hong Kong and show up in the data as Hong Kong investment. Parent companies located in China sometimes channel investment from their subsidiaries back into China, or even create subsidiaries for this purpose: so-called round-tripping. Chinese firms may be motivated by the desire to gain access to concessionary tax and other advantages enjoyed by foreign-invested firms, as well as to the autonomy and anonymity that come from channeling funds through Hong Kong subsidiaries. But here we must be careful. One of the peculiarities of the Hong Kong economy is that it has long been the headquarters of a number of large firms that are owned by Beijing. Firms such as China Resources and China Merchants (owned by the Chinese Ministry of Commerce and Ministry of Transportation, respectively) have been active in Hong

Kong for 50 years. These firms are big investors in China, but it would be a mistake to reduce their activities to simple "round-tripping." The relationship is in fact a more complex one with a much longer history. Recently these relationships have become even more complicated with the rise of investor companies headquartered in offshore tax havens. Increasingly global companies are sometimes difficult to pin down to a single home economy.

17.5   THE CHINA CIRCLE

The close economic association among the economies of the PRC, Hong Kong, and Taiwan warrants calling them the China Circle. The basis for the emergence of the China Circle was the success of Taiwan and Hong Kong in developing labor-intensive manufactured exports during the 1960s and 1970s, particularly to the U.S. market. Both economies produced an enormous range of light, labor-intensive manufactures: beginning with plastic flowers in Hong Kong, extending through a vast range of sporting and travel goods, to the huge garment and footwear sectors. This success had an important demonstration effect on China from the beginning of the reform era, because Chinese policymakers observed their success and sought to emulate and repeat it through economic reform. The export success of Taiwan and Hong Kong began to have a much more direct effect on the mainland in the mid–1980s, when it began to drive a restructuring of East Asian production networks. Exporters found increasing wages and costs (including land costs) and currency realignments creating "push" to move production to lower-wage locations. At the same time, capabilities were rapidly upgrading in both Taiwan and Hong Kong: educational levels soared, supply of engineering and scientific manpower increased, and commercial and financial experience accumulated rapidly. Attracted to higher-skill and higher-remuneration occupations, they were "pulled" away from traditional labor-intensive manufacturers, whose managers had no choice but to look around for other locations.

The opening of China to foreign investment at this time created a dramatic opportunity to transfer labor-intensive export production to the PRC. This development, described in the preceding chapter, was part of a worldwide trend toward increasing intraindustry trade. The trend toward the geographical dispersion of production chains leads to an increasing share of international trade that is made up of intermediate and capital goods, and to increasing FDI to build the required networks. This process was particularly powerful in the China Circle because transaction costs for Taiwan and Hong Kong firms to operate in the PRC were low. Proximity, aided by common language and customs, made doing business on the mainland easy and cheap, once the mainland's economic system opened up. Moreover, low transactions costs made it possible to initially move only the most labor-intensive—typically low-skilled—stages of production onto the mainland, while retaining other activities in Hong Kong or Taiwan. Production chains were quickly created that crossed political boundaries and allowed Hong Kong and Taiwan to specialize in high-value services and technology-intensive production while much of the ordinary manufacturing moved to the PRC.

This restructuring moved remarkably quickly for traditional labor-intensive manufacturing, such as garments and footwear, and was basically completed by the early 1990s. For example, Taiwan firms moved their footwear production to the mainland, and in the United States imported shoes from China "displaced" imported shoes from Taiwan. A similar restructuring of the electronics industry began around 1990. It has been followed by many successive waves of relocation, of which the most recent—and one of the most dramatic—has been the transplantation of the notebook computer industry during 2002–2003. In the personal computer (PC) and components industry, production of keyboards and power supply units (the most labor-intensive products) were the first to move to the mainland, because the cost advantages were most marked. They were followed by production of monitors and motherboards, and a steadily expanding range of IT hardware products.

The previous chapter pointed out that foreign-invested firms accounted for 88% of China's high-technology exports. A look at the largest high-technology exporters can give us further insight into this process. Of the top 10, shown in Table 17.1, nine are foreign-invested firms. All of the foreign firms are from either Taiwan (four) or the United States (five). In fact, both U.S. and Taiwan firms are linked in the same global production networks. For example, Dell is the seventh-largest high-tech exporter, but No. 1, Quanta, from Taiwan, is also

Table 17.1
Top exporters of high-tech products, 2003

Chinese company	Parent company	Parent home	Export value (billion U.S. dollars)
1. Tech-Front Shanghai	Quanta	Taiwan	5.2
2. Hongfujin Precision Industry	Hon Hai	Taiwan	4.2
3. ASUStek Computer Suzhou	ASUStek	Taiwan	3.2
4. Motorola China	Motorola	U.S.	2.8
5. Great Wall International	Great Wall/IBM	China/U.S.	2.6
6. Dongguan Export Processing	Dongguan	China	2.6
7. Dell China	Dell	U.S.	1.7
8. Mingji Diantong	BenQ	Taiwan	1.7
9. Intel Shanghai	Intel	U.S.	1.6
10. Seagate Wuxi	Seagate	U.S.	1.5

"Export value" refers to value of high-technology exports only.

the largest single external supplier of computers to Dell. Moreover, with the exception of Motorola, all these high-value exporters are engaged in assembling valuable components into high-value final products. Computers and laptop computers make up a big share of the total; contract manufacturing of a range of final products accounts for most of the rest. Even Intel operates a testing and packaging facility in Shanghai and imports the actual chips that are processed there (Jiang 2004).

As manufacturing production has moved to the China mainland, the southern coastal provinces have been industrializing rapidly, while Taiwan and Hong Kong have to some extent deindustrialized. The Hong Kong industrial labor force, which peaked just below one million, had declined to 172,000 by June 2003. In Taiwan the manufacturing labor force reached a peak in 1987 of 2.8 million, but then leveled off and was at 2.59 million at the end of 2003. Meanwhile, in the two provinces of Guangdong and Fujian the industrial labor force increased from 6 million in 1985 to 11 million at the end of 2001. Between them, Hong Kong and Taiwan have lost about a million manufacturing jobs, while Guangdong and Fujian have gained about five million. In fact, these data probably understate the total number of new manufacturing jobs in Guangdong and Fujian. There have been major flows of immigrants from other parts of China into these provinces, and some immigrants working in the informal sector are not captured in official employment statistics.

Hong Kong and Taiwan have both experienced substantial success in upgrading to higher-skilled activities, while simultaneously experiencing steadily rising incomes and relatively low unemployment. Hong Kong's restructuring has been especially thorough, as it has shed many industrial functions altogether and moved into greater specialization in services, particularly finance, transport, and telecommunications. In Taiwan restructuring within the manufacturing sector itself has been the most impressive feature. Total manufacturing value added has continued to grow, even as manufacturing employment has dropped. Taiwan has moved into technologically more sophisticated products while shedding low-technology products. Thus the upgrading of skills occurred in opposite and symmetrical ways in Hong Kong and Taiwan. Hong Kong moved out of manufacturing and into a variety of business services, such as finance, marketing, and accounting. Taiwan has been quite successful in improving technological capacities and moving into production and export of commodities at much higher technological levels, yet it seeks also to become a business-operations and financial center. Both experienced dramatic success through the late 1990s; both were buffeted by the economic turbulence of the late 1990s and post–2001 global economy; both seem to be recovering today.

17.6   FDI IN CONTEXT

The preceding pages have made clear that FDI has had an enormous impact on China, transferring manufacturing capability, jobs, and export markets to China. The close integration of China and other East Asian economies especially the China Circle economies of Taiwan and Hong Kong—has created extremely competitive, flexible, and low-cost manufacturing networks. Looking to the future, the challenge for China will be to expand the benefits receiving from openness to foreign investment. That expansion should come in terms of the sectors open to foreign participation and the modes of foreign participation.

17.6.1   Sectoral Composition of FDI: The WTO Impact

Manufacturing is a much larger part of FDI inflows into China than it is for FDI inflows in the rest of the world. Manufacturing accounted for 70% of Chinese FDI inflows in both 2003 and 2004. Manufacturing accounted for only 38% of the stock of FDI in developing countries at the end of 2002 (and even less, 32%, in developed countries), while services accounted for 55%. By contrast, services in China accounted for only 27% of FDI inflows in 2003. Moreover, other kinds of investment—portfolio investment and bank lending—have been relatively unimportant in China through the present. Manufacturing accounted for 62% of registered foreign capital at the end of 2002. To a large extent, this emphasis is explainable in terms of the restrictions that China has maintained on foreign entry into the most important service sectors. China's accession to the WTO involves commitments to dramatically lower most of these barriers. Indeed, arguably, the impact of WTO membership will be most dramatic in opening service sectors, even more than the impact on trade, which had already been substantially liberalized by the time of accession. However, this impact is not yet evident in the investment numbers. On the contrary, the share of investment in manufacturing has actually increased slightly in recent years. As Chapter 6 noted, China's comparative advantage in manufacturing has remained strong while, in parallel fashion, India's momentum in service exports is accelerating.

Three service sectors that account for large proportions of FDI inflows in all developing countries (and their shares in total inflows 2001–2002) stand out: wholesale and retail trade (7.4%), transport and telecommunications (8.0%), and finance (11.5%). In China, by contrast, incoming FDI in the service sector is highly concentrated in real estate, specifically in property development. This sector accounted for 10% of total investment in 2003. By contrast, wholesale and retail trade (2.1%), transport and telecom (1.6%), and finance (0.4%) are clear underperformers. These three sectors together account for 27% of world developing-country inflows (including China) but only 4% of inflows into China itself (SYC 2005; 648; UNCTAD 2004).

These are the sectors where WTO commitments will have the biggest impact. Wholesale trading rights—previously off-limits to foreign firms—were being granted during the 2003–2005 period. Transport and telecommunications sectors are being opened to minority foreign ownership during the 2005–2008 period. Financial sectors are being progressively opened to foreign participation, with an important milestone coming in 2007, when the banking market is opened to foreign participation. These changes will drive further expansion and significant structural change in Chinese FDI inflows. A new wave of internationalization and restructuring will begin.

17.6.2   Modes of Capital Inflow

In the early 1980s borrowing from governments and international organizations was the most important form of capital inflow to China, and banks have been important since the mid–1980s. But since 1993 these have been overshadowed by FDI. One reason for the predominance of FDI, of course, is that until very recently China's financial markets were virtually closed to portfolio investment (Chapter 19). In addition, though, Chinese policy-makers initially displayed a preference for direct investment, primarily because it brought technology and commercial expertise as well as capital. As a result—and because of concern that foreign debt might not be well managed—China maintained strict controls on foreign borrowing through most of the 1990s. As a result, foreign borrowing has been a small part of overall capital inflows. At the end of 2003, China's total foreign debt was a manageable $194 billion (14% of GDP), compared to $403 billion in foreign-exchange reserves. Of the total debt, $77 billion was short-term borrowing (considered more risky) and $52 billion was borrowed from governments or international organizations (considered the least risky, and often borrowed at concessionary rates).

China has maintained restrictions on capital account convertibility. That is, while an exporter or importer can freely convert RMB to foreign exchange with presentation of trade documents, individuals and businesses cannot simply buy or sell large amounts of domestic or foreign currency. In theory, therefore, we should expect other kinds of capital flows reflected in the balance of payments to be quite small. However, this expectation is false. Despite the nominal lack of convertibility on the capital account, liquid capital flows to and from China are in fact quite large. Inspection of the balance of payments reveals that there is considerable fluctuation in the direction and also the relative size of different payments components. In part, this reflects the fact that data on specific components of the balance of payments are simply not very accurate. But in part it reflects the fact that individuals and businesses, in the absence of capital account convertibility, utilize many different channels to move money into and out of China. The standard way to look at the balance of payments is to break it down into the current account (payments for goods and services) and the capital account (transfers of assets). When there is a surplus in the private transactions in the balance of payments, it must (by definition) be equal to the accumulation by the Central Bank of official foreign exchange reserves. If collected data do not show this equality, a term for "errors and omissions" will be added to the data to make it balance. In China, errors and omissions are large and change direction (Prasad and Wei 2005). Moreover, China's foreign exchange reserves have soared from U.S. $286 billion at the end of 2002 to $819 billion at the end of 2005.

One way to simplify this complexity is to divide the balance of payments in a nonstandard way into three components: the balance of trade in goods and services, inflows of foreign direct investment, and everything else. In this classification, we have fairly reliable data for the first two components, and the third component is checked by the definitional requirement that all the components of the balance of payments equal official reserve accumulation. This third component, then, includes everything from the capital account except FDI inflows, plus two items from the current account (remittances and profit from investments), as well as errors and omissions. It covers all the flows of liquid capital into and out of China. These three components are expressed, as a percentage of GDP, in Figure 17.4. The result is quite striking. The balance of trade has been positive and above 2% of GDP since 1996, but jumped in 2005. FDI inflows have been stable, around 3%–4% of GDP since 1996. But the "all other" component has been huge and highly volatile. From 1997–2000, this corresponds to net outflows of liquid capital over 6% of GDP annually. Then, remarkably, flows turned around, and in 2003 surpassed 5% of GDP inflow. Capital outflows, by this definition, were $80 billion in 1997, and capital inflows were $72 billion in 2003. Clearly, these flows are influenced by expectations of devaluation (in the outflow period) or appreciation (since 2003). These flows resemble those experienced by the countries of East Asia afflicted by the Asian financial crisis (1997–1998) in their size and instability. The difference is that those countries, to varying degrees, all have open capital accounts. The remarkable thing is that the capital flows from China look just like those from other countries, notwithstanding the fact that theoretically China has capital controls. Obviously, the capital controls do not work. The most powerful argument for China to liberalize its capital account is not that

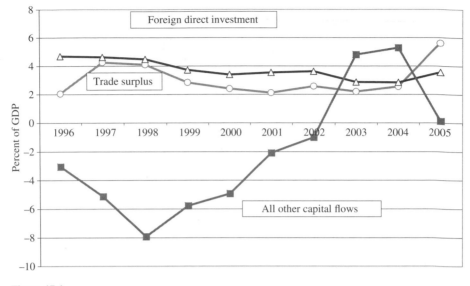

Figure 17.4
China's balance of payments

capital account liberalization is necessarily better, but that a legal, regulated open capital account might function better than a hidden black or grey market with de facto openness (Prasad, Rumbaugh, and Wang 2005).

17.7 CONCLUSION

The volatility of capital flows during the Asian financial crisis of 1997–1998 highlights another aspect of China's reliance on FDI. Even though China was exposed to volatile flows of financial capital like other East Asian economies, China enjoyed a more reliable inflow of FDI at the same time. The investors behind FDI inflows had made a long-term commitment, and in any case their assets were not of a type that could be quickly liquidated. The greater share of "patient capital" in China's foreign investment left it less vulnerable to financial crisis.

The challenge for China over the next five years will be to move to a greater openness while maintaining some of the advantages the existing regime has provided. The predominance of FDI among China's external capital sources is exceptional; it implies that China's "openness" as measured by exposure to FDI is greater than its openness in other dimensions. We should be wary of excess reliance on a single indicator, and we should anticipate that further waves of liberalization are ahead. Those waves will make China's service sectors more open to investment and also make China more susceptible to potentially destabilizing flows of liquid capital. At the same time, global manufacturing networks will continue to use China as a production base with steadily expanding capabilities.

BIBLIOGRAPHY

Suggestions for Further Reading

Gaulier, Lemoine, and Ünal-Kesenci (2005) is a good overview of investment as well as trade. Prasad and Wei (2005) is an excellent, up-to-date account of China's use of foreign capital. On elements of the balance of payments and capital flights, see Gunter (2004). A number of different approaches have been taken to assessing the differences among investors in China by national origin. See, for example, Fung, Iizaka, and Siu (2003); Fung, Lau, and Lee (2004); and Liu, Xu, and Liu (2002) for varying approaches.

The Ministry of Commerce hosts an excellent Web site, in English, on foreign investment in China. See http://fdi.gov.cn/main/indexen.htm.

Sources for Data and Figures

Data cited are for actually utilized incoming foreign direct investment, including "other" investment which is part of EP contracts or compensation trade. (Overseas share issuance has not been included.) For international comparisons of foreign investment see UNCTAD. UNCTAD (2004) provides the comparative data on services. Source does not give 2005 figure for "other" investment, which has been estimated, and equals about 5% of total FDI.

Figure 17.1: *SYC* (2005, 644–45) and earlier volumes. Updated from fdi.gov.cn.

Figure 17.2: *SYC* (2005, 643) and earlier volumes.

Figure 17.3: *SYC* (2005, 643) and earlier volumes. Updated from fdi.gov.cn.

Figure 17.4: Balance of payments tables in standard formats are available at *SYC* (2005, 82) and www.pbc.gov.cn. Service trade, investment income, and remittances have been consolidated with all capital flows, except FDI and errors and omissions, to create a single conglomerate category. See text for discussion. Updated from SAFE (2006).

Table 17.1: Ministry of Commerce, Department of Science and Technology. "Top 50 Exporters of High-Technology Products in 2003." Accessed April 4, 2004 at kjs.mofcom.gov.cn/article/200403/200403001923071.xml.

References

Chan, Thomas, E. K. Y. Chen, and Steve Chin (1986). "China's Special Economic Zones: Ideology, Policy and Practice." In Y. C. Jao and C. K. Leung, eds., *China's Special Economic Zones: Policies, Problems and Prospects*, 87–104. Hong Kong: Oxford University Press.

Chu, David K. Y. (1986). "The Special Economic Zones and the Problem of Territorial Containment." In Y. C. Jao and C. K. Leung, eds., *China's Special Economic Zones: Policies, Problems and Prospects*, 21–38. Hong Kong: Oxford University Press.

Fung, K. C., H. Iizaka, and A. Siu (2003). "Japanese Direct Investment in China." *China Economic Review*, 14(3):304–15.

Fung, K. C., Lawrence J. Lau, and Joseph Lee (2004). *United States Direct Investment in China*. Washington, DC: American Enterprise Institute (AEI) Press.

Gaulier, Guillaume, Françoise Lemoine, and Deniz Ünal-Kesenci (2005). *China's Integration in East Asia: Production Sharing, FDI and High-Tech Trade.* CEPPI Working Paper 2005-2009. Paris: Centre d'Etudes Prospectives et d'Informations Internationales.

Gunter, Frank R. (2004). "Capital Flight from China, 1984–2001." *China Economic Review,* 15:63–85.

Jiang Xiaojuan (2004). "2003–2004: Zhongguo Liiyong Waizi de Fenxi yu Zhanwang." In Liu Guogong, Wang Luolin, and Li Jingwen, eds., *Zhongguo Jingji Qianjing Fenxi 2004 Nian Chunji Baogao* [Blue Book of China's Economy (Spring 2004)], 202–27. Beijing: Shehui Kexue Wenxian.

Liu Minquan, Luodan Xu, and Liu Liu (2002). "Foreign Investment in China: Firm Strategies." In Shang-jin Wei, Guanzhong James Wen, and Huizhong Zhou, eds., *The Globalization of the Chinese Economy.* Cheltenham: Edward Elgar.

Prasad, Eswar, and Shang-Jin Wei (2005). "The Chinese Approach to Capital Inflows: Patterns and Possible Explanations." Working Paper 11306. Cambridge, MA: National Bureau of Economic Research. Access at http://www.nber.org/papers/w11306.

Prasad, Eswar, Thomas Rumbaugh, and Qing Wang (2005). "Putting the Cart Before the Horse? Capital Account Liberalization and Exchange Rate Flexibility in China." IMF Policy Discussion Paper, Asia and Pacific Department PDP/05/1. Washington, DC: International Monetary Fund.

SYC (Annual). *Zhongguo Tongji Nianjian* [Statistical Yearbook of China]. Beijing: Zhongguo Tongji.

SAFE (2006). State Administration of Foreign Exchange, International Payments Analysis Small Group. "2005 nian Zhongguo guoji shouzhi baogao [Report on China's international payments in 2005]" Beijing: SAFE, April. Accessed at http://www.safe.gov.cn/model_safe/tjsj/pic/20060428215218906.pdf

UNCTAD (Annual). United Nations Conference on Trade and Development. *World Investment Report.* New York: United Nations. Accessed at http://www.unctad.org/Templates/Page.asp?intItemID=1485&lang=1

VI MACROECONOMICS AND FINANCE

Headquarters of the People's Bank of China, Beijing 2006.

Effectively managing macroeconomic policy during the transition to a market economy is demanding and difficult. Fiscal policy and monetary policy are both subject to extraordinary challenges. Many of the transitional economies of Eastern Europe and the former Soviet Union underwent periods of severe macroeconomic instability that contributed to large recessions. By contrast, China has generally been able to navigate around the largest macroeconomic pitfalls. To be sure, significant macroeconomic cycles have marked the transition process: three inflationary cycles occurred through the mid–1990s, and since the mid–1990s significant deflationary pressures have been prominent. However, hyperinflationary episodes have been quickly controlled; household financial savings have generally maintained their value; and, most importantly, expectations about the future have not been plagued with the extreme uncertainty that follows from serious macroeconomic disruption. This chapter addresses the basic features of the macroeconomics of China's transition.

First, the chapter examines the broad structural changes in national saving that underlie macroeconomic balances. China's gradual transition achieved macroeconomic consistency: decision-makers in the household, business, and government sectors were able to adjust their saving and investment decisions gradually. The expectations upon which saving and investment decisions were based were consistent with the way the economy actually evolved. Most important, the saving and investment decisions made were consistent with stability and sustained growth of the economy. Second, the chapter examines the government budget, which is an important actor in the long-run shifts in saving and investment behavior, and the agent of fiscal policy. Ordinarily, fiscal policy would be one of the most important instruments for influencing the macroeconomy. However, in China the context of fiscal decline and reconstruction has limited the effectiveness of fiscal policy. The chapter discusses the overall context of fiscal policy by assessing reforms in the fiscal system to date. The fiscal and tax reform of 1994 emerges as one of the crucial milestones of the entire transition process. Despite that reform's success, shortcomings of the fiscal system, particularly in local rural finances, are still challenging. Finally, the chapter considers credit and monetary policy, which have been the main drivers shaping the macroeconomic policy in recent years. A clear, cyclical pattern is evident in the macroeconomic data.

18.1   TRENDS IN NATIONAL SAVING

In China, national saving was high under the planned economy, and it remained high during (and since) the reform process. However, the composition and institutions of saving have changed dramatically. It is conventional to divide economies into household, business, and government sectors. Each of these sectors receives income, and each sector consumes, saves, and invests. Economy-wide saving and investment is the sum of saving and investment in the three sectors and, after funds are transferred among sectors, total saving equals total investment.[1] Under the planned economy, government-run businesses (SOEs) did nearly all the saving. This business sector was not autonomous, of course, and it turned over its surpluses to the government, which planned and carried out most of the investment. Household incomes were low and growing relatively slowly, and household saving was also low. Thus the most important transfers of saving, along with the overall balance of saving and investment, took place within the state sector. The tax system was not terribly important, nor was the banking system's role in intermediating funds very important.

These relationships began to change rapidly with market transition. Most important, household saving quickly began to increase from the very low levels that characterized the planned economy.[2] Financial saving (additions to cash and bank deposits) tripled in a short time, increasing from 2.3% of household income in 1978 to an average of 6.8% in the years 1980–1983. Moreover, after

1. This statement is true as an identity. If saving exceeds voluntary investment, unsold goods will accumulate as inventory, or involuntary investment. However, for each individual sector saving and investment will typically differ, and they need never converge.

2. It is perhaps surprising that households saved little under the planned economy: there was very little to buy and ration coupons were required for many items when they were available. It is natural, perhaps, to expect that there would be "forced saving" and "monetary overhang" as consumers searched for goods to buy. However, there is abundant evidence that saving was in fact low. This fact will be less surprising when we remember that accumulating cash for transactions purposes is only one objective of saving, and not the most important one. More important is whether there are expected future opportunities or risks that warrant putting aside money and deferring consumption today.

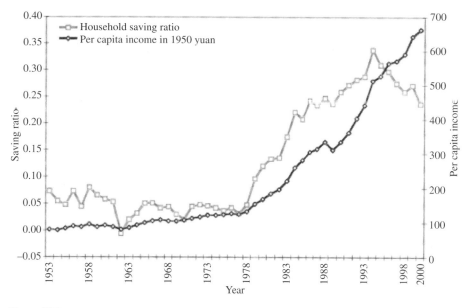

Figure 18.1
China's household saving ratio and per capita income, 1953–2000

this initial surge, household saving rates continued to increase. Figure 18.1 shows a reconstruction by Modigliani and Cao (2004) of China's annual household saving rate between 1953 and 2000. As of 1995 households were generating 70% of domestic saving, over 25% of GDP (*SYC* 2001, 79). The literature suggests three reasons for the dramatic increase in household saving: (1) income growth accelerated; (2) working-age households had less security in old age, given the decline in the number of offspring following stringent birth-limitation policies; and (3) household investment opportunities exploded (Modigliani and Cao 2004). Definitive research on Chinese household saving behavior has not been done, but it is clear that behavior changed dramatically after 1978: high household saving was not a "cultural" characteristic before 1978.[3] It is valid to stress the importance of the changed economic environment after 1978. Households had reasonably stable expectations of the future, and Chinese households never had the experience of seeing the value of their bank deposits wiped out by inflation, as occurred in the Soviet Union. More important, the scope of household business and housing investment grew

3. The increase in household saving rates cannot be explained simply by the more rapid growth in household income during those years either. Instead, saving behavior shifted upward in response to the changed environment.

dramatically. Chinese households responded to this new opportunity by setting aside more money for the future.

The increase in household saving was particularly important because of the decline in saving by the traditional workhorses of the Chinese command economy, the SOEs. As discussed in Chapter 13, SOEs lost their protected markets and their high profitability in the wake of entry and competition from TVEs and private firms. Naturally their ability to save declined as well, as did the volume of surplus turned over to the government. The result of these trends was a dramatic shift in the locus of national saving away from the government and toward households. Household saving picked up the slack left by declining SOE saving; the result was a "soft handoff" as overall national saving remained high. High saving funded high investment, which kept growth on track. With reasonable stability of growth, household expectations about profitable investments were realized, and the overall system achieved intertemporal consistency.

Under the emerging system, the household sector as a whole developed a large surplus of saving over investment. Households placed their financial surpluses in the banks, which lent the funds to enterprises (including, but not limited to, SOEs, which became heavily indebted, or leveraged) and to the government, which began to run deficits for the first time. As a result the banking system, through its lending decisions, increasingly held the key to macroeconomic stability. Moreover, the government budget rapidly declined as a share of GDP, and became less central in determining overall macroeconomic balance. In fact, the rapid decline in government budgetary revenues potentially threatened macroeconomic stability. When government officials were unable to raise sufficient revenues directly through the taxation authorities, they would resort to the banking system to provide inflationary financing of government activities. The following sections, then, first discuss the overall fiscal system and its reform, and then the banking and monetary systems.

18.2   THE FISCAL SYSTEM AND FISCAL REFORM

Figure 18.2 shows the dramatic changes in the budget as a share of GDP. From 1978 onward fiscal revenues declined steadily, setting off alarm bells by the early 1990s. Ultimately, budget revenues reached a minimum at 10.8% of GDP in 1995; given a budget deficit equal to 1% of GDP, expenditures were 11.8% of GDP at all levels of government (central down through county). By comparison, in a sample of 22 developing countries in the late 1980s,

Figure 18.2
Budgetary share of GDP

government expenditures were 32% of GDP on average (Hofman 1998).[4] Faced with this challenge, policy-makers had to address critical problems with the fiscal system. As argued in Chapter 13, this same budget crunch led to a big shift in policy toward state-owned enterprises, and obviously the budgetary challenge required fiscal and tax reforms as well. The key event in this process was the fiscal reform of 1994. This reform largely replaced the traditional revenue remittance system with a tax system that resembles the Western system in many ways; it allowed enterprises to compete on a more equal footing, reduced the scope of government involvement in the productive sector, and allowed the government to focus more on the delivery of

4. Following IMF practice, Chinese data have been adjusted (raised) slightly to include subsidies paid to loss-making state enterprises. These subsidies are excluded in the analysis of central and local government budget shares. Chinese statisticians have also revised their own historical data to include most types of subsidies, but I have used alternative estimates of historical enterprise subsidies. In addition, however, Chinese fiscal data exclude certain types of expenditures carried out by quasi-governmental entities that ought to be considered fiscal outlays. Most obviously, pensions and health benefits paid by SOEs are excluded from fiscal data, although they are virtually indistinguishable from government social security programs. These exceed 2% of GDP. In addition, some types of fixed investment funded by government extrabudgetary funds ought to be consolidated into government expenditure. A plausible estimate is that these amount to 3%–4% of GDP. Thus, at their low point, Chinese budgetary expenditures, broadly defined, probably surpassed 17% of GDP but were still well below the 32% developing-country average cited in the text.

public goods and services. At the same time, fiscal reform has consistently sought a formula for an appropriate relationship between central and local government authorities.

Before 1978 the government had raised revenue through profit remittances from SOEs; there were no personal or enterprise income taxes and, indeed, no real tax policy at all. After 1979 the government introduced a variety of profit-retention systems in order to give SOEs stronger and better incentives. As discussed in Chapter 13, the systems adopted were not standardized, and each SOE ended up negotiating a revenue-retention rate with its own supervising agency. These systems achieved some success in facilitating industrial reforms, but they saddled the budgetary authorities with a complex system that negotiated tax rates on a case-by-case basis. Even nominal rates of enterprise taxation varied by ownership type, and various tax exemptions and special cases were rife. In the early 1990s about 60% of GNP was accounted for by the nonstate sector, but almost 80% of tax revenues were derived from SOEs. Relationships between central and local governments were also negotiated on a case-by-case basis, with each provincial government given a revenue target and long-term sharing rule tailored to that province's economic conditions. Besides being problematic in their own right, these mechanisms obviously failed to halt the problem of fiscal erosion.

In response to this situation and these concerns, in 1994 the Chinese government enacted a sweeping reform of the fiscal system. The new system assigned different categories of taxes to the central and local governments, similar to the federalist system used in many Western countries. The fiscal reform had three crucial elements: new taxes, a tax assignment and sharing system, and a new central government taxation agency. The most important of the new taxes was the VAT levied on most manufactured goods at the uniform rate of 17%. Very small private enterprises without regular bookkeeping systems were to pay a tax of 6% of gross sales in lieu of VAT. In addition, a 33% profit tax was introduced, with uniform rates for state, collective, and private enterprises. The system of personal income taxes was unified and made slightly more rigorous. A "consumption tax" (actually a luxury or excise tax) was introduced for cigarettes, alcohol, and a few other luxuries. A number of minor local taxes were introduced (or more accurately, regularized). In return, the previous system of industrial and commercial taxes was abolished, and the SOE profit contract system was eliminated.

These new taxes were assigned to various levels of government. The central government had complete claim on the consumption tax, customs duties, and most direct and indirect taxes on central-government-controlled sectors (e.g., railroads, financial institutions, and some large centrally controlled enterprises). Provincial governments had direct control over direct taxes on local enterprises, as well as a number of relatively modest taxes, including real estate and property taxes, and pollution and resource fees. The key provision was the designation of most VAT revenues as "shared income," with 75% going to the central government and 25% to the local government. In order to collect these taxes, a new central government taxation authority was created. Under the previous system, most tax revenues had been collected by local government tax bureaus, and localities had then transferred funds to the central government. Under the new system, the central government first collected the bulk of revenues—including all VAT revenues—and then shared them with the provinces. To manage such a system, a central government tax agency was created and given substantial authority.

18.2.1   Reversing Fiscal Erosion

As Figure 18.2 shows, tax reform did stabilize and then increase budgetary revenues. From 1996 through 2005, budgetary revenues increased as a share of GDP every year, a remarkably strong showing. By 2005 budgetary revenues were 17.5% of GDP. Expenditures were 18.6% of GDP, which, when allowance is made for quasi-fiscal expenditures, places China close to, though still below, the group of developing countries cited earlier. The recovery in overall expenditure since 1995 has been accompanied by a remarkable shift in the composition of expenditure. As Figure 18.3 shows, most of the reduction in expenditure from 1978 through 1995 was accommodated by a reduction in investment and subsidy outlay. Since 1995, however, most of the increase in budgetary expenditures has come in the form of current expenditures for the civilian economy. Outlays for administration, education, and pensions and social security have all increased rapidly. Thus, just as China's budget increasingly raises revenues in forms resembling a developing-market economy, so its budgetary expenditures increasingly fund activities that converge to government roles in other market economies.

18.2.2   Broadening the Tax Base: Horizontal Equity

The need of the fiscal system to broaden the tax base and make taxes lower and more uniform was consistent with the need to create a level playing field to enhance competition among enterprises. The tax reform succeeded in eliminating at least four major sources of horizontal inequity, that is, inconsistent treatment that distorted resource allocation by treating different taxpayers differently. Enterprise profits, which had been treated differently depending on their ownership (SOEs, collectives, and private firms), and on the enterprise's

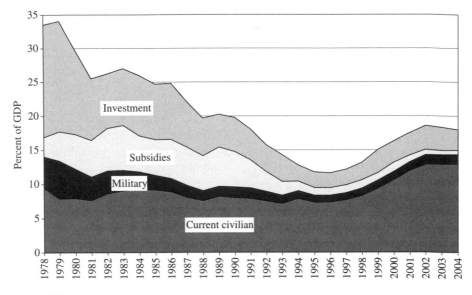

Figure 18.3
Types of fiscal expenditure

profit contract, were unified into a basically uniform profit tax regime. (Widespread profit tax exemptions, especially for foreign-invested firms continued, though, despite government exhortations to scale back or eliminate tax breaks.) Multiple similar taxes with different tax bases and tax rates, including the product tax and business tax, were merged into the VAT, which had only two different rates for the VAT. This significantly reduced the variation in tax burdens due to differential tax rates. Finally, the movement of the VAT to the central government level improved the uniformity of application of tax and improves geographic equity. Local governments are rarely able to give VAT tax relief to favored enterprises (Ball 1999, 37–45). These changes make the tax system more transparent, less costly to administer, and easier for the public to understand. Because compliance is simpler, tax administration officers can be reallocated to handle the more important issues of assessment, collection, and audit.

18.2.3   Restructuring Central-Local Relations

The 1994 reform dramatically boosted the center's share of revenue collected. Excluding borrowing, central government collections, as a share of GDP, more than doubled in 1994, while local collections dropped in half (SYC 2005; 276). Figure 18.4 shows that since reforms began, China has had three different

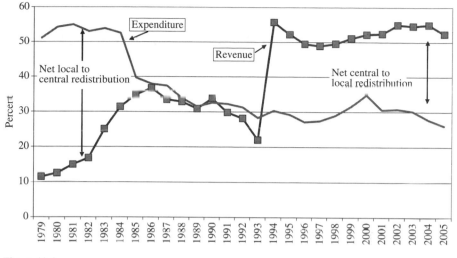

Figure 18.4
Central government share of budgetary revenue and expenditure

systems linking central and local budgets. At first, the central government was dependent on revenues transferred from local governments, making more than half of expenditures but collecting less than 20% of revenues. This was a legacy of the Maoist decentralization of the Cultural Revolution period. During an intermediate period, 1985–1993, the central government spent about the same share of outlays, 30% or more, as the share of revenues it took in. Although there were transfers in both directions between center and localities, they balanced out almost exactly. Since the 1994 tax reform, however, the central government has been largely in control of initial tax collections, taking in a little over 50% of all revenues. The central government spends directly about 30% of all expenditures. Local governments are now dependent on central government transfers that pass on about 20% of total revenues to them. This arrangement enhances the central government's overall position and gives it a stronger bargaining position vis-à-vis local governments.

The actual increase in central government bargaining power depends on the central government's command of an effective tax collection agency. This control took time to establish since tax offices had traditionally been subordinate to provincial governments. Gradually, though, control over revenues has been recentralized through changes in the organization of tax administration and assignment of collection of the most important taxes to the central government. Moreover, the central government retains the power to set rates and define bases for all taxes remains with the central government, giving the central government pervasive control over the budgetary process. However, local governments continue to control the bulk of all expenditures. As Figure 18.4 shows, central government expenditures spiked in 2000 but generally have drifted below 30% of all budgetary outlays: local governments, then, make 70% or more of all budgetary outlays, and this proportion increased in 2004 and 2005. Local governments make more expenditures, even as the central government achieves more leverage over local governments through its control of revenue collection and redistribution.

18.3   THE FISCAL SYSTEM TODAY

The reforms of 1994, in conjunction with administrative reforms that reduced the size of the central government bureaucracy, largely resolved the central government's fiscal dilemmas. However, the same cannot be said for the fiscal system at the local level, particularly in the countryside.

18.3.1   Intergovernmental Fiscal Relations: Principles

Since almost all countries have more than one level of government, they necessarily all have some kind of intergovernmental fiscal system and share certain problems: Who should do what? Who should collect what taxes? How should vertical imbalances be rectified? And what should be done about horizontal imbalances? Large countries have more complex and formal systems of intergovernmental finance. Developing countries face problems associated with technical capacity and administrative capabilities. Countries that are in transition from a central-planning to a market-oriented environment have problems with respect to privatization and the allocation of assets among governments (Bird and Chen 1998, 152). China is a large, developing, transitional country and thus tends to have all these problems in its intergovernmental fiscal system.

As China's central government has specific policy objectives that can be achieved only through the actions of local governments—such as to foster the development of particular infrastructure or to provide basic education and health services equally throughout the country—it may be a better idea to adopt specific, conditional transfer formulae designed to achieve these results by altering the incentive structures, together with a healthy dose of direct central intervention and significant monitoring capacity. Indonesia, for example, achieves this aim basically by collecting all revenues centrally and doling them out regionally in accordance with central designs (Bird and Chen 1998, 174).

In fact, the 1994 reform can be considered as a step in this direction—toward centralization rather than decentralization of decisions in some important respects. Perhaps surprisingly, though, budgetary expenditures are still relatively decentralized in China. Overall, as a share of GDP, local government expenditures have increased steadily since 1996, and in 2005 they were 13.7% of GDP, while central government expenditures were only 4.8% of GDP (Table 18.1). These figures represent greater decentralization that is found, for example, in India, where during the 1990s local government expenditures were 14% of GDP, but central government expenditures were 16% of GDP (Goyal, Khundrakpam, and Ray 2004). If social security expenditures are one day incorporated in central budget accounts, they would increase central expenditures by 3% of GDP. Relatively decentralized management would still characterize the Chinese system.

Should China's budgetary system be shifted to a more decentralized system of fiscal federalism? Decentralization is generally held to be a good thing, because government that is closer to the population being served is more likely to be responsive to popular wishes in extraction and allocation of resources. However, it should be noted that effective decentralization makes extensive demands on the quality of local governance. Effective decentralization requires (a) accountability of local government, (b) autonomy of local government operation, (c) clarity and transparency of central government mandates and entitlements given to local government, and (d) capacity of local government to collect revenues and deliver services efficiently, combined with central government capacity to monitor and audit. In each of these areas China has made some progress but does not yet fulfill the requirements for genuinely effective decentralization (Bahl 1999, 131).

18.3.2 Inadequacy of Local Government Revenue in Rural Areas

Formally, then, the Chinese system remains highly centralized. No local government has the right to levy new taxes or change rates on existing taxes. In practice, rural local governments are highly constrained in the types of taxes to which they have access. In areas where the agricultural collectives collapsed or did not spin off moneymaking subsidiaries, there are few regular sources of income. There is a widespread rural budget crisis (Chapter 10). Responses to the weak rural fiscal system have come both from localities, in the form of extrabudgetary funds and irregular fees, and from the center, in the form of earmarked transfers.

Table 18.1
Budgetary Expenditures and Balance (as percent of GDP)

Year	Expenditures		Balance
	Central	Local	
1994	3.6	8.4	−1.2
1995	3.3	7.9	−1.0
1996	3.0	8.1	−0.7
1997	3.2	8.5	−0.7
1998	3.7	9.1	−1.1
1999	4.6	10.1	−1.9
2000	5.6	10.4	−2.5
2001	5.3	12.0	−2.3
2002	5.6	12.7	−2.6
2003	5.5	12.7	−2.2
2004	4.9	12.9	−1.3
2005	4.8	13.7	−1.1

18.3.3   Extrabudgetary Funds, Levies, and Charges

A crucial issue relating to the evolution of government finances, and specifically to the relation between central and local government, is the future role of extrabudgetary and off-budget revenues at all levels of government. Extrabudgetary funds (EBFs, *yusuan wai zijin*) are distinguished from budgetary funds by two features: (1) they come under decentralized management and allocation by different agencies and organizations, and (2) they are earmarked for specific uses (Wong 1998, 193; Wong 1997; World Bank 2002).

At present, the most important fully authorized components of EBF fall in to four categories (West and Whiting 1998): fees collected by public institutions and administrative agencies, the township unified levy and village retained fund, contributions to social insurance funds, and fees collected by local finance bureaus. It is possible to view EBF activities as a way for local governments to claw back some autonomy, to free expenditures from strict central mandates, and to increase the overall rate of revenue mobilization (Bahl 1999, 84). However, there are several negative elements:

• Reliance on extrabudgetary funds creates further inequities across regions and across government agencies. These inequities arise because regions differ in their ability to generate extrabudgetary revenues and because extrabudgetary revenues are not subject to redistribution across regions.

• There is a considerable inducement for local governments to engage in fiscal manipulations to increase the amount of these extrabudgetary revenues. The more locally raised money that can be channeled into either of these accounts, the less local government will be required to share with the center. The result is a kind of tax avoidance practiced by the local governments against the center.

• There is an uncontrollable proliferation of fees and levies that the government has found impossible to curb despite repeated calls. For example, one survey in Hunan Province found that TVEs were subjected to more than 100 types of fees, paid to 60-odd administrative units and agencies. Given the fact that EBFs are irregular and imposed at local discretion, there is little to prevent a corrupt local official from arbitrarily imposing a new fee to fund his own administrative expenses.

The central government has tried to address these issues by abolishing specific items of illegal and unjustified fees. The central government has clearly reacted to the fact that collection of taxes, fees, and charges in rural areas became a major source of peasants' discontent. Although some fees are unreasonable, others go to the improvement of services, like schools and hospitals, and it is difficult for peasants to tell the difference. The best solution would be to make finances transparent and involve rural residents in decisions with regard to township finances, including what kind of services peasants want and how they are going to share the burden. Indeed, this objective is a significant motive behind the Chinese government's otherwise rather tepid support for village-level democracy.

18.3.4   Abolishing Local Taxes and Stepping Up Transfers

In the first decade of the 2000s, a relatively consistent approach to the problem of rural finance has gradually emerged from the Chinese central government. Essentially that approach relies on increased transfers from higher levels of government and reduced local taxation of the farm economy. This approach perhaps first became evident during the Western Development Program (WDP). As part of the WDP, higher-level budgetary authorities began providing direct subsidies for administrative personnel and education to poor counties in the western regions. The greatest part of these subsidies goes to urban personnel. Central money is used to cover deficits in local social security funds, bring government personnel wages up to national standards, and pay relief to unemployed workers. These transfers redistribute budgetary income geographically but do not directly address the urban-rural gap or the problems in rural local finance. However, this approach has been steadily expanded to rural areas. Transfers have been expanded to reach rural education and basic health insurance in some of the poorer provinces. The central government has made a commitment in principle to bring rural education into the formal budgetary system nationwide by 2010, which would necessitate a major increase in central government transfers (Budget Report 2006).

During 2004 a major policy initiative emerged with the abolition of agricultural taxes in several Chinese provinces. In 2005 this initiative was spread to 22 of China's 31 provinces. Ending the agricultural tax substantially reduces the tax burden on farmers, and also significantly shrinks the tax base of local governments. Obviously, abolishing this tax is possible only with a significant commitment to transfer funds to local governments from higher levels. In principle, such transfers ought not to be difficult, since the agriculture tax, at around 60 billion yuan, only accounts for 2.2% of budgetary revenues. But it is not necessarily so easy to ensure that the money actually reaches its preferred target. The role of the county fiscal authorities has been strengthened, and county-level bureaucracies were already somewhat overgrown and sometimes overbearing. It is not enough to increase tranfers: they must also be administered effectively.

18.3.5   Arbitrary Nature of Transfers

Overall, the central government's new budgetary power, derived from the fiscal reform of 1994, has been used in a pragmatic, but not very consistent, fashion to resolve problems as they have emerged. As the central government has dispensed with adequate financial resources, it has used them to fund a steadily increasing array of transfers to local levels. The main force behind transfers is the rebate of taxes, something that was agreed to in the implementation of the fiscal system but that favors provinces that paid larger sums to the center in the past. Of central-local transfers in 2000, 47% were this type of rebated taxes. Another 4.3% of rebates were rule-driven, systemic transfers, tied to a specific formula and purpose. That left fully 48.7% of transfers that are discretionary, ad hoc payments from center (Zhang and Martinez 2002; Wong 2005). Many of these discretionary payments are earmarked for good purposes: western development, education, social security, and government wages in poor areas are all prominent justifications.

However, this system has a number of disadvantages, two of which are most significant. First, since the transfers are not guided by an overall developmental framework, they are not very effective in transferring income to lower-income regions. The impact of transfers to poor regions is swamped by the impact of other special purposes and tax rebates to richer areas (Wong 2005). Second, because transfers are not rule driven, they have perverse incentive effects. Local government officials have strong incentives to be seen as needy by upper levels of government. They do not have the confidence that they will continue to receive budgetary support if they improve the governance and living conditions of their populations.

18.4   FISCAL DEFICITS AND FISCAL POLICY

Fiscal policy has the ability to shape macroeconomic conditions, primarily through the ability of budgetary authorities to run deficits (stimulating demand and the overall economy) or surpluses (restricting demand). In general, given the overwhelming pressure of fiscal erosion until recently, Chinese fiscal policy has tended to adapt to macroeconomic conditions, rather than shape them. Chinese budgetary deficits have generally been modest. After an initial bout of deficit spending in 1979–1980, China tried to keep deficits around 1% of GDP in most years of the 1980s and early 1990s. After 1998, however, fiscal policy shifted gears as China was faced with the rising unemployment resulting from state-sector downsizing and the external effects of the Asian financial crisis. Against this background, the Chinese government began to implement expansionary fiscal policies. Undoubtedly encouraged by trends with respect to budgetary revenues, which indicated that overall government finances were being placed on a sounder basis, the government risked an increased deficit well over 2% of GDP from 2000 to 2002 (see Table 18.1). However, as the Chinese economy surged forward and overheated after 2002, deficits were cut back to 1.1% of GDP in 2005.

An important limitation to deficit spending today is the concern about a possibly unsustainable increase in government indebtedness. China faces a challenging set of future spending demands, including the restoration of capital to debt-ridden state banks and welfare payments to pensioners and the unemployed. Currently the overt public debt in China is modest: at the end of 2005 official government debt was only 17.9% of GDP (Budget Report 2006). However, many types of government obligations are not included in official debt tallies. A recent attempt by the Chinese Ministry of Finance to account for all types of government obligation came up with a much higher figure of 55% of GDP (O'Neill 2002; Kynge 2000). This figure included special bonds issued to recapitalize the banking system (see Chapter 19) and other domestic obligations, as well as foreign debt owed to the World Bank, the Asian Development Bank, and foreign governments. This more realistic figure indicates some of the problems China faces. With total budgetary revenues still less than 20% of GDP, though increasing, the ability to fund a government debt significantly larger than this cannot be taken for granted. Thus the decision to promptly reduce budget deficits from the peaks 2000–2002 is prudent.

Moreover, to meet the needs of funding future debt levels, China needs both to push through reforms to its tax system and create more vibrant capital markets, which would allow it to raise more money through taxation and private-sector financing.

18.5   INFLATION AND MACROECONOMIC CYCLES

Overall, inflation in China has been moderate since the reform era began, particularly in comparison with other transitional economies. Nevertheless, China has been troubled by persistent "boom-bust" cycles, in which periods of unsustainably rapid, inflationary growth have been followed by periods of macroeconomic austerity and slower growth. Figure 18.5 shows the three early inflationary cycles, as well as the post–1998 period when deflation was significant.

China's macroeconomic cycles show clear signs of fitting into a broader pattern of political-economic business cycles. Expansionary phases have generally been accompanied by significant decentralizing reforms and relaxed supervision of the industrial and financial systems. This relaxation phase has often been marked by significant institutional reforms. However, relaxation/ expansion has often been followed by inflation and other signs of macroeco-

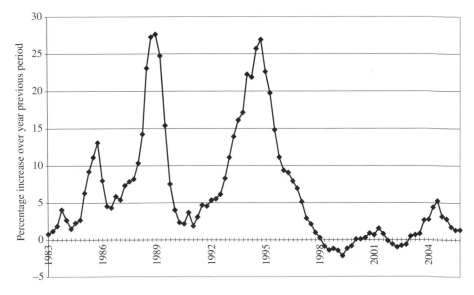

Figure 18.5
Consumer price inflation (quarterly)

nomic imbalance. Transport or energy bottlenecks, for example, or balance-of-payments difficulties have frequently accompanied inflation. In response to these "warning signs," policy has typically shifted to a more cautious stance, with institutional reforms scaled back or even reversed, while macroeconomic austerity measures are put in place. Such contractionary phases are often characterized by a politically more conservative policy line as well. Only after this "tightening-up" phase controls inflation and causes economic growth rates to plummet does the policy environment change in a way that facilitates further reforms and renewed growth. While cycles recur and are costly, they also seem to demonstrate that policy-makers can control inflationary impulses when they respond vigorously to inflationary warning signs.

China underwent an inflationary crisis during 1988–1989 that shook the foundations of its political and economic system. Inflation jeopardized the economic-reform process and fueled popular discontent, thereby contributing to the political crisis that culminated at Tiananmen Square on June 4, 1989. High inflation occurred in spite of repeated expressions by the Chinese leadership of their determination to hold inflation rates below 10% and in spite of traumatic historical experience with inflation. China had experienced hyperinflation in the 1940s and two years of serious inflation in the early 1960s, following the collapse of the GLF. However, these historical memories failed to prevent the collapse of macroeconomic discipline during the late 1980s. Moreover, another inflationary outburst occurred in 1993–1994, though with far less dire consequences. In this later inflationary outburst, incomes rose rapidly enough that most residents experienced real improvements in living standards notwithstanding the inflation. Still, the experience was sufficient to evoke a renewed commitment to fighting inflation from the Chinese government.

After the inflationary surge of 1993–1994, Chinese policy-makers declared their intention to achieve a "soft landing." Looking back on China's experience of macroeconomic cycles and recognizing that overly harsh contractionary policies were as much to blame for the cyclical pattern as overly expansionary policies, macropolicy shifted toward the objective of a gradual elimination of inflation over two years. Instead of stomping on the brakes, policy-makers tried to tap the brakes repeatedly. By the end of 1997 a soft landing had been achieved, as inflation was brought down virtually to zero. Since that time, overall price stability has been achieved. Nevertheless, policy-makers have frequently struggled to find effective policy settings in the face of rapidly changing conditions. China fell into deflation between 1998 and 2002. Consumer prices declined for 26 months during 1998–2000 and again for 14 months in 2001–2002. In the entire five-year period, by the end of 2002, overall consumer prices declined 1.5%. Beginning in 2003, however, the macroeconomic environment shifted into a new expansionist phase. A surge of inflation during 2004 put an end to the deflation but it was not sustained, and by 2005 the consumer price inflation had fallen back to modest levels (see Figure 18.5).

18.6 MONETARY POLICY

Under the planned economy, the uses of money were circumscribed by the plan, while, conversely, households faced frequent shortages of consumer goods, so money did not carry the full range of purchasing options it carries in a market economy. During market transition in the former Soviet Union macroeconomic policy was viewed primarily through the lens of monetary policy's role in stabilizing the economy. "Big bang" transitions were also "big bang" stabilizations. Prices were rapidly liberalized, so it was essential that the money supply be stable and strictly controlled to prevent runaway inflation. The results included big fluctuations in the real economy—including large recessions—while the real economy adjusted to completely new monetary and macroeconomic relationships.

In China monetary policy adopted more gradually to the needs of a market economy. Households increased their demand for money, even for the narrowest definition of money, currency in circulation. From 5.8% of GDP in 1978, currency in circulation climbed steadily to 16.9% of GDP in 1993, before finally stabilizing near that level. In other words, the velocity of circulation of money declined, as households were satisfied to hold large money balances. Demand for broader definitions of money, such as M2, increased even more rapidly (discussed in Chapter 19).

A full discussion of monetary policy in China is beyond the scope of this section. Chapter 19 discusses financial institutional reform in China, with most attention given to the banking system. For current purposes, it is sufficient to note two basic characteristics of Chinese monetary policy. First, by definition, monetary policy has accommodated the cyclic phenomena described in the previous section. Clearly "relaxation," decentralization, and systemic liberalization can only lead to inflation if demands for real resources are accommodated by credit policy. In fact, each of the expansionary cycles has been accompanied by an acceleration in the pace at which credit is extended to the real economy. Conversely, during each austerity phase the rate of credit creation has been brought down to near or below the rate of inflation.

Monetary policy has been driven by the same political-economic forces that drive the business cycles as a whole.

This fact is somewhat striking because the formal institutions that make monetary policy have undergone substantial change during the period under review. A central bank has been created, and management of monetary policy nominally accorded to the bank's board of governors. The instruments that govern credit supply and money creation have gradually shifted toward a system of reserve requirements, with central bank lending augmenting the resources of commercial banks when necessary. Rather than recounting those changes, it is sufficient to note that none has yet been sufficient to serve as an effective check on the cyclic process.

In part this failure may be due to the fact that interest rates have never been deregulated, and thus have never been free to play a stabilizing role. Interest rates have been adjusted in an attempt to keep them in a reasonable range. However, adjustments have never been quick enough to fully reflect the range of cyclical factors. Thus real interest rates (nominal interest rates minus the rate of inflation) have been significantly negative during times of high inflation and significantly positive during times of minimum inflation. In a sense, such interest rates act as automatic *destabilizers*. During inflationary periods when policy-makers are most interested in curbing demand for credit, low real interest rates actually stimulate credit demand; conversely, when the economy slows and policy-makers might be looking for a revival of investment, high real interest rates discourage firms from borrowing. Not surprisingly, with fixed interest rates, bank officials repeatedly imposed credit ceilings to reinforce the control they exercise through reserve requirements and central bank discounting.

18.7 CONCLUSION

Neither fiscal nor monetary policy can be said to have effectively driven China's macroeconomy to a stable equilibrium. Instead, both have adapted gradually to the evolving conditions of China's increasingly market-based economy. Monetary policy was expansionary and accommodative during the first 15 years of transition. Since 1998 monetary policy has tried to moderate the deflationary impact of real economic conditions without reigniting the cyclical inflationary dynamic that had become familiar in preceding years. Thus far, China has been able to maintain a remarkable level of macroeconomic consistency, underpinning the high-investment, high-growth economy that has become so characteristic of China today.

BIBLIOGRAGHY

Suggestions for Further Reading

Bahl (1999) and Brean (1998) are good overviews of the fiscal system, while Lu and Wiemer (2005) highlight the single most striking recent change. Wong (2005) lays out the way the system may be changing at present. OECD (2005) has a good discussion of the interaction between budget and government administration.

Sources for Data and Figures

Figure 18.1: Modigliani and Cao (2004, 146).

Figure 18.2: *SYC* (2005, 271) and earlier volumes.

Figure 18.3: *SYC* (2005, 272–75) and earlier volumes.

Figure 18.4: *SYC* (2005, 276) and earlier volumes.

Figure 18.5: Compiled from monthly consumer price index from the National Bureau of Statistics, published in various venues. *China's Latest Economic Statistics; China Monthly Statistics*. NBS Web site: http://www.stats.gov.cn/tjfx/jdfx/t20051110_402290694.htm

Table 18.1: *SYC* (2005, 271) and earlier volumes, with adjustments. Budget Report (2006).

References

Bahl, Roy (1999). *Fiscal Policy in China: Taxation and Intergovernmental Fiscal Relations*. San Francisco: The 1990 Institute.

Bird, Richard M., and Duanjie Chen (1998), "Intergovernmental Fiscal Relations in China in International Perspective," *Taxation in Modern China*, edited by Donald J.S. Brean. London: Routledge, pp. 151–86.

Brean, Donald J.S., ed. (1998). *Taxation in Modern China*. London: Routledge.

Budget Report (2006). Ministry of Finance. "Report on the Implementation of the Central and Local Budgets for 2005 and on the Draft Central and Local Budgets for 2006." March 5. Beijing: Tenth National People's Congress.

Goyal, Rajan, J.K. Khundrakpam and Partha Ray (2004). "Is India's public finance unsustainable? Or, are the claims exaggerated?" *Journal of Policy Modeling*, 26, 3, pp. 401–20.

Hofman, Bert (1998). "Fiscal Decline and Quasi-Fiscal Response: China's Fiscal Policy and System 1978–1994," in Olivier Bouin, Fabrizio Coricelli, and Francoise Lemoine (eds.), Different Paths to a Market Economy: China and European Economies in Transition. Paris: OECD.

Kynge, James (2000). "China's Fraught Fiscal Future", *Financial Times*, Jan. 11.

Lu, Mai And Calla Wiemer (2005). "An End to China's Agriculture Tax." *China: An International Journal* 3, 2 (September): 320–30.

Modigliani, Franco and Shi Larry Cao (2004). "The Chinese Saving Puzzle and the Life-Cycle Hypothesis." *Journal of Economic Literature*. Vol. XLII (March), pp. 145–70.

Naughton, Barry (1987). "Macroeconomic Policy and Response in the Chinese Economy: The Impact of the Reform Process." *Journal of Comparative Economics*, XI:3 (September).

OECD (2005). *Governance in China*. Paris: Organization for Economic Cooperation and Development. Chapters 6–8. Available at: http://www.sourceoecd.org/governance/926400842X

SAC (Annual). *Zhongguo Tongji Zhaiyao* [Statistical Abstract of China]. Beijing: Zhongguo Tongji.

SYC (Annual). *Zhongguo Tongji Nianjian* [Statistical Yearbook of China]. Beijing: Zhongguo Tongji.

West, Loraine and Susan Whiting (1998). "A Study of Extrabudgetary Revenues and Expenditures" Seattle: University of Washington, Manuscript.

Wong, Christine P.W., ed. (1997). *Financing Local Government in the People's Republic of China*. Hong Kong: Oxford University Press.

Wong, Christine P.W. (1998) "Fiscal Dualism in China." In Donald J.S. Brean, ed., *Taxation in Modern China*, 197–208. London: Routledge.

Wong, Christine P.W. (2005). "Can China Change Development Paradigm for the 21st Century? Fiscal Policy Options for Hu Jintao and Wen Jiabao after Two Decades of Muddling through." Berlin, Germany: Paper prepared for the Asia Department, Stiftung Wissenschaft und Politik.

World Bank (2002). *China: National Development and Subnational Finance: A Review of Provincial Expenditures*. Washington, DC: World Bank.

Zhang, Zhihua and Jorge Martinez (2002). "The System of Equalization Transfers in China." International Studies Program Working Paper, Andrew Young School of Policy Studies, Georgia State University.

Until very recently China's financial system lagged behind the rest of the economy in the transition process. The banking sector has been one of China's most protected industries, overregulated, dominated by state ownership, and protected from international competition. It is not that institutional innovation has been lacking in the financial sector. Quite the contrary: China has fundamentally restructured its banking system and experimented with numerous financial innovations. But these innovations have often failed and new institutions have not yet been allowed to play the dynamic and independent role that financial institutions can play in a market economy. Meanwhile, economic growth and the development of a market economy are posing new demands on this financial system.

The financial system is currently the focus of a great deal of attention from policy-makers, and it is in the midst of a period of rapid change. Heretofore, financing was dominated by banks, especially state-owned banks. China's financial system can thus be characterized as "deep but narrow" (Box 19.1). Chinese banks will be exposed to increased competition as China phases in its commitments as a member of the WTO. Most importantly, China has agreed to allow foreign-owned banks to provide domestic currency services to domestic residents without geographic restrictions beginning on December 11, 2006. In the meantime, China's capital markets, including stock markets, are also in the midst of a difficult period of reform, regulation, and retrenchment. These features lead to worries that the financial system is lagging behind other aspects of China's economic development and may become a source of economic vulnerability.

Section 19.1 provides an overview of China's financial system. It reviews the process of financial deepening, while stressing that the system remains relatively narrow. While the institutional foundations for a more diverse financial system have been laid, those institutions have generally not been allowed to take on a prominent role, and the financial system has remained dominated by banks, especially state-owned banks. Sections 19.2 and 19.3 examine the

Box 19.1
Financial Deepening and Financial Broadening

Financial development in any country can be usefully decomposed into *financial deepening* and *financial broadening*. Financial deepening is defined as an increase in the ratio of financial assets to national income, or GDP. The ratio of financial assets to GDP is a measure of the extent to which past saving has been transformed into investment through the intermediation of financial institutions. Financial deepening occurs both because more wealth has been created, relative to income, and because a larger share of wealth is held indirectly, in the form of financial claims on the entities that control physical assets. Financial deepening indicates how effectively financial institutions have performed their primary function, mobilizing saving for investment.

Financial broadening refers to an increase in the variety of financial institutions and instruments. Financial broadening occurs as capital markets develop with a variety of participants buying and selling stocks, bonds, and other instruments. Financial broadening is associated with the increasing importance of new types of market traders, such as stockbrokers. Even more important, it is associated with the growth of institutional investors such as insurance companies, pension funds, and mutual funds that themselves hold financial assets while also selling assets with new characteristics to their customers. Financial broadening implies a greater choice for savers and for investors, which allows the financial system to more efficiently match up different uses with various sources of funds. In developed economies, investors and firms are moving toward reliance on capital markets rather than banks as the primary form of financial intermediation, and financial innovation continues unabated, particularly the creation of new types of securities.

Together, financial deepening and broadening are integral to the growth of an economy. An effective financial system facilitates the sharing of information between investment projects and potential investors. It makes possible an efficient allocation of risk, permitting an appropriate balance between the saver's need for liquidity (short-term access to savings) and the need for long-term commitment of resources to productive projects while balancing the varying appetites for risk that different market participants may have. An effective financial system also contributes to corporate governance and effective monitoring of borrowers. The complex of interacting markets provides multiple channels for revealing and responding to economic shocks, as well as moral hazard. Because it broadens the capital base and allows greater investment, as well as contributing to higher efficiency through selection of better investment projects, financial development is associated with faster sustained growth in an economy (King and Levine 1993). Financial broadening, combined with effective financial market regulation, implies that in the long run the financial system should be more stable and robust. The diversity of financial markets and instruments allows the system to respond quickly to economic changes as they emerge and to shift some of the riskiest investments to those parties most able to afford them.

banking system in particular, focusing on the twin problems of institutional reform and nonperforming loans. Section 19.4 discusses equity (stock) markets that have been created but remain underdeveloped, with a lack of transparency and high volatility, and of moderate size. The next section briefly examines informal and curb markets, and the importance of retained funds. Then we look briefly at the problem of financial system risk. The Asian financial crisis of 1997–1998 revealed that rapidly growing economies with financial-system shortcomings similar to those in China were vulnerable to significant economic disruption.

19.1 THE FINANCIAL SYSTEM IN THE PLANNED ECONOMY AND UNDER REFORM

The financial system under the planned economy was remarkably shallow. The government-run banking system made up virtually the entire financial system, which provided trade credit and payments services to facilitate the exchange of goods. Credit enabled firms to hold inventories, but there was no long-term lending for investment projects and, of course, no stock or bond markets. The financial system was purely "passive," meaning that important economic decisions were never based on financial considerations: Decisions about which investments to undertake were made by planners and financed from the government budget; banks merely accommodated the physical flows that the planners arranged. However, there was a large retail banking network, including rural credit cooperatives in nearly all townships (market towns) that provided households the opportunity to put savings safely in the bank, if they had any to begin with. And a system of trade credit, albeit highly inefficient, was in place to support transactions beyond local areas. These were nontrivial accomplishments for the low-income economy that China was at that time.

Today China has virtually all the institutions of a modern financial system. The central bank, the People's Bank of China (PBC), sets monetary policy and provides credit to the commercial banks. The banking system has grown and diversified, and now includes a full panoply of commercial banks, government policy banks, and independent banking institutions. Capital markets have developed, particularly after the establishment of the Shanghai and Shenzhen stock exchanges in 1992. Financial and institutional innovation has been nearly continuous since the 1980s. However, the basic features of the evolution of the financial system can be captured in two points: first, the financial system has gotten much deeper (Figure 19.1). However, the system remains quite "narrow," in the sense that it continues to be dominated by the banking system (Table 19.1). We examine each of these points in turn. As China marketized, households and unincorporated businesses increased their saving, and those savings predominantly flowed into the banking system (Chapter 18). The banking system was transformed, becoming an important channel for household surpluses to be invested by businesses, and taking on the role of intermediation typical in a market economy. The money measure M2, consisting of currency plus demand and savings deposits, increased steadily from 32% of GDP in 1978 to 162% in 2005 (Figure 19.1). This is much higher than most other economies, and higher than East Asian economies, such as Japan. The most important component of China's financial deepening

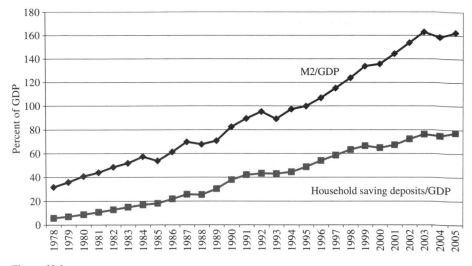

Figure 19.1
Financial deepening—M2, household deposits (percent of GDP)

Table 19.1
Sources of funds raised in domestic financial market (percent)

Year	Bank lending	Treasury bonds	Corporate bonds	Stocks
2000	72.8	14.4	0.5	12.3
2001	75.9	15.7	0.9	7.6
2002	80.2	14.4	1.4	4.0
2003	85.2	10.0	1.0	3.9
2004	82.9	10.8	1.1	5.2
2005	78.1	9.5	6.4	6.0

was the increase in household balances: household saving deposits increased from 6% to 77% of GDP between 1978 and 2005. The substantial increases in both these ratios meant that financial resources were available for investment in China.

The steady deepening of the financial system in China contrasts with the experience of other transitional economies. It would be reasonable to anticipate that the transition from a socialist to a market economy should lead to financial deepening—after all, a huge demand suddenly opens up for previously unavailable financial services. But in fact, in many of the European transitional economies the sudden release of prices in the face of pent-up inflationary pressures led to a surge of inflation that wiped out the value of accumulated financial balances. Many households found that their life savings had become worthless. In Russia, for example, broad money [M2] declined from 80% to only 20% of GDP between 1990 and 1993. At the same time, the economic disruption that accompanied the "big bang" caused incomes to drop, and new saving declined even more. In those economies, financial systems shrank even more rapidly than the overall economy declined, and they had to be rebuilt from the ground up.

China's more cautious approach to transition averted this kind of financial demolition. Savings held in the banking system have been protected. During periods of high inflation (at the peak of the macroeconomic cycles described in Chapter 18), household term-saving deposits have been given supplemental interest at the rate of CPI increase, protecting the value of deposits. As a result, China has a far "deeper" financial system than any other major transition economy.

Yet this achievement also has costs. With a banking system flush with cash, government officials have naturally been tempted to tap into bank surpluses to fund their clients and pet projects. As described in Chapter 13, financing for SOEs shifted strongly toward reliance on bank financing during the mid–1980s. In part, this change was a conscious policy response to the decline in budgetary revenues and represented an attempt to shift investment financing from costless budgetary grants to interest-bearing, repayable loans. However, bank financing was also used to prop up numerous loss-making SOEs. Indeed, the "soft-budget constraint" described in Chapter 13 has as its counterpart the virtually unlimited access to bank lending on the part of loss-making firms. In a broader sense, the entire period of "reform without losers" depended upon the ready supply of bank credit to nonviable firms. As this type of lending continued through the 1980s and much of the 1990s, an enormous stock of nonperforming loans built up in the state-owned banking system. For a long time policy-makers were loath to acknowledge this problem, preferring to continuously draw resources out of the banking system to prop up the state-enterprise sector. Only at the end of the 1990s, as discussed in section 19.3.1, did policy-makers begin to grapple with the real costs of strengthening the banking system.

This reliance on the banking system had further repercussions in the hesitancy of policy-makers to allow other types of financial institutions to play an important role in the financial system. Policy-makers have been very sensitive to financial innovations that might draw a substantial amount of funds from the banking system. After all, they have been reliant to a significant extent on the supply of funds through the banks. Therefore, policy-makers have been careful to maintain control over the overall financial system, and they have tried to maintain robust flows of saving into the banking system. This orientation doubtless helps explain the second of the major characteristics of the Chinese financial system: it has remained dominated by the banking system, and capital markets have remained relatively underdeveloped. Capital markets represent an alternative to bank financing and contribute to the development of a diverse, or broad, financial system. Firms may finance investment directly, raising funds by selling stock or bonds. China's stock markets took off quickly during the early 1990s, but they have remained hobbled by governance and transparency issues. Issuance of corporate bonds has been even more severely restricted. As Table 19.1 shows, banks have maintained their dominance of the financial system in China, and they even tended to increase their share of the market somewhat. Banks have accounted for around 80% of the funds transferred through formal financial institutions during the 2000s. Corporate bonds accounted for only 1% of funds raised, until the initial emergence in 2005 of significant corporate borrowing. The stock market (discussed later) fell below 4% of funds raised in 2003, and has remained a modest source of funding so far in the decade. China's financial system remains narrow and bank dominated. Other East Asian economies have large banking systems, but because China's most important banks are state owned, China's financial system is also state dominated.

19.2   THE BANKING SYSTEM

Today (2005), the Chinese banking system consists of a core of state-owned institutions, most of which are descended from the institutions of the planned economy. Table 19.2 shows the main banks and their share of total banking assets. Total assets in 2003 were 28 trillion RMB, more than twice GDP. The first three categories—the Big Four state-owned commercial banks, joint-stock commercial banks, and city banks—are the focus of government restructuring efforts and receive the most attention. Together they account for three-quarters of total banking system assets.

19.2.1   State-Owned Commercial Banks

The four state-owned commercial banks are the direct descendants of the planned-economy bank system. They are huge organizations, each with hundreds of thousands of employees and ranking among the top-50 largest financial institutions in the world in terms of assets. In the days of the planned economy, these banks were subdivisions of a single government bank, sometimes dubbed the "monobank" because it was a single organization with a

Table 19.2
Assets of banking institutions

	2003		2005	
	Billion yuan	Percent	Billion yuan	Percent
I. State-owned commercial banks ("Big Four")	15,194	55.0	19,657	52.3
II. Joint-stock commercial banks	3,817	13.8	5,812	15.5
III. City commercial banks	1,462	5.3	2,036	5.4
IV. Other	7,166	25.9	9,962	26.6
(State-owned) policy banks	2,125	7.7	—	
Rural credit cooperatives	2,651	9.6	3,721	9.9
Rural commercial banks	38	0.1		
Urban credit cooperatives	147	0.5		
Nonbank financial institutions	910	3.3		
Postal savings	898	3.3		
Foreign-funded financial institutions	397	1.4		
Total: all banking institutions	27,639	100.0	35,964	100.0

virtual monopoly on financial business. The monobank kept the books on transactions that were mainly among divisions of the state-run economy, serving as accountant and cashier. During the 1980s the "monobank" was broken up: Four state-run commercial banks—the "Big Four"—were carved out of the monobank and given independent identities and assigned sectors of operation.[1] The largest in terms of assets is the Industrial and Commercial Bank of China (ICBC), which took over lending and deposit taking in the cities. The Agricultural Bank of China (ABC) did the same in the countryside; it has the largest staff and 44,000 branch offices. The Construction Bank (CCB) focused on project financing and took over many of the relatively skilled personnel who had been involved in investment planning in the old system. The Bank of China (BOC), which had actually maintained some overseas branches throughout the planned-economy period, handled foreign-trade and foreign-exchange transactions. It has a smaller, more qualified staff and fewer branches than the others, but the second-highest level of assets. The four have quickly displayed separate personalities: the CCB and BOC possess higher levels of expertise and have restructured most rapidly. The ABC faces the most challenging economic environment, operating as it does in the lower-income rural sector. All four are burdened with the legacies of the old system, however: overstaffing, lack of skills, and absence of a business orientation. Most critically, each was accustomed to providing credit on demand to government and

1. In 1984 the People's BOC was also carved out of the rest of the monobank, as the first step in its long process of conversion into a true central bank.

party officials in the local and national bureaucracies. Inevitably, the banks' political subordination to government officials led to a steady build up in unrecoverable loans.

The Big Four today are in the midst of a major program of restructuring (discussed in section 19.3.3). A concerted effort was made to place the Big Four on a commercial basis during a round of banking reforms in 1994 through 1998 (coinciding with the beginning of the second phase of economic reform, Chapter 4). New laws were passed to provide charters for the central bank and for commercial banks, providing some protection for independent decision-making on the part of commercial banks. In order to remove banks from the pressure and influence of local government officials, the power of national bank headquarters was strengthened, and personnel power centralized in Beijing. The People's BOC (the central bank) organized a system of regional branches similar to the U.S. Federal Reserve banks. The national credit plan, by which the government directly influenced lending decisions, was finally abolished in 1997. Reserve requirements for the commercial banks were reduced, and central bank lending to the commercial banks was cut back as well. All these changes gave the Big Four much greater autonomy, while at the same time tying their fortunes much more closely to the central government. From this time on, all important changes of the Big Four, for better and for worse, were determined from Beijing. The Big Four state-owned commercial banks are still the most important part of the entire financial system, accounting for 53% of total banking system assets in 2005. Whether they can be successfully restructured is the most important challenge facing the Chinese financial system.

19.2.2 Joint-Stock Commercial Banks

The joint-stock commercial banks (JSCBs) present a sharp contrast to the Big Four. There are 11 JSCBs, which were set up between 1986 and 2001. Each JSCB is a new entrant and thus is relatively unburdened by baggage from the planned economy era.[2] The JSCBs have younger, more highly trained staffs and considerably lower amounts of bad loans on their books. The JSCBs have introduced a welcome element of competition in the banking system, and they have steadily gained market share, surpassing 15% of total banking-system assets in 2005.

However, the JSCBs are not as free from entanglements as might at first appear. Each of the JSCBs is special: each one has a unique history and a

---

2. However, the largest of the JSCBs, the Bank of Communications, is the reincarnation of a bank originally founded in 1908.

unique set of relationships with government officials and interest groups, usually at a local level. While the JSCBs are not owned by the national government, they are typically owned by diverse groups of SOEs, government agencies, and non–state-owned enterprises. Typically, local governments retain substantial influence. Several of the joint stock banks are listed on the stock exchange, so a minority of shares is held by the public. One, the Minsheng Bank, claims to be private, since no government agencies hold shares in the bank. However, the principals of the bank have a long history of close and complex links to government and party officials in both Shanghai and Beijing.

19.2.3   City Banks

About 100 city banks were created from urban credit cooperatives that had been set up to provide lending services to small-scale urban firms. Mostly dating from 1998, city banks are predominantly controlled by local governments and generally operate on a local scale. Compared to JSCBs, the city banks are smaller in scale and generally have weaker management and lower asset quality. A few city banks stand out for better quality, though, including the Bank of Shanghai and the Nanjing City Commercial Bank.

19.2.4   Other Banks

Chinese data frequently lump all remaining banks into a large "other" category, accounting for about one-quarter of total assets. This approach can be quite misleading, however, because the institutions in this category have very different characteristics. The two largest institutions in the "other" category are both legacies from the planned economy period, but they are very different in nature.

19.2.4.1   Policy Banks

When the state-owned commercial banks were chartered to operate as commercial businesses, three policy banks were set up to take over lending in support of government policy objectives. The idea was to free the commercial banks from pressure to undertake politically popular projects. The three policy banks have taken different roads: the China Development Bank has expanded its portfolio of large-scale infrastructure projects in an aggressive and entrepreneurial way; the Export-Import Bank has settled into a normal export-promotion role; and the Agricultural Development Bank has foundered, trying to define a role for itself in an increasingly marketized rural economy. Put together, the three policy banks are quite large, accounting for nearly 8% of total assets in 2003.

19.2.4.2   Rural Credit Cooperatives

RCCs were developed during the 1950s as part of the overall system of collective organization in the countryside (Chapters 5 and 10). The RCCs were only loosely integrated into the state financial system—they were never part of the "monobank"—and they played an extremely positive role in bringing trade finance to the countryside and allowing farmers to purchase modern inputs crucial to higher agricultural productivity. Moreover, the RCCs thrived during the early phase of reform in the countryside. The RCCs channeled local savings into TVE development at a time when TVEs were highly profitable. The resources and revenues of the RCCs grew dramatically during the 1980s.

However, in the intensified competitive environment of the 1990s, the RCCs ran into serious difficulties. TVE profitability plummeted and many RCC clients had trouble repaying loans. Interest rates on RCC loans were fixed below market rates, so profitability was low while village leaders often steered loans to their own favored projects. In China's more mobile society, traditional community oversight no longer worked well. By 2002, China's RCCs had a negative net equity and hundreds of billions of RMB in nonperforming loans, although the accounts were in too much disarray to know the true state of affairs.

In 2003, policy-makers finally began to grapple with the serious issues confronting the RCCs. A broad program of restructuring was introduced. Money has been pumped into the RCCs, modest amounts by the standards of the urban financial bailout, but large relative to China's rural economy. New lending programs, including microcredit groups, have been introduced to the RCCs (Gale and Collender 2006). The RCCs have been amalgamated into county-level bodies, and some have been converted into joint-stock banks. By the end of 2005, the bank regulator was able to report that the RCCs had positive equity (165 billion RMB) and a much reduced NPL burden of 325 billion RMB, or 15% of outstanding loans. A beginning has been made in reviving a rural institution of potentially pivotal importance (CBRC 2006).

19.2.4.3   The Fringe

Besides the five categories already described, remaining players in the Chinese banking industry are quite small. A postal saving system, patterned, ironically, on Japan's now-troubled system, is the largest single component. Foreign-funded banks play a role, but a quite modest one; in fact, foreign-funded banks actually account for a smaller share of bank assets in 2003 than they did in 1997, as domestic firms have become more competitive in foreign-exchange lending and as obstacles to foreign-bank expansion have continued to be formidable. An important development at the end of 2005 was that permission was given to start-up genuinely private banks in 20 localities. This marked the first time the Chinese government explicitly permitted private banking, although private banks had been informally tolerated during some periods and places. In the future, foreign-funded and private banks are both likely to play a significant role in China's banking sector.

Through the present, however, most of the "fringe" of China's banking industry looks more like the wreckage of failed experimentation than like the embryos of future financial giants. The nonbank financial institutions referred to in Table 19.2 include a range of failed experiments. Some are investment companies. One variety was the international trust and investment companies, but these were sharply retrenched following the 1998 default and bankruptcy of the Guangdong International Trust and Investment Company (GITIC). Domestic trust companies proliferated during the 1980s but were cut back sharply in the mid–1990s. Enterprise investment companies still exist but have been subject to increasing control. The urban credit cooperatives were another failed experiment: Initially set up everywhere, the more successful ones were captured by municipal governments and converted into "City Banks," while those remaining did not qualify for conversion because their scale and asset quality were inadequate. In sharp contrast to other areas of the economy, institutional experimentation has been largely unsuccessful in China's banking sector. Repeatedly, dramatic liberalization programs have been attempted, only to be scaled back in subsequent years. New financial institutions have been created, only to be shut down or restructured into more modest organizations.

Overall, then, China's banking sector is still dominated by government-controlled entities. In 2003, 72% of assets are in three classes of organizations that were legacies of the planned economy: the Big Four, the three policy banks, and the rural credit cooperatives. Another 19% of assets were in new banks, predominantly set up under the tutelage of local governments (including JSCBs and city banks). That leaves 9% of assets on the fringe, including new foreign and (now) private banks, as well as the hulks of yesterday's past experiments. China's banking system needs a great leap forward to move into the modern competitive economy.

19.2.5   Central Bank and Regulatory Apparatus

In April 2003, China established an independent regulatory body, the China Bank Regulatory Commission (CBRC). The CBRC was instructed to keep regulatory oversight independent from the monetary-policy functions of the central bank (PBC). This was an important administrative step on the way to establishing an arm's-length, regulatory relationship with a diverse group of banks. This is necessary to fulfill China's WTO commitments, but also essential for the next stage of financial-sector reform in China.

19.3   WEAKNESS OF THE BANKING SYSTEM

The Chinese banking system entered the twenty-first century woefully unsuited for the demands of a sophisticated market economy. In part, this inadequacy was a result of the fact that the banking system that was created under the planned economy simply did not have the skills, incentives, or culture required to make an effective commercial banking system, and it was inevitable that it would take time and resources to build up those capabilities. But in part, the banking system's lack of capacity was the result of the function the banks played during the transitional period.

During the period of "reform without losers" (1978–1993), the banking system played the key role in buffering workers in inefficient firms from the consequences of increased competition. Soft budget constraints implied continuous bank lending to unviable clients. Many "zombie firms" were kept alive by steady infusions of credit from the state banking system. These firms had no hope of repaying their loans, and a large buildup of nonperforming loans (NPLs) inevitably occurred. In addition, of course, NPLs increased because of ordinary government control over the lending process. Given the pervasive politicization of the economy and the continuing rule of the Communist Party, it was inevitable that many unproductive projects were funded for patronage or showcase purposes, or from simple lack of economic analysis. Clearly, these practices led to extensive resource misallocation and heavy burdens on the banking system. At the same time, the protections put in place for savers—particularly the protection of savers' balances during high-inflation phases—meant that the banks were paying a relatively high price for the savings they controlled. The "spread" between lending and deposit rates was narrow, and often negative. For example, during 1995 the banks were paying 24% annually for long-term deposits while charging 14% annually for long-term loans. Inevitably the banks found their profitability impaired and their capital steadily eroded. By the mid-1990s, then, the banking system was in desperate shape (Lardy 1998, 92–127).

These processes led to a steady buildup in NPLs, combined with a steady erosion in the banking system's own ability to generate funds to pay off their own bad loans. In the most generous interpretation, the bad-loan burden reflected the costs of transition. The political system had used the resources in the banking system to compensate groups that would otherwise have been losers, keeping the process of economic transition on track. But such a process could not be sustained forever. Bad loans continued to increase, so that by the late 1990s they were around 40% of total lending. This is a huge number: an international comparison might indicate that a maximum of 5% of total lending as NPLs might be considered a benchmark of economic health. The banks were staggering under a heavy burden. Moreover, the banks had nowhere near the resources necessary to resolve the problem. The international benchmark of whether a bank has adequate financial resources to deal with unexpected adverse events is the Basle standard, which requires that banks have owned equity capital equal to 8% of (risk adjusted) assets. When the Big Four were carved out of the monobank in the mid–1980s, they met this standard. The ICBC had a capital adequacy ratio (CAR) of 10%, and the ABC had a CAR of 12%. However, as the banks were forced to write off various kinds of loans, their CARs plummeted to around 5%, while the share of NPLs soared. The banks were technically insolvent and unable to resolve their problems.

Finally, at the end of the 1990s policy-makers shifted gears and recognized that the fragility of the banking system was a huge potential problem. Undoubtedly their recognition of the dangers was brought home by the magnitude of the Asian financial crisis in 1997–1998, which plunged previously well-performing economies such as Korea, Thailand, and Indonesia into enormous difficulties, with huge real costs. Chinese policy-makers began to recognize that rather than looting the banking system, they needed to inject substantial resources into that system in order to avert a potential economic crisis. Since 1998, perhaps the highest priority of policy-makers has been to strengthen the financial system. The challenge of the banking sector can be best understood by examining nonperforming loans from the standpoint of the "stock" problem and the "flow" problem. The stock problem refers to the difficulty of clearing up the existing stock of bad loans already on the bank's balance sheets: it primarily reflects the legacy of past costs. The flow problem refers to the need to prevent new lending decisions from creating new nonperforming loans, and instead making current lending decisions on a commercially sound basis: it primarily reflects the need for the banking system to maintain healthy practices, currently and in the future.

19.3.1   Measures to Reduce the Stock of Nonperforming Loans

Because the outstanding volume of bank lending is large, bad loans, default risk, and costs of recapitalization of the banking system are all large relative to GDP. China began to publish reasonably informative data on NPLs at the end of 2002 (Table 19.3). For the two most important categories of commercial banks—the Big Four plus JSCBs—the data show the total value of NPLs declining from 2.3 trillion RMB (19% of GDP) in 2002 to 1.2 trillion RMB in 2005 (6.7% of GDP; see Table 19.3). As discussed subsequently, the data should be regarded with appropriate skepticism, but they can provide a benchmark and be used to build up a realistic description of the resources Chinese policy-makers have already committed to their banking system.

Starting in 1998 the Chinese government had already begun a massive effort to recapitalize the banks. It began with the issuance of 270 billion RMB in special bonds to help the Big Four boost their CARs. This was followed in 1999 by the most important single policy in the recapitalization, the establishment of four state-run assets-management companies (AMC), one for each of the Big Four. The AMCs purchased nonperforming loans at face value from the Big Four commercial banks. The loans they purchased were those made before 1996; there was thus an attempt to erect a kind of "firewall" between the bad old lending decisions made before the downsizing of the SOE sector and the newer lending, which in theory at least should be relatively better and more responsive to the market. Thus the creation of the AMCs was an intregal part of the enterprise reforms (described in Chapters 8 and 13), as well as bank restructuring per se. However we look at the creation of the AMCs, note that the 1.4 trillion of NPLs were removed from the Big Four bank balance sheets *before* the 2002 accounting shown in Table 19.3. This fact implies that total accumulated NPLs in the Big Four *before* the AMC buyout were about 3.5 trillion RMB (2.1 plus 1.4 trillion), almost exactly one-third of GDP. Remov-

Table 19.3
Nonperforming loans in China's banking system

Year	State-owned banks		Joint-stock banks		Total percent of GDP
	Billion yuan	Percent of loans	Billion yuan	Percent of loans	
2002	2,088	26.2	203	11.9	19.0
2003	1,917	20.4	188	7.9	15.5
2004	1,575	15.6	143	4.9	10.7
2005	1,072	10.5	147	4.2	6.7

ing a large part of this enormous NPL burden from the banks averted a liquidity crisis and prepared the ground for more fundamental banking reform.

The job of the AMCs is to recover as much value as possible from the NPLs they bought from the banks by selling the loans to third parties, foreclosing on assets and auctioning them off, or swapping loans for equity (Ma and Fung 2002). To pay the Big Four for the loans, the AMCs themselves had to assume 1.4 trillion RMB in debt (which they did by issuing 820 billion in new interest-bearing bonds, backed by the Ministry of Finance, and taking over from the Big Four 580 billion in debt to the central bank.) The AMCs have become important players and innovators in China's financial markets, and by the end of 2005 the AMCs had disposed of two-thirds of their total NPLs, and recovered 177 billion RMB in cash, about 13% of the total. That is a respectable recovery rate for NPLs. However, it is unlikely that there will be much in asset recoveries beyond this level, and the Chinese government will have to assume the bulk of the AMC debt as the AMCs wind up operations.

In theory, the Big Four were not supposed to receive any further government bailouts after the AMCs. Bailouts undermine the efforts to create a hard budget constraint for the banks themselves and to force them to bear responsibility for their own lending decisions. However, an end to bailouts was simply not realistic given the magnitude of the problem. The solution adopted was to provide a further infusion of capital to individual banks, but only in conjunction with a broader restructuring designed to make each of the Big Four stronger and more independent commercial banks. To qualify for the restructuring, the banks had to first make a credible effort to write-off recently generated NPLs using their own financial resources (profits and loss provisions). Thus in 2003, the CCB sold off 130 billion RMB in bad loans for 50% of their face value and wrote off another 60 billion RMB, reducing its equity capital by 125 billion RMB. Moreover, they had to significantly improve internal management and controls. The CCB laid off a quarter of its staff, closed one-third of its branches, and invested heavily in information technology and a more tightly managed organizational structure. At the end of 2004 these actions by CCB, and parallel efforts by BOC, were deemed to have been sufficient, and the two banks received US$45 billion for a further stage of recapitalization. In this case, the funds came not from the Ministry of Finance, but from China's foreign exchange reserves (thus, ultimately, from the Central Bank). The cash infusion was used as equity capital from a new bank holding company, the Huijin Corporation, which became the ownership agency with authority over the banks (Huijin is thus parallel to SASAC in the industrial and commercial sphere.) The other two of the Big Four hoped to follow as soon as possible. These measures are part of a program to strengthen the banks' current operations and convert them into publicly listed joint-stock companies (discussed in the following sections). They have been quite effective in the short run in reducing the stock of NPLs. As Table 19.3 shows, the Big Four state-owned commercial banks had brought their NPLs down to 10.5% of outstanding loans by the end of 2005. The CCB and BOC have done still better, bringing NPLs down below 5% of lending and CAR above 10%, both near or above international benchmarks. But this achievement has cost the Chinese government a healthy sum. Adding together the various rounds, including projected recapitalization of the ICBC and ABC, the Chinese government will have injected a sum equal to about 2.4 trillion RMB (US\$300 billion), just into the Big Four, in order to provide them with the basis of financial health. To build on this resource commitment, the banks will have to dramatically improve the operation of the banking system.

19.3.2   The "Flow" Problem: Ensuring Good Lending Decisions

It is insufficient to deal with the "stock" problem of nonperforming loans. All the money the Chinese government has spent to recapitalize the banks will be in vain unless the banks are able to create the proper incentives so that the "flow" of new lending is shaped by market return and a prudent attitude toward risk. Indeed, reducing the stock problem even makes it *more* difficult to resolve the flow problem, because today's bailout raises the likelihood of additional bailouts in the future and signals that bank managers may not be held responsible for today's decision-making. Conversely, if the money results in a healthy financial system, it will have been well spent.

In fact, Chinese banks still operate at relatively low levels of efficiency. Margins and costs are high. Poor lending decisions continue to be made, and transactions are slow and procedures cumbersome. Studies of regional bank markets indicate that despite the creation of interbank markets for funds, funds do not systematically move to regions with higher rates of return (Park and Sehrt 2001; Boyreau-Debray and Wei 2005). It is unlikely that the system does a very effective job of channeling funds to projects with the highest returns. Any banking system has two main jobs: financial intermediation and provision of liquidity services—that is, providing funds to enable transactions (Meek 1991). The Chinese system does both its jobs, but with relatively low efficiency and at high cost.

Some of the most important issues shaping the improvement in Chinese bank efficiency include the following:

Redefining the Scope of Bank Business. In developed economies banks have increasingly moved away from a focus on lending and toward a "fee for service" model. But in China, fee income in 2004 was only 0.17% of assets, one-quarter to one-fifth the level in other Asian economies. Because of low fee income and high bad-debt expenses, total return on assets for Chinese commercial banks was only 0.44% in 2004, about one-third the level in other Asian economies. Among the potential areas of expanded fee earning, perhaps the most lucrative is credit cards. Although Chinese banks have issued hundreds of millions of debit and cash cards, slow development of credit bureaus and clearing networks has slowed the growth of the credit card business.

As a result, almost all the net income of Chinese banks comes from the interest spread between deposit and lending rates. Fortunately, since 1998 overall price stability has created an environment in which deposit rates could be reduced while lending rates have been kept fairly high. Banks have made good profits from the interest spread. Moreover, bank assets have diversified. A decade ago the bulk of bank assets consisted of loans to SOEs. Today consumer lending plays a significant role: Mortgage lending, a new business since the housing privatization of the late 1990s, has increased steadily and accounted for about 9% of total credit outstanding at the end of 2004. Government and banking system bonds constitute a large and growing share of bank assets. The banking system's more diversified portfolio gives it greater resilience in the face of economic shocks.

Internal Oversight. Oversight of lending decisions still appears to be seriously deficient. Loan officers have a great deal of decision-making power with respect to individual loans and bear most of the responsibility for identifying credit risk. Once a loan is granted, oversight weakens further. Although credit departments classify loans according to repayment status, procedures for assessing changes in creditworthiness or projected cash flows are limited. There are few departments specializing in the proper classification and addressing of doubtful and nonperforming loans. Yet loan officers, and even top managers, earn low regular salaries. Excess discretion and lack of controls over lending decisions has led to a number of serious scandals. Indeed, *both* of the immediately previous heads of the Bank of Construction—generally considered the best run of the Big Four banks—were implicated in corruption scandals, lost their jobs, and faced prison sentences or criminal charges. Indeed, corruption has surely been an important cause of NPLs in the first place.

Incentives. Loan officers have been given employment contracts rewarding them for increasing revenues and maintaining low default rates, but not for accurately assessing future risks or making provisions for future defaults. (It is extremely difficult to design contracts that provide adequate risk sharing, and this has certainly not been done in the Chinese case.) Given the ease with which individual loan officers may roll over loans, postponing problems indefinitely, no individual has the incentive to carry out the overhaul of administration and procedures necessary to improve operations. During certain periods (e.g., 1998–2001) bank incentives systems were tailored to reducing the absolute value of NPLs outstanding, and credit decisions became more cautious. During other periods incentives focused on NPL ratios, providing a strong incentive to increase the base of new lending.

Skills in Business Appraisal and the Development of a Credit Culture. Credit personnel are seriously lacking in training relating to due diligence issues such as the proper analysis of cash flow and assessment of repayment ability and risk. Reporting of problem loans follows subjective and inconsistent criteria. These characteristics mean that the ability of the banks to discriminate between good and bad loans on commercial principles is still quite limited.

19.3.3   Current Bank-Reform Program and Prospects for the Future

During 2005 a comprehensive bank restructuring and reform program got under way, based on the reasonable degree of success achieved in writing off NPLs and recapitalizing the banks. The timing of the program was also influenced by the looming beginning of foreign-bank entry, mandated for December 11, 2006, by China's WTO accession agreement. As described earlier, at the end of 2004 the two best of the Big Four, the CCB and BOC, were restructured into joint-stock corporations wholly owned by the Huijin Corporation, an arm of the central government. Then CCB took the next steps, first selling stakes to strategic international investors, then listing a portion of its shares on the Hong Kong stock exchange. Specifically, CCB sold 8.7% of its shares to the Bank of America and 6% to Temasek, an investment company that is an arm of the Singapore government, and then it sold another 12% of its shares in an initial public offering. The successful offering valued CCB at an enormous US$67 billion. Although the CCB remains more than 70% owned by the central government, it has received a major infusion of money and skills, and it now has a share price that will track its every move. The Bank of America, which has the option to raise its stake to 19.9%, has pledged to be an active partner, dispatching a 50-person technical assistance team to CCB headquarters and gaining a seat on the board of directors. These steps, represent a new phase in the development of commercial capabilities at CCB, and in the internationalization of the Chinese banking system. The BOC is poised to follow the CCB's lead during 2006, having negotiated the sale of strategic stakes to the Royal Bank of Scotland (10%), among others.

However, while the CCB achieved remarkable success through the end of 2005, and while the other Big Four banks will attempt to follow the same path, future outcomes will likely be highly diverse. The other Big Four banks may have a harder time finding foreign partners, since they are less attractive than the CCB, and the Chinese government may be less eager to make concessions to draw in strategic partners. Indeed, some foreign banks have chosen to partner with JSCBs, regarding them as more dynamic and less burdened by legacy costs than any of the Big Four. Most notably, Citibank and HSBC, two of the world's largest banks, have both elected to partner with JSCBs: HSBC has taken a 19.9% stake (the maximum permitted by current law) in the Bank of Communications, the largest of the JSCBs, and Citibank has a smaller stake in Shanghai Pudong Development Bank and appears to envisage development of its own network of bank branches after 2006. Significantly, both HSBC and Citibank have gained entry into the credit card business through their strategic alliances. Clearly, by 2010, China's banking landscape will have changed dramatically, with heightened competition and with foreign banks playing a large role through their stakes in the Big Four, through their cooperation with JSCBs, and through their own subsidiaries.

How will the Chinese banking system adapt to this new competitive environment? First, besides the Big Four and a few of the JSCBs, much less progress has been made in other areas of the banking sector. The RCCs are deeply troubled, notwithstanding a major government effort to restructure them. The policy banks have a significant NPL burden, and very little information has been available lately on the evolution of their NPL rates. These institutions, which account for a quarter of total assets in the banking system, probably have over US$100 billion in NPLs and no clear plan for resolution. Second, the Chinese government will almost certainly impose "soft" market barriers on foreign-bank expansion in China, limiting the rollout of branches through capital requirements and regulatory delays. Thus we should expect to see an extended period of shakeout, in which some of China's banks fail but others succeed. While the risks are significant, the possibility of a positive outcome is also substantial.

19.4   STOCK MARKETS: LEARNING TO CRAWL?

China's stock markets were initiated with the help of local government policy entrepreneurship. The municipalities of both Shanghai and Shenzhen, in competition, invested resources in building stock market institutions in the late

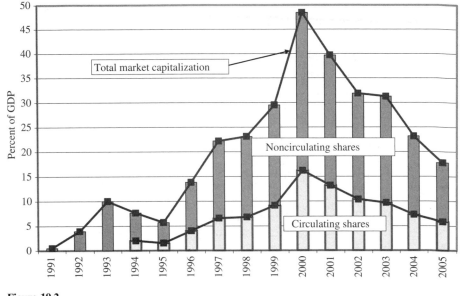

Figure 19.2
Stock market capitalization as share of GDP

1980s, before the central government gave the go-ahead for a formal market setup. Not until 1991 did the central government gave its blessing, along with the accelerated development of Shanghai's Pudong Special Zone. Once they got the go-ahead, the markets in both Shanghai and Shenzhen grew rapidly, and by 2000, China had the second-largest capital market in Asia, after Japan, at least by some measures. The creation of stock markets was a significant achievement, but there were shortcomings that made the achievement much less substantial than it might initially appear. After 2000 those shortcomings became increasingly apparent to market participants in China, and the following year the market began a sustained decline that lasted more than four years. Between mid–2001 and mid–2005, China's GDP increased by more than 50%, but stock market capitalization decreased by more than 50%. Clearly, something was seriously wrong with the market that led it to become so thoroughly detached from the dynamism of the Chinese economy. Figure 19.2 shows the rise and decline of China's stock markets in relation to GDP. Why does the Chinese market display these trends?

19.4.1 Birth of the Market: Raising Funds for the State Sector

Chinese stock markets were given the go-ahead by the top political leadership—and especially by the premier at the time, Zhu Rongji—because of the role they could play in reforming the state-enterprise sector. As described in Chapter 13, the conversion of traditional SOEs to joint-stock and limited-liability corporations was the centerpiece of SOE restructuring and downsizing during the 1990s. As part of this policy approach, the development of stock markets for former SOEs seemed promising: "partial privatization" through sale of a minority stake in a listed firm would introduce new shareholders into the firm, provide a channel for better information disclosure, and perhaps lead to further privatization. Privatization through several successive tranches of stock sales had been successfully adopted in several Western European countries. Most important of all, however, stock market listing also promised to create a new source of funding for SOEs. When Chinese enterprises listed on the stock markets, the revenues from the initial public offerings (IPOs) almost never went to the national treasury. (That is, SOEs were never "sold" by the government.) Instead, virtually all the sales proceeds went to the listing firm itself or to its immediate parent. Government officials accepted this arrangement because of their worries about the financial position of SOEs. The enterprises of course welcomed listing because the result was a large new source of relatively unencumbered funds.

For the first decade of stock market development, more than 90% of the firms listing were SOEs. Indeed, almost all of the largest non-defense-related state industrial enterprises have been listed on the exchanges. By the end of 2004 there were 1,377 firm listed on the markets in Shanghai and Shenzhen, most of them still government controlled. Initial development of the markets in China was thus clearly part and parcel of the process of state-enterprise reform, rather than being an alternative funding channel for independent and private firms. This would not necessarily have been a bad beginning, if initial listing had led quickly to more thorough privatization. Instead, this subordination to the state-owned economy became a congenital defect, and stock market reforms became stalled. They present a classic example of the way in which a gradualist reform can get "stuck" halfway through the process of change.

19.4.2   Characteristics of the Market

19.4.2.1   Circulating and Noncirculating Shares

In almost all cases, when an SOE was listed on the market, the government and the parent of the enterprise retained a majority of the equity in the firm. Given the desire for speed, combined with worries about control and profiteering from insider privatization, the shares that were retained by government and other sponsors were simply not allowed to circulate. Although the proportion of shares that could circulate increased gradually through 2000, at a maximum only one-third of the total shares were allowed to circulate. Since 2001 policy-makers have attempted to break down the distinction between circulating and noncirculating shares, but with no success until 2005. As a result of this paralysis, the status of circulating and noncirculating shares was basically unchanged through at least 2004.

Table 19.4 gives more information on the ownership types of all Chinese shares. The government directly owns the largest proportion of total stock, 46% at the end of 2001, in its capacity as sponsor of IPOs. "Sponsor legal persons" are usually the state-owned corporations that are the parents of the listed firms, or in some cases holding companies established to manage government shares. Government-owned and "sponsor legal person" together make up direct and indirect government control, and "legal person" ownership reflects the continuing interest of the firms that sponsored the listing in the first place. Although the "legal person" shares, by definition, cannot be sold on the market, they can be transferred through private placements, and 5.3% of total shares have been sold in that way by the end of 2005. A small proportion of nonnegotiable shares were issued to workers in the firm, but these shares have now virtually disappeared.

Even the circulating shares trade in segmented markets. A-shares, which are the primary type of shares traded, are denominated in Chinese currency and available only to Chinese citizens. B-shares are denominated in foreign currency and were originally reserved for foreign investors, although Chinese citizens may now hold them as well. H-shares are shares listed by Chinese companies on the Hong Kong stock exchange or on other markets outside

Table 19.4
Capital Structure of Listed Firms

	Percent of total shares	
	2001	2005
I. Noncirculating shares	65.3	61.8
IA. Sponsors' Shares	59.8	53.4
Government-owned	46.2	—
Sponsor Legal Person	12.7	—
IB. Private Placement of Legal Person Shares	4.7	5.3
IC. Worker Shares	0.5	0.1
II. Circulating shares	34.7	38.2
A-shares	25.3	29.9
B-shares	3.1	2.9
H-shares	6.4	5.4

China.[3] Originally this market segmentation was due to the inconvertibility of the RMB. Chinese policy-makers wanted to collect Chinese household saving but also tap into foreign capital without exposing themselves to the possibility of destabilizing capital flows. Prices differ in these market segments: typically A-shares are priced higher than B-shares or H-shares, presumably due to the limited investment options available to Chinese households. More generally, segmentation causes market inefficiencies: disclosure standards, regulations, trading volume, and risk premiums differ across markets; and liquidity and pricing efficiency are lower.

19.4.2.2 Low Contestability

By far the most important consequence of the segmentation of share types and markets is the low contestability of control. Since majority control of most listed companies remains firmly in government hands, private shareholders have no possibility of gaining control over a company. In such a situation, the market can only rarely serve to discipline the management of existing firms, and the stock market's role in improving corporate governance is minimal. The Chinese stock exchanges have not served until now as a market for corporate control. Moreover, under such a government-dominated ownership system, stock market listings have only led on to privatization in a minority of cases, in which legal-person shares have been placed with private investors.

19.4.2.3 Rationing of Listing Opportunities

Because listing is so lucrative for an SOE, the demand for permission to list is very large. Regulators have formally or informally rationed the right to list on the exchange virtually since the beginning. It is not enough that a firm meet the requirements for listing; it must also compete for the favor of regulators in gaining permission to list. This necessity produces a further distortion of the market's ability to value companies accurately.

19.4.2.4 Thin Markets

The market is "thin," meaning that the supply of desirable shares is quite limited, and as a result, prices (especially for A-shares) have tended to be very high. At the market's peak in 2000, Chinese shares were extremely expensive,

---

3. In August 2005, 117 firms had issued H-shares, and all but two were listed on the Hong Kong stock exchange. The two exceptions are listed in Singapore only. Seventeen of the H-share companies have joint listings in New York or London, and 32 have issued both H- and domestic A-shares. Chinese start-ups listed on NASDAQ are not included in the H share count.

with a price/earnings ratio above 40. (In comparison, the U.S. S&P 500 price/earnings ratio has historically been between 15 and 25.) Of course, rapidly growing companies should have higher price/earnings ratios to account for higher expected future earnings. But even accounting for China's high growth rate, Chinese A-share valuations have traditionally been very "rich." When noncirculating shares are sold through private placement, by contrast, they sell for a very large discount because of restrictions on their liquidity. The stock markets are also characterized by rapid turnover and relatively high volatility. Annual turnover is typically above total market value in both Shanghai and Shenzhen. Restricting the comparison to the one-third of shares that actually circulate, annual turnover is typically more than three times market value. The Chinese markets are also relatively volatile.

19.4.2.5 Weak Disclosure and Regulation; Multiple Related-Party Transactions

Until 2001, Chinese disclosure and regulation standards were extremely poor. Since that time, there has been a sustained effort to improve disclosure. Corporate reports must now be posted on the Internet in a timely fashion; accounting standards have improved; and a competitive business press improves transparency. Despite these improvements, disclosure standards and reliable information still lag far behind the standards of developed-economy markets. In particular, since the regulatory system was crafted with an eye to protecting the rights of the government as owner of companies, protections for minority shareholders are weak. But of course, in this market virtually all holders of circulating shares are limited to minority stakes.

These realities are especially problematic because of the form in which most state-owned firms are listed on the market. Typically, a state firm consolidated some or all of its income-earning assets into a subsidiary that was to be listed. The parent firm retained most of the shares, and also retained direct management of the nonproductive or loss-making assets. In some cases the parent companies transformed themselves into empty shell companies, with no productive assets at all, living off the dividend payments made by the subsidiary. In other cases, productive assets were divided among parent and subsidiary. An example of the latter case is CNPC, the China National Petroleum Company, the parent of Petrochina, which is China's biggest oil producer. Petrochina is an H-share-listed company, but only 10% of its shares circulate. CNPC retains some of the oil fields (though not Daqing, the largest), most of the social-service organizations, and all of the oil-field-service operations. Thus CNPC sells goods and services to Petrochina, while it is also completely dependent on the profit that it derives from its 90% stake in

Petrochina. At the same time, CNPC is entangled with the government regulators who, among other things, impose pricing regulations on Petrochina's extensive retail operations. Given the multiple related-party transactions between CNPC and Petrochina, a (minority) holder of Petrochina shares really has no way of knowing what he will get for his holding or of assuring that his rights are protected in transactions overseen by the dominant shareholder.

19.4.2.6   Policy-Driven Market

Given the limitations on individual company information and shareholder control, the Chinese stock market inevitably is driven primarily by changes in government policy. Studies have shown that market fluctuations are better explained as reactions to government policy changes, particularly those that affect liquidity on the markets, rather than as reaction to changes in underlying fundamentals of individual companies. Morck, Yeung, and Yu (1999) studied 40 emerging stock markets and found that individual firm share prices in the Chinese market were much more likely to move together in a given week than those in other markets. In essence, investors in the market are forced to gamble that the Chinese government will favor the further development of the stock market and hope that parent companies will choose to foster the share value of the their subsidiaries.

19.4.2.7   Insider Control and Manipulation

Worldwide, most stock exchanges are self-regulating organizations. Market participants set up cooperative structures to police each other for mutual benefit. Unfortunately, in the Chinese market, at least until recently, widespread opportunities for collusion have inhibited the evolution of institutions for self-regulation. Three types of agents are most important to the Chinese market: managers, securities companies, and regulators. The managers of state-owned firms, as discussed earlier, have a strong interest in securing a listing opportunity. Securities companies have a monopoly over trading and listing procedures. All the securities companies until 2002 were 100% state-owned companies, typically owned by local governments. Securities companies had the flexibility to put parties together to make deals while also holding substantial stakes themselves. The China Securities Regulatory Commission, the CSRC, holds the ultimately scarce resource of permission to list, as well as regulatory approval of various transactions. At its worst the market has been manipulated to the advantage of these three parties. Such manipulation is seen most clearly in the process of the initial public offering (IPO). Chinese IPOs have traditionally been more severely underpriced than in other markets, guaranteeing that any party lucky enough to be allowed to buy into the IPO would make a hefty (and quick) profit. The securities companies would guide SOEs through the listing process, rewarding interested parties with the right to buy the newly listing share and keeping a portion on their own account. The CSRC doled out positions in the listing queue, the SOEs would pay to get a place in line, and the securities companies managed the transaction that brought all parties together. This kind of insider manipulation drove market dynamics for many years.

In addition to the chronic, institutionalized manipulation of the market, there have also been a number of egregious market manipulation scandals involving individual stocks. Given the thinness of many markets, informal investment funds were able to manipulate prices and profit from them. It is sometimes said that the Chinese market is dominated by individual investors, since there are 73 million individual accounts of market investors (2005). However, more detailed studies have repeatedly shown that the various investment funds control a large number of accounts and transactions. Public money is often channeled into speculative investments. The odds on gambling are greatly improved by the asymmetry of the bargain: individuals can keep a portion of any windfall profits, while posting all losses to the public account. The unpredictability of the market and the ease with which it is subject to manipulation led one of China's most famous reformist economists, Wu Jinglian, to declare that China's stock exchange was "more like a casino than a market."

19.4.3   Reform Initiatives: Selling Down the State Share: Changing the "Split Share Structure"

A concerted effort to reform China's stock market was begun in 2001. There were two main strands to the policies adopted. The first was to begin the process of selling down the state's noncirculating shares by requiring that 10% of all new listings be sold to benefit the social security fund. The second was to dramatically increase transparency and information disclosure. These two measures together triggered the beginning of the long market decline described earlier. Although the policy to sell down the state's shares was quickly reversed, the regulatory measures were maintained. Market participants concluded, probably correctly, that the days were over in which the government provided an implicit guarantee to prop up the market. Moreover, as information disclosure improved, a series of scandals made the public increasingly aware of the reality of market abuses and manipulation. An exodus from the stock market began.

The most common interpretation is that the market is allergic to measures that will increase the supply of state shares, since, with demand unchanged, such measures will drive down the values of the existing shares. While this is part of the explanation, the remarkable fact of the post–2001 period has been that the market has declined steadily *without* any increase in the supply of state shares. Given the importance of policy and momentum in the market, the slump in the market became self-reinforcing as expectations were continuously revised downward. Moreover, the securities companies have always been major players in the market. In the bull market through 2001, securities companies were the primary beneficiaries. During the bear market since 2001, securities companies were caught out and have suffered severe financial losses. Most of the securities companies are technically insolvent, and many cannot redeem their clients' accounts. With liquidity of the securities companies severely constrained and no obvious reason for the market to change direction, the market entered a prolonged slump.

It was not until 2005 that policy-makers finally devised a way to begin to reduce the volume of noncirculating shares. The solution found was to allow each listed company to devise its own program for converting the status of noncirculating shares. In each company the shareholders of the circulating shares had to agree to the company's specific proposal. In practice, this meant that each company had to reward holders of its circulating shares with bonus shares (typically on the order of three bonus shares for every 10 circulating shares held) as compensation for permitting the conversion to circulating status. At the same time, (predominantly) government holders of noncirculating shares had to agree to actually sell no more than a small proportion of their shares for a further three-year lockup period. This approach finally broke the logjam surrounding noncirculating shares, and by the end of 2005 more than 200 firms had passed proposals to convert their noncirculating shares. Potentially, by the end of 2005 the long decline of the Chinese stock market was nearing an end, and a period of growth, on healthier foundations this time, could reemerge.

19.4.4 Institutional Investors

The limitations on China's stock market development have naturally had an effect on the development of institutional investors. Institutional investors, such as mutual funds, pension funds, and insurance companies, benefit from a healthy market, but they also contribute to the healthy development of the market. Institutional investors are often large shareholders with an interest in monitoring enterprise performance and serving as "patient" owners with a long-term interest in improving corporate governance and performance. The stock market reforms of 2001 envisaged the government social security fund beginning to play a major role in the stock market as an institutional investor. The failure of this effort left China without a significant long-term institutional presence of the market. Since 2001 there has been a steady growth of institutional investors, but from a small base. The number of mutual funds has grown, but in the first six months of 2005 their purchases were only a little over 2% of total market transactions. The most interesting development has been the permission granted at the end of 2002 for qualified foreign investment institutions (QFII) to invest in the market. These are mutual funds operated by foreign banks or brokerages. Each fund has a specific quota of foreign-currency investments it can accept; the fund is then allowed to invest in RMB-denominated A-shares up to the limits of its quota. This system—pioneered in Taiwan and Korea—enables foreign investment in the domestic stock market while still retaining control over capital inflows and outflows. At the end of 2004 total quotas of US$3.25 billion had been approved. China's insurance companies have begun to participate in China's stock market, but stock holdings are limited to a small proportion of their assets for prudential reasons. In all these cases the legal form for new institutional investors has been created, and investment flows have begun, but so far the amounts are very small relative to the market as a whole. The prolonged decline in the market of course inhibits the pace at which institutional investors seek to enter the market.

19.4.5   Comparative Evaluation of China's Stock Market

With the previous discussion, we are now in a better position to evaluate the comparative development of China's stock markets. As Figure 19.2 showed, China's stock market reached a peak in 2000 when total market capitalization approached 50% of GDP. Such a figure would have marked China's stock market as comparable in size to other large developing countries, shown in Figure 19.3. But that figure was actually quite misleading. In the first place, valuations were inflated and not sustainable, and four years later total capitalization had fallen to 23% of GDP. As Figure 19.3 shows, China in 2004 was at the bottom of a group of comparable developing countries, equal to Mexico. Yet even this comparison is misleading, because it assumes that noncirculating shares have the same value as circulating shares, whereas in fact they sell at a discount, when they are traded at all. The value of circulating shares alone is only 7% of GDP. The figure to be used for comparison should be somewhere between total market capitalization and that of circulating shares alone. This would put China at the bottom of the large developing countries and, of course, far below the level of developed economies.

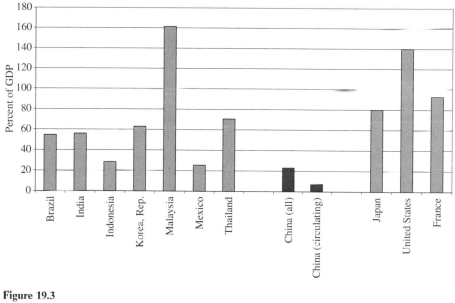

Figure 19.3
Chinese stock markets in comparative perspective, 2004

19.5   BOND MARKETS

Fixed-income securities play a very restricted role in China, relative to the banking system, and even relative to the stock market. Government bonds do serve as alternative assets for households, companies, and financial institutions. The total stock of government treasury bonds outstanding at the end of 2003 was 2.26 trillion RMB, amounting to 19% of GDP. Further, outstanding policy bonds, issued by policy banks and used to support large infrastructure projects, amount to 10% of GDP. These sums are probably not large enough to create a liquid, well-functioning market for government bonds, because the total includes a substantial volume of government debt that was allocated to different organizations—including banks—by government command rather than by market means. Only a portion of this figure circulates among domestic actors voluntarily seeking to diversify their asset holdings. The market for corporate bonds is even more underdeveloped. After numerous incidents with improper issuance of enterprise bonds, the government in recent years has authorized the issuance of an extremely small number of domestic bonds. Through the end of 2004 issuance of government-authorized corporate bonds never exceeded 36 billion RMB, which is virtually insignificant. However, the scope for corporate bonds began to expand in 2005. In late 2005 firms were authorized to issue short-term commercial paper for the first time. In sum, bond markets in China are extremely limited and lag even further behind the needs of the economy than does the stock market. There remains a huge scope for development in this area.

19.6   OTHER FINANCIAL MARKETS

Informal financial markets in China are large, important, and little studied. Three tiers of informal financial markets can be distinguished. At the "bottom," informal rural credit mechanisms—including credit clubs, moneylenders, and unregistered private banks—are very significant, particularly in the countryside. In a recent court case it was decided that private moneylenders were not usurious so long as interest rates were not more than four times officially regulated lending rates. According to estimates based on household surveys, in 1986 rural informal financial markets surpassed formal rural institutional lending in size (Xu Xiaobo et al. 1994, 218–20). At the "middle level," many state and collective firms have issued various kinds of promissory notes, "stocks," and other IOUs that are not formally recognized by the government (or included in the statistics in this chapter). These IOUs exist in a legal gray area, with the ability of lenders to collect essentially dependent on local government willingness to enforce specific contracts. Finally, at the "top," many local governments dispose of significant funds that are not included in the formal budget but are available for investment purposes. For example, government statistics on fixed investment reveal that "other" financial sources of investment (outside of bank lending, government funds, or private or enterprise-retained funds) equal about 4% of GDP annually, about half as much as formal bank lending. Most of these funds are controlled by local government officials or by entities set up under their patronage (such as local investment corporations or investment funds). Thus there is a large amount of financial intermediation occurring in China that is captured very imperfectly—or not at all—by officially reported statistics.

19.7   CONCLUSION

China's financial system faces two unique challenges. The first is to avoid instability while navigating imminent financial development and opening. This challenge relates primarily to the stability of the banking system. Figure 19.4 shows the comparative size of the Chinese banking system by showing M2 (currency plus bank demand and term deposits) as a share of GDP. Figure 19.4

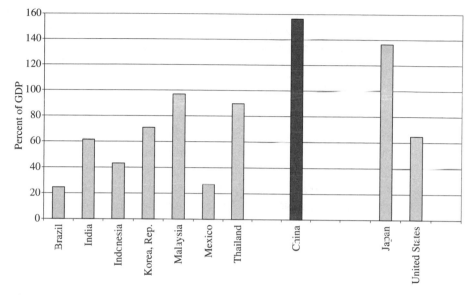

Figure 19.4
Chinese monetary depth in comparative perspective: M2 as a share of GDP, 2004

is in the same format as Figure 19.3, but the results of the comparison are reversed. China has much greater monetary depth than any other large developing country, and even more than Japan. It is the tremendous size of the banking sector that contributes to worries about China's financial stability. Even with the remarkable recapitalization of the banking system and the write-off of literally trillions of RMB in nonperforming loans, the potential for further losses is still significant. Simply because the banking system is so big—because the financial system is deep but narrow—the volume of bad loans and default risk, relative to GDP, is still fairly large. Unacknowledged debts within the Chinese system are still significant. Worries are persistant about both commercial banks and other financial institutions.

First, the performance of the commercial banks probably looks better than it actually is. Between 2002 and 2005, China went through the expansionary phase of a macroeconomic cycle, with extraordinarily rapid growth of credit and the economy. In such a conjuncture, a large proportion of total lending is new lending, and with favorable economic conditions very few new loans are nonperforming. However, in the downturn of the cycle, a significant proportion of those loans could turn bad, particularly if the cyclical fluctuation is large. Indeed, while the government has bailed the banking system out of a large potential crisis, government bailouts have also created long-term costs for the operation of the financial system, because of moral hazard. In fact, this issue of moral hazard permeates all layers of the banking system from the credit analyst who makes a "bad loan" because he knows the government will cover bank losses in the long run to the borrower who defaults because he knows the government will cover bank losses. The other worry is that unacknowledged debts in other financial institutions (other than the commercial banks) may be large. It is known that the volume of nonperforming loans at the rural credit cooperatives and the Agricultural Development Bank (among the policy banks) is quite large. Other areas where accounting for debt is weak include securities firms and local-government-guaranteed development projects. Given relatively low total government debt, these problems can be managed as long as policy-makers remain focused on prudent financial management. However, if policy-making veers off in a reckless fashion, financial problems could quickly emerge and snowball.

The second challenge is to develop the virtuous cycle that can be created through a well-functioning financial system. Financial oversight is a crucial component of improved corporate governance. In turn, accumulation of reliable financial markets is essential to the process by which citizens build up their stock of wealth. China needs the security of that accumulation to protect the interests of a population that will be aging rapidly in 10 to 20 years. Intermediaries such as pension funds and mutual funds, can provide social security to large segments of the population, ensuring that their economic gains over the past decades are not endangered. Pension funds, mutual funds, and insurance companies can perform their functions effectively only if they have efficient capital markets in which to invest. As discussed in Chapter 7, the unique demographic structure of China will cause rapid population aging, which will in turn place extreme pressure on the pension system in the coming years. This coming population aging challenges China to create a broad and deep financial system in a relatively short period of time. Chinese citizens do not have enough investment options to plan for their futures and are forced to rely too heavily on the government to provide pensions; it is only through further reforms to the financial markets that citizens can begin to invest and sufficiently provide for their future well-being. China's financial system still needs to undergo several further steps of development before it can really serve these diverse needs. When it does so, it can expect to find that improving institutions in different financial arenas reinforce each other's beneficial effects, creating a more transparent and more stable system.

With China's accession to the WTO in December 2001, the clock began to tick on a dramatic removal of restrictions on the activities of foreign banks. On December 11, 2006, China is scheduled to allow foreign banks to offer services in RMB to Chinese customers, without geographic restrictions. Adjusting to this change will be difficult, even after five years of preparation. Competition within China's contemporary banking industry is weak, and its role in improving banking efficiency has been limited. It can be expected that Chinese banks will be able to draw on their vast national retail networks for some time, giving them superior access to funds. However, foreign banks will likely compete aggressively for the most attractive borrowers, especially those in the most advanced coastal cities. We can anticipate rapid change in the banking sector in the wake of intensified competition. At the same time, it is entirely possible that the moribund Chinese stock market will spring back to life. Much of the excess valuation in the market has been worked off during the five-year downturn, and institutions and policies have been adopted that will serve to clear away much of the underbrush that has obstructed the development of a healthy market. If China is able to maintain financial stability over the next decade, we can anticipate an extraordinarily rapid phase of financial development as the financial sector quickly broadens, diversifies, and begins to meet the needs of a dynamic Chinese economy.

BIBLIOGRAPHY

Suggestions for Further Reading

For the comparative context of financial system and economic development, see Levine (1997) and Allen, Chui, and Maddaloni (2004). There are excellent and well-written introductions to China's stock markets: Green (2004a, 2004b) and Walter and Howie (2003). Lardy (1998) first demonstrated the parlous condition into which Chinese banks had descended in the 1990s. Hoshi (1995) describes how Japan dealt with a huge bad-loan problem after World War II. OECD (2005) is a good update.

Sources for Data and Figures

Data on European transitional economies comes from Dittus and Prowse (1996) and Caprio and Levine (1994, 16). Comparative Asian economies for 2001 are from CSFB (2002). Hong Kong, because of its interregional financial functions, has a much higher M2/GDP ratio (281%).

Figure 19.1: PBC Research (1992); *SYC* (2005, 675).

Figure 19.2: China Securities Regulatory Commission, at www.csrc.gov.cn/en/statinfo/index_en.jsp?path=ROOT>EN>Statistical%20Information

Figure 19.3: World Development Indicators.

Figure 19.4: World Development Indicators.

Table 19.1: PBC (2002, 30; 2003, 13; 2004, 18; 2005, 18). Accessed at www.pbc.gov.cn/english/huobizhengce/huobizhengcezhixingbaogao/

Table 19.2: China Bank Regulatory Commission, at www.cbrc.gov.cn. 2003: www.cbrc.gov.cn/english/module/viewinfo.jsp?infoID=726; 2004: infoID=966; 2005: infoID=1329

Table 19.3: China Bank Regulatory Commission, 2004 data at www.cbrc.gov.cn/english/con_tgsj/tgsj.jsp?moduleRegID=5&infoLANG=2//

Table 19.4: China Securities Regulatory Commission, at http://www.csrc.gov.cn/cn/homepage/index.jsp

References

Allen, Franklin, Michael Chui, and Angela Maddaloni (2004). "Financial Systems in Europe, the USA, and Asia." *Oxford Review of Economic Policy*, 20(4): 490–508.

Boyreau-Debray, Genevieve, and Shang-Jin Wei (2005). "Pitfalls of a State-Dominated Financial System: The Case of China." NBER Working Paper No. 11214, (March). Cambridge, MA: National Bureau of Economic Research. At http://www.nber.org/papers/w11214.pdf

Caprio, Gerald, Jr., and Ross Levine (1994). "Reforming Finance in Transitional Socialist Economies." *World Bank Research Observer*, 9(1), January, pp. 1–24.

CBRC. China Bank Regulatory Commission. www.cbrc.gov.cn

CBRC (2006). "The Achievement of Rural Credit Cooperative Reform Are Evident." www.cbrc.gov.cn/mod_cn00/jsp/cn004002.jsp?infoID=2279&type=1

CSFB (2002). Credit Suisse First Boston (Hong Kong) Equity Research. *China Financial Landscape: Metamorphosis-incomplete.* Hong Kong: CSFB, December 5.

Dittus, Peter, and Stephen Prowse (1996). "Corporate Control in Central Europe and Russia: Should Banks Own Shares?" In Roman Frydman, Cheryl Gray, and Andrzej Rapaczynski, eds., *Corporate Governance in Central Europe and Russia*, vol. 1: *Banks, Funds, and Foreign Investors*, 20–67. Budapest: Central European University Press [Distributed by Oxford University Press].

Gale, Fred, and Robert Collender (2006). "New Directions in China's Agricultural Lending." USDA WRS-06-01. www.ers.usda.gov/publications/WRS0601/WRS0601.pdf

Green, Stephen (2004a). *Enterprise Reform and Stock Market Development in Mainland China.* Frankfurt: Deutsche Bank Research, March 25.

Green, Stephen (2004b). *The Development of China's Stock Market, 1984–2002.* London and New York: RoutledgeCurzon.

Hoshi, Takeo (1995). "Cleaning Up the Balance Sheets: Japanese Experience in the Post-War Reconstruction Period." In Masahiko Aoki and Hyung-Ki Kim, eds., *Corporate Governance in Transitional Economies: Insider Control and the Role of Banks*, 303–59. Washington, DC: World Bank.

King, Robert G., and Levine, Ross (1993) "Finance and Growth: Schumpeter Might Be Right." *Quarterly Journal of Economics*, 108(3), August, 717–38.

Lardy, Nicholas R. (1998). *China's Unfinished Economic Revolution.* Washington, DC: Brookings Institution.

Levine, Ross (1997). "Financial Development and Economic Growth: Views and Agenda." *Journal of Economic Literature*, 35(2), June, 688–726.

Ma, Guonan, and Ben S. C. Fung (2002). *China's Asset Management Corporations.* Basel, Switzerland: Bank for International Settlements. (BIS Working Papers No. 115, August.)

Meek, Paul (1991). "Central Bank Liquidity Management and the Money Market." In Gerard Caprio, Jr., and Patrick Honohan, eds., *Monetary Policy Instruments for Developing Countries*, 17–19. Washington, DC: World Bank.

Morck, Randall, Bernard Yeung, and Wayne Yu (1999). "The information content of stock market: Why do emerging markets have synchronous stock price movement?" *Journal of Financial Economics* 58, 215–60.

OECD (2005). *OECD Economic Surveys: China*, Issue 13. Chapter 3: "Reforming the Financial System to Support the Market Economy," 137–76. http://hermia.sourceoecd.org/vl=2758661/cl=12/nw=1/rpsv/~3805/v2005n13/s1/p11

Park, Albert, and Kaja Sehrt (2001). "Tests of Financial Intermediation and Banking Reform in China." *Journal of Comparative Economics*, 29: 608–44.

PBC (Various years). People's Bank of China, Monetary Policy Analysis Group. *China Monetary Policy Report*. Beijing: China Financial Publishing House.

PBC Research (1992). People's Bank of China, Research and Statistics Department, *China Financial Statistics (1952–1991)*. Beijing: Zhongguo Jinrong.

SYC (Annual). *Zhongguo Tongji Nianjian* [Statistical Yearbook of China]. Beijing: Zhongguo Tongji.

Walter, Carl, and Fraser J. T. Howie (2003). *Privatizing China. The Stock Markets and Their Role in Corporate Reform*. New York: Wiley.

Xu Xiaobo et al. (1994). *Zhongguo Nongcun Jinrong de Biange yu Fazhan 1978–1990* [Chinese Rural Finance Change and Development, 1978–1990]. Beijing: Dangdai Zhongguo.

VII CONCLUSION: CHINA'S FUTURE

Shanghai 2005, from the Jinmao Tower in Pudong.

For centuries the pressure of population on China's limited natural resources has led to severe environmental degradation. A hundred years ago most of China had already been stripped of forests. Modern economic growth has created another set of challenges, creating massive pollution and apparently unsustainable demands on natural resources. Many regions of China present a picture of rapid economic growth and severe environmental damage. How serious are China's environmental problems? Do they threaten to undermine the progress being made toward a higher quality of life for the majority of Chinese citizens? This chapter provides an introduction to China's environmental problems without attempting to provide a definitive answer to these questions.

Economists frequently view environmental issues through the lens of the "environmental Kuznets curve." According to this conception, pollution and other environmental problems worsen during the early stages of economic growth and then begin to improve as a country reaches middle-income status. There are technological and preference-related arguments for this pattern. In terms of technology, early stages of industrialization often involve rapid spread of relatively crude production techniques that, while relatively easy to master, produce lots of by-products and pollution. Subsequently a broader technological capability gives access to cleaner and more efficient production techniques. In terms of preferences, poor people understandably place priority on economic growth to increase income and consumption. Public environmental quality is a "luxury good," and demand for environmental quality at low income levels is therefore initially limited, but it increases rapidly as incomes grow above a certain level. This viewpoint implies a certain degree of optimism about environmental problems, because it suggests that countries will develop the means and the will to tackle their own environmental issues as they develop.

There is considerable debate as to whether the environmental Kuznets curve accurately describes the variety of developing-country experiences

(Stern 2004). Nevertheless, it is a good tool for organizing a brief discussion of China's environmental problems. Clearly, China has experienced significant environmental deterioration over the past 20 years. Thus there is evidence to support the idea that China is on the downslope of the Kuznets environmental quality curve. But the Kuznets curve reminds us of that ultimate environmental quality is the outcome of many contending economic, technological, and social forces. There have been significant areas of environmental progress in China over the past 20 years, and there is growing concern among the population and in government policy-making circles about environmental problems in China. The capability to analyze environmental problems and the ability to implement and pay for cleaner and more efficient production techniques have grown. It is sometimes said that China's breakneck growth has been purchased at the cost of the environment but this contrast is far too simple. Growth has worsened many environmental problems but development has also brought China the means to address other environmental problems. We cannot yet discern whether these contending forces have enabled China to turn the corner to the upslope of the environmental Kuznets curve.

Emblematic of the growing environmental awareness in China is the growth of a national environmental policy and administrative structure. Environmental agencies were created during the 1980s, and the National Environmental Policy Agency (NEPA) gained administrative independence in 1988. During the March 1998 government downsizing, environment bucked the small-government trend, and the renamed State Environmental Policy Agency (SEPA) was promoted to ministerial status. Local governments down through the county level all have environmental bureaus. NEPA (1993) laid out a daunting list of China's major environmental problems, all of which are likely to have long-term effects both on natural ecosystems and on economic growth.

We can divide environment problems into two broad groups (Figure 20.1). The first group refers to pollution in the broad sense. Pollution causes the largest current costs. Urban air pollution causes more than 100,000 excess deaths annually, and millions of dollars in health costs. China's air is dirty, and getting dirtier. At the same time, pollution is the aspect of the environment most susceptible to a degree of optimism based on economic development and changing population preferences. China's urban air today is not dirtier than the air in major Western cities in the 1950s, and China's citydwellers are beginning to demand improvements in the air they breathe. The second group refers to the sustainability of resource use. In these cases, economic activities result in impairment of the natural system's ability to replenish itself, but the costs of this resource depletion are not necessarily apparent in today's economy.

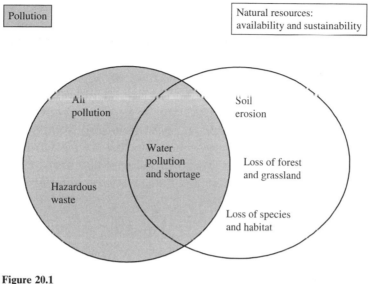

Figure 20.1
Pollution and resource sustainability

Indeed, some degree of depletion of resources might never lead to problems. However, because we do not know exactly where the boundaries of excess depletion begin, or what the carrying capacity of the system will turn out to be, these sustainability issues might present the greatest long-run challenges to well-being. Water is the critical resource in both groups, because it is highly polluted and currently being exploited in an unsustainable fashion. Water is the most important area of intersection between pollution and sustainability concerns. The other area of greatest long-term concern is the impact on the atmosphere from China's enormous and growing reliance on coal for energy production. Even though China has greatly improved the efficiency with which it uses coal, its rapidly growing economy will steadily increase that amount of coal it uses, produce more local air pollution, and contribute to greenhouse gases and global warming.

20.1 POLLUTION

Air and water pollution are damaging to human health, worker productivity, and agricultural output. As the scale of the economy has grown, total waste production has grown. Coal use has doubled since 1990, with production over 2 *billion* tons in 2005. Coal burning discharges particulate matter, sulfur dioxide, and greenhouse gases into the air. Energy consumption, in the form of coal, biomass, and petroleum products, is responsible for most air pollution. At the same time, some efforts to control pollution have begun to have an affect.

20.1.1   Air Pollution

In China's cities today, particularly the larger ones, trends in air quality are shaped by offsetting forces. Air quality has been improved by industrial emission controls and by the shift in household fuel use away from coal. But the growth of industry and the growth of automobile transport are causing an increase in pollutants. The resulting outcomes have differed across cities and specific pollutants.

A major source of improvement in air quality has been the reduction in household use of coal. Until recently even urban households burned coal for heating and cooking, but household use of coal has dropped off dramatically from its peak in 1988. Eighty percent of the urban population now has access to gas for cooking. Indoor air quality in many urban households has improved significantly as gas, electricity, and central heating have spread. In rural areas, indoor air pollution is still a severe problem. About half of the rural population has unimproved stoves that burn raw coal and wood and produce particulates, sulfur and nitrogen oxides, carbon monoxide, and other pollutants. Indoor air pollutants contribute to high rates of respiratory disease, the leading cause of death in rural areas and the third-leading cause in cities.

Ambient (outdoor) air quality has improved in many cities, particularly due to the reduction in total suspended particulates (TSP). Despite the increase in the use of coal, the primary source of particulates, TSP concentrations have declined due to controls and change in the way coal is exploited. A much larger proportion of coal is now burned to generate electricity, in larger and better-equipped facilities. Sulfur dioxide emissions have remained roughly constant, however, because sulfur control measures have not been effective enough to offset growing coal use. Ambient concentrations of particulates and sulfur dioxide in many Chinese cities are among the highest in the world and are significantly above World Health Organization (WHO) guidelines and Chinese air quality standards.

The biggest negative impact on air quality has come from the dramatic increase in trucks and automobiles. The total number of vehicles in China soared from 5.5 million in 1990 to 43 million in 2005 (including 11.5 million motorized tricycles and other low-powered vehicles). Motor vehicles emit particulates, sulfur, carbon monoxide, nitrogen oxides, and volatile organic compounds. Lead is an especially pernicious pollutant because of its irreversible effects on children's intelligence and aptitudes, and China did not eliminate leaded gasoline until 1999. Nitrogen oxides, a major byproduct of the internal combustion engine, have increased steadily since the 1980s. Nitrogen oxides contribute to the formation of ozone, photochemical smog, and greenhouse gas. The European Space Agency recently completed a global mapping project, in which satellite instruments were used to map nitrogen oxide densities for 18 months from 2003–2004. The largest global concentration of nitrogen oxides is the North China Plain, with the area around Beijing in particular standing out. North China now surpasses the northeast United States, where nitrogen oxide emissions are large, but stable (Beirle, Platt, and Wagner 2005). Overall, Chinese cities have become smoggier but less gritty in the past 20 years.

20.1.2   Water Pollution

Since 1980 the quality of China's surface water and groundwater has deteriorated significantly under the pressure of rapid industrial development, brisk population and urban growth, and increased use of chemical fertilizers and pesticides. As a result, water pollution is now a serious problem for urban and rural drinking water. Main sources of pollutants include the following:

Industrial Waste. Pulp and paper, metallurgical, and chemical factories are the worst polluters. Processing of farm products contributes to oxygen-demand pollution, in which water is depleted of oxygen and loses the ability to support healthy plant growth. There has been major progress in cleaning up large-scale factories, and today 90% of industrial wastewater from regulated (large-scale) industries receives some kind of treatment. However, smaller factories, including township and village enterprises, often have no treatment facilities at all.

Municipal Waste. A decade ago almost no municipal sewage was properly treated. A major push has been undertaken to improve sewage treatment, but still only a reported 42% of municipal wastewater was treated in 2003.

Agriculture. Intensively used nitrogen fertilizers and pesticides are a serious source of water pollution. Poor-quality fertilizers, excessive use of nitrogen fertilizers (relative to phosphorous and potassium), and especially widespread use of cheap ammonia bicarbonate fertilizer, which is readily soluble and easily washed out to streams, lakes, and aquifers, add to the impact. Pesticide use, more widespread in recent years, has been implicated in species loss (birds) and has polluted some important water bodies. Animal waste from livestock farms is another major source of biological oxygen-demand and coliform pollution. The ecological balance of Hangzhou Bay is seriously threatened, primarily by agriculture-related runoff, which, according to one study, contributed 88% of chemical oxygen-demand pollution.

As a result of these pollutants, water quality is poor, especially in the water-short northern regions. Table 20.1 summarizes the available data. Water quality below class V means that the water is literally toxic: obviously unsafe for human contact, it is unsuitable even for irrigation, and cannot be safely purified for human uses. In the Liao, Hai, and Huai systems, half the water is in this category, as well as a third of the Yellow River. (See Figure 20.2, which shows these river systems.) These rivers have all three of the biggest pollution problems. Waters turn eutrophic from biological oxygen demand and chemical oxygen demand: depleted of oxygen, waters can only support bacteria and flagellates, and no higher life forms. Persistent heavy metals, such as chromium, mercury, and lead, build up in the water and riverbeds. Chlorinated hydrocarbons (such as PCBs and DDT—banned but still used) build up and are also highly persistent. Class IV waters can be used for industrial and some recreational purposes but is not fit for direct human contact. Class III is the standard for direct human contact, and also for intake into purification for drinking water. Class I is pristine. In northern China the water in only about one-third of the river length meets the standard for human contact. Moreover, this is the entire river system; quality is much worse in the downstream, urban areas where most people live.

Water shortage in the north severely compounds the pollution problem. During dry periods local water-use agencies keep water dammed up to retain water for local users, but in doing so they trap all kinds of pollutants. When the first rains come, gate operators open the dam gates and flush their sections of the river, but in so doing they send a highly polluted waste stream into the main river channel. In recent years authorities have reinforced regional coordination to reduce this problem and ensure continuously flowing (and flushing) rivers. As of 2004 the Yellow River had flowed without interruption for

Table 20.1
Water quality class of main river systems, 2003

	River length (kilometers)	Percentage of total distance in each quality class					
		Class I	Class II	Class III	Class IV	Class V	Below V
National	134,593	5.7	30.7	26.2	10.9	5.8	20.7
Songhua	11,135	0.9	9.2	35.5	32.4	5.2	16.8
Liao	4,529	1.6	8.8	17.6	8.6	13.5	49.9
Hai	10,719	3.1	17.3	18.2	6.1	2.8	52.5
Yellow	13,721	7.6	14.1	11.8	17.7	16.8	32.0
Huai	11,621	2.1	8.8	16.8	15.4	8.0	48.9
Yangtze	38,513	8.9	37.3	31.3	6.4	5.8	10.3
Pearl	16,061	2.0	47.2	25.7	9.2	2.1	13.8

five years, reversing the previous pattern in which the river water would be exhausted most dry seasons. Yet these efforts have not yet produced significant improvement in the overall quality of the Yellow River.

The experience in the Huai River basin has been especially alarming. A surge of polluted water on the Huai River in 1994 killed massive numbers of fish, caused widespread illness, and forced municipal and industrial water intakes along the river to shut down. Economy (2004) describes how this event shook up central government leaders and induced them to launch a massive program to clean up the river. Premier Li Peng declared that the Huai would be clean by 2000. Some 60 billion RMB ($7.2 billion) was poured into pollution control in the Huai River over the next decade. However, this expensive program failed utterly to meet its ambitious goals. Indeed, as Table 20.1 shows, the Huai is still one of the most polluted rivers in China. Despite the money made available, local governments protected their local industries and shielded them from costly upgrades or shutdowns. Water quality improvement has been imperceptible.

Southern rivers are less polluted, largely because of the region's more abundant water and the rivers' larger assimilative capacity. Nevertheless, there are many seriously polluted areas. The section of the upper Yangtze River near Chongqing was found in 1993 to have failed NEPA standards for chemical oxygen demand, chromium, mercury, lead, ammonia nitrogen, petroleum, acidity, and coliform. One of the worries associated with the Three Gorges Dam is that it will trap pollutants around the densely populated Chongqing area.

20.1.3   Costs of Pollution

Air and water pollution damages the health of people exposed to it, lowers the productivity of workers, and degrades natural resources. What are the costs of these damages, and which damages should worry Chinese policy-makers the most? A number of studies have attempted to quantify the costs of pollution to the Chinese economy, without achieving much consensus.

World Bank (1997) was an ambitious attempt to calculate the costs of pollution in China. According to this study, total air and water pollution costs were estimated at $54 billion a year, or roughly 8% of GDP. These costs do not make the growth rate lower or less meaningful; instead, they are ongoing costs that reduce the well-being of China's population in every year. The largest losses were due to

• Health losses associated with urban air pollution—particularly debilitating chronic bronchitis

• Health losses associated with indoor air pollution

• Chronic disease from water pollution—especially heavy metals and toxins

• Crop and forestry damage from acid rain

• Nervous system damage and reduced intelligence among children exposed to high levels of lead.

The study calculated that the total health and productivity losses associated with urban air pollution, including hospital and emergency room visits, lost work days, and the debilitating effects of chronic bronchitis, cost more than $20 billion a year, making them the single largest pollution cost in China today. It would be possible to avoid 178,000 premature deaths each year if China met its own class II air pollution standards, and 4.5 million person-years are lost because of illnesses associated with urban air pollution levels that exceed standards. Estimates based on conservative assumptions about indoor air pollution suggest that it causes 111,000 premature deaths a year. The health problems caused by indoor fuel use are on a scale roughly comparable to that posed by smoking. Water pollution damages human health, fisheries, and agriculture (from polluted irrigation water) and increases spending on clean water supplies. Improvements in water supply and sanitation can substantially reduce the incidence and severity of diseases, such as hepatitis, as well as the infant mortality associated with diarrhea. Surprisingly, though, water-related diseases are less common in China than in other developing countries, and they appear to be a less significant cost than respiratory diseases plausibly related to air pollution. There are other hidden costs to pollution. For example, China is estimated to have at least 5,000 so-called brownfields—chemical- or solid-waste dump sites. Virtually none of these have been cleaned up, and little is known about the potential costs.

20.1.4. Pollution Control

China put into place a significant pollution-control effort during the course of the 1980s. The resources actually flowing into that effort, stepped up considerably after 1997–1998, when the combination of government reorganization (which made SEPA into a national ministerial-level organization) and a series of environment-linked disasters, including flooding on the Yangtze, increased the priority given to the environment. Overall, Chinese official data indicate that 1.4% of GDP went into investment in pollution control in 2003, a substantial sum. The bulk of this went for urban infrastructure, with water and sewage the largest chunk, followed by greenification. Lesser amounts go to abate industrial pollution and fit new factories with pollution control equipment (Environmental Statistics 2004, 7, 96).

China was an early adopter of a system of fees for discharges of pollutants. That system has generated a steadily increasing flow of funds that are earmarked for pollution abatement. The total sum surpassed 6 billion RMB (about $750 million) in 2002. Pollution fees have some obvious benefits, since they encourage firms to find least-cost methods to improve their environmental performance. Chinese fees have been criticized, however. Fees are frequently rebated to the polluting firm in order to fund investment in pollution abatement, but oversight of actual spending is weak. Corruption and diversion of fees have been a problem in some areas—moreover, local environmental officials actually have an incentive to keep polluters polluting, since allowing these practices to continue generates revenues for them. Nevertheless, some important achievements have been made. Generally speaking, the abatement of industrial wastes from large factories has been a relatively positive part of China's environmental policy. According to SEPA (2004), total wastes have stabilized even as industrial output has grown sharply. Total industrial pollution of water, as measured by chemical oxygen demand, has declined somewhat. Industrial heavy-metal pollution has declined very significantly since 1997, and discharge of petroleum products has been significantly reduced. If maintained, these are significant achievements.

20.2 SUSTAINABILITY

Not all environmental problems can be traced to pollution, nor can they be appropriately evaluated in terms of their current costs or expressed as a percent of GDP. Critical environmental problems in China relate to the coordination of enormous demands on China's natural resources. These problems are more difficult to quantify because a large but unknown share of costs are deferred to the future. There are no markets that reflect the true costs of activities. In some cases, designing such markets would be difficult or impossible. In other cases, because China is a transitional and a developing economy, markets are simply incomplete. There is a significant danger that slowly increasing costs might suddenly reach a "tipping point"; Rather than increasing in a linear relation with demands on resources, costs may increase qualitatively once the level of "carrying capacity" of an environment is reached.

20.2.1 Broad Impact of Pollution and Global Warming

As China's economy has become large, the implications of Chinese pollution and resource use have also grown. Air pollution, for example, has regional and global consequences. When fossil fuels are burned, oxides of sulfur and nitrogen combine with other chemicals in the air to form sulfuric acid and nitric acid, which precipitate as acid rain. These gaseous emissions can stay in the atmosphere for several days and travel hundreds or thousands of kilometers before falling back to the earth's surface as acid rain. Acidity is highest in southern China, particularly in Sichuan, Guizhou, Guangxi, and Hunan, both because of extensive use of high-sulfur coal and because of naturally acidic soils.

China is a significant contributor to the problem of global warming. China is the second-largest source of greenhouse gases, after the United States, and its carbon emissions are growing rapidly. By most estimates, China accounts for about 15% of global carbon emissions, compared to 23% for the United States. As described in Chapter 14, the breakdown of Chinese statistical reporting led to a significant underestimate of coal use at the end of the 1990s, which led to excessive optimism about China's ability to limit carbon emissions. We now know that total carbon emissions have continued to grow. Assuming that Chinese statistics for 2005 accurately measure total coal production, as seems likely, then China's production of coal energy—and thus carbon emissions—have been growing since 1996 somewhat *faster* than they were growing before 1996, at 5.1% annually compared to 4.6%. At this growth rate, China will catch up with the United States and become the largest single contributor of carbon dioxide emissions some time between 2015 and 2020.

There is significant debate about China's role in a global climate-control regime. In the Kyoto Treaty, developing countries including China and India are not required to control their carbon emissions. Critics of the treaty argue that no global regime can be meaningful without Chinese and Indian participation. Chinese policy-makers have argued, in the general spirit of the environmental Kuznets curve, that development should come first, and that developing countries should be unconstrained during the development process, deferring their contribution to this global public good until a later date. They also point out that even when Chinese carbon emissions catch up with those of the United States, per capita carbon emissions will only be one-quarter the level of the United States. In the middle ground are those who point out that China, since it contains pockets of extremely backward technique, presents opportunities for reduction of carbon emission at potentially extremely low cost. An international regime that would create incentives for China to abate, either through tradable emissions credits or through alternative mechanisms, would be in the interests of all parties.

China continues to be a relatively energy-intensive economy. As described in Chapter 14, China in 2002 required about 0.23 kilograms of oil equivalent to produce one dollar of PPP-adjusted GDP. That figure compares to about

0.15–0.25 kilograms for a number of large lower- and middle-income industrializing countries. China's energy efficiency is likely to continue to improve,
since over the past 25 years China has been steadily reducing the amount of
energy input required to produce a given value of GDP. There are still many
opportunities to improve energy efficiency. However, it is likely that China will
remain a comparatively energy intensive economy. The fundamental problem
is China's enormous dependence on coal for power generation (Chapter 14).
Coal is cheap to burn, but much more expensive to burn cleanly. Some areas
of coastal China will shift to imported petroleum products, and there is scope
for alternative and less-polluting techniques. However, most parts of China
will continue to be dependent on coal for the foreseeable future. Improvement, therefore, must rely on a combination of more-efficient coal use (especially through concentration in larger and cleaner electricity-generation
facilities) combined with larger investments in pollution-control equipment.
In addition, the fact that China has such an extraordinarily large share of its
total output in industry (Chapter 6) also inevitably implies higher energy use
per unit of GDP. Industries such as steel, cement, and chemicals are by far the
largest users of energy in an economy. It seems inevitable that Chinese greenhouse gas emissions will continue to grow and eventually make China the
largest single contributor to global warming. In the meantime, global warming
is already a reality.

20.2.2   Sustainability of Land and Water Resources

Further broad issues of sustainability relate to the intertwined questions of
sustainability of land and water resources. Since China has virtually no unexploited potentially arable land, any reductions in existing farmland must be
viewed very seriously. At the same time, the productivity and value of existing (and remaining) farm land has been increasing. Simple land availability is
unlikely to be the major obstacle to agricultural output or food availability. In
addition to conversion of agricultural land to nonagricultural uses (housing,
roads, and factories), degradation of farm land is a substantial cause of the
reduction in farmland. Pollution is significant, but by no means the most important factor. Rather, issues relating to appropriate water supply dominate the
problem of land degradation. Too much water in the wrong times and places
causes erosion, and too little causes desertification (Table 20.2). Erosion is concentrated in western regions of China, where overall water supply is deficient,
ground cover is sparse, and seasonal rainfall causes huge soil losses due to
erosion. Serious flooding on the Yangtze in 1998 was directly linked to the
degradation of the upstream environment due to deforestation and erosion.

Table 20.2
Major causes of arable land degradation

	Percent of total
Erosion	48
Desertification	18
Salinization and waterlogging	7
Pollution	12

20.2.2.1 Desertification

Desertification is an enormous problem. China, as stressed in Chapter 1, is an arid country. West of the Aihui–Tengchong line much of the land is desert. However, the desert has been moving east, primarily because of the impact of human activity in China. The overexploitation of grass and forest lands has greatly reduced the regenerative capacity of the land's plant cover. With weakened biological buffer zones, deserts have spread significantly. The State Forestry Administration did large-scale surveys of desert areas in 1994 and 1999, and discovered that deserts had grown by 52,000 square kilometers in just that five-year period. One of the most dramatic results has been an increased frequency of sand and dust storms. In March 2002, two huge dust storms blew across northern China, reducing visibility for days and pushing airborne particulate matter over the top of all measurement scales in Beijing. These storms blew clouds of dust beyond China, affecting Korea and Japan, causing school closings, and coating some cities with a thin layer of dust.

The single most important factor aggravating desertification in recent years has been overgrazing in the grasslands of Inner Mongolia and other pastoral regions of northern China. The dissolution of the collectives in these areas led to the distribution of herds of grazing animals to individual households and an explosion in the size of herds. The "tragedy of the commons" was exacerbated as each individual household sought to maximize its own individual income from animal husbandry. Vast areas of China are classified as grasslands: over 40% of the entire land area. The impact of intensified exploitation on marginal grasslands on the edge of the desert has been catastrophic in some areas. Chinese policy has recognized the danger of desertification for more than 20 years, but policies have not been sufficient to arrest the advance of the deserts. "Shelter belts" of planted trees seek to halt the encroaching desert. Indeed, the expansion of the desert during 1994–1999 came despite the successful rehabilitation of 5,700 square kilometers through reforestation, grass seeding, and expanded irrigation. Most of the rehabilitation took place in central China, in areas not too distant from major watercourses. Most of the spread of the desert took place in northern China, especially in the vast border areas populated by herders.

20.2.2.2   Forests and Grasslands

Away from the frontiers of expanding deserts, the efficacy of Chinese sustainability policy has been substantially better. For many years tree planting has been emphasized as a government policy, as a civic responsibility, and, on several occasions, as a campaign of mass mobilization. Over the long term this consistent emphasis has had a significant payoff, and China's overall forest cover has grown substantially over the past 40 years. The sixth national inventory of forest resources, over the 1999–2003 period, found that forest cover had grown to 18.2% of the national territory (175 million hectares), up substantially even from the 16.6% in the previous (1994–1998) inventory. Indeed, the lowest forest cover was found in the first such national inventory, in 1962, which found that only 8.9% of China was forested (Roumasset, Wang, and Burnett 2004). But these statistics obscure a substantial deterioration in the quality of forestland. The newly planted forest cover tends to be composed of a relatively small number of fast-growing species, scattered through densely settled parts of China. At the same time, considerable acreage of old-growth forest, with diverse species and big trees, has been lost. In 1998, Chinese policy-makers prohibited logging in a broad swath of forests in Southwest China. They were reacting with alarm to devastating floods of the Yangtze that were linked to erosion and deforestation in the upstream reaches of the river. This drastic measure slowed the exploitation of China's largest remaining natural forests. However, in the long run, protection of these forests depends on further developing a system of property rights, rules, and rewards that give local residents incentives to protect forestlands.

Since the turn of the millennium the Chinese government has encouraged the conversion of marginal farmlands to forest or grassland through a variety of programs. The most important program is "grain for green," which provides farmers compensation for five to eight years when land is converted from grain farming to forest or pasturage, while also allowing the farmer to maintain ownership of the land. Pilot implementation began in three western provinces of Sichuan, Shaanxi, and Gansu in October 1999, and farmers in those provinces removed a total of 1.24 million hectares from grain production through the end of 2001. Nationwide, the amount taken out of agriculture in this way was over 2 million hectares in 2002 and 2003, before dropping to only 733,000 hectares in 2004 (because of higher farm prices and less enthusiastic implementation). Altogether, this program has taken almost 5% of China's cropland out of production, providing a recuperative opportunity for a significant area of China's marginal lands.

20.2.2.3   Water Availability

The interplay of land and water resources is also shown by the fact that irrigation remains by far the biggest human use of water in China, accounting for two-thirds of total water use, although the proportion is slowly declining. Particularly troubling is the fact that to date China has been forced to rely on numerous unsustainable practices to maintain current supplies of water to its cities and agriculture. We have already referred to the intense demands on the rivers of northern China and the intense pollution that already afflicts them. A related serious problem is the overexploitation of groundwater. Using underground water supplies (aquifers and ground water) in such a way that they are gradually depleted is sometimes known as "mining water." This is a very serious problem in northern China (Cheng 2002, 52–63). Large amounts of water have been withdrawn from underground sources beginning in the 1970s for tube-well irrigation in the North China Plain. The water table underneath Beijing fell from only five meters below the surface in 1950 to 50 meters in 1994. It has become more difficult and costly to extract water from these underground sources. Private entrepreneurs now dig deep wells and sell the water, increasing supply but increasing the long-run threat to the sustainability of water supply. The problem is most severe with respect to wheat, which requires water outside the normal rainy season and is thus dependent on irrigation (Lohmar and Wang 2002). Conceivably, the North China Plain might stop growing wheat if food prices stay low and water costs continue to rise.

Cities have been extracting increasing amounts of water. As a result, many cities are now experiencing difficulties extracting water, as well as subsidence of land. Coastal cities including Tianjin and Shanghai have experienced major subsidence problems. Depleted aquifers allow saltwater to intrude into water sources near the coast, requiring the abandonment of thousands of wells. These are very serious problems, and solving them will be expensive. Efficiency improvements are possible at nearly every point in the chain of collecting, storing, and delivering water. Currently, charges to farmers for irrigation water cover an estimated 36% of the cost of supplying the water (Lohmar et al. 2003). Higher prices would help economize on water and shift it toward higher-value nonagricultural uses. However, there is no guarantee that effective measures will be adopted in a timely fashion. China's agriculture is so small-scale, with more than 200 million farms, that charging for volume of water delivered is costly and probably inefficient. Problems with water availability may be compounded by deteriorating dams and irrigation facilities. Many of the facilities in the most populous and prosperous parts of China were constructed in the 1950s. Some are made of earth or brick; they are heavily silted, and need repair and upgrading urgently. According to Nickum, "The primary pressure on irrigated area now, and probably for some time into the future, is project obsolescence within the irrigation sector itself" (1998, 890).

These concerns will probably require larger government investments in water management facilities. In northern cities, the past pattern has been over-exploitation of rivers and surface reservoirs, followed by overuse of underground water resources, and finally recourse to long-distance water transfer (Smil 2003, 157). One major initiative, tentatively approved by the Chinese government, is to pump southern water northward to alleviate stress in the North China basin. There are three feasible routes (Figure 20.2). The western route is most expensive but might provide the best water quality; the eastern route is cheapest but provides the lowest water quality. The middle route may be the best compromise, and preparatory construction work is underway. Eventually, the middle route would be connected to the reservoir on the

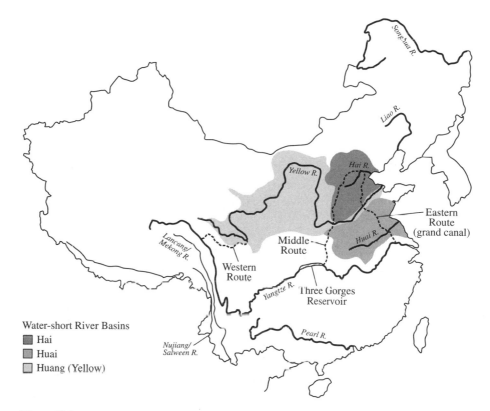

Figure 20.2
South–north water-transfer routes

Yangtze above the Three Gorges Dam. A large volume of water could then be transported north, about twice as much as is shipped to California from the Colorado River in the United States. These grand infrastructure projects are expensive and, in the long run, less important than the hundreds of thousands of small-scale improvements in the efficiency with which water is used, as delivery systems are upgraded, and consumers are given stronger incentives to conserve water.

20.3   CONCLUSION

Environmental degradation has imposed serious costs on the Chinese economy and reduced the well-being of the Chinese population. Moreover, there is increasing public concern about environmental issues, and that concern has increasingly been publicly articulated. A milestone of sorts was reached in February 2004, when Premier Wen Jiabao suspended work on a series of dams projected for the Nujiang (Nu River or Salween) in Yunnan. This river flows through a beautiful, rugged area where the upper reaches of three great rivers (the Yangtze, Mekong, and Salween) flow in parallel less than one hundred kilometers apart. It is naturally an area of enormous biodiversity, as well as being the home of several different ethnic groups living in these remote highlands along the border with Myanmar. The release of plans for a cascade of dams along this river triggered significant protests within China, as well as abroad. The government's responsiveness to these protests will be a bellwether of its willingness to let public opinion serve as an input into economic decision-making.

China is currently engaged in a large-scale program of dam building to generate electricity that will be essential if China is to restrain the growth of its fossil fuel use. By far the largest part of China's hydropower potential is in the Southwest. The case of the Nujiang thus represents an ongoing conflict between the needs of economic growth and the obligation to protect biological and human diversity. To navigate this conflict, China will urgently require public input and discussion in the decision-making process. China already has requirements for environmental impact statements: if such statements are to fulfill their potential role, they must be available for public inspection and comment, which has not often been the case in China. The case of Nujiang thus provides an ideal opportunity to give environmental impact statements their proper role. This kind of role for public opinion is also indispensable if something like the environmental Kuznets curve is to prove a reality in China. Perhaps environmental quality is a luxury good, and demand for it increases more than proportionately as income grows. Even so, if citizens have no way to convert their preferences into effective demand and command over society's resources, it is hard to see a consistent motive force behind environmental improvement.

The challenges of water availability, resilience of the natural environment, and atmospheric degradation and climate change are among the most serious that China confronts. In each case it is easy to see that current practices are unsustainable, but it is hard to project when the obvious costs that these practices impose will force serious change. There is still an opportunity for improved environmental policy-making to make a significant difference before further environmental catastrophes develop.

In its most recent planning exercise, the five-year plan for 2006–2010, the Chinese government called for a reorientation of the economic growth model toward a sustainable growth with a lighter environmental impact. By itself, of course, mere adherence to a particular approach to development planning will not dramatically change the quality of China's environment, no matter how friendly to the environment it is proclaimed to be. But this shift in viewpoint suggests that government policy might slowly begin to become one positive element in the complex mix of factors that determine China's environmental trajectory. In combination with many other social, technological, and economic factors, that could turn China in the direction of gradual environmental improvement.

BIBLIOGRAPHY

Suggestions for Further Reading

World Bank (2001) and the special issue of the *China Quarterly*, no. 156: "China's Environment," December 1998, though slightly dated, are still useful balanced introductions to China's environment.

Smil (2003) collects his original pioneering work on the Chinese environment, along with a retrospective reassessment. Though the shifts in time perspective are occasionally bewildering, overall it is an astonishingly rich and stimulating volume that effectively demonstrates the author's prescience.

SEPA, the State Environmental Protection Agency, has a good English-language Web site, http://www.sepa.gov.cn/english/, with annual reports on the environment posted. There are also daily air pollution readings from more than 80 Chinese cities.

An excellent online bulletin on China's environment is put out by the U.S. embassy in Beijing. See the Beijing Environment, Science, and Technology Update at http://www.usembassy-china.org.cn/sandt/estnews020802.htm. The discussion in the chapter on desertification drew on the issues of February 8, and March 29, 2002. Estimate of funds spent to clean up the Huai River from issue of June 30, 2004.

The China Environment Series of the Woodrow Wilson International Center for Scholars China Environment Forum has published regular issues with short pieces on specialized environmental topics.

Sources for Data and Figures

Figure 20.2: Map of south–north water transfer routes. Liu (1998, 902).

Table 20.1: Environmental Statistics (2004, 18).

Table 20.2: Ash and Edmonds (1998, 860).

References

Ash, Robert F., and Richard Louis Edmonds (1988). "China's Land Resources, Environment and Agricultural Production." *China Quarterly*, no. 156, pp. 836–79.

Beirle, S., U. Platt, and T. Wagner (2005). "Potential of monitoring Nitrogen Oxides with satellite instruments," Heidelberg: Institut für Umweltphysik. Accessed at http://avdc.gsfc.nasa.gov/ST&WG/ST/ST_200511/Posters/Beirle_aura_poster.pdf

Cheng Shengkui, chief ed. (2002). *2002 Zhongguo Ziyuan Baogao* [2002 China Natural Resources Report]. Beijing: Shangwu Yinshuguan.

Economy, E. (2004). *The River Runs Black: The Environmental Challenge to China's Future.* Ithaca, NY: Cornell University Press.

Environmental Statistics (Annual). National Bureau of Statistics, Population, Society, and Science & Technology Statistics Division. *2004 Zhongguo Huanjing Tongji Gaiyao* [China Environmental Statistics Compendium 2004]. Beijing: Zhongguo Tongji.

Liu Changming (1998). "Environmental Issues and the South-North Water Transfer Scheme." *China Quarterly*, no. 156 (December), pp. 899–910.

Lohmar, Bryan, and Jinxia Wang (2002). "Will Water Scarcity Affect Agricultural Production in China?" In U.S. Department of Agriculture, Economic Research Service, *China's Food and Agriculture: Issues for the 21st Century*, pp. 41–3. Washington, DC: USDA.

Lohmar, Bryan, Jinxia Wang, Scott Rozelle, Jikun Huang, and David Dawe (2003). *China's Agricultural Water Policy Reforms: Increasing Investment, Resolving Conflicts, and Revising Incentives*, U.S. Department of Agriculture, AIB-782, March. http://www.ers.usda.gov/publications/aib782/

NEPA (1993). National Environmental Protection Agency. *Environmental Action Plan of China.* Beijing: China Environment Press.

Nickum, James E. (1998). "Is China Living on the Water Margin?" *China Quarterly*, no. 156, (December), pp. 880–98.

Roumasset, James, Hua Wang, and Kimberly Burnett (2004). "Environmental Resources and Economic Growth." Pittsburgh: University of Pittsburgh draft paper.

SEPA (2004). State Environmental Protection Agency, Environmental Information Center, "Analysis Report on the State of the Environment in China." At http://www.sepa.gov.cn/english/SOE/analysis/index.htm

Smil, Vaclav (2003). *China's Past, China's Future: Energy, Food, Environment.* London: RoutledgeCurzon.

Stern, David I. (2004). "The Rise and Fall of the Environmental Kuznets Curve." *World Development*, 32(8): 1419–39.

World Bank (1997). *Clear Water, Blue Skies: China's Environment in the New Century.* Washington, DC: World Bank.

World Bank (2001) *China: Air, Land, and Water.* Washington, DC: World Bank.

Index